Living Dangerously

A Biography of Joris Ivens

In memory of my brother Ad

Living Dangerously

A Biography of Joris Ivens

Hans Schoots

Amsterdam University Press

Translation: David Colmer

This is a slightly abridged and revised translation of *Gevaarlijk leven. Een biografie van Joris Ivens*, (Amsterdam 1995).

The publication of this translation was financially supported by:
The *Stichting Prins Bernhard Fonds*
Thuiskopiefonds
The Dutch Film Fund
The Foundation for the Production and Translation of Dutch Literature

Cover illustration: Mark Kolthoff, Gemeentearchief Amsterdam
Cover design: Korpershoek Ontwerpen, Amsterdam
Lay-out: JAPES, Amsterdam

Isbn 90 5356 388 1 (paperback)
Isbn 90 5356 433 0 (hardback)

e-mail adress of the author: hschoots@wxs.nl

Contents

Introduction

I first became aware of Joris Ivens in the late sixties after seeing his Vietnam films during protest meetings in a cellar at Tilburg University, known in those days as Karl Marx University. I met Ivens himself in 1986 when I visited him in Paris several times to interview him for the Dutch weekly *De Groene Amsterdammer*. I was fascinated by his attempts to come to terms with his life story, interwoven as it was with the history of Communism. After I sent him my article – 'I Clung Too Long to my Utopias' – he telephoned and said: 'You've just written up what I said. I'd been hoping you'd bring some order into it.' It was something he himself had felt unable to do. I had felt the temptations of totalitarianism myself and had formed a definite opinion about my own experiences, but how could I know what Joris Ivens wanted to say?

I began toying with the idea of writing his biography. I had long been interested in the uncomfortable relationship between art and political commitment, and Ivens had spent much of his life on the interface between the two. A biography of Ivens presented an opportunity to throw light on the century's great ideological clashes through the story of one individual. At the same time it would be more than the life story of a fascinating character, it would be an account of socially committed artists and documentary film-history in general.

I was dissatisfied with the various books about him that already existed. There were several good studies of specific aspects of his life and work; the general accounts went no further than the sixties, and so much was left unsaid. Ivens's own memoirs, *Joris Ivens on La mémoire d'un regard*, published in France in 1982, were the most honest, but also showed most clearly how much more there was. Early in 1990, I began work on this biography.

A book written with the slogan 'In the footsteps of...' was a scarcely tenable proposition. Joris Ivens filmed in twenty-one countries and on every continent except Antarctica. Fortunately, all the important archives relating to the filmmaker are located in Europe, and most of the main characters who were still alive had settled there.

I was able to establish fairly systematically what kind of documents were available elsewhere in the world. Institutions in Australia and the Americas sent me overviews of relevant material. Prominent examples are the FBI in Washington and the Ernest Hemingway Collection in Boston.

There are several places where further documentation presumably exists. First of all, China. Recognizing the central place this country occupied in Ivens's career, I had initially resolved to go there, but the reactions to my letters and telephone calls were so discouraging that I changed my mind. I fear that the bureaucracy in such a country is not susceptible to the personal touch, and after speaking to Santiago Alvarez of Cuba, I was doubly convinced that I could expect nothing but official rhetoric. (All Alvarez could tell me was that Ivens 'was an eagle, looking out over history and the revolutionary struggle with his sharp eyes'.) I took comfort in the knowledge that I had visited China and Cuba in earlier years and could imagine how foreign visitors like Joris Ivens had been treated there. Fortunately, quite a lot of documentation about Ivens's period in China can be found in the archives of the Europese Stichting Joris Ivens in Nijmegen, Holland.

Two archives that probably include new information are those of the KGB and the Stasi. The KGB insisted that it did not possess an Ivens file, whereas access to the Stasi archives required difficult formalities and a waiting period of several years. I wish any subsequent Ivens biographers every success.

This book is based on original documents: letters, notes, diaries, reports and scenarios. These are suffused with the spirit of the times in which they were written, and the information they include has not been colored by memory. Often there were several documents and letters about the same subject, each able to complement the picture with its own perspective. At a rough estimate, I would say that I read two thousand letters and worked through fifteen to twenty thousand pages of other documents, including many not previously studied. I see the interviews as a supplement, albeit an essential one. The very fact of meeting someone who has played a role in the story is a tremendous bonus. There is nothing new about the dangers of interviews as a historical source: all memories are selective and in the least favorable scenario the interviewer is deliberately misled. I believe that comparing the information from various sources allowed me to avoid the worst pitfalls.

Although Ivens undoubtedly lived many years of his life convinced that he was consistently on the side of freedom, the inverse was often true, and in his latter years he began to recognize this. My book includes many facts that will distress his friends and be enthusiastically welcomed by his enemies. So be it. I would like, however, to take this opportunity to anticipate the discussion and defend Ivens against the worst excesses of criticism. Ivens was a hardened Communist, a party man; I believe that no one will be able to doubt that after reading this book. But does that disqualify him from his title as Knight in the Order of the Dutch Lion? I prefer to assume that he was decorated for his significance as a filmmaker. Most of his films from the twenties and thirties were and still are mileposts in documentary history. From a cinematic point of view, Ivens's postwar films were no longer so remarkable, but they remained well-crafted and sometimes spectacular, as was 17TH PARALLEL, filmed in the middle of the Vietnam combat zone when he was sixty-nine years old. His last film, A TALE OF THE WIND, made with his wife Marceline Loridan, represented a surprising new turn in his work. His unflagging enthusiasm for the medium was an inspiration to many filmmakers.

During my research into the historical events, the peaks and troughs of Ivens's film career, and the turbulence of his private life, I was perhaps most struck by an anecdote from Jan de Vaal, former director of the Dutch Film Museum. It was the early sixties and, after many years abroad, Ivens returned for the first time to view the Amsterdam museum's collection of his films. RAIN, which he had made in 1929, was screened. When the lights went up, he said: 'The dog was missing.' It was a shot of a few seconds, perhaps less, without any particular significance. Just a dog walking through the picture. In this story I felt the love and dedication with which Ivens approached filmmaking.

It is time for more objectivity in our view of this honored and maligned but indisputably extraordinary figure. This remained my goal as I followed Ivens through the heights and the depths of the twentieth century.

Those who contributed to the making of this book are listed in the acknowledgement. This English translation is a slightly abridged version of the Dutch original. Readers seeking more detail on Ivens's bureaucratic wrangling with the Dutch government should refer to *Gevaarlijk leven*.

Amsterdam, October 2, 1999

I   The Boss's Son (1898-1921)

By the standards of the late nineteenth century, Friday November 18, 1898 was an unremarkable day. The newspapers described the Spanish-American War in the Philippines, from Tangiers came reports that 'three French columns are advancing toward the Moroccan border and the scene of the uprising', and Chinese rebels had attacked and looted a town on the upper reaches of the Yangtze. The Dreyfus case dragged on in the courts and, elsewhere in Paris, work was proceeding on the new bridge over the Seine, the first stone of which had been laid by Czar Nicholas II of Russia. In The Hague, despite rumors to the contrary, the weekly auditions of the Dutch Minister of Colonial Affairs continued as always.

Early that morning the child who would become famous as Joris Ivens was born George Henri Anton Ivens in Nijmegen, a city in the east of the Netherlands. His mother, Dora Ivens-Muskens, gave birth in the parental home at Van Berchenstraat 15 and there were no complications to speak of. She had just turned twenty-eight; Kees, his father, was one year younger. They had been married for four years and George was their second child. Their oldest son was named Wim, and they had three more children after George: Hans, Thea and Coba – five, eight and eleven years his junior.

No one could have guessed that little George would one day participate in another Spanish war, or be sent off by the American authorities with the request never to return, and then be refused entry to the Philippines. He would dedicate years to the Chinese revolution and, as a resident of Paris, he would make a film featuring Czar Nicholas's bridge. By that time the Russian monarch himself was long dead, shot by rebels who would later be on very good terms with this story's restless main character. Relations with the successors of the Dutch Minister of Colonial Affairs would be less cordial.

Nijmegen is an old city, founded by the Romans and famed for the Valkhof, a castle Charlemagne built on the hills overlooking the Waal. In the second half of the nineteenth century most of Nijmegen's walls and gates were demolished in order to reshape the city in the mold of an ordinary Dutch town, but Joris Ivens remembered the city fondly and recalled it as 'not really a Dutch town... a place where Mediterranean influences are still visible'.[1]

Every year, thousands of ships sail past Nijmegen on the Waal, transporting cargo between the Ruhr and Rotterdam. Flowing through a broad landscape of summer and winter dykes, levees and water meadows, the ancient river evokes thoughts of distant and unknown places. George's maternal grandparents, the Muskenses, lived down on the riverbank, ten minutes' walk from the Van Berchenstraat. There, amid other merchants, his grandfather traded in grain and seed.

George's paternal great-grandfather, Heinrich Ivens, had been a cabinetmaker in Efferen, a small town a few miles southwest of Cologne, and had apparently been involved in the revolutionary movement of 1848.[2] Efferen was also the birthplace of George's grandfather, Wilhelm. An enterprising young man, Wilhelm Ivens moved to Nijmegen around 1867 to learn the trade of photography from one of the two German photographers who had already established themselves there.

In 1871 Wilhelm opened his own 'Photographic Studio' in Nijmegen. He enjoyed a high professional standing and was granted a royal warrant. The drive to achieve was second nature to the Ivenses, and Wilhelm was active in the city and beyond, both as the first chairman of the Dutch Photographers' Association and as the secretary of the Humanitas Society, a charitable organization in aid of orphans and young vagrants.[3]

In 1891 Wilhelm handed the management of his studio over to his son Kees, who was more interested in the technical and commercial side of photography and turned the studio into a 'Phototechnical Agency and Dealer in Photographic Articles'. On May 17, 1894 he opened a new business and married Dora Muskens. More than forty years later, he still referred to May 17 as 'the day of days'.[4]

Business flourished and branches were soon opened in Amsterdam, Groningen and The Hague. The company was renamed Capi, after the managing director, C.A.P. Ivens (Kees is short for Cornelis). Although not particularly creative himself, Kees Ivens still had a broad interest in culture. He played Schubert on the piano for his family and took them to the theater to see concerts, plays and motion pictures. The artists Jan Toorop, Eugène Lücker and Han Pieck visited the family home.

Like his father, Kees Ivens was a driven, committed man: he sat on the town council for the progressive, liberal and Catholic 'Justice for All'; was on the board of the Dutch Amateur Photographers' Association; and was a member of 'Faith and Science', a debating society for Catholic intellectuals. There, he once said: 'We must keep an open-minded perspective, knowing what we want and honestly admitting it, we must be mild in our assessment of others, not fanatical in religious matters. Tolerance is, after all, the basic principle of community.' Joris Ivens, who once called his father 'a man with rigorous morals',[5] became acquainted early in life with the concept of work-

ing for the general good. Kees Ivens read the liberal *Algemeen Handelsblad*
and had an unshakable nineteenth-century belief in progress. He launched
plans for a Meuse-Waal Canal and a Waal Bridge to replace the ferry service, then put in years of hard work until both projects were finally realized.
On the completion of the bridge, he saw the improved connection between
Nijmegen and Arnhem – less than twenty miles apart and finally linked by
road – as nothing less than a step toward a more peace-loving humanity,
with a more international and continental perspective. 'Our hope is that a
conflict between two nations will one day seem as ridiculous as a war between two cities would seem to us now.'[6] He would be made a Knight and
later an Officer of the Order of Orange-Nassau in recognition of his efforts.
In the *Provinciale Geldersche & Nijmeegsche Courant* he wrote enthusiastically
about new technical inventions: 'Today it is Roentgen, tomorrow Edison,
the day after Raoul Pictet, and then Lumière, all demanding our attention
for *noch nie dagewesene* things.'[7] Even the jubilee of his own business fitted
into Kees Ivens's greater vision. In a brochure marking the occasion, he
went back centuries into Nijmegen's past to prove that history was moving
irresistibly forward toward a better future. In 1939, moved to despair by the
premature death of his son Wim, commercial setbacks and the imminent
world war, he wrote in his diary: 'The only thing that can sustain us is the
unshakable conviction that everything leads, along immense pathways invisible to us mortals, to one final goal.'[8]

Out walking with George, he must have used stirring phrases like these
to describe his ideals. Later, we hear their echo when, toward the end of a
filmmaking career that had spanned sixty years, Joris Ivens speaks of his
film A TALE OF THE WIND: 'We want to film the wind. It is the memory of all
things; everything that has been said is in the wind. Perhaps I also see the
wind as the great onward flow of humanity that – irrespective of the smaller
streams, of fascism and empires, of declining civilizations – leads to something better.'[9]

Kees Ivens was both a convinced liberal and a dominant, interfering
character. Some Capi employees – he called them Capians – saw him as a
stern and superior man with overblown ideas. Within the family his word
was law. 'He never pounded on the table, but when he said something it
had to happen,' explained his daughter Thea. He talked people round until
they did what he wanted of their own accord. Joris Ivens described his father as 'on the one hand very protective but, on the other, extremely demanding.'[10] Kees Ivens dreaded chaos and the unexpected. 'Order is the
soul of every business,' he believed, but his organizing extended far beyond
the commercial sphere. George once received a letter from his mother 'without Dad having read it', in which she remarked that his father 'has always

been so keen on having everything arranged and settled, and wants everyone to follow a predetermined path. That only works with puppets, not with people.'[11] George did not have his father's passion for organizing others, but time would show that he was easily his match when it came to sticking to certainties.

George's dynamism came from his father and his grandfather; he got his gentleness from his mother. Dora Ivens was a smallish, rather plump woman, who generally wore her dark hair in a bun. Photos invariably show her with a friendly, even-tempered expression. She was sensitive, capable and creative; husband, children, grandchildren and Capians agreed. No one ever heard an improper word from her lips. Jan Toorop, who twice painted her portrait, once said during a reading: 'She is a woman with taste – artistic, calm and intelligent.' Kees Ivens noted in his diary: 'One of those present applauded in his heart.'[12]

In his memoirs Joris Ivens wrote that he loved his mother deeply, but later events suggest that the reality was less simple. Why was he so slow to get in touch after the war? Why did he wait until sixteen months after Germany's capitulation and thirteen months after Japan's before writing his first postwar letter to his mother, even though he had been overseas for eight years: a period in which his father had died, his mother had gone through difficult years of war, and Thea's husband had been shot dead on the eve of liberation? When he finally reached Nijmegen in 1947, he dropped by for two quick visits, 'just long enough to see my mother, hug her and talk a little. Just long enough to brush my memories with my fingertips and turn away from them again.'[13] When she died fourteen months later, he was abroad again and had not seen her in the meantime. What made him turn away so quickly? And what inspired him to write to a friend at age twenty-three: 'Especially when I think about the marriages I saw everywhere around me, I know very well that I go along with many of Strindberg's ideas – and see women as the main cause of marital unhappiness.'[14]

Ivens's mother seemed to live in the shadow of her broad-minded and dominant husband. In the evening she would place his slippers before the chair only he was allowed to sit in. George 'gnashed his teeth' while witnessing what he would later call her subservience. 'At meals he would always be served first and given the best pieces. If there were seconds, he would go first again; everyone else always had to wait. I was furious about all those privileges, but I didn't let it show.' Did little George feel compelled to somehow protect his mother? Dora was virtually the embodiment of goodness. It was almost impossible to refuse her anything and she deserved to be surrounded by constant care. Some psychoanalysts believe that it can have far-reaching consequences for a young child to feel responsible for its mother at an age when it needs so much care and freedom itself. The child feels an urge to flee, and later in life continues to see intense relationships with others as threatening.

Dora Ivens was a devout Catholic who took her children to Sunday Mass. When they were older, however, she told them: 'If you think you don't need to go to church, don't feel obliged to do it just to make me happy.'[15] The children responded by doing it to make her happy. Toward the end of his life, Joris Ivens summed up his childhood in Nijmegen with the words: 'I was young there. I had a happy life there.'[16] The earliest memory he cites in his memoirs is of a train journey. He was five, and he and Wim were pulling faces at strangers to stop them entering their compartment: 'We did everything we could to protect the intimacy of our family from the outside world.' There is no doubt a great deal of truth in this image of a childhood in sheltered surroundings, where the children are taught to have a broad perspective on the world, with Father providing the material comforts and Mother the warmth, but there was another side to the picture. Their home in the Van Berchenstraat had to be the scene of constant harmony, no discord was allowed. 'You had to suppress everything. Never openly argue, that was the rule.'[17] Inevitably, tensions and frustrations were hidden beneath that gleaming façade.

A photo from 1905 shows George as a well-behaved six-year-old in a sailor suit. In another photo of him dressed up as a sailor, he is holding the Dutch flag. It is 1909 and a princess has been born: Juliana, the future Dutch queen. The Ivenses are resolute royalists.[18]

George was a model son in other regards as well. A childhood friend later reminded him about playing together outdoors: 'The annoying bit was that around four-thirty you'd grab me by the coat and tell me that we had to hurry, because you didn't want to miss Benediction in the church on the Graafseweg... No matter what I said or did, I never talked you out of going to Benediction.'[19] George Ivens remained a faithful churchgoer until late in his teens.

At an early age, he showed technical insight and an enterprising streak that was worthy of his father and grandfather. After witnessing a demonstration flight by the aviator Jan Olieslagers, who took off from a field outside Nijmegen, George decided to build his own flying machine and, with Wim's help, the contraption was parked in their garden just three months later. It didn't fly, but photos show a not unsuccessful half-size replica of a

Blériot. Another three months later, an improved version with a joystick and moving flaps was completed.

In 1911 George was sent to the school his father had attended, the Municipal High School, on the Kronenburgersingel. His mother would have preferred a Catholic school but Ivens family tradition and business interests prevailed. Kees Ivens considered a municipal education superior to a Catholic one because of its broader outlook, and he favored a high school to a Gymnasium because George needed to be prepared for taking over the business. As the oldest, Wim was first in line for the succession, but he had proven such a promising pupil that he had been allowed to go to the Gymnasium, so that he could later go on to university. Without any further ceremony, George was singled out as his father's future successor. He must have been nine or ten when the decision was made to send Wim to the Gymnasium. In his memoirs Joris Ivens wrote that his father had 'always' seen him as his successor and added laconically: 'I accepted the decision without worrying too much. I had a fairly carefree character and, all things considered, it was not an entirely uninteresting future.' In the 1940s, however, he felt very differently and reproached his father for never having considered 'his responsibilities in regard to his children's ages, their rights, personalities and talents.'[20]

As a young boy he was faced with the prospect of bearing a heavy responsibility for his parents and family. He was too young to either resist or grasp the consequences. It must have been a source of self-confidence and, as the chosen successor in a prosperous family, he must have wanted for little, but it was a particular kind of self-confidence, dependent upon his father's approval. George paid for the freedom to do his own things in his spare time by following the prescribed educational path; he was a fidgety foal in a fenced-off field.

George was none too diligent and his results were mediocre. He enjoyed sports the most and he was good at physics, geography, history and Dutch, but regularly failed math, French, German and English.[21] He had little feeling for abstract thinking and preferred spending his time camping, playing soccer or organizing school socials and stage shows. He had inherited the natural exuberance of the Limburgers and the Rhinelanders, people who can always find an excuse for a party. Joris Ivens never lost his taste for the good life, which he expressed in a predilection for good food and pleasant evenings spent drinking with friends.

James Fenimore Cooper's *The Last of the Mohicans* and Indian stories by the German writer Karl May were George's favorite reading, and when the fair came to town he liked to visit Alex Benner's traveling movie theater or

George with his homemade flying machine. In the cockpit, his sister Thea (1911).
EUROPEAN FOUNDATION JORIS IVENS (EFJI)

Jean Desmet's Imperial Bio to see films like A REDSKIN RAID ON A FARM or A REDSKIN'S GOOD HEART. Kees Ivens occasionally asked staff members to film his family and the family also produced the home movie that has gone down in history as Joris Ivens's first film: WIGWAM. The opening title of a copy in the Dutch Film Museum, presumably added by Ivens himself in 1931, gives the shooting date as the spring of 1912 and continues: 'How the fourteen-year-old scout saw Jonkerbosch and Kwakkenberg.' This date was backed up by Thea Ivens, who started school in 1912.[22] Capi instrument maker Piet Rutten operated the camera and Ivens later recalled that the script he had written included close-ups and other technical directions.[23] He was obviously inspired by the cowboy films shown in Nijmegen's theaters.[24] George played the lead role of the good Indian, Flaming Stream, and the whole family joined in, with cocoa-smeared faces where necessary. George caused considerable damage maneuvering a horse through the hall of a house in the Jonkerbosch. Perhaps WIGWAM should primarily be seen as an extension of the Ivens family's much-loved fancy dress parties. George was more interested in the heroic lead than the filming as such. Kees Ivens screened WIGWAM in 1915 during a meeting of the Dutch Amateur Photographers' Association. The script, as he informed the audience, was by

George, 'future member of the Ivens Company', while the Capi managing director had taken charge of the direction himself.[25]

The future member of the Ivens Company showed little interest in photography. Piet Rutten was given the job of familiarizing George with photographic techniques, but never saw him with a camera. He took the odd photo, wrote Ivens himself, but had no creative urges. He never felt the slightest inclination to 'develop a particular sense of composition or framing' and he was never 'tempted by a landscape or a beautiful tree. Never.'[26]

He preferred swimming in the Waal with friends. He was a small, finely built, athletic boy, nicknamed Spunky by his family. Throughout his life, he seldom suffered from a lack of energy. After a soccer injury degenerated into a case of periostitis, his parents forbade him from playing soccer, but he kept on playing in secret. The games were written up in the local paper and legend has it that he first called himself Joris to conceal his identity on the soccer field. But years later Kees Ivens wrote in his diary: 'Joris, to use the name De Jonge first gave him'. Broer de Jonge was one of George's boyhood friends, but his father does not go into detail about the circumstances in which the new name was introduced.[27] By the time George went to university, the name Joris was in common usage among his fellow students, but his parents stuck to George until their deaths.

Long before his high school graduation in 1917, it had been decided that he would go to Rotterdam to study at the Dutch College of Economics in preparation for his future in the photographic trade. Shortly after arriving in that city at the end of the summer vacation, however, he was called up for military service. 'The three brothers didn't all need to join the army. My oldest brother had already started studying medicine and the other one was too young. What's more, I had the strongest constitution, so it was decided that I would do military service in the name of my family.'[28] Holland was neutral, but elsewhere the world war was in full swing. A good part of a generation was being slaughtered on the battlefields of Russia and Western Europe. In the north of France, the battles of Verdun and the Somme alone cost the lives of 1.7 million soldiers. While still at school, Joris Ivens had traced the hostilities on a map with little flags, and military service did not make his existence any more martial. As a former high school student, he was sent to Ede to the Training School for Reserve Officers of the Mounted Artillery. In his official portrait, his uniform, sword, riding boots and leather gloves look impressive, but he still has the eyes of a naive schoolboy. His unit was stationed in North Brabant, close to the Belgian border, where German deserters seeking sanctuary in Holland had to be disarmed. He volunteered for aerial reconnaissance and divided his military service between 'horse riding, maintaining the materiel, and flying over our territory in a bi-plane'. The aircraft was a two-seater: the pilot sat in the front with Ivens be-hind him as observer, spying out the surroundings with binoculars.

The end of the world war brought great social upheaval. As the war pro-gressed, disgust at the bloodshed grew all over Europe, and the Russian and German revolutions had a radicalizing influence on the labor movement and the intelligentsia in Holland. There were food riots and major strikes and, in November 1918, Social Democrat leader Troelstra made his famous call for revolution. Joris Ivens's unit was apparently put on alert, but in the end the task of intervening went to the military police.[29] Joris Ivens scarcely noticed the political turbulence.

After being discharged from the field artillery as a reserve second lieutenant in March 1919, he took a room in downtown Rotterdam at Zwarte Paardenstraat 87a and resumed his studies at the College of Economics. His subjects included the banking, credit and monetary systems but, as at school, Ivens preferred spending his time elsewhere. This time his interests were tennis, rugby and the student associations. He joined the Rotterdam Students' Fraternity. The high-spirited photographer's son was popular and, as a sportsman, partygoer and reserve officer, he must have soon won favor in Rotterdam student circles. He was treasurer of the Rotterdam Stu-dents' Society after six months and within a year he was fraternity chair-man, complete with gavel, white bow-tie and a board member's badge on a ribbon around his neck.

Ivens became friends with another fraternity member, Arthur Müller-Lehning. He too had been sent to the College of Economics so that he could take over his father's business, a textile company in Zeist. A pacifist and ad-vocate of social change, Arthur Lehning was a member of the Theosophical Practical Idealists' Association and also sympathized with the Clarté Move-ment, which the French writer Henri Barbusse had founded in 1919.[30] His political ideas were a major influence on Ivens, especially after the comple-tion of their studies in Rotterdam.

On weekends Joris Ivens regularly returned to Nijmegen, where he one day appeared with his first girlfriend, Welmoedina Welsch or 'Quick'. Quick was blonde, more than two years his junior, and a fellow student in Rotterdam. Ivens considered her beautiful, cheerful and lively, and his sis-ter Thea thought she was great fun.[31] Ivens established what he described as intimate relations with Quick and in Nijmegen there was talk of marriage. But he was Catholic and she was Protestant, and his parents wanted him to promise to have his children baptized. 'Issues like that were completely irrelevant to Quick and me. We made the promise and got back to loving each other.'[32]

After the war, university students all over Europe felt a longing for solidarity and reconciliation. In Holland the need for a national student association was being discussed on all the campuses, including at the Rotterdam Students' Fraternity. Arthur Lehning was a natural proponent of the new association and, under his influence, Joris Ivens became one of the founders of a new local student federation and a board member of the national student organization. But family duties called. In January 1921 he lay down his administrative functions in time to pass his exams, and in July he left the College of Economics with his bachelor's degree in commercial economy. 'By the skin of my teeth', as he described it, 'but that's all you need'. [33] After the summer vacation he left for Berlin to study photographic techniques, the next stop on his way to the board of Capi.

2   Ragmop (1921-1927)

Mass strikes, assassinations by right-wing extremists and the declaration of a state of emergency set the political stage during Joris Ivens's first year of study in Berlin. Germany's defeat and the revolutionary uprising of 'workers and soldiers' in 1918 had plunged the city into turmoil, and the formation of the Weimar Republic had done little to restore order. Rejecting the world of the parents who had failed so miserably, young people experimented with sex and drugs. Dadaists and Expressionists set the tone in the art world. More than just an art movement, Expressionism stood for an exalted awareness of life and the hope that a new, purified, broadminded and cosmopolitan man would arise from the rubble of war. The Expressionists saw the Weimar Republic as a gray democracy, led by excessively moderate politicians who bowed to the interests of the old imperial elite, which was still anchored in the army and judiciary. The chaos of Berlin would put an end to the tidiness of Joris Ivens's life.

In autumn 1921 he began studies at the Technical University in Charlottenburg, where Kees Ivens had studied thirty years earlier. Joris Ivens was twenty-two, he had led student organizations and was an officer in the reserve, but his father still arranged everything. Joris moved in with an elderly couple who lived close to the university on the Am Kniesquare, the present-day Ernst Reuterplatz, and Kees informed his business associates of his son's arrival. Joris visited them dutifully, but his father's acquaintances were unable to talk about anything except lenses and tried to foist their marriageable daughters on him, so he soon abandoned the practice.

The brick building of the Photochemical Institute was located on the sprawling university campus near Bahnhof Zoo. That year there were only five first-year students in photography. Ivens took eight subjects over four semesters, including cinematography with *Geheimrat* Prof. Forch and photochemical practical classes run by Prof. Otto Mente. Head of the institute was *Geheimrat* Prof. Adolf Miethe, an internationally renowned scientist who lectured in Berlin dialect on general photography and introductory photographic optics. Instead of sticking to his professional field, Miethe digressed inspirationally into the philosophy of science and Einstein's theories, and made a profound impression on Ivens. During an excursion to the Sendlinger factory in the suburb of Zehlendorf, Ivens bought a second-class train ticket in order to sit with the professor. Much to the amusement of the other students, the great man himself bought a third-class ticket. Miethe took cocaine and snorted it openly during lectures. The widespread drug use was just one expression of the feverish Berlin atmosphere.

Ivens became 'tremendously confused'. He would stay in bars with the other students until three or four a.m., then end up with a woman in a hotel room or brothel. He became a regular at Club Libelle, got drunk, took cocaine occasionally, and began 'seriously going off the rails'. 'When I went out onto the street the next day, I no longer knew what I was supposed to be doing or where I wanted to go. I got onto the first tram that came along and rode it to the terminus. When I came back I didn't have any money on me. I had spent it all, but I couldn't remember what on.'[1] He had come from a world where everything was organized, and the transition was too much for him. Four years earlier his father was still sending him off to church, now suddenly nothing was certain. 'It is only later that you realize you'd lost your way. It's then that you see that there was no deliberate maliciousness in the things you did or thought,' he wrote.[2]

Amid all the confusion, he was soon suffering most from a lost love, probably Quick, who moved him to write that there was 'a woman I loved and still love terribly', who 'might be leaving' his life, because of the kind of calculation 'our era instills in everyone'. Had Quick's parents insisted that she look for a better match? 'Maybe you see now why I throw myself into everything new – the newness great people and artists feel so intensely, because they break with materialism and insensitivity – things that took away from me the dearest thing I had and can have.' It convinced him that some people needed to hold onto ideals, to 'uphold idealism in the face of everything mechanizing in our bourgeois society', and he felt the 'pure sensation of wanting to be a good person'.[3]

In the spring of 1922 he returned to the parental home in Nijmegen in such a state of confusion that his father advised him to see a psychiatrist, a suggestion he rejected, along with the family doctor's sedatives. He withdrew into himself. He cycled to the woods near Oisterwijk and spent five weeks camping beside what he called the 'Joris Fen'. He described what he did during this therapeutic vacation in his memoirs: 'Exactly the opposite to someone who wants to analyze and understand something that has just happened to him. I had no urge to think things over or read, it was enough for me to come closer to nature, like an animal, and to let myself be carried along by nature and by the elementary sensations it imposes: hunger, thirst, tiredness, sleep.'[4] In time he was able to face the inhabited world again and found comfort with a girl from Rotterdam who was staying at her uncle's in Oisterwijk, nineteen-year-old Miep Balguérie-Guérin. They walked through the woods without saying a word. When a friend of Miep's made remarks about this, Ivens wrote: 'I'm so scared that people will start gossiping about you – and denigrate the genuine pure friendship I feel for you.'[5] She traveled to Italy soon after, and he wrote: 'I would love to know how you feel inside a big, round carriage looking out through big spacious windows at the surrounding countryside. That grand feeling of progressing, the longing to walk to the engine, to take everything into your own hands, twice as fast and further. Shoveling coal into the fire – the people in the train rely on your determination, they're not afraid, they can't be. Don't you ever have that longing?'[6]

He still wasn't his old self and he had not forgotten his lost love. One summer evening in Nijmegen he bumped into a boyhood friend who later wrote to him: 'I found you vastly changed in comparison to the friend I had known so well. You spoke with a soft, rather flat voice, were somewhat depressed, and acted as if all the world's worries were on your shoulders, at least that was my impression. It was like humanity, this humanity, had disappointed your expectations. Knowing you, I realized that that would happen one day, because in your younger years you had a childishly pious belief in the Church and the World, which would inevitably be disappointed one day.'[7]

He returned to Berlin, determined that the chaos would not overwhelm him again. More than fifty years later he would say in an interview: 'You could say that I want to encounter reality... But I'm scared of reality, you have to keep it under control.'[8] He took two first-floor rooms in Schöneberg at Martin Lutherstrasse 42 and began practical training at Goerz, a factory for photographic products.

Balguérie-Guérin hoped for a steadier relationship and made plans to move to Berlin. She had attended a boarding school in Lausanne and was as much of a searching soul as Ivens himself. He compared the two of them to drivers approaching each other in the night: they could sense the person sitting behind the headlights on the other side of the road even though they couldn't see each other. She wrote: 'Joris, do you believe that someone who has lost his way badly a few times can become good again?' He answered: 'Miep, I definitely do believe that, and you should actually ask whether someone who has lost his way a few times can *stay* good.' He was still full of restlessness and afraid of feeling that she was trying to tie him down. 'Because I know very well that feeling bonded would kill something in me.' He warned her that he was dangerous for her, and would ask too much independence of her if she came to Berlin, but she hoped his fears would turn out to be exaggerated and, in the end, he was glad when she did come. But scarcely three weeks later they were eating their farewell dinner at Brechler on the Kurfürstendamm – Balguérie-Guérin wrote 'last meal' on the back of the bill – and she returned to Rotterdam disappointed.

In the following years, she would make accusations and tear up letters, the contact would be broken and, to her joy, Ivens would make renewed efforts to reestablish it, because he valued their friendship so highly – until the final, angry parting of the ways in 1927. Although Miep Balguérie-Guérin married three times, she burnt all her husbands' letters and only kept the ones from Joris Ivens. He would marry four times, with a fifth wedding called off at the last moment.

He was convinced that people considered him strange and eccentric. It was a time 'in which I felt misunderstood and thought that everyone else was hard. Almost as if I were playing the martyr for myself.'[9] The loneliness was, however, soon alleviated. During his first year of study, he had bumped into his clever but perpetually-frowning friend Arthur Lehning in the Schauspielhaus, where Max Reinhardt's company was performing Strindberg's *A Dream Play*. To Lehning's amazement, the former fraternity chairman was wearing a black pullover. Lehning was only visiting Berlin, but their friendship revived in September 1922, when he moved there with his girlfriend Annie Grimmer. Ivens became a regular dinner guest at their apartment on the Schaperstrasse and occasionally borrowed a shirt. Arthur Lehning was studying at Friedrich Wilhelm University and working at the publisher Die Schmiede, where he made numerous contacts in the Berlin art scene. He had become an anarchist, and in Berlin he met renowned Russian kindred spirits such as Alexander Berkman, Emma Goldman, Alexander Shapiro and Gregori Maximov.

Hendrik Marsman, who went on to become a leading Dutch poet, also spent a long time in Berlin in 1922 and 1923. Ivens met him through Lehning, who had been friends with Marsman since primary school. Rejecting any borders beyond those of the cosmos, the poet declared: 'Truly, the new, vast optimism has leapt upon us, we experience the vitality, the dynamism, the excitement, we believe in the juices of the earth, the pregnancy of nights, in the flaming seed.'[10] Marsman himself did not adhere to this philosophy of life for all too long, but in a sense Ivens remained true to it his whole life. Even later, after becoming a confirmed Communist, he still retained something of the 'vitalistic', adventurous nomad.

The friends plunged into the nocturnal world of entertainment and culture: bars, theaters, galleries and clubs. There was plenty of choice: on one particular evening there might be a play directed by Max Reinhardt, another by Erwin Piscator – with a set by a famous Expressionist painter – and a revue in the Apollo Theater – where naked women on the stage demonstrated the arrival of a new era. The motion-picture theaters showed films by Wiene and Murnau, and the notorious gallery Der Sturm – always willing to display new extravagances – exhibited the latest fruits of the Dadaists and Expressionists' fertile imaginations.

Ivens was open to all that was new. He read Einstein, Freud, Bakunin, Marx, and Lenin, albeit relatively superficially. He read a few of Marx's pamphlets, but found *Das Kapital* too theoretical, and when others claimed to have read it, he only half believed them.[11] His friends were unanimous, Ivens was never very inclined toward intellectual reflection; his view of the world was practical and intuitive. His first political reading was not Marx, but the works of the nineteenth-century anarchist Mikhail Bakunin. Influenced by his Russian friends, Arthur Lehning had become a great admirer of Bakunin, and he undoubtedly recommended him to Ivens. Ivens and Lehning even discussed plans to found a publishing house to publish Bakunin's works and a magazine inspired by *Die Aktion*, a cultural and political magazine Franz Pfemfert had founded in 1911. By the early twenties, *Die Aktion*, a platform for Expressionist thought, was attempting to establish links with radical Communists, anarchists and other groups to the left of the Communist party.[12] Presumably Lehning and Ivens also intended to publish misunderstood poets, because Lehning was also involved in Marsman's self-publication of his first volume, *Verzen.*

At a party at Arthur Lehning and Annie Grimmer's in the spring of 1923, Ivens met a small, rather sloppily dressed woman with black wiry hair and a somewhat coarse, round face. Her name was Germaine Krull. He was not very large himself, but his relatively powerful build, gentle open face, brown eyes and wavy dark-brown hair appealed enormously to Germaine. Like his friends, he generally wore a suit with a white shirt and tie. The two of them clicked at once and a great all-consuming love began. Ivens's new girlfriend was very different from Balguérie-Guérin, who had needed to ask her parents' permission to go to Berlin. Krull was twenty-five, a year older than Ivens, and had lead an adventurous life in a world whose existence he did not even suspect. Whereas Ivens still had to move toward Communism, she had already become a dissident.

Luise Germaine Krull was born on November 29, 1897 in Wilna, which lay in German Posen at the time of the birth and in Polish Poznan after World War I. Her father was an engineer. Soon after her birth, the family moved to Paris, and then later to Munich. In 1917 Germaine completed her training at the Munich Photographic School and Research Institute and opened a photographer's studio. Towards the end of World War I, she became active in a group of left-wing Social Democrats in Munich that was centered on the writer and journalist Kurt Eisner, who became president of the Bavarian revolutionary republic in 1918. Eisner was murdered by a royalist officer in February 1919. According to police reports, Germaine worked as a Communist party courier between Munich and Berlin, but she

Joris Ivens and Germaine Krull PHOTO GERMAINE KRULL, EFJI

soon rejected the party in favor of a group of radical leftist dissidents led by her lover, the economy student Samuel ('Mila') Levit. After the Reichswehr drowned the Munich uprising in blood, Germaine helped a number of revolutionaries escape to Austria, and warrants were issued for the arrest of her and her mother. She was tried on charges of rendering aid to fugitives early in 1920. Although acquitted, she was deported from Bavaria soon after. Levit was sentenced to fifteen months' imprisonment for using false papers.[13]

In 1921 Germaine Krull went to Soviet Russia with Mila Levit. As members of the 'opposition' they were in trouble with the police from the moment of their arrival. Levit soon became disillusioned with the Soviet experiment and described the Russian Revolution as 'even worse than capitalism'. He was invited to serve as a translator at the Third Congress of the Communist International in Moscow, but on their arrival in the city both he and Germaine were arrested and imprisoned in the Lubyanka, the security forces building. Germaine was led to the interrogation room at gunpoint. 'Do you think your ideas are better than those of Comrade Lenin? Do you think we need your help?' was the only explanation she was given. After a while they were released. Levit was given an exit visa and a distraught Krull was left behind in Moscow. It turned out later that Levit had promised to have nothing more to do with politics, and from that moment she considered him a traitor. After she declared during a subsequent interrogation that the Communist party leadership had betrayed the Munich Revolution, she was deported from Russia as a 'counterrevolutionary of the left'. In Berlin two friends from Munich took her under their wing, Fritz Pollock and Max Horkheimer, later co-founders of the Frankfurt School.[14]

When Ivens met her, Krull was working at a photo studio in the Kurfürstendamm. In May 1923 they spent the Whitsun vacation together at Krummhübel in the Giant Mountains, on the current Polish-Czech border, and from then on they were inseparable. Germaine called Ivens 'Hoi Hoi' – what they had said to each other upon first meeting – and her nickname since Munich had been 'Zottl', Ragmop. Despite the playful pet names, it was no easy relationship. Ivens described her as unstable and oversensitive, ebullient phases alternating unpredictably with bouts of depression. Germaine wrote: 'I felt strangely attracted towards him. The simple way he looked at things won my trust. I told him everything. I had such a need to talk! And he listened to me. I told him about my great love for Mila, our struggle for the working class, Russia, prison... Joris listened, not saying a word, but holding my hand. I could feel his empathy for me.'[15] She became friends with Marsman as well, and her depressive moods are reflected in her letters to him. 'Your affectionate rascal has so many damn worries, they've made her all sick! – Thanks for your book, I'm so alone and cried out and burnt out that I can't write a thing.' According to Ivens she was obsessed with death and suicide, and marked by her experiences in Russia. He was her savior and protector: 'She leans on me and I draw her toward me.'[16]

Germaine combined a vulnerable nature with a life experience that was almost beyond his grasp. She knew more about all the things that had confused him so much. She was his 'introduction to revolution, art and life'. With Germaine he discovered love. 'I mean that extraordinary relationship between two creatures, an erotic and sexual relationship, of course, but also a deeper one, characterized by a sensitivity you recognize and share, with the feeling, so uncommon and moving, that you are discovering the world and rebuilding it together. A relationship in which your ideas, taste, passions and hope suddenly surface and miraculously merge with the other person's ideas, taste, passions and hope. I can readily say that I was a complete stranger to all of this. Germaine opened up this new universe for me.'[17]

She knew a lot of people and introduced him to her friends in the Romanische Café, a quasi-Romanesque building opposite the Gedächtniskirche. The Expressionists had their own table to the right of the entrance and the chess players sat on the balcony; at the time it was the most important meeting place for Berlin artists and intellectuals. Germaine's old acquaintances from the days of the Munich Revolution also came here, at least when they weren't in prison.

In late 1922 the French decided that Germany was failing to meet the enormous reparations that had been imposed after World War I. As a punitive measure, they occupied the Ruhr in January 1923, again wounding German national pride. The mark had been gradually declining in value, but now it began falling at a dizzying rate and society rapidly polarized. Faith in the government plummeted with the currency. Support for extreme right-wing groups increased and the German Communist party, the KPD, gained tens of thousands of new members. Strikes, demonstrations and unemployment riots broke out all over the country. On June 3 the Berlin Communists organized a major demonstration against the extreme right. Soon after, they declared that civil war was unavoidable, and in August a general strike in Berlin brought down the government. In October the KPD was preparing an armed insurrection, but this was cancelled at the last minute, and a month later the party was banned. Around the same time Hitler's beer hall putsch failed in Munich. Finally, at the end of December, monetary reform stopped the devaluation of the mark, and the threat from radicals from both sides of the political spectrum subsided.

Germaine Krull and Arthur Lehning coaxed Joris Ivens along to demonstrations where he soon concluded that their political ideas were beautiful but very unpractical. 'My anarchist friends said: Lenin betrayed the revolution, Bakunin was the greatest writer, anarchists are being executed in the Soviet Union.' Perhaps, but compared to their chaotic and impulsive behavior, he found that the Communists 'acted methodically and efficiently' during confrontations on the street.[18] They took a clear line at least, and were practical and effective. And so, almost without noticing, he switched from a permissive, Expressionist attitude to power politics and the logic of Communism. For now, he only thought it applicable to nations in crisis, like Germany, and not to orderly countries like France or Holland. This explains why, after returning to Holland, he did not feel any inconsistency in writing to the anarchist Lehning with proposals for their mutual publishing house.[19]

Ivens did not suffer a bit from the inflation in Berlin. His hard guilders were worth more and more, and by late 1923 one guilder could be exchanged for a billion marks. Food was a more valuable medium of exchange than banknotes, wealthy foreigners bought entire streets in Berlin for next to nothing, and the rent of Ivens's own one-bedroom apartment shrunk to a symbolic amount. Thanks to his guilders, he no longer needed to book for the theater, he simply showed up at the last moment and took the most expensive seats. One of Germaine's friends went to Amsterdam to work in a cabaret, and on her return exchange rates were so favorable she was able to buy a farm, complete with stock. In their affluence, Lehning and Ivens organized a party and, in perfect keeping with the prevailing sense of doom, called it 'Europe's last party'. The guests included the poets Alfred Wolfenstein and Johannes R. Becher and well-known Expressionist writers like Rudolf Leonhard, author of the aphorism: 'Poetry can only be extravagant, because poetry begins with the superlative'.[20] Becher joined the Communist party around this time, and when Ivens met him again after World War II he was the East German Minister of Culture.

In December 1923 the stabilization of the mark brought an end to the good life. In his autobiography *The Camera and I*, Ivens later made a cryptic remark about this: 'My financial situation became very tight and I had to leave the University.'[21] But his father paid for his education. Had he raced through his money too quickly after all? Or was he no longer interested in his studies? After four semesters at the university, he had already qualified for a certificate. He didn't really need an engineering degree, since he was only doing the course as preparation for the photographic trade.[22]

At the start of 1924 he did practical training at Ica and Ernemann in Dresden, two factories for photographic and film equipment which welcomed the son of a good Dutch customer with open arms. In the cinematic research laboratory of Professor E. Goldberg, inventor of the 35mm Ica Kinamo hand-held camera, which had been on the market since 1921, he was given a thorough grounding in this camera's construction. This stood him in good stead later as a filmmaker and ardent Kinamo user. At Ernemann he was on a workbench for projectors and carbon lamps.

He felt isolated in Dresden, 'that's putting it mildly... It was such a big change for me, such a different world, that I didn't establish contact with anyone.'[23] Dresden was the center of red Saxony, a stronghold of the workers' movement. In October 1923 a revolutionary government of Communists and Social Democrats even held power there for ten days, until the central authorities in Berlin sent the Reichswehr to put down the insurrection. Towards the end of these disturbances, the workers in his factory took Ivens to a demonstration for higher wages where the police opened fire on the crowd, an event that made a great impression on him. Communists asked him to take a film about a demonstration from Breslau to Berlin; since the party had been banned, foreigners made safer couriers. With a first-class train ticket and his Dutch passport in his pocket, Ivens made several of these journeys.[24] He rounded off this period of approximately six months of training in the lens-making workshop at Zeiss-Jena.

Ivens and Krull spent the summer in Holland. They stayed in Nijmegen, where Germaine's presence almost led to a conflict between father and son. She wrote to Marsman: 'His father lives in a very latent state of war with me and I have to make sure that Hoi Hoi doesn't lose his temper.'[25] The messy revolutionary didn't appeal to Kees Ivens at all, and Joris's seventeen-year-old sister Thea was similarly unenthusiastic about big brother's new love, even if deeply impressed by Germaine's black lingerie.[26] His mother was more tolerant. 'I don't mind if you go and sleep with her in the guest room, but there is no need to let people know,' she said. The couple later set up house outside the city in the family's wooden country home.

Joris Ivens remained true to the family business, despite his belief that young people 'have to surrender material things to achieve their ideals. If they don't, they live in agreement with 'Dad and Mom'... if they don't rebel, they lack the new creative insight, and don't deserve a different life that rises above the same old rut of their parents' lives.'[27] He started at Capi Nijmegen and, in the autumn of 1924, after familiarizing himself with the working methods there, was made head of the technical department and branch manager of the Capi at Kalverstraat 115 in Amsterdam. His father wrote an enthusiastic letter to friends in the Dutch East Indies: 'There is no question of me withdrawing from the business. On the contrary. Now that we have George, I can really get down to things. Hopefully, we are heading for a period in which all fields will flourish and pick up.'[28] His son moved into a room at Amstel 190, a grand house with a double staircase leading up to the front door and large windows with a view out over the river Amstel. Germaine returned to Berlin at the end of the summer, but in 1925 she rejoined him in the room on the Amstel.

At night they went off into the city in search of the worldly atmosphere of Berlin. With Hendrik Marsman, painter Charley Toorop, writer Jan Slauerhoff and others, they spent whole evenings debating the world in the bars around the Leidseplein: starting at the Art Deco bar of the Hotel Americain or the traditional Dutch bar of Café Reynders, then moving on to the artists' club De Kring, where they stayed until three or four a.m. In the bleary-eyed mornings, Ivens hurried to the Kalverstraat. The store was his father's pride: in 1916 Kees Ivens had commissioned a number of leading Symbolist and Art Nouveau artists to turn the store into a *Gesamtkunstwerk*. With its stained glass overhead lights, murals, carvings and Art Nouveau frontage, the building was a genuine monument, albeit one that fell prey to modernization after World War II. In these first years Ivens took his work extremely seriously. He wrote about amateur photography for several magazines and in 1928 he joined the staff of the magazine *Het Lichtbeeld*. He gave a lecture at the Hague International Exhibition of April-May 1928 and was twice nominated for a lectureship in photography at Technical University Delft, a post which was finally left unfilled.[29]

The Berlin publishing house project with Arthur Lehning had shrunk to a plan to publish a magazine, and in the first half of 1926 Lehning, who now lived in Paris, came to Amsterdam to discuss this with his friend. Early in 1927, however, he launched the *Internationale Revue i10* alone, apparently because Ivens was too busy with Capi.[30] In retrospect this avoided a great deal of unpleasantness, because Lehning didn't want any Communist editors and Ivens developed in just that abhorrent direction soon afterwards.[31] A few years later they were so alienated from each other politically that they broke off contact without further ado. When they met again as old men in the 1980s, their only subject of conversation was how best to preserve their personal archives for posterity. The prominent modern Dutch architect J.J.P. Oud joined *i10* as architecture editor, composer Willem Pijper was responsible for music, and Laszlo Moholy-Nagy covered photography and film. An impressive number of leading modern artists from all over Europe participated in this unique magazine.

In Amsterdam Germaine Krull took semi-abstract photos of harbor machinery, and these were published a few years later in her photography book *Métal*. But Holland was too small for her ambitions and in 1925 she moved on to Paris. She rented an attic in Montmartre and Ivens began commuting between Amsterdam and Paris, sometimes even flying, a means of transport that really was reserved for the elite in those days.

Krull met Sonia and Robert Delaunay, the celebrated Parisian husband and wife painters, who introduced her to the Paris art scene. Within no time she was photographer to the fashion houses of Lanvin, Lelong and Poiret, even though she still attached more importance to her experimental photos of metal constructions, which Robert Delaunay exhibited with his own work. On publication, *Métal* was welcomed as an important contribution to modern art. Krull became the star photographer of the illustrated magazine *Vu*, produced photo novels, and did commercial advertising for Peugeot.[32] When Belgian cineaste Henri Storck met her in Paris in the early thirties, Ragmop had metamorphosed into 'a scintillating person, elegantly dressed, with many friends, a star'. Dutch writer and composer Lou Lichtveld viewed her with less sympathy. He stayed with Ivens at Krull's home on the Boulevard Saint-Michel in 1931 and found her 'a frightening woman. She knew exactly what she wanted, no nonsense. A spider that gobbles up males after mating.'[33]

At first her departure for the French capital seemed to change little in their relationship. Although they had not married, she had stationery printed with the name Germaine Krull-Ivens and the addresses '78 bis Rue de Maistre' and 'Amstel 190'. But estrangement was imminent. In October 1926 Germaine wrote to Marsman asking her 'sweet pony' to drop in on Hoi Hoi, who was all alone. In spring of the next year her tone became more emphatic: 'Go straight to Hoi Hoi – he needs you badly. He doesn't have anyone to talk to apart from you. Please. It's just awful and I can't help him. You understood me when we spoke. I can't act any other way. I'm in love with someone and Hoi Hoi is suffering terribly because of it, me too, and so is the other person.' She had told Joris everything and complained that it was hard 'knowing that the person who is dearest to you suddenly doesn't understand and tries not to feel', possibly suggesting that she had been thinking of a three-way relationship. She gave notice of her arrival in Amsterdam and asked Marsman to be present during her conversation with Ivens.[34]

Who was 'the other person'? In her memoirs Krull wrote: 'I had never loved a woman before but I was tremendously happy with Elsa and she felt happy as well. Were we lesbians?' But Elsa left Paris and Germaine never saw her again. A brief but tumultuous affair with a man followed – 'I was like a bird hypnotized by a snake' – after which she met Eli Lotar, a handsome youth with a Greek profile, black eyes and such a gentle expression that 'it almost hurt to look at him'. Lotar was a Jewish Rumanian who began as her photographic assistant and was soon promoted to lover. 'I knew that Joris was much better. I could have kicked myself, but my senses were too strong.' Ivens came to Paris and quarreled violently with Lotar – a very unusual experience for Ivens – but they settled their differences relatively quickly.[35] Eli Lotar later worked as a cameraman for Ivens and for Luis Buñuel.

On April 2, 1927, with emotions running high and their relationship about to end, Joris Ivens and Germaine Krull married in the town hall of the Eighteenth Arrondissement in Paris.[36] Krull's insecure status – due to the changes in the borders around her birthplace – had caused legal problems and the marriage entitled her to a Dutch passport. In his memoirs Joris Ivens described it heroically: 'From my perspective I had left my life with Germaine far behind me, but now she was Dutch.' Within a week of the wedding, Krull had already sent a thank you note to Marsman for being so quick to lend the bridegroom moral support at his home on the Amstel. On May 21 she wrote that it 'was going terribly with Joris. He won't and can't understand and I'm despairing.' In a letter to Marsman dated July 11, she concluded: 'Joris was here for a few days and I don't think it's brought him one step further.'[37]

Ivens had lost one great love in Berlin and now it had happened to him again; another reason to be careful about establishing strong personal ties.

Perhaps one of the attractive sides of his relationship with Krull had been the fact that they had been apart for more than half of the time: he was in Dresden or Jena while she was in Berlin, she was in Berlin or Paris while he was in Amsterdam. At any rate, events in his subsequent relationships proved that geographic distance suited Joris Ivens's needs.

Ivens's life was becoming increasingly inconsistent with the career his father had mapped out for him. The free atmosphere of Berlin, the friends with artistic ambitions and outspoken political ideas, Germaine Krull's unconstrained lifestyle, all these experiences had left their mark and stimulated his urge for independence. Although he continued to faithfully fulfil his duties to the family business, he began straying from the preordained path.

3 A Time of Daily Discoveries (1927-1929)

After making WIGWAM under his father's direction, many years passed without Joris Ivens giving any sign of a particular interest in cinema. In Berlin he was a regular patron of the motion-picture theaters, but this was just part of a broad interest in the city's overwhelming cultural life. Presumably, his frequent theater visits continued in Amsterdam. He definitely saw VARIETY by the German filmmaker E.A. Dupont in spring 1926, because Marsman's poem 'Salto Mortale' was inspired by their discussion of the film.[1] Dutch artists, writers and architects were fascinated by the medium's phenomenal artistic potential. It was an inexhaustible topic of discussion in the bars on the Leidseplein and in De Kring, and Ivens was swept up in the general enthusiasm.

After the Lumière brothers' first cinematic demonstration in 1895, film rapidly became a standard carnival attraction. In these inauspicious surroundings the medium developed, and in certain circles there was a growing belief that motion pictures could be more than mere entertainment and were worthy of a place in the realm of high culture. At the same time the avant-garde movement, which had been active in all fields of artistic endeavor, also turned to the cinema. The international cinematic avant-garde of the 1920s lived in a whirl of excitement and daily discoveries. Joris Ivens and his friends felt the attraction of the avant-garde. They believed in films that did not set out to depict reality, let alone tell a cheap romantic story, but instead created a world of their own through rhythm and movement, qualities they believed to be the essential characteristics of the medium. They did not want anything to do with movies designed to entertain the populace.

Postwar Berlin was a center for compulsive innovation in all fields. Film audiences were astounded by Expressionist works like Friedrich Murnau's NOSFERATU, Fritz Lang's BETWEEN TWO WORLDS and Robert Wiene's THE CABINET OF DR. CALIGARI, with its malevolent doctor adrift in an uninhibitedly fantastic set. In the mid-twenties a new generation of Soviet filmmakers emerged. One of them, Lev Kuleshov, discovered the 'Kuleshov effect'. In a famous experiment, he juxtaposed a shot of the actor Mozzhukhin's face with shots of a bowl of soup, a dead woman and a girl at play. It was always the same shot of the actor, but the audience was impressed by how powerfully Mozzhukhin was able to express peace, grief, and joy. In short, the meaning of a shot could be changed completely by combining it with another shot, and images could be manipulated at will at the editing bench. The Soviet filmmakers concluded that editing was the essence of cinema.

Armed with this vision and an unbridled revolutionary zeal, Sergei Eisenstein made STRIKE in 1924 and, one year later, THE BATTLESHIP POTEMKIN, about the 1905 uprising of the sailors of Russia's Black Sea Fleet. While Eisenstein based his work on ideas and crowds, Vsevolod Pudovkin worked on his audiences' emotions by concentrating on individual heroes. In 1926 he completed MOTHER, based on Maxim Gorki's novel with the same title, a moving account of the tragic experiences of a working-class woman. In the Ukraine, cinematic poet Alexander Dovzhenko was making his masterpieces ZVENIGORA (1928) and ARSENAL (1929). As an alternative to these fiction films, generally based on themes drawn from the history of the revolution, Dziga Vertov advocated pure documentary that showed reality as it was, at least according to its maker. His CINEMA EYE came out in 1924; several years later THE MAN WITH THE CAMERA was released. These incredibly creative works from the Soviet Union shook audiences in theaters and projection rooms all over Europe, often at private viewings for film lovers, because Western authorities regularly banned Soviet films as revolutionary propaganda.

German Expressionism was as good as dead and Neue Sachlichkeit was the new trend in Berlin. Besides a number of abstract films, its primary cinematic expression was Walter Ruttmann's BERLIN, SYMPHONY OF A BIG CITY (1927), a documentary study of motion with impressions from twenty-four hours in the life of the city. In Paris, cinema was influenced by Surrealism and its associations with the subconscious. The Spaniards Luis Buñuel and Salvador Dali showed the provocative UN CHIEN ANDALOU and, according to Buñuel, the first screenings were responsible for two miscarriages, which is quite possible, because the famous sequence in which editing creates the illusion of a living person's eyeball being sliced open is only one of the film's hair-raising images. The greatest French pioneer of cinematic technique was Abel Gance, whose NAPOLEON (1927) included spectacular experimentation with camera movement and editing.

In the United States, Hollywood had developed into the world capital of the popular movie, although the dividing line between popular films and real cinematic art was nothing if not vague. Even D.W. Griffith, maker of the highly praised BIRTH OF A NATION, was a Hollywood man. The unrivalled Charles Chaplin made his films there, and even the most inveterate Hollywood haters were unable to deny his genius. Elsewhere in America, one-man-band Robert Flaherty was pioneering the documentary. His first film, NANOOK OF THE NORTH (1922), about the lives of Canadian Eskimos, remained a documentary benchmark for decades.

The Dutch premiere of Eisenstein's THE BATTLESHIP POTEMKIN in an Amsterdam theater in September 1926 was an unimaginable sensation. People left the auditorium in tears and film critic Mannus Franken wrote: 'Here a tension is evoked that goes far beyond the false entertainment that is usually presented in motion-picture theaters, here a man is speaking who – in his own imagery, with his own expressions and at his own pace – says something that cannot be misunderstood. I still remember the impression the film made on me... The tension was so great that I had to leave the theater halfway through the film. It wasn't until the third viewing that I succeeded in watching the film through to the end.'[2]

One of the first film reviewers to expressly see his task as art criticism was L.J. Jordaan, political cartoonist and one of the editors of the weekly *De Groene Amsterdammer*. His supporters included four of the editors of the student magazine *Propria Cures*: art students Henrik Scholte, Menno ter Braak and Dick Binnendijk, and law student Hans Ivens, younger brother of Joris, who had contact with the group through him. Ter Braak had already written to Jordaan with the proposal to put together a catcall squad to express their disapproval in the theaters when bad films were shown,[3] but this was too disreputable for Jordaan's taste, and in 1927 they began developing more substantial ideas to advance the cause of avant-garde cinema.

Early in May of that year, the friends watched Pudovkin's MOTHER at a private viewing. The film had just been banned by the mayors of the main Dutch cities, but Scholte wrote in his diary: 'This is without a doubt the best film I have ever seen. What does the Soviet propaganda matter?' They decided to defy the ban by screening the film at De Kring, and Scholte proposed 'founding an association to enable us to show all kinds of banned films or strongly avant-garde products for a select audience'. His friends agreed and on that very day, May 11, 1927, they decided during a meeting in Café Americain to found the 'Amsterdam Filmliga'. The entry in Scholte's diary for that day also states: 'Americain and De Kring have been on edge for the past few days because of the sensational airplane flight from New York to Paris', a reference to Charles Lindbergh's transatlantic flight.[4]

Joris Ivens was not present at the gathering in Americain, but on the night of May 13 he served as projectionist for a showing of MOTHER. The film was preceded by a speech by Scholte launching the new Filmliga. The idea of the Filmliga was greeted enthusiastically by writers, artists and architects, and the Filmliga developed into a national organization with several thousand members.

A few days after the so-called 'night of MOTHER', a provisional Filmliga board was formed. In addition to Scholte, Ter Braak and Hans Ivens, the board members included Jordaan, painter Charley Toorop, actor Hans van Meerten and Joris Ivens. That same day Scholte presented his oft-quoted manifesto: 'Once in a hundred times we see cinema, the rest of the time we see movies. The herd, the commercial regimen, America, kitsch. At this juncture, cinema and movies are natural opponents. Our belief in pure, autonomous cinema, in film as art and as a future, is pointless unless we take matters into our own hands.' [5]

'I have to confess that I was one of the most orthodox members. In my eyes the manifesto was as precious as the Bible,' wrote Ivens.[6] In theoretical issues, he was more a follower than a leader. He never forgot the Filmliga's conviction that a filmmaker should be an Artist before all else, and decades later he still took it very seriously when someone suggested that one of his films might not be a real work of art.

Despite being one of the five editors of the magazine *Filmliga*, Ivens only wrote seven articles in four years, several of which were less than a page long. The editorial board confronted the outside world with fierce polemics and passionate debate, convinced as they were that they were living 'in a time of crisis, when new insights were doing battle with routine and tradition. Making noises of level-headed wisdom would have been both meaningless and ineffectual,' as Jordaan wrote later.[7]

While the intellectuals published profound essays, Ivens's involvement with the Filmliga was more practical. In spring 1927 he had moved from the Amstel to an attic at Damrak 46, opposite the stock exchange. The room was up under the roof beams and sparsely furnished, the walls were hung with enormous film posters. Ivens founded a modest library there for Filmliga members. He and distributor and Filmligamember Ed. Pelster arranged the Filmliga film acquisitions, and Capi's third floor projection room in the Kalverstraat virtually became a branch of the organization. The board members met there to subject film after film to their critical appraisal. In his enthusiasm Ivens drew Capi employees into the Filmliga activities. Correspondence clerk Helene van Dongen was entrusted with the Filmliga's international communications. She also translated the introductory speeches visiting foreign filmmakers gave when showing their films, and sometimes operated the Ernemann projectors during board meetings. Salesman Joop Huisken peddled the *Filmliga* magazine, which also published an acknowledgement of the assistance of Capi staff in dispatching the films.

Ivens's work for the Filmliga had a very enjoyable side because as 'First Technical Officer' he made the most trips abroad.[8] Largely thanks to his efforts, many leading figures in the international film world visited the Filmliga in the late twenties. Filmmakers Walter Ruttmann, Hans Richter, Germaine Dulac, René Clair, Alberto Cavalcanti, Sergei Eisenstein and Vsevolod Pudovkin did the ritual rounds: starting with welcoming drinks at the Schiller Hotel on the Rembrandtplein, proceeding to the Capi projection room, putting in an appearance at the Filmliga screening on Saturday afternoon, visiting De Kring in the evening, seeing the canals, the new Plan South housing development and the monumental Tuschinski motion-picture theater, then ending with a farewell at Central Station. The enthusiasm in the Filmliga and numerous stimulating encounters in various European capitals encouraged Ivens to plunge into filmmaking himself. His library included theoretical works on cinema and, with his characteristic drive, he began studying films at the editing bench. In a *Filmliga* article he described a scene in MOTHER: 'This street battle is constructed along strictly mathematical lines: one movement to the right (running horses, duration 1 second); one movement to the left (saber cut, duration 1 second); one movement directly toward the camera (a person falling forwards, duration 1/2 second), etc.'[9] He tried to uncover the principles the great filmmakers had developed for shooting and editing. With a psychiatrist, he discussed the emotional effect of movements from left to right in comparison to movements from right to left. He wondered whether Chinese viewers, who read downwards from the top of the page, would be similarly affected. His conclusions on this point were not saved for posterity.[10]

Later Ivens could not remember when he began filming, but it must have been earlier than is generally accepted. The first datable attempt at a film – after WIGWAM and some unambitious home movies – is mentioned in Henrik Scholte's diary, in the entry of May 16, 1927, three days after 'the night of MOTHER'. Scholte notes Ivens's intentions of making a film with Charlotte Köhler as the female lead. Köhler, a former girlfriend of Scholte's, had already had a minor role in the German film MANON LASCAUT and was on her way to becoming one of Holland's greatest stage actresses. Later that month Scholte wrote about Ivens's 'serious and reliable plans' to 'compose a Dutch avant-garde film' based on a script by Marsman, in which Charlotte Köhler would play the 'young role'. Together with Köhler and several others, Scholte went to Capi on Saturday May 28 to view the test shots. They were not disappointed: 'Despite all kinds of mistakes in the direction, camera work, make-up etc., it was still a complete success for Lottie. Her film presence was extremely expressive. In her movement, and especially with her plain but intense face, she has proven herself 'photogenic' in every way. Joris Ivens was very serious and will now definitely persevere.'[11]

More than six months before starting on well-known films such as THE BRIDGE and RAIN, Ivens had already taken the first steps in the production of a fiction film. The script Scholte was referring to was probably based on Marsman's 1923 prose poem 'The Flying Dutchman'.[12] The production does not seem to have proceeded any further, but Ivens continued to speak of his plans to film 'The Flying Dutchman' into the early thirties, and returned to the idea in the late fifties, when once again the project did not go beyond the planning stage.

Prior to his shots of Charlotte Köhler, Ivens had already done some technical film studies as part of his work at Capi, and in 1927 he also shot the lost footage[13] known as FILMSTUDY ZEEDIJK, which was not actually filmed in the Zeedijk, but around the corner in Heyens's boarding-house at Oudezijds Voorburgwal 8. 'The bar was deserted, or as good as deserted, the few men sitting at the tables hardly looked up when I came in, there was an intense atmosphere and the light was beautiful,' mused Ivens later. Piet Kruijff, the landlady's grandson, remembered it differently. Ivens pointed his camera at Piet, his brother and his two sisters, 'but he was mainly interested in the girls, very pretty fashionable girls, about twenty or twenty-two years old. They had to walk back and forth for a while. Up and down the stairs.' Ivens himself called these unedited shots his first film. In the eighties he attached quite a bit of importance to this 'emotional and intuitive' piece of work, but this could be seen as mythologizing. At the time he considered the shots 'less appropriate for public screening: they serve as study material.'[14]

Menno ter Braak described another lost short: 'A simple, didactic, documentary account of the laying of a road: that was Ivens's film debut.'[15] The fledgling filmmaker is known to have filmed paviors in Amsterdam. The estate of writer Jef Last included a notebook of film scripts, including one for a children's film entitled 'Die Strasze' – presumably with an eye to German publication – which explained that streets did not appear out of thin air, but were the product of workers' labor. 'Filmed in part by G. Ivens,' is written beneath the script. Had Ter Braak only seen this 'part', or was there a completed film of Last's script, ending with the declaration: 'Worker and child shake hands'?[16]

At the time Ivens's political sympathies were still in a state of flux. Together with artist and flamboyant Mussolini-devotee Erich Wichman he worked on a film called THE SICK CITY. They actually shot part of this film, but the footage has been lost. Wichman's scenario reserved the leading roles for Wichman and Ivens themselves and in the film they wandered disparagingly through Amsterdam pointing out signs of decay, among them the new buildings erected by the socialist municipal administration. According to THE SICK CITY, the solution to Amsterdam's problems could be found in the brochure *Voor afbraak* ('Destroy') by anti-democrat Robert Groeninx van Zoelen, who agitated against 'national decay'. Wichman was not the only Dutch artist to feel the attraction of Fascism in the twenties. In Italy Marinetti's Futurism had proven highly compatible with the politics of the far right. Dutch artists were more attracted by the longing for a 'grandiose and gripping' life, than by Mussolini's political theories. Marsman too had sympathized for a time with Fascism. The great separation of the minds on the extremes of the political spectrum did not take place in Holland until 1928-1929, when Ivens too became organized, on the side of the Communists.[17]

In late 1927 and early 1928, Joris Ivens and actor Hans van Meerten made an in-depth study of what they called the 'first-person film', but which is usually referred to as subjective camera. In an article for *Filmliga* Van Meerten optimistically announced 'a new era', in which the camera would no longer be outside the action of the film but would become an actor itself, and not just incidentally, but consistently throughout the whole film. Ivens backed him unreservedly and pressured his fellow editors to print the article in its entirety to give 'Van Meerten a kind of moral patent on his idea.'[18]

A striking example of their method was a shot they made of the drinking of a glass of beer. Looking into the glass, the camera observes the beer level sink slowly until the interior of the bar becomes visible through the bottom of the glass: the camera takes the place of the beer drinker. Although Van Meerten believed that 'up to now no one in the avant-garde centers has seen the potential of the 'first-person film', Abel Gance had experimented with the subjective camera as early as 1915, Dupont's VARIETY included shots showing the world through the eyes of a trapeze artist, and Dziga Vertov had also experimented with the subjective camera. Van Meerten's proposal of maintaining this point of view through an entire film had doubtlessly been considered by others as well. There was however little enthusiasm for applying the method with such rigor. Viewers would eventually want to see the person whose eyes the camera was looking through. In 1946 Robert Montgomery directed LADY IN THE LAKE, a film in which he sustained the subjective camera from start to finish, but even he cribbed by showing the main character, played by Montgomery himself, looking in the mirror.

Ivens and Van Meerten thought that the similarity between eye and camera could be further perfected if the camera followed the jiggling movement the eye naturally makes when walking. The young investigators constructed a platform on four bicycle wheels and attached the camera to a rod that moved up and down while being wheeled along, like a long-necked bird nodding its head. They pushed this contraption through the streets with the camera rolling and projected the results two days later. We had the choice of two interpretations, explained Ivens: 'Drunken, I walk through the Kalverstraat' or 'the Kalverstraat seems to be flooded and I'm rowing to the Dam.'[19] It made the viewer seasick. After this experiment Ivens published his own treatment of the 'first-person film' in April 1928, a piece that arouses the impression that the duo's primary goal had been the rejuvenation of the fiction film. Ivens hoped that the Filmliga might found an independent studio for experimentation with the first-person film.[20] but this came to nothing and he and Van Meerten ended their collaboration.

In autumn 1927 Joris Ivens traveled to Berlin to invite Walter Ruttmann to visit the Filmliga. 'From our perspective in faraway Holland, Ruttmann was an artistic giant, but when I saw him at close hand, wrestling with an old, poorly equipped camera, and limited by a lack of craftsmanship, I realized that from a technical point of view I was more than his equal,' Ivens wrote. He became aware that the works of art he so admired were products of practical craftsmanship. Ivens saw Ruttmann's latest film, BERLIN, SYMPHONY OF A BIG CITY, which must have impressed him deeply, as its influence on his work over the years that followed is unmistakable.[21] Previously, Ruttmann had made short, purely abstract films, but he had now wedded his sense of form to a concrete subject, the life of the city of Berlin. Encouraged by meeting Ruttmann, Ivens made his first film in the first months of 1928, THE BRIDGE.

On the night of October 30, 1927, under the watching eye of workers and engineers, the first train had rolled over the new lift bridge over Rotterdam's Koningshaven. The bridge was a no-nonsense industrial product and its completion was a source of universal satisfaction. A railroad architect pointed out its cinematic potential to Joris Ivens. Its numerous sliding and rotating components made the steel construction perfect for capturing the pure rhythmic movement that the Filmliga had declared the essence of cinema. Germaine Krull's abstract photos of machinery might have also influenced Ivens to begin filming the bridge, but at the same time there was a very practical reason for his choice: 'I needed to fit the project into my ordinary work, so I needed a theme I could work on one day, leave alone the next, and come back to without it changing.'[22] For the film critics THE BRIDGE was an abstract or absolute film. 'The iron construction disintegrates into hundreds of separate images from which the material has disappeared,' wrote the authoritative Hungarian film theoretician Béla Balázs,[23] but scrambling over the construction, Ivens felt as though his subject 'had a personality like an ancient giant's, so that it became a film of the bridge after all, instead of a pure composition of movement', because the construction of the film was 'determined by the functions of the bridge itself'. Trains and passing ships make up the 'general psychological line'.[24] This perspective tied Ivens in to another feeling among modern artists, for whom this kind of construction was a living symbol of a great new future. In the words of Marinetti, the Italian futurist Marsman admired so much: 'We shall sing the nocturnal trembling glow of arsenals and workshops, torched by fierce electric moons; insatiable stations, devourers of smoking snakes; factories hung from clouds by spiraling plumes of smoke; bridges like gigantic gymnasts leaping over rivers, glimmering in the sun like gleaming knives; adventurous steamships testing horizons.' Dutch filmmaker Hans Keller later illustrated the same emotion in his documentary OVER THE BRIDGE by associating Ivens's film with László Moholy-Nagy's work *Die große Gefühls-maschine.*

Ivens was working on microscope films for Capi at Leiden University. During generous lunch breaks, he would arm himself with a Kinamo and occasionally with a De Vrij camera as well and catch the train from Leiden to Rotterdam some fifteen times. The handheld Kinamo was not widely used by professional filmmakers and thus, without really being aware of it, Ivens became a pioneer of filming 'off the shoulder'. He even took shots en route: 'I quickly detached the lock to the coupling, and went and stood in the open air between two cars to make various close-ups of the movements of the buffers.'[25]

For someone with a primarily technical bent like Ivens, editing THE BRIDGE must have been a revelation. Film enabled him to transform the bridge's familiar mechanisms into something of a completely different order: into art. His cinematic experiments brought the twenty-eight year old into unfamiliar territory, a realm where anything was possible and there were no fathers laying down the law.

Meanwhile his fellows at the Filmliga were far from convinced that his efforts would amount to anything. Jordaan felt 'somewhat alarmed' to hear that Ivens planned to show his own work at one of their matinees. Although Ivens was 'an industrious colleague, a level-headed and businesslike organizer and a good friend', the results of his film work were awaited 'apprehensively'.[26] With the exception of Cor Aafjes's modern HANDELSBLADFILM and a number of scientific shorts by J.C. Mol, the Filmliga had not programmed any Dutch films. This made the response all the more enthusiastic when THE BRIDGE really did turn out to be something special. The filmmaker showed his work to the Filmliga selection board with accompanying music specially written by pianist and Bach aficionado Hans Brandts Buys.[27]

Soon after, on May 5, 1928, THE BRIDGE premiered during a Filmliga screening in Amsterdam's Central Theater. Ivens bowed while cheers rang through the auditorium. Menno ter Braak saw THE BRIDGE as the successful conclusion of 'a process of years' in which its maker had experimented behind closed doors, the press was jubilant, and Jordaan called the premiere 'an important date in the culture of a nation'. He wrote that 'at a particular moment in time, THE BRIDGE was able to provide a positive, concrete answer to many vague but pressing questions. No matter what the judgement about Ivens's later work might be – the fact that THE BRIDGE was made then and in that form will never decline in significance.'[28]

In the preceding years there had been few hints that Ivens would enjoy a cinematic career spanning more than six decades. Despite minor deviations in and after Berlin, he had remained a dutiful dealer in photographic articles and his father's successor. Superficially, it seemed quite implausible that he of all people should become the leading figure of a new generation of Dutch filmmakers. His relationship to art had always been that of an observer, not a creator, but through Hendrik Marsman, the Berlin poets, Germaine and his friends from the Leidseplein, he had begun to feel increasingly at home in the art world, and had realized that, when it came to film, his Berlin education and training gave him possibilities that were virtually beyond the reach of others. The equipment he needed was there for the taking in his own store.

Artistic trends like De Stijl, Neue Sachlichkeit and Constructivism were striving to integrate esthetics, technology and functionality. This ambition fitted exceptionally well with Ivens's way of thinking. Whereas many modern artists hesitantly entered the technical arena in order to achieve a synthesis of art and the modern age, Ivens was a technician who had stumbled upon art. Writing in *Filmliga*, Jordaan encapsulated this aspect of THE BRIDGE: 'The audacious idea of consistently sticking to the inspiration, drawing exclusively on the structural, logical beauty of a work of engineering, is extremely Dutch. It is the instinctive, atavistic urge of a morass dweller, who sees a board over a ditch as a thing of beauty.'[29]

At the very start of his film career, social issues emerged as an important theme in Ivens's work. An anonymous criticism of THE BRIDGE advised him to 'abandon the ivory tower and listen to the tremendous class struggle',[30] but by the time he received it, such admonitions were no longer needed.

Many artists in his circle admired the artistic innovation in the Soviet Union. They inclined toward socialism emotionally, and were favorably disposed toward the Soviet state. The Communist Party initiated the formation of the Netherlands-New Russia Society as a forum through which nonparty intellectuals and artists could sympathize with the USSR in a relaxed but organized way. Joris Ivens joined and became film correspondent for the magazine *Nieuw Rusland*.

Even before the premiere of THE BRIDGE, preparations were being made in the seaside village of Katwijk for the following project: the fiction film BREAKERS, based on an idea by Jef Last, directed by Mannus Franken, and with Ivens behind the camera. Jef Last – a former student of Chinese who had worked as a miner, fisherman and sailor out of sheer love for the ordinary people – was just finding his feet as a writer. Mannus Franken was another former student, from the Technical University Delft, who had gone to Paris to write. His contacts with leading figures in the French cinematic avant-garde had led the Filmliga to appoint him as its Paris representative.

In BREAKERS an unemployed fisherman loses his sweetheart to a rich pawnbroker. The melodramatic story was meant to illustrate 'how losing work that has become an essential part of one's identity can also lead to a loss of inner certainty and everything one holds dear,' according to Jef Last, who played the lead role himself.[31] Just as in the much-admired Soviet films, the actors were amateurs and, in the spirit of socialism, the film crew sounded out the opinions of the locals. 'When viewing the rushes in the evenings we invite as many Katwijkers as we can pack into the alcove, and make the most of their criticism,' Ivens explained to Jordaan, who visited the crew on location.[32] The locals even provided good advice during the actual filming, as with Shot 237 in the dunes: 'Jef – lie down next to her first and play with the skirt of her pinafore,' called out Franken, 'then shyly and carefully slip your arm in behind her back and look up at her imploringly.' The watching fishermen found it an insipid display and vented their criticism loudly. At the director's request, they demonstrated how a real Katwijker would go about it.[33]

BREAKERS was meant to be more than just a socially-aware drama. Ivens declared that he and Franken did not want the people appearing as actors, but in the service 'of the editing and the image'. Drawing inspiration from the French avant-garde, Franken's chief hope was to evoke moods, and appeal to the subconscious through 'invisible associations'.[34]

The trio could not agree about the end of the film and two versions were made. Franken thought it should end with the tragic hero walking out onto the jetty and there, amid spraying foam and towering waves, contemplate suicide. This sequence was filmed and Ivens's brilliantly dynamic editing made it the highlight of the film, but Ivens himself, in his incorrigible optimism, wanted to add a hopeful continuation in which Jef Last, suddenly and inexplicably in possession of a fishing boat, sails off toward distant horizons.

The filmmakers had to work with modest means but, more importantly, they had no experience with fiction films and, according to the critics, showed little talent for the genre. Ivens's positive contribution was limited to a number of visually successful sequences. Franken showed little psychological insight, and Last was no more successful as a fisherman. Menno ter Braak called BREAKERS a 'failure, but not bad for that'. At any rate the makers of this avant-garde film were a notch above the Dutch producers of popular movies, whose works were only good as a 'digestive aid'. With BREAKERS you could at least see that the intentions were good, he wrote.[35] In retrospect the critics of the day did not do the film justice. Visually, the film has a lot to offer, and the way the actors flesh out the story is nowhere near as bad as was claimed, but that was an achievement that the leading lights of the Filmliga did not rate highly at the time.

Ivens knew Last from Capi, where he bought supplies for the Workers' Film Service, which he headed. Last was a member of the left-wing opposition in the Social Democratic SDAP, and became a Filmliga board member in Rotterdam. Filmmaker and writer got along well. Ivens liked hanging around in bars until late at night, and Last felt most at home in the company of hustlers and other lowlife. It was while wandering through the back streets around Amsterdam's Zeedijk with Last that Ivens met Cheng Fai, a Chinese sailor who had jumped ship and whom he employed as household help and general dogsbody.

While still living at Amstel 190, Ivens met the woman who would make him forget Germaine Krull: Anneke van der Feer. She had short blonde hair and remarkably light-colored eyes. Rather than an exceptional beauty, she was a modern easy-going girl. Friends remember the blonde Frisian in a blue turtleneck sweater, blue skirt and blue stockings, with the whole complemented by a blue beret – the outfit was cobbled together but stylish. Born on December 25, 1902, Anneke van der Feer was almost four years younger than Ivens, but – almost sixty years later, he still cited it as an important detail – 'a little taller'.[36] In her hometown of Sneek her businessman father had forced her to attend the domestic science school, but she wanted to be an artist and moved to Amsterdam in 1924. There she joined the artists' group The Independents. She was a fairly good artist but not a great one. She made woodcuts and painted cityscapes and portraits, all in a somewhat angular style. Later she designed the poster for Ivens's PHILIPS RADIO, but otherwise kept a careful distance from his film work. This made her one of the few people in his surroundings to resist his tendency to involve others in his work, which did not prevent her from sharply criticizing his films when necessary. They had what is known as a free relationship, but their friends were convinced that this noncommittal surface concealed a great love. In letters she called him 'Kiddo' or 'Dearest Monkey'; her pet name was 'Puppy'.

After World War II, when their own relationship was long over, Van der Feer wrote to Ivens: 'I've got a boyfriend as well, but I think that eventually my work always forces me to give these things up because I want or need to be alone. Something like the way you felt when we had just met, and at the

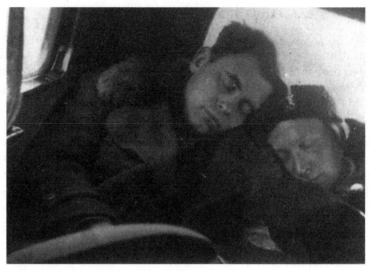

Joris Ivens and Anneke van der Feer. EFJI

time I didn't fully understand. Now I do.'[37] Despite many resolutions to the contrary, Ivens did not manage to rein in his aversion to commitment until he was past retirement age.

He and Anneke came into a fixed orbit around the Dutch Communist party after joining the Association for People's Culture (the Vereniging voor Volkscultuur or VVVC), which aimed at producing socialist propaganda through all cultural means, including film. Party leader Leo van Lakerveld set up the VVVC at the start of 1928 as a subsection of the Dutch division of International Red Aid, a support organization linked to the Communist International. The VVVC board included a familiar face: painter and illustrator Han Pieck, who had been visiting the family home in Nijmegen ever since Ivens was a boy. Pieck was on good terms with Joris's father and occasionally acted as an intermediary when conflicts arose between them, something that would happen more and more often as Joris gradually lost interest in Capi. The illustrator was a longstanding party member. Recruited by the Soviet secret service in the early thirties, he later played a prominent role in an espionage scandal centered on the British Foreign Office.[38]

The depth of Joris Ivens's own political involvement in the late twenties is shown by the fact that he requested an official discharge from his commission as a reserve officer, a function he had previously carried out with pleasure. After completing his military service in 1919 he had, as was usual, retained his rank, and in March 1923 he was promoted from second to first lieutenant of the Fifth Field Artillery Regiment.[39] Shortly after beginning work as a correspondence clerk for Capi at the start of 1927, Helene van Dongen saw an unfamiliar officer enter the store and announce: 'I'm Mr. George.'[40] This was what the staff called Joris Ivens. He had probably just come back from military exercises. Two years later he wrote to inform the Ministry of War that he resisted all forms of militarism and no longer wished to be an officer.[41] In Communist circles, anti-militarism as a concept was sharply differentiated from pacifism: it consisted of resistance to capitalist military forces, but sympathy for the Red Army. The Ministry of War was unperturbed. Without further ceremony, it granted him an honorable discharge at his own request, although he remained liable for call up as an ordinary soldier until October 1938.[42]

Van Lakerveld initiated a 'co-production' of Red Aid and the VVVC, both of which he headed: the short film POVERTY IN THE BOGS OF DRENTHE. It became Ivens's first socially-motivated documentary. In February 1929 he traveled with Van Lakerveld, Communist parliamentarian Louis de Visser and Han Pieck to Drenthe, the poorest Dutch province. 'Unemployment everywhere. But even those who are working have to live in hovels, patched together from sods of peat, slats of wood, crates and cardboard boxes. Up to ten or twelve people often have to live and sleep in one stuffy room. Lacking the bare minimum of food, prey to crippling disease and tuberculosis. The suffering that human beings are subjected to here is indescribable,' states one of the film titles.[43] The prevailing conditions in Drenthe must have made a deep impression on the son of a wealthy businessman and the experience can only have strengthened him in his Communist sympathies. Van Lakerveld ensured that the film paid sufficient attention to the VVVC and the party. During World War II the film was presumably dumped in an Amsterdam canal to prevent it from falling into German hands.[44]

The Communist movement had been quick to recognize the propaganda value of the cinema. Lenin had declared that film is 'the most important of the arts',[45] and Comintern board member Willi Münzenberg, head of International Workers' Aid, had made filmmaking the key task of his organization. Workers' Aid had begun as a support organization, but had evolved into the Comintern's main propaganda machine. In the propaganda field, Münzenberg was probably the greatest genius the Communist movement ever brought forth. From his international headquarters in Berlin, Red Willi lead a press empire that included the newspaper *Die Welt am Abend*, the magazine *Arbeiter Illustrierte Zeitung* and a series of other magazines. With a combined circulation of millions, his publications reached a much wider readership than the official party organs. He founded the film production company Prometheus and the international distribution company Welt-film, and created the Mezhrabpom Film Studio in Moscow – named after the Russian abbreviation for International Workers' Aid – with Pudovkin as the studio's star director. In Holland, a 1926 split in the Communist party re-sulted in Red Aid rather than Workers' Aid being involved with film[46] and it was Van Lakerveld who maintained contact with Münzenberg in Berlin.[47] Münzenberg's international construction of companies, magazines, organi-zations and illegal networks was answerable to the Comintern and the national parties had no jurisdiction over his activities. By working for the VVVC, Joris Ivens entered this world, which operated according to the motto: everything for the party, but nothing in the name of the party.

4 Exactly How We See It Too, Sir (1929)

In the spring of 1929, Joris Ivens moved from his attic on the Damrak to the two top floors of a canal-side house at Singel 399. To get to his apartment, visitors had to climb a number of flights of stairs through what most resembled a musty old office building. At the top they found a living area so stark that 'simple' was an exaggeration. Ivens cared nothing for homemaking or furniture, and the place was empty except for a couple of beds. It looked like a tramp's hideaway. 'He was actually an incredibly primitive guy,' according to his colleague Willem Bon. 'I could hardly believe my middle-class eyes.'[1] At the back was the Filmliga library, which consisted of a magazine table and an old bookcase full of books, periodicals and photos.

The top floor was one big room with an editing bench against one of the walls. On the opposite wall were horizontal slats of wood with nails from which to hang the strips of film during editing. To accentuate that this was a workplace, Ivens had painted several of the beams aluminium-colored. He would walk around between the highly-flammable nitrate film calmly smoking. The darkroom was in the back corner, and there was a barrel organ that shook the whole house. 'It made a tremendous noise and George would play it to keep himself awake when working through to edit a film,' his father wrote in his diary.[2]

His Chinese assistant, Cheng Fai, moved from the Damrak to the Singel with him. He helped with an umbrella during the shooting of RAIN, used a Primus stove (between the strips of nitrate film) to cook a murky black mushroom soup with supposed medicinal qualities, performed librarian's duties, and did voluntary work at Capi, where he mastered the photographic trade to such a degree that he was able to set sail for the Dutch East Indies in 1929 and start his own photography business there. Cheng Fai's departure meant the end of the last semblance of domestic order in Ivens's home. His assistant Mark Kolthoff found that Ivens had a marked aversion to domesticity. He virtually never cooked and became annoyed when others wanted to cook in his apartment. He breakfasted in the cafe on the corner and would eat dinner at friends' homes, in a restaurant or in a nearby soup kitchen. Ivens moved through life with 'the flair of a student', according to Kolthoff.

Ivens had plenty of drinking mates and acquaintances, but looking back it is impossible to identify any truly close friends. He and Germaine had broken up, his political differences with Arthur Lehning were becoming irreconcilable, and his friendship with Hendrik Marsman was fading away. He did not form any long-term bonds with the people he met at the

Leidseplein or the other Filmliga board members, and his promising collaboration with Mannus Franken did not last. Around 1929 a completely new group of co-workers arose around him and he found political allies in the Dutch Communist party, but a few years later he had left virtually all of these behind as well. Not because he was unable to raise any affection for them, on the contrary, many of them were convinced that they were Ivens's best friend. He was able to make people feel that they were important to him. For the duration of an encounter, no one existed for him beyond his conversational partner, but afterwards he moved on. He remained a loner.

The activities he pursued in his spare time clashed increasingly with his work for Capi. As early as June 1927, he had complained in a letter to Arthur Lehning that 'that nickel-and-dime work at Capi has got such a hold on me'. He had just thrown himself into the Filmliga and had made his first film plans, but 'all kinds of fields that arouse my love and interest lie before me, and I can't reach them. Must change.'[3] This happened. 'I used stuff from the store. Fortunately I got along well with the Capi staff. They didn't report it and they kept it off the books as far as possible.'[4] When Mr. George was absent for long periods, Helene van Dongen copied his signature so that the mail could be sent off, and when his father telephoned from Nijmegen, the store manager would say: 'Your son is out demonstrating cameras.'[5] His parents realized that George's career was developing in an unintended direction. Joris Ivens and his father argued on the telephone. 'But you mustn't imagine that there was any shouting or slamming of doors,' said his sister Thea. The proprieties were observed.[6]

A commercially interesting film commission from the Dutch construction workers' union in May 1929 gave big brother Wim the opportunity to negotiate a compromise. A doctor attached to the Queen Wilhelmina Hospital in Amsterdam, Wim Ivens cut a fashionable, if portly, figure, wore his hair slicked back and was the proud owner of an enormous, gleaming Lancia. He confronted his father with George's determination: 'He transforms his expertise, his technique, into art, not trade.'[7] Kees Ivens allowed himself to be convinced and agreed to set up the Capi Film Company. Henceforth the absence of the Kalverstraat branch manager could be explained with the words: 'Unfortunately film obligations make it impossible for Mr. Ivens to call at your residence at that time on Wednesday.' Wim took charge of the business contacts with the commissioning companies, and Joris began work, sincerely intending to make a go of the film company, which actually operated from his house at Singel 399.

'It's high time we had a clan of Dutch film workers who take the 'trade' seriously,' he wrote in March 1929 to Jan Hin, a Benedictine priest from Ant-

Joris Ivens takes to the air for ZUIDERZEE. PHOTO JOHN FERNHOUT, NEDERLANDS
FOTO ARCHIEF (NFA)

werp who had once marched into his store in full regalia, more enthused by
cinema than by the Word of God. Ivens's suggestion that they needed to
start from scratch was incorrect. There were talented filmmakers working at
the Polygoon Studio for newsreels and documentaries, but he probably
didn't count them because they were not part of the art scene.

With his commission from the construction union, he was able to contribute toward the creation of the envisaged clan, because he needed a number
of co-workers. Ivens was wildly enthusiastic about filmmaking and inspired everyone he knew. 'He drew you in when you were working with
him,' found photographer Eva Besnyö. 'Some people really set out to exercise influence, but I don't believe Joris was like that.'[8] 'He had the women at
his beck and call, and the men too for that matter,' recalled co-worker,
writer and composer Lou Lichtveld. Other people did a lot for him because
he had 'a certain gentleness'.[9]

No one was more eager to help than Helene van Dongen, the small, dark-
haired Capi secretary with the rather sharp face. According to Ivens they became close 'in business matters first and then emotionally'. Helene Victoria
Rosa van Dongen was born in Amsterdam on January 5, 1909. She was

raised a Catholic and her father was fond of saying: 'Sissy's going to be a nun.'[10] In 1927 she applied for a job with Capi as a correspondence clerk. Soon she was not only Mr. George's secretary, but also his right hand for various aspects of his film work. Later she was prone to exaggerating her role in this early phase, sometimes claiming that she edited Ivens's work from the very beginning. Another time, however, and more truthfully, she said of THE BRIDGE: 'I stored the scenes of the film... in the compartments of an egg carton. Beyond that I just watched and listened.' She was probably accurately describing the situation in the late twenties when she wrote: 'We didn't have the money for a professional lab. There were no funds available to employ a special assistant to help Joris with his film work either. For Joris the simplest solution was to nominate me as voluntary assistant.'[11] Her contribution grew gradually until 1931 and PHILIPS RADIO, when she shared the editing credit with Ivens. In the ten years that followed, she edited most of his films. Many of Ivens's co-workers found Helene bossy, but this criticism is not entirely fair: Ivens was fond of having his wife or someone else delegate unpleasant tasks so that he could remain nice. Nonetheless, friend and foe agreed that Helene van Dongen had a difficult character.

The relationship between Ivens and the ten-year-younger Helene began in the early thirties. Looking back, Ivens wrote that their love was based on 'really sharing life: the hope, the difficulties, the disillusion, but also the successes and the joy'. The reality obscured by this phraseology is suggested by what he said at the end of their long relationship: it had been a 'fifteen-year friendship'.[12] Ivens saw Helene as a 'gentle and dependent' woman whose knowledge of life did not go far beyond what 'the nuns who raised her had taught her'.[13] In fact, she had been no more raised by nuns than he by Catholic brothers. More than anything else, his statement betrays something about himself. After his mother and Germaine, it was now Helene who needed his care, he thought.

Their relationship had a strongly professional basis. Ivens soon recognized Helene's exceptional qualities. She developed from complete ignorance of film and technology into the talented editor of a number of his most important films, a person who later taught sound editing in Moscow and enjoyed a first-rate reputation in her field in the United States, partly because of her work on some of the best films of the grand old man of the documentary, Robert Flaherty. In his reference book on film history, *The Film Till Now*, Paul Rotha called the collaboration of Ivens and Van Dongen 'one of the most fruitful in film history but which has tended to obscure Helen van Dongen's own quite distinct talent'. And American documentary specialist Richard Barsam called her 'one of the most gifted, creative, skilled editors in nonfiction film history'.[14]

The new relationship with Helene did not end his relationship with Anneke van der Feer. Ivens now began a long-term triangular relationship, with the possible underlying motive being the freedom of not having to commit himself fully to either. The two sides of Germaine were now divided between two girlfriends. Anneke was the woman of the world, living among activists and artists. Helene was the 'gentle and dependent' companion in his film work. Van Dongen was not happy with the situation: 'There were always other women in the background and I had to accept that. I'm old-fashioned, I love one man and that's it.'[15] Van der Feer, who 'didn't fully understand' his reserves when she first met him, turned necessity into a virtue and began a second relationship with the poet Halbo C. Kool. Ivens referred to him as 'your boyfriend'; she spoke to him of 'little Helene'.[16]

At the start of 1928, Ivens also began another long-term collaboration, with Johnny Fernhout, later known in the USA as John Ferno, the troublesome younger son of painter Charley Toorop. Ivens had met Toorop in the mid-twenties when she had an affair with Marsman, and in Amsterdam they moved in the same artistic circles centered on De Kring, the Filmliga and the Netherlands-New Russia Society. She asked Ivens to take on the fourteen-year-old Johnny as an apprentice because his school results had hardly been encouraging. During a visit to Toorop's studio, Ivens obliged by asking Johnny if he would like to become a camera assistant. He cleaned the film cassettes while Ivens filmed THE BRIDGE, was the crew's short-trousered assistant on the set of BREAKERS, and cycled around Amsterdam with Ivens on the back of his bike: 'He filmed the wheel, handlebars and lamp over my shoulder in the pouring rain.'[17] With WE ARE BUILDING Fernhout's career began taking on a more serious form, henceforth he operated the camera himself.

WE ARE BUILDING became Ivens's first film about the workers' movement and manual labor itself. The main component of the extensive project was construction work, shot by Ivens and his co-workers at locations all over the Netherlands. In the first section, distributed separately under the title PILE DRIVING, he concentrated on the formal experimentation that had characterized THE BRIDGE, a tendency which is also present in some other sections of WE ARE BUILDING. In the rest of the film, he stuck to a strict realism that demonstrated his remarkable sensitivity to the work process.

By far the most beautiful of the major parts of WE ARE BUILDING was ZUIDERZEE WORKS, subsequently adapted for separate distribution as ZUIDERZEE, and reworked a number of times as land reclamation progressed in the years that followed.[18] Taking advantage of his military training in aerial reconnaissance, Ivens took to the skies in a navy trainer to film the construction of the dykes. At one stage the pilot lost control and the aircraft went into a steep dive. Ivens discovered just in time that he had jammed his camera bag up against the dual controls.

The final extended and revised version of ZUIDERZEE became NEW EARTH, which allocates a central place to the closure of the Vlieter, the last open section of the IJsselmeer Dam. That at least is the suggestion: the sequence of fast-flowing water, masses of mud, and cranes with enormous buckets was actually put together from shots of various closures in the Wieringermeer Dyke and the IJsselmeer Dam. Ivens was only half lying when he told how he had filmed the historic event as a struggle between man, land and water, each represented by one camera, whereas he was actually on the other side of the Urals when the Vlieter was closed on May 28, 1932. The camera operators at the Vlieter were John Fernhout, Helene van Dongen and Capi salesman Joop Huisken.[19] The edited sequence became one of the most impressive in Ivens's work.

In Holland trade union films could generally count on a large degree of public interest. 1930 also saw the release of TRIUMPH and FISTS OF STEEL, both made by the Polygoon Studio. Jo de Haas's FISTS OF STEEL in particular could compete with WE ARE BUILDING in terms of quality and had the advantage of a greater unity. Nonetheless, the esthetic qualities of some parts of Ivens's film still impress today, and at the time it was screened very successfully to construction workers all over the country. According to the Social Democratic newspaper *Het Volk*, politically close to the construction union that had commissioned the film, the premiere was the most important event 'to ever take place in Dutch cinematic life'. A jubilant union chief seized another reporter from the same newspaper by his lapels: 'Come and see it! It's terrific... No, don't go making excuses, come to Utrecht with me and hear how much our boys love the movie!' Ivens himself said that he was 'tickled pink' when, after showing PILE DRIVING, he was approached by two pile drivers who said: 'That's exactly how we see it too, sir!'[20]

Writing from Paris in October 1927, Mannus Franken sent Ivens a proposal for a poetic short film with impressions of Amsterdam in the rain. 'Returned from a trip to Berlin and Dresden to find your two letters about RAIN,' Ivens wrote back. 'Seems to me to be an excellent plan.' And a week later: 'Rain scenario, I walk around in the rain here thinking about it, and look and look. I'll shoot some of it in the coming days.'[21] Two months later Henrik Scholte saw the first fragments, 'that were shown in a circle of intimate friends and turned out to be magnificent'.[22] For more than two years Ivens worked on the twelve-minute short between other projects. He designated 'rain spotters' to alert him to appropriate images and kept an oilskin, boots and two

Helene van Dongen, Amsterdam. PHOTO MARK KOLTHOFF, GEMEENTEARCHIEF
AMSTERDAM

loaded cameras ready, so that he could turn out the moment the first drops
fell. He even filmed some shots from his bed. He said: 'I slept with Anneke
and with my camera.'[23]

But friction soon arose between Ivens and Franken. In February 1928
Filmliga technician, Ed. Pelster wrote to Franken that he didn't like the way
'that people here think that it is his film [Ivens's] alone and that he doesn't
do anything to dispel that impression'. Franken answered that he had no
ambitions on that score, despite having provided the concept and the main
part of the scenario. However, he continued: 'Deep down it does actually
annoy me – it was work from the two of us and now it's almost too late to
broach the subject.'[24] Franken's complaints were probably justified. In any
case, Ivens later claimed that he had conceived it all himself: 'The idea behind RAIN occurred to me when we were filming BREAKERS,' he said in his
memoirs.[25] Whereas work on BREAKERS only started six months after

Franken's first letters. They continued to collaborate, corresponding about RAIN and visiting each other several times to discuss progress. In spring 1928 Ivens wrote to Franken telling him that the completion date for the film was now July, or otherwise September. In October he wrote that 'it will be soon be finished'. But in June 1929 he was still saying: 'I've made some more progress with RAIN.' Ivens was dependent on the weather and 'fell in love with the material', so that during editing he couldn't bring himself to throw anything away.[26]

The smoldering dissatisfaction between Franken and Ivens flared up again when a number of magazines described RAIN and BREAKERS as Ivens films, without any mention of his partner. Replying to Franken's complaints, Ivens wrote: 'You know damn well what I want: to be the cameraman and together, under the direction of the director, to make a good film. I have every confidence in you, and tell everyone so, and challenge every attack on your work. If you no longer believe that, then we shouldn't work together any more. Your letter makes it sound as if I deliberately make sure that it doesn't say Franken next to BREAKERS and RAIN, that's not the case. But from now on, when they ask me something, I'll emphasize it much more.' He published a rectification in *Filmliga* pointing out Mannus Franken's role, and informed Franken that the rain film was 'totally based on your idea'. At the same time he also asked: 'Is there any chance of your spending more time here? Why didn't you ever ask about the filming? We watched the rushes together, but I had the feeling 'Mannus is just letting it slide'... RAIN will turn out best if the cameraman and writer collaborate closely – including with the shooting itself.'[27]

Franken had apparently already decided to adopt a low profile, perhaps because he sensed that Ivens was too talented to just operate the camera, perhaps because Ivens really was claiming too much credit for himself, a tendency later co-workers would also complain about. The result was predictable; RAIN did end up being primarily an Ivens film. Although Mannus Franken was responsible for the idea and the scenario, he was generally in Paris, whereas in Amsterdam Ivens wrote a shooting script, did the filming and completed the lion's share of the editing. The course of events must have helped convince him to take on the role of director more explicitly in the future.

After various screenings of incomplete versions in Amsterdam, Paris and Berlin, the film finally premiered on December 14, 1929 in Amsterdam in the Filmliga's new theater, De Uitkijk. It still convinces as a poetic impression of Amsterdam as seen through the eyes of an introvert observer wandering through the city during a rain shower. 'One has to surrender to it with the calm of an opium smoker awaiting the consequences of his intoxication,' was the apt summary of the Paris correspondent of the daily *NRC*.[28]

Despite everything, Mannus Franken and Joris Ivens had collaborated fairly intensively in 1928 and 1929, on BREAKERS, on RAIN, and on Franken's *D 16 MM*, a Constructivist, total theater performance for the anniversary celebrations of the Delft student fraternity. In October 1929, Franken declared in an interview that he had written a script for THE FLYING DUTCHMAN, a project he aimed to realize together with Ivens. The script was 'based on H. Marsman's short, concrete novella, which is a modern conception of the highest order. We have a clear vision of the theme and its adaptation. We could begin at any time.' After this a further estrangement seems to have taken place silently – neither of them were given to direct confrontation. Ivens must have continued hoping for a revival of the collaboration for quite some time. At the start of 1931, he told the *NRC* that he still anticipated filming THE FLYING DUTCHMAN with Franken, but by this time Franken had already gone his own way.[29] He filmed JARDIN DU LUXEMBOURG in Paris and went on to make numerous films in Holland and the Dutch East Indies.

The estrangement of Joris Ivens and Mannus Franken encouraged the film critics to consider their separate talents. Decades later, L.J. Jordaan summed it up concisely: 'It is still a mystery to me why the combination of the two cineastes was ever broken. Personally I still believe that for both Ivens (despite the heights his career later reached) and Franken it would have been a blessing had they remained together. After all, Ivens represented practicality, painstaking technique and restless activity. In Franken one found the fertile mind, subtle poetry and lofty ideals.' Jordaan had already expressed similar sentiments in his 1931 booklet *Joris Ivens*. At that time he found that, with all their failings, BREAKERS and RAIN 'possessed a delicacy and an allure whose absence in the '100% Ivens' films is sometimes painfully obvious', with which he was referring to films like WE ARE BUILDING, ZUIDERZEE and PHILIPS RADIO, which came out in 1931. 'RAIN in particular is shrouded by mildness and a soft, melancholy romanticism. This elevates the somewhat gruff realism of Ivens's conception to another plane, that of individual emotion.' Filmliga board member Henrik Scholte wrote that, in his predilection for unadorned documentary, Ivens was an engineer more than a poet. *Filmliga* also reprinted an article from the magazine *De Gemeenschap*, written by 'Close-up', pseudonym of the critic A. van Domburg – *Filmliga* went so far as to add 'an excellent reviewer' – who distinguished two kinds of Ivens films: 'the ones he has made himself and the ones he has produced in collaboration. They're all skilful. Only the latter are inspired.' Ivens's work demands admiration, according to Van Domburg, but with his dour spirit and cool intelligence he lacks fantasy and playfulness: 'He doesn't know delight, he does know dedicated attention.' Lou Lichtveld, who provided the music and sound for Ivens's PHILIPS RADIO in 1931, concluded that music mattered to Ivens when it was in the service of film but hardly interested him as an art in itself. Lichtveld saw it as a tendency: 'Joris was mad about Russia, but he wasn't interested in Soviet literature, nor in any other literature. That was why he couldn't be a good fiction film director. He didn't see the dramatic side. He had a tremendous feeling for cinematic rhythm and editing but not for psychology.'[30]

Ivens definitely left his mark on the poetic RAIN and was thus not entirely bereft of poetry, but it was true that his natural tendency was in another direction. Mechanical movement, industrial production and human labor were the dominant elements in his early films. When he came up against the limitations of Neue Sachlichkeit, which was in danger of becoming stranded in sterility, he did not turn to poetry but opted for a strict, socially-committed realism. In the course of his life he made a number of distinctly poetic films and traces of poetry can also be found in many of his other films, but in his oeuvre as a whole it remained a secondary element.

Nonetheless, the start of his filmmaking career was marked by preparations for the fiction film THE FLYING DUTCHMAN, and into the eighties he kept up his plans to make a film based on this romantic story, in which Captain van der Decken is doomed to sail the seas in search of salvation. The project represents what Ivens would have liked to have been: a wandering poet.

5 You hear me, Father, Mother, Charnel House! (1930-1931)

After the Berlin premiere of his film STORM OVER ASIA in January 1929, Soviet director Vsevolod Pudovkin traveled on to Amsterdam to give a lecture for the Filmliga. Board member Joris Ivens went to Berlin to accompany him on the last leg of his journey, and took the opportunity to attend the party that Dadaist painter and cineaste Hans Richter had organized in Pudovkin's honor in the suburb of Grunewald. The guests included Walter Ruttmann, Erwin Piscator, Béla Balázs and the Danish actress Asta Nielsen, one of the silent era's greatest stars.[1]

Besides being a chemical engineer and one of the great innovators of Russian cinema, Pudovkin was also a faithful follower of Lenin. In the Soviet Union of the 1920s, avant-gardism and Communism still seemed compatible. The October Revolution had ushered in a period of cultural freedom in which Futurists, Suprematists, Constructivists and other avant-gardists experimented with film, theater, music, literature and the visual arts. It was only after Stalin had established his position in the early thirties that artistic innovation was really put to an end. Failure to conform to the Great Leader's populist perspective on culture led to poor work prospects at the very least.

In the AMVJ building on the Leidseplein, Pudovkin spoke on the significance of editing in modern film. The Dutch authorities had forbidden any discussion of politics, and although Pudovkin did not defy their ban, he did defend himself against the accusation that Soviet cinema invariably portrayed capitalists as scoundrels, whereas workers were without fail the embodiment of virtue. In the works of Dickens too, the heroes were always poor and the villains rich, but 'one could hardly accuse him of Bolshevism'.[2]

During breakfast at the Hotel Schiller on the Rembrandtplein, Ivens made a proposal that appealed to Pudovkin. Several months later Ivens wrote to the VOKS, the Soviet association for cultural relations with foreign countries. 'At the time I proposed to Pudovkin that a young director or cameraman could come to Holland for four months. As he can stay at my apartment, the only expense involved will be traveling costs. I could subsequently come to Moscow for four weeks in the same fashion.'[3] In reply he received an invitation, with a note undertaking to partially reimburse his traveling costs and provide accommodation in Moscow. No further mention was made of the visit in the opposite direction. Before actually embarking, Ivens met other Soviet artists elsewhere in Europe, among them Dziga

Vertov in Frankfurt and the writer Ilya Ehrenburg in Paris. With 'the permission of the CPH', the Communist party of Holland, as noted in a party document,[4] Ivens finally boarded the long-awaited train to Moscow, film mecca, on January 13, 1930.

He was already favorably disposed toward the Soviet Union, but what he saw there surpassed his wildest expectations. He felt revolutionary fervor everywhere he went. He met with many fellow filmmakers, his work was reviewed in the press, and there were numerous discussions with the public. His reception closely resembled an organized campaign of manipulation, but he didn't see it that way himself and the ideological unanimity among the people he met probably did make organization superfluous.

In an icy Moscow, he was put up in Sergei Eisenstein's modest apartment. The famous director himself was in Amsterdam giving a lecture for the Netherlands-New Russia Society. Ivens would meet Eisenstein later, in Paris, where they would roam the city with Germaine Krull, and film in several bars. Eisenstein's assistant and future wife Pera Attasheva was Ivens's guide and interpreter in Moscow. For Ivens 'it was like a fairy tale'.

His first public appearance was before an audience of two hundred and fifty in the Museum of the Revolution on the Tverskaya. The house was full and hundreds had been turned away. The meeting was introduced by Pudovkin, who also summarized his vision of the Dutch guest in an article. He believed that RAIN and THE BRIDGE showed that Joris Ivens was a serious filmmaker who had done a good job of capturing the images and had an outstanding purity of form, but that it was only with ZUIDERZEE that life and blood appeared in his work, because he had broken free of his former vague, esthetic principles and made the transition to a work of living reality.[5]

The films Ivens showed in the Soviet Union included THE BRIDGE, RAIN, PILE DRIVING, ZUIDERZEE WORKS and a number of films by Dutch colleagues. He had BREAKERS with him as well, but was less certain of its quality and preferred not screening it for an audience of Muscovite film connoisseurs.[6] Every day in Moscow he would give one or two screenings at diverse social organizations, from the Business Club to the Club of the Red Seamstress. In the latter venue employees of the transport organization were gathered for the occasion. After returning to Holland, Ivens told a reporter that the invariably closed meetings were like 'a kind of test'.[7] They were always run the same way: a committee on the stage, speech with film screening, incisive questions from the audience and, finally, a vote on diverse resolutions in which those present expressed their opinion of the presented works. During these meetings the Dutch guest was subjected to a deluge of alternating praise and disapproval. The Soviet press also swung between being highly affectionate and extremely critical: 'Ivens cuts and edits his films in an attic. The screen he uses when editing is scarcely larger than a postage stamp. As a result his production is limited... Of course, Ivens's works are very interesting for Soviet cineastes and audiences because the concepts behind his films are simple and they have been filmed with great craftsmanship. We must study Ivens's films carefully because he has an original working method and original ways of filming, and his films are cheap nonetheless,' wrote one magazine, but another stated: 'Ivens is not interested in people. He is infatuated with the cold beauty of industrial objects. Ivens elevates the cult of objects to fetishism, almost to mysticism. His BRIDGE is like an industrial God.' The reporter wondered 'on which side of the barricades Ivens would stand' and warned him to choose 'the class that is struggling to liberate humanity'.[8]

Ivens was sensitive to this kind of criticism. During his presentation at the Museum of the Revolution, where he went into detail on the emergence of the Filmliga and typified THE BRIDGE and RAIN as exercises, a member of the audience began by pointing out that ZUIDERZEE WORKS showed little of the living conditions of the workers. He defended himself by saying that he had had no choice as the film was made under commission to the Social Democratic union leadership. The report of the meeting stated: 'Comrade Ivens is proud of the fact that this film depicts neither managers nor engineers, but only workers. He had to go against the Social Democrats to achieve this, and in Holland it is seen as extraordinarily revolutionary.' In Holland he was faced 'with the dilemma of whether to continue working as he had up to now, or to directly pursue a revolutionary path. And with an eloquent gesture, he illustrated what would then happen to him. Thus he has no choice but to carry on doing what he has done up to now, or else to stay here and work here.'

Ivens explained that filming under capitalist conditions was subject to such great constraints that it was questionable whether there was any point to it at all. 'Instead of displaying the contradictions of bourgeois society, it would be more important to show the workers in Holland the development of the USSR,' he stated to loud applause. During a meeting with students from the film school, which he presented with a Leica camera, he said that people could not expect 'a Dutch director to depict what he saw, because he would be immediately thrown out of the country'. He tried to smuggle images into his work that intensified the contrast between the classes but added that you couldn't remain a smuggler for long. 'Either the circumstances in Holland will change, or I'll have to leave.'[9]

It was true that the Central Commission for Film Censorship exercised a certain control over public screenings in Holland, but apart from very exceptional cases, any film could be shown at a closed screening, even to audiences of five hundred or one thousand. And for none of Ivens's films such a close screening was necessary. Ivens said what his Soviet audiences wanted to hear, but he must have also believed himself that the situation in Holland was as black-and-white as he claimed in Moscow. At a point when his popularity as a filmmaker was at a peak in Holland, he thus propounded for the first time two ideas that were to be a major influence in his further career: that there was no longer a place for him in his own country and that it would be more meaningful to work in the Soviet Union.

The discussions following the screenings for Soviet workers underlined what his fellow filmmakers and the newspapers were saying. Audiences asked why he showed so few faces and left out information about social issues such as the wages of the laborers on the Dutch dams, the destinations of the trains crossing THE BRIDGE, and – Five-Year-Plan ritual – the number of tons being carried across it. On February 6, seven hundred construction workers gathered in Moscow's The Builder hostel to watch ZUIDERZEE WORKS. It must have been here that a member of the audience declared that the film could not possibly have been made by a bourgeois, because the work had been shown on the screen through the eyes of a worker. Ivens was especially delighted by this comment. Those present passed a resolution: 'Despite the impossibility of capturing the workers' lives in their entirety, the film gives a clear picture of the extraordinarily heavy conditions under which Dutch construction workers are forced to labor, bearing in mind the bourgeois laws and the betrayal of the Menshevik union leaders. After having the situation explained to us, we now see clearly that conditions are incomparably better for the working class in our technically backward country.'[10]

Stroika, the newspaper of the building federation, which had considerable funds at its disposal, asked Ivens to make a film about one of the major construction projects being undertaken in the USSR, such as the dam on the Dnieper. He promised to return to the Soviet Union to do so as soon as possible and, shortly after, while spending several weeks in the south of the country, he made a two-day visit to assess the planned location. He made an agreement with Sovkino to return in October to make a documentary of his own choice. It is unclear whether this referred to the same project.[11]

Decked out in a long black leather coat, the standard garb of a genuine Bolshevik, he spent two months touring the country with his films. He went to Leningrad, Kiev, Kharkov, Rostov, Odessa, Batumi, Tbilisi, Yerevan and Baku, and visited film studios, factories, sovkhozy, schools and theaters. During the trip he wrote to the VOKS in Moscow: 'I'm learning to view Western Europe through better eyes and with the necessary distance. How

Joris Ivens, Valja Millman (VOKS) and Vsevolod Pudovkin in Moscow (1930). EFJI

dry and futureless everything is there, and how lively and human here.'[12] In Leningrad's Moskovska-Narvsky House he showed his films to the cadres of the glorious Putilov factory, but they were less enthusiastic than their fellow workers at The Builder. 'Our workers are themselves very familiar with dredging operations and dam construction,' concluded the ever-present observer. They found the films unsatisfying because they did not include 'the special aspects of Western technology that are unfamiliar to us. I also notice that with Ivens the cult of industry and the machine has a decided tendency to take on a typically intellectual character... Such a view of the machine is naturally foreign to a worker and forms a barrier to his acceptance of the film.' The Dutch guest had more success with an intellectual audience at Leningrad's Lenarch House. Director Leonid Trauberg introduced the films and applause sounded repeatedly during the screening. The report stated that 'the formal qualities of a number of films were especially appreciated, in particular RAIN.'[13]

The highlight of his visit to the Ukraine was a meeting with the great poet of the screen Alexander Dovzhenko, who was unexpectedly enthusiastic about BREAKERS and gave him the third reel of EARTH in exchange for a copy. In Tbilisi he spoke with Mikhail Kalatozov, who became world famous with his film about the Second World War, THE CRANES ARE FLYING. The Georgian would later be one of the witnesses at Joris Ivens and Helene van Dongen's marriage in Los Angeles. During a tour of the Georgian film factory, one of the proletarian extras heard the Dutch visitor speaking French. Back in Holland, Ivens described the incident: 'He immediately addressed me in that language, fluently and excitedly discussing all kinds of things and finishing off by saying that he was glad to have a chance to speak French again. Afterwards the director told me that the person who had done me the honor was a former Caucasian grand duke or something like that.'[14]

The Georgians were the first people to be moved to tears by RAIN, and audiences in Armenia gaped in astonishment at ZUIDERZEE WORKS. One labor functionary asked Ivens how much a land reclamation project like that cost. Upon hearing the amount, he did not hesitate to offer an equally large tract of land in Armenia for half the price, with an invitation to all seven million Dutchmen and women to come and live there.

To his regret Ivens had to return home; his work at Capi was calling and unfinished films were waiting. 'But perhaps the most important reason was... the desire to tell my own people about Russia. Something like the spirit of a crusader.'[15] He had shot some film with his Kinamo during his travels, and in Amsterdam he edited this together with some old footage to make the eight-minute short NEWS FROM THE SOVIET UNION. He also asked the VOKS to provide some Soviet films for him to use during lectures in Holland: 'Could you please protect my semi-political work with a cover of artistic films. You understand me.'[16]

On April 6, 1930 Ivens returned to Amsterdam, where both the Filmliga art lovers and the ardent VVVC supporters were eagerly anticipating his account of his travels. The Filmliga members were catered for by a talk in De Uitkijk and an interview in *De Groene Amsterdammer*. The interviewer was board member Jordaan who met Ivens 'in the Filmliga library' at his home on the Singel. 'The samovar starts steaming and Ivens presents me with a glass of hot tea with a splash of vodka.' The traveler related that his total impression of the Soviet Union was one of feverish activity and 'strict simplicity of morals and the environment'. The only primitive thing left was the streetcar service. Speaking of the Five-Year Plan, he said: 'As far as I could tell, everyone was full of it and ready to participate in it.' The Western press was already publishing substantially-true horror stories about the forced collectivization, then in full swing. Ivens declared: 'I don't have anything to do with politics and, as a result, I had neither the desire nor the occasion to go into such matters.' He was 'a filmmaker and that's all' but thought that 'the mania for meetings and discussion would be more likely to encourage freedom of speech rather than suppress it... as long as it's public. The only thing the Soviet authorities seem scared to death of is underhandedness – what we'd call 'intrigues'.'[17]

Two weeks after his return, he addressed a crowded auditorium at the VVVC matinee at the Cinema Royal in Amsterdam. The communist daily *De Tribune* noted that 'Comrade Ivens' praised the close collaboration between Russia's film artists and the mass of the workers, spoke of the immense enthusiasm for the Five-Year Plan, and declared that he would like to return to Russia to make a film about the spectacular socialist development. Ivens also gave lectures about his trip in other parts of the country, including at his old school, the College of Economics in Rotterdam, where he covered the wall of the lecture theater with Soviet statistics and informed his audience that he was glad that Marx had some influence, even though he had heard nothing but bad things about him during his studies.[18] Some of his Amsterdam friends had now begun speaking of 'Boris' Ivens.[19]

Ivens had probably told Jordaan that he had nothing to do with politics because he didn't want to offend his Filmliga friends, but the use of the term 'Comrade Ivens' in *De Tribune* shows that the CPH already counted him as one of their own. He became even more active in party-linked organizations such as the VVVC. In the winter of 1930-1931, acting on Leo van Lakerveld's instructions, Ivens edited VVVC NEWSREELS as an alternative to traditional newsreels. They were partly intended for screening at the Sunday matinees Van Lakerveld organized in several large Amsterdam theaters.

The first VVVC NEWSREEL was put together from newsreels borrowed from Polygoon. Ivens recut them to create the desired political impact, then returned them to their original state after screening and sent them back to their owners. Later VVVC NEWSREELS covered subjects such as the work of International Red Aid, the life of Lenin, the Russian and German revolutions and, according to *De Tribune*: 'the war-mongering powers; the global terror; the International Red Aid demonstration of March 8 and the police behavior on the Leidseplein; fascism (Mussolini, Hindenburg and the Pope); the counterrevolution and a gas attack; development in the Soviet Union; the Red Army on the alert.'[20]

In the autumn of 1930, Ivens also initiated a VVVC-based workers' photography collective. 'I tried to set it up with Jef Last and a few Communist workers. We'd give workers a camera and send them into the Jordaan or the Dapper neighborhood and we'd organize – without their knowing – some kind of occurrence: a squabble between neighbors or two fishwives going at each other.'[21] He did not persevere for very long. He didn't really believe in photography and was never able to raise much interest in it. 'Grandfather was a baker, father was a baker, and now the son doesn't want to bake any more rolls.'

Ivens had doctrinaire beliefs, according to Lou Lichtveld, who collaborated intensively with him in this period, but strangely enough you didn't notice it in day-to-day contact. He never tried to whip up support, but simply found it self-evident that you would join Netherlands-New Russia. 'If you didn't, you were a bit of a dope.'[22]

In Moscow Ivens had sold a large number of copies of THE BRIDGE, RAIN, ZUIDERZEE and several other parts of WE ARE BUILDING to Sovkino's distribution company for 3,200 dollars,[23] and new clients approached him soon after his return to Holland. The head of publicity at the light bulb company Philips, a fellow member of the Filmliga, asked him to make a film for the company. He was now faced with a difficult choice. He could begin work in the Soviet Union in October, but the commission from Philips gave him a chance to justify the formation of the Capi Film Company to his father. He decided to accept the Philips job, even though working in the Soviet Union remained his ideal. In early 1931 he sent new proposals for films to Moscow and received a new invitation in response. He wrote back that he was delighted to come 'this time as a co-worker instead of a guest'.[24] The work for Philips took longer than anticipated and he also accepted a second commercial commission, so he was not able to actually leave for Moscow until autumn 1931.

Left-wing artists of the day found nothing unusual in the combination of political and commercial work. Dutch Bauhaus architect Mart Stam, for instance, worked on both the famous Van Nelle factory in Rotterdam and the steel town of Magnitogorsk in the USSR. With his Philips film, Ivens decided to avoid the conflict between his political convictions and the nature of the commissioning company by giving a neutral picture of the production process. It was to be the 'cinematic expression of a, rather, *the* twentieth-century production line manufacturer', as he apparently explained to an *NRC* reporter. He wrote a scenario of a little over one hand-written page and, together with John Fernhout and Mark Kolthoff, left for Eindhoven, 'where the new great work of Holland's cinematic avant-garde would be filmed by Joris Ivens and his assistants'.[25] Dressed in brown overalls, Ivens and his crew set up great batteries of lights in the production sheds: the 'Nine Eye', the 'Jupiter', the 'Americans' and the 'Weinerts'. The film crew had advanced technology at its disposal and Ivens was able to give full rein to his craftsmanship. The sharp lines and rhythmic movements of the industrial surroundings gave him every opportunity to further develop the esthetics of THE BRIDGE. As energetic as ever, Ivens worked so hard in

Eindhoven that his assistant Kolthoff went to bed totally exhausted every night, only to be kept awake by the sound of his director enjoying himself with an unidentified local woman in the room above his.[26]

The media spoke of a film 'by Joris Ivens and Lou Lichtveld' because the latter provided music and sound effects. PHILIPS RADIO became the first Dutch film with sound. A number of journalists in their wake, the filmmakers traveled to the sound-film studio Films Sonores Tobis in an old cloister in Épinay-sur-Seine, near Paris. There 'volunteers also assist with the grinding stone, the windlass, the oxygen tank, or on any other noise-making device that can be dragged in. A Filmliga spokesman drives back and forth in a small electric cart as if re-enacting the chariot scene in BEN HUR. And outside the studio, where a microphone has been placed on the quiet lawn, the amused manager of a Dutch weekly drives up and down in his car to engender the desired 'background noise'.'[27]

PHILIPS RADIO had been planned as a silent film and the decision to add sound was only made after the visual material had been shot. This caused special technical problems. In Eindhoven they had filmed at 18 to 20 frames per second, but the soundtrack had to be recorded at 24 frames per second. When screening, it was impossible to have both tracks running at the correct speed. Accordingly PHILIPS RADIO has been called 'a hybrid, if not an amphibian film', with one foot in the silent era, and the other in that of the sound-film.[28]

During the premiere of PHILIPS RADIO in Amsterdam's Tuschinski Theater on September 28, 1931, a Philips engineer mounted the stage to hang giant laurel wreaths around the necks of Joris Ivens and Lou Lichtveld, an event which, in the light of Ivens's political convictions, was not entirely devoid of irony. Commenting on the words of praise from the 'gentleman from Philips', the party daily *De Tribune* sniggered: 'Meanwhile we have the presumption to believe that we saw more in the film than did the bourgeoisie in the auditorium.' The evening's program also included the first screening of Hans Richter's short film EUROPA RADIO, another Philips commission. Earlier Ivens had written to Jan Hin: 'As you know, I do not have a very high opinion of Richter's working method.'[29]

The Dutch reviews of PHILIPS RADIO were favorable but far from jubilant. A striking number of critics complained that Ivens showed an excessive interest in the machinery and too little interest in the people who worked at it. 'Ivens didn't see any people in the factories,' wrote *Het Volk*, and even spoke of a *'document inhumain'*.[30] The filmmaker himself developed an ambiguous attitude to this piece of work. He sometimes liked considering it a documentary version of Chaplin's MODERN TIMES, but although Ivens also showed man as an appendage of the machine, he lacked Chaplin's critical approach. At other times Ivens simply said that the film gave an impression 'of what a cineaste who is sympathetic to the product sees'. More than anything, his film shows his enormous respect for modern technology, an admiration that was consistent with the aim of the film. During shooting Ivens explained to an *NRC* journalist: 'The audience has to be fascinated by what it sees, it has to be impressed by the company, so that it goes away thinking: a company with a set-up like this must make a good product.'[31] He had made a company film in pure Neue Sachlichkeit style, something no one could reasonably object to. Although there were apparently some dissenting voices, the management of Philips was generally satisfied and the screening even brought tears to the eyes of old Mr. Philips. A company press release spoke of a 'good modern film', and Philips proudly referred to 'our Ivens film' in letters to the Commission for Film Censorship.[32]

This did not stop the film from being cut for screenings in Rotterdam and Nijmegen. The film was too long to be part of a double feature within a normal program, and as a concession to the theater operators, Philips arranged for it to be shortened. The abstract, experimental ending took the brunt. Philips even went so far as to give Rotterdam's Thalia Theater written permission to cut the film at its own discretion. Joris Ivens was already in Moscow, but there was a heated exchange of letters between Wim Ivens and Philips, followed by correspondence between their lawyers. The conflict was finally settled amicably, with company heads Kees Ivens and Anton Philips personally assuring each other that they valued an ongoing cordial business relationship.[33]

In 1932, after his experience with PHILIPS RADIO, Ivens wrote to Helene van Dongen and Lou Lichtveld from Moscow, asking them to make a sound version of RAIN with music composed by Lichtveld. Van Dongen and Lichtveld traveled to Épinay for the recordings, but the critical reception of this sound version was mixed and, looking back later, Ivens himself found that the 'power of the silent film was somewhat impaired by this Debussy-like music'.[34]

By the time PHILIPS RADIO premiered, Ivens's other commercial film had already reached an advanced stage of production: CREOSOTE, an educational film for the Continental Commission for the Propagation of Creosote. A byproduct of chemical factories and iron and steel plants, creosote was used for impregnating railroad sleepers, telegraph poles, and other wooden products. The Creosote Commission had already worked out the main line of the film, the locations had been chosen, and Ivens called in French cineaste Jean Dréville to help with the work. Shooting took place in the spring and summer of 1931 in the forests of Polish Silesia, on the Vistula River – one photo shows Dréville and Ivens on a timber raft in coat and tie and surrounded by workers – and at further locations in France, Belgium, Germany and Holland. The result was a professional educational film that fully satisfied the requirements of the commissioning body.

Disagreement later arose over the credits for CREOSOTE. Although Ivens remarked in *The Camera and I* that he shared the direction with Dréville, his filmographies state that he was solely responsible for direction and editing and list Dréville as cameraman. In turn, Dréville claimed to have directed the film alone, and said that Ivens was too busy with PHILIPS RADIO and only lent an occasional hand. According to Dréville, Ivens's only actual role was that of producer. Dréville also claimed to have done the editing. In fact Ivens traveled to Épinay to work on the Philips film several times during shooting; Helene van Dongen, who was involved in the editing, referred to it as 'Dréville's film' in the *festschrift* for Ivens's sixty-fifth birthday; and Ivens did not wait for the completion of the work before returning to the Soviet Union. CREOSOTE premiered in The Hague on January 26, 1932, three and a half months after Ivens's departure. [35]

Late in 1930 the newspapers had reported the foundation of Studio Ivens, with Joris Ivens providing leadership and technical supervision for his co-workers, 'with due regard for their artistic independence'. Ten months after this proclamation, however, the supervisor departed to the Soviet Union for more than a year and later declared: 'I don't know how that studio ended, it never actually existed, I provided some space.' Mark Kolthoff said: 'Studio Ivens was just a name, it was nothing,' and Helene van Dongen attributed the pompous title to the courtesy of the press more than anything else. [36] Studio Ivens was basically the Capi Film Company, the company that was owned by Ivens senior and employed Ivens junior, and had produced WE ARE BUILDING, PHILIPS RADIO and CREOSOTE.

Kees Ivens later decided that he had been wrong in consenting to the foundation of the film company. In 1935 he wrote in his diary: 'Capi plucked and plundered enough by George's methods. The F.C. [film company] has brought Capi to the brink of ruin.' Although things were going badly for the family business, it is questionable whether a real commitment from Joris Ivens would have made much difference as there were serious structural problems. In 1924 the Maas-Waalsche Bank, where Capi had a revolving credit of 250,000 guilders, went bankrupt, and 'from then on the problems began', as Kees Ivens wrote in a more realistic mood. Wim had sacrificed his entire capital to Capi, and George had worked hard as well, but the fundamental issue remained insufficient working capital.[37] In the course of the 1930s, Capi became an incorporated company, and control passed largely into the hands of others. It must have been scant consolation for Kees Ivens that the Capi Film Company had allowed his son and various other Dutch documentary filmmakers to learn the trade in the days when there was no Dutch film school.

After October 9, 1931, when Joris Ivens departed for the Soviet Union, thirty-five years would pass before he worked in Holland again. In the intervening decades he would make a long journey through the international communist movement.

'Before you could become a party member, the mass organizations checked whether you were serious,' said Ivens.[38] He was judged suitable and a document in the former Central Party Archives in Moscow confirms that in 1931 he joined the CPH – rechristened the CPN in 1935 – and was still a member in 1936. According to that same document, he was not an 'activist' in Holland but had, as a filmmaker, 'done a lot of work for the Dutch section of International Red Aid and the Friends of the Soviet Union'.[39] Mark Kolthoff, who also moved in CPH circles, believed that, in contrast to the usual practice, Ivens was not part of a cell – the basic party unit in a factory or neighborhood – and was thus an outsider within the party. Ivens's party mentor was Gerard Vanter, a former editor of the party newspaper *De Tribune*, chairman of the Friends of the Soviet Union, and one of the key players in the party's links with Moscow. Joris was in awe of Vanter according to young Lou Lichtveld, who served as go-between for the two in Amsterdam.[40] Ivens consulted with central committee member Alex de Leeuw on ideological questions, and his dues were collected by Arie van Poelgeest, a barge hand who later fought in Spain. Whenever the CPH was holding one of its many financial campaigns, Van Poelgeest would call on Ivens: 'He was a milk cow, we asked him for money a lot.'[41]

Joris Ivens's admission to the CPH and his departure for the USSR represented a breach with his family; furthermore, his departure came down to a de facto resignation of his position with Capi. The success of his film work had long convinced him that there were alternatives to a future as a dealer in photographic equipment, but he found it very difficult to cut his ties to his family, especially as his job at Capi offered him financial security and provided opportunity for cinematic experimentation. From an early age he had learnt to accommodate his parents, and they had always assumed that he would eventually take over the business. When his interests began devel-

oping in another direction, his father had seized every opportunity to impress his responsibilities upon him. Seeing his work for the liberation of the
proletariat as a higher task might have helped him to finally cast aside the
shackles of family.

It is uncertain whether he explicitly informed his parents of his decision
to leave Capi or simply departed for Moscow without saying whether or not
he would be returning. After all, this was the path he took later when wanting to break with a wife, girlfriend or political ally: years of evasive circling
were preferable to a confrontation. No matter how radical his political
standpoints, in personal relationships he had an extreme need for harmony
and avoided any discussions that could lead to differences of opinion.

Now that he had finally stopped letting his father have his way, the reaction was furious. 'George (Joris) turned out to be unsuitable for steady, te-
dious, solid work,' wrote Kees Ivens in his diary. 'I pointed that out to him.
He claimed things were all right. Then went off roaming after all and deserted the Capi ranks. The long-term result was the loss of the whole Capi
structure. We were supposed to make George's capacities productive
through the Film Company. The idea fascinated Wim. Mountains of gold
were promised and it turned into a fiasco. George couldn't stick it out and
went to Moscow. Forgetting his obligations to his parents, his family, Wim
and the Capi shareholders. With 'Moscow' George has hastened the collapse (May 1935) of the Hague Capi store.' Elsewhere in the same diary, his
father expressed himself even more forcefully: 'Antagonized everyone with
his unprecedented nonchalance... Annoying the Managing Director of Capi
and hurting his parents greatly with everything. Causing severe damage to
Capi with his social stance... Oozing nonchalance, naive selfishness, messi-
ness, antisocial egocentricity. But good at heart with all of that.'[42]

Kees Ivens had started out believing in the Capi Film Company, and
when the front page of the newspaper *De Telegraaf* showed photos of
George working on PHILIPS RADIO, he had proudly had it framed. This
made his disappointment all the more bitter. Despite being able to admit
that George was 'good at heart', he still tended to blame him for all his problems. Joris Ivens never forgot his father's angry outburst: 'You've only
made one real film in your life, THE BRIDGE, and you won't make any more
in the rest of your life either.'[43] He even remembered them as his father's
words of farewell. They weren't, but it shows how much this rejection
stung. Father and son met occasionally without the slightest animosity
throughout the thirties, and it wasn't until April 17, 1939, when Joris Ivens
interrupted his international wanderings for a lightning visit to Nijmegen,
that the two saw each other for the last time. His father found their conversation 'particularly frank' and kept hoping for a miracle. In the Capi annual

report for 1939 he still spoke of Capi's 'Assistant Director Joris Ivens, whose cinematic work has taken him to America. Naturally 'without cost to Capi'... His work has made him very well known, if not famous, over there, and that also benefits Capi here.' On May 4, 1940, six days before the German army crossed the Dutch borders, Kees Ivens made a last attempt to convince George to retrace his footsteps: 'Together we now need to reach a definitive decision, not only in our interest, but in your interest. You're constantly fostering goodwill for your name as a cinematic artist, but that could take so long that, by the time your name is established, your body will no longer be able to stand up to your bohemian lifestyle.'[44] Kees Ivens never stopped deluding himself that the prodigal son would one day return.

Upon joining the Communist movement, Joris Ivens felt 'a new emotion, that was stronger and more essential, namely that I was part of an international community and a generation that formed the vanguard of world revolution'.[45] He was incapable of fully committing himself in personal relationships and it seems likely that his utopian beliefs were a partial substitute for this. He now had one constant bond to which he could devote himself. His relationship with the Communist party came to resemble the situation in his childhood. Where his parents had once lovingly mapped out his life and expected him to subordinate himself to the interests of the family, this role was now fulfilled by the party and the working class. In return he gained a sense of security, the experience of belonging, and a reassuring conceptual framework that explained the world. 'I'm not crazy about doubt. I need my certainties to be able to live,' he wrote in his memoirs. He derived a phenomenal amount of energy from his participation in the movement, from a political commitment that remained a strange combination of almost childlike faith and first-hand knowledge of the suspect mores within the Communist apparatus. Rather than being a marginal figure on the edge of the movement, he was right in the middle of it and, as a filmmaker, helped to shape it. Ivens's character was not suited to the role of unattached fellow traveler; he was too practical, more interested in deeds than in theoretical reflections.

In the thirties many intellectuals and artists shared his Communist convictions. It was the era of the great ideologies of the left and the right. Organized labor was a powerful factor within society and the choice between capitalism and socialism seemed urgent. The history of Communism was relatively new and the full scope of its consequences had not yet become apparent. Not unreasonably, Ivens later invoked the *air du temps* to explain his position, but it is also true that he paid little heed to the opinions of friends like Arthur Lehning and Germaine Krull, people who had recognized the inevitable consequences of the teachings of Lenin and Stalin.

During their walks in Nijmegen, Ivens's father had told him about the liberal ideal of progress and about technology in the service of mankind. Wasn't the development of socialism in the USSR actually a logical extension of his father's ideas? Hadn't his father taught him that building a steelworks was a step toward the salvation of humanity? And the Five-Year Plan that the Soviet proletariat devoted all its energy to, wasn't that just the systematic fulfillment of that dream of progress? In Russia the working man was shaping the new era, and Ivens's technical background gave him a particular affinity for this side of affairs. The discussions with Soviet workers, who were able to express their visions so clearly and succinctly, had confirmed his faith in the historical mission of the proletarian class. 'A callused palm is the passport to the Soviet Union,' he declared during his lectures after his first trip to the USSR.[46]

His position was similar to that of affluent youth in the sixties: the miserable circumstances of the poor contrasted so sharply with their own affluence that they made it seem somehow despicable. He too had been born on easy street and was able to look forward to a life of boredom. For Ivens, Marsman's words lost none of their validity: 'Spectacular and moving is the life I want! You hear me, Father, Mother, world, charnel house!' A life by the side of the proletariat would not only require sacrifices, it also held the promise of excitement and adventure.

Since his first visit to the Soviet Union, he had been convinced that his future as a filmmaker lay there and nowhere else. In the *Revue des Vivants* he wrote: 'Because of an excess of individualism and an overly artistic attitude, Europe is not open to the social effects of the documentary. Consequently I think that the development of my concept, of my cinematographic ideal, can only be achieved in Russia.'[47]

6 The Magnetic Mountain (1932)

Anneke van der Feer, Helene van Dongen, Filmliga boardmember L.J. Jordaan and several others gathered on a platform at Amsterdam's Central Station on October 9, 1931 to see Joris Ivens off. On the way to Moscow, he made a short stopover in Berlin to attend the International Proletarian Film Conference at Willi Münzenberg's Weltfilm. The participants included Münzenberg himself, Hans Richter, Béla Balázs, and the Italian Francesco Misiano – head of the Mezhrabpom Studio where Ivens would be working. Ivens gave a speech about the problems confronting socialist filmmakers in capitalist countries.[1]

He was not the only Western filmmaker on his way to Moscow. In 1930 the Soviet regime's specialist for culture, Anatoly Lunacharsky, had written: 'The well-known film company Mezhrabpom has been given the job of aiming a considerable proportion of its production at the Western market, in the first instance for working-class audiences in those countries. We assume that, with the help of revolutionary writers and other European artists, Mezhrabpom will be able to honorably acquit itself of this task.'[2] In the year that followed Mezhrabpom invited not only Ivens, but also Balázs, Richter, Ruttmann, stage director Erwin Piscator, the German-Czech author and journalist Egon Erwin Kisch, and the Austrian composer Hanns Eisler.[3] Despite his Communist sympathies, Ruttmann preferred to stay in Germany, where a few years later he made a prologue for TRIUMPH OF THE WILL, Leni Riefenstahl's film about the Nazi party rally in Nuremberg. Piscator had left for Moscow in the spring, and Richter had started work on his film METAL in the Ukraine.

After arriving in the Soviet capital, Ivens confided to the daily *Vechernyaya Moskva*: 'Here I can work the way I want to. Being here gives me a new lease of life both personally and artistically... The time has come to apply all the knowledge and experience we have acquired abroad on the front of the revolutionary film in the Soviet Union.' He showed PHILIPS RADIO, but the Soviets followed the Dutch press in remarking upon the minimal role of people in this film. Just five weeks after the gala premiere in Amsterdam's Tuschinski Theater, Ivens felt obliged to declare: 'Between you and me, the left-wing school of cinematography and businessmen (who commissioned the film) are eternal enemies.' He added that the commissioning company had 'strictly restricted' him to 'mainly filming the machines in the factory and to a much lesser degree the workers'.[4] In reality the only limitation Philips set was that the shooting had to take place within the factory gates.

In Amsterdam Wim Ivens was shocked to find extensive quotes from his brother's statement in *De Tribune*. He wrote to Philips that 'we are convinced that Joris Ivens would never have even thought the perfidious opinions attributed to him in that article, let alone voiced them... We are still negotiating with *De Tribune* about the possibility of a rectification.' Philips engineer Halbertsma, who had hung a wreath around Joris Ivens's neck in the Tuschinski, now visited Kees Ivens in Nijmegen. Halbertsma reported the long-suffering father as saying that his son's 'only relationship with the Soviets was in his capacity as filmmaker' and that his son 'did not share their revolutionary convictions'. At the insistence of Wim Ivens *De Tribune* finally published a rectification informing readers that 'the name Philips was not mentioned' in the Russian article. This made little difference, and in the light of Ivens's earlier statements about the filmmaker's place in the West, one can assume that *Vechernyaya Moskva* had rendered his words faithfully.[5]

Ivens left Helene van Dongen behind in Amsterdam and moved into a very modest Moscow apartment with Anneke van der Feer. They too were affected by the omnipresent poverty in Moscow. 'There were shortages everywhere... We mostly ate in the film club canteen, which was a frugal meal, and sometimes treated ourselves to a luxury restaurant.' Ivens and Van der Feer led an artistic life Moscow-style with his studio colleagues. They drank vodka, smoked *papirosy* and 'worked through the whole world's repertoire of revolutionary songs until early in the morning'. Van der Feer arranged some work for herself in the form of drawings from Moscow for leftist Dutch magazines.

In 1932 the first Five-Year Plan was drawing to a close. Soviet industry was being built up at a phenomenal rate and the collectivization of agriculture had been imposed by force, with the 'liquidation of the kulaks as a class' as strategic objective. 'Kulak' was a term of abuse for wealthier peasants, but since countless others also resisted collectivization, the name was often extended to include all those who raised objections. The liquidation of the 'class' amounted to a death sentence for hundreds of thousands of peasants, with millions more deported or condemned to forced labor. The policies led to a famine that claimed millions of victims, especially in the south of the Soviet Union. Ivens could not know everything, but when confronted with unpleasant facts he told himself that they were a necessary evil. Revolutionary development demanded sacrifice. 'I considered that life had been turned upside down by this change, that chaos and anarchy were unavoidable, and resistance too, and that the most important thing was the general line,' he wrote as an old man.

In search of inspiration, he spent several months touring the Soviet Union, visiting numerous industrial projects and the Baltic Fleet. 'It is tremendous to see that in big factories of ten or twenty thousand workers, even the most junior worker is interested in the factory as a whole and knows everything there is to know about the production process and the organization,' he wrote to Henrik Scholte in Amsterdam.[6] Ivens produced a script about the role of young people in socialist development, an all-encompassing epic, set in the northern Caucasus, the Urals and Central Asia. Mezhrabpom director Pudovkin considered the plan unworkable and advised him to focus it. Ivens opted for the construction of blast furnaces in the new steel town of Magnitogorsk, in the Urals, where the youth organization Komsomol played a major role. A collective was formed under Ivens's artistic leadership, with the political responsibility in the hands of the Moscow Komsomol, who gave Ivens a 'concise Bolshevik education'.[7] A young man called Andreyev joined the crew as their representative, and the Komsomol group from the capital's N-1 factory adopted the film. Iosif Skliut was appointed scriptwriter and Englishman Herbert Marshall was made assistant director. Marshall was studying at the Moscow film school (GIK), where Ivens was an occasional lecturer. Marshall and Skliut became good friends, and it wasn't until years later that the Englishman discovered that Skliut reported to the security services about him.[8]

In the Mezhrabpom film factory, monthly meetings were held for the entire staff of some five to six hundred, with sessions of criticism and self-criticism and a committee on the stage. Ivens sat in on a 'comradely hearing about someone who had been pilfering in the kitchen'.[9] The tone of these meetings was reflected in the text supporting his film plans, which he submitted to Litotdel, the studio's all-powerful literary office: 'As a party member, I naturally reinforced my subjective impressions with a political education in Marxism-Leninism, and my daily small revolutionary activities enabled me to better carry out my responsible film work.'[10] In fact he never studied Marxism-Leninism very thoroughly, and his announcement that he would base his film 'on dialectical materialism' meant little, unless the label can be affixed to every cinematic use of antithesis.

In the Soviet Union of 1932, obtaining permission to carry out a film project was an arduous process. Pudovkin summarized the state of affairs in deferential terms in the Western magazine *Experimental Film*: 'The State has given the cinema an educational role, in the broadest sense of the term. It is not possible for any person to film anything he pleases. Each script, before entering production, is submitted to the various departments which pass judgement upon its cultural, artistic, and ideological values. If any details are found amiss, the writer is called in, and, together with the head of the department in question, he corrects his work.'[11] In reality the departmental intervention went far beyond the details, but by February Ivens had nonetheless gained the approval of the Muscovite Komsomol committee, the Litotdel and the Mezhrabpom management, and he and his crew were able to leave by train for the Urals on March 25, 1932.[12] Anneke van der Feer apparently stayed behind in Moscow. The film crew had signed a 'contract of competition' with the crew of director Boris Barnet, who was working on OUTSKIRTS. The contract committed them to completing their film by October 22, three weeks earlier than planned, so that it could be screened at the fifteenth anniversary of the Moscow Komsomol.[13]

Magnitogorsk was built near Mount Magnitaya, a deposit of iron ore so vast it made compasses go wild even at a distance. It had been a hamlet of a hundred souls in the middle of the steppe, but now a city was being built around an enormous blast furnace complex, reputedly the world's largest. It was an enterprise of epic proportion, a concentration of faith in the belief that a new world could be built by human hands. Jef Last too had been deeply impressed. That summer, during a train journey through the Urals with the Frenchman Louis Aragon and other writers, he had noted his impressions of the pioneer town: 'A year ago the train station at Magnitogorsk was nothing more than a furnished freight car. Now there is a wooden shed, in two years there will probably be a brick building with a steel roof. Surrounding the station is a howling wilderness where the newly arrived workers who have not yet been housed in barracks have built filthy black huts from peat and mud.'[14] The city, with a population of almost two hundred thousand, lay on a desolate gray plain that was covered by a thick layer of snow and ice for months on end in the winter, and could turn into a sea of knee-deep mud in the spring and autumn. The first blast furnace had already been completed and the second, the Komsomolska, was under construction. 'The earth has been torn open along a length of miles,' wrote Last. 'In the chasm-like gashes the workers lay the black snake of gigantic pipes. From the depths of round craters, they pass the excavated earth up through three rows. Our road passes over veritable mountains of piled up planks and iron. In an empty plain six massive, heavy chimneys rise up to the heavens, rows of freight cars thunder towards them over a concrete viaduct. Glowing walls of coke fall hissing into the waiting cars, the white steam from the blast furnaces covers the horizon like a gigantic curtain.'[15] The construction of the blast furnaces had been supervised by American engineers and the city had been planned by Ernst May, municipal architect of Frankfurt. In Magnitogorsk Joris Ivens undoubtedly met the Dutch architects Mart Stam and Johan Niegeman, May's assistants.

Ivens and his crew set up camp in a wooden barrack without toilet facilities. In three months they became hardened pioneers. 'Our skin was tanned by frost and sun, we had become used to hunting lice and cockroaches the whole night through, we didn't have an ounce of superfluous fat, we could say with pride that we had stood the test of the elements. All the same, I had terrible problems with my asthma and I had the first symptoms of typhus.'[16] The enthusiastic workers and the Komsomol youth who went to Magnitogorsk to build a new world, the workers sent there by their superiors and the foreign advisors all suffered great deprivations, but conditions were far worse for the approximately thirty-five thousand political prisoners who were forced to carry out the heaviest work, such as the excavations Last described so heroically. They were families who had resisted collectivization, been transported in packed freight cars, given a patch of barren land to live on, and were escorted to work each day under armed guard. The first group arrived in May 1931 and in the first six months of that year many of them died, including more than five thousand children. In Magnitogorsk the former 'kulaks' lived in four special settlements, where the principle 'those who don't work won't eat' was rigorously enforced and the sick were doomed. Their conditions did not improve until several years later.[17] Ivens was aware of the prisoners but does not seem to have given them much thought. In his memoirs he wrote open-heartedly: 'I cursed them now and then, the way you curse weeds in your garden.' Whenever there was a power failure, the habit was to blame it on the kulaks, just as everything that went wrong in the USSR at that time was attributed to sabotage. Later, Ivens still wrote: 'In the daytime they dug, at night they committed sabotage.'[18]

Instead of the fate of people like these, Ivens concentrated on the great ideal as personified by the model workers of Magnitogorsk, whose names were renowned throughout the Soviet Union. There is no mention of forced labor in his film, although prisoners are presumably visible in some shots. Ivens was swept along by the heroism of those workers who really had volunteered to labor to build socialism, the revolutionary proletariat striving on the work front. Cameraman Shelenkov recalled his director continually exclaiming: 'They are heroes! They are real heroes!'[19]

At Ivens's request, Otto Katz, the director of the German division of Mezhrabpom, contracted the composer Hanns Eisler to write the film music. Ivens knew Eisler from Berlin. A brilliant pupil of the Viennese composer Arnold Schönberg, Eisler had broken with the master in order to dedicate himself to socially-committed applications of music. The small, portly man, who was as bald as a billiard ball by the age of twenty-one, had written scores for plays by Bertolt Brecht, film music for KUHLE WAMPE (a production of Willi Münzenberg's Prometheus Film) and, above all, militant songs known by workers all over the world. In May 1932 Eisler took the train from Berlin to Magnitogorsk, where he was immediately given a pair of overalls. He used a graphophone to record the industrial sounds and immersed himself in the local folk music.

Late in May, the crew traveled to Kusnetsk, more than a thousand miles to the east, to film the transportation of coke to the blast furnaces. At a station *en route* a telegram arrived from Moscow informing them that, on the basis of the work report, the crew had officially been declared a Shock Brigade. The crew members were presented with prestigious red Shock Brigade books – with portraits of Lenin and Stalin in the front – which entitled them to somewhat better meals at public restaurants and a number of other privileges. In Kusnetsk, according to Ivens, 'there was a barber shop, which was equipped with several ordinary chairs but had only one professional barber chair. Our Shock Brigade books gave us the privilege of sitting in this special chair for a haircut.'[20]

In July he made a lightning trip to Western Europe, gave a speech at the International Congress for Photography in Leipzig, visited Amsterdam, and filmed demonstrations in London and Berlin for the prologue of his Magnitogorsk film. The film, called SONG OF HEROES, 'dedicated to struggling proletarian youth', starts with these images of crisis and conflict in the capitalist world, then moves on to the triumphant development of socialism. The different phases in the construction of a blast furnace are shown in a bedlam of fire and noise in which purposeful and dedicated workers fulfil their tasks. Insert titles such as 'We must become a land of Steel and Iron. We must catch up with the capitalist countries and surpass them (Stalin)', the stirring passages in Eisler's music, and the omission of essential information make SONG OF HEROES dubious and propagandistic, but stylistically it is a fine example of Neue Sachlichkeit, building on ZUIDERZEE and PHILIPS RADIO.

Even before leaving for Magnitogorsk, Ivens had become entangled in a heated conflict at Mezhrabpom over the direction the film was taking. Pudovkin had advised him to use the experiences of a single worker as his main storyline, thus giving the audience an opportunity for identification, but when Ivens submitted plans based on that method, he was attacked by adherents of the theories of Dziga Vertov, who believed that documentaries had to be objective and completely rejected the direction of action. Those concerned were supporters of the RAPP, the Russian Association of Proletarian Writers, who strove to proletarianize the art world and organize it into production units, but were stylistically so experimental that their work was incomprehensible to the average worker. Their final hour came in February 1932 when the magazine *Proletarskoye Kino* launched a fierce attack on their 'documentarism'. In April the party decided to disband the RAPP and all related organizations and place the art world under its direct control.[21] The tide had turned in favor of what later came to be called Socialist Realism.

Ivens joined in the debate and, in late February and early March, turned against the so-called 'documentarist' beliefs which, he added in conciliatory tones, had once been his own. He found them too rigid, because they failed to satisfy 'the conditions appropriate to the progress of socialist development in the Soviet Union' and led to 'formalism and a schematic approach... One does not become involved with the documents.'[22] For the first time, Joris Ivens had explicitly distanced himself from the avant-garde movement in which he had been prominent since THE BRIDGE, and embraced the theory of reconstruction – the re-enactment and staging of events – which he would defend for the rest of his life. There was actually nothing particularly surprising about any of this as the films of American documentary pioneer Robert Flaherty were well known in Russia and were largely based on re-enactments, the real new element was that other schools were now banned by the state.

In a *Filmliga* article in late 1932, Ivens sketched the changed atmosphere: 'The new Russian film concentrates on the tribulations of a single person' and documentaries had become 'a combination and interweaving of acted passages and argumentation'.[23] While filming SONG OF HEROES, he explained to a reporter that he was also working that way. 'We're not filming a fiction film but a documentary film in which a large number of so-called organized episodes take place.' Members of the Tram Group of Magnitogorsk, the local workers' theater, acted out the experiences of an ignorant peasant who is reshaped into a skilled worker.[24]

When Ivens returned to Moscow with his material, however, the Socialist Realists, who were now calling the tune in Moscow, attacked the formal Neue Sachlichkeit elements in SONG OF HEROES. As with PHILIPS RADIO, the preponderance of images of machinery was criticized.[25] Ivens's film itself was still heavily 'documentarist', and although he had promised beforehand that 'the material would not overshadow the political perspective',[26] this had happened: the form dominated the contents. He had not succeeded in building up a convincing story around the Kirghiz peasant worker Afanasyev. This was hardly surprising: he had virtually no experience with actors and needed two interpreters to communicate with his amateur lead, one from German to Russian and one from Russian to Kirghiz.

The bureaucrats also objected to the music. Eisler wrote the *Magnitogorsk Song* and the *Ballad of the Komsomols* to lyrics by the writer Sergei Tretyakov, who seems to have also traveled to Magnitogorsk. 'I remember you driving the whole floor of the Metropol Hotel mad,' Ivens wrote to Eisler. 'Tretyakov had written a poem that went 'Ural, Ural, magnitaya gora...' A piano was brought up to the room. Then you played the song on the piano, but so passionately that it had all the power of the Komsomol and Magnitogorsk in it. Everyone on the floor opened up their doors at the birth of the song *Magnitaya Gora*.' The songs were rejected by the music publisher's censors, but later accepted after all.[27] Tretyakov was suspect because he had been a long-time adherent of futurism and subsequently practiced what was known as the 'literature of the facts', a style that provided an 'objective' view of everyday events. In other words, he practiced a literary version of the detested 'documentarism'. Around this time Eisler and Tretyakov were also working on an opera about Magnitogorsk, which seems to have suffered the fate that originally befell their songs. The premiere in the Bolshoi Theater was announced in the newspaper but never took place.[28]

SONG OF HEROES was ready on October 1, but because of the criticism it was unable to premiere at the fifteenth anniversary celebrations of the Muscovite Komsomol as intended. On November 13 Tretyakov informed Eisler: 'Still unable to ascertain what has happened to prevent the release of Ivens's film. They say that the film is not a success, but I haven't been able to investigate this because Ivens is ill.'[29] Sometime in the 1920s, Ivens began suffering from recurring bouts of asthma. He had withstood the climate of the Urals only to be laid low by difficulties in Moscow, because nothing could make him so ill as being kept from his work. Finally, on January 2, 1933, SONG OF HEROES premiered in Moscow.

Several years later the film was shelved in the Soviet Union because it included lyrics by Tretyakov. Soviet film historian Drobashenko later wrote: 'SONG OF HEROES is the only film by Joris Ivens that was filmed with Soviet material. That makes it all the more insulting that audiences were not allowed to see it at the time.' It wasn't until December 1961, long after Stalin's death, that excerpts from the Magnitogorsk film were again shown, this time on Moscow television and accompanied by an interview with the filmmaker.[30] According to Ivens he only heard about the Soviet ban on the film in Eastern Europe in the fifties, and he did not discuss it publicly until shortly before his death.[31] Sergei Tretyakov and his wife were arrested as 'Japanese spies' in 1937. After a period of internment in a Siberian prison camp, he was executed in 1939.

On January 13, 1933, after a long train journey from the Soviet Union, Ivens was back at Amsterdam's Central Station. He enthusiastically related his experiences in the East to the waiting journalists and announced that he would be returning to the USSR in six months for another film. 'I will be accepting a new commission from Mezhrabpom to make a film about the culture brigades among the small obscure tribes in Kamchatka, where there are people who are hardly aware that there has been a world war. No one knows what kind of awesome future awaits in those regions and I find it attractive technically: the sound of pioneers amid the utter silence of the north, where every word becomes doubly pregnant. That is, after all, the ultimate – being an idealist on the basis of a concrete grasp of reality.' He was radiant, remarked the reporter from *Het Volk*. That same newspaper later called SONG OF HEROES 'the most beautiful symphony of work ever compiled', and in general the Dutch press was favorably disposed toward the film.[32]

As an ironic coincidence immediately after his return, Ivens was one of several filmmakers to receive an invitation from the 'Made in Holland' Association, in conjunction with the Ministry of Economic Affairs and Employment, to submit a scenario for a short film with the slogan: 'Don't buy foreign products when you can buy Dutch'. Ivens responded with a plan but the commission went to collegue Max de Haas. Nonetheless, it showed that Ivens's stay of more than a year in the USSR had not disqualified him from semi-governmental jobs.[33]

In Amsterdam numerous small revolutionary activities awaited him. In his absence, *De Tribune* had already announced that he would be one of the instructors at the Marxist Workers' School on the Prinsengracht. His first lesson there dealt with the question of how filmmakers could participate in the class struggle. In his notes we read: 'From the working class. Class conscious. Politically educated. Marx, Lenin. Revolutionary. Want class struggle – don't avoid it. But take a pure, sharp stand against capitalism – not becoming a Social Democrat who obscures the struggle – mobilize yourself in the revolutionary struggle of the proletariat under the leadership of the Communist party. This also applies to filmmakers who have not emerged from the working class. Herein lie dangers. With many artists it is only a particular revolutionary temperament that moves them to take the side of the workers. They are fiercely opposed to the rottenness of all bourgeois and capitalist conditions. But that's as far as it goes. They are too vague, anarchistic in their thinking – or religious.'

Although he might not have said so himself, he was a textbook example of this category that was, in his own words, 'poisoned from childhood and through many years of education with bourgeois ideology'. The solution for

cinematic workers was to ally themselves 'with the day-to-day revolutionary struggle, with the masses, with the organizations'. His lectures also covered Soviet cinema, the usefulness of the film medium in the class struggle,
and Western film, in which love served as a diversionary tactic to make
'class differences matter less', and a 'deceptive' appeal was made to family
feelings.[34] As far as his remark about the family was concerned, this had
more to do with his own situation than with the lives of his working-class
audience: they saw the family as the cornerstone of the proletarian community.

He also participated in a campaign against the German film DAWN
by Gustav Ucicky. On January 30, 1933 Adolf Hitler had come to power
in Germany, and in March the Rembrandt Theater on Amsterdam's
Rembrandtplein programmed DAWN, about a heroic World War I U-boat
crew. When their submarine is hit after a successful mission, two of the crew
members offer themselves up to save the rest, declaring: 'We Germans
might not know how to live, but how to die, that's something we know!' Political organizations to the left of the Social Democrats saw the film as milita-
ristic German propaganda and formed a committee in which Joris Ivens and
Jef Last played an important role. By that time Last had become a CPH
member. A week of riots on the Rembrantplein and demonstrations in the
theater followed. During the screening, slogans were shouted, stink bombs
were hurled, and Ivens released white mice, causing some of the ladies in
the audience to leap up screaming. Last and Ivens were banned from the
theater, but DAWN was dropped from the program.[35] Amsterdam was, however, only an intermezzo. There was work to do in Paris.

7 Socialist Realism (1933)

Joris Ivens's reputation as an avant-garde filmmaker had been established in Paris since the late twenties, but when he showed RAIN, PHILIPS RADIO and part of ZUIDERZEE in Studio 28 in the winter of 1933, a good month after his return from the Soviet Union, it was obvious how much he had changed. In his introduction he criticized his early work so harshly that *Filmliga* correspondent Hans Sluizer wondered why Ivens had shown these films at all. Sluizer identified most of the audience as Ivens's political sympathizers and described the discussion that followed as a long-winded process of saying all kinds of things that 'added up to complete agreement with the opinions of the esteemed speaker'.[1]

Annoyed by Sluizer's article and its claim that he had adopted the role of 'Russian propagandist', Ivens sent the *Filmliga* editors a response in which he declared that the journalist had 'understood nothing of my talk'. Two thirds of his speech 'covered the development of the documentary, and it was only in conclusion that I related something of the working methods of our collective for the youth film I made in the Soviet Union'. He denied having declaimed 'dogmas of Russian art criticism' or the 'working principles from the Russian art front'. He had merely explained the points of view that were currently taking root in Moscow, points of view he happened to agree with. 'I outlined the guidelines that can free the documentary from its ossified form, doing so in the light of the youth film I directed in Magnitogorsk. I defended the right of audiences to documentaries that go beyond mere generalization.' In other words, he criticized the objective, Vertov-style documentary and argued for the use of staged scenes. Although Sluizer may have given a somewhat biased picture of the Paris meeting, he had touched upon the essence of the matter: after the discussions in Moscow, Ivens now confirmed his turn to Socialist Realism and his departure from the avant-garde.[2] His reaction to Sluizer's piece was probably primarily motivated by shock. Although rapidly distancing himself from the old Filmliga ideals, he still wanted to be part of the club. Sluizer's piece proved to be no barrier to further good relations with *Filmliga*.

In spring 1933 Ivens and Helene van Dongen settled in the French capital for a longer period, staying in small Left Bank hotels such as the Michelet on the rue de Vaugirard. Ivens only saw Anneke van der Feer during trips to Holland. A new political commitment was growing among artists in Paris, especially after the Reichstag Fire in Berlin, the symbolic end of German democracy. Joris Ivens soon established himself in the artists' circles centered on the French Communist Party, the PCF, and the artists' organization Association des Écrivains et des Artistes Révolutionnaires, the AEAR. He met the writers Louis Aragon and André Malraux – both leading figures in the AEAR – and members of the AEAR film section, among them film historian Georges Sadoul, Spanish Surrealist filmmaker Luis Buñuel, and the young French cinematic genius Jean Vigo. The Belgian filmmaker Henri Storck, then living in Paris, was also a member of the AEAR, but did not see Ivens there once in six months of faithfully attending meetings.

That summer Buñuel, Vigo, Storck and Ivens frequented the Closerie des Lilas on the corner of the boulevard du Montparnasse and the boulevard Saint-Michel, one of the big Left Bank artists' cafés. With their caps on the table in front of them and glasses in their hands, they discussed the state of the world. Ivens combed his dark-brown hair straight back and wore a coarsely woven suit coat with a sweater or a white shirt with a casual checked tie. Buñuel – with the face of a gangster – described the isolated Spanish mountain villages from which he had just returned; Vigo – mussed up hair – looked around nervously; and Storck – small black-rimmed glasses with round lenses – drew back imperturbably on the cigarette permanently dangling from the corner of his mouth.

Luis Buñuel had just completed the film LAND WITHOUT BREAD in Spain, filmed by Ivens's old rival Eli Lotar and paid for by an anarchist friend who had won twenty thousand pesetas in a lottery. Storck, a former Ostend shoe salesman with contacts in the West Flanders art world, had joined the avant-garde in the late twenties. He had made short films like IMAGES OF OSTEND and assisted Jean Vigo with his film ZERO FOR CONDUCT.

Ivens had already met the writer and adventurer André Malraux through Germaine Krull, who had also introduced him to the writer Vladimir Pozner, always easy to spot because of his dark, brilliantined pompadour. Pozner and his wife Ida were to become two of Ivens's most faithful friends, and in the decades that followed Pozner would regularly write speeches for him in France, the USA, and the GDR.[3] Born in Paris to Russian parents, Vladimir Pozner had attended university in Leningrad and now translated Russian literature and wrote short stories and novels. He joined the editorial staff of the illustrated magazine *Regards* – set up according to the formula of Münzenberg's *Arbeiter Illustrierte Zeitung* – and also worked on *Commune*, the AEAR magazine. He joined the PCF in the early thirties and remained a member until his death in 1992. In the mid-thirties he was briefly involved with the famous Soviet spy Alexander Rado, who set up an obscure press agency, presumably as a cover for other activities, and manned it with Pozner and the writer Arthur Koestler.[4] During World War II Rado headed the Red Army's espionage network in Western Europe. Ida

Pozner was a German whose KPD cell in Berlin had included the writer Anna Seghers and the 'raging reporter' Egon Erwin Kisch.

During his stay in Paris Ivens was sick with asthma half the time and often had to receive his friends in his hotel room. Storck related: 'We would sit around his bed.' Van Dongen too kept watch at his bedside.[5]

The new left-wing zeal in Paris could also be felt at the Pathé-Nathan Studio in Joinville, where Ivens, Van Dongen and Hanns Eisler were working on NEW EARTH, an adaptation of ZUIDERZEE. Ivens had originally planned two reels, but took on Eisler's suggestion at the last moment and added a third reel with a political message.[6] After the damming of the Zuiderzee, the reclamation of new land in the Wieringermeer Polder and the first harvest, the narrator – Ivens himself – leveled an accusation against the capitalist Depression: why all this work when the hunger afflicting the entire globe is not alleviated, and the workers go hungry after completing the dam? 'We are being choked with grain!' he cries in a strident voice, and the viewer sees the valuable product being dumped into the water. The Brazilians had apparently dumped coffee at sea, vegetables were left to rot in Holland and grain was burnt in the United States to keep prices artificially high, but no grain from the new Dutch polders had actually been thrown away and none had been tipped into the water in the vicinity of Paris either. Ivens held a collection among the studio staff, bought three bags of flour and shook them out into the Seine for the cameras. In the film this was accompanied by Eisler's *Ballad of the Sack Dumpers*, performed by a Catholic chorister. 'When I told Brecht about it, he laughed so hard tears came to his eyes,' said Hanns Eisler. He wrote to Brecht: 'Of course, Uncle Hanns also provided the ending with text in the good old Brecht style.'[7]

The addition of a political finale was not a stylistic improvement. A film that had formed a superb unity had been extended with an extra reel in which both editing and commentary were glaring and obtrusive. Ivens had sacrificed the form to the message. He realized that it lacked cinematic unity, and hoped to compensate this with 'the uniting strength of the ideas'. Later he admitted that 'for an economist my position is primitive; the film is an appeal to justice, humanity, common sense.' Eisler, on the other hand, was wildly enthusiastic and wrote to Brecht that, in comparison to NEW EARTH, Eisenstein's POTEMKIN was 'a sickly, rightist-reformist, yes, almost petit bourgeois, *concoction*.'[8]

The work in Magnitogorsk and Paris had brought Ivens and Eisler closer together. In a small café near Metro Vaugirard they had their cognac tree: 'After the first three glasses we had circled the base of the tree... By the twentieth glass we were already sitting on the second bough. By the twenty-fifth we were right at the top... This cognac tree was sometimes very important to our collaboration.'[9] Eisler was the real connoisseur of cognac, Ivens preferred Dutch gin. After World War II, he once sent special instructions to Paris from Eastern Europe for the purchase of Dutch gin, available in the rue Monsieur Le Prince, if possible, Oude Papegaai.

Ivens was very enthusiastic about his collaboration with Eisler, whom he credited for teaching him a great deal about the relationship between film and music. 'Take my film NEW EARTH for example. It shows the construction of a dam. The dyke is closed from two sides and the Zuiderzee gets rougher and rougher, because the gap keeps on getting smaller. And finally, when the distance between the two sides of the dam has been reduced to approximately a hundred and fifty feet, neither the engineer, nor the worker, nor anyone else knows whether it will take six hours, six days or six weeks to close the dam. It depends on the wind. And I had filmed with three cameras that visually express the dynamics, the power of the opposing forces. But how can I show that uncertainty? Whether it will take six hours or six days? I can't show it with pictures, but Eisler can do it with music. So I said to him, 'Make a nervous sequence for me. Show that the result is uncertain...' Because I can't get it across by myself, and he can't get it across by himself, but together we have one hundred percent success. That is art, that is the value of music in film.' It wasn't about 'making a bit of music to go with it', said Ivens. 'The music has a function, doesn't it? Perhaps its task is being silent? Or its task is to partly introduce the element of time. Filmic time passes more quickly, perhaps the music should only represent normal time? Time is tremendously important in film, people always forget that... After all, you have the sound, the text, the music and the picture. And these four columns mustn't ever combat each other or want to take priority. And when one has priority, the director has to give instructions for that. 'Now the music has priority and the picture can be very restrained because the picture is very rhythmic.' Or, 'Now the music has to be silent because the original sound is much more beautiful. And later the music can shape the sound.' It's a simple rule, but most people still transgress against it. The composer who is brought in doesn't understand it.' Ivens also explained that he valued his friendship with Eisler especially highly, because in Holland he had always been a loner who seldom found discussion partners.[10] This was unfair to Lou Lichtveld, who had immersed himself in the theory of film music and produced a very modern soundtrack for Ivens's PHILIPS RADIO.

When NEW EARTH was completed, Eisler, Brecht and Kisch viewed the results in a private showing. The Czech expressed his doubts about the scene with the grain, whereupon Brecht declared: 'Kisch, this is a classic masterpiece, you're talking rubbish!'[11] On December 14, 1933 the film premiered in the Cinéma des Champs-Elysées.

In Paris Ivens maintained his contacts with the apparatus of Comintern functionary and Workers' Aid boss Willi Münzenberg. Red Willi had left Nazi Germany in time to rebuild his empire in France. It now revolved around the World Committee for the Victims of German Fascism, with sections in numerous countries and links to a complete solar system of sub-organizations and committees. Münzenberg had drawn an incredible number of leading intellectuals from all over the Western world into his organizations. Joris Ivens was one of two hundred artists and academics to join the Dutch division of the World Committee.[12] He visited Münzenberg at 65 Boulevard Arago, where Ida Pozner worked in the German Freedom Library. She saw Ivens and Münzenberg disappear into the office at the back of the library. 'The female employees followed Joris with their eyes because he cut a handsome figure,' said Ida. She knew that secret matters were discussed in the back office but not which. The German Richard Gyptner worked there as the illegal Western European representative of Comintern head Georgi Dimitrov, and the office was later used as a Workers' Aid international liaison center.[13]

In Paris Ivens and Eisler also visited their old acquaintance Otto Katz, who had headed the German division of Mezhrabpom during the making of SONG OF HEROES and was now living in a hotel close to the Tuileries.[14] As Münzenberg's right-hand man, he was entrusted with the World Committee's contacts with the film and theater worlds. Katz was also the main author of the famous *Brown Book of the Hitler Terror and the Burning of the Reichstag,* published by Münzenberg's propaganda machine to prove that the Reichstag Fire in Berlin had been the work of the Nazis themselves and not of the Communists. It has now been established that the fire was a desperate act of individual resistance by an unemployed Dutchman from Leiden, Rinus van der Lubbe.[15] Distributed in large editions in seventeen languages, the *Brown Book*'s analysis of the fire was a combination of half-truths and inventions, with an enormous impact on public opinion.

Katz delved into Van der Lubbe's background while researching his *Brown Book.* In his unpublished memoirs, Jef Last wrote: 'Soon after the Reichstag Fire, Joris Ivens suddenly showed up at my place. 'Was it true that Freek van Leeuwen had known Rinus personally?' I confirmed that. 'Did you know he was homosexual?' I said that I had suspected it. 'Not that it makes any difference to me personally,' said Joris... 'Richard [Otto] Katz (He spoke the name with a certain degree of respect) is here for the International. He's preparing a big counter-trial with the best international lawyers in London. Katz believes that Van der Lubbe was lured to Berlin by the homo clique centered on Röhm. It would be a terrible blow to Hitler if he could prove it... Do you think that Freek would be willing to speak to Katz?' I traveled to Leiden and explained what was involved to Freek. 'It's against fascism.' To my surprise but also, I must say, to my delight, Freek declared his willingness to travel to Amsterdam. The interview with Katz himself was held in De Kroon with Anneke van der Feer as interpreter, but I wasn't there for that myself.'[16] Freek van Leeuwen, a leftist writer who has now been forgotten even in Holland, traveled to London for the counter-trial but was only able to state that he 'had the feeling' that Van der Lubbe was homosexual. Katz then made up some extra information for the *Brown Book* himself, because there was no factual material establishing any kind of link between Van der Lubbe and the homosexual SA leader Ernst Röhm.[17] 'After his return Freek's circle of friends in Leiden met him with hatred and icy contempt. He fled to Antwerp,' Last continued.

On August 19, 1933 Henri Storck visited Helene van Dongen in Paris. His notes referred to her as 'Joris Ivens's secretary'. He asked her to ask Ivens whether he wanted to collaborate on a film in the Walloon coal basin the Borinage.[18] Ivens was not there: he was camping in the North Brabant fens with Anneke van der Feer, no doubt on the 'Joris Fen'.[19]

In Brussels preparations for the Borinage film were already in full swing. It was a project of the Belgian Communist movement and the idea had originated with André Thirifays, founder and secretary of the Belgian Club de l'Écran, a more politicized sister-organization of the Filmliga. Key figures in the production were Club de l'Écran chairman Piet Vermeylen, who was also chairman of International Red Aid in Belgium, and Gaston Vernaillen, national secretary of Workers' Aid. To assess the local situation, Storck traveled to the mining region with Vernaillen, Workers' Aid chairman Beublet and a Communist parliamentarian, Lahaut. Also involved were Dr. Paul Hennebert, who was active with International Workers' Aid, and the lawyer Albert van Ommeslaghe, a member of Red Aid.[20] The modest starting capital personally contributed by these initiators covered little more than the raw stock, but an anonymous patron later donated twenty thousand francs. It was not until 1974 that Henri Storck discovered that this generous contribution had been made by Maurice Calmeyn, a Communist sympathizer from an enormously wealthy family on the Belgian coast. Calmeyn apparently died on his way to the premiere, and his gigantic gravestone in De Panne, complete with star, hammers, sickles and the inscription 'Égalité', would not have been out of place in an elite cemetery in Moscow.[21]

Storck discussed a provisional scenario with Luis Buñuel and Vladimir Pozner in Paris, and Ivens arrived at the Gare du Nord in Brussels one month after receiving Storck's invitation. The Belgian was glad that Ivens had come as he had too little experience himself. They left at once for the mining region, where dumps and winding towers overshadowed the dark brick houses on the cobblestone streets. The Walloon provinces had suffered greatly from the Depression. The mines were small and obsolete, and some of them were only operating a few days a week: the coal reserves were impossible to sell. The owners had cut wages more than once and the miners' living conditions had deteriorated. In 1932 there had been major strikes, whereupon the government had declared martial law and attempted to violently suppress the workers' protests. Communist leaders, who had actually only played a marginal role, were arrested and accused of preparing a revolutionary uprising. After four months, the conflict was resolved by an agreement between employers and unions that virtually ignored the miners' demands.

One year after this strike, Storck and Ivens filmed the conditions in the area. BORINAGE became a silent film, which did not prevent Hanns Eisler from coming from Paris to visit the crew. Dr. Hennebert, who made weekly house calls to miners, and the lawyer Jan Fonteyne, who defended prosecuted strikers, were their guides. As the police tried to hinder their work, the film crew was constantly on the move, changing hotels and moving from one worker's home to another. Ivens in particular had to ensure that the police did not catch him with a camera, as he could be deported as an undesirable alien. The police searched his room but did not find a thing. 'Questioned by the Belgian secret service in the café at Jemappes,' wrote Storck in his notebook on September 29.[22]

They filmed the gray landscape, the funeral of a miner who was killed in an accident, impoverished homes, and miners and their wives searching for pieces of coal on the mines' dumps. Sometimes the miners tried to conceal their woeful circumstances from the camera. 'As a result the people searching the dumps for coal in front of the camera pick up clearly visible chunks of coal instead of the minuscule pieces they usually find,' related Fonteyne.[23] The film revolves around the vicissitudes of the families of a number of revolutionary miners who are living in the most wretched conditions. 'We were incensed,' said Henri Storck, 'by the humiliating situation in which the men, women and children lived, by the ruthlessness of the economic oppression, and by the police violence they were subjected to. The management of the mines exacted a cruel revenge by evicting workers who had been prominent in the revolutionary struggle, without paying any regard to their destitution or their families.' Since the electricity had been cut off in most of the houses, the film crew brought in acetylene lamps, these generated heat that attracted masses of vermin from every nook and cranny. At the home of the Mouffle family, Storck discovered a number of religious objects, crucifixes and such-like, hidden away in cupboards, 'doubtless with an eye to our visit'.[24]

The filmmakers tried to avoid esthetic effects that might distract attention from the conditions under which the miners lived. They wanted 'to destroy a particular superficial beauty', and much later Ivens could still get very angry with people who insisted on seeing BORINAGE as an esthetic work. 'When people came up to me after a screening saying, 'Magnificent, how did you manage it? That distance, that diffident camera, it really is unprecedented for the era.' I really felt like answering, 'Please just shut up! You don't know what you're talking about.'' Nonetheless, he sometimes wondered whether he and Storck had gone too far in their anti-estheticism. He wrote that BORINAGE might possibly have been 'too extreme a break' with formalism, in other words, that he might have neglected the exterior form too much after all.[25]

After the editing, Club de l'Écran and Red Aid chairman Piet Vermeylen proposed the removal of several scenes that linked the film too closely to the Communist movement, among them the re-enactment of a portrait-carrying march in Wasmes commemorating the fiftieth anniversary of the death of Karl Marx. Vermeylen hoped to show the film in public theaters, and also rejected as too provocative a meeting of the Unemployed Miners' Committee with a newspaper clipping with a photo of Lenin on the wall. Ivens 'vigorously opposed' the suggestions, according to Storck, who first shared Ivens's point of view but later made a number of futile attempts to change his mind.[26] Only a few captions about the position taken in parliament by the Communist representative Jacquemotte were removed. Storck wanted to call the film MISÈRE AU BORINAGE, the title under which it premiered, but Ivens preferred BORINAGE. Rather than evoke pity, he wanted to mobilize public opinion against the system.[27] Storck in turn thought that BORINAGE misleadingly suggested that the families they had filmed were representative of the region's mining population, whereas they had shown the specific circumstances of a number of activists.

Despite the disagreements, the first screening took place on March 6, 1934 in Brussels, in the official presence of Social Democratic Party leader Émile Vandervelde. Subsequently the film was only shown at private screenings. Ivens later stated that BORINAGE was banned in Holland, but the film was never actually submitted to the censorship commission.[28] Perhaps because he was apprehensive about their conclusions, or perhaps because there was no time – he left for Moscow six weeks after the premiere and spent most of that time in Paris – but most probably for the simple reason that the Dutch distributor defaulted on payment and never received the film.

Henri Storck continued to make films until the late 1980s. In the course of the 1930s, his political persuasion swung toward Social Democracy. He and Ivens remained friends and met regularly at festivals and meetings of documentary organizations after World War II. Storck reported some tense moments, such as after a screening of Borinage in the Salle Pleyel in Paris, when Ivens was called up onto the stage as the director even though co-director Storck was also present. Ivens was preparing to receive the applause when Storck said to him: 'All well and good, but then I'm coming up onto the stage with you.' 'Oh, yes. Yes, of course...' replied Ivens.[29]

The major Dutch critics gave Borinage average-to-positive reviews. Predictably, the conservative daily *De Telegraaf* saw the film as nothing more than a plea for Communism. The Social Democratic press was also critical of the film's Communist message. This was understandable; when the Social Democratic newspaper *Het Volk* asked Ivens why the film ignored the activities of the socialists, who had dominated the strikes, he answered: 'As I didn't want to become involved in the political struggle, or to put it better, since I didn't want to show the entire course of the activities of the various political parties during the strike, I limited myself to the party that bears my political convictions.' He added that his film could be seen as 'an attack on the De Man Plan', the Belgian Social Democrats' program for the Depression.[30]

More remarkable than the criticism was the praise that various socialist newspapers and magazines expressed for Borinage. *Het Volk* remained distinctly well disposed to Ivens throughout the thirties. On his departure for the Soviet Union, the newspaper deplored Dutch industry's failure to help him and his colleagues find work, overlooking the fact that Ivens was actually leaving because he wanted to stop making films for Dutch businesses. Later, when he returned from Spain or China for brief visits to Holland, the reporters of *Het Volk* hung on his every word and invariably reported them positively in the columns of their newspaper.[31] The *NRC* was disappointed that Borinage abandoned avant-garde principles for simple realism, but the critic was still 'greatly impressed' by the results: 'His aim of providing a convincing portrait of far-reaching social misery has been fully achieved.'[32] *De Groene Amsterdammer*, the weekly that had demonstrated great affinity with the Filmliga over the years, called the miners' film 'a great work' and observed that 'with this work, our only truly imposing cinematic artist bids farewell to his country and his people. Because Borinage, with its humanity and idealism, will not reach Dutch audiences... The times do not favor it!' The magazine spoke regretfully of the imminent departure of 'the man who has consistently dared to pursue his solitary path!'[33]

NEW EARTH, with its pronounced social tenor, was also favorably reviewed by most critics. After the premiere, the *Handelsblad* correspondent in Paris defended Ivens in advance against the prospect of 'oversensitive' criticism of the film's tendency. *Het Volk* had nothing but praise and, remarkably enough, *De Telegraaf* was extremely positive as well.[34] Despite this general approval, Ivens later made a great deal of fuss about how Holland, specifically the film critics and the Filmliga, dumped him in response to BORINAGE and NEW EARTH.

The Filmliga descended into a state of chaos in 1932-1933 and was disbanded in the summer of 1933. There were numerous factors involved, but neither BORINAGE nor NEW EARTH played any role in this final phase, because shooting had yet to begin on one film and the other was not yet completed. In the general confusion within the Filmliga, Ivens too must have been the target of occasional criticism, and some of his old friends in the organization regretted his political radicalism and his swing to realism. The Communist *Tribune,* the newspaper of Ivens's own party, seized on Hans Sluizer's critical article from Paris to ease the filmmaker away from Filmliga circles with a piece entitled: 'Joris Ivens in disgrace'. For convenience's sake *De Tribune* took the article Sluizer had written in a private capacity as proof that Ivens had been rejected by the Filmliga in its entirety. When he returned from the Soviet Union 'the gentlemen' thought 'in their broken Dutch that no worker can make head nor tail of' that there would be 'some cinema for them to drool over', wrote the newspaper. 'But the person who came back wasn't the Joris of the gentlemen of the Filmliga, he was 'Our Joris'. And that doesn't seem to overly please the gentlemen.' *De Tribune* suggested that the Filmliga rejected SONG OF HEROES, and excitedly countered Sluizer's piece by stating 'that there is not one country in the world, not a single one, where artists can so perfectly express themselves, so fully dedicate themselves to art, as that very land where Ivens made his KOMSOMOL'.[35]

Many Filmliga members remained well disposed to Ivens. When *Filmliga,* which continued as an independent magazine after the organization was disbanded, reviewed SONG OF HEROES, it did not object to the film's Communist tendency. On the contrary, the criticism was that the filmmaker got caught up in images 'of sometimes unprecedented beauty', without succeeding in 'reshaping them, subordinating them to a time-tested conception'.[36] These doubts were strikingly similar to the criticism Ivens had received in Moscow. In a review of New Earth, *Filmliga* again aimed its criticism at the chosen form, while explicitly endorsing the tenor of the film. The third reel was called 'a feverish film reportage' and the review posed the question: 'Can Ivens square all the elements of this indictment with his talent?' Only to conclude: 'The questions do not, however, need to be answered at this moment. It's good that these things are being rammed home,' referring to the fierce agitation against the Depression at the end of the film. The author expressly defends Ivens's departure from the old Filmliga principles: 'The avant-garde film has come to a standstill, that's old news. Ivens was left with no other option, and all those who have cinema's best interests at heart should support him.'[37]

In April 1934 Ivens was finally able to leave for the Soviet Union. His work on Borinage and New Earth had delayed his departure for nine months. With the passing of the years he became increasingly convinced that he had not left of his own free will but had been forced into exile. He wrote that Holland had adopted a 'hostile attitude' toward him. Borinage had received bad reviews in the Dutch press and the political ending of New Earth was 'the straw that broke the camel's back'. According to Ivens the reaction of the press could be summed up as: 'What is Ivens actually doing staying in this country?' His father is supposed to have added: 'They're right.' Ivens: 'Overnight I found myself in a political ghetto without any possibility of appeal.' He drew his conclusions. 'I calmly let the Dutch express their dissatisfaction, then turned my back on them. Holland had slammed the door on me.'

In fact, the reviewers and his friends in the film world had approached him in a completely normal fashion from beginning to end, and had given him no cause for emigration. Nonetheless, it is possible that he already felt misunderstood at that time. It does not seem coincidental that he cited critical reviews and the rejection of his father in the same breath. In his mind, father and fatherland became increasingly entangled over the years. 'This insult,' he wrote later, 'moved me to make decisions that I had been postponing for a long time. Without further ado, I shrugged off all the things I had been dragging around with me for years: my father, my responsibilities, my obligations, my roots.'[38]

With Borinage, Ivens had concluded an era. From his first test shots around 1927 through Song of Heroes in 1932, formal experimentation and social commitment had co-existed in his work, but social commitment had gradually become the dominant factor and this process had culminated in his choice of emphatic realism in the miners' film.

Films like THE BRIDGE, RAIN, ZUIDERZEE/NEW EARTH, PHILIPS RADIO and SONG OF HEROES made Ivens's avant-garde period a highlight in his more than sixty-year career as a filmmaker. The modernist regard for film as a goal in itself, as an art form that did not serve as a 'reflection' of the outside world, but created a world of its own through the possibilities inherent to the medium, was most clearly present in THE BRIDGE and RAIN, although Ivens also anchored these films in reality. In PILE DRIVING, ZUIDERZEE, PHILIPS RADIO and SONG OF HEROES a new element appeared that tied in exceptionally well with Neue Sachlichkeit: industrial labor or, as he put it himself, the struggle between mankind and nature.

In 1929 he had also made simple realistic documentaries, POVERTY IN THE BOGS OF DRENTHE and parts of WE ARE BUILDING. Formally, this was the least interesting work of his first period, but the Drenthe film in particular was a forerunner to BORINAGE and what followed, born as it was of the need to be accessible and politically convincing for working class audiences. As early as October 1929 he stated in an interview: 'On the other hand, I see a danger, not an artistic danger, but a social danger in experiments that, like the work of many French cineastes, concentrates too much on the comprehension of a small group of intellectuals.'[39]

In 1930 Pudovkin believed that there was a clear break in Ivens's work between THE BRIDGE and RAIN on the one hand and ZUIDERZEE on the other. This temporal dividing line was, however, incorrect, since older films such as POVERTY IN THE BOGS OF DRENTHE, BREAKERS and parts of WE ARE BUILD-ING had already dealt with the social aspects Pudovkin found lacking in THE BRIDGE and RAIN. Nonetheless, his observation was apt for other reasons. According to Pudovkin, THE BRIDGE and RAIN were 'uncharacteristic' for Ivens because, despite their beauty, they were merely empty formal conceptions.[40] This shows Pudovkin's psychological insight because Ivens was searching for spiritual certainty in an unreliable world, something he could only temporarily find by filming raindrops or bridge mechanisms. Even from a cinematic perspective, he must have welcomed the possibility of associating his work with a social objective as a means of escaping the tendency to sterility that some critics had noted. ZUIDERZEE, PHILIPS RADIO and SONG OF HEROES thus united the ideal – progress through production – and the form.

At that time Ivens still saw himself as an avant-garde filmmaker, albeit within the definition Soviet cineastes gave to the term: the form was important, but one also had to be a 'representative of the masses' on the alert for 'an excess of individualism'.[41] In a speech at the International Congress for Photography in Leipzig in 1932, which he attended during the shooting of the Magnitogorsk film, he used unabashed Filmliga language to describe the task of the independent filmmaker as 'responding to the nature of film: image and movement', but went on to say that documentaries needed to activate.[42] These are the words of a communist cineaste who is still torn between film as an autonomous medium and Socialist Realism. This ambiguity was visible in his epic about the blast furnaces in the Urals, a film that sang the praises of the revolution in the language of Neue Sachlichkeit.

After BORINAGE his cinema was fully at the service of the revolutionary cause and the form was subordinate. In an interview during filming, Ivens and Storck stated that they strove to depict the life of the working class as faithfully as possible, declaring: 'We have continually found our inspiration in the greatest reality.' They explained that the avant-garde inevitably led to 'a sterile impasse of empty aesthetics'.[43] In late 1934 Ivens concluded a speech in Moscow with the appeal: 'Let us work in the spirit of Socialist Realism.' He further distanced himself from his first work, THE BRIDGE: 'I didn't concern myself with politics at that time and thought that that made my art apolitical as well, whereas I was actually supporting bourgeois ideology through these apolitical films without being aware of it. I pretended to myself that I was combating bourgeois ideology by making a work of art that was revolutionary in its form.' In the case of BREAKERS: 'I had become clearer in my political convictions, but my film work lagged behind these insights and gained a sentimental, bourgeois humanist tendency.'[44]

He now wrote a plea for films with a 'simple line' and an 'exciting story about people', in which he declared that 'the documentarist theories of film, the fact fetishists in literature, and the so-called objective and naturalist schools of painting' had to be defeated, because they opposed 'a clear vision in our art'. His piece was pervaded by the spirit of the first All Union Congress of Soviet Writers[45] that was held in August and September 1934 and which he presumably attended. The theoretical basis of Socialist Realism had been presented at the congress and, in a major speech, party functionary Karl Radek had condemned the work of Western writers such as James Joyce and John Dos Passos. Ivens followed his example, although it was unlikely that he had read either Joyce or Dos Passos. In his opinion they made 'mangled art' and presented reality as chaos. For Joris Ivens this was an alarming idea.[46]

8 Sidetracked (1934-1936)

No other phase of Joris Ivens's adult life has remained as obscure as the time he spent in Moscow from April 1934 to January 1936. The main reason was his own reluctance to speak about this period, and it even seemed as if he wanted to suppress his memories of it. During an interview in 1976, for example, his generally very accurate memory did not prevent him from saying: 'I made two trips to the Soviet Union, in 1930 and in '32. I then made my film about the Borinage, and in '35 I left for America for seven years.'[1] Twenty-one months in the USSR had disappeared. This period is completely absent in his autobiography *The Camera and I*, even in the drafts he wrote in the early forties, and his later memoirs *Joris Ivens ou la mémoire d'un regard* ('A Vision Remembered') cover it in just over two pages, mangling the facts and dates so much that his stay there comes out about a year shorter. He parried questions on the subject with either friendliness or annoyance. In the eighties, when he had more or less broken with Communism, he explained his silence by saying that he didn't want to continually be seen as a Stalinist.[2] What had happened in Moscow?

In Paris in the summer of 1933, Ivens and André Malraux had written a scenario based on Malraux's novel *La condition humaine*, about the bloody suppression of the revolutionary uprising in Shanghai in 1927. Preparations were begun for a fiction film with documentary elements that would be filmed in China, and the project attracted a great deal of attention from the French press. After negotiations with a French producer collapsed, Mezhrabpom in Moscow declared its willingness to take on the project. Josip Skliut, the scriptwriter of SONG OF HEROES, was to write a screenplay, and Ivens hoped to be able to collaborate with the Muscovite theater director Vsevolod Meyerhold, who had plans for a play based on the same novel. Ivens also hoped to prepare a Russian adaptation of BORINAGE in Moscow and still had older commissions from Mezhrabpom for a documentary about Soviet aviation and a major film about Kamchatka, the peninsula in the far east of Siberia.[3] With no less than four productions in the offing, Ivens left for Moscow in mid-April 1934, accompanied by Anneke van der Feer. The press stated that he would be taking the boat from Antwerp to Leningrad, but they secretly went by train via Switzerland, Austria and Czechoslovakia.[4]

In late June, Helene van Dongen was still hesitant about joining him. 'That depends entirely on what and when Joris is going to film,'[5] she said. Nevertheless, soon after she too left for the Soviet capital, where Ivens continued his relationships with both women. Van der Feer was officially made a *Vsekomchudozhnik*, a Communist Artist, and a member of the Moscow Artists' Union.[6] Van Dongen was less enthusiastic about Soviet socialism. During Ivens's previous trip to the USSR, she had written to Jan Hin: 'Speaking confidentially, I think it's a terrible shame that he gives his great capacity for work for that modern fashion 'Communism'.'[7] Despite this she fitted in. She took some classes with the great Soviet filmmakers at the Moscow film school, taught sound editing there herself, and collaborated with Ivens on several distinctly propagandistic films at Mezhrabpom. Anneke and Helene seem to have done their best to accept each other's presence. In later years the terms in which they referred to each other in letters were not unfriendly, and they sometimes even wrote to each other.[8]

Two days after arriving in Moscow, Ivens came down with asthma and severe bronchitis and had to be admitted to the Kremlin Hospital, usually reserved for the Soviet elite.[9] There Dr. Ignati Kazakov treated him with Lysat. Four years later during the big show trial of the old Bolsheviks Bucharin, Rykov and nineteen others, Kazakov was sentenced to death for his involvement in the 'murder' of writer Maxim Gorki and for participating in a conspiracy to get rid of Stalin and other Soviet leaders during medical treatment, partly by administering the very same Lysat. The accusations were completely unfounded and in his memoirs Ivens described with appropriate self-mockery how the transcripts of the trial scared him out of his wits when they reached him in China. 'Not for a second did it occur to me that these people might have been tortured and worked over until they agreed to sign their confessions. When I read the transcripts I didn't have the slightest doubt that they had turned traitor.' Ivens sent a telegram to his brother Wim, who was still working as a doctor in Amsterdam. 'What do you think about this Lysat? I was treated with it and now this Dr. Kazakov has confessed that it was sabotage.' The answer was brief: 'No, you're not at risk.'[10]

Discharged from hospital with his health intact, Ivens was confronted by an unpleasant surprise when André Malraux arrived in Moscow in June 1934 in order to collaborate with Sergei Eisenstein on a scenario based on *La condition humaine*. This new attempt got no further than the previous scenario with Ivens, as Eisenstein was hardly popular with the regime and Malraux permitted himself too many critical remarks,[11] but the course of events so frustrated Ivens that he later denied ever having worked on a project with Malraux. 'They were just rumors made up by journalists,' he said, forgetting that he and Malraux had been interviewed by French, Belgian and Dutch newspapers.[12]

The plans for films about Kamchatka and aviation also evaporated for no obvious reasons and Ivens's main activity now became a short anti-Nazi film in collaboration with the German Communist author Gustav Regler, another new arrival in the USSR. Its title was probably SAAR PLEBISCITE AND SOVIET UNION, although this is not entirely certain as the film itself has disappeared.[13]

After World War I, the German region of the Saar had been placed under the governorship of the League of Nations as a no-man's land between Germany and France, and a plebiscite was to be held in January 1935 to allow the population to decide whether to go *heim ins Reich*. Hitler saw this as the first step toward the unification of all Germans in the Third Reich, and the plebiscite campaign became a confrontation between supporters and opponents of Nazism. 'At that time it was very important to me,' said Ivens, 'there were a lot of smear campaigns about the Soviet Union in Europe, especially in Hitler's Germany, and I wanted to combat these lies by showing everyday life in Moscow... Then Gustav Regler approached me with a proposal. He was thinking of a campaign in the Saar, a propaganda campaign, and wanted a film he could use. I thought it was a fantastic idea and agreed to collaborate on it, because at the time we thought the Saar was tremendously important for the antifascist struggle in Europe as a whole.'[14]

SAAR PLEBISCITE AND SOVIET UNION was meant to praise Communism as an alternative to Nazism and, according to Regler, Ivens explained to him that there was no place for subtlety. 'Only a bad propagandist covers too many aspects. Simplicity is what works. Listen: 'The Nazis lie, the Russians tell the truth.' That's what we have to say, nothing else!' Regler had his doubts, at least according to his autobiography, until Ivens took him to the editing room and presented a dazzling vision of Soviet socialism: after Red Square a desolate steppe appeared, and in this impressive vastness a mirage of a modern farm with combine harvester and silo emerged, approached and became reality. The film ended in a grandiose apotheosis. 'Just as many streams merge to form one river, happy workers hurried toward cheerful peasants, villages met cities, the river swelled and then flooded onto Red Square as if the dam of life had burst: gymnasts and runners, wrestlers and high jumpers – could a famished state bring forth so much health? – singing girls, dancing children, the rowers, the skiers, the mountaineers, the amateur pilots, all lithe and supple-limbed. And the lens panned down Lenin's mausoleum and the round face of Dimitrov appeared! He raised both arms, embracing youth, faith and victory.'[15] The Bulgarian Georgi Dimitrov had just been made general secretary of the Communist International. Some of these shots were probably filmed on July 27, 1934 when one hundred and thirty thousand Muscovite sportsmen and women marched past under the watchful eye of Joseph Stalin himself. Regler was so overwhelmed by the edited sequence that his doubts evaporated, but three years later he noted in his diary: 'It was just like the German fairy tale, you say the magic word and the table's covered with food.' Elsewhere he simply called SAAR PLEBISCITE AND SOVIET UNION a 'film of self-deceit'.[16]

The responsible Comintern functionary began by refusing to release the film for public exhibition. The official concerned was Béla Kun, legendary leader of the Hungarian revolution of 1919. When Regler asked Kun what he thought of the film, he was apparently told that it was an overly aggressive, black-and-white presentation. But when Regler later bumped into the Hungarian in the Moskva Hotel, Kun released the film after all with a nonchalant gesture. Regler traveled by train to Saarbrücken, where the first screening was held on December 16, 1934 in the beer hall Der Stiefel. It was both première and final screening, because while Hitler advanced, Regler's fellow German Communists were worried about Stalin's absence from the film. The German Communist party on the Saar rejected Regler's explanation that it was important to reach as wide an audience as possible and banned further showings.[17] Soon after, ninety percent of the population of the Saar voted for reunification with Germany.

Although Regler returned to Moscow after the debacle in the Saar, Ivens said that he had never heard of the German Communists' ban,[18] which is scarcely credible because even if he hadn't met Regler again in Moscow, he saw him in Madrid in 1937. It is more likely that he preferred not being reminded of one more humiliating experience. In the Soviet Union he seemed to be at the mercy of forces beyond his control.

The Moscow film world had become hopelessly frustrating. Eisenstein was constantly being thwarted and was virtually unable to work from 1932 to 1935. Kalatozov and Vertov met with similar difficulties and the latter wrote in his diary: 'How to fight bureaucratic replies with instructions which are not decisions but postponement, decisions with an endless 'tomorrow'? How to explain impatience to the talented, patience to the untalented?'[19] Foreign guests of the regime fared no better. Hans Richter had left in 1933 without having been able to complete his film METAL. Erwin Piscator, who was on friendly terms with Ivens, had been brought to Moscow to film Anna Segher's *The Revolt of the Fishermen*, but when Piscator's film was finally completed after three years of setbacks, it was shelved after a few weeks in the theaters and its maker was accused of 'formalism' and 'vulgar sociology'. The insidious thing about this kind of criticism was that it always had a grain of truth. Later Joris Ivens also criticized Piscator: 'With him nothing went through the soul, through the heart. He saw art as very cerebral, a matter for the mind.'[20] Another foreign guest, Béla Balázs, completed THE TISZA BURNS in the spring of 1934. The film was banned even before the premiere. 'This was the bitterest period of my life,' wrote Balázs. 'Morally the most humiliating, spiritually the most barren, and physically, too, the most exhausting – and the most unsuccessful... During these three years my hair turned gray. And I ruined my heart for good.'[21] This did not prevent him from remaining true to the Soviet Union.

Of the four projects that had brought him to Moscow, Joris Ivens only completed one, the new version of BORINAGE. He added the finishing touches at Mezhrabpom in fall 1934. The main line of the film was now the contrast between workers' lives under socialism and capitalism. He filmed an encounter between Belgian proletarians visiting the Soviet Union and Russians working on the construction of the Moscow subway. Seated at a lavish table, the Belgians retold the story that had been shown in the first version of BORINAGE, but now with more bravura. Their fellow-workers in Moscow were in complete agreement: 'Yes, that's how it must be. Your words clearly show how you fight your struggle. The concept of taking them by storm grows in the consciousness of the masses... Comrades, they could not prevent our victory and they will not prevent yours.'

The commentary was by Dimitrov's secretary, Alfred Kurella, a German writer whom his fellow immigrants suspected of spying for the Soviet secret service. In his 1947 book *Ich lebe in Moskau* he was appropriately enthusiastic about the work of the secret police: 'Just as a surgeon cannot limit himself during a cancer operation to only removing tissue directly affected by the malignant growth, it is also necessary in this kind of operation against life-threatening diseases of the social organism to take a broad perspective on the circle of people you hold responsible.'[22] At the end of the film, images of the old Ukrainian miners' village Sobatshovska were intercut with flashes from the revolutionary period, followed by the climax: the modern miners' settlement of Gorlovka, seen from the air and most resembling an exclusive residential neighborhood. The interior shot of a beautiful apartment with a big cake on the table shows that nowhere else are miners as well off as they are in the Soviet Union.

The editing was the work of Helene van Dongen, who was becoming increasingly flexible as far as 'that modern fashion 'Communism'' was concerned. The twenty-three-year-old American Jay Leyda had been assistant-director. Leyda attended the Moscow film school, went on to work for Vertov and Eisenstein, and became a leading film historian. Henri Storck found the Russian BORINAGE 'rather ridiculous, but there you go'.[23]

A great honor was conferred upon Ivens when BORINAGE was shown immediately after Dziga Vertov's THREE SONGS ABOUT LENIN for the foreign delegates at the Comintern's seventh world congress, held in August 1935 in Trade Union House in Moscow,[24] but the film does not seem to have reached Soviet theaters. Two years later Ivens submitted a complaint to a Moscow film functionary: 'I still haven't heard whether the films BORINAGE and NEW EARTH, of which Russian versions have been made, have already been shown in Moscow theaters. Could you make some inquiries with the distribution department? When they were made the Dutch and French censors, and now the American censors... banned or cut these films because they were such powerful and open-hearted documents of the workers' struggle, all the more reason to show them uncut in the Soviet Union.'[25]

1935 was a year of hope for Moscow. Prosperity was growing, for the first time the rationing of bread and other food was lifted, and portraits of Stalin took pride of place among the new articles in the shopwindow of Gastronome 1, just as they did in all the stores. The nightlife was picking up, and maps of Moscow were available for the first time in ten years, albeit ones of little practical use, since they only showed what the city would be like in 1945 upon completion of the ten-year construction plan. Stalin announced a constitutional change that promised more democracy. The prevailing belief was that 'the worst is over'.

That same year, however, the run-up to the great terror of 1936-1938 began. Since the late twenties, a bloody repression had claimed millions of victims, particularly in the countryside, but this oppression now turned on the party and the new elite itself. In December 1934 Leningrad party leader Sergei Kirov was murdered in circumstances that have yet to be clarified and a wave of arrests followed, known in the penal camps as the 'Kirov flood'. In January 1935 revolutionary veterans Zinoviev and Kamenev were subjected to torrents of abuse in the press and sentenced to long terms of imprisonment, and accusing randomly selected people of being involved in Kirov's assassination became habitual practice. Immediately after his death, meetings of mourning and self-criticism were arranged in factories and institutions everywhere and became scenes of mass confession. Between May 1935 and September 1936, another major purge of the party took place, with yet more meetings at which every member was expected to give a public account of himself. Under the pretence of mass democracy, the country was falling into the grip of organized collective hysteria, and the word 'vigilance' echoed everywhere.

Ivens later wrote about this period after the assassination of Kirov: 'Afterward suspicion and mistrust dominated the scene, the most contradic-

The only known photo from Ivens's stay in Moscow in 1934-1936. Ivens, Gustav von Wangenheim (standing) and actors from FIGHTERS receive French writer Romain Rolland in the Mezhrabpom Red Front Studio. BUNDESARCHIV/FILMARCHIV

tory, whispered rumors did the rounds. Some people claimed that Stalin had organized this tragic event, others categorically stated the opposite. It was difficult to get to the truth, it was difficult to understand it, it was difficult not to feel that the regime was going through a turbulent period. The state and socialism were under threat and there was a split between those who wanted to destroy them from within and those who remained unconditionally true to them. The threat was the Trotskyist conspiracy and faithfulness was personified by Stalin and the party.' Ivens himself did not hesitate: 'We stood behind Stalin, we were for the Soviet Union, for the revolution.'[26]

A favorite pastime in Ivens's circle of friends were *vechera*, parties with black bread and tea and plenty of vodka. He did not like to miss such occasions and spent pleasant evenings in Moscow with Béla Kun, Erwin Piscator, German central committee member Heinz Neumann and many others.[27] He, Anneke and Helene became good friends with Hans Rodenberg, the director of the German branch of Mezhrabpom, and his wife, and Ivens also had contact with several Dutch citizens who were working for the Comintern in Moscow.

During the purges of 1936 these innocent *vechera* could suddenly become terrifyingly important, because if one of those present was later unmasked as an 'enemy of the people', almost anything was enough to drag others down in the victim's fall. Several *vechera* in late 1934 became a subject of discussion eighteen months later in the German party group of the Writers' Association, when the suspicious activities of some of the comrades were being traced. At least seven of the party-goers Ivens met were executed or died in imprisonment in the years that followed: Béla Kun, Heinz Neumann, the writers Heinrich Süsskind, Ernst Ottwalt and Maria Osten, Münzenberg's associate Kurt Sauerland, and the journalist Julia Annenkova.[28]

Toward the end of 1934, Mezhrabpom made Ivens director of the film FIGHTERS, Russian title BORTSY, and he started work enthusiastically as it was to be a documentary about Comintern chief Georgi Dimitrov, a man he admired greatly. Like Rinus van der Lubbe, Dimitrov had been arrested in Berlin in 1933 on suspicion of involvement in the Reichstag Fire, but after Münzenberg and Katz's *Brown Book* had first mobilized world opinion, Dimitrov gave his judges in Leipzig such a reply that they felt obliged to release him. In Moscow he was given a hero's reception. Ivens had met Dimitrov in the early thirties in Berlin and got to know the Comintern leader better while Dimitrov was taking a rest cure on the Black Sea. 'In the course of our conversations he impressed me deeply... Our relationship was almost disarmingly simple. Dimitrov could be warm and was able to give you his undivided attention. He had the gift of putting the people he worked with at their ease. This simple manner contrasted sharply with his heavy responsibilities. Within the regime, Dimitrov had a lot of power at his disposal.'[29]

Together with Vladimir Pozner, who had come from Paris and was staying with Maxim Gorki, Ivens began gathering documentation about the Reichstag Fire trial. He wrote a scenario that was apparently unable to be executed because there wasn't enough documentary material in the film archives, but perhaps the real reason was that the slogan 'film for the millions' had just been made the guiding principle of Soviet film. It was necessary to reach the greatest possible mass of viewers, and experience had shown that fiction was the most appropriate means to achieve that end.[30] After heated discussion between documentary and fiction advocates in the FIGHTERS group, they decided to make a fiction film.[31] This change of course cannot have been a prohibitive objection for Ivens, as he himself had entertained similar ambitions ever since THE FLYING DUTCHMAN. LA CONDITION HUMAINE was to have been partly fictional, and in 1933 he and Henri Storck had met writer Paul Gustave van Hecke in Brussels to discuss a film of Charles de Coster's *Till Eulenspiegel*. He also submitted plans to Mezhrabpom for fiction films based on B. Traven's novel *The White Rose* and, again, *Till Eulenspiegel*.[32]

More objectionable was the way he was gradually nudged out of the production. He first lost control of the scenario, which was taken over by the German stage director Gustav von Wangenheim and Dimitrov's secretary Alfred Kurella. In January 1935 they sent their first synopsis to Maxim Gorki, who had the status of an oracle in the Soviet Union at that time. On April 9, Von Wangenheim, Ivens, Kurella and Mezhrabpom director Samsonov gave Gorki a reading of a complete script, now the story of a young German worker called Fritz who is definitively converted to socialism by Dimitrov's speech during the Reichstag Fire trial. 'I can only congratulate you!' was Gorki's response.[33]

By this time Ivens had been demoted to co-director with Von Wangenheim,[34] who ended up taking sole directorial credits. Ivens found Von Wangenheim authoritarian and there seems to have been serious friction between them, but Ivens continued to work with the German until his departure for America in January 1936, probably for the simple reason that, as an employee of Mezhrabpom, he had no choice.

Von Wangenheim also clashed with Bertolt Brecht, who was in Moscow at the time and was infuriated by the director's refusal to give the female lead to his girlfriend, Helene Weigel. The role went to Lotte Loebinger, an actress from Von Wangenheim's own Deutsche Theater/Kolonne Links. At a party meeting the director related that Brecht had accused him of anti-Semitism. Von Wangenheim was Jewish himself and considered it 'infamy dressed up as politics'.[35]

All the scenes for FIGHTERS were shot twice in Mezhrabpom's new Red Front sound film studio, once in German and once in Russian. Georgi Dimitrov visited several times to check progress, and in the summer of 1935 Ivens and Von Wangenheim showed the French writer Romain Rolland around the studio. Rolland was in Moscow as a guest of honor at the seventh Comintern congress, and they took advantage of his presence by having him give a speech and using it in the film.

Hanns Eisler was to write the film music, but late in 1935 Von Wangenheim approached Dimitri Shostakovich instead. Around the same time Stalin personally launched an attack on the unfortunate Shostakovich in *Pravda*, so he was no longer an option either,[36] and in the end the German Hans Hauska wrote the music.

Helene van Dongen was assistant director and took charge of the editing. Despite all their work neither Ivens nor Van Dongen is included in the credits of FIGHTERS. Was it their choice, or did Von Wangenheim omit their names out of spite? Four months after Ivens's departure for America, the film was completed. Full of Socialist Realist cliches, it was passed by the Executive Committee of the Comintern and on December 1 the Russian version premiered in Moscow theaters.[37]

In the pathological fantasies of Stalin and his security functionaries, Kirov's murder was linked to the foreign powers' meddling in Soviet affairs. A general xenophobia arose. A number of foreigners had been arrested in spring 1935, and during the filming of FIGHTERS the security service came to the studio to pick up one of the crew. 'While Dimitrov was there, can you imagine that?' exclaimed Von Wangenheim during a party meeting.[38] Foreigners in the Soviet Union were faced with the choice: become a Soviet citizen or leave. Foreign Communists were admitted to the Communist Party of the Soviet Union, the CPSU, after a ballot, or otherwise generally deported.[39]

Ivens's status was also subjected to an investigation. 'Conclusion of the commission: it is imperative that he remain a member of the CPN and a Dutch citizen, without concurrent membership of the CPSU. We request permission for him to stay in the USSR to work in his specialty.' The report, dated June 5, 1936, was signed by Dutch engineer Anton Struik, one of the leaders of the CPN. By that time, Ivens himself had already left on his 'official journey to America'.[40] Even if Ivens had wanted to become a member of the CPSU, the admission requirements were exacting. 'In Russia it was very difficult to become a member,' he said. 'You had to be nominated by five people and then spend two years as a provisional member.'[41] Judging by similar cases, he would have been unlikely to qualify for CPSU membership because he was only a recent member of the CPH/CPN by Soviet standards, was of suspect bourgeois origins, and was not fluent in Russian.[42]

Ivens's departure for America in January 1936 on an official journey or 'creative vacation' did not void his contract with Mezhrabpom, and he was told to return to Moscow after five months of study, lectures and screenings in the United States. It is impossible to say whether he really planned to do so, but both Helene and Anneke stayed behind in the Soviet Union and returning must have been a serious option. Mezhrabpom director Samsonov, with whom he had arranged his trip to America, seems however to have deliberately provided him with an escape clause by giving him permission to remain in the United States if he was able to make a film there.[43]

Once in New York, Ivens wrote to Hans Rodenberg, director of the German branch of Mezhrabpom, requesting him to release Helene from her contract and send her to the United States to assist him on a film about Harlem. Once FIGHTERS was as good as finished, she followed him across the

Atlantic. Von Wangenheim later claimed that he had edited the film himself in a few days.[44]

In the summer of 1936, Ivens requested a six-month prolongation of his stay in America but at the same time inquired about the chances of the film proposals he had submitted to Mezhrabpom: the films based on *The White Rose* and *Till Eulenspiegel* and a documentary about the sea route through the Arctic Ocean. In a letter to Rodenberg he wrote: 'You realize that, like everyone else who has worked in the Soviet Union, I am often overcome by a great desire to be back there, surrounded by the mighty, socialist Soviet life. On the other hand, you know how much there is to do here and that we are both working toward the same goal.'[45] Was he trying to keep Moscow on the back burner? Although his faith in the Soviet Union was untarnished, it is difficult to accept that he was willing to subject himself to the Moscow labyrinth of killing bureaucracy, ideological sniping and purges. A few years earlier he had announced that the Soviet Union was the only place he could realize his cinematic ideal. That expectation had been brutally dashed. Fifteen years would pass before he returned to the USSR.

Anneke van der Feer remained in the East for a few more years, and apparently even married there, presumably a Serb Communist she called 'The Flip', a name she might have derived from Filipovic.[46] Ivens saw her again in the late thirties in Paris, where she was studying art. She told him that 'terrible things' had happened in the Soviet Union and added: 'It's good that you didn't stay there, you would have been sure to get into trouble.'[47] Van der Feer returned to Amsterdam, and 'Kiddo' and 'Puppy' did not meet again until after World War II.

Ivens left the Soviet Union just before the great reign of terror. Six months later fear had a firm grip on the people he had left behind. On June 1, 1936 Von Wangenheim made a severely incriminating statement about one of his actresses, the popular Carola Neher, who had been a great success in Germany as Polly in Brecht and Weill's *The Threepenny Opera*. She was arrested and died in a camp six years later.[48] Gustav Regler soiled his hands by editing the official reports of the show trial where Zinoviev and Kamenev were sentenced to death, although he himself had been a friend of Kamenev's.[49] Erwin Piscator left the Soviet Union for a short visit to Paris and was on the point of returning when he was saved by a telegram from an acquaintance in Moscow: 'Nicht abreisen, Reich.'[50] Several of Ivens's German émigré colleagues from FIGHTERS fell victim to Stalinist oppression in the years that followed. Bruno Schmidtsdorf, who had played the hero Fritz, was arrested and disappeared in the Gulag; actor Gregor Gog was exiled to Siberia; the well-known painter and set designer Heinrich Vogeler starved to death af-

ter a forced evacuation in the steppes of Kazachstan; composer Hans
Hauska was deported; and the actor Alexander Granach, who had played
Dimitrov, was arrested in 1937 but released after the German writer Lion
Feuchtwanger, who lived in Paris, intervened on his behalf.[51] Scriptwriter
Alfred Kurella was one of those who came through unscathed and later, as
the Secretary of the Central Committee of the East German Communist
party, represented the hard line in cultural policy. Von Wangenheim also
played a leading role in GDR cultural life after the war.

Dutch residents of the Soviet Union did not escape Stalin's reign of terror. Engineer Dirk Schermerhorn, who had been in charge of the construction of the Turksib railway line, was arrested in October 1936 and executed a
year later after a fifteen-minute trial. Wim Rutgers, son of engineer Sebald
Rutgers, leader of the international colony in the Kuzbass and an acquaintance of Ivens's, was sent to a camp during World War II and never returned.[52]

Ivens himself did not get anywhere as a filmmaker in Moscow. He had
only made the pamphleteering Saarland short, which disappeared in internal conflicts in the party, and a lamentable propaganda version of
BORINAGE, which probably did not even reach Soviet theaters. His involvement in FIGHTERS vanished without a trace. His activities for the international Communist movement, and especially his status as an employee of
Münzenberg's Mezhrabpom Studio, had lured him into a position of de-
pendency. His films were being screened for Communist audiences or not
at all, and he was economically tied to the movement. On top of all this, his
friends were dying in the Gulag. It is difficult to say when he became aware
of this: the big trials in Moscow were reported in all the papers; reports
about less-prominent victims spread by word of mouth within the Communist movement and at the latest he must have been informed by the numerous acquaintances from Moscow he saw in Spain in 1937. In retrospect,
there was nothing good to say about his years in Moscow, and stubborn
suppression was the only way to keep the faith. As the German writer and
Communist Anna Seghers answered when asked about the Moscow trials:
'My method: I successfully forbid myself from thinking about such things.'

With his departure for America, Ivens traveled to freedom. Fifty years later
he summarized the situation by saying: 'Of course, the poor in the United
States had a hard time, but as a filmmaker you at least didn't get letters of instruction and you could do what you liked.'[53] He was still a member of the
CPN, and for a time the party continued to consider him as such, but presumably he ended up being quietly dropped from the list of members for
not paying his dues. It is not known whether he, in accordance with Comin-

tern statutes, joined the Communist Party of the United States, the CPUSA, after settling more or less permanently in that country. He did, however, maintain good contacts with Earl Browder, the General Secretary of the CPUSA, and with Gerhard Eisler, the Comintern representative in the United States. It did not really make much difference whether he was an actual member because, even as what his Polish wife Ewa Fiszer later called a 'freelance Communist', he remained absolutely faithful to the party, its organization and its political line. This was how he was able to create a certain degree of artistic freedom for himself within the movement: his position was beyond question. Under the party's protective wings, and with the sense of belonging fostered by the party's global network of contact persons and bases, he could go off in search of adventure. In an interview he once said: 'Some Communists say altruistically: 'I work so that my children will be happy, for a beautiful future.' But I work to be happy myself, for immediate results.'[54]

9 Land of Opportunity (1936)

With a suit and a pair of shoes as his only luggage, Joris Ivens landed at New York on February 18, 1936. From Moscow he had traveled via Amsterdam and Paris to the French port of Le Havre, where he set sail for the New World on the liner *Île de France*. In Amsterdam a Dutch engineer he knew from the Soviet Union had given him the two hundred and fifty dollars he needed to show American immigration officials to gain entry; he himself had nothing.[1]

Like every European seeing New York for the first time, he was over-whelmed and exhilarated and realized 'that America was going to turn out quite a bit more complicated and astonishing than I had first thought.'[2] He could not have come at a better time, as the political climate of the day was particularly receptive to his message. In an attempt to extricate the country from the Great Depression, Democratic President Franklin D. Roosevelt had introduced his New Deal, and a movement had arisen among writers, journalists, photographers and filmmakers to document the harrowing conditions prevailing in mining areas, working class neighborhoods and impoverished rural communities. There were also fears that Nazism might spread to the United States. The Communists were pursuing the relatively moderate antifascist policies they introduced all over the world in the mid-thirties. They were sympathetic to Roosevelt and had become very active in the cultural arena. Although the American working class maintained its traditional mistrust of Communism, the party's support among artists and intellectuals was growing.

Ivens had to regularly report to Mezhrabpom about his activities in the United States and he sent bulletins to Moscow in May, August and September. In the meantime he kept Verlinsky of the Soviet film distribution company Amkino in New York informed of his activities. Ivens had agreed with Mezhrabpom director Samsonov that the purpose of his trip to America would be threefold. First he hoped 'to stimulate independent film production and the film movement for the popular front' through lectures and screenings, during which he would steer clear of workers' associations and unions, 'because I had been advised not to make myself too vulnerable, so that my work and activities would not give rise to political complications'. He would also study advanced American film techniques, so that they could be deployed in the Soviet Union, and lastly he would, if possible, make a film in the United States.[3]

Ivens stayed with acquaintances in Greenwich Village for the first few months. The two hundred and fifty dollars from Amsterdam were essential because Moscow neglected to dispatch his films on time and his lectures, which were his main source of income, had to be postponed. At a congress for modern theater groups in Philadelphia he did give a speech in the name of the International Association of Revolutionary Theater, which was still being run from Moscow by Erwin Piscator.[4] Six weeks after arriving, Ivens was finally able to hold his first lecture with a film screening at the New School for Social Research in Greenwich Village. He went on to give further lectures in New York and the nearby university towns of Buffalo, Dartmouth and Syracuse for extremely attractive fees ranging from one hundred to two hundred and fifty dollars per evening. At New York University he spoke about 'the development of independent cinema'. After showing RAIN he remarked: 'That was RAIN. It rains. That's all.' He thought that filmmakers would be better off linking their work to 'the movement of the masses'. He interpreted the concept 'independent' in his own way, not as meaning that cinematic artists needed to be autonomous in their work, but that they should operate outside the commercial film industry and locate themselves in the class struggle. As examples of his own attempts in this direction, he showed PHILIPS RADIO, parts of the Russian version of BORINAGE, and NEW EARTH. During the screening of this last film, the audience was so enthused by the sequence of the closing of the IJsselmeer Dam that it applauded loudly when the caption 'CLOSED' appeared on the screen.[5]

Ivens's reading tour was organized by the New Film Alliance, which aimed to stimulate quality political films. It was one of many groups centered on the Communist party that had been cooked up according to Willi Münzenberg's tried and tested recipe: a board and an advisory council comprised a few Communists, a number of sympathizers and some liberals, with the actual work being done by a few party activists who stayed in the background.[6] The New Film Alliance was closely linked to Nykino, a group of progressive documentary filmmakers with an office on 12th Street on the Lower East Side. Compared to Europe, American documentary filmmakers were behind the times. Robert Flaherty had made his classic first films years earlier, but his compatriots had been slow to follow his example, and he himself had been living abroad for years. At the time, the leading documentary filmmaker in the United States was Pare Lorentz, who had just completed THE PLOW THAT BROKE THE PLAINS. Nykino was 'a small group of young, independent cinema enthusiasts... There are a number of good craftsmen in this group, mainly camera operators,' wrote Ivens, reporting back to Moscow.[7] He got to know the triumvirate that headed Nykino: Leo Hurwitz, Ralph Steiner and Paul Strand. Hurwitz remained active as a documentary filmmaker, Strand and Steiner later became known as photographers.

Ivens's reputation had preceded him. The fact that he had lived in the Soviet Union and had filmed SONG OF HEROES appealed to the Nykino members' imaginations. 'We immediately became friends,' said Leo Hurwitz, who called Joris Ivens 'a model'. According to Nykino member Irving Lerner, Ivens's arrival was 'a turning point... a shot in the arm... It was assistance from a recognized filmmaker who confirmed the theories of Nykino.' Willard van Dyke recalled that 'if a political question arose, Ivens was often the one who was consulted'. Jay Leyda, who had assisted with BORINAGE in Moscow and had returned to New York some time before Ivens, said that his moral support, organizational experience and craftsmanship were of great importance to Nykino.[8] Nykino was one big family. 'All of our personal affairs were known to one another, we had no separate lives,' related Ben Maddow. The members shared the same political convictions and, as beginners and fringe filmmakers, they were all in the same, unsteady boat.[9] Ivens did not become a full member of the family; he was neither a beginner nor a fringe filmmaker.

The National Board of Review of Motion Pictures agreed. This national organization of film critics rated NEW EARTH as second best foreign film of 1936, after Jacques Feyder's CARNIVAL IN FLANDERS and before Alexander Korda's REMBRANDT. The American authorities were less enthusiastic about his work and demanded cuts in BORINAGE and NEW EARTH. Among other things, they demanded the removal of the commentary accompanying the march with the portrait of Marx and the lines: 'Mr. Legg, president of the American Farm Board says, 'One active useful pig eats as much wheat as a family of five. Give the wheat to the pigs. Wheat is too cheap.'' [10]

That summer Ivens traveled to Hollywood with Helene van Dongen. *En route* he gave a lecture in Detroit and visited the Ford factory. They bought an old Pontiac and Helene did the driving. Ivens never got his driver's license. After a trouble-free journey they arrived in Hollywood, according to Ivens, 'the world's greatest center of agitation and propaganda'.[11] They were welcomed by the actor Fredric March and the directors King Vidor, Josef von Sternberg, John Ford, John Cromwell, Ernst Lubitsch and Rouben Mamoulian: definitely an illustrious gathering. March and Lubitsch were committee members of the Hollywood Anti-Nazi League and the others were simply liberals, with the exception of King Vidor, who was a self-declared conservative and anti-Communist. The press reports about the documentaries the remarkable European had screened in New York must have aroused curiosity in Hollywood, especially since left-wing ideas were coming into fashion there. The Anti-Nazi League had just been founded, partly through the efforts of Münzenberg's associate Otto Katz, who had been in Hollywood the year before under the pseudonym Rudolf Breda. The league immediately attracted considerable support and a branch of the Communist party was soon formed in the movie capital.[12] Some of the members made for peculiar political activists: they met by the poolside at their mansions, entertained themselves at parties that raised thousands of dollars for good causes, and were, in their own way, nonetheless genuinely concerned about the fate of the poor and the menace of Nazism. Ivens and Van Dongen stayed with radical director Frank Tuttle and his Russian wife. Tuttle was most famous for the silent comedies he had made for Paramount.

Ivens could hardly believe his eyes when he saw the unsurpassed techniques and efficient organization in the West Coast film factories. He visited director Frank Capra on the set of LOST HORIZON and Vidor, Mamoulian and Lewis Milestone showed him around their studios.[13] He screened his films at parties, and in July he presented his work in Hollywood's Film Art Theatre. He told his very interested audience that for him, 'a Dutchman of bourgeois origins, raised as a Catholic', progress, morality and the people's happiness had better chances in a society where egoism and personal profit had been defeated, as they had in socialist Russia. He admitted that one 'still saw traces of the old regime' there, but explained that, 'despite all the faults, all the imperfections and the occasional abuses of power, Soviet society was on a higher level than American society'.[14]

During his stay in California, Ivens immediately became involved in a short fiction film about an unemployed worker, MILLIONS OF US, a production of a number of Hollywood residents who were united in the group American Labor Films. 'Owing to personal conflicts the film had not been completed. The material was extremely good and I helped the group to finish the film,' he wrote to Moscow. Ivens scouted out locations in San Francisco Bay for the groups following project.[15]

In his article 'Notes on Hollywood', published in the magazine *New Theatre* that October, Ivens sharply criticized the film industry. Nowhere in the world were conditions so favorable, and still they only produced four or five good films a year. As positive exceptions he listed THE INFORMER by John Ford, MODERN TIMES by Charles Chaplin, MR. DEEDS GOES TO TOWN by Frank Capra, FURY by Fritz Lang, and PASTEUR by Wilhelm Dieterle. These were all films that rose above the general mediocrity but also touched upon some social issue or other. Ivens thought that cinematic artists of integrity should follow the example of New York's independent cineastes by immersing themselves in the reality of everyday life and taking account of the needs of peace groups and labor organizations. He also suggested the foundation of an 'experimental studio for a systematic examination of the fundamental laws of the art of film', where test footage that the big studios refused to finance could be shot – an old dream from his Filmliga days.[16] In Hollywood there was no longer anything unusual about Ivens's political beliefs, but the film production continued as ever. 'When one of those cele-brated directors happened to use the word democracy three times in his script, he saw himself as a revolutionary,' he mocked.

After returning to New York, Ivens and Van Dongen rented a large one-room apartment in Greenwich Village, at 46 Washington Square. By the standards of the Village, gathering place of America's bohemians, their ac-commodation was modest; after all, six-bedroom apartments were avail-able for just 85 dollars a month, less than Ivens received for one lecture.[17] Unfortunately he didn't give many lectures and their financial position in America remained problematic. When Vladimir Pozner came over from France that year and stayed with them, he and Ivens had to share an over-coat; in cold weather only one of them could go out at a time.[18]

Greenwich Village was familiar territory to Ivens because, as Allen Chur-chill put it in his book about the neighborhood: 'while the nation went Dem-ocrat, the Village went Communist'.[19] He met John Dos Passos, the left-wing author of the highly-praised modernistic novels *Manhattan Transfer* and *U.S.A.*, which Ivens had disapprovingly called 'mangled art' two years ear-lier in Moscow. Their conversations resulted in a synopsis for a documen-tary about the American film industry, though Ivens did not expect it to ever be able to be filmed, 'because it was scathing and one hundred percent anti-Hollywood'.[20]

His efforts to get a film off the ground in the United States suggest that he was not all too anxious to return to the USSR. That spring he had made a short film about the Russian school in New York under commission from Amkino, and he had also begun work on a major project: a film about Har-lem. The financing of this 'Negro film' had seemed settled, but new money problems had arisen and the production was no longer certain, as he wrote to Moscow in September. The film was not mentioned again. Ivens and the successful popular science author and bacteriologist Paul de Kruif, whose book *The Microbe Hunters* had sold more than a million copies, collaborated on a film adaptation of his latest book, *Why Keep Them Alive?*, about the de-plorable healthcare for the poor of Detroit. This film was not realized either. Finally, he received a commission for an educational music film, to be made with the Boston Symphony Orchestra. Ivens and Van Dongen wrote a script, but it is doubtful that the film was ever made.[21]

Driven by financial necessity, Ivens and Van Dongen accepted work in November from the Progressive Education Association, an institution that worked with New York University and was financed by the Rockefeller Foundation. Their task was shortening Hollywood movies to about thirty minutes for use in the education system as a catalyst to discussion of social issues. In an interview with a Dutch reporter, Ivens explained: 'The informative value of this kind of film is of secondary importance and its esthetic significance is completely irrelevant. But Americans, despite their superficially easy-going and jovial character, are very restrained. Under the direct stimulus of one of these films, their innate reserve yields and a fruitful exchange of ideas is possible.' [22] The first film they worked on was Fritz Lang's FURY. After seeing the short version, Lang apparently complimented himself. 'What a good story I wrote,' he told Van Dongen.

Van Dongen continued working for the Education Association for a year or two; Ivens left within two months and was replaced by Joseph Losey. Losey's background was in the theater, but after World War II he became famous as the director of films such as THE DAMNED, THE ACCIDENT and THE GO-BETWEEN. At the time he was unfamiliar with the medium and Helene van Dongen must have taught him the first tricks of the trade.[23] They edited at least twenty-five educational films together and Van Dongen tested them out on the students of a New York high school.

In New York, Joris Ivens started feeling the same oppressive atmosphere he had disliked so much back in Holland, one of 'left-wing circles, stopgap solutions and curbed expectations', as he later described it.[24] He wanted his expectations to be realized. He dreamed of sweeping panoramas, unlimited adventures and revolutionary heroics.

That summer, civil war had broken out in Spain. On July 17, 1936, officers of the Foreign Legion in Spanish Morocco had started a rebellion against the Republican government of Spain. They were acting under orders from a group of right-wing generals, among them Francisco Franco. The rebels were supported by garrisons in the mother country, but the quick *coup d'état* they had hoped for failed because hastily formed people's militias defended the center-left government, which had attempted to push through social reforms against the interests of the big landowners and the all-powerful Catholic church. Hitler provided the generals with aircraft to fly troops from Morocco to Spain, and a bloody war raged for more than two and a half years. The war and its aftermath would cost some half a million lives. Whereas the rebels received extensive support from Germany and Mussolini's Italy, the government had to make do with much more modest aid from the Soviet Union and insignificant Mexico. International volunteers

thronged to Spain to take up arms against Fascism and Nazism. For Joris
Ivens the Spanish Republic symbolized a people's struggle against tyranny
and poverty.

In the United States the most important organizer of support for the
Spanish Republic was the North American Committee for Spain, a branch
of an international committee that had been formed, once again, by
Münzenberg in Paris. In the fall the first Americans left for Spain to fight in
the International Brigades and the group Film Historians Inc. asked Helene
van Dongen to edit newsreel material into a film to use in campaigns in aid
of the Republic. The short was called SPAIN AND THE FIGHT FOR FREEDOM,
and Van Dongen quickly combined it with an Amkino compilation film entitled No PASARAN! The whole was now called SPAIN IN FLAMES. The commentary was the work of the writers John Dos Passos, Archibald MacLeish,
Ernest Hemingway and the Spanish author Prudencio de Pereda.[25] Ivens
was also involved in the production, but pointed out to the enthusiastic
group that something scraped together from archive material could only
have limited powers of persuasion, and that only filming on the spot could
achieve their goals, adding that he would be willing to go to Spain himself
to make the film.

What was the state of his contractual obligations with Moscow?
Mezhrabpom had been dissolved on June 5, 1936. The high concentration of
foreigners in the studio had become a thorn in the flesh of the Soviet authorities, and Moscow had long been intent on reining in Willi Münzenberg's
powerful political machine, of which Mezhrabpom was a part. After this,
Ivens had sent his reports straight to the head of the Soviet film industry,
Boris Shumyatsky, whom he again asked for permission to stay longer in
America. It is not known whether he received a reply. What is certain is that
the plan for the Spanish film exceeded Mezhrabpom's hopes of a year earlier, when the decision was made that 'if given an opportunity to make an
important film here, that I should most definitely accept that work'.[26]

For the production of the Spanish film the organization Contemporary
Historians Inc. was now founded, with the involvement of MacLeish, Ivens,
Dos Passos and Hemingway, the playwrights and scriptwriters Lillian
Hellman and Clifford Odets, and the theater producer Herman Shumlin –
the last three big names on Broadway. Ivens could have sought the assistance of the diligent workers of Nykino, but the stars of Contemporary Historians made for better publicity. Events around History Today, a group
formed in 1937 to make a Chinese film, will be discussed in Chapter 11, and
in the light of those facts one can assume that Ivens maintained tight control
over Contemporary Historians and worked in close consultation with party
and Comintern functionaries.[27]

With the exception of Hemingway, all the Historians belonged to the entourage of the American Communist party. The charming liberal Archibald MacLeish was a committee member of the League of American Writers, which had been founded by the CPUSA as a means of binding progressive writers. Odets and Hellman were members of this organization as well and had also joined the Hollywood Anti-Nazi League. Shortly afterwards they, together with Dos Passos, joined the advisory council of Frontier Films, the name Nykino adopted in March 1937. Ivens himself was appointed to the Frontier Films production staff, but never really worked for the organization. It was probably just a way of taking advantage of his name.[28]

The total costs for the Spanish film comprised some eighteen thousand dollars and were primarily raised from the members and sympathizers of Contemporary Historians. Most of them gave five hundred dollars, while Ernest Hemingway and the North American Committee for Spain each provided four thousand dollars.[29] As soon as there was enough money to cover the initial costs, Ivens wired his old protégé John Fernhout at Keizersgracht 522 in Amsterdam: 'Magnificent opportunity can you come to Spain January February poor wages important film telegraph answer Joris.' Ivens himself was not going to be paid, but his cameraman was to receive a modest reimbursement. John Fernhout did not need to think it over. He wired his 'yes' to New York, and a few days later Ivens sent a letter with further details. The plan was 'a kind of documentary about the lives of the various members of a family in a village between Valencia and Madrid: two sons at the front, one son with the fleet, and mother, daughter and one son in the village.'[30]

Ten months after arriving in New York from Moscow, Ivens sailed back to the old continent on the liner Normandy. Helene van Dongen was less keen on dangerous expeditions and stayed behind in New York.

10 The Spanish Labyrinth (1937)

The Normandy sailed into the port of Le Havre on New Year's Eve 1936 and Joris Ivens met John Fernhout soon after in Paris. He also met with another acquaintance, Luis Buñuel, now based at the Spanish embassy on the rue de la Pépiniere as the Paris representative of the Ministry of Propaganda of the Republic. Ivens signed a contract giving Buñuel the right to check the content of the film material shot in Spain before it was sent to the United States.[1] Presumably he also visited Willi Münzenberg, who was coordinating aid to Spain for the Comintern, and Otto Katz, who now headed Agence Espagne, the press agency that Münzenberg and the Spanish Minister for Foreign Affairs, Alvarez del Vayo, had set up together in Paris.[2]

With almost four hundred and fifty pounds of baggage, including three cameras, Ivens and Fernhout flew from Toulouse to Valencia, where the Republican government had relocated after the military situation around Madrid had become too precarious. On January 21, 1937 they shot the first footage of the film Archibald MacLeish would later christen THE SPANISH EARTH. They then left the coastal orange groves behind them and headed for Madrid by car. Speeding through the dry, grayish-brown landscape of the Castilian plateau, they were stopped in dusty villages by militant sentries who demanded to see their papers. The three safe-conducts they were carrying – one Communist, one Social Democrat and one anarchist – now came in useful. Republican Spain was divided into all kinds of factions, everyone was armed and the best way of avoiding difficulties was to present the right safe-conduct. Ivens had been advised to pay careful attention to appearances. When the villagers were wearing red shirts, he could assume that he had arrived in an anarchist stronghold; if things were well organized, the Communists were running things; and if it was quiet, the Social Democrats were in charge.[3] Seven hours after leaving Valencia, the travelers reached the Spanish capital safely.

They worked from a building on the Calle de Velázquez, the headquarters of the International Brigades and the 'Fifth Regiment'. This Fifth Regiment was the militia of the Spanish Communist party, the PCE, and the Brigades were also Communist-led. Ivens and Fernhout slept in the Florida Hotel on the Plaza Callao.

Spain's ancient capital was under siege. By early November 1936 the rebel advance had reached the outer suburbs. In a fit of bravado, Nationalist General Mola ordered a cup of coffee at Café Molinero on the Gran Via over the radio, but the defense of Madrid was rapidly organized and the rebel advance was halted. Months later Mola's coffee was still sitting untouched on a table, much to the amusement of the Republican guests. There was constant shelling, people were dying in the streets every day, and there was fighting on three fronts around the city.

In New York Ivens and MacLeish had written a three- or four-page scenario, a complicated story requiring a large cast and mostly staged scenes. On arrival in Spain, however, Ivens realized that 'there is no place here for directing, here the direction is in the hands of life and death'.[4] In preparation for their film, he sought the advice of two important Communists in Madrid, Michail Koltsov and 'Commandant Carlos'. The Republic was dependent on the Soviet Union for military supplies and party functionaries, Soviet generals and Comintern representatives were able to exercise a power that bore no relation to the Communist party's modest support among the population.

Ivens knew Michail Koltsov from Moscow. He was the Soviet Union's most influential journalist and *Pravda*'s correspondent in Spain, and a confidant and direct representative of Stalin, to whom he reported weekly by telephone.[5] He advised Ivens to not just show the war but to show ordinary life as well. Koltsov fell out of favor with Moscow three years later and was sentenced to death after a twenty-minute trial.

Commandant Carlos and Carlos Contreras were pseudonyms for the Italian Communist Vittorio Vidali, political commissar of the Fifth Regiment. He personified the two faces of Communism in Spain: he made a great contribution to the defense of Madrid, but was merciless to those he saw as his enemies. The *New York Times* correspondent in Madrid, Herbert Matthews, himself an unambiguous supporter of the Republic, wrote: 'The sinister Vittorio Vidali spent the night in a prison briefly interrogating prisoners brought before him and, when he decided, as he almost always did, that they were fifth columnists, he would shoot them in the back of their heads with his revolver.'[6] As a Comintern agent in Mexico and the United States, Vidali had already been implicated in the murder of the dissident Cuban Communist Julio Antonio Mella in 1929. In Spain he was involved in the liquidation of the Spanish politician Andrés Nin, leader of the POUM, a small semi-Trotskyite party and thus an object of hate for Stalin. Recently released KGB files confirm that Soviet agents murdered Nin, and rumors that Vidali pulled the trigger himself have circulated since 1937. A few years later he was one of the organizers of the first attempt to assassinate Trotsky in Mexico, and it is possible that he was also responsible for the 1943 murder of the Trotskyite Carlo Tresca in New York.[7] Vidali thought that Ivens's film should focus on the struggle of the Spanish people as a whole for parliamentary democracy. After World War II, Vidali sat in the Italian senate for the

Italian Communist party. When in Italy, Ivens had occasional contact with him then as well.[8]

Soon after arriving in Madrid, Ivens and Fernhout filmed an important sequence for THE SPANISH EARTH, a meeting in the Salle de Goya on the occasion of the abolition of the party militias, which were to be incorporated into the government army. Ivens showed a number of speakers: Enrique Lister, Vittorio Vidali, José Díaz, Gustav Regler, and Dolores Ibárurri. The commentary identified them as: a stonemason who had become a military commander, another commander, a printer who had become a member of parliament, a German writer who had come to fight for his ideals, and the renowned 'La Pasionaria', who had inspired the Spanish people to defend the Republic. This was all true, but another world remained hidden to the unsuspecting viewer. Lister was a Spanish worker who had become a military commander after training at a military academy in the USSR, and became a member of the central committee of the PCE. José Díaz was the general secretary of the PCE and made half-hearted attempts to resist the overwhelming Soviet influence in his country. He fell out of a window in Tbilisi in mysterious circumstances in 1942 and was succeeded as Spanish party leader in exile by one of the other speakers: Dolores Ibárurri. Gustav Regler had come to Spain from Moscow to fight in the International Brigades as a political commissar, but left the party after his experiences in the Civil War. And lastly Ibárurri, a hard-liner who always dressed in black and had won international fame with the slogan 'It is better to die on your feet than to live on your knees!' Like Lister, she would flee to Moscow after the Republican defeat, and thereafter fulfil the role of mouthpiece for Stalin.

Rather than dawdle in Madrid, Ivens and Fernhout headed for the frontlines. On February 12 they filmed a new twentieth-century innovation in the village of Morata de Tajuña: the bombing of the civilian population, carried out by Franco's airforce. 'After the explosions there was complete silence in the village. We thought the people would come back now. Then we realized that they were listening to see if the planes would return and bomb again. Silence between two people may be dramatic, but you should hear the silence of five hundred people after the crash of bombs,' wrote Ivens.[9]

After four weeks in Spain, the duo was back in Paris on February 21 to view the first results of their work, and Ivens showed his rushes to about one hundred invited guests, including Vladimir Pozner and the director Jean Renoir.[10] Around the same time Ernest Hemingway also arrived in the French capital. Hemingway was the author of novels such as *A Farewell to Arms*, about World War I, and *The Sun also Rises*, about America's 'lost generation' in 1920s Paris, and was otherwise chiefly known as a lover of bullfighting, African big-game hunting, and deep-sea angling. Although he generally avoided politics, he felt strong ties to Spain because of earlier trips and was on his way there as a war correspondent. As a member of Contemporary Historians, he and MacLeish had agreed in New York that he would write the commentary for Ivens's film, and he was doubtlessly planning to join the film crew in Spain.[11] Legend has it that Hemingway and Ivens met in café Au Deux Magots near Saint-Germain-des-Prés. Ivens claimed that Hemingway had not yet seen the necessity of choosing between the two Spanish camps, but in the United States the writer had already paid the fares for several American volunteers on their way to fight in the International Brigades and had single-handedly financed two ambulances for the Republic.[12] 'Hem' is supposed to have only seen the light once they were in Madrid, where it turned out that 'he found all his friends on the right side. All the bullfighters and barkeepers he knew were with the Republican army. It made it easier for him to choose our side.'[13] In reality the owner of Chicote, Hemingway's favorite Madrid bar, was on the other side of the front and, to his sorrow, many matadors and bull breeders had also taken the side of the generals. Nonetheless, Ivens's belief that his friend did not see things clearly can be explained to a degree because he himself thought in the unambiguous categories of Communist politics, whereas Hemingway did not embrace any single concept and most resembled a Boy Scout, driven by a simple sense of justice and occasionally sighing that every war was inhuman, a sentiment Ivens considered naive. He did his best to provide the American with a political education and Hemingway's biographer, Carlos Baker, referred to him as 'Ernest's Political Commissar'.[14]

A few weeks after Hemingway, John Dos Passos also arrived in Paris. Archibald MacLeish, in his capacity as editor of *Fortune,* had arranged a job for Dos Passos as a correspondent in Spain, where he planned to join Ivens's crew.[15] In contrast to adventurers like Hemingway and Ivens, Dos Passos was a typical intellectual, a thoughtful, bald-headed cigar-smoker who was nevertheless capable of extreme emotion. The fourth member of Contemporary Historians to head for Spain was Lillian Hellman, but she got stuck in Paris with pneumonia and did not reach the Iberian peninsula until long after the film was completed.

Ivens and Hemingway traveled from Paris to Valencia, which they reached on March 17, 1937, and immediately drove on to Madrid, where Hemingway joined Ivens in the Florida Hotel. Dos Passos did not cross the lobby of the Florida until mid-April, after traveling to Valencia via Perpignan in a truck, then driving the rest of the way with André Malraux, now a colonel in the international air squadron Escadrilla España.[16]

John Fernhout (Ferno) filming SPANISH EARTH (1937).
NFA

The Florida Hotel had become the headquarters of the international group of reporters, intellectuals and artists who had been drawn to Spain by their solidarity with the Republic.

Already present were Martha 'Scrooby' Gellhorn, journalist and Hemingway's lover, the photographer couple Robert Capa and Gerda Taro, the American writer Josephine Herbst and the French author Antoine de Saint-Exupéry, and many other celebrities were to follow. Ivens and Fernhout were far too busy to hang around their hotel. Joris Ivens impressed Martha Gellhorn as hardworking and concentrated. She was very positive about him. He was 'funny, persuasive, absolutely not boring', but always stayed calm and never spoke rashly, even though things never stopped going wrong and agitation and raised voices were part of everyday life in the Spanish Civil War.[17] A few minutes' walk from the Florida was the Gran Via Hotel, where journalists, writers, volunteers, Soviet advisers and diverse shady characters met in the anarchist-run restaurant and dinner guests never knew if they would be served the cheapest rotgut or a bottle of

Château d'Yquem 1904 from the looted cellars of King Alfonso XIII. At the Gran Via Ivens and Fernhout bumped into Jef Last, who had joined the Fifth Regiment and would later become a captain in the Spanish army.[18]

Hemingway was a great help to the film crew. With a flask of whisky and raw onions in his pockets, he lugged equipment and arranged transport. Ivens generally wore battle dress and a black beret. Hemingway went as far as the beret but otherwise stuck to civvies. Although he rarely wore glasses, he almost never took them off in Spain, clear evidence of the seriousness of their task. They were given safe-conducts granting them freedom of movement in the combat area because, as one of the documents stated, they were there to make 'international antifascist propaganda'. Later Hemingway would often recall their work: 'The first thing you remember is how cold it was; how early you got up in the morning; how you were always so tired you could go to sleep at any time; how hard it was to get gasoline; and how we were always hungry. It was also very muddy and we had a cowardly chauffeur. Nothing of that shows on the screen except the cold when you can see the men's breath in the air in the picture.'[19] He drew on his experience in the Great War to lecture his Dutch friends about the excessive risks they were taking. Even during the Vietnam War, at the age of seventy, Ivens was never deterred by danger.

They were soon on familiar terms with the party functionaries at the front, among them the political commissar of the 12th International Brigade Gustav Regler, who had worked with Ivens on the Saarland film. Regler later wrote: 'He filmed the impact of the shells from dangerously close by, and told me afterwards that in the film he intended to follow the shells with images of explosions; it had to look like the shells of this war could break dams, water would flow, bringing fertility to vineyards that had been neglected by their wealthy owners for decades; the filthy landowners gambled away their money in Hendaye; Ivens would go there too to show them, gorged, weary from doing nothing; he was still unafraid of being accused of making a black-and-white portrait.'[20]

Sometimes Ivens doubted the value of their work, because what use were you in the trenches when a wounded comrade was lying next to you and you were unarmed? But he gradually lost this sense of operating 'at the expense of their courage, their heroic fight'. As he wrote in the weekly *De Groene Amsterdammer*: 'It is as if the camera takes on a trigger and a barrel.'[21] It was probably the first time that he used this oft-repeated comparison of camera and gun. On the other hand, the camera could also create moments of peace. 'There were peculiar moments,' related Ivens, 'when hostilities were momentarily suspended because friend and foe wanted to pose for the film. For the sake of Spanish vanity, the war would be briefly put aside while they posed in fraternal unity for particular scenes I was filming. Once it was over, everyone ran back to the trenches and opened fire.'[22]

From the Florida Hotel it was only eight minutes' walk to the western front on the Casa de Campo, where Ivens, Fernhout and Hemingway filmed on April 9 from inside an abandoned building in the combat area, which consisted of a number of university buildings that had been shot to pieces. The American described it in his daily news report: 'Just as we were congratulating ourselves on having such a splendid observation post and the non-existent danger, a bullet smacked against a corner of brick wall beside Ivens's head. Thinking it was a stray, we moved over a little and, as I watched the action with glasses, shading them carefully, another came by my head. We changed our position to a spot where it was not so good observing and were shot at twice more. Joris thought Ferno had left his camera at our first post, and as I went back for it a bullet whacked into the wall above. I crawled back on my hands and knees, and another bullet came by as I crossed the exposed corner. We decided to set up the big telephoto camera. Ferno had gone back to find a healthier situation and chose the third floor of a ruined house where, in the shade of a balcony and with the camera camouflaged with old clothes we found in the house, we worked all afternoon and watched the battle.'[23]

Martha Gellhorn considered Joris Ivens unusual for a Communist because he didn't play the Messiah or try to convince you.[24] All the same, he clearly made work of Hemingway. There was an obvious affinity between the two men and they soon grew toward each other. And winning the writer over would be a tremendous propaganda coup for the Communist movement. Ivens suggested that 'Comrade' Hemingway could write an article about 'the great and human function of the political commissar at the front', because 'some people think that we could do it now without pol. commissars'.[25] These functionaries were controversial in the Republican army, since they were virtually all Communists and had their very own perspective on unity and the maintenance of the troops' political morale.

Ivens took Hemingway to the Soviet headquarters in Madrid, the Gaylord Hotel, where Michail Koltsov and the Soviet generals stayed, and where Ivens himself was free to come and go. Ivens said: 'That gave him an edge and with it came more confidence, which for him was very important, because other correspondents did not have this access. So through me he was able to get accurate, first-hand information. I didn't keep any secrets from him. 'Yes, here are Russians.' For many people the Gaylord Hotel was some kind of secret center. I had a plan for Hemingway, and I think I used the right tactics. For this kind of man. I knew how far he could go and that he was not a traitor. I didn't introduce him to the Russians when he first asked me. But after four weeks. I thought, now, he is ready to make that step, and it worked.'[26] After the Civil War was over, Hemingway gave the Gaylord an important role in his novel *For whom the Bell Tolls*. 'It was there you learned how it was all really done instead of how it was supposed to be done... At the start when he had still believed all the nonsense it had come as a shock to him. But now he knew enough to accept the necessity for all the deception.'[27]

Ivens also wanted to show the war's social background. To do this he chose the wine-growing village of Fuentidueña de Tajo, a few hundred houses in the shadow of the ruins of a Moorish castle, some forty miles from Madrid on the road to Valencia. The peasants, almost all members of the Social Democrat union, had formed an agricultural co-operative and were cultivating land the landowners had left fallow for years. The extra produce was sold in Madrid and thus benefited the war effort. Dos Passos in particular preferred immersing himself in the social side of the war to pursuing the hostilities, whereas Hemingway showed no interest in Fuentidueña. Together with Ivens and Fernhout, 'Dos' temporarily settled in the union meeting room at the back of the village pharmacy. He translated the conversations with the peasants, as neither of the Dutchmen spoke Spanish.[28]

The images filmed in the village show daily life behind the lines: the bakery, household chores, farm labor, digging an irrigation ditch. As a link between the war and the peasants, Ivens allocated a role in the film to Julian, a young man from Fuentidueña who goes to fight near Madrid and returns home on leave. Unfortunately the crew was unable to locate him in the trenches and they were left with the flimsiest of storylines, thus repeating one of the flaws of SONG OF HEROES.

In New York, Helene van Dongen received few signs of life from Madrid. Hemingway wrote to his mother-in-law: 'It seemed as though the world were in such a bad way and certain things so necessary to do that to think about any personal future was simply very egoistic. After the first two weeks in Madrid I had an impersonal feeling of having no wife, no children, no house, no boat, nothing.'[29] He neglected to mention that in the Florida Hotel at night Martha Gellhorn was doing her level best to encourage this feeling. It must have been genuine all the same, and three years later, on a quiet day in Camagüey in Cuba, Hemingway wistfully contemplated those days in Spain: 'We were even unconditionally happy, because when our people died, we thought that the cause justified their deaths and made them unimportant. They died for something they believed in that would one day become reality.' Ivens was in complete agreement. He saw the Spanish struggle as a new beginning for a 'race that knows no war' and considered the truth in Spain to be 'dramatically simple': it was a people's struggle against fascism.[30]

Sadly the truth in Spain was far from simple. The Republic itself was divided into two camps. A moderate Popular Front of Republicans, Social Democrats and Communists, supported by part of the influential anarcho-syndicalist movement, were working together in the government. But many anarchists, left-wing Social Democrats and revolutionary socialists believed that the socialist revolution needed to be immediately put into effect in the struggle against Franco, and in several regions they began socializing agriculture and industry, thus alienating the Republican center. It was difficult to find a middle ground between the two main streams, so the Communists under the leadership of Comintern and Soviet functionaries began resorting to imposing unity by force. They executed political opponents, or those they took to be their political opponents, and in Barcelona in May 1937 a civil war broke out within the Republic. The small splinter party POUM in particular suffered badly. Stalin's aversion to the Comintern's favorite bogeyman Leon Trotsky and other presumed conspirators now spread through the entire international Communist movement.

The film crew of THE SPANISH EARTH also became acquainted with the violence within the Republican camp. After arriving in Valencia, John Dos Passos went looking for his friend José Robles, who had taught Spanish language and culture at Johns Hopkins University in Baltimore and now held the rank of lieutenant colonel and worked as interpreter for the Soviet General Goriev. Dos Passos wanted to ask Robles's advice, because 'I knew that with his knowledge and taste he would be the most useful man in Spain for the purposes of our documentary film.'[31] He found Robles's wife alone at home, desperate because her husband had been taken in for questioning and had not returned. Dos Passos made futile inquiries with various authorities, and finally Robles's son was informed that his father had been executed by a 'special section'. The circumstances were never clarified and an official charge was never made. Robles had presumably fallen victim to a Communist liquidation. In Madrid Dos Passos made further attempts to uncover the details, but Hemingway told him that his inquiries were endangering the film and that his concern was naive. Robles had been shot dead, therefore he must have been guilty, according to Hemingway. One of his biographers remarked that he would have felt differently if it had been one of his friends.[32] It was not the first time the two writers had clashed and their friendship of almost twenty years now came to an end. Soon after, Ivens wrote to Hemingway from Valencia: Dos Passos 'is running here for the same cause as he did in Madrid – it is difficult. Hope that Dos will see what a man and comrade has to do in this difficult and serious wartime.'[33] Minister

Ernest Hemingway and Joris Ivens beside the film crew's car, just hit by enemy fire (Spain, 1937). PHOTO JOHN FERNHOUT, NFA

of Foreign Affairs Alvarez del Vayo, a long-time Soviet sympathizer, did not tell Dos Passos what had happened to Robles but promised to send his wife a death certificate so that she could obtain a pension. She received neither.

In a letter to Hemingway less than two years later, Ivens called Robles 'the friend-translator-fascist of Dos Passos'.[34] And early in 1938 he had written: 'I still get angry when I think of the fact that Dos after being with us went into the POUM office in Barcelona – it is not only the worst political thing to do – but more: dirty disloyal to all of us.' He now referred to Dos Passos as an 'enemy'.[35] All this because Dos Passos had interrupted his return journey to France to stop in Barcelona, where he had spoken with POUM leader Andrés Nin and the British author George Orwell, who had fought in a POUM militia on the Aragon front and as a result had to flee the country soon after to avoid arrest.

After '1968', when Joris Ivens was taken up by a new revolutionary generation with somewhat less esteem for the Soviet Union, he was regularly asked which position he had taken on the violent clashes between the different factions in Republican Spain. 'I didn't witness them and I never heard anything about them,' he answered. 'If I had known about it, I would not have accepted it.' In the same breath, however, he defended 'the law of half truths'. He believed that 'if you're in the domain of class struggle or a war of liberation and a particular truth is in the way of events, then you have to progress beyond that truth if you want to get anywhere. If you don't, you run the risk of blocking your own capacities. Of course, this brings dangers with it, but I believe that you have to accept this law of half truths.'[36]

On April 27, 1937 he flew from Valencia to Paris, and a week later he sailed out of Le Havre for New York on the Île de France. A few days later a remarkable incident took place in Paris on the platform of Saint-Lazare Station, where Dos Passos was boarding a train for Le Havre. Hemingway approached him and asked in menacing tones what he intended to write about Spain, adding that there were only two possibilities: for or against. Dos Passos shrugged, at which Hemingway held a fist under his nose and warned him that the critics would crucify him if he didn't change his attitude.[37] In New York, Dos Passos informed Archibald MacLeish that he still wanted to be involved in the film, and Archie wrote to Hem that Dos was 'extremely anxious to cooperate in any way he could' and that he was no Trotskyite, despite Hemingway's bland assertions to the contrary.[38] But the breach was final. In a *New York Times* interview in July, Ivens named everyone else who was involved in THE SPANISH EARTH, up to and including the errand boy, but did not even mention Dos Passos.[39] Although he did not go public with the José Robles affair until much later, Dos Passos's point of view on Spain came fairly quickly into line with that of George Orwell, who continued to support the Republic, but expressed the fear that a police state would emerge if the Communists had their way.

After Spain Ivens had difficulty adjusting to ordinary life 'with its peace and indifference'. He felt as if he had returned from another world where he had been marked by war. Now he was back in daily reality where 'the details of life, friendship and even love had lost their vigor'.[40] For who else other than Helene could his love have lost its vigor?

Spain had distanced him even more from everyday life. He now became the frontline filmmaker of world revolution, throwing himself with equal energy into the Chinese struggle, the fight against U-boats in the Atlantic during World War II, the Indonesian independence movement, the Communist reconstruction of Eastern Europe, and the Cuban and Vietnamese revolutions.

Meanwhile, he and Helene worked on the editing of THE SPANISH EARTH in New York's Preview Theatre, assisted by Prudencio de Pereda. There was no room for frills. Van Dongen: 'We simply didn't have time to ruin things with beauty.'[41] With only Ivens and Hemingway's stories to go by, they created astonishingly realistic war noises in the studio. Marc Blitzstein and Virgil Thomson compiled film music from Spanish folk songs, but made the mistake of putting Catalonian music to pictures of peasants in Castilian Fuentidueña, whereas Catalonia did not appear in the film at all. In the Spanish situation, where regional chauvinism played a crucial role, this was a serious error, and during the Civil War it was magnified by the fact that Catalonia, in contrast to Madrid, was intensely anarchistic.

Hemingway wrote a commentary without realizing that many of the images spoke for themselves. Upon seeing Ivens's red scribbles on his pages, he shouted furiously: 'You God-damned Dutchman. How dare you correct my text?'[42] Finally, he admitted that he was wrong and returned home to Key West to write a more concise commentary. When Hemingway came back to New York with a revised version, everyone was satisfied except for one person: Orson Welles, who was supposed to record it. If Welles's memoirs are to be believed, he and Hemingway quarreled violently. 'There were lines as pompous and complicated as this: 'Here are the faces of men who are close to death', and this was to be read at a moment when one saw the faces on the screen that were so much more eloquent. I said to him: 'Mr. Hemingway, it would be better if one saw the faces all alone, without commentary.' This didn't please him at all and, since I had, a short time before, just directed the Mercury Theatre, which was a sort of avant-garde theatre, he thought I was some kind of faggot and said, 'You ---- effeminate boys of the theatre, what do you know about real war?' Taking the bull by the horns, I began to make effeminate gestures and I said to him, 'Mr. Hemingway, how strong you are and how big you are!' That enraged him and he picked up a chair; picked up another and, right there, in front of the images of the Spanish Civil War, as they marched across the screen, we had a terrible scuffle. It was something marvelous: two guys like us in front of these images representing people in the act of struggling and dying... We ended by toasting each other over a bottle of whisky.'[43] According to Prudencio de Pereda, this was a total fabrication and Welles and Ivens made several critical but friendly comments about Hemingway's text.[44] Ivens was satisfied with Welles's work and the film was shown in Los Angeles and Hollywood with his voice on the soundtrack. There, Welles's voice was criticized for being overly detached. Hemingway was asked to record the commentary himself, and this became the definitive version.

Ivens spent three days in Florida visiting Hemingway and his wife Pauline, after which the two men flew from Miami to New York to attend the second congress of the League of American Writers in Carnegie Hall. It was a historic high-water mark in the alliance between American literature and Communism. The opening night was chaired by Archibald MacLeish and speeches were given by the general secretary of the U.S. Communist party, Earl Browder, and by Joris Ivens and Ernest Hemingway. Ivens screened a silent provisional cut of THE SPANISH EARTH and declared: 'This picture is made on the same front where I think every honest writer ought to be.' He appealed to his audience: 'Life is ahead of you. Catch it.' Later history would ask: 'Where were you in 1937? Only talking in the New School?' This was a reference to the left-wing New School of Social Research in Greenwich Village. Hemingway announced that only one political system was incapable of producing good writers: fascism.[45]

On July 8 Ivens, Hemingway and Martha Gellhorn visited the White House at the invitation of the First Lady, Eleanor Roosevelt. Gellhorn had become friends with the president and his wife while working with Roosevelt's adviser Harry Hopkins. The president appeared for dinner, a meal Hemingway described as 'the worst I've ever eaten'. He detailed the menu as including 'rainwater soup followed by rubber squab'.[46] More important was the screening of THE SPANISH EARTH, for which some thirty viewers gathered in the White House projection room. The Roosevelts were impressed by the film, which had turned out especially well, and after the screening FDR said: 'Why didn't you stress more the fact that the Spaniards are fighting not merely for the right to their own government, but also for the right to bring under cultivation these great tracts of land which the old system forcibly left barren?' He called the makers over to discuss the film. Ivens and Hemingway had consulted intensively with Contemporary Historians about what to say. They had settled on a plea for the suspension of the American arms embargo, which did not differentiate between the Spanish government and Franco's rebels. But Roosevelt dominated the conversation and did not allow them to say their piece. He was on the side of the Republic, but was neither willing nor able to change American policy. Later in the evening, when Harry Hopkins remarked that the Republicans would win, Hemingway replied that if the Republic did not get any weapons he was not so sure that they would. 'We had tried and we were quite proud that we had,' said Ivens.[47] In her daily column 'My Day', syndicated in a number of newspapers, Eleanor Roosevelt praised him as an extremely artistic and fearless filmmaker. The fact that the film had not been made out of self-interest had made a deep impression on her.[48]

Two days later Hemingway and Ivens flew to the West Coast, and on July 12 they screened their film in Hollywood at the home of actor Frederic March. March had played the male lead opposite Greta Garbo in Clarence Brown's ANNA KARENINA and was now acting with Janet Gaynor in William Wellman's A STAR IS BORN. There were seventeen guests: the directors Ernst Lubitsch, King Vidor, Fritz Lang, Anatole Litvak, Lewis Milestone and John Cromwell, the actors Robert Montgomery, Luise Rainer, Errol Flynn, Miriam Hopkins and Joan Bennett, and the writers Scott Fitzgerald, Dorothy Parker, Lillian Hellman, Dashiell Hammett, Donald Ogden Stewart and Marc Connelly. This all-star audience included some members of the Hollywood branch of the Communist party; others were only in the Anti-Nazi League. After the screening, Ivens gave a speech that was un-adulterated Hemingway. 'Now you have seen what it looks like. There are some things that we could not get in. The way the ground rocks and sways under your belly and against your forehead when the big bombs fall. That does not show. Nor the noises kids make when they are hit, also there is a sort of foretaste of that when the child sees the planes coming and yells, 'Aviacion!'' He talked about dead comrades on the front and continued: 'These men all knew what they were fighting for. You all know what they were fighting for. It is an old story and we do not have to go over it again. It is our fight as much as it is theirs.' He went into the issue of medical treat-ment. 'I don't know whether you have ever been wounded. It differs from an operation in that there is no anesthetic and you never know whether your stomach is full or empty when it happens. The chances are it is empty. At the moment that it happens, unless the bullet or the shell fragment hits a nerve, and even then it may numb it, it is not very painful. It is more like be-ing knocked down by a club and you can be clubbed in the belly or the legs or the neck or the shoulders or the feet or almost anywhere. If you are clubbed in the head you don't know anymore about it at the time... Ivens concluded his account with a remark that out-Hemingwayed Hemingway: 'I know that money is hard to make but dying is not easy either.'[49] Dorothy Parker was in tears and they collected no less than seventeen thousand dol-lars, enough for seventeen ambulances. Ivens and Hemingway personally ordered the chassis from Ford in Detroit and the bodywork was done in Spain.[50] Everyone made a donation except Errol Flynn, who escaped through the bathroom window.

The following day Scott Fitzgerald sent a telegram to Hemingway: 'The film was beyond praise and so was your attitude.' Fitzgerald detected 'something almost religious' in the enthusiasm of Hemingway, who had given Ernst Lubitsch a dressing down for suggesting improving the film Hollywood-style. Ivens gave private screenings of THE SPANISH EARTH at the homes of various other celebrities as well: John Ford, Darryll F. Zanuck and Joan Crawford, who apparently asked him to warn her 'if the film be-comes too horrific' so that she could close her eyes.[51]

On July 13 the Committee of Film Artists for Spanish Democracy orga-nized the first public screening in the Philharmonic Auditorium in Los An-geles. People fought for tickets. British writer Anthony Powell reported that three thousand five hundred people crowded into the aisles and on the stairs. Another two thousand five hundred were turned away. After the film Hemingway gave a speech. Ivens said a few words as well and then gave the stage to film director Herbert Biberman. His 'manner and methods would have cleared any hall in England in ninety seconds, but I believe they were the traditional ones of American preachers beginning 'Is there anyone here who will give one hundred dollars?' and working down to dimes and nickels.' Biberman, who fell victim to Senator Joe McCarthy's Communist hunt during the Cold War and spent six months in prison, raised two thousand dollars – another two ambulances.[52]

Money was not the only purpose of this expedition to the West Coast. Contemporary Historians aimed to distribute THE SPANISH EARTH in the commercial theaters and hoped that the Hollywood greats would intervene on the film's behalf. Despite their support none of the big distributors was willing to take the risk, and finally it was left to the small leftist distributor Garrison/Prometheus to release the film. Ivens was deeply disappointed, but the market was difficult for documentaries that dealt with a sensitive political theme and took sides so blatantly. That the makers of THE SPANISH EARTH had been fairly restrained, that the Communists who appeared in the film were not named as such, that there were few ideological lectures and no theatrical flag-waving, and that the military exercises shown were touchingly chaotic was not enough. During a reading at New York University, Ivens went into the subject 'Documentary Film and Propaganda' at length. He asked: 'Mention a film that has no propaganda. Not so much in a political sense, but in a moral sense.' What was the Hays Office, which monitored the morality of all Hollywood films, if not 'an excellent agency of propaganda for existing morals and the existing social order?'[53]

The official premiere of THE SPANISH EARTH took place in the Fifty-fifth Street Playhouse in New York, and the film went on to show in three hundred theaters in the United States and in thousands of smoke-filled halls on the labor union and action committee circuit.[54] The film critics' organization, the National Board of Review, declared it one of the three best American films of 1937. It was, after all, a film with superior photography and, what's more, one of the first fully-fledged war documentaries filmed completely on location.

In Holland the daily *Het Volk* praised the makers of THE SPANISH EARTH for their 'noble attitude' and the Central Commission for Film Censorship concluded that 'there are no grounds for denying to adults this depiction of a piece of global suffering, which shows reality as it is without adding or removing anything'. This did not stop them from ordering a number of cuts to preserve 'a maximum of neutrality to both sides'. [55] The film was cut in England as well, and finally THE SPANISH EARTH also fell victim to Ivens's self-censorship. After World War II the GDR authorities erased Gustav Regler from history because the once-so-valued writer had turned dissident around 1939. While living in Eastern Europe, Ivens accepted the removal of a shot showing Gustav Regler and the accompanying text.[56]

Hemingway returned to Spain and wanted to show the film to the troops on the front, but there is no evidence of the film actually reaching the country where it was shot. Ivens suspected Luis Buñuel, the Republic's propaganda representative in Paris, of 'keeping the print away from Madrid', or that there was some 'kind of sabotage somewhere in the embassy – too many party people in the picture'.[57] As time progressed, Republican politicians tried increasingly to force back the excessive Communist influence in Spain.

The Spanish Civil War continued to occupy Ivens. On January 28, 1938 a letter he wrote to Hemingway included an ominous sentence. Referring to his visit to Amsterdam in December, he now wrote that 'a cleansing action is hard work, specially if it regards people who were once your good friends'.[58] Who were the good friends who no longer made the grade? He was most likely referring to Jef Last, with whom Ivens had made BREAKERS and planned other films, explored Amsterdam's nightlife, set up a photography collective, campaigned against the German film DAWN, and who he had recently seen in Madrid. In 1936 Jef Last had visited the Soviet Union with the French writer André Gide. On his return Gide had published the moderately critical *Retour de l'URSS* and been branded a traitor. Last was already in Spain, where his fellow party members urged him to distance himself from Gide at a writers' congress. In his speech, however, he avoided the issue, and in later articles he occasionally returned to it in an extremely outspoken way. In late July 1937 he was summoned to the CPN political commissar in Madrid – there were hundreds of Dutch volunteers fighting in Spain – and the CPN daily *Volksdagblad* warned: 'Inasmuch as Jef Last values being seen as a comrade in the ranks of the working class and not as a turncoat, he will urgently recant these Trotskyite-derived jeers at the Soviet Union.'[59] According to Last, he was court-martialed in autumn 1937 on the fatal charge of collaboration with the POUM but released soon after. To avoid further difficulties, the Republican government sent him to Scandinavia on a propaganda trip.[60] Last's crisis of faith deepened, and in February 1938 he cancelled his CPN membership, in all likelihood narrowly avoiding expulsion. The CPN clearly still viewed Joris Ivens as a member because it is inconceivable that he could otherwise have been involved in an internal purge. The parallels between Jef Last and John Dos Passos were obvious and explain Ivens writing to Hemingway about the events: he too had given up friends for his ideals.

On April 1, 1939 the Spanish Civil War ended in the defeat of the Republic. The victorious General Franco had tens of thousands of Republicans shot and three hundred thousand Spaniards fled the country. 'Yes, Marty,' Ivens wrote to Martha Gellhorn, 'A hard blow to take with so many cowards in England and America, who could have prevented it without even courage – just a little decency and honesty is all we ask... A pity you are not here now, we could talk and swear. A hell of a fight ahead, for all of us.'[61]

11 Chinese Poker (1938)

Joris Ivens was fond of enlivening meals by describing his culinary adventures in China. Catherine Duncan, a friend of Ivens after World War II, recounts: 'When at a dinner party the talk turns on food and the merits of different national cuisines, Joris caps all the reminiscences of exotic dishes with his account of a feast given in his honor in China. Chinese cooking, he insists, is the most refined and recherché in the world. An official dinner with its procession of forty or so dishes, its skilful blending of tastes, is designed to flatter esthetic as well as gastronomic appreciation. He cites the gilded duck, as an example, where only the skin of the duck is eaten and the rest thrown away. But even this was only a preparation for the pièce de résistance which came at the end of the repast. Here Joris's eyes begin to sparkle wickedly. 'At the end of the meal,' he says, 'a live monkey was brought in and placed on the table. With a little hammer the monkey's skull was cracked open and the brain served still hot and palpitating to the assembled guests. Not even the truite au bleu or the rainbow death of the salmon can equal this dish in its sublime refinement.' After this story, as the others usually find they have lost all appetite for a second helping of dessert, Joris finishes the platter.'[1]

In the fall of 1937, Ivens's Chinese adventures had yet to begin. He had just announced that his next film would be shot in China, where the Sino-Japanese war was raging. Japan had occupied Manchuria and was preparing to conquer all of China. Nippon was an expansive, reactionary power, and anti fascists equated the struggle in China with the war in Spain. At the same time, resistance to Japan was of vital importance to the Soviet Union. Japan, Germany and Italy had formed the Anti-Comintern Pact, and the Soviet Union felt threatened from both east and west. An important motive for the Comintern's support of China's struggle against Japanese aggression was thus the conviction that the Soviet Union had to be defended at any price. There is no doubt that Ivens shared this belief: every Communist, wherever in the world he might be, was obliged to defend the first socialist state as if it were his own fatherland – no, the state the great Lenin had founded *was* the fatherland of all workers.

The Middle Kingdom was in a state of chaos. A republican movement had dethroned the Chinese emperor in 1911 and the country had been ravaged by self-interested warlords ever since. The political arena was dominated by the Nationalist Kuomintang led by Chiang Kai-shek and the Communists under the leadership of Mao Zedong. Their armies had been entangled in a life and death struggle, and they did not form an uneasy alliance until the Japanese threat became impossible to ignore. Chiang Kai-shek was made commander-in-chief of military operations against Japan, and in return he accepted the existence of Communist base areas.

Even Ivens's friends were surprised by his decision to go to China. At the Hollywood presentation of THE SPANISH EARTH he had declared that he would soon be returning to Spain.[2] Nonetheless, a Chinese connection with 46 Washington Square was not entirely new. Helene van Dongen had promised to edit a film being shot by a Chinese crew in the Red base areas. This work in China had been delayed because of 'changes in the military situation' and 'our lack of experience in 'documentary work'', as M.T. Yuan wrote to her in January 1937. 'Personally as a friend I hope you can be just a little patient with us.' Yuan went on to say that 'a number of leaders' agreed fully with her proposal to shoot three-quarters at the front and one-quarter in the hinterland and thanked her for her generous help both present and past.[3] This particular film does not seem to have been completed, and this might partly explain Ivens's reorientation toward the Far East.

Hemingway was disappointed to hear of Ivens's new plans. 'So, you're going there! It's all over with Spain, the Third International is now turning its attention to China!'[4] Martha Gellhorn said: 'In New York we were promoting THE SPANISH EARTH as if the whole world depended on it. What always astounded me was that Joris did not return to Spain. Ernest and I went back there, he didn't. I believe he wasn't that emotionally involved after all.'[5]

Hemingway was right in presuming that the change of course had not originated with Ivens himself. A few months later, a letter from Ivens confirmed his suspicions. 'Such a sudden change in assignment, a shift to another front, is not easy... Had to shift my work to China.' He explained that it was 'my job to get the money and to organize the project'. After explaining the preparations at unusual length, he concluded: 'confidential of course, tear this letter up'. Hemingway didn't, thus preserving a rare source of information about Ivens's working methods. Ivens's letter made clear that the original intention had been to shoot a Chinese Communist party financed film in a revolutionary base area. After forming a united front with the Kuomintang in September 1937, however, the party decided to make Chinese unity against Japan the film's main theme, whereupon Ivens tried to find ways of collaborating with the Communists' new allies.[6]

The letter to Hemingway explained that he had initially tried to arrange financing without involving the Contemporary Historians. He contacted Chinese business people and artists in Hollywood, but his plans met with a cool reception and the Chinese aid committees he contacted had passed 'out of our control'. Initial attempts to gain the support of the Nationalist embassy in Washington also failed. Ivens concluded that the backing of rich Chinese could only be won if they were approached by an 'organizational front' of well-known intellectuals and writers, and approached Contemporary Historians after all. He actually believed that this group first needed to be 'cleaned', as Dos Passos was still a member and could cause problems. 'The Chinese people who gave the money' did not need 'to know everything about me'. After 'a long talk with my people', he called a meeting of Contemporary Historians and 'forced a decision' to make a Chinese picture, even though none of those present were enthusiastic, only MacLeish a little bit.

The China film was now presented publicly as an initiative of the actress Luise Rainer, who was married to Contemporary Historians member Clifford Odets. Rainer, an Austrian immigrant, had become popular with the Chinese community through her role as a Chinese in the film THE GOOD EARTH, based on the book by Pearl S. Buck. An elaborate dinner was organized for wealthy Chinese – Van Dongen and the Pozners were also present[7] – but due to 'some intrigue or other by Chinese government officials' they were unable to raise any money. Later the Nationalists came round, and by the time Ivens left for China he had the support of their embassy.[8]

He first traveled to Paris with Helene van Dongen in a futile attempt to raise funds. In the same letter to Hemingway, he wrote: 'our own funds are too tightened up with Spain and other things'. Ivens discussed the China project in detail with 'M.', who was apparently known to Hemingway and can scarcely have been anyone other than Willi Münzenberg, who controlled the cash flow to countless Comintern aid organizations from his Paris base and had maintained intensive contacts with China through the League against Imperialism and diverse committees since 1925.[9] The idea of making a film in China may have even originated with Münzenberg. This must have been Ivens's last meeting with this exceptional figure. Münzenberg broke with Moscow in the course of 1938, and in 1940 he was found dead under a tree in the South of France with a noose around his neck. It could have been suicide, but there was a widespread belief that he was murdered by Comintern agents. He disappeared from Communist histories and Ivens's memoirs make no mention of him either, despite the important role Red Willi had played in his career.

In Paris Ivens had numerous discussions over numerous Chinese meals, and his enthusiasm for his expedition to the Far East grew: 'What a story, what a people, what a struggle.' He arranged for John Fernhout and the photographer Robert Capa to accompany him to China. Capa was in a deep depression after the death of his girlfriend, the photographer Gerda Taro, who had died in an accident in Spain. China was about as far away as he could get, and the expedition would also satisfy his longstanding wish to learn more about film.

In mid-December, Ivens traveled from Paris to Amsterdam for the above-mentioned purge, and took the opportunity to visit his parents in Nijmegen. On Sunday, December 12, 1937, his father wrote in his diary: 'He is a big kid and a good bohemian. His film about Spain and his celebrity in America are making him famous... No one believes that he doesn't make an awful lot of money. And no one will lend me money. Telling me to ask my 'rich' son. Poor too.'[10] In Amsterdam Joris saw Wim, the brother he was closest to, for the last time. Wim died of a brain tumor in the fall of 1938 at the age of forty-three. Joris Ivens received the news of his death in America, where his sorrow was all the more intense, 'because up till that moment I had believed that I was immune to such reactions. I wasn't able to work or do anything coherent at all. I stood with my forehead against the wall and my fists clenched, and gave in to my tears. 'Where could all these tears come from?' I asked myself.' He sent a letter to his parents and his father answered, but he 'only wrote about his own difficulties and said almost nothing about Wim... It was a ghastly reply and terribly hurtful. My father was indeed very distant.' But perhaps Joris Ivens was just as distant with his father. The entries about Wim in his father's diaries are heartbreaking and anything but indifferent.[11]

Back in Paris, Ivens received an unexpected telegram from Archibald MacLeish informing him that they had raised the money they needed for the Chinese film. A number of Chinese had undertaken to make contributions totaling fifty thousand dollars, the amount of Ivens's budget. The financiers insisted however that Luise Rainer be given a role in the film, and that the script be submitted for their approval before filming.[12]

Since Contemporary Historians continued to doubt the success of the enterprise, according to Ivens's letter to Hemingway, he now founded a new group: History Today Inc., with a board comprising himself, MacLeish and Broadway producer Herman Shumlin, with 'no Dos Passos or so'. He advised Hemingway to immediately quash any attempts by Dos Passos to use the now dormant Contemporary Historians to make a film of his own. During a dinner in the Port Arthur Restaurant in New York's Chinatown, Ivens presented a one-page scenario he had hastily put together with Lillian Hellman. Their table companion was their most important sponsor, K.C. Li, a Chinese-American importer who supported the Kuomintang. Not for a moment did Ivens intend to follow this scenario. He had learned his lesson in Spain and planned to postpone decisions until he was in China. Through the Nationalist Chinese ambassador in Washington, he arranged his visa, diplomatic introductions and a considerable financial contribution. Chinese Americans ended up supplying twenty-two thousand dollars, while twenty thousand was raised from unknown sources within China.[13] Ivens had never been so busy. As he wrote to Hemingway: 'You are right, we sometimes do too much, but we have not yet enough trusted people for special work.' Ivens was in the heart of the Communist machine and urged Hemingway: 'If there is something you like to talk over with one of our leading people, do it, Helen van Dongen will fix the rendezvous for you.'[14] She too was fully at home in party circles.

In his letter to Hemingway Ivens wrote things that he would definitely not have revealed to most of the other members of Contemporary Historians. Although their work together in Spain had turned the American into a loyal sympathizer with the Communist movement, Ivens's confidences might nonetheless have gone a little too far. Hemingway faithfully continued to visit Spain until the Republic's final defeat, and he must have seen Ivens's neglect of his earlier promises regarding Spain as a form of desertion. Now he read: 'Once and for all, know that we are not impatient – we trust you.'[15] In other words, you haven't really figured things out yet, but you will. That was not the kind of thing Hemingway liked to hear; getting to the heart of things was his role, and he had once written that he admired Communists when they were soldiers but hated them when they played the priest. Furthermore, Ivens's remarks about several other members of Contemporary Historians might have led him to suspect that he too might be viewed in a similar way. People like Lillian Hellman helped wherever they could, wrote Ivens, and he looked on that as a positive thing, particularly since they were unable to do any harm because they were not in a leading position. They weren't to blame for not having the correct insight. In his characteristically skewed English, Ivens explained that they had been 'unhappy and in the wrong way alone after their puberty years'.

In late January 1938, on his way to China, Ivens wrote from the Moana Seaside Hotel in Honolulu suggesting that it might be a good idea for Hemingway to join him. By the end of March however, he still hadn't received a reply. He now wrote from Hankou in China that Hem's arrival was extremely important, but the letter did not reach Key West until June, and the writer did not come.[16] He was still concentrating on Spain. After Ivens's return from China, he and Helene van Dongen paid a last visit to the Hemingways in Cuba, where the two men went marlin fishing in Pilar, Hemingway's yacht.

Two years later Hemingway published *For whom the Bell Tolls*, in which he was unexpectedly critical of the course of events in the Spanish Republic. He believed that the fight against Franco had not been dictated by abstract ideals – for which one could read Communism. Anyone whose heart was in the right place had simply not had a choice. The Communist press in America saw the book as an attack on the Republican cause, but Ivens said later: 'With him it was never a betrayal. He returned to his old point of view.'[17] In 1948 Hemingway and Dos Passos settled their differences, forgiving and forgetting their clash in Spain. Three years later Ivens had a chance encounter with Hemingway in Lyon, France, at a screening for a local film club. Passing through the city, the writer spotted the film posters, stormed into the foyer of the theater, embraced Ivens and exclaimed: 'And, are you still at it?' Hemingway shot himself in the head with his hunting rifle in 1961. In 1963 his widow, Mary Hemingway, sent her congratulations to Leipzig, where Ivens was celebrating his sixty-fifth birthday: 'To my knowledge, Ernest admired him greatly.'[18]

On January 21, 1938 Ivens left San Francisco for Hong Kong aboard a Pan-American Airways seaplane. Ivens realized that the expedition to China was hazardous. Before departing he wired his parents in Nijmegen, who immediately dispatched a farewell telegram in reply. Back home in Nijmegen, people had their own ideas about George's enterprises. His father confided to his diary: 'On the afternoon of January 16, 1938, I met Mr. and Mrs. de Jonge, formerly George's best friends... Mr. de Jonge said: 'He must have put together a pretty penny by now.' Unfortunately, I had to disabuse him. After I had told them a thing or two, Mrs. de Jonge said: 'He always was a dreamer and an idealist.' 'Be that as it may,' said her husband, 'that doesn't mean he has to be a fool as far as the future's concerned. How old is he now?'[19] Ivens tendency to give priority to working for the cause might have kept him busy, but it had hardly made him a wealthy man.

On board the USA Clipper, Ivens suddenly wrote to his girlfriend from the Oisterwijk fens, Miep Balguérie-Guérin. He had been carrying an unanswered letter from her around with him for a year. Now he related his wanderings to her and prompted her to write back. She did: 'Years and years ago, someone once told you that your life should be like a flag! Remember? It seems to me now that your life is like a flag in a storm. It flaps and blows until it's tattered and torn, but does it ever hang still? That's sometimes necessary for essential repairs, otherwise it will wear out so fast!'[20]

Above the Pacific, a blocked fuel line forced the aircraft to return to San Francisco. Three days later it made a new attempt to cross the ocean. 'Of course, there was something peculiarly heroic about it', according to Ivens, 'because the aircraft before ours had disappeared, leaving nothing but an oil slick.'[21] He felt like a real Flying Dutchman. During the stopovers he went in search of drink. 'Guam... In the hotels of Pan-American Airlines, no liquor.

Found some in the little native village near the airport in a tiny café... Manila. Walk with Baker. Got very drunk together.' After all kinds of delays, Ivens arrived in Hong Kong on February 8, 1938 and took a room in the Metropole Hotel. 'I'm in the ring now, and no longer nervous.'[22]

Equipped with all necessary film equipment, Robert Capa and John Fernhout had meanwhile sailed from Marseilles on board the passenger ship Aramis. Also on board were the English writers W.H. Auden and Christopher Isherwood. Their account of the journey describes how Ivens's assistants' coarse antics and jokes about whores caused uproar in second class. 'Capa is Hungarian, but more French than the French; stocky and swarthy, with drooping black comedian's eyes.' Fernhout was 'as wild as Capa, but slightly less noisy'.[23] The two Englishmen might have been given a photo of Gerda Taro. Capa had stacks of them in his suitcase and handed them out to anyone who was willing to listen to the story of Taro's death in Spain. Eight days after Ivens, the Aramis arrived in Hong Kong.

In the British Crown Colony, a mysterious contact took Ivens to Madame Song Qinling, the widow of Sun Yat-sen, the Chinese revolutionary leader who had inspired the 1911 overthrow of the imperial regime, founded the Kuomintang, and hoped for a more-or-less Social Democratic China. Unfortunately Sun had died in 1925, and under the leadership of Chiang Kai-shek, the Kuomintang had developed in a rightist and nationalistic direction. Madame Song was extremely active politically, and many Chinese saw her as the personification of her husband's ideals. She maintained good relations with the Chinese Communist party and was close to Willi Münzenberg, who she had met in Berlin in 1925. She had given him permission to use her name in the letterheads of any of his committees. Song Qinling had lived in Moscow for a considerable time, she was a board member of the League against Imperialism, and she had participated in the congress of the 1932 Amsterdam-Pleyel movement for peace, organized by Münzenberg.[24] Madame Song was about forty years old at the time of her meeting with Ivens and she impressed him deeply. Some seven years later he would call her the 'most wonderful woman I ever met in my life'.[25] She explained the country's complicated political relationships and warned him about her sister Song Meiling, the wife of Chiang Kai-shek, while also providing him with a letter of recommendation to her. A third sister was married to the director of the National Bank of China. Ivens had no idea about the scheming world he was about to enter. 'In the midst of it all the Song family carries on its intrigues which sometimes disgust me completely,' remarked America's Ambassador Johnson.[26]

In Hong Kong Ivens also established contact with Dutch consul Van Woerden. The film material sent to America during Ivens's stay in China went through the consulate. Lastly, he also met with Edgar Snow, the American journalist and lifelong sympathizer with Chinese Communism. In 1936 Snow was the first Western reporter to visit – with a letter of introduction from Song Qinling – the Communist base areas. He wrote the famous book *Red Star over China* that same year. As part of his preparation for his expedition, Ivens had read the book on the plane from San Francisco.[27] In 1971 Snow was given a hero's funeral in Peking.

Less than a week after Fernhout and Capa's arrival in Hong Kong, the trio flew to Hankou. They set up in the Lodge Hotel on the northern bank of the Yangtze, where French gunboats were moored at the door. The European buildings were downtown: consulates, warehouses, offices and banks, British and American stores, theaters, churches and clubs. The Chinese city radiated out from the center in a tangle of lanes that led out onto the Hubei Plain. The winters were Siberian and the summers subtropical.

Hankou was the seat of the Nationalist government and Song Meiling sent the film crew an invitation to tea in Chiang Kai-shek's headquarters on the opposite side of the river. Passing through a stone gate flanked by painted lions, they reached the villa where the reception was to be held. Ivens described the conversation with Song Meiling as being 'as banal as any other chit-chat', but Auden and Isherwood, who she received in audience a few weeks later, went into more detail. 'She is a small, round-faced lady, exquisitely dressed, vivacious rather than pretty, and possessed of an almost terrifying charm and poise... She can become at will the cultivated, westernized woman with a knowledge of literature and art; the technical expert, discussing aeroplane-engines and machine-guns; the inspector of hospitals; the president of a mothers' union; or the simple, affectionate, clinging Chinese wife. She could be terrible, she could be gracious, she could be businesslike, she could be ruthless; it is said that she sometimes signs death-warrants with her own hand.'[28] The filmmakers were introduced to Generalissimo Chiang Kai-shek himself, who listened to their plans without giving the slightest sign of approval or disapproval. Song Meiling appointed Ivens with an escort: Huang Renlin, Chiang's adjutant and one of the leaders of their political 'New Life' movement. Definitely not just anyone. The film crew was under constant surveillance from Song Meiling's spies, and she liked to casually impress the fact upon them. 'Did you have a good time at so-and-so's last night?' she would ask.[29]

Huang Renlin supervised every aspect of the film work. After reading in their budget that they were only being paid fifty dollars a week, he refused to believe that they were a professional crew and Ivens was forced to ask Luise Rainer and other Hollywood associates to telegraph that he really was a person to be taken seriously. Didn't the crew include Robert Capa, a photographer for *Life*, a magazine that was well known even in China? By using these arguments, however, Ivens may have miscalculated, because by convincing the authorities that the film really was serious, he gave them even more reason to keep a close watch on him and his crew; the Kuomintang was very concerned about its image abroad. Huang informed Ivens that he would be accompanied on his wanderings by General Theodore Du and an extra cameraman, who would be equipped with a 16mm camera and would keep a check on them by filming everything Fernhout filmed. This job was given to Chiang Kai-shek's court photographer 'Chuck'.

Looking back on this patronizing behavior a few years later, Ivens said: 'I never understood completely,' but mainly saw himself as a victim of censorship whose chief target was the Western film industry, which had a predilection for showing the Chinese as comical people with bound feet and pigtails. 'I explained to Madame Chiang Kai-shek the fundamental misunderstanding of our purpose in coming to China. They saw our project as a commercial venture, and because of that it had to follow the procedure of motion picture companies previously operating in China.' Strangely enough, in his eyes, his biggest problem was 'not with a military censorship, which should have full control in wartime, but with a narrow civil censorship of the most human aspects in and behind the front – ordinary crowds of people, single faces, ordinary streets and landscapes. The fiction films usually made about China have certainly justified their care in this matter, but I regret this loss every time I see the completed 400 MILLION.'[30]

There is no doubt that the Nationalists in Hankou were aware of Ivens's political inclination. Informed circles in the United States knew all about Ivens and still Chiang Kai-shek's embassy had provided him with financial support, which proves that the Nationalists really were willing to work with him. At the same time they wanted to see China presented abroad as a modern nation, and thus subjected him to the restrictions that applied to all foreign filmmakers.[31]

Chiang Kai-shek and his wife fiercely opposed their Dutch guest's plan to cross over into the territory of their Communist archenemies. Portraits of Chiang Kai-shek and Mao Zedong hung beside each other in fraternal harmony in the streets of Hankou, and such things probably contributed to Ivens's underestimation of the nest of intrigue in which he found himself. His knowledge of Chinese politics was based solely upon *Red Star over China*, Malraux's novel *La Condition humaine*, and some conversations. Ivens's openness in Hankou about his intentions of visiting Mao Zedong's Eight Route Army in the Communist base area of Yan'an was rather ill advised. During one of the daily press conferences given by Chiang Kai-shek's press chief Hollington Tong, Auden and Isherwood heard that Ivens's film crew was going to film a 'little red devil', one of the child soldiers of Mao's army.[32]

Negotiations with Huang Renlin about the film crew's working conditions dragged on for more than four weeks. Fernhout in particular was sometimes on the point of exploding with anger, but Ivens realized that such a breach of etiquette would only make things worse. 'You never get angry in China, it is indecorous, you lose face, you don't dare get angry. You must remain calm. They have been doing that for three thousand years. Keeping calm.'[33] Capa too was becoming severely frustrated. Registered as a member of the film crew rather than as a photographer, he was not allowed to do any reportage outside the city. He and Fernhout killed the time drinking and womanizing in the Dump Street bars: Mary's, the Navy Bar, The Last Chance. Ivens would join them after yet another hopeless discussion with Huang Renlin.

A peculiar trio had found its way to one of the far corners of the globe, only to end up in a sleazy bar. Ivens was an inspired loner; Capa believed that the world was absurd and treacherous; Fernhout's main motivation was a thirst for adventure. Ivens was thirty-nine; both Capa and Fernhout were under twenty-five.

At the office of the Communist Eighth Route Army in the Chang Gai, better known to the people of Hankou as 'Eighth Route Street', Ivens discussed his plans with Zhou Enlai, the Communist party's representative in China's provisional capital, a member of Chiang Kai-shek's National Military Council, and the future premier of the People's Republic of China. In Hankou Ivens also met the American writer Agnes Smedley, who sympathized with the Red Army, organized humanitarian aid to China, and edited a newspaper that was financed in its entirety by the Comintern.[34]

On April 1 Ivens and his companions were finally able to leave by train for the front. The group now comprised the Chinese business manager Jack Young; the chief censor Theodore Du; the shadow cameraman Chuck; Tsao, Ivens's personal assistant, who was attached to China's Military Council and reported daily to Chiang Kai-shek's headquarters, but was also a secret member of the Chinese Communist party; and lastly the servant Piao, who wore yellow shoes and carried a rifle in a suitcase. The other passengers included Irving Epstein from United Press and Captain Evans Fordyce Carlson, an American army observer who was also a Quaker. They reached their destination two days later, after a journey of almost six hundred miles.

'Our luggage was unloaded and distributed among soldier bearers who filed off in a long serpentine column into the night. We must have looked

something like a Hollywood cinema group going on location, what with tri-
pods, cameras and other photographic paraphernalia,' Carlson wrote. Two
hours later they reached the farm near Tai'erzhuang where General Sun
Lien-chung of the 35th Division had established his field headquarters.
Midway between Shanghai and Peking, Tai'erzhuang was a walled town
and the site of an important railway station. They were received cordially
by General Sun, an officer who held no political ambitions and taught his
troops to treat the civilian population with courtesy. 'It was a lazy sort of
battle', wrote Carlson, 'for the Japanese were on the defensive, and the Chinese preferred to conduct their assaults at night'.[35] The peasants continued
to plant their crops in the daytime, while artillery batteries exchanged fire
from a great distance and the occasional stray shell exploded in their fields.
At night Ivens and Fernhout gave renditions of Dutch folk songs, Carlson
played harmonica and Capa contributed songs from the Hungarian
steppes.

Two-thirds of Tai'erzhuang was already in Chinese hands, and during
the night of April 6 the Japanese were driven out of the rest of the town in a
fierce street battle. It was the first Chinese victory since the start of the war.
In the morning the filmmakers and journalists rushed to the town. Carlson
noted: 'Climbing over sand-bag barricades and stepping gingerly through
barbed-wire barricades, we entered a city of the dead. The Japanese had not
had time to bury all of their killed compatriots, though black patches of
ashes here and there indicated a last minute attempt to incinerate some of
the bodies. At one place an elderly Chinese peasant lay sprawled in the
street, the feet of a pair of geese still clutched in his lifeless hand. Farther on
was the body of a woman, an unborn child protruding from her ruptured
abdomen. It was all too ghastly for words.'[36] The crew stayed in the town
filming with Carlson, Jack Young, Chuck and the journalist Epstein until
darkness fell. On their way back to headquarters, flames from burning villages lit up the horizon.

Robert Capa tested his abilities as a cameraman at Tai'erzhuang, but as
far as Ivens was concerned he wasn't really cut out for it. Ivens believed that
motion picture and still photography had next-to-nothing in common, and
Capa's failure confirmed this opinion. Photographers thought in terms of
static images rather than movement and were too impatient for the long
production time required by film. Capa was not especially happy in Ivens's
crew: 'In general, I am the 'poor relation' of the expedition, and this is causing me plenty of difficulties... They are very fine fellows, but the movie is
their private affair (and they let me feel that), and the still pictures are completely secondary... The pictures of Tai'erzhuang are not bad, but it really
isn't easy to photograph well if you have a big film-camera at your back,

four censors around, and then have to help the film operator.' He would have preferred returning to Paris immediately.[37]

That evening General Sun gave a dinner to celebrate the victory. Theodore Du performed songs he had written for the occasion and everyone sang along. Ivens befriended Carlson, who would later become famous as the commander of 'Carlson's Raiders'. In his legendary World War II campaign on the Pacific island of Guadalcanal, Carlson put the guerrilla tactics he picked up from the Chinese Red Army into practice against the Japanese.

Censor Du was constantly interfering with the filming. On April 11, Ivens noted in his diary: 'This morning at three o'clock when we were sound asleep a loud and noisy guy came in and yelled a couple of words in Chinese. We swore back, of course. Had we only understood him, he was from the Ninety-first Division that passed the headquarters to reinforce the front, and wanted to take us there. But Mr. D. told him that we didn't have enough film. We had thousands of feet for our hand cameras and Mr. D knew it, but he hates the front. A hundred times I told him we were ready to go, every minute. I hate him.'[38]

Du had shown his fear of hostilities on previous occasions as well, but he was not the only reason that few battles were filmed. Ivens also accused the officers in the area of not allowing him to go to the front because of excessive concerns on his behalf. Furthermore, neither Du nor the commanding officers could oblige the crew by changing the nature of the war. It remained, as Carlson had observed, 'a lazy sort of battle' that mostly took place after dark. The team spent another week working near Tai'erzhuang. In the evenings while playing cards with General Sun, Ivens kept on asking himself: 'Am I here to play poker?' He continued to feel as if the Chinese were stringing him along.[39] On April 14 the crew resigned themselves to traveling back to Hankou. The Japanese retook Tai'erzhuang soon after and resumed their march southward.

In Hankou, Ivens prepared with Zhou Enlai for his journey to the Eighth Route Army in Yan'an, via Xian where a truck would be waiting to take him to the Communist base area. He now made a concerted effort to rid himself of Theodore Du. The authorities consented but appointed as replacement a charming teacher called Deng, who was no less bothersome. Ivens obtained official permission to leave for Xian and, together with Fernhout, Capa and the others, boarded the train that would take them to Zhengzhou and on to the northwest. Xian was a walled city in Shaanxi, dusty from the winds of the Gobi Desert, and the travelers took rooms in an unexpectedly luxurious hotel, known to foreign visitors as the Xian Guest House. The authorities, however, had no intention of allowing them to travel any further. The

Kuomintang officers in Xian, presumably acting on instructions from Song
Meiling and Huang Renlin, forbade them to travel on to Yan'an, ten days'
march to the north. Ivens received a telegram from Hankou on May 11, in
which Huang Renlin and Chiang Kai-shek's press officer Hollington Tong
requested his immediate return to the capital on a transparent pretext. The
director wired back that his work precluded returning and tried to outsmart
them by submitting a request to film at the Great Wall, which in the north
runs toward Yan'an. Instead he was treated to a long journey in a rattling
bus through sandstorms to another part of the Wall, three hundred miles to
the west, near Lanzhou. 'Capa went slowly mad,' Ivens wrote, describing
this journey. 'On the third afternoon he came to me very happy, said, 'Do
not talk to me. I am going to think backwards.' Two days later he said, 'I
arrived at my birth, please talk to me.''[40] Near Lanzhou there were only a
few crumbling ruins of the Wall left. Ivens filmed them anyway, and used
the shots later as an image of the collapse of ancient China.

Despite everything, he still hoped to be able to reach Mao's base area, or
to be able to arrange for it to be filmed in some other way. While trying to
keep Hankou happy by forwarding a rather peculiar scenario about the adventures of a girl student at the Great Wall,[41] he also wrote detailed directions for the filming in Yan'an. These guidelines were never put into
practice, but provide an insight into his utopian mentality. Despite never
having set foot in a Chinese Communist area, he could already imagine it in
detail, something that was all the more remarkable considering that he had
concluded in Spain that even a rough scenario could only be written on location. His plan lists sixteen themes, including: students on their way to
Yan'an 'talking to the peasants'; lessons in which theory and practice are always closely linked; political education – discussing Spain and America;
commandants and soldiers discussing the course of a battle after the fighting; soldiers assisting peasants at harvest; the churches are spared ('if possible American church'); the civilian populace assisting the guerillas. In
summary: 'Emphasize in the picture the important and excellent relations
and close contact between army and population.'[42]

A number of these subjects are found in Edgar Snow's *Red Star over China*
and Ivens apparently discussed the content of his film with Zhou Enlai. All
of these fine things were aspects of the declared policy of the Chinese Communist party, although people did not always cooperate voluntarily.
Wealthier peasants in particular, at least those who hoped to come through
alive, could expect an existence full of humiliations and arbitrary injustice.
Skepticism, however, was not part of Ivens's make-up, and his efforts to
reach Yan'an were rooted in his determination to film his dream, irrespective of the factual situation he might encounter.

On May 21, Hankou sent a new telegram that could not have been clearer: 'Guerrilla units can be found anywhere stop madame wants me to inform you China has only one army under Generalissimo's command in your production you are cautioned not to publicize any particular unit.'[43] Madame was, of course, Mrs. Chiang Kai-shek. The Communist party, whose local headquarters was in a settlement just outside the city walls of Xian, now decided to cancel the journey to Yan'an in order to avoid endangering the collaboration with the Kuomintang. Ivens's memoirs infer that Zhou Enlai was in the city at that point and had to deploy all his powers of persuasion in order to convince him that this was the right decision. It was a bitter pill, but nothing Ivens could say weighed heavier than unity in the struggle against Japan. He now made a forced decision to film in Xian and its surroundings, which he did under close observation from censor Deng, who sometimes held a hand in front of the lens when he thought there was a risk of China being depicted in an unfavorable light. The poor, the crippled and the elderly were unsuitable for foreign consumption. The military command in Xian arranged a parade especially for the film, for which Ivens was not particularly grateful. Not because it was staged, but simply because he would have preferred filming a 'little red devil'. He incorporated the parade sequence in THE 400 MILLION, but changed its meaning by intercutting it with shots of his heroine Song Qinling as a symbol of progressive China.

After an extended stay in Xian brought on by catching the mumps, Ivens was back in Hankou at the end of June. On July 4 he filmed a meeting of the Military Council under the chairmanship of Chiang Kai-shek. It was the first time a camera had been permitted at one of these gatherings. He was back in favor by virtue of his submittal to the Kuomintang yoke. Nonetheless, Ivens still managed to shake off his censors on a couple of occasions. He filmed a meeting of Communist leaders, and in a taxi in a dark street he handed over a Bell & Howell Eyemo camera with a number of reels of film to Wu Yinxian, who much later became vice-president of the Peking film school. The camera was intended for the Yan'an Film Group and, after many years of faithful service, ended up in a glass case in the Museum of the Revolution in the capital of the People's Republic of China.

On July 25 Ivens and his co-workers arrived by train in the southern Chinese city of Canton, the film's last location. They moved into the top floor of the city's tallest hotel in order to have a good view of the bombing that was ravaging the city. Later Ivens recalled the chilling scenes he saw in the streets. 'Two little kids were weeping and there was a little cross on the floor and some blood and our translator asked, 'Why are you weeping?' And the kids said, 'That is our mother.' There are things you cannot film. You cannot describe it. That happens a lot in documentary film because you go deeply into human suffering and sometimes the medium is not big enough to tell it.'[44]

After a stay in Hong Kong, where they again visited Song Qinling, Ivens and Fernhout traveled on to the United States. On August 21/20, 1938, they crossed the International Date Line on board Pan-American Airways' Philippine Clipper on their way to San Francisco. Robert Capa went back into China, finally free to return to his own work. The great photographer died in Vietnam in 1954 after stepping on a landmine during the battle of Dien Bien Phu.

'All exterior shots in sunny weather.' With these words Ivens concluded a summary of his Chinese diary for the *New York Times*.[45] But once he had seen the results of seven months in China, he was so discouraged that he seriously considered destroying the negatives, and wrote to History Today board member Herman Shumlin that going ahead with the China film endangered his reputation as a filmmaker.[46] A number of people viewed the rushes and encouraged him not to lose heart, among them Dashiell Hammett, detective novel author and Lillian Hellman's husband; John Howard Lawson, scriptwriter and chairman of the Hollywood branch of the Communist party; and Dudley Nichols, chairman of the scriptwriters' union and the writer of John Ford's STAGECOACH and THE INFORMER.[47] Nichols provided a commentary for THE 400 MILLION, but a commentary for a documentary is not the same as a script for a fiction film, and Ivens and Frontier Film member Ben Maddow had to drastically rewrite it.[48] In spite of this Nichols's name appeared on the credits and Ben Maddow's did not; Nichols was famous and it was all for the cause. According to Ivens, the final completion of THE 400 MILLION was largely due to the expertise of Helene van Dongen.

The result of all this effort was a weak film. It included beautiful shots but, with the exception of the section about Tai'erzhuang, it had clearly been compiled from disconnected material. Ivens elaborated further on his old idea of enlivening documentary with an individual story. In the absence of his 'little red devil', a certain Sergeant Wong was now conjured up in the editing room from a few, probably coincidental, close-ups of some soldier. After SONG OF HEROES and THE SPANISH EARTH, this third attempt to build up a storyline around a character again failed to meet Ivens's expectations. Still he insisted that the concept of a story was 'correct ten times over'.[49] Hanns Eisler, who had fled Europe for the United States at the start of 1938, wrote the music. He shared Ivens's doubts about the quality of the whole and accordingly suggested they call it: 'Notes towards a Film on China'.[50]

After a preview in Hollywood for the American Friends of the Chinese People, the film premiered on March 7, 1939 in New York's Cameo Theater. Meanwhile, political tension had been growing in Europe and interest in China had been decreasing accordingly. The only people to attend the film in large numbers were Chinese Americans encouraged by the many posters hanging in Chinese restaurants and laundries. The message was nothing new to them, according to a disappointed Ivens. He left things in the hands of Garrison Films, the distributor of THE SPANISH EARTH, and set sail with John Fernhout on the passenger ship Normandie for a six-week visit to Europe.

On April 14, 1939 they arrived at Amsterdam's Central Station, where they were met by journalists from *Het Volk*, the *NRC* and other Dutch newspapers. In the Noordhollands Koffiehuis they told the reporters about their Chinese adventures. Ivens announced that he would be making a film in the Amazon basin about Roosevelt's policies in Latin America, and Fernhout informed them that he had submitted plans in the United States for a film about the Burma Road in South China.[51]

After two days in Amsterdam, Ivens traveled on to his family in Nijmegen. His father wrote: 'It was a comfort having him with us. Spent very many hours talking about Wim, about Ma, about Capi.' The old gentleman noted hopefully that George himself now realized 'that he has to settle down and end that Bohemian life. He hopes to have well-paid regular work within three months. He will also finish his book about China.' But overcome with doubt he added: 'Will things really turn out that way?' In any case, the book about China, working title: 'Today is Tomorrow', never appeared. Kees Ivens was happy with the visit: 'George was especially warm, as far as the loss of Wim is concerned as well.'[52] The next day he took George to Nijmegen Station, and there they saw each other for the last time. Kees Ivens would die in 1941. His son traveled to Paris, breaking his journey in Amsterdam to visit Wim's grave at Zorgvlied Cemetery.

THE 400 MILLION only screened sporadically outside the United States and did not reach Holland until late in 1939. In the few months remaining before the outbreak of war, it was only shown at private screenings. It was not until September 1945 that the film was submitted to the Dutch censors, who released it uncut.[53]

12 Ivens's Interbellum (1939-1941)

In the summer of 1939 a shock wave went through left-wing America. On the night of August 23, a nonaggression pact had been signed in Moscow by the foreign ministers of Nazi Germany and the Soviet Union, Von Ribbentrop and Molotov. Throughout the 1930s, thousands of Western artists and intellectuals had supported Communism because they saw the USSR as a bastion against Nazism. Now newspapers featured a picture of a cheery Joseph Stalin patting Joachim von Ribbentrop on the back. Indignation grew when it became clear that the pact was more than a diplomatic formality. In a secret protocol, the new allies had demarcated their spheres of influence: the Wehrmacht occupied the west of Poland and Soviet forces marched into East Poland and the Baltic States. 'One swift blow... first from the German army and then from the Red Army, and there was nothing left of this abomination from Versailles,' was how Molotov summarized the liquidation of the Polish state to the Supreme Soviet.[1] The further consequences of the Molotov-Ribbentrop Pact became apparent more gradually. West of the new border the Nazis were brutal in their treatment of the Poles – who they saw as an inferior race – while in the east, nine hundred thousand Polish citizens and two hundred thousand prisoners of war were deported to the Soviet Union in eighteen months, mainly in stock cars. All anti-Nazi propaganda was cancelled in the Soviet Union. FIGHTERS was just one of the films that were no longer allowed to be shown. As a goodwill gesture to Hitler, Stalin plucked a number of German Jewish Communist refugees out of his prison camps and handed them over to the Gestapo: a squalid affair that was snatched from oblivion by the testimony of one of the victims, Margarete Buber-Neumann, whose murdered husband Heinz Neumann was known to Ivens from Moscow social gatherings. Around this time, her now renegade brother-in-law, Willi Münzenberg, concluded: 'The traitor, Stalin, is you.'[2]

Joris Ivens later recalled a heated discussion about the pact in New York, with Hanns Eisler and Earl Browder, the leader of the American Communist party. Ivens remembered Bertolt Brecht as also being present, but he was still in Europe at the time. Although Ivens did not say so in so many words, Browder and Eisler were diametrically opposed. Speaking on Soviet-German relations shortly before, Browder had declared: 'There is as much chance of agreement as of Earl Browder being elected president of the Chamber of Commerce,'[3] yet once the impossible pact had been sealed, he wasted no time in backing it. The Jewish Austrian Hanns Eisler, a faithful supporter of the Communist movement since the twenties, did not want to submit to the new fraternal relationship between Hitler and Stalin. Ivens took the Moscow line: 'I saw this pact as an unavoidable strategic choice, and in the absence of a more rational explanation, this thought allowed me to sleep easy.'[4]

Some people outside party ranks were also able to accept the Molotov-Ribbentrop Pact. Ernest Hemingway recalled that only the Soviet Union and Mexico had supported the Spanish Republic, while the United States, England and France remained idle. 'When the International Brigades were fighting in Spain there was no pact between the Soviet Union and Germany. This alliance was only born after the Soviet Union had lost all faith in the democracies,' he asserted, and Ivens agreed: 'Many of us think the same way as you.'[5] However, it was France and England that now had declared war on Hitler, while Stalin waited on the sidelines in the hope that the Western powers would destroy each other.

Ivens might not have been entirely at ease with Moscow's policies, but they barely caused a ripple on the surface of his calm certainties. After seeing 'the destruction of the Kulaks as a class' in Magnitogorsk, the Communist operations in Spain, and the persecution in Moscow, he was familiar with the saying often used in Communist circles: you can't make an omelet without breaking eggs. The Moscow trials hardly touched him. The charges seemed irrefutable to him, and at the same time the reports about the trials were 'like arrows flying over my head that I kept out of the way of', as he wrote in his memoirs.

Leftist America now split along ideological lines. Liberals who had sympathized with Communism distanced themselves from it, and only a small group of faithful followers were left. While resignations poured into the office of the Hollywood Anti-Nazi League, the hardcore members decided to adapt to the new Soviet policy, drop the 'anti-Nazi' and change the name to Hollywood League for Democratic Action.[6] Internal conflicts broke out within the scriptwriters' union and other unions and the Communists became isolated. They, in turn, turned on their dissidents. Hanns Eisler's wife Lou Jolesch later related how party members shunned her husband for almost two years for criticizing the pact. They no longer said hello to him on the street.[7]

The news of the Molotov-Ribbentrop Pact reached Joris Ivens on location in Ohio in the small town of St. Clairsville, where he was working on his new film POWER AND THE LAND. He had first tried to find work in Mexico. The Eislers had moved there temporarily after the expiry of their residency permit for the United States, and Ivens had visited them with Helene early in the summer of 1939. Socialist President Cardenas was in power and had made his country a haven for thousands of German and Spanish émigrés. Eisler's house in Mexico City became a gathering place for countless acquaintances from Europe. Ivens submitted a plan for a rural documentary to the Mexican Ministry of Agriculture, but 'it took too long to get any definite answer... so I got impatient and left'. Afterwards the Mexican government apparently accepted his proposal after all. In late 1939, he announced that he would soon be starting work on the film, although he never did.[8]

Ivens had just come back from Mexico when he was telephoned by Pare Lorentz, America's most important documentary filmmaker after Robert Flaherty. Lorentz had made socially critical films like THE PLOW THAT BROKE THE PLAINS and THE RIVER with a subsidy from the Roosevelt administration, whose New Deal was accompanied by active cultural policies. After the success of the first Lorentz films, Roosevelt founded the United States Film Service with Pare Lorentz as director. In this capacity, he now asked Ivens to make a film about the electrification of American farms. The offer was a very welcome one, if only because, after Spain and China, he would now be paid for a change. The idea of employing Ivens had originated with Lorentz's regular cameraman, Floyd Crosby, who was the chairman of the Motion Picture Guild, a group dedicated to the production of socially-aware films, which had been founded in Hollywood earlier that year by people such as Lillian Hellman, Dudley Nichols, Frank Tuttle and others who knew Ivens well.[9]

POWER AND THE LAND was to be an educational film for the Rural Electrification Administration (REA), which fell under the Department of Agriculture. The REA perspective was that the REA program was able to provide farms with cheap and abundant energy, but the farmers were technically, physically and psychologically incapable of using it in a way that really raised their standard of living. It was hoped that a film would change this. Even before Ivens started work in June, REA officials had already sketched out a rough script.[10]

After searching the Midwest, Ivens settled on the farm of Bill and Hazel Parkinson. Located in a photogenic landscape of rolling hills, the farm was close to St. Clairsville, a village about fifty miles south of Pittsburg. The Parkinsons, who had four sons and one daughter, kept seventeen dairy cows and a few other animals on their two-hundred-acre farm, and grew most of their own feed, plus crops for their own consumption. Their income was one hundred and forty-five dollars a month. The film crew thought of it as an average farm, but the figures were later scrapped from the commentary at the request of the REA, because it turned out that the average American farmer only owned one cow and earned just twenty-nine dollars a year.[11] Parkinson was a member of the local electricity cooperative and already had mains power, this made the basic principle of the REA scenario possible: first a day on the farm without electricity, then a day with it.

Ivens and crew moved into a hotel in St. Clairsville in late July and roared out to the farm every morning in a big Packard. The tripod on the car gave rise to wild speculation among the locals, and the sheriff finally came out to investigate whether it really was intended for a machine gun and whether the obscure group led by indeterminate Europeans really was engaged in espionage. Ivens showed his government documents and the matter was settled. He quickly won the hearts of the Parkinsons. The farmer called him 'Dutchy' and invited him to move out to the farm. Ivens screened Lorentz's film THE RIVER for the local farmers in order to gauge its impact on the target group.

The filming was arduous. Cameraman Arthur Ornitz was inexperienced, and Pare Lorentz was dissatisfied with the rushes he received in New York. Ivens was taken aback by the poor results and the problem was not resolved until October when Floyd Crosby came to reinforce the crew.[12] Crosby had already worked with Robert Flaherty and F.W. Murnau and became one of Hollywood's most sought-after camera operators.

Ivens saw major shortcomings in the scenario imposed upon him. During a lecture in New York he explained: 'The real drama of rural electrification in the United States is the conflict with the private utilities, who refuse to put up lines to farmers, but who fight any attempt by farmers to put up their own. In our film on this subject, we had a task into which this natural drama did not fit as a main line, but it will be there – in a short passionate speech by one angry farmer.'[13] Competing for customers, private companies laid cables next to the government power lines, and this sometimes led to outbursts of violence and arson, nothing remarkable in the folklore of the United States, where gunfights between strikers and company guards were a regular occurrence. To illustrate this aspect of the social struggle, Ivens filmed a barn that had been set alight for the occasion. A strong wind was blowing, however, and burning pieces of the roof ended up in a nearby field, which also caught fire. The film crew and the people who had gathered to watch succeeded in subduing the flames, but one of the farmers had a heart attack on the spot.[14]

Lorentz found that Ivens ignored earlier criticism and continued to take too many liberties. With the shooting almost completed, the producer still felt compelled to write: 'One point we must be clear on: while I am perfectly willing to agree that you might make a very exciting documentary film from the material you have, unless that film is specifically enough like the original outline approved by the men who gave me the money and who trust me to see that such a picture is made, I feel it would be an unfortunate thing for both of us.'[15] Ivens had little scope to express his political vision.

In another area, however, he was able to realize a long-cherished ambition. Of all the documentaries he made in his career, POWER AND THE LAND is one of those with the most acting in it. BORINAGE had included a number of successful re-enactments and there had been clumsy attempts in SONG OF HEROES, THE SPANISH EARTH and THE 400 MILLION, but with this farming family, he was now able to dedicate himself to serious direction. From the outset, half of the film needed to be staged because it was set on a farm without electricity, whereas the Parkinsons were already connected to the mains. During a lecture in New York, Ivens described his experiences with non-professional actors: 'The writer must employ his imagination to manipulate the real, personal characteristics of the new actors – searching them with seemingly careless observations. He must learn thereby, for example, that the farmer takes special pride in the sharpness of his tool blades, and therefore suggest a toolshed scene which will make use of that fact. The key to this approach, I think, is that a real person, acting to play himself, will be more expressive if his actions are based on his real characteristics.'[16] He told students at Columbia University that it was necessary to take the limitations of amateurs into account, because 'if you ask a farmer to show despair because his horse died, you would just be surprised what you would get! It simply cannot be done.' Actors are able to rehearse a role, but 'with non-actors, it is just the opposite. They may be bad to start with, but after two or three attempts they are simply awful!' He fervently defended the realism of his method. 'We lived on the farm for two months, and we can safely invite you to go out there and see for yourself, if you don't believe our film.'[17]

The re-enactment of events is generally accepted by documentary filmmakers, assuming that the director at least tries to present original events as faithfully as possible. Ivens often stuck to this principle but, particularly with the films he made in the socialist countries, he sometimes went a step further and set up reconstructions that might have coincided with his dreams but had little to do with the facts. An example is the Russian version of BORINAGE, which presented an abundant meal and a modern home as if there were nothing more ordinary in the Soviet Union, whereas the country had just undergone disastrous famines and the public housing problem was never resolved.

After returning from St. Clairsville, Ivens received a letter from Hazel Parkinson. He was so proud of it that he included it in its entirety in *The Camera and I* and quoted from it again in *Joris Ivens ou la mémoire d'un regard*. Ivens had presented the family with an electric mixer and the response clearly shows how taken they were with him.

'Dear Dutchy,

We certainly were surprised to receive such a wonderful gift from the crew and I find it very difficult to express our appreciation in words. We sincerely hope you will come back sometime and help us eat some of the things I intend to prepare with it. The boys had a wonderful time in New York. They thought you and Ed were good entertainers. The neighbors have all asked about you and they all have a word in your favor. The compliments vary from 'Mr. Ivens is a mighty fine man' to 'well, he is a damn good Dutchman.'...
Bip and Ruth often speak of you and wish you were here. In fact we all do. I am sure Bill would like to see the warm fire in the grate with you tonight but you are probably doing something far more interesting than talking to farmers...
We all join in sending you our best wishes for a Merry Christmas!

Sincerely,
The Parkinsons.'[18]

Ivens's sojourn on the farm seems to have stimulated a yearning for an idyllic and harmonious family life, an existence far removed from his unattached lifestyle. The family was hospitable and he showered them with gifts. Bip thanked 'Dear Dutchy' on illustrated note paper: 'I take good care of the knife you gave me, the football and helmet are nicer than any thing I got for X-mas. Tom is still working on the airplane.' If only the film crew's Packard could return and save him from his school tests, sighed Bip.[19]

In December 1939 Ivens and Van Dongen made a first cut of POWER AND THE LAND in New York. As far as Pare Lorentz was concerned, Van Dongen need not have been there at all. He considered her 'probably the most banal and redundant film editor ever to handle motion pictures, particularly important and sometimes beautiful films.' He couldn't understand what Ivens and Flaherty saw in her.[20] Lorentz's standpoint was at odds with the general assessment of Van Dongen's skills. After the picture editing, work came to a standstill for three months because Lorentz wanted to write the commentary himself but was too busy with other things. 'A good film director but no organizer,' judged Ivens, who received no salary while waiting.[21]

The differences of opinion about the Molotov-Ribbentrop Pact were apparently no barrier to Ivens asking Hanns Eisler to write the music for POWER AND THE LAND,[22] though in the end the job went to composer Douglas Moore. In 1941 Eisler worked on his last Ivens film. Together with the philosopher Theodor Adorno, Eisler participated in the experimental 'Film Music Project', writing a composition to accompany RAIN entitled *Vierzehn Arten den Regen zu beschreiben*, 'fourteen ways of describing rain'.

Eisler considered these variations for a quintet as his best chamber music and also referred to them as 'fourteen ways of being sad in a civilized fashion'. Eisler and Adorno summarized the results of their project in the book *Composing for the Films.*

POWER AND THE LAND premiered in St. Clairsville on August 31, 1940 with the Parkinsons as guests of honor. The first New York screening followed on December 10 in the Rialto Theater on Times Square, where the thirty-minute film was shown together with the Western TRAIL OF THE VIGILANTES and a Donald Duck cartoon. POWER AND THE LAND was a likable film that satisfied the REA guidelines. Richard Barsam, one of America's leading writers in the field of nonfiction film, was surprised that it 'could have been made by a foreigner and yet emerge as wholly American as a painting by Edward Hopper'. He called this 'a tribute to the subject and to the vision and sensibility of the director'. According to incomplete figures from the U.S. Department of Agriculture, more than six million people saw the film between 1940 and 1968, mainly at educational meetings.[23]

Helene van Dongen finished POWER AND THE LAND by herself after an acquaintance from the Sloan Foundation invited Ivens to make a film about the social significance of new technology. The Sloan Foundation, named after General Motors president Alfred P. Sloan, financed films produced by New York University's Educational Film Institute. There, in the spring of 1940, Ivens and the German émigré publisher Wieland Herzfelde started work on what they called 'the frontier film'. Herzfelde had participated in the Berlin revolutionary movement of 1918 and had been one of the first members of the German Communist party. With his brother, photomontage artist John Heartfield, he had also been a member of the Berlin Dada group. In 1939 he had been forced to flee Prague for the United States.[24]

The concept of 'the frontier', crucial to the history of the United States, referred to the western border the pioneers were constantly pushing forward. It evoked deep emotions and was thus an appropriate vehicle for consideration of comparable subjects. After all, one could also identify frontiers in social development. '1. The 1840 Episode (The Land Frontier). 2. The 1890 Episode (The Industrial Frontier). 3. Present-Day Episode (The New Frontier).' According to Ivens, atomic energy and socialism were waiting beyond this last frontier. However, just as with POWER AND THE LAND, the sponsor thought differently. Ten weeks before the start of shooting, Ivens wrote to Ernest Hemingway: 'I have to stay at the techn. frontier, for social frontiers no Sloan money.' He decided to insert his beliefs into the film anyway by including a madman who would make the requisite statements about the evils of capitalism.[25]

In May 1940 he flew to Denver, Colorado with Floyd Crosby and the rest of the crew. They planned to continue shooting until mid-September and began by filming some strange scenes. 'In a bizarre landscape of red mud, where uranium 235 is mined, a man wants to kill himself because he no longer believes that humanity has a future. Two boys pull him out of the sludge. He is furious. The man wanted to take his life in a place where the future of humanity lies: the raw material for the atomic industry. The other characters are a young engineer who builds dams but is unable to find work on the East Coast and leaves New York to head west over the Rocky Mountains in search of a new existence, and a farm boy from the West who can't see a future for himself and crosses the Rocky Mountains headed for New York, where he thinks he will have a better chance in life. They meet in the Rocky Mountains. The engineer stands uphill and the farm boy stands downhill. They shout their plans to each other.'[26] Ivens progressed no further than these two sequences. In June the Sloan Foundation ended its financial support of the Educational Film Institute. Three completed films had to be withdrawn from circulation, including John Fernhout's documentary about the inhabitants of the mountains of Kentucky AND SO THEY LIVE. The two crews on location were recalled. Besides Ivens's crew in Colorado, the other was a crew led by Fernhout, who was working on a new film in Illinois.[27] In the US Fernhout used the name John Ferno.

The magazine *Film News* reported on the reasons for the Sloan Foundation's withdrawal of its support. 'There is a report, however, of dissatisfaction with the critical tenor of films and scripts on hand in view of changed world conditions. War and national defense, it is said, make necessary a more constructive approach to economic material.' The threat of war was all too real. Germany had already occupied Norway, Denmark, Holland, Belgium, Luxembourg and half of France, but the American Communist party supported the Molotov-Ribbentrop Pact and argued for non-involvement in the 'imperialist war' in Europe. Instead the party was trying to intensify the domestic class struggle, a course it maintained until Hitler's invasion of the Soviet Union a year later. Thereafter, the party even refused to distribute films about social conflicts, using the very same arguments the Sloan Foundation had put forward in 1940. Ivens, Fernhout and a number of their colleagues took New York University and the Sloan Foundation to court and won payment of several months' salary, but were unable to force the return of their work.[28]

For Joris Ivens a new period began about which he later wrote: 'To be frank, I was at a complete loss and went through a profound crisis.'[29] Besides being unemployed and isolated because of his political position, his relationship with Helene van Dongen was at an all-time low. Soon after his return from Spain, when their love had, in his words, 'lost its vigor', he began giving Miep Balguérie-Guérin a new return address: 'C/o Edw. Kern, East 57 Street, New York'. This might have been to avoid jealous reactions from Helene, but by spring 1940 the family in Nijmegen was also writing care of Edw. Kern. While Van Dongen simply stayed at the old address on Washington Square, Ivens had obviously moved elsewhere. Late in the summer of 1940, Joris Ivens left Helene and New York behind him and departed for an extended stay on the West Coast, hoping that this would hasten a resolution of their problems. In the years that followed, they saw each other even less than before. Their relationship revived in 1943 when they made their last film together, and Helene van Dongen remained hopelessly in love with her 'Bubi' until the dramatic end.

While Ivens was without work, she had her hands full. After the educational films for the Rockefeller Foundation, Van Dongen, Joseph Losey and Hanns Eisler had made a puppet film in 1939 for the combined American oil industry, PETE ROLEUM AND HIS COUSINS. That same year, she had also worked on the uncompleted documentary WE WHO MADE AMERICA. The next year she worked on THE MAKING OF AMERICA and in 1940-1941 on Robert Flaherty's THE LAND, a film that Ivens called a masterpiece and Flaherty himself considered his most profound work.[30] Authors of documentary guides agree that THE LAND owes its power to a significant degree to Helene van Dongen's editing. She increasingly began to see herself as an American and permanently changed her name from Helene to Helen. Later she even developed an aversion to using Dutch.

Upon arriving in California, Ivens discovered that 'Hollywood was completely closed' to him. He stayed with Andries Deinum, a Dutch friend who said: 'He had a very hard time of it. They didn't want him there.'[31] After studying sociology and film at Stanford University, Deinum became a lecturer at the University of Southern California, but was later dismissed after being questioned by the House Un-American Activities Committee. 'One of the problems was that I knew you,' Deinum wrote to Ivens at that time, and 'to tell the truth, I'm rather proud of that'.[32] Deinum's house was always open to Ivens.

The studio bosses did not look kindly on people who stuck up for their rights, and taking the Sloan Foundation to court had not made Ivens popular. There was a more important reason for Hollywood's cold shoulder though, one that had affected other Communists as well: the Molotov-Ribbentrop Pact.[33] The liberals who had worked with them in earlier years now accused them of betraying the anti-fascist cause, and Ivens was open to an even graver charge, as his own fatherland had been occupied in May 1940 and he did nothing.

In an airplane above Colorado he had received the news of the German invasion of Holland, 'while telling myself it left me cold'. Around the same time he happened to write to Archibald MacLeish about some practical matter. His ally from THE SPANISH EARTH and THE 400 MILLION returned his letter with a furious note on it. 'What do you think of your Nazi friends now? How, *how* can you keep up that faith of yours in the light of this horror? How CAN you?' It wasn't until six months later that MacLeish sent a conciliatory letter saying that he was sorry 'if the words I wrote hurt you. I think you will believe me when I say that if they hurt you it was because they also hurt me to write them. The Moscow-Berlin Pact was, to me, like a personal affront – an affront to every decency.'[34] MacLeish's links with the Communist movement were over.

In the year preceding the occupation of Holland, Ivens corresponded unusually frequently with his family in Nijmegen. Because of guilt feelings about his peculiar political stance? Or simply because his parents were in serious financial difficulties and their health was ailing? After the German invasion of Holland on May 10, 1940, the exchange of letters ended abruptly. His family continued to dispatch letter after letter to New York but received no reply, despite there being a normal mail service between occupied Holland and neutral America – only the telegram service was blocked at the Dutch end. Eventually the family began to worry and wrote to Helen van Dongen at Washington Square to ask how Joris was. She wrote back that he was fine and that he had sent a number of letters and telegrams to Nijmegen, but she didn't give his parents any more information and neglected to mention that she herself hardly saw him. On December 8, seven months after the last sign of life, his mother and father wrote: 'Have you become such a wanderer that Kern doesn't always know your address either? We're almost starting to think that something is wrong. And if there is something wrong we would like to know all about it, rather than remain uncertain... Honest to goodness, son, we don't know what to make of it. Are you that sick?'[35]

Even though Ivens had moved to Hollywood some time earlier and might not have received this mail from Nijmegen until later, it is still extraordinary that he did not write at a time when his family was being subjected to trying wartime conditions. It is most likely that he didn't write any letters at all in this period because not one arrived, whereas Helen's mail reached Nijmegen promptly. He might have sent telegrams, but they were

not delivered in Holland. His spirits were low, and when he reluctantly fulfilled his responsibilities as a correspondent, he usually did so by telegram.

The fact that nothing was heard from Ivens in Nijmegen during the first
seven months of the German occupation despite an operative mail service is
perhaps the clearest indication of the seriousness of the crisis he was going
through. 'Are you that sick?' might not have been too far from the truth. He
didn't start writing again until 1941. 'Financially everything is going terribly. I hung around Hollywood for a few months, then went back to New
York, tried to get work in Washington, now I'm back in Hollywood. I have a
free place to stay here. It's always the same story: a great artist, they say, exceptional talent, some good publicity, but no work. Will probably stay like
this forever.'[36]

At the end of 1940, he finally got a job through the agent J. Walter Thompson, a member of the Association of Documentary Film Producers, an
American interest group for documentary filmmakers that had elected
Ivens as chairman. It was a standard advertising short for Shell, but he
couldn't afford to refuse the job, which further emphasizes the straits he
was in. Shell had placed great importance on the medium ever since 1933,
when British documentary filmmaker John Grierson had founded the Shell
Film Unit in London. Ivens was nothing more than a functionary in a production that had been mapped out from A to Z. On November 11 he started
his directorial work at the Shell research laboratories in Emeryville, California, and the prints were to be delivered on schedule eight weeks later. A car
came to pick him up from his hotel in the morning, the lights were ready
when he arrived, he gave his directions, and at five o'clock he could call it a
day. The film was called OIL FOR ALLADINN'S LAMP and this title was ex-
pounded upon in typical Shell style: *Facts are sacred; comment is free.* The
script included lines like: 'Ammonia, derived from gases, is bottled in cylin-
ders in gaseous form and bubbled into irrigation water to make more and
better quality oranges for your morning's glass of orange juice... Bigger and
better lettuce for your noonday salad and more and richer potatoes for your
evening meal.' The accompanying camera directions stated: 'Close-shot
large glass of orange juice; close-up of different foods.'[37] Ivens later said that
he never saw the film in its completed form, and it is certain that he would
not have wanted to see it.

At the start of 1941 Ivens was taken a little more seriously and was given
a job on the art and science faculty of the University of Southern California
at Los Angeles, lecturing on his experiences as a filmmaker each Monday
and Friday until the summer. In the same period he started on an autobiography, dictating his memories to film historian Jay Leyda. The book's type-

scripts include Leyda's questions. 'I don't like writing,' said Ivens. 'I wrote
The Camera and I because I was unemployed.'[38] In 1943 he signed a contract
with the New York publisher Harcourt, Brace and Company, but the book
did not appear under the above title until 1969, when it was published by
Seven Seas Books in East Berlin and the affiliated International Publishers in
New York. There are remarkably few differences between the original text
from the early forties and the final version. His perspective on most matters
had hardly changed in the intervening twenty-eight years.

   His isolation in Hollywood encouraged Ivens to look for work abroad,
and in the first half of 1941 he sent a plan to the government of Bolivia for a
film that would 'counteract the popular misconception which the United
States may have about the people of your country'. The American State Department and the Rockefeller Committee on Latin American Affairs were
willing to support the project as part of Roosevelt's Good Neighbor Policy,
and Donald Ogden Stewart, one of Hollywood's great scriptwriters, wrote a
synopsis entitled JIMMY JONES – GOOD NEIGHBOR, in which facts about
Bolivia were 'concealed in a human-interest story with comic digressions'.
It basically came down to a fellow called Jimmy Jones going to Bolivia to
make a film and, through his adventures, gradually coming to a better understanding of the country and its people.[39]

   On June 22, 1941, Ivens and Stewart suddenly lost interest in Bolivia.
Stewart, chairman of the League of American Writers and former chairman
of the now dissolved Hollywood Anti-Nazi League, was a fellow supporter
of Soviet policy. He wrote about that date in his autobiography: 'I was driving alone... It was a beautiful clear, calm, star-filled night, and I was listening to some dance music on my radio. It was a Cole Porter tune... Suddenly
the music stopped. After a moment: 'We interrupt this program to tell you
that this afternoon the German armies invaded the Soviet Union and a state
of war now exists.' I listened, and I unexpectedly began to cry. Not with pity
for the Russian people: I wept with joy and relief. I was once more on the
'right' side, the side of all my old friends. Now we were all fighting Fascism... It was one of the happiest nights of my life. I could continue believing
in my remote dream, the country where the true equality of man was becoming a reality under the philosophy of Marxism and Leninism and the
leadership of the great Stalin.'[40]

   Joris Ivens could not have put it better.

13 Glamour Boy of the Revolution (1941-1944)

Early in October 1941, Joris Ivens received word from Nijmegen that his father had died on August 29. Kees Ivens had spent his last years a sick and disappointed man. In the childhood memories of his granddaughter Annabeth he was an old grump in a dark room. He stuck to his post until the end; the cause of death was bronchitis contracted at the opening of the Arnhem-Nijmegen electric railway.[1] Shortly before his father's death, Ivens had written to his parents: 'My thoughts often dwell on you and my childhood and everything you did for me and meant to me. And I put a lot of that into my work and will continue to do so.'[2]

The funeral was on September 1, long before he heard the news. After it reached him he wrote to his mother.[3]

'New York, Oct. 5, '41
Dear, dear Ma,

Received your letter dated July 29. [Must have been August 29.] Pa is no longer with us. The date of his death already seems long ago. Time races on. My dear, dear Ma, I am with you with all my sympathy and all my supportive thoughts. The hardest thing is not being able to come over now to help you through this difficult time. In your letter I read that Pa died calmly and gently. That is good after such an active, full life. The throes of death could have been hard.

Looking back on Pa's life, I see that he achieved many things through hard, hard work, and all those things have been lost in the last few years. In financial and business terms, Pa has been an example to me of energy, perseverance and vitality. Many of the things I do in my work come from that. The strange thing is that Pa couldn't always see that. Years ago I wrote to him that he could be proud, not only of the businesses and his great work for the community in Nijmegen, but also of us, his children, your children...

All kinds of thoughts race through my mind, e.g. the certainty that we will see each other, even if it takes a year or two, and the certainty that I will be able to help you then. I know that Hans and Thea and Uri [Nooteboom, Thea's husband] and Coba are giving you tremendous support. And I would give everything, everything, to be able to walk into that quiet street and take you in my arms. The sense of being together and the faith you always gave me tell me that you will be able to cope with this hard blow. Our last farewell still feels as though it were an hour ago. Pa was filled with worries about you, and I was more worried about him...

The many walks, trips and conversations I had with Pa are passing through my mind. The less important ones fall by the wayside, the differences of opinion about business fall aside, and a man, a person, a friend, a father stands before me. And then I see that at times Pa was a great man, an honest person, a best friend, a caring father – and that at times there were also differences of opinion, and blemishes – but despite that, in the end, the pure qualities won out...

Hans will be a good support to you. I know that he is now fulfilling my duty, because I am too far away. Do not doubt that all of us are with you in our thoughts, that we shall help you, because you are our mother and Pa knew that we would stand by you if you were left alone...

Experiencing such a loss from a distance is terribly unreal. But the sorrow it causes is real, and I am filled with an intense and powerful awareness of the love and sympathy I feel for you. Know that I am thinking of you, of Pa and of everyone very, very much. I hug you tight and face the future with you. You are elderly and we are in the prime of our lives – we want to have you with us for a long long time, until we are old ourselves too, and able to look back on our lives the way you can, my dear, dear Ma.

All my love, all my best wishes, wishing you every strength, your son,

George'

The letter took a whole month to reach Nijmegen and his mother wrote back: 'You wrote with such sensitivity and well and truthfully, everything Pa meant to us... I'm glad you wrote it the way you did. It is such a support and comfort to me. I thank you for it.'[4]

Ivens doubtlessly meant every word he had written, including the conciliatory words about his father. His 'in the end, the pure qualities won out' recalled what Kees Ivens had once written about his son in a moment of anger: 'But good at heart'. The enormous mutual frustrations had not destroyed their appreciation of each other.

But was it true that Ivens was prepared to 'give everything, everything, to be able to walk into that quiet street and take you in my arms'? He must have been convinced of it himself, with an Atlantic Ocean full of U-boats between him and Nijmegen, and with a mail connection that would soon be broken. After the war, however, when all the connections were re-established, it took him a very long time to get in touch.

After the German attack on the Soviet Union, Ivens contacted the Dutch authorities in New York, presumably the Netherlands Information Bureau, to offer his services as a filmmaker. Holland had been occupied for more than a year and the Dutch were not eager to make use of his services. As he wrote himself, forty years later: 'My patriotism coincided too much with the Soviet political line.' The Dutch authorities did respond to his suggestion of using NEW EARTH for propaganda. A much-shortened version produced by Dutch government editors – even featuring Prince Bernhard – was released around 1944. 'Cut to pieces', concluded Ivens after seeing the result.[5]

Ivens was in Hollywood when the German Wehrmacht marched into the Soviet Union, but rushed to New York in the expectation that he might be able to make himself useful there. A new address appeared on his letterhead: '433 East 21st Street', in Manhattan's East Village, fifteen minutes' walk from what had now become Helen's apartment on Washington Square. Ivens made work of re-establishing his contacts in New York. This is shown clearly by a list of appointments on three randomly chosen days, based on a piece of scrap paper and elaborated upon here.[6]

Wednesday

11:00 – 12:00	Edwin Locke, scriptwriter POWER AND THE LAND.
12:30 – 14:00	Edgar Snow, journalist, sympathizer with Chinese communism.
14:00 – 16:00	Joseph Losey, director, active for Russian War Relief.
17:00 – 18:00	Van Stappen, probably an official from the Dutch legation.
19.30 – 20:00	Hans Richter, German Dadaist painter and filmmaker, knew Ivens from the Filmliga days and from the Soviet Union, working in New York at the New School of Social Research.

Thursday

Telephone: Jerry; Luise Rainer, actress, involved in THE 400 MILLION; Luis Buñuel, old drinking buddy from Paris, made Spanish version of POWER AND THE LAND for distribution in South America.

9:00 – 10:30	dentist
15:00	Fiedler, from the J. Walter Thompson Company, Ivens's agent for the Shell film.
16:00	Hans Richter and Robert Flaherty.
17:00	Association of Documentary Film Producers, Ivens chairman.

Friday

9:30	Richter.
10:00	Fitelson, legal advisor for the Shell film.
11:00 – 12:00	Tom Brandon, owner Garrison/Prometheus Films, distributor of THE SPANISH EARTH and THE 400 MILLION.
12:00 – 14:30	Paul Strand, documentary filmmaker, head of Frontier Films.
19:00	Richter.

The great Robert Flaherty had returned to the United States in the summer of 1939 after nine years in Europe and Asia and was now working on THE LAND with Helen van Dongen. He was a romantic who idealized a harmonious life amid the wilds of nature, the opposite of Ivens's industrial progress. 'For hours at a time we talked, I tried to convince him, he resisted, telling me that I was an idealist and returning to his original line of thought: 'Science murders man, it robs him of his dignity.'' They met regularly in New York. 'Bob took me to the Explorer's Club and taught me how to drink Irish whiskey. He was always the same generous friend and brother-in-arms. Sometimes his eyes could flash blue arrows when he talked of some producer or banker or backer who tried to limit his liberty as an artist, or tried to press some economy on him that Bob thought would lessen the artistic quality of his work. Yes, generous, emotional, Irish Bob could also be militant.' Ivens occasionally visited Flaherty and his wife in Vermont. 'The house was deep in a thick blanket of snow. The living room was enormous, a proper setting for Flaherty's movement, voice, thinking, visions, generosity. The picture window was the size of a cinerama screen – before we had ever seen such a screen in a theater. The fireplace looked like a small room, stone-walled and big enough to require railroad ties for its fuel. Towards evening I remember how Bob played in the snow with a great white shaggy dog that circled him and leapt at him. Though no films were shown that day, I felt that I had come closer to understanding his film work.'[7]

The East Coast was also home to the Soviet embassy, the Soviet distribution company Artkino, and the head office of Russian War Relief, which collected humanitarian aid for the beleaguered Soviet Union. Late in the summer, Ivens started a compilation film for Russian War Relief, produced by Artkino, which was 'responsible for content to embassy'.[8] It was, in other words, a film under commission to the Soviet government.

Frontier Films' Ben Maddow wrote a script under the pseudonym Dave Wolf[9] and Ivens edited the film, which came to be called OUR RUSSIAN FRONT. It became an account of the Russian battles, primarily compiled from Soviet newsreels. Jay Leyda and Joseph Losey were also involved.

With the USSR at war, Ivens's thoughts turned more than ever to his Soviet colleagues. He had no difficulty painting a romantic picture of how they had adjusted to the new situation in just two days: 'How could they do that so quickly? Not because of some kind of mysterious power. Directors, officials, writers, actors, cameramen, they were all actively involved with the world around them. They were productive and vital. They built up their own film industry, together with the people of their country, together with the Red Army that stands guard for them. I know what the meetings at which the film industry was attuned to the war effort must have been like. They're familiar to me. I know how free and open you feel when having your say in your own studio, in the presence of everyone, directors, functionaries, cameramen, authors, carpenters, the staff from the reproductions section, stenographers. During meetings like that you often achieve a lot more than you would sitting at a cleared, tidy desk.' [10]

By late October, film and commentary were ready and there was an outline for the music.[11] Ivens now flew to the West Coast to find some famous Hollywood director willing to symbolically add the finishing touches so that his name could be used in the publicity. A week had been allocated for this final work. He stayed with Andries Deinum in Los Angeles and on October 29 he screened the film he had put together in New York for the directors William Wyler, Lewis Milestone and Anatole Litvak. Wyler had directed dozens of feature films since the twenties, including WUTHERING HEIGHTS. Milestone's reputation rested primarily on his film ALL QUIET ON THE WESTERN FRONT. Litvak was something of a lesser god but still eminently suited to the purpose at hand. He had already given a conditional promise to complete the film. The Hollywood directors were not willing to dance to just any tune though; they had definite opinions and the screening was a failure. Ivens noted: 'Did not like script. Want to do it all over again.' After much discussion, Ukrainian-born Lewis Milestone undertook to finish the film, with Litvak providing studio facilities. Wyler decided not to participate.

A few weeks later, much to Ivens's annoyance, little had been done. Piqued, he wrote: 'Go back to N.Y., or do it myself' but that was impossible; the star-directors would be 'insulted'. Lewis Milestone took 'full charge' and Ivens had hardly any further influence over the final results. He was sidelined by a promotion to production coordinator and made responsible for contacts with Artkino and Russian War Relief.[12] Hollywood author Elliot Paul adapted Ben Maddow's commentary, and actor Walter Huston recorded the narration in one night at the Fox studios.

The text for OUR RUSSIAN FRONT was politically delicate. Artkino's Nick Napoli wrote to Ivens: 'I trust you will be careful in eliminating those words and lines in the commentary which make a direct or indirect appeal for an AEF.'[13] 'AEF' must have stood for American-European Front, the so-called second front in Europe that Stalin would spend the coming years constantly demanding. For the time being, however, the Kremlin needed to show restraint because the United States was still neutral. These were months in which international relationships were changing at lightning speed. The USSR had remained aloof from the conflict and had been attacked by Germany. America was still neutral but had already begun supplying Britain with arms. Now Stalin was waiting impatiently for the Americans to become active participants in the war.

Litvak considered Elliot Paul's commentary 'obvious and propagandistic'. He supported humanitarian aid to the Soviet Union, but not an appeal for tanks and airplanes. Neither was he convinced that the Red Army struggled 'for freedom for other people'. Artkino, Ivens and Milestone refused to bow to these criticisms and the conflict caused new delays. Soon after Nick Napoli was able to write to Ivens: 'I sure am glad you got rid of Annie.'[14] Annie was Anatole Litvak, whose criticism became obsolete on December 7, 1941, when Japan devastated the American naval base at Pearl Harbor in Hawaii. The United States had been drawn into the war, the Soviet Union had become an ally, and the American man in the street's image of Stalin changed overnight to a gruff but goodhearted figure: Uncle Joe.

Around New Year's, a few weeks after Pearl Harbor, the 38-minute film OUR RUSSIAN FRONT was completed. Instead of taking a week, the Hollywood stars had fiddled with it for two months and unrecognizably altered the original version. Ivens could at least take comfort in the success of the results. The film broke all box office records at the Rialto Theater, 'The House of Hits' on New York's Times Square, where it screened for more than twenty hours a day.[15]

Even before the completion of OUR RUSSIAN FRONT, Ivens was considering new work. He wrote to Archibald MacLeish, now head of Roosevelt's 'Office of Facts and Figures', outlining the potential of documentaries for MacLeish's organization. They were able to give 'a penetrating picture of facts, to show the deeper meaning, to dramatize in human terms, to make clear the motives of our government behind the facts and to shape the mass of unrelated facts to a body of well-organized facts of the day-to-day war position.' He enclosed a number of concrete proposals, such as one for a series of short 'Film Letters to the President', in which American citizens told about their everyday life in wartime. He had already written a sample scenario for a 'letter' from a railroad engineer. Another plan proposed 'A Day in the United States', in which hundreds of camera operators all over the country would take shots on the same day, a concept that had already been used to make a film in the Soviet Union. The date he suggested was noteworthy: May 10, 1942, the anniversary of the German attack on Holland and other neighboring countries.[16] MacLeish no doubt remembered the date and the furious note he had sent Ivens. Although interesting, the proposals were never executed.

In his letter to MacLeish, Ivens spoke of the American government as 'our government'. Now that the United States was at war, he was at pains to

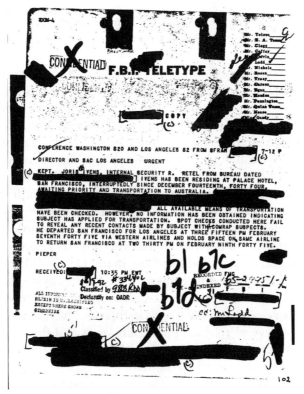

One of approximately 650 pages in Ivens's FBI file.

emphasize his loyalty, and on January 13, 1942 he even sent a letter to the FBI in which he 'offered assistance... whenever needed'. He received an acknowledgement from FBI director J. Edgar Hoover[17] on February 6, but this notorious Communist hater was not anxious to accept Ivens's help. On the contrary, according to a report from the Bureau itself, the Dutchman had been under observation 'intermittently' since July 1940, when he started working for the government on POWER AND THE LAND. The FBI file on Ivens at that time only amounted to some ten or so pages mainly compiled from newspaper reports but also including several of the 'Subject's' personal documents, which had come into the possession of the FBI through what one agent described as an extremely confidential source. In other words, someone had stolen papers from Ivens and handed them over to the Bureau. The gleanings of this mysterious theft turned out to be a kind of advertising text praising Joris Ivens as a filmmaker.[18] In the years to come, the Ivens files at American intelligence agencies would expand to some six hundred and fifty pages.[19] As a comparison: this was almost twice as much as the dossier about the writer Dashiell Hammett, who was imprisoned for five months as a subversive element during the Cold War.

After the New York presentation of OUR RUSSIAN FRONT, Ivens returned to Los Angeles to run a workshop at the University of Southern California, where short educational films related to the war effort were being made. It was a full-time job with a regular salary. To his horror he suddenly received 'an urgent service call from the Dutch government'. It was not as bad as he feared. The 'service call' turned out to be 'for consultation only and some articles about film from time to time, that was all'. Ivens wrote to university colleague Frank Judson: 'I am happy. Your letter helped me in my conversations to keep me out of a regular service job, because defense-film-production in Los Angeles is important for all countries.'[20] Ivens no longer had such a great commitment to Holland. He felt very much at home in the United States and was considering settling there permanently. When he did leave, in 1945, it was because the government of the Dutch East Indies had offered him an extremely attractive position. At the same time, it is not entirely clear what 'regular service' could have been in this case. Ivens had resigned as an officer of the reserve in 1929 for political reasons and things like that were not usually forgotten, although it is possible that the relevant documents were out of reach in occupied Holland.

Ivens's workshop became a new testing ground for the personal drama he advocated in documentaries. For example, the commentary for a film about emergency relief for civilians in wartime: 'Any other time you'd never know them as heroes in the making. Dr. Bowman, the Senior Air Raid Warden, is one of the most respected men in our sector. His two colleagues in the neighborhood have volunteered with the emergency medical service. He lives next door to me and always mows that middle strip of lawn between our places.'[21] It was for a good cause, but for a director with some ten major films to his name it was far from challenging. Since POWER AND THE LAND, Ivens had not been able to derive much honor from his work: a promotional short for Shell and OUR RUSSIAN FRONT, which Lewis Milestone had appropriated artistically, Ivens's final credit as co-director notwithstanding.

Less than two months after taking up his job at the university, Ivens was asked by Hollywood director Frank Capra, now Major Frank Capra of the U.S. army, to join his propaganda-film production group. Before they could come to an agreement, he also received an invitation from John Grierson to come to Canada to make a navy film. The Canadian government had appointed Grierson, the great pioneer of the British documentary, to head the National Film Board and organize the production of government films.

When the country followed Great Britain in declaring war on Germany, his organization became a weapon in the struggle against Hitler. Ivens opted for Grierson, stopped work at the university and arrived in Ottawa in the second half of April. The sight of the girls waiting for his autograph at Canadian naval headquarters must have cheered him up. He was dressed for the occasion in a fashionable pinstriped suit.

Except for a number of short trips to New York, Ivens stayed in Canada for the rest of the year. The long-suffering Helen van Dongen was in Washington working on the compilation film RUSSIANS AT WAR for the U.S. State Department and now had to make do with letters and telegrams from Canada signed Bubi or 'All my love and kisses, Joris B. Ivens'.

Ivens had been hired to make a film about the Canadian navy, the exact subject however remained unclear for a long time. Even six weeks after the start of filming, no one was sure whether they were making a general overview of naval operations or two short films, one about the navy on the East Coast and the other about capturing a German submarine.[22] It ended up being a film about a corvette accompanying a transatlantic convoy.

One of the leading lights of Canadian literature, Morley Callaghan, wrote a scenario. Ivens was disappointed with the results. He considered Callaghan a competent author and a nice guy, but unsuitable for the job: he had no film experience; he questioned things that had been debated to death years before; he was overly critical and cynical; he was too soft and was infatuated with his own script. Ivens kept parts of Callaghan's original and rewrote the script himself.[23]

Filming started on June 16 in the seaport of Halifax in Nova Scotia. Never one to miss an opportunity for a plane ride, Ivens took a few shots from the gun-turret of a Catalina seaplane. On board the corvette Port Arthur, he sailed to the other side of Nova Scotia with a small crew. 'We have to escort a Dutch submarine to Pictou. She keeps her distance – a small thin line and the conning tower seems small and dangerous. She gets playful and dives. We all try to guess when she will surface. Tension – waiting – where? Then you realize what the sea around you is like – sealed like the lips of a merciless man with a treacherous secret. Finally the O-15 surfaces, far behind us. Anticlimax.' The following day he complained about the equipment Ottawa had sent: 'Grierson seems too remote from field work. He doesn't realize that modern photographic and optical technology is very different to what it was like ten years ago.' In a progress report he wrote that the National Film Board was not sufficiently attuned to the production of long documentaries.[24]

The capture of a German submarine was enacted before the harbor of Pictou. The Dutch O-15 under the command of Lieutenant Quint was given the enemy role and the number on the conning tower was changed to U-15 for the occasion. In an attempt to make this reconstruction as realistic as possible, Ivens put together a thick folder of clippings and notes with all kinds of details of real confrontations with U-boats.

In mid-August shooting resumed on the East Coast. Together with his cameraman, an assistant and 'a fifty-year-old camera without filters or a lens hood', Ivens embarked on a six-week journey on the Port Arthur, a small, maneuverable ship with a gun at the front, depth charges on the after-deck and a crew of sixty. The Port Arthur accompanied convoys to Europe. These sea-going merchant marine caravans brought the Allies essential supplies from North America but were vulnerable to attack from submarines. The shadows of dozens of ships glided through the fog in the chilly waters of the north Atlantic. Now and then, there would be the flash of a flare, or a torpedo would surge through the water and explode. The escort vessels turned back halfway with a convoy traveling in the opposite direction. 'We lived alongside the crew, as if we were part of it. Just like them we had to be at our posts within twenty-five seconds of the alarm for 'action stations' being given. We challenged each other and had friendly competitions: who could be at their post first, and whether or not we could make it in twenty-three seconds. Sometimes it took us twenty-seven seconds. We had a spot opposite the guns and were always ready straight away because we slept in our clothes and kept everything close at hand. When you make documentaries, you need to adapt to each different situation.'[25]

ACTION STATIONS! became the title of the film, and Ivens continued to work on it in a studio in Ottawa until the end of 1942. It was a professional, well-made documentary and a gripping portrayal of the war at sea. But Ivens himself was not very enthusiastic. He told Californian students: 'I don't think this film is as powerful as THE SPANISH EARTH and THE 400 MILLION. It also doesn't show my personal opinion of the Royal Canadian Navy. It is more the work of a professional documentary director who has been asked to do his bit for the war effort.'[26] No further information about Ivens's personal opinion of the Canadian navy was supplied.

The National Film Board made a short version of ACTION STATIONS!, cutting the film from fifty to twenty-two minutes. It was given the title CORVETTE PORT ARTHUR and included in the film series CANADA CARRIES ON. This shortened version was shown all over Canada and also reached the Commonwealth countries Great Britain, Australia and New Zealand.[27]

After the Canadian premiere in early 1943, Ivens returned to Los Angeles and the home of Andries Deinum. Deinum drove Ivens wherever he needed to go. Places like Burbank, where Walt Disney had invited Ivens to show his films and been especially impressed by RAIN. Or to the Academy Awards presentation in the Ambassador Hotel, the annual climax of Hollywood glitter, where John Grierson received an Oscar. The Academy of Motion Picture Arts and Sciences had dedicated a special retrospective to Ivens's work in 1941, and he became a member of the Academy's documentary jury.[28] In Hollywood Ivens was a sought-after speaker for both large and small meetings. According to Deinum Ivens was popular, people found him interesting and friendly, and he was considered an exceptional filmmaker, 'despite being vaguely suspect, because he had thrown himself into all those wars, in Spain and in China'. They called Ivens the 'glamour boy of the revolution'. He knew everyone. In his company, Deinum met John Huston, who was working on war documentaries for Capra, Dorothy Comingore, who had played Susan Alexander in Orson Welles's CITIZEN KANE, and the director Jean Renoir. Deinum recalled that Ivens had an enormous capacity for alcohol, something Renoir had also noticed. 'Joris Ivens helped me with my English correspondence. Every evening when we sat down to eat, he would make the same joke: 'And now we're going to eat at Ciro's.' Ciro's was a nightclub that was fashionable at the time. Harry and Grace, my servants, made a vain attempt to save my cellar. The devotion with which they defended my interests was all the more praiseworthy in light of the fact that they were both strict teetotalers.'[29] Ivens's culinary requirements were not always so refined. He had been known to astonish dining companions by simply making a sandwich of a chocolate bar.

At lectures on documentary film at the University of Southern California, he told his students that he believed that America was behind the times because its film production was monopolized by the entertainment industry. He proposed that Washington could alter this by following the example of the Canadian National Film Board and appointing one or more Film Commissioners. Perhaps he thought of himself as a suitable candidate for such a position.[30]

Again, Ivens's activities on campus were of short duration. He finally joined the production group of multiple-Oscar-winner Frank Capra, who had been promoted to the rank of Lieutenant Colonel in the meantime. Capra's unit was the 834th Signal Service Photographic Detachment and was a part of the Signal Corps. Housed in the old Fox Studio on North Western Avenue, popularly known as 'Fort Fox', the detachment made propaganda documentaries for the forces in the series WHY WE FIGHT, KNOW YOUR ALLY and KNOW YOUR ENEMY. Capra could use an old hand like Ivens; his own experience was limited to fiction films and he had once disparagingly summarized documentaries as 'films about polar bears sliding on their asses down mountainsides.'[31] For years documentary filmmakers had searched for audiences and now, rejoiced Joris Ivens, 'an audience of ten million people is demanding our work. They need us.'[32]

In his memoirs, Capra boasted that he was 'the first Voice of America' and considering the enormous influence of his films at home and abroad, he was not far from the truth. The films were mandatory viewing for every American soldier; after seeing them they even received a stamp in their ID booklet. Not that the GIs were easily fooled. An acquaintance in the army wrote to Ivens about the first film in the WHY WE FIGHT series, PRELUDE TO WAR: 'I saw the film many times, together with many thousands of men, in three different army camps. The reaction, almost verbatim, was always about like this: 'Swell... Really, this film has pep despite the fact that there is no story. But, of course, propaganda...''[33] Capra films such as PRELUDE TO WAR and BATTLE OF CHINA included shots from THE SPANISH EARTH and THE 400 MILLION.

When Ivens started working for Capra as a civilian, he insisted on engaging his own assistants, a demand that led to discussion among the commanding officers but was finally accepted. He chose Helen van Dongen for the editing and Corporal Carl Foreman as scriptwriter.[34] After the war, Foreman went on to write HIGH NOON and THE BRIDGE ON THE RIVER KWAI and to produce THE GUNS OF NAVARONE.

Helen van Dongen came over to the West Coast, and a period of nine months of intensive collaboration began. In the fall of 1943 they moved into a modest wooden house with a veranda, a small living room, a small kitchen, one bedroom and a garden the size of a large handkerchief. The address was 2045 Stanley Hills Place in Laurel Canyon, in the hills above Hollywood. Rents in Laurel Canyon were low, which explained the presence of large numbers of European refugees, including Vladimir and Ida Pozner a few doors up. Pozner's attempts to find work as a writer in Hollywood failed and he was forced to take a job in a shipyard as a steel bender.

Ivens, Foreman and Van Dongen were given their own office in a small film factory on Lillian Way, where they started writing the scenario for the compilation film KNOW YOUR ENEMY: JAPAN. They selected the visual material from hundreds of Japanese and American newsreels, fiction films and shorts. The Capra group took liberties that must have even startled someone as broadminded as Ivens. They had no scruples about inserting bits of fiction films into their documentaries. The definitive version of KNOW YOUR ENEMY: JAPAN, for example, completed after Ivens was no longer involved, included a sequence showing the Tokyo earthquake as recreated in Hollywood for the melodrama PENNY SERENADE.[35]

Ivens had more difficulties with the use of films from the hostile camp: 'I got the Japanese footage... When a Japanese soldier is killed he goes straight to heaven because he dies in the service of the Emperor. The Japanese Emperor, you see, is the basic thing. So when the soldier is killed, the Japanese send the package with the ashes to their country. To Japan. Of course, then they make a big memorial service over there – they call in the widows, relatives and sisters, and they receive the package in an impressive ceremony. But, of course, we knew from the information we received that these were frequently not the ashes of the man they said it was at all... They were just plain ashes, or maybe the ashes of some other people, and that was not too fair on the family. Then I started to use this material, to say – 'Look, it's a scandal!'... And when we came to the editing, and we showed the mothers, the sisters and the wives receiving what they think are the ashes of their husband, their brother or their son – they were moved, terribly moved. And it was so moving that I left out the whole sequence... They were such honest, straight people. They were – they were fooled, but still their feelings were of great integrity and profoundness. So... there are limits to compilation editing.'[36]

Ivens had the Walt Disney Studio make an animation sequence in which the Japanese emperor came down out of the sky in a kamikaze dive during which his regal robes gradually changed into a military uniform.[37] Ivens reserved the main role in KNOW YOUR ENEMY: JAPAN for Emperor Hirohito. He saw him as a war criminal, an instrument of the Japanese militarists, politicians and industrialists, who subjugated the Japanese people by appealing to the divinity of the emperor. '*These* people, the *real* rulers of Japan – the power-hungry generals and admirals, the money mad industrialists, the grinning hypocritical politicians – want to rule the world,' according to the commentary written under his direction.[38]

By late 1943, a three-and-a-half-hour provisional version of KNOW YOUR ENEMY: JAPAN was ready and Frank Capra took it to Washington to show it to the American General Staff. They watched it once and then informed him that the tenor of the film was unacceptable. A fierce debate was raging in America about how to deal with Japan after victory. The State Department saw the Japanese as singularly and sentimentally receptive to magnanimity and shows of respect and concluded that a generous treatment of the Japanese emperor could have a positive effect on postwar developments.[39] In KNOW YOUR ENEMY: JAPAN, Ivens too aimed for reconciliation with the Japanese people but by other means, namely by mobilizing the Japanese people against their ruler, the militarists and the capitalists. Lastly, some officers within the supreme command argued for 'virtually the total eradication of the Japanese as a race.'[40] Ivens's approach clashed with both American points of view. After nine months of work, both he and Helen van Dongen were fired by Capra on January 7, 1944.

Carl Foreman stayed and became entangled in a rearguard action over KNOW YOUR ENEMY: JAPAN. Capra himself embraced the simple vision: the only good Jap is a dead Jap. Novelist Irving Wallace, who had been brought in to help, declared: 'You can believe me when I say that Foreman and I fought this terribly, persistently, because it was all wrong.' In Wallace's eyes, it began looking very much like racism: 'How could we indict an entire people in our film?' Even in 1945, however, Pentagon hawks still thought that the film needed changing because it showed 'too much sympathy for the Jap people'. A few days after atomic bombs were dropped on Hiroshima and Nagasaki, KNOW YOUR ENEMY: JAPAN was released for screening to the troops, but the supreme commander in the western Pacific, General Douglas MacArthur, thought this was going too far and left it on the shelf. It was not shown publicly until 1977.[41] Nowadays it is sold on video as a 'film by Frank Capra and Joris Ivens', although Ivens made a point of distancing himself from the final version 'because of its completely different tenor'.[42]

Capra's dismissal of Ivens could have had deeper causes than a difference of opinion about this one film. American conservatives were terrified of Communist influence on the film medium in general and on Capra's army unit in particular.[43]

From the spring of 1943, when he started working for Capra, Ivens was regularly subjected to what Bureau jargon called 'physical surveillance': FBI agents followed him. A major part of the 1943 FBI reports about Ivens is still classified, the reasons given being the protection of the privacy of third parties, the protection of sources, and national defense and foreign policy considerations. There is no doubt that the FBI mistrusted his activities. Soon after Pearl Harbor, the Communist party in Hollywood set up so-called 'Writers Clinics' for training scriptwriters. Carl Foreman was one of the students and Ivens gave a number of classes there in the summer of 1943; among other things, he told his students that the documentary 'is part of the ideological superstructure of the economical system and is changing with this basis'.[44] Apart from this ritual turn of the prayer wheel, he discussed his own experiences in his work since the late twenties, something he had done numerous times in speeches and lectures. Many of the students were employed by the studios and the course would have promoted rather than damaged America's national interest, but it must have all looked extremely suspicious from an intelligence point of view. The war had suddenly given Hollywood a propaganda task it was unprepared for. The Communists were old hands and thus became involved with 'an impressive number of top-quality war films which made a positive contribution to the government's war information program', according to one study.[45] At the time the differences of opinion between the American Communist party and the White House were not so great, despite the Communists' constant calls for the war effort to be sped up more than was reasonably possible. In 1944 the CPUSA finally abolished itself for a time, convinced as it was of its own superfluousness, but conservatives viewed even this action with suspicion.

On October 18, 1942 the FBI had already noted Ivens's presence at a large meeting of the League of American Writers in New York's Carnegie Hall, where a plea went up for the 'immediate' establishment of a second front in Europe. The organizers assumed that the Western Allies were deliberately postponing landing on Europe's Atlantic coast until the Soviet Union had taken care of the dirty work, a suspicion that was most prevalent in the Kremlin. British policy definitely lent credence to such an accusation. Roosevelt and the American high command however were working at full capacity on the preparations for a second front, something that presented enormous logistic problems. The German grip on the Atlantic through their submarines was a serious barrier to a military build-up for a European invasion, and it was only in the course of 1943 that this control began to weaken.

The speakers at Carnegie Hall included Orson Welles, Charles Chaplin and Joris Ivens, who was down from Ottawa where he was still working on ACTION STATIONS! On the same stage where he had given a speech about Spain for the same organization five years earlier, he now declared that his greatest wish was to be 'in liberated Holland, in my fatherland, to film the rise of the great city where I received my professional training and which is now flatter than a gravestone: Rotterdam'.[46] In a speech that Ivens watched with astonishment, Chaplin made a fierce plea for more aid for the Soviet Union. 'Pointing into the auditorium exactly where the people we needed were sitting, he said, 'I don't want to talk to you, I'm speaking to the balcony. Comrades! Friends!'... His feelings were justified but his tactics were wrong.'[47] The conservatives made Chaplin pay. He remained the public's darling and THE GREAT DICTATOR drew full houses everywhere, but Chaplin was no longer welcome in society circles.

Three weeks later Ivens was in New York for a congress for Soviet-American friendship, and in early October of the next year he participated in a writers' convention organized in Los Angeles by the University of California and Hollywood Writers Mobilization, a successor organization to the Hollywood Anti-Nazi League. At the opening ceremony, messages from President Roosevelt and the Republican presidential candidate Wendell L. Willkie were read out and the speeches, by speakers including Thomas Mann and Darryll F. Zanuck, were dutiful and patriotic.[48] Joris Ivens spoke about morality in documentary films and met a few old acquaintances, among them the guerrilla specialist Lieutenant Colonel Evans Fordyce Carlson, and the guest of honor the Georgian filmmaker Michail Kalatozov, who had shown him around his studio in Tbilisi back in 1930. Patriotic or not, the conservative Californian senator Tenney denounced the congress as a sinister Communist gathering. For some Americans Joris Ivens was becoming an undesirable alien.

14 War Under the Palm Trees (1944-1945)

On New Year's Day 1944, a justice of the peace presided over a simple marriage ceremony at Wilton Place in Los Angeles. Helen van Dongen and Joris Ivens were the happy couple, Michail Kalatozov was the witness, and one of the few guests was Andries Deinum.[1] There was something strange about the marriage, because neither bride nor groom would later admit to the date. Helen van Dongen did not contradict others when they claimed in her presence that she had married Ivens in the thirties,[2] and Ivens refused to be drawn into statements on the subject. Filling in a form at the Dutch embassy in Paris in the fifties, he gave his date of marriage as '1941 Los Angeles USA' and put down 'Nevada USA 1943' as the date of his divorce from Van Dongen.[3] Why this incorrect information? Was it a desire to erase the past? Or was it because he was worried about his third wife, Ewa Fiszer, discovering the truth?

The truth was that two days after the marriage ceremony, he happened to bump into a cheerful, elegant thirty-year-old American brunette of his acquaintance, Marion Michelle.[4] They had lunch together and went to Players, director Preston Sturges's popular club on Sunset Boulevard. Within two weeks they were lovingly referring to each other as 'Mr. and Mrs. Pumpkin'. For Marion Michelle, Joris Ivens was 'a very romantic figure. He was very handsome and charming with his European *savoir-vivre*.'

It took a while before Michelle discovered to her horror that her new flame was also a newlywed. Nothing at his home in Stanley Hills Place had suggested the presence of a woman. Helen was already far away on the East Coast, making the compilation film NEWS REVIEW NO. 2 for the Office of War Information. Ivens explained to Michelle that in the puritanical American environment, Helen felt more comfortable as a married woman, but that 'in a certain sense' their relationship was 'over'.[5] This excuse was not entirely fictitious. Dutchwoman Frenny de Graaff, who had spent years in Moscow as a translator and was an occasional visitor to the apartment on Washington Square, had witnessed how upset Van Dongen became when Ivens received yet another invitation for an event she could not attend because they were not married.[6] This, of course, was not Van Dongen's real motive for marrying. The following years would show clearly that her feelings for him were anything but 'over' in 'a certain sense'. She must have hoped that taking the plunge might save their shaky relationship, and Ivens too might have fleetingly believed that a justice of the peace could perpetuate their relationship. Or was he was so compliant that he did it just to please her? Their relationship had lasted for almost fifteen years, and all that time he had shied away from fully committing himself. For years there had been a three-way relationship with Anneke van der Feer, after that he had spent more time away than at home, and finally he had moved out to live alone. When he allowed himself to be drawn into a marriage nonetheless, the result was predictable: he promptly threw himself into someone else's arms.

About Helen van Dongen he later wrote: 'Over these years she had been the tender, faithful and efficient woman every man hopes to meet in his life,' a description that seems more suitable for a secretary than a lover. In a letter he wrote in 1944 he called their relationship 'a fifteen-year friendship' and confided that Helen 'doesn't realize that the love that gives warmth and great happiness is not there'.[7] A confession with sweeping consequences, because the unavoidable conclusion was that he had been fooling Van Dongen and probably himself the whole time.

Ivens kept his involvement with Marion Michelle from Van Dongen for more than a year, something that presented no great practical difficulties as she was spending most of her time on the East Coast. Ivens met Michelle long before things between them became serious. Around 1940 she had been a member of the Association of Documentary Film Producers in New York. Ivens was the chairman, but according to Michelle they did not have any personal contact at that time. This changed around 1943 when she introduced him to her father, the lawyer Koblitz, who had many clients among Hollywood's European émigrés. Ivens needed legal assistance to arrange a divorce with Germaine Krull. He and Germaine had begun divorce proceedings in 1937, the process had not been completed though and she was now in Congo-Brazzaville and impossible to reach. He applied for a Mexican divorce at the start of 1943 and it was finalized on August 27; all Ivens needed to do was honestly declare that he had had no contact with his wife for years.[8] That same year Ivens, who was still working for Capra, helped Marion Michelle's husband, Joseph Vogel, to get a job with a Signal Corps camera team.[9]

Marion Michelle herself was working in the censorship section of the Office of War Information. This section, in the Taft Building on the corner of Vine and Hollywood Boulevard, checked America's entire film output during the war, and it was here that Michelle and Ivens bumped into each other on January 3. The letters Ivens wrote to Michelle in the New Year show that he was capable of passion in word and deed. But for how long? And how realistic were the dreams they discussed during a romantic weekend on a

Marion Michelle. PHOTO JORIS IVENS, COLL. MARION MICHELLE / EFJI

Californian beach? 'Three acres of land on a hilltop, a simple house, even children, boys and girls...'[10]

Marion Michelle Koblitz – she later dropped the surname – was born into a prosperous middle-class Jewish family on June 19, 1913 in Cleveland, Ohio. Her parents were academics and she studied literature. To foster her general development her parents sent her off on the traditional Grand Tour of Europe in 1933. She opted for a 'social tour' of Russia and later gave talks on the effervescent vitality she had witnessed in Moscow. After graduating from university she became a photographer, and in 1939 she published a photo-book for children, *Peg and Pete See New York*. She had moved to this city herself some time before, and had been trying to carve out a place for herself at Frontier Films. She made the stills for Leo Hurwitz and Paul Strand's NATIVE LAND and experimented with 16mm film. In 1941 she went to Mexico with a letter of recommendation from Strand and began work on a film about rural schools for the Mexican Ministry of Education. Disagreements arose between her and the commissioning body, however, and the film was never completed.[11] Together with her husband, she then tried her luck in Hollywood, where she became a 'very assistant' editor at Universal Studios before ending up at the Office of War Information.

'Drop me behind the lines in Yugoslavia then,' was apparently Joris Ivens's response to his dismissal from Capra's group. This was definitely not meant as a joke because he volunteered for the OSS, the Office of Strategic Services, forerunner to the CIA, whose agents' zone of operations included the Balkans. He convinced Andries Deinum to volunteer for the OSS as well, and in the end Deinum was accepted and Ivens was not. Deinum believed that his friend was rejected because he was a Communist, but the OSS research department employed other leftists such as the German philosopher Ludwig Marcuse, and the service even accepted party members, on the condition that they were open about their membership and suspended activities for the party for the duration. In retrospect this did not always happen and the results of some OSS work ended up in Moscow. With the liberation of Western Europe approaching, the OSS had a shortage of Dutch speakers, and in January 1944 Deinum was sent to London, where the Dutch were both allies and a target for espionage. 'They were all spying on each other there in London,' according to Deinum, who returned to California at the end of 1944.[12] It is unclear why Joris Ivens wanted to join the OSS. Did he hope to gather intelligence for the Soviet Union? Or did he simply wish to contribute to the Allied war effort and settled on the OSS because he already felt half-American?

By 1944 the Red Army had reconquered large parts of the Soviet Union, Allied troops were advancing on Monte Cassino in central Italy, and Japan was retreating in the Pacific. The Allies were on the offensive everywhere, but there were no openings for Joris Ivens. 'Here I sit, under the palm trees, while there's a war on,' he philosophized dejectedly. 'He was fairly unhappy in Hollywood,' according to Marion Michelle. 'But not really unhappy,' she added, 'you couldn't be in that glittering world, where everyone was writing scripts and hoping they would be worth a fortune'.[13]

Partly through the work of Capra's unit, interest in documentaries was growing in Hollywood. Fiction films were becoming increasingly realistic, and real soldiers were being used in war films, a complete innovation. Ivens hoped to play a role in stimulating this development, and in January 1944 he made preparations with his longstanding acquaintance from Frontier Films, Leo Hurwitz, for a large seminar on the 'craft problems of the realistic film', to be held at Consolidated Film Laboratories. Thirteen sessions would cover the consequences and requirements of realism throughout the production process, from directing and acting through to exhibition.[14]

Ivens was able to engage with these matters on a more practical level after being employed as an advisor by the producer Lester Cowan, who was hoping to strengthen the documentary and realistic aspects of his fiction films. Cowan was making THE STORY OF GI JOE, based on the Italian adventures of renowned war correspondent Ernie Pyle. Ivens proposed actually following Pyle on the Italian front with a six-man film crew, but this idea was torpedoed by the officer responsible, General MacNair, who thought that the battlefield was not there to serve as a backdrop for the movies.[15] The film finally became a fiction film about Pyle's experiences with the troops in Italy, filmed in the United States. Sixteen scriptwriters worked on GI JOE, and Ivens supervised their work to make sure it was realistic enough. Directed by William Wellman, with Robert Mitchum in one of the leading roles and with one hundred and fifty soldiers added to the cast to re-enact their battle experiences, it became a film without phony heroics, photographed in documentary style and praised by film critic James Agee as a work of art that would stand the test of time.[16]

Cowan used Ivens for a multitude of duties and when journalist Virginia Wright interviewed him she was surprised that he 'has no desire to be identified with any one phase of production. He is even strangely indifferent to credits.' Ivens was happy just being involved at a high level with so many aspects of major Hollywood productions. One of Cowan's plans was to have Ivens direct a film about the life of the Chinese revolutionary leader, Sun Yat-sen, deceased husband of Ivens's Hong Kong heroine Song Qinling.[17]

'A Russian ship with a female captain and an all-female crew put into the port of Los Angeles. A large meeting praising the indissoluble bonds of Soviet-American friendship was held in the Shrine Auditorium. Charlie Chaplin gave a speech and kissed the cute curvaceous captain,' wrote Salka Viertel, scriptwriter and bosom friend of Greta Garbo. This gave Lester Cowan an idea. He invited Viertel to lunch at the Beverly-Wilshire Hotel and asked her if she could write a script about a female captain, to be played by Garbo. Cowan made an agreement with the Norwegian embassy in Washington that the story would be set in the world of the Norwegian merchant marine during the war. Working title: WOMAN OF THE SEA.

Greta Garbo was present at the next lunchtime meeting. The reclusive Scandinavian beauty had withdrawn from the film world several years earlier. Although she had considered accepting a number of roles since then, she had always ended up declining. 'Garbo was clearly fascinated and emphasized that she was fully convinced that I would write a good script,' according to Viertel, who had provided the scripts for a number of successful

MGM films for the Swedish star. This time Garbo did not want to sign a contract until the screenplay had been completed. Lester Cowan began production and in April 1944 he appointed Ivens as co-producer. 'I had known Joris since he visited Hollywood with Hemingway,' related Viertel, 'and I was delighted at the prospect of working together. We soon became good friends.'[18]

According to Viertel the original idea was to adapt a story by C.S. Forester, but the Norwegian embassy bombarded her with inspiring newspaper clippings, including a report of the hijacking of the coaster Galtesund by a resistance group, who used it to sail to England. Joris Ivens remembered things differently and said that the idea for WOMAN OF THE SEA originated with his friend Vladimir Pozner.[19] Either way, Greta Garbo was to become the Galtesund's heroic Captain Dagny.

Ivens took charge of the practical preparations. With Marion Michelle he shot preparatory footage in San Francisco harbor on board the Norwegian freighter Thor I, which according to expectations would be made available for the film by the Norwegian government.[20] As location, he selected the west coast of Canada, which shows some similarity to the coasts of Norway and Scotland. He contacted John Grierson in Ottawa in order to assure himself of his co-operation and Grierson wrote back: 'I saw the news of you tying up with Lester Cowan Productions and I hope you soaked the boys with the fleshpots and got you plenty of flesh. You're a piker if you took anything less than two thousand a week.'[21]

Ivens had taken much less, and Michelle had also told him that he needed to up his demands. He was a veteran of film history with a place of honor among the pioneers of documentary film, but he had no money to show for it. Whereas Cowan inhabited a mansion on Las Palmas Boulevard, he was living in a poky house on Stanley Hills Place. He once wrote to his mother: 'It's such a shame that I can never get anything that will get me anywhere. I sometimes earn good money for a short time, but that's always followed by another period between two film productions, sometimes six to twelve months, in which I earn next to nothing... I believe that Pa was right when he said that I didn't have much of an instinct for business.' Acting on Michelle's instructions, he withdrew to Palm Springs in May and wired Cowan that he demanded a raise to 450 dollars a week from June 1, going up to 750 once shooting began, and separate payment for GI JOE. In addition, as co-producer for the Garbo film, he wanted his name in a separate credit, not just in a list. 'If it had gone wrong I would have been in a fix, but Marion didn't want to hear a word about that. She was convinced it would work.' And it did. Cowan agreed by return, and a relieved Ivens wired back that there were still a number of things to be settled but that he would be back the next day.[22]

On April 24 Cowan hired Vladimir Pozner to help Salka Viertel develop the screenplay. According to Viertel, she, Ivens and Pozner formed 'a harmonious collective'. 'Pozner, his attractive wife Ida and their two children became good friends and we stayed friends for many years. We worked at my place and Garbo often dropped in 'to inspire us'.'[23] Viertel's home on Mabery Road in Santa Monica was the focus of the German artistic community in Hollywood. On Sundays she hosted *gemütliche* salons, regularly attended by such luminaries as Thomas, Heinrich, Klaus and Erika Mann, Lion Feuchtwanger, Alfred Döblin, Bertolt Brecht, Ludwig Marcuse, Hanns Eisler, and Charles Chaplin. Marion Michelle's father also occasionally hosted parties attended by German émigrés. She recalled seeing Thomas Mann, writer Franz Werfel and Lotte Lenya, the star of Brecht's *Threepenny Opera*.[24]

In the second half of May, Pozner and Viertel gave Greta Garbo part of the screenplay to read. She considered it 'wonderfully written'. There were discussions about who would provide the costumes and which stills photographer would be used – sensitive issues for Hollywood stars – and who would be the most appropriate director. Leslie Fenton, who had the advantage of having served as a Royal Navy officer, was brought in to fulfil this last task. On June 20 Garbo was given the first half of the screenplay to read, along with a scenario for the second half. A few days later she phoned Viertel to tell her that she didn't like the story and would not be acting in the film.[25]

Those involved went to great lengths to make her change her mind, but she kept a low profile and could only be reached through her agent, Leland Hayward. As she had already agreed to the outline – the Norwegian embassy had even officially announced her participation – Cowan proposed bringing in different authors to write a new screenplay.[26] She was adamant, and Leland Hayward added that as the war was ending anyway, the film would be outdated by the time it came out.

Ivens defended the project once more in a letter to Lester Cowan. 'A picture, just like a book, does not become timeless through avoidance of any direct reference to a given period or locale; only if it succeeds in uncovering in a very concrete situation elements common to all periods and all locales, has it a chance to survive. If you take any screen classic, from BIRTH OF A NATION to MODERN TIMES you will see that this is correct. Keeping all this in mind, let's now examine our film. Of course, it has a war background – what else could one expect from a story abut the Norwegian Merchant Marine? The important point, however, is... whether the story it tells has a meaning, a significance, an importance valid yesterday, today and tomorrow. What is our story? It is the story of what war does to human beings, not in terms of battles, but in terms of personal relationships. It is the story of separations and reunions, a basic human theme, which will be even more important after the war is over than it is now.'[27]

It was all true and all in vain. Garbo's withdrawal meant the end of WOMAN OF THE SEA. But what was the real reason for her withdrawal? The most likely explanation was her unwillingness to return to the silver screen, because she never accepted another role. According to Ivens, however, other forces were at play. Garbo had sought the advice of her ambassador in Washington, 'an old, reactionary Swede', who told her: 'You would be taking a very high risk, it doesn't even occur to these people that the Germans might win the war. Incredible!' This sounds like a highly distorted version of the story told by Salka Viertel: 'I couldn't believe it when I heard that people had convinced Greta that Norway would be Communist within a few weeks and that I myself was 'under the influence of the Reds'... The two 'Reds', Pozner and Ivens, had been engaged for the movie by Lester Cowan. As foreigners, they did not get involved in any official political activities and privately they had a right to their own opinions. We agreed on some points, on others we didn't, but neither Volodja nor Joris defended fanatical Marxist principles to me, in contrast to many of my American friends.'[28]

In a final attempt, Ivens and Pozner sent Garbo a letter. Only two artists had survived Hollywood without compromising, they wrote, Chaplin and Garbo. Millions of people over the whole world would soon be wondering what their heroes had done during the fearful days of the war. Chaplin had made THE GREAT DICTATOR. For Greta Garbo 'the story of Dagny would have been the answer – Dagny who could be French or Chinese, Spanish or Polish – Dagny who stands for millions of women fighting today so that their children might be free – Dagny whom we wanted to have your face and your voice. We are sorry you have decided otherwise. We, too, have great respect and a great admiration for Greta Garbo.'[29]

Vladimir Pozner began work on a new project with Viertel and Bertolt Brecht, a scenario for the film SILENT WITNESS, and Ivens went back to routine work with Lester Cowan. After KNOW YOUR ENEMY: JAPAN, he had now missed out on another film project that would have been important to his career.

On a September day in 1944, a telegraphed invitation for an interview with a representative of the Dutch East Indian government in exile was delivered to Stanley Hills Place. Ivens accepted and met with Charles van der Plas at San Francisco's Palace Hotel later that month. A lean man with a downy beard, Van der Plas looked more like an intellectual than an administrative officer, but was in fact the Dutch delegate to Allied Supreme Command and the right hand of the Lieutenant Governor General of the Dutch East Indies, Huib van Mook. He now asked Ivens to become Film Commissioner of the Dutch East Indies, a post comparable to Grierson's position with the Canadian National Film Board.

'His words were beautiful and very progressive,' thought Ivens. 'A real new Indonesia had to be built, and first conquered in a united action of course. Question. Why do you ask me? 'We think something great in history will happen, the liberation of a great people. We want that filmed by an artist, by a man with vision, imagination... who knows how to film world events and give them perspective. You did a film in Spain.' 'Spain? Many times, it stood in the way of my getting work.' 'Because you did Spain, an antifascist film, a freedom film, *we want you*. Your government wants you.'' Two years later Ivens remembered wondering: 'Why the hell are they making up with me?' But in September 1944 there was nothing to make up for. He might not have been received with open arms in 1941 when, more than a year after Germany's occupation of Holland, he offered his services to the Dutch government, but, as his correspondence with Frank Judson showed, he hadn't been enthusiastic about serving his fatherland himself either. At most, his conflict with 'Holland' was shadowboxing, with his country standing in for his father and a few critics who had offended him. There was no real conflict with the Dutch authorities until late 1945.

Nonetheless, it was still surprising that the government of the Dutch East Indies should approach a left-wing filmmaker. 'Have they grown up to real progressive ideas?' he asked himself. In the Palace Hotel, Charles van der Plas enthused about freedom and equality, whereas before the war, as Resident of East Java, he had been known for his harshness. Together with many others, he cherished high expectations of a postwar period in which everything would be different. In the 1941 Atlantic Charter, Roosevelt and Churchill had declared that each nation had a right to self-determination, and the Americans in particular had turned against old-style European colonialism. Queen Wilhelmina of the Netherlands had promised Indonesia equal participation in the realm and independence in domestic affairs, and in 1942 Van der Plas had co-authored the propaganda guidelines promising the postwar Dutch East Indies 'unity in diversity', 'a community in which Indonesians, the Dutch, the Chinese and Arabs can feel equally at home', perhaps even a society 'which can serve as an example to the world'. Van der Plas made radical statements: 'Our propaganda has always been dominated by entrepreneurialism and technology. It might appeal in business circles, but entrepreneurs will only stand by us as long as doing so serves their interests better than opposing us would.'[30] It was crucial to spread the news of imminent change in the East Indies in the mighty USA, and Van Mook and Van der Plas hoped to underline the seriousness of their intentions by appointing Joris Ivens.

Ivens and Van der Plas signed a contract on September 28, 1944. Since a military rank was a prerequisite for admission to the war zone, Ivens was made a pro forma public relations officer in the Royal Dutch East Indian Army.[31] Instead of falling under the army's information service, however, he was directly responsible to Governor General Van Mook. Three weeks later Ivens's appointment was made public during an elaborate press conference at Holland House in New York. In his dealings with the press in the months to come, he never failed to mention the freedom and democracy awaiting Indonesia, or to say that part of his task was to convince the Dutch and the Indonesians through his film work that 'in the Indonesia of the future they could and would have to work together on a basis of complete equality, mutual respect and mutual appreciation', as stated in his contract.[32]

He ordered equipment for his film unit in New York, and John Grierson promised him a Canadian cameraman. Before Ivens's return to the West Coast, the Museum of Modern Art organized a farewell reception where guests from the film world mingled with the acting ambassador of the Netherlands, American army and airforce officers and the Dutch, Soviet and Chinese consuls.[33]

Ivens began preparing for his departure to Australia, where he would organize his film unit before joining the Allied troops who were about to liberate the Dutch East Indies from the Japanese. He still needed an assurance from the American authorities that he would be allowed to re-enter the country when the time came, as he was dependent on laboratories and editing facilities in the United States for the completion of his films. On November 10, 1944 he submitted his application for a re-entry permit.[34]

FBI agents still followed Joris Ivens from time to time, and his correspondence was checked at local post offices. Early in 1944 the surveillance of Communists and suspected Communists was intensified in Hollywood. Ivens was subjected to special attention and that summer the head of the Los Angeles FBI had proposed to headquarters that he be placed on the Security Index, the list of persons who were a danger to domestic security. The proposal was accepted and he was not deindexed until 1956.[35]

After Ivens submitted his application for a re-entry permit, the FBI applied to the Attorney General for permission to tap his telephone (Hempstead 5026); this was granted without further formalities. Hoover sent an 'urgent' letter to Los Angeles instructing his agents to proceed.[36] It was already too late, because Ivens was already spending most of his time in San Francisco, ready to board the first available military flight to Australia after receiving his re-entry permit. When the permit didn't come, he asked Archibald MacLeish, who had risen to the post of assistant secretary of state, to intervene. MacLeish did what he could, as evidenced by Hoover's drunken scrawl at the bottom of an otherwise blacked out page in Ivens's file: 'Typical of MacLeish's double-talk! It would be charitable to say he is gullible but I doubt if he is that dumb.'[37] The visa section of the State Department received a negative recommendation from the FBI, and on February 13, 1945 Ivens heard from Washington that he had been refused a re-entry permit.[38] If he left the country, he could presume that he would not be re-admitted.

The FBI did not trust Ivens at all. In his file he was described as a 'dangerous Communist' who was 'strongly suspected of being a Soviet espionage agent', and was in any case an 'outstanding pro-Soviet propagandist in the motion picture field' who maintained dubious contacts with the Communist party in California.[39] However, the parts of the FBI file that have been declassified do not show anywhere why he was dangerous or that he had been spying. When the Dutch Information Service inquired about the issue a few months later, the Americans answered that Ivens was 'one of most dangerous Communists in United States' and a 'member of Communist party in both Russia and Germany and friend of Soviet vice-consul for Pacific Coast'. This time there was no mention of espionage.[40]

It is unlikely that Joris Ivens was a member of the Communist Party of the Soviet Union, since he had not been admitted to this party during his long stay in Moscow. It is difficult to ascertain whether he was a member of the KPD, the German Communist Party. German émigrés in the United States and Mexico kept the KPD going in exile, and Ivens knew several leading members, including Gerhard Eisler, the most important party functionary in North America, and Otto Katz, whose pseudonym 'Breda' appears in Ivens's notes from 1941. Katz was in New York at that time and later settled in Mexico.[41] There is no clear indication of why the FBI believed that Ivens was a KPD member. In this context, the file only refers to contacts with the so-called Free Germany Movement.[42] In July 1943 the KPD leadership in Moscow, together with other emigrants and captured German officers, had founded the Nationalkomitee Freies Deutschland, which argued for the postwar reconstruction of a democratic Germany. In retrospect, this was the first step toward the formation of the German Democratic Republic. Bertolt Brecht tried to form an American counterpart to the Moscow committee and organized a meeting at Salka Viertel's home on August 1, 1943. Those present included Thomas and Heinrich Mann, Lion Feuchtwanger and Herbert Marcuse. Thomas Mann distanced himself from the initiative a few days later after hearing from the State Department that it was a Communist cover organization.[43] Again the FBI does not commit itself to stating what Ivens's actual contacts with Free Germany involved.

Vladimir and Ida Pozner did confirm that Ivens knew a Soviet vice-consul in California. They had also known him well, but they could not recall his name.[44] The USSR had consulates in San Francisco and Los Angeles, with Grigori Kheifetz and Peter Ivanov as the most active vice-consuls. Kheifetz knew Bertolt Brecht and Hanns Eisler, and was probably the person the Pozners and Ivens knew as well.[45] A cheerful Jew, he spoke a number of languages fluently, had a technical background and kept up with cultural matters. He was also the secret resident, in other words the boss, of the NKVD in San Francisco, a man with a long career behind him, first as secretary to Krupskaya, Lenin's wife, and in the thirties as a GPU agent in Italy and Germany.[46] The GPU and the NKVD were the forerunners of the KGB.

The FBI even investigated Ivens's contacts with the suspects in the 'COMRAP Case', which presumably refers to the Soviet attempt at atomic espionage through the radiation laboratory of atomic researcher Robert J. Oppenheimer. Working from Kheifetz's consulate in San Francisco, Peter Ivanov attempted – through George Eltenton of the Shell laboratory in Emeryville and Professor Haakon Chevalier, researcher at Oppenheimer's laboratory in Berkeley – to approach Oppenheimer himself for information about America's secret nuclear research. Shortly afterward, this research was concentrated in the desert at Los Alamos under Oppenheimer's leadership. Eltenton and Chevalier were friends of Oppenheimer's and all three of them sympathized with Communism, which did not stop Oppenheimer from reporting the matter to the authorities in 1943.[47]

Vladimir Pozner was a good friend of both Chevalier's and Oppenheimer's. 'I can still see the big party in Chevalier's garden before me,' he wrote, 'in aid of Russian War Relief, attended by people from all parties, all unions, all faculties and, not forgetting, the Oppenheimers and, it goes without saying, the Soviet consul, whose daughter was an army doctor in Stalingrad.' Pozner also remembered the going away party that 'Opje', as he called Oppenheimer, gave at his home on Eagle Hill in San Francisco in the spring of 1943. Oppenheimer was leaving for Los Alamos, but their friends did not know this and did not ask any questions, according to Pozner. The Oppenheimers left their children's toys behind for the Pozners, and Vladimir was given Goethe's *Faust*, with a dedication from 'Opje' in the front. Pozner was later incensed by Oppenheimer's declaration 'that our dear

Joris Ivens on Laguna Beach, California, awaiting departure for Australia (1945).
PHOTO MARION MICHELLE. COLL. MARION MICHELLE / EFJI

friend Haakon Chevalier was a Soviet agent.' That was a lie on the part of 'my comrade Oppenheimer', wrote Pozner.[48]

There was a whole subculture in which Communist artists, Soviet agents and atomic scientists mixed freely. Naturally, these entanglements drove the FBI to distraction, and the Bureau never really succeeded in separating the sheep from the goats. Ivens lived next door to the Pozners and met them, Brecht and Eisler at Salka Viertel's on Sunday afternoons; he regularly visited Brecht at home, sometimes together with Marion Michelle; and presumably met privately with Kheifetz, just as Brecht and Eisler did. It is very likely that he would have at least discussed the political situation in Hollywood with a Soviet official in Kheifetz's position. After all, in 1936 he reported on the American film world to both Moscow and Verlinsky in New York. Helen van Dongen was also under FBI surveillance, which again noted very close links to another Soviet vice-consul, this time from Los Angeles.[49]

Without a re-entry permit, Joris Ivens was in a difficult position, and he had dug himself into a hole with his women as well. Who should he take to Australia with him? Helen? Marion? Both perhaps? The Dutch East Indies government had given Van Dongen, doubtlessly with Ivens's approval, a contract as a member of his film unit, but she still wasn't aware of his relationship with Michelle. Michelle, in turn, thought that Ivens should finally choose, and informed him that she did not want to see him again until he had made a decision, an ultimatum she soon withdrew. The situation became even more complicated in late November when Helen came over from New York to live with her husband on Stanley Hills Place, who bought a car for her, a bluish-green Lincoln Zephyr Coupé 1938. He began commuting between the two women. He stayed in the Palace Hotel in San Francisco with Michelle, and in between times with Van Dongen in Hollywood.

Report from two FBI agents, Hollywood, December 14, 1944: 'Special Agent X and the writer observed the subject [Ivens] and his wife leave home at 9:40 a.m. They carried with them two suitcases, airplane luggage, and one briefcase. They stopped at the Hollywood Knickerbocker Hotel in Hollywood and left the two suitcases with the Bell Captain there. Ivens told the Bell Captain that he would call back later for them. They then proceeded to a parking lot on Vine Street north of Hollywood and went on foot to the Taft Building, 1680 North Vine Street, where the Office of War Information is located... At 11:45 a.m. both the subject and his wife proceeded to the General Service Studios on Las Palmas where they separated. At 12:05 Ivens left the General Services Studios and proceeded to the lunchroom at the corner of Santa Monica Boulevard and Las Palmas Avenue and made a telephone call. He then proceeded on foot to the corner of Hollywood and Santa Monica Boulevards two blocks west. At 12:45 p.m. he was picked up by xx [Marion Michelle] in a 1939 Pontiac sedan. She drove directly to the Hollywood Knickerbocker Hotel where she picked up Ivens's luggage and drove quickly to the Lockheed Airport in Burbank. Both the subject and xx departed from Los Angeles at 2:00 p.m. on Western Airlines, flight #36, for San Francisco.'[50]

At the end of January, Van Dongen still did not know that Ivens was planning to take not only her but also Michelle to Australia with him. He was afraid of hurting her and thought, paradoxically enough, that it was his responsibility to be extra supportive because of the bad news hanging over her head. Michelle wrote in her diary: 'What a set-up. I go to Australia as the villain of the piece, live like an orphan in another city, some fun. While he tries to get her to *like* the idea of giving him up.' He told her that he had discussed things with Helen, but Marion did not believe him and wrote: 'I know his indirection + his history.'[51]

The powder keg blew at a Hollywood party when Van Dongen realized that Ivens was planning to take Michelle to Australia with him as well. She was shocked and distraught. The Pozners who witnessed the drama had little solace to offer.[52] It was a hard blow for Helen van Dongen in more than one respect. Not only her marriage but also her work was completely disrupted, despite the fact that Ivens would spend the next six months claiming that there was no reason for her not to come to Australia as well.

FBI wiretap report dd. March 2, 1945: 'Ivens and his wife engaged in a lengthy conversation according to x. This discussion concerned the possibility xx [Helen van Dongen] getting an early departure for Australia. She stated that she would not be released by the Office of War Information until the film on which she is working is finished... xx told her husband that xxx of the Office of War Information was coming to Los Angeles on Saturday, March 3, 1945, and she would attempt to prevail on him to get an early departure date. She was not very hopeful, however, and felt that the best she could do would be about the middle of April. The above conversation was in the Dutch language and the translator Special Employee xxxx reported that the tone of Ivens's conversation indicated that he was not anxious for his wife to join him in Australia.'[53]

Five days later and without a re-entry permit, Joris Ivens boarded a military aircraft and took off for Australia from the Fairfield airforce base. On the personal orders of J. Edgar Hoover his baggage was subjected to a thorough search, 'with the exception of three small packages which bore the seal of the Dutch government'. Nothing unusual was found.[54] Marion Michelle followed by sea some time later. Helen van Dongen never made it to Australia. Soon after his arrival in Australia, Ivens received a telegram from Hollywood: 'Very happy with all the beautiful flowers. Helen.' Marion too had received flowers from Australia that day with lots of love.[55]

15   Indonesia Merdeka (1945-1946)

After a flight of more than fifty-three hours via Honolulu, Christmas Island, Canton Island and Fiji, Joris Ivens reached Brisbane, home to the main Dutch East Indian colony in Australia. 'No Van der Plas,' he ascertained and traveled on south to Melbourne, where he took a room in the Menzies Hotel, the former headquarters of U.S. General Douglas MacArthur. Ivens developed an immediate aversion to the stuffy city of Melbourne, where women wore respectable hats, men dressed in dark suits, and everyone tried to imitate England whenever possible.

The Dutch authorities in Australia received him enthusiastically. Two weeks after his arrival, the Dutch consul general organized a festive welcoming reception in the Usher Hotel in Sydney and the military commander Lieutenant General L.H. van Oyen dispatched a circular to all sections requesting their full cooperation with Ivens. When the Allied supreme command granted him accreditation as a war correspondent, allowing him to join MacArthur's headquarters in the Philippines on May 1, it seemed as if nothing could go wrong.[1]

During a day at the beach, he explained his plans to Charles van der Plas. The Joris Ivens Film Unit would make a feature film in black-and-white and two shorts in color, all shot in the combat zone. Two more short films would follow, and an agreement had already been reached in America with the Dutch Minister of Education P.A. Kerstens for a series of twenty educational programs for use in the East Indies after liberation.[2]

Ivens traveled to Columbia Camp in Brisbane, where the Dutch community awaited the reconquest of the East Indies. Here he began to realize that not all of his countrymen embraced the ideals of Charles van der Plas. In their temporary accommodation under the gum trees, all kinds of colonials waited impatiently to regain possession of their plantations and mines and resume their prewar routine. Shell, the KPM shipping company and other corporations ran their own intelligence services and their representatives viewed Van der Plas as a destructive fool. In turn, Van der Plas believed that the Dutch exiles' little world 'suffers from all the ailments such a community brings with it, unfortunately including the old colonial delusions of grandeur, which are painfully ridiculous in the light of the position we occupy here'.[3]

Meanwhile, forces opposing Ivens were at work behind the scenes. The Netherlands Forces Intelligence Service, NEFIS, under the charge of Colonel Simon Spoor, later General and commander-in-chief in the Dutch East

Indies, submitted a request for official information on Ivens to his American colleagues. On April 20, 1945 he received a report from General MacArthur that Ivens was 'one of most dangerous Communists in United States'. Spoor felt sufficiently informed and wrote to General Van Oyen that 'giving Ivens an official function in the Dutch organization must be judged to be highly undesirable' considering that the United States was apparently 'delighted to be rid of him and was evidently planning on staying rid of him'. He concluded that Ivens's movements should be 'monitored and immediately reported to the USA security organization' and ended by proposing 'denying approval for accreditation of Ivens'. Although 'it might be permissible in peacetime to allow the cinematic artist Ivens to indulge his world view to his heart's content, I believe that in the present time of war it would be inadmissible for the Dutch side to promote an officially accredited filmmaker who is in disrepute with our Allies and who they do not wish to have anything to do with'. On April 25, the following telegram was sent to MacArthur's Philippine headquarters: 'NEFIS desires Ivens not repeat not be accredited as war correspondent.' The answer was not slow in coming: 'Boris Ivens will not be accredited by Uncle Sugar Army as war correspondent. He will also be barred from entry into Philippine territory.'[4]

MacArthur's telegram was the beginning of the end. The Allies were preparing to conquer the Indonesian archipelago from New Guinea and from the north, but the combat zone was off limits to Joris Ivens, despite the fact that filming the liberation of Indonesia was his most important task as Film Commissioner.

For Van Mook and Van der Plas, the men who had appointed Ivens, the decision of MacArthur's headquarters came as an extraordinarily unpleasant surprise. In an internal memo they wrote of 'a Dutch loss of face', but they remained unimpressed by the 'disconnected facts' the Americans presented against Ivens, and continued to back him fully. He was, 'with his strong socialist tendencies, an idealist, but above all, a mild man, who does not begrudge his fellow men their freedom to judge and to act and, as he has repeatedly stated, rejects equally the violent methods of Communism and fascism'.[5] Had Ivens really renounced world revolution before these well-meaning politicians? It was highly likely; it was a time of tremendous optimism about the new world that would be built up after the war. When Ivens left the United States, the American Communists were pursuing a policy that general secretary Earl Browder summarized in the words: 'Capitalism and Socialism have begun to find the way to peaceful coexistence and collaboration in the same world', and Moscow too seemed to have struck revolution from its agenda. Ivens had also been inspired by the book *One World* by Republican presidential candidate Wendell L. Willkie, a passionate plea for international cooperation across ideological borders.[6]

There is no doubt that he shared his superiors' hopes for Indonesia's future and they had reason to trust him. Accordingly, Van Mook, Van der Plas and the Dutch embassy in Washington continued their attempts to obtain a belated re-entry permit for Ivens. When this failed, Van Mook suggested that, if necessary, they could get him into the United States on a diplomatic passport, enabling him to complete his films there after all.[7] In the expectation that the problems would settle, they reconfirmed the orders for supplies in New York, and continued to develop plans for the work in Indonesia. Ivens's charm even disarmed the war-horse Colonel Spoor. After meeting the feared agitator in person a few months after his fatal telegram to MacArthur, he wired General Van Oyen: 'My personal impression however not unfavorable.'[8]

Ivens was sidelined again. In his Melbourne office at 170 Latrobe Street, work continued on the educational program and he gave camera lessons to a number of enthusiastic Indonesians, but things were hardly as he had imagined them.

Meanwhile Helen van Dongen was still in Hollywood. She had not been given a re-entry permit either. When she booked a passage to Australia anyway in early May, Ivens hurriedly wired her that she should stay in America, and in June he again strongly advised her to wait until she had received the coveted documents.[9] There were practical arguments for this course of action: there was little to do in Australia and if he eventually began work after all, she would be able to take care of the processing and editing in America. The circumstances were also very convenient. Without any effort on his part, he was able to avoid a new situation of having to navigate between Helen and Marion. Even the FBI had realized that he wanted to unburden himself of Van Dongen, and now 'forces beyond his control' had resolved this difficult problem.

For some time Van Dongen continued to carry out supportive activities in New York – tasks such as collecting footage from the film archives – but she heard less and less from down under. In April of the next year she sighed: 'I don't know why I still write to you, I haven't received any replies since December.'[10] Thereafter the radio silences only grew. In 1947-1948 she tried in vain to meet up with Ivens when she was in Europe.

It is not known exactly when she divorced Ivens. In May 1950 Helen van Dongen married the sixty-year-old Kenneth Durant, another husband with a remarkable career behind him. With his colleague John Reed, Durant had witnessed the Russian Revolution. On his return to the United States, he became the secretary of the unofficial ambassador of the unrecognized Bolshevik state. He remained in the diplomatic service, and from 1923 to 1944 he headed the American branch of the Soviet press agency Tass, as well as various other Soviet organizations in the United States. His first wife, the poet Geneviève Taggart, died in 1947. Durant came from a very wealthy family, and he and Helen van Dongen moved to an estate in Vermont, where they withdrew from their former activities. They managed their woods and streams, and wrote a book about a variety of boat in use in the Adirondacks, the area they lived in. Kenneth Durant died in November 1972.[11]

Van Dongen did not see Joris Ivens again until 1978. 'I went away with the gratifying feeling that we had said goodbye as true friends,' she wrote afterwards in the Dutch film magazine *Skoop*, but this impression passed quickly when she saw the French publication of Ivens's memoirs in the early eighties. As far as she was concerned, he had told nothing but lies about her. She responded in an interview: 'He is a great artist, but as a human being, you can have him.'[12] She did not provide any striking examples of his lying, and in reality it was probably not the lies that had stung so much as the truth: his memories of the years they spent together were detached and far from loving.

On July 6, 1945, Marion Michelle sailed from Los Angeles on board the MS Tabian with an official posting from the government of the Dutch East Indies, and on August 1 she arrived in Melbourne, where she joined Ivens's Film Unit.[13]

Ivens moved his unit to Sydney on August 31.[14] Almost five hundred miles northwest of Melbourne, Sydney was an improvement in many ways. The climate was warmer and the atmosphere was lively and cosmopolitan. It was the center of Australia's modest film world, there was a vibrant political scene and it was home to most of the country's Indonesians. He and Marion moved into Birtly Towers, a dingy apartment building whose main feature was a sweeping harbor view.

The Joris Ivens Film Unit was now complete. From Canada, there were Donald and Joan Frazer, cameraman and editor respectively, and two of Charles van der Plas's Indonesian protégés had also joined the team. One was John Sendoek, who had been imprisoned as an Indonesian nationalist during the thirties, but had spent the war working for the Dutch radio station in California – because it was 'better than being beaten' – and would later work for the Ministry of Information and the diplomatic corps of the Republic of Indonesia. The other was John Soedjono, a former soldier in the Royal Dutch East Indian Army who had fled to Australia after the Japanese

victory. He had been a dancer at a Javanese court and sometimes gave im-
promptu performances of graceful traditional dances in his baggy army
uniform.[15]

During the Japanese conquest of the East Indies in 1942, the Dutch had
found the time to transport thousands of interned Indonesian nationalists
from prison camps on the Upper Digul in New Guinea to Australia in order
to imprison them again there. After protests from the host country, however, many of the Indonesians had to be released and a number of these en-
listed with the Allies. The result was the establishment of a large Indonesian
community of well-organized Islamic nationalists and Communists in Australia. Shortly after arriving in Australia, Ivens had met Catherine Duncan, a
charming twenty-nine-year-old actress and radio play author, who said of
herself: 'I was on the left, that is, the Communist party.'[16] She introduced
Ivens to Maskoen, an Indonesian who had spent twelve years in the camps
on the Upper Digul. He also met Soendardjo, another veteran from the
camps, and Soeparmin, the secretary of the Indonesian Seamen's Union.
Ivens brought them into the educational film project and must have felt immediately that they were kindred spirits. Like him, they were driven and
willing to make great personal sacrifices for their political ideals. 'I saw the
courage and conviction of the Indonesians who, after having been a colony
for 350 years, were now demanding their freedom. Spoken to many Indonesians here, officers, soldiers, clerks, sailors, all of them spirited, educated
people, civilized. Not the extremists the press is so fond of calling them. The
only extremists here are the Dutch colonial businessmen, who seem to decide all government policies.'[17]

On August 6, 1945, the Americans dropped an atomic bomb on Hiroshima.
Three days later they dropped another on Nagasaki. A week later Emperor
Hirohito announced Japan's surrender over the radio after the Allies had
declared that they did not want to destroy the Japanese nation or the Japanese people, only their militarism. They hinted that the emperor could stay
on.

At the time of the Japanese capitulation, Indonesia was still largely occupied and the Allies commanded the Japanese forces to maintain order in the
country. It took another six weeks before British forces under General
Mountbatten, who had taken over the regional supreme command from
MacArthur, arrived on Java. In this twilight situation Soekarno and
Mohammad Hatta succumbed to pressure from young radicals and proclaimed the independent Republic of Indonesia on August 17 with Japanese
consent. A civil-war-like situation developed and in the next few months

thousands of Indonesians, Japanese and British soldiers and Dutch citizens died in fighting and raids.

During this chaotic period, Ivens was asked on September 24, 1945 to extend his one-year contract with the government of the Dutch East Indies.[18] It was a difficult choice. On the one hand, it seemed as if his chances of reaching Java had improved now that the area was no longer under General MacArthur's command, and there was even talk of including Ivens in the colonial staff, completely freeing him from the requirement of military accreditation. On the other hand, the slowly spreading news of the independence movement was beginning to occupy his thoughts.[19] In Australia an anti-Dutch mood was growing: Prime Minister Chifley's Labor government adopted an attitude of non-cooperation with Dutch nationals present in the country; the trade union movement was distinctly sympathetic to the Indonesian Republic; and Indonesians began making their presence felt with demonstrations in Australian cities. After much hesitation, Joris Ivens decided to sign for another year.

His champion and supporter Charles van der Plas had been on Java since September 15. Unbeknown to Ivens, his capricious ally was now the author of a plan to arrest the Republican leaders and dissolve Soekarno's Republic. Van der Plas wanted other 'democratic Indonesians to genuinely take on authority and responsibility', but it was too late for such compromises. The Republic was a fact, and a few weeks later Van der Plas himself became the first Dutch official to openly call for negotiations with Soekarno.[20]

Ivens realized how much times had changed on October 1, when Huib van Mook also departed for Batavia without taking him with him. Van Mook had run a risk by engaging Ivens and had continued to support him through all the difficulties, but history had now taken a turn Van Mook had not expected. He supported equality between the Dutch and the Indonesians, and advocated Indonesian independence in domestic affairs, but as part of the Kingdom of the Netherlands. Ivens who too had believed in a great task for Holland in the East Indies, now quickly transferred his loyalties. He was already in touch with Republican Indonesians and his longing for simplicity and certainty now allowed him to look beyond the complications. To discredit the Republic, the Dutch were fond of drawing attention to Soekarno's collaboration with the Japanese. Ivens simply did not believe these stories, and far away in Sydney he was not influenced by atrocities inflicted on Dutch civilians by young Indonesians. It is likely that the reports of these abuses hardly even reached Australia. Ivens went straight to the heart of the matter: it was an authentic liberation struggle that deserved his support.

What to do? He was torn, and on September 23 a month of serious bronchitis and asthma attacks began.[21] A few weeks after extending his contract, he was already wiring Helen van Dongen: 'Considering violent situation Indies my position now impossible stop drastic decision on my part rapidly unavoidable.'[22] His departure from government service was only a matter of time.

In the last week of September the Indonesian conflict became visible from Ivens and Michelle's own window in Birtly Towers. On the docks where Dutch shipments to Indonesia were being prepared, waterside workers and crews began a boycott in support of the Republic. This boycott rapidly spread to all Australian harbors and enjoyed the support of virtually the entire Australian trade union movement as well as several foreign seamen's unions. Despite slackening occasionally, it continued until 1949.

Over the months that followed, Ivens's choice for the Republic grew into a conflict between him and the Dutch government that would pursue him for years to come. As the exact dates from these months played a role in the later controversy, it is important to give them in detail.

In Sydney on October 13, Ivens and cameraman John Heyer made some shots of the departure of the Esperance Bay, a ship bearing more than one thousand four hundred Indonesians which was setting sail for one of the ports in the hands of the Republic.[23] These turned out to be the first shots for a film, but it was only in the weeks that followed that Ivens decided to make the short agitational film about the boycott campaign, which came to be called INDONESIA CALLING! Between October 24 and 27 he and Marion Michelle worked on a scenario, on the 28th a production schedule was written, and two days later Michelle noted in her diary: '1st day shooting.'[24] On the second day of shooting, November 4, shots were made in Sydney Harbour of the troop-ship Stirling Castle, which was on its way from Amsterdam to Batavia loaded with Dutch soldiers. From a small boat an appeal for solidarity with Indonesia's struggle for freedom was made by loudspeaker to the Dutch sailors and soldiers. The reply from the decks consisted of catcalls, patriotic songs and a fusillade of empty bottles, vegetables and pieces of iron and wood.[25]

The next morning a scene that had actually taken place three weeks earlier on the departure of the Esperance Bay was staged on a dock. Ivens: 'Was quite a stunt. We got about 30 Indonesians with suitcases, as if they were leaving Australia, plus Elliott, Secretary of the Seamen's Union. We got them in a taxi through the gate'. With British filmmaker Harry Watt, in Australia working on his film THE OVERLANDERS, Ivens filmed at the Lido, the KPM seamen's hostel in North Sydney which was full of Indonesian and Indian sailors. Three operators came and went in those first days. After that, Michelle did the camerawork herself. Shooting continued until November 16.[26]

It was an exciting time. The whole harbor was monitored from the office of the Waterside Workers' Union, and the moment news came in that something was happening it was off to the scene by car or motorboat, sometimes followed by the police. 'We had to duck publicity. This film was a mystery for the press. They tried to find out who was making it, but could not. Nobody talked.'[27] There were good reasons for secrecy: filming was forbidden on the docks; there were military zones; and, no matter how reluctantly and ineffectively, Ivens was still in the service of the Dutch East Indian government. Publicity could not be avoided for long. A report in *The Melbourne Sun* of November 5 came to the attention of Dutch officials who suspected, not unjustly, that Joris Ivens was behind the mystery film. They launched an investigation. 'It was decided to engage Mr. Manderson... who is well and favorably known to Colonel Spoor', according to the report. Manderson set off for Sydney and what his overheated report described as a week of 'extraordinary and revealing investigation' in a 'web of celluloid intrigue'. He made discreet inquiries in the film world, mixed with Indonesians and trade unionists, and visited Australian intelligence, but received his most important tips from a taxi driver called Charlie, who had driven Joris Ivens, Marion Michelle and a cameraman to the harbor and the Lido on November 5.[28]

Manderson talked to so many people that Ivens must have caught wind of his activities, but even without this stimulus, it was high time for him to quit his position as Film Commissioner. His beautiful dream of witnessing the liberation of the East Indies and taking charge of film production for a progressive government had evaporated. Now that he was filming in Sydney Harbour, it was likely that he would even be dismissed. He wrote to Helen that he 'had to make a fast move, to get in the first blow', and in an interview he later remarked: 'Things had started leaking out.'[29] Ivens did indeed get in the first blow. On Wednesday, November 21, 1945, he publicly resigned his position.

That day he sent a long telegram to the government in Batavia: 'The present situation in Indonesia makes it impossible for me to continue my work as Film Commissioner and producer of documentary films according to the principles specified in my contract. You asked me to do this work according to the objective specified in my contract: 'Furthermore it is considered of vital importance to the war effort of the Allied nations and to ensure permanent peace in the southwest Pacific that these films demonstrate the building of a future Indonesia in which Dutch and Indonesians can and must cooperate on a basis of mutual respect and mutual appreciation for the

Ivens and British director Harry Watt with representatives of the Indonesian Seamen's Union (Sydney, 1945-1946). PHOTO MARION MICHELLE. COLL. MARION MICHELLE / EFJI

benefit of the great Western ideals of freedom and democracy.' The ideals of freedom and democracy have been expressed in the Atlantic Charter, which respects the right of all peoples to choose the form of government under which they shall live, and in my opinion the peoples of Indonesia have every right to expect a realistic application of this Charter in order to obtain their national independence... I believe that the present attitude of the government of the Dutch East Indies only serves the interests of a small group in Holland.'[30]

He timed the delivery of the text to the post office so that Java would not receive the message until after he had held a press conference. At the same time he mailed a personal letter to Charles van der Plas in Batavia, explaining the step he was taking and expressing his respect for Van der Plas and Van Mook.[31] After returning from the post office, he prepared his press conference statement at home, then went to the Usher Hotel to await the zero hour. Marion Michelle had already made her way to the Australia Hotel, where the international press had been invited. No Dutch officials had been notified and they only became aware of the situation after the event. Ivens arrived in the Kent Room of the Australia Hotel at six o'clock and announced his resignation in a short statement. A minor uproar ensued. Reporters ran for the telephones, and the story appeared the next day in several leading European and American dailies. It even made the front page of *The New York Times*, a detail Ivens was later fond of mentioning.

After the press conference, he went out for a meal at Romano's with Marion Michelle, Harry Watt and several other supporters. A few tables away sat an unsuspecting Alfred Schuurman, the head of the Dutch publicity department and a drinking companion of Ivens's from the Dutch Club. Ivens and his cohorts ended the day by downing a bottle of Johnny Walker Red Label at Birtly Towers. Everything had gone according to plan.[32]

The next morning the rest of the Joris Ivens Film Unit submitted their resignations. Ivens wired Andries Deinum in Los Angeles asking him to mobilize support.[33] His old friends stood by him: the Hollywood Writers Guild, Hollywood Writers Mobilization, Dudley Nichols, Lewis Milestone and Jean Renoir made declarations of solidarity, and from Europe he received declarations of support from the English Association of Cine-Technicians, the French Syndicat des Travailleurs de l'Industrie du Film and the director Jean Painlevé.[34]

There was one note of discord: John Fernhout denounced Ivens's move. Before leaving for Australia, Ivens had informed the American press that, in addition to Van Dongen, he also wanted to take Fernhout with him. Fernhout had made various documentaries in the United States and since early 1942 he had headed the film section of the Netherlands Information Bureau in New York. He had accompanied Princess Juliana as adjutant on several of her journeys. In late 1944 and early 1945, Fernhout had filmed in the liberated south of the Netherlands. He had repeatedly pressed his superiors for a detachment to Ivens's team in Australia and plans in this direction were well advanced. Ivens's resignation put an end to them.[35] The fact that he was suddenly no longer needed in Australia would not have been the only thing bothering Fernhout. He had become a moderate, and it is likely that he had interpreted Ivens's appointment to the post of Film Commissioner as a sign that his former mentor had also turned his back on extremism and rediscovered an affection for his fatherland.[36]

The friends had been growing apart for some time. When his former wife Eva Besnyö saw Fernhout again in Amsterdam after the war, she noticed immediately that something was wrong. 'When I met up with John again he didn't want to talk about Joris.' The only thing he occasionally let slip was: 'Joris claimed all the honors for himself.'[37] What was he referring to? The last film they collaborated on was THE 400 MILLION. The contract between Fernhout and History Today Inc. states: 'Our understanding is that you will, in accordance with such instructions as shall from time to time be given to you by Mr. Ivens, photograph scenes and persons to portray the rise of the new China.' Ivens himself signed on behalf of History Today.[38] The opening credits for the film, however, state: 'A film by Joris Ivens and John Ferno', the name Fernhout used in America, and a 1940 catalogue also noted their shared responsibility for script and direction. Ivens apparently changed his mind later, because in postwar filmographies prepared under his supervision Fernhout has been demoted to cameraman. At John Fernhout's funeral in 1987, a short, autobiographical text was read out. Some of those present immediately noticed one striking detail: there was no mention of Ivens. 'He really had renounced Joris,' explained Besnyö.[39]

Neither Van Mook nor Van der Plas reacted to Ivens's resignation or, to his regret, to his letters,[40] but some of the Dutch colonial officials in Australia were furious. Press chief Alfred Schuurman must have felt personally betrayed. He declared – and felt 'extremely sorry to say' – that by taking this stance the Film Commissioner had become a 'traitor to queen and country'. 'While Indonesian and Dutch leaders in Java are doing their utmost to find a mutual basis to solve the problems, Ivens states that he doubts the good intentions of the representatives of his own nation.' Schuurman pointed out that Van Mook had met with Indonesian Prime Minister Soetan Sjahrir just four days before Ivens's resignation. On the day of Ivens's press conference itself, Queen Wilhelmina had reiterated that Indonesia would become an independent member of the Kingdom of the Netherlands. Schuurman accused Ivens of casting doubt upon this promise, and thus making himself 'an outcast in the eyes of every sincere Dutchman'.[41] But Ivens was not casting doubt upon Wilhelmina's promise; he disagreed with it and supported the Republic's demand for unconditional independence.

He was later accused of starting work on INDONESIA CALLING! while in the service of the Dutch government and this was true: the first shots were taken five weeks before his resignation and he started systematically working on the film one week later. It has also been suggested that Ivens used government money and supplies for his film. Beyond the fact that he continued to receive his modest salary, this is incorrect. He began work with a camera and film stock from an Australian government body and later used a shabby, borrowed Kinamo hand camera that failed to meet the most elementary amateur demands and was definitely not Dutch property. In his report, governmental sleuth Manderson had already stated that Ivens was not working with Dutch equipment or material, and Australian intelligence confirmed this conclusion.[42] Several days after his resignation, Ivens discussed the transfer of the film unit's books with a government official, whose impression was 'that Mr. Ivens views the winding up as a matter of honor'. A government bookkeeper also carried out an audit and declared that he 'had no reason to think that there was anything wrong with the financial side of the Unit'. Consul-general J.B.D. Pennink, who had earlier angrily suggested confiscating Ivens's passport, was satisfied and considered further Dutch action against Ivens superfluous.[43]

A certain normalization of relations took place, because although Ivens had announced his resignation, he was obliged to give two months' notice. He remained an employee of the colonial government until January 21, 1946, and not just officially. The educational program was further developed in consultation with officers from the Department of Education. He was still meeting with them as late as January 1946.[44] He even went for a meal with one of his opponents, who told him that Van der Plas had resigned on Java for the same reasons as Ivens.[45] It was all very gentlemanly and it seemed as if the affair would have no further consequences, although it must be said that INDONESIA CALLING! had not yet been released.

Two weeks after the press conference in the Australia Hotel Ivens resumed work on the film; history does not wait for periods of notice to expire. 'Since I had just broken with the Dutch but still had two months of my contract to serve, it was necessary to work in secret. The same thing applied to Marion Michelle, the camera operator and assistant director.'[46]

The climax of the film would be the story of the steamship Patras, a freighter manned by Indians and Dutch soldiers that managed to break the boycott and sail from Sydney Harbour with a load of ammunition on October 26. In the Tasman Sea the Indians reconsidered and stopped the engines. With the ship drifting in the surf and the rugged Australian coast to port, the officers had little choice but to accede to the mutineers' demands and return to Sydney. On October 29 the Patras was back where it had started. The seamen's solidarity was celebrated with a festive meal of chicken curry, and the Australian authorities turned a blind eye. This was fortunate for the Indians because martial law was still in force and their actions could have met with harsh punishments.[47]

Ivens had missed these spectacular events and decided to stage a re-enactment. 'We go out with two launches... covering shots, just circling around with camera launch and shooting. Outgoing ships are all too fast to shoot. Found ship at anchor with some Indians aboard, coal loading. We avoid the coal crane. Swoop camera from ship to launch, from launch to ship to get some movement. Pan along ship to fake the movement of the ship.'[48] A perfect description of the sequence about the returning ship in INDONESIA CALLING!, although Michelle was not fully successful in her attempt to hide the coal crane from view. The rest of the sequence was cut together from shots they had made of several different ships.

Some supplementary shots for INDONESIA CALLING! were made early in February 1946, but editing had been in full swing since January 8.[49] The tiny editing room of the Supreme-Sound Studio had neither windows nor ventilation and the equipment dated from cinematic prehistory. According to the studio's owner, H. Murphy, the really primitive thing was the rushes Ivens showed up with. He apparently went so far as to declare that he would film a new version of BEN HUR in his backyard if Ivens could turn the material into a film. Nonetheless, despite the half-broken camera, a minimal amount of film of varying quality and the most elementary editing equipment, the result was a serviceable political pamphlet.

The picture editing of INDONESIA CALLING! was only just finished when Ivens came down with another serious attack of bronchitis and asthma in late February. Kept going by a nurse who administered adrenaline and penicillin injections, Ivens dragged himself to the studio to add the sound-track but was unable to go on. Marion Michelle and Catherine Duncan completed the work, and in late March Ivens was admitted to hospital in a critical condition and needed to go on a resuscitator. He identified two causes for his collapse: stubborn sinusitis and 'overstrained nerves, possibly caused by years of work without a vacation. Exciting work, Spain, China, Canada, USA, and the backlash from the resignation.'[50] An attractive future of years of important work in Indonesia had dissolved into nothing, leaving him on a continent on the edge of the world where there were more sheep than people. He was forty-seven years old and suddenly started turning gray.

According to Michelle, he was not really dispirited. 'I never saw Joris really depressed. He wasn't that kind of person. I don't believe that he was ever really bored or unhappy.'[51] He always had an essential conviction that things would turn out. The doctors prescribed rest and mountain air, and after a brief first vacation in the Blue Mountains, he and Michelle returned there to settle for almost six months in Blackheath, a small town some two and a half hours west of Sydney by train. From their house 'Haslemere' they looked out over a serene valley with pines and wattle trees, and in the evening they had an uninterrupted view of the sunset, but for the lively Michelle this exile was not exactly an unqualified pleasure. Culturally the area was as good as dead, despite the lecture Ivens gave at the local Rotary club. They scarcely saw any neighbors and the convalescence proceeded slowly. After a month at Haslemere she wrote in her diary: 'I've had to do most of the work and it's plenty – big iron stove, fireplace, wood to chop, dusty house – don't feel like writing in diary even if I had time. Events of the gloomy month are few.' Later she did not have many beautiful memories to look back on. 'Presumably we were not unhappy, but it's a blind spot. As if you spent a while somewhere and absolutely nothing happened.'[52] Even so, there were occasional idyllic moments. They grew radishes and celery in their own garden and went walking in the mountains. Visitors up from Sydney could find Ivens with a cat on his lap. Marion's carefree character must have been a great support to him in this difficult period and soon after he wrote to his brother Hans in Amsterdam: 'I have new wedding plans.'[53]

As he regained his strength, Ivens began writing up his experiences from the last year for his autobiography. In the end, however, the chapter written in Blackheath was not included in *The Camera and I*.

One of the few occasions they went down to Sydney was for the premiere of INDONESIA CALLING! on Friday August 9, 1946 in the Newsreel Theatre in Kings Cross. The secretary of the Waterside Workers Union, Jim Healy, who had been one of the group's mainstays during the making of the film, sang a stirring song for the occasion, after which Indonesian, Chinese and Australian singers all did their bit to add to the festive atmosphere. A representative of the Indonesian government was ceremonially presented with a copy of the film for President Soekarno, in reality an empty can as there were no copies. Even at the premiere, the names of the makers of INDONESIA CALLING! were not made public. The film was screened without credits and *The Melbourne Sun* could only guess at the identity of the director.[54]

A telegram from Ivens's mother in Nijmegen reached Australia in July 1945,[55] but Ivens didn't get around to writing back until August 1946. It was fifteen months after V-E Day and the war in Asia had been over for a year. Even though the mail services were functioning normally, the only signs of life from Australia had been a number of short telegrams and a few Red Cross packages without an accompanying letter. His mother was still delighted, and after one of the packages reached her in her old people's home, Sancta Maria, she wrote that 'it was like a magic box'. Another six months passed before he replied. In the meantime, his mother corresponded with Helen van Dongen in New York, who kept quiet about how little contact she now had with Ivens. The resulting correspondence had a somewhat unreal quality. Dora Ivens would ask questions like 'Were you able to settle in Australia?' and Helen would answer evasively. In September 1946 Dora Ivens wrote to Helen: 'I don't ask Joris to write to me, so don't you either.' But in a letter to Ivens in April, Van Dongen had already commented: 'Your mother is very anxious, couldn't you have written as well, instead of just sending a package?'[56]

A few days after his mother's unspoken reproach, the letter she had almost given up on finally arrived from Blackheath. In no less than twenty-
two pages, Ivens described at length everything that had happened to him
in Australia. Despite his long silence, he still seemed to place great importance on his mother's approval and continued to swing between a need for
her appreciation and an urge to distance himself. About his relationship
with Helen, he wrote: 'The last eighteen months things haven't been so
good between us. All kinds of reasons. Mostly my fault and restlessness... I
don't think that it will ever come good between us again. It's a shame, because it hurts both parties, but it wouldn't be good to drag on something
that has no vitality or future either. It seems that Helene hasn't mentioned it
to you and she doesn't want to, not to anyone. So please don't let on in the
letters you write to her either. It is all very difficult, especially for her.' He
didn't add that he already had a new long-term girlfriend and wrote
vaguely: 'I was living in a boarding house but was well looked after.'[57]

His mother answered straight away: 'How happy I was to get your letter.' She also comforted him: 'As far as your opinion about the Dutch East
Indies is concerned, it is shared by a lot of Dutch men and women, believe
you me.' She thanked him for the two hundred and fifty dollars he had sent
her, but told him that before sending anything else he needed to look after
himself 'PERFECTLY WELL'. 'You won't forget now, will you?'[58] Jitske van
de Berg, the former manager of the Kalverstraat branch of Capi and virtually one of the family, informed Ivens: 'Ma perked right up after receiving
your letter and we discussed it over and over... She really did suffer a great
deal from your poor correspondence. That's not meant as a reproach. We all
know what a bad writer you are and how well-meaning you are and what
with the war and the bad connections.'[59]

'Hardly a week passes without the rattling of a Dutch skeleton in the Federal parliament,' wrote the Australian newspaper the *Sunday Times* on August 18, 1946, and this time the skeleton was INDONESIA CALLING! The
Australian censors had allowed domestic screenings of the film, but banned
its export for diplomatic reasons. The Liberal opposition expressed their
doubts about Ivens's latest product, while Labor minister Frazer declared
laconically: 'I have seen the film and there is no Communist propaganda in
it.'[60] Three months later, the Labor Party won new elections and the entire
cabinet viewed INDONESIA CALLING! and revoked the export ban.

One of the first countries to buy the film was the Soviet Union. Tom
Brandon of Garrison Film, the New York distributor of THE SPANISH EARTH
and THE 400 MILLION, took charge of international sales. INDONESIA CALL-
ING! reached unions and leftist organizations, but Ivens was more con-

cerned about the film being shown in Indonesia itself and dispatched two copies to Java by courier. Ivens would have preferred to go there himself as well. In March he informed the Indonesian government that he would welcome an invitation. He heard nothing in reply. After he and Marion Michelle tried and failed to book a passage to Europe on November 1, he again asked the Indonesians to provide an answer by January 1, 1947.[61] By the end of 1946 there was still no news from Java, and he now decided to accept the offer of work that had reached him through Tom Brandon in New York: a documentary for the Czechoslovak government, based on Maurice Hindus's book praising the rapid development of the new Czechoslovakia, *Bright Passage*.[62] Hindus was an American who had made a name for himself before the war with laudatory books about the Soviet Union. Ivens decided to return to Europe and travel on to Prague after first re-establishing his contacts in London, Amsterdam and Paris.

He had been in Australia for almost two years and Sydney's Woolloomooloo Quay was the scene of an emotional farewell as he and Marion boarded the Otranto. Australian and Indonesian friends waved goodbye. Standing by the railing on the upper deck, Ivens took the cover from the book *The Ten Best Filmplays* – red on the outside, white on the inside – tore it in half and held the two halves up side by side to make the flag of the Republic of Indonesia. 'Merdeka!' the slogan of Indonesian independence, sounded from the quay.

The Otranto, an old tub full of Italian POWs, had been at sea for one day when an invitation for Ivens to visit Indonesia reached Australia. The message was conveyed to him when the Otranto put into Melbourne. Although torn, Ivens decided to stay on board and travel to Indonesia after fulfilling his obligations in Czechoslovakia.[63] The Otranto sailed on to Perth and Colombo, and Ivens used his time on board to develop detailed plans for the organization of the Indonesian film industry. He explained his proposals in two long letters to Prime Minister Sjahrir. The plan had two key features: the foundation of an Indonesian National Film Board on the Canadian and Australian models, and the organization of an International Film Brigade to convey expertise and organize foreign support for the Republic. It also included proposals for educational and instructional films, the formation of mobile projection units and countless other practical matters. Ivens offered his services as co-ordinator for the execution of this plan.[64]

Conditions on the Otranto were primitive. 'No bar, no alcohol,' noted Ivens. He had to share a small cabin with twelve men, Michelle slept in a crowded women's cabin, and for the Italian prisoners the conditions were even worse. Using a few old records and the loudspeaker system, Michelle organized a daily hour of classical music. While the sounds of violins dissipated over the waves of the Indian Ocean, Australia and Indonesia disappeared further and further behind the horizon. Temporarily, thought Joris Ivens, but he would never see Indonesia with his own eyes.

16 The Uncle Behind the Iron Curtain (1947-1950)

'A sharp face, lightly tanned and used to the outside air. Bushy hair, dark, with touches of gray. Hardly aged. This is how Joris Ivens appears before us at a press conference at the Schiller... He speaks thoughtfully, tentatively, with difficulty even,' according to one of the journalists. Another referred to Ivens's blue and red tie, which 'went well' with his 'brown American-style suit'.[1]

After four weeks on the Otranto and a week in London, Ivens and Michelle arrived at Amsterdam Central Station on February 22, 1947. They took a room at the Schiller on the Rembrandtplein, and for several weeks Ivens was too busy to take a nostalgic stroll through the city.

He met with his brother Hans, who was working in Heineken's legal department and was on the verge of leaving for a three-year detachment in Egypt. Hans had become a great admirer of his older brother and had postponed his departure in order to see him. In Nijmegen, Ivens and Michelle spent a few nights at his sister Thea's, and twice visited his mother at her old people's home. For Ivens it was 'just long enough to brush my memories with my fingertips and turn away from them again'.[2] Mother and son spoke Dutch, so Marion Michelle wasn't able to follow the conversation. She was still rather impressed by this self-confident seventy-six year old. Dora Ivens gave her son's new girlfriend a warm welcome but told Thea: 'I think it would be better for George not to get married anymore, it always goes wrong anyway.'[3] Fourteen months later she died. In that time Ivens wrote to her regularly and sent money, but he postponed plans to drop by again until it was too late.

Ivens had received mail from his old love, Anneke van der Feer, in Australia in 1945, and they had gradually begun writing to each other more frequently. Anneke confessed 'that you're my best friend in all the world and all the things from the old days are still there, and are good the way we see them. I knew that, of course, but it's clearer to me now. Bye love, I have lots of plans and am busy working and hope that things are like that for you too. Lots of love, I sit up and wag my tail. Your Puppy.'[4]

While still on board the Otranto, Ivens had wondered about the political situation in Amsterdam and decided to entrust the publicity surrounding his arrival to Van der Feer. He would discuss the 'tactics and contents of speeches and special articles' with her after arriving. Van der Feer's studio on the fourth floor of Oudezijds Achterburgwal 192 was one of the first addresses Ivens and Michelle visited in Amsterdam. From the Otranto, Ivens had written to Hans: 'In Holland I don't want to represent just one party, but promote unity between the progressive parties.'[5] This position coincided with the policy of the CPN, the Communist party of the Netherlands, which aimed for collaboration between Communists and Social Democrats. Ivens's goal was more precisely defined. 'All indications are that I'm coming at the right moment: there's a crisis in the documentary film world in Europe and I will help give it more direction for the future.' Leftist artists and intellectuals had been disillusioned by the lack of political reforms after the war. 'There is something of an international crisis among artists: some are creeping back into their shell, others are returning to *l'art pour l'art* – but there are some who are more active with their art and their work, and want to do their bit for the development of their country.'[6]

During his short stay in London, Ivens had brought himself up to date on the British film world. He visited Ealing Studios, where the directors Alberto Cavalcanti and Harry Watt worked, and spoke with John Grierson's most faithful disciple, Basil Wright, who later characterized the British documentary of the day by saying: 'Like all movements in the arts, you start by being wild men, then you become established, and then you become old-fashioned... I think by 1946, 1947, we were over the peak.'[7] 'We' being the documentary filmmakers of Grierson's school.

What did Ivens have to say to his fellow documentary filmmakers and artists in Holland and Europe in these difficult circumstances? Speaking to a full house in Amsterdam's Kriterion Theater, he stuck to the documentary's social and admonitory roles, as illustrated by THE SPANISH EARTH and THE 400 MILLION. He saw the main scope for improvement in formal aspects, and spoke approvingly of the narrowing gap between fiction and nonfiction that had taken place during the war in Hollywood and also in England, where more and more documentary filmmakers were now making fiction films that were firmly anchored in reality. He cited David Lean's BRIEF ENCOUNTER as a good example of such a film. Inversely, documentaries needed to take on elements of the fiction film if they were to become more than just 'illustrated dryness'. Harry Watt's THE OVERLANDERS could serve as a model: it was 'a documentary, but with the pace and dramatic structure of a fiction film'.[8] Since Ivens had just returned from faraway Australia, he had probably not yet seen the marvelous works of the Italian neorealists. The fame of Rosselini's OPEN CITY was only just beginning to spread in Western Europe.

Although the presentation at the Kriterion was co-sponsored by the Holland-Indonesia Association, Ivens wanted to avoid new difficulties with the

Dutch authorities and showed part of ZUIDERZEE and Paul Rotha's film about housing in England, LAND OF PROMISE, instead of INDONESIA CALL-ING! He only showed INDONESIA CALLING! for cadres of the CPN, and in the artists' club De Kring.[9]

Ivens reported the CPN members as being less enthusiastic about INDO-NESIA CALLING! than he had expected. Communist writer Theun de Vries met with Ivens at the time but was later unable to recall the course of events surrounding the Indonesia film. He did say: 'The Dutch abroad, especially artists, escaped from the tutelage of the party and were viewed with some degree of suspicion.'[10] Although Ivens's return might not have been met with jubilation, the party was favorably disposed and the party daily *De Waarheid* printed no less than four articles about him in just two weeks. Un-der the headline 'Freedom's Filmmaker' it approvingly described his deci-sion to resign as 'the only logical conclusion' given the situation in Indonesia. Other papers, such as the *Algemeen Handelsblad, Het Parool* and *Het Vrije Volk*, were unequivocally positive about his visit to Holland. They did not write about the Indonesia film for the simple reason that, beyond a select few, no one in Holland knew of its existence.[11]

In the memoirs he wrote as an old man, Ivens misrepresented this visit to Amsterdam: 'I could not stay in Holland for long. In Amsterdam I was a pa-riah, a traitor. With my resignation I had snubbed the queen, with INDONE-SIA CALLING! I had betrayed my country. I was attacked and slandered from all sides. Even the Dutch Communist party disagreed with me. To them I was nothing more than an adventurer.' The very friendly reception he en-countered was incompatible with his growing conviction that he had been vilified in Holland since the early thirties. Although the important Amster-dam dailies had not published a word of criticism about his work, he com-plained only six months later in a letter to his mother about 'spiteful, short-sighted film critics in Holland' who only saw him as a political figure. 'And they don't even know what kind of films I am still going to make, with more artistry and permanent worth than they would ever be capable of under-standing.'[12] Had his devout mother sent him a clipping from some Catholic newspaper or other, or was he still referring to the critics from the thirties?

Even the Dutch authorities did not place the slightest obstacle in his path. In Australia, of course, a number of Dutch officials had raised a furore about his resignation, and others had set their minds on vengeance, but these things only became apparent later, when the Cold War was in full swing and INDONESIA CALLING! had become a stick to beat the Communist dog. In early 1947 the Ivens issue was already the subject of machinations behind the scenes in The Hague, the seat of Dutch government. Even before he landed, the Ministry of Foreign Affairs had written to the Ministry of Justice: 'Possibly there are grounds for the instigation of a judicial procedure for anti-Dutch activities against the involved upon his arrival in the Netherlands.'[13] Nothing happened though, and in The Hague Ivens met with the permanent secretary of the Ministry of Arts and Science, who 'virtually invited' him 'to return to Holland to help get the film industry back on its feet', as Ivens wrote at the time. He considered it 'not for me, it's a penpusher's job, and I want to go on making films myself'. The offer surprised him. He remarked to the permanent secretary that it was 'quite a leap' for the government to make. More Dutch offers followed. Nederlands Volksherstel, an aid organization for national recovery, asked him to make several short films about the Dutch West Indies, but he answered dryly that he had declined 'in the East only last year'.[14] And he still had his commission in Czechoslovakia.

After stopping at Paris *en route*, Joris Ivens and Marion Michelle traveled on to Prague, where they moved into the Alcron Hotel. They were ready to make their contribution to building socialism in Eastern Europe.

At the end of the war, Roosevelt, Churchill and Stalin had divided the continent into spheres of influence, leaving the Soviet Union free to play a dominant role in the countries the Red Army had won from the Germans. The Allies had agreed that free elections would be held, but small Moscow-backed Communist parties used manipulation and terror to seize power in Bulgaria, Rumania, Hungary and Poland. Events took a different course in Czechoslovakia, which had been a modern industrial nation and a parliamentary democracy before the war. In free elections held in 1946, the Communist party won 38% of the vote and a coalition was formed under Communist leadership. Czechoslovak democracy remained operative until February 1948, when it was suspended on the orders of the Kremlin. Tito's Yugoslavia was Communist as well. There the Germans had been driven out without the Red Army and this allowed the country to adopt a more independent position.

While the East came under Soviet control, Western Europe oriented itself toward the United States and was reconstructed along capitalist lines with aid from America's Marshall Plan. In the course of 1947 the estrangement between East and West changed into outright hostility. 'Give my love to everyone, all my nephews, from their uncle 'behind the iron curtain', as shortsighted Americans and Englishmen call this part of the world,' wrote Ivens to his mother.[15]

From Prague, Ivens traveled with Lubomir Linhart, the director of Czechoslovak State Film, to the May 1 celebration in the Yugoslav capital Belgrade.

Ivens showed INDONESIA CALLING! and wrote to a friend in Australia: 'You will be happy to know that Marshall Tito has seen the film and that he said it was very good.'[16] Delegates from all over Eastern Europe had come to Belgrade for the festivities and a plan was hatched to expand the film about Czechoslovakia with parts about Yugoslavia, Bulgaria and Poland. Béla Balázs made unsuccessful attempts to involve Hungary in the project.[17] From Yugoslavia, Ivens and Linhart went straight to Sofia for further negotiations. They were received there by Ivens's old acquaintance Georgi Dimitrov, now head of the People's Republic of Bulgaria. Ivens explained the project with gusto and Dimitrov smiled: 'I can almost see the film before me.' He promised his undivided support.[18]

Prague became the base for a four-country project with the working title, 'Four New Democracies', later changed to THE FIRST YEARS. 'The whole enterprise as such was under the control of the party,' according to Ivens.[19] He was made director and Michelle became the scriptwriter. It was to be a four-part film consisting of a poetic depiction of agriculture in Bulgaria, an epic account of Yugoslav youth, a docudrama about Polish industrialization, and finally a didactic section about the history of Czechoslovakia.

The first leg of this Eastern European tour began in July 1947 in Radilova, a poor Bulgarian peasant village with white cottages surrounded by tobacco and sunflower fields, near Pestera at the foot of the Rhodope Mountains. The story was based on the daily hardships of the farmer Todor, his wife Stojna and their family. Like the other inhabitants of Radilova, the family struggled with drought. But then the village dreamer lay his ear to the ground and discovered underground water. The hydroelectric dam the government had built nearby enabled them to pump up the water with electric pumps. As the commentary explained: 'the water has waited centuries for socialism to come and make it possible to tap it'. The cameras captured an idyll of poor peasants in an ancient village being touched by the ideas of a new age.

From Bulgaria they went straight to Yugoslavia. In accordance with his trusted formula, Ivens traced the experiences of a main character, Marko. After filming in Marko's fishing village on the island of Vis, the film crew set up at a railway bridge under construction on the Bosna River, sixty miles north of Sarajevo in the mountains of Bosnia. Here two hundred thousand young workers were building the Sarajevo-Samac railroad. 'A typical Yugoslav group comes down the road,' wrote an onlooker. 'Colorful and vibrant, a column of young men and women in gray and brown overalls, marching along, with their shovels bouncing on their shoulders and singing at the tops of their voices. Above their heads a riot of colorful material, bright flags of red, white and blue and the five-pointed star. By the side of the road, a group of young men momentarily stop work to greet the newcomers. Some-one is playing an accordion. Someone shouts and the others take up the cry, 'Long live Tito!' and *'Brastvo Jedinstvo'*, fraternity and unity. Ivens and his men are there to film it. Now follow the eye of the camera to the next scene, a glimpse of the struggle for the bridge, as convincing as reality itself. You see the barracks wall, a youth from a new brigade on his knees by his baggage, stroking his shaven head with his hand somewhat regretfully– his wavy locks fell into the dust a few minutes earlier at the hands of a youthful bar-ber and under the all-seeing eye of Ivens's camera.' The reporter continued: 'Beyond the laundry on the line is the actual subject. The Bridge, tall con-crete columns, wooden scaffolding, iron girders, going up and down, hang-ing in balance, somehow ending up in place, pushed and pulled without the help of cranes, young men pushing wheelbarrows, young men driving piles with primitive wooden stampers, whereas machines are used for most modern bridges. Beneath it, the Bosna, a narrow stream after a hot sum-mer.'[20]

Even in the forests and mountains of Yugoslavia, Ivens kept up with world politics and wondered anxiously: 'Will we be on time with our film? The American newspapers are full of war, war and war. France could tip the balance. Us here, the four democracies, working for our plans and our fu-ture. Strong, healthy people who believe in themselves and not in the help of selfish gentlemen from the stock exchanges.'[21]

Traveling along the Adriatic coast, an incident led Ivens to see himself as a victim of sabotage. The crew's truck had gone into a garage in Split for re-pairs on the brakes, but when they tried to drive up a hill afterwards, the steering malfunctioned. 'We were almost killed,' said Michelle.[22] It was a fact that right-wing extremist Croats were doing everything they could to undermine Tito's regime.

In Belgrade they met Anneke van der Feer, who had come in search of 'Flip', her Serb lover from before the war, who now occupied a high post in Yugoslavia. 'I heard that he has remarried and that was awfully horrible for a while,' she wrote to Ivens, 'but it won't stop me from continuing our good comradeship if I get a chance'.[23] Back in Amsterdam she mounted a small ex-hibition about Yugoslavia, with her own watercolors and photos of the youth brigades and the reconstruction of Sarajevo. Her later work, mainly made in summery Zeeland, was painted in a somewhat Impressionistic style. She remained a faithful member of the CPN and died in Amsterdam of heart disease in January 1956.

The film crew moved on to Warsaw, a city that had been almost completely destroyed in the Second World War. Seven hundred thousand inhabitants had died, and after the 1944 uprising the Germans had blown up the houses and buildings one by one. 'From my window I see nothing but devastated buildings – the whole city is leveled. No matter how much one had heard of the terrible destruction, the reality comes as a great shock,' Marion Michelle wrote[24] Under these conditions the drive and spirit of the reconstruction were all the more impressive. The population lived in cellars and ruins, but were surprisingly well dressed. Visitors coming to the city from Czechoslovakia were astonished by the food on sale; three years after the war, next to nothing was available in Prague and the atmosphere was somber and drained.[25]

In the Polish episode of THE FIRST YEARS the idea of a documentary with a storyline centered on one individual was taken to an extreme. It actually became a fiction film experiment, a docudrama, with semi-professional actress Jadwiga Wolanska taking the main role against a documentary and realistic background. In Amsterdam at the start of 1947, Ivens had defended a point of view that scarcely recognized a boundary between fiction and nonfiction. Now he endeavored to put these ideas into practice.

From his earliest cinematic attempts, Ivens's ambitions had extended to fiction film. In the twenties he had planned THE FLYING DUTCHMAN, and BREAKERS was followed by a series of unexecuted plans for fictional or semifictional films: TILL EULENSPIEGEL, LA CONDITION HUMAINE, THE WHITE ROSE. Fiction was also an important element in the uncompleted 'frontier film' for New York University. In 1941 he and Donald Ogden Stewart did preparatory work in Hollywood for the semi-fictional JIMMY JONES – GOOD NEIGHBOUR; a few years later he was involved as a consultant in THE STORY OF GI-JOE and as co-producer in WOMAN OF THE SEA. It was as if he were merely waiting for an opportunity to cross the boundary into genuine fiction. Despite this, he still called the Polish part of THE FIRST YEARS a documentary and the leading lady was not even given a credit.

In Poland he was immediately confronted with a major directorial problem. He didn't speak Polish and Wolanska did not speak any foreign languages at all, so he had to do everything through an interpreter. The film's story was about ordinary people overcoming personal problems by committing themselves to socialist development. The main character is a piano teacher who lost her home, her husband and her child in the war. In the first sequence she walks through the ruins of Warsaw and visits a trial where, to her satisfaction, war criminals are sentenced to death. Then on to Katowice in Silesia, a region from which almost the entire German population was expelled after 1945. A number of members of the Polish film crew actually refused to go there, convinced as they were that the heart of Poland lay in Warsaw and not in the former German territories.[26] Wolanska is deeply af-

fected by her losses and feels little enthusiasm for her new job in the laboratory of a steelworks. The workers are highly motivated, because their steel
will be used to reconstruct the devastated capital. The gloomy widow shuts
out her workmates but thaws when she sees the dedication with which they
try to make up for the lost production caused by an accident in Furnace 3.
The magnificent images of the genuine blast-furnace accident only emphasize that Ivens is at his best as a documentary filmmaker and not as a fiction
director. The film moves on to an engagement party. Someone plays bun-
gling piano. Wolanska strikes a chord to show how it should be done, then
makes her way through the darkness to the factory to see how Furnace 3 is
holding up. The end.

Ivens ran the work in Katowice from his room in the Polonia Hotel,
where the wall was covered with schedules and lists. He got up every morning between six and six thirty to plan the day. He liked to drink until the
early hours and was the life of the party, but in the morning it was time to
work. After breakfast the crew left for the factory in the back of a truck.

Far away in Nijmegen, Ivens's mother suffered an acute cardiac thrombosis
on May 12, 1948. Thea Ivens did not know that her brother was in the south
of Poland and sent a telegram to director Elmar Klos's film company in
Prague, an address Ivens had provided. Presumably Klos was unable to
read the Dutch telegram. Dora Ivens died that night and the funeral was
held two days later. A new telegram – 'Ma died suddenly May 13, Thea' –
was now sent to Ivens's own office in Prague at Jindrisska 34, an address
probably found on one of his letters to his mother. Both telegrams were for-
warded to Warsaw but Ivens did not receive them until May 24, by which
time he was back in Warsaw at the Bristol Hotel. He wired Nijmegen at once
and Thea answered with a detailed letter about the circumstances of their
mother's death. 'I didn't know where to reach you, but you must take solace
in the fact that you could never have got here in time, it all happened much
too quickly.'[27]

Accordingly the most remarkable passage in Ivens's memoirs reads: 'In
1949 [Should be 1948, HS] while in Poland shooting THE FIRST YEARS – I was
filming in the vicinity of Wroclaw – I received a letter from the Dutch government requesting that I report to the embassy in Warsaw. I immediately
thought of my passport. [At that time there were no problems with his passport.] But no, it was about my mother, she had died two weeks earlier. For
two weeks they had done nothing to alert me. Even though it would not
have been difficult for them to locate me, they only needed to telephone the
Polish Ministries of Education or Culture to find out where I was. They had,
however, neglected to take any steps at all. If I had been alerted on time,

Director Ivens and cameraman Ivan Fric filming near the bridge over the Bosna for the ill-fated Yugoslavian section of THE FIRST YEARS (1947). PHOTO MARION MICHELLE.COLL. MARION MICHELLE / EFJI

they could not have refused my right to go to Nijmegen for the funeral. As far as Holland was concerned I was still a traitor, a dangerous man whom they mistrusted.'[28]

What could have happened? Although Thea did not mention it in her letter to Joris of May 28, the family may have contacted the Ministry of Foreign Affairs after not receiving a reply from Prague. But even the most diligent of diplomatic services could not have succeeded in finding Ivens in a remote corner of Poland when the family did not even know which country they should look in. Was Ivens's sense of guilt about not being with his mother when she died so great that he needed a scapegoat?

After completing the Polish section of THE FIRST YEARS in the summer of 1948, Ivens and Michelle lived in Prague for one and a half years. They moved into the former Turkish embassy, a large villa in Badeniho, where other guests also found accommodation. Catherine Duncan, their friend from Australia who now lived in Paris, moved in with them for seven months to write the commentary for THE FIRST YEARS, and that summer Bertolt Brecht and Hanns Eisler also came to stay. In the United States they had been questioned by the House Un-American Activities Committee and had left rather than await further developments. They would both settle in East Berlin soon after. Prague was the scene of a heartfelt reunion. Also present was Willi Münzenberg's former right-hand man, Otto Katz, alias Breda, alias André Simone, now a press functionary for the Czechoslovak Ministry of Foreign Affairs and one of the editors of the party newspaper *Rude Pravo*.

Ivens, Eisler, Brecht and Katz: in the preceding two decades they had taken virtually the same route, with stops in Berlin, Moscow, Paris and Hollywood. For Otto Katz Prague was the end of the line, a few years later he would be sentenced to death in the infamous Slansky Trial, along with ten other, mainly Jewish, top functionaries of the Czechoslovak Communist party. After more than twenty years' faithful service to Moscow, Otto Katz was hung on December 3, 1952.

Things had not progressed that far in the summer of 1948, but the Communists had seized power in Prague in February of that year and effectively put an end to the democracy. Stalin had had more than enough of that bourgeois nonsense in Czechoslovakia, and furthermore an opinion poll had indicated that the Communists were likely to suffer serious losses in the upcoming elections. Non-Communist ministers were removed from the cabinet, party militias roamed the streets, and the popular Minister of Foreign Affairs, Jan Masaryk, son of Czechoslovakia's founding father and the target of an earlier Communist bomb attack, was found dead beneath his window in the Czernin Palace one week after the coup. Jumped, according to the Communists; pushed, according to the rest of Czechoslovakia. Some people named Otto Katz as one of those involved in Masaryk's death.[29] Events in Prague in February 1948 caused great indignation in the West, but Joris Ivens fully backed the political changes, and Marion Michelle stood behind Joris. 'We were terribly naive,' she said later.[30]

During the decisive days in Czechoslovakia, they were in Poland with the film crew. On March 10 Ivens wrote to his mother: 'Don't let the newspaper reports about the countries here disturb you, things are going very well. The masses feel better now than they did before the war and have much more scope. Only a small group feel that their days are over and scream loudly that all the new things are bad.' In an earlier letter he had written: 'People will say they're just Soviet satellites. It's not true, Ma – a powerful and magnificent new national life is emerging here. A rebirth of fabulous, optimistic people longing for a free and undisturbed life.'[31] He commented on the Prague takeover in the Czechoslovak part of THE FIRST YEARS. Images of bourgeois politicians consulting in the lobby of the parliament were accompanied by the words: 'They were making plans for an old-time betrayal... And we understood when the anti-planners [opponents of the Five-

Year Plan] provoked a political crisis, it was their last attempt to restore the old order.' Images of workers' militias followed: 'Our people came from the factories, from the fields and workshops. From the Tatra to the Bohemian forest, we came out to defend the Republic.' It was true that the Communist seizure of power went together with big demonstrations, but in reality the sly 'anti-planners' were sidelined politicians, and they were only dangerous because they still enjoyed the support of a significant portion of the population. Ivens simply saw wicked oppressors against whom the masses rose up as one man.

The Czechoslovak section of THE FIRST YEARS was made up of three parts. A cinematically uninteresting history of the country up to 1918, composed mainly of shots of old prints, was followed by 'A Lesson about Shoes' about the nationalization of the Bata factories in Zlin. A curiosity from another era was the elevator with built in boardroom, which slid from one part of the factory to another at the push of a button to allow the director to take control on the spot. The commentary mentioned the omnipotent Bata's Nazi sympathies, but not the fact that his workers had been the country's best paid and had worked the shortest hours before the war. The third section, 'Liberation', was a heavy-handed propagandist apology for Communist policies in postwar Czechoslovakia. A fourth section – an animated sequence in which puppets made by Jirí Trnka and one of his pupils seem to have ridiculed the Marshall Plan – was rejected by the authorities for unspecified reasons. The reaction of Soviet cineaste Michail Chiaureli to the puppet section is on the record. He told Ivens that making jokes about important and dangerous issues like the Marshall Plan was unacceptable, Chaplin had already made a similar mistake in THE GREAT DICTATOR. Ivens was not particularly impressed by the reprimand, but Trnka's work was not allowed to be used.[32]

Although THE FIRST YEARS closely followed the party line, the production in Prague was still very sluggish. Lubomir Linhart left State Film and thereafter the required material was either delayed or withheld completely. Finally, Ivens complained to the new Minister of Foreign Affairs, Vladimir Clementis.[33]

In the summer of 1948, filmmakers from twelve countries from East and West founded the World Union of Documentary in the Czech town of Mariánské Lázne, with prominent members including Joris Ivens, Henri Storck of Belgium and John Grierson, Paul Rotha and Basil Wright from Great Britain. Ivens had always been a firm advocate of some kind of association of documentary filmmakers. In New York in the summer of 1939, he had already been elected chairman of the Association of Documentary Film

Producers, which vanished without a sound during the war. The World Union of Documentary collapsed soon after its foundation due to conflicts originating in the Cold War. In the sixties, when the antagonism had subsided somewhat, the Association Internationale des Documentaristes was founded, whose committee members included John Grierson, Henri Storck, Joris Ivens and Richard Leacock, with Marion Michelle editing the organization's magazine. Most documentary filmmakers however were probably too busy and too individualistic to really become involved in organizational work. They knew each other from conferences and festivals and belonged to a fairly close-knit network, that only occasionally took on an organized form.

Meanwhile preparations were being made by the Dutch government in The Hague for a cold war against Ivens. In the course of 1947, the Ministry of Justice began investigating whether he was guilty of an offence that justified a reduction in the period of validity of his passport or even its confiscation. Memoranda about the conflict in Australia passed from desk to desk and officials formed opinions based upon dubious information. There was only a hazy understanding of what had happened in Australia. One document circulating – entitled 'Information concerning Joris Ivens' and written by a major in military intelligence – contained no less than eighteen factual errors in just forty-three lines.[34]

The conclusion reached was that it was impossible to prosecute Ivens, since any possible offences had been committed in Australia and not in the Netherlands. A decision about his passport proved more difficult. On May 1, 1948 the Ministry of Justice inquired whether the Ministry of Foreign Affairs had taken a position, and on September 28 of that same year, Foreign Affairs described the confiscation of Ivens's passport as 'inopportune'. The same correspondence continued: 'Of course, measures could be taken against Ivens when he returns from abroad and is in our country,' but did not specify what measures these might be.[35]

Joris Ivens noticed almost nothing of this consternation in officialdom until July 1948, when INDONESIA CALLING! was withdrawn from the program of the Locarno Film Festival because of pressure from Holland.[36] Hostilities stepped up on October 20 that year when Ivens applied to the Dutch legation in Prague for an extension of his passport. Passports were normally extended for two years, Ivens was only given three months: orders from The Hague.[37] He asked the secretary of the legation, M.J. Rosenberg Polak, if he might be informed of the grounds for the Dutch government's objections so that he could defend himself. He explained that events in Australia were being presented unfairly in The Hague, and that the accusations against him were either untrue or distorted. Rosenberg Polak asked the Ministry of Foreign Affairs what he should tell Ivens and received the following reply, which he read out to Ivens: 'The activities abroad of the party in question have had, in certain respects, a detrimental effect on the interests of the Kingdom. Some of his actions could have been liable to prosecution if he had committed these actions in Indonesian territory. Accordingly, we see no grounds to provide the party in question with the same facilities as other Dutch citizens abroad whose actions are not detrimental to the interests of the Netherlands and Indonesia.' Somewhat superfluously, Rosenberg Polak added: 'You have a lot of enemies in The Hague.'[38] Foreign Affairs explained to the envoy in Prague that the limited validity of Ivens's passport would allow his location to be monitored. The authorities were worried that he might even pop up in Indonesia, where the struggle was still raging unabated.[39]

The prosecutable actions the ministry was referring to were covered by what was known as the 'hatred-sowing clauses' in the East Indian penal code: 'The public expression of feelings of hostility, hatred or contempt for the Governments of the Netherlands or the Netherlands East Indies is punishable by a term of imprisonment not exceeding seven years.'[40] This gross breach of freedom of speech had been chiefly used to gag rebellious Indonesians, but had now, for the occasion, been declared applicable to Joris Ivens.

In the Cold War atmosphere of the day, The Hague's actions against Ivens were presumably motivated by more than just the issue of Indonesia. In the wake of the indignation about the Communist coup in Prague, politicians in The Hague had begun searching for ways to ensure that nothing comparable happened in Holland. The cabinet discussed the necessity of anti-Communist measures and the general concern was understandable. The CPN had celebrated the Prague takeover with a triumphal meeting in Amsterdam's Concertgebouw, and speaking on behalf of the Communist party, parliamentarian J. Haken had even made the reckless prediction: 'Things will reach that stage here too.'[41] It might not have been coincidental that eight months after 'Prague' – and in that same city – Ivens only received a three-month passport extension. Either way, until spring 1950 his passport was only extended for a few months each time. After this, the skirmishing entered a new phase.

While a long drawn-out conflict developed between the Dutch government and Joris Ivens, he distanced himself remarkably enough from the initial cause of contention, the Republic of Indonesia. In line with the standpoint of the Communist movement, he became convinced that the populist Soekarno government was too right-wing. In September and October 1947 he was still hoping for an imminent departure for Java; the date of departure was later put forward to "next spring".[42] Subsequent developments in Indonesia convinced Ivens to abandon his travel plans.

In the former Dutch colony, negotiations alternated with periods of war, but a tenuous settlement between The Hague and the Republican leaders was approaching. In Madiun on Java a leftist uprising against Soekarno's policies of compromise broke out. The Indonesian Communist party under the leadership of Musso, who had just returned from Moscow, backed the uprising, which was put down by Republican troops. The CPN and Moscow supported their sister party in Indonesia and denounced the transfer of sovereignty to Soekarno, which finally took place in 1949, as 'reinforcing the imperialist grip on Indonesia'.[43] At a screening of INDONESIA CALLING! that same year, Ivens had referred to the beautiful past, 'when the Republic really was an expression of the struggle for the complete independence of Indonesia'. On other occasions he called the country 'a vassal state of American and Dutch capitalists'.[44]

Ivens now turned his attention to China, where the revolution was taking a more favorable course. The Red Army was increasingly forcing the Kuomintang onto the defensive and the Communist party was on its way to absolute power. In the summer of 1948, Ivens wrote to his old acquaintance Zhou Enlai, who would soon become the first premier of the People's Republic of China. 'I would like to come once more to China and see on the spot what are the film needs of Free China and what help could be given to ensure a regular film production, and possibly I could make a documentary film myself, for I have not forgotten my promise to return to your country.'[45]

Such a journey was only possible after the completion of THE FIRST YEARS. Ivens had begun by calling the film 'so ambitious... I might even say sensational, it will be something so completely new in the history of film' and 'the most exciting and profoundest material I ever made for a film'. But with the project approaching completion he said: 'I made a resolution never to make such a film or work that way again.'[46] He was at the mercy of Eastern European bureaucracy and less and less was left of THE FIRST YEARS as time progressed.

The problems began when Stalin excommunicated Yugoslavia in June 1948, as a punishment for Marshal Tito's daring to think for himself. The other Eastern Bloc countries cut off all contact with the 'Titoists' on the Adriatic. Ivens declared to the newspaper *De Waarheid* that when Yugoslavia 'really does go the way of the Marshall countries... well, then I'd have to drop one of my four murals, because it would no longer coincide with reality'.[47] A few minutes of the rushes of the Bosnian railroad were rediscovered in ar-

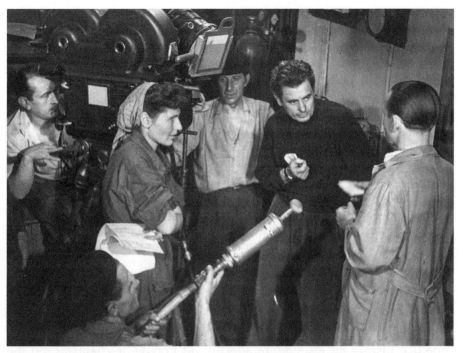

Shooting THE FIRST YEARS in the steelworks of Katowicze in Poland (1948).
Marion Michelle with scarf, Joris Ivens in dark sweater. COLL. MARION MICHELLE / EFJI

chives in Prague in 1996, the rest is still lost. In Czechoslovakia, Jirí Trnka's
puppet sequence was rejected, and the Bulgarians went so far as to demand
a completely new version of the section about their country, claiming that
the picture Ivens gave was not optimistic enough.

In June 1949, Ivens traveled from Prague to Sofia to discuss the Bulgarians' criticism. He could no longer count on an appeal to Georgi Dimitrov,
who was seriously ill in a Soviet sanatorium. The Bulgarian cultural functionaries began by exhausting themselves with self-accusations: it was their
fault that the film hadn't turned out the way they would have liked. They
should have sent better people along with the film crew, people who would
have helped Ivens and his co-workers to see the country 'through other
eyes, looking more toward the future'. Now it was all in minor, whereas it
should have been in major. One of the things that bothered them was the depiction of a birth in Radilova. Ivens showed, as he later explained, 'not the
birth itself, but everything leading up to it. While the pregnant woman lies
in her bed, a restless cow walks around the yard and you see an older
woman boiling water and pacing back and forth excitedly. I showed that the
child was being born in a farmhouse.' The apparatchiks thought that impos-

sible because there were maternity clinics in the villages. 'I said, "Maybe there are, but I didn't see any in that province." That didn't put off the functionaries, who replied, "You have to film the future, that is the reality."'[48]

Ivens was 'not so happy about all their criticism and objections' and found that they were 'not understanding of our cinematographic style', but his dissatisfaction was tempered by the friendliness, warmth and personal attention surrounding him. After all, Bulgaria was 'a young, fresh country'. He was faced with a dilemma. Although he could sympathize with the Bulgarians' wishes to display the newest locomotives, dams and medical posts, he was also attached to his original work, which had concentrated on showing socialism as a new mentality in a primitive village that really existed, and with a storyline that couldn't just be interrupted. Ivens aimed for a compromise. He did not want to 'lose the good formal qualities of the old film' but it had to be 'politically correct'. The Bulgarians conceded that a completely new film was impossible and accepted a solution involving drastic changes to the existing version. Ivens then began making supplementary shots in the countryside with a film crew.[49]

He accepted far-reaching violations of his artistic integrity, but all his disappointments were compensated by his firm conviction that Eastern Europe had history on it's side. In a lecture in Prague he characterized the cinema of capitalist countries as 'decadent, cynical, sexual, cosmopolitan', as 'blunt propaganda' that 'lowers the morale of the masses' and whips them 'up against the Soviet Union and the people's republics', whereas the USSR and the new democracies were the very places where there was hope for art.[50] The most remarkable word in this summary was undoubtedly 'cosmopolitan', which Stalin had introduced as the key word in the anti-Semitic persecution of 1949, which included a number of Ivens's colleagues in the Soviet film world among its victims.[51] Presumably Ivens, the cosmopolitan *par excellence*, only had a vague idea of what Moscow actually meant by this term. He just howled along with the other wolves.

THE FIRST YEARS finally premiered in December 1949 in Prague. That same month Ivens developed severe pneumonia and had to spend a few weeks in a Prague hospital before leaving with Marion Michelle for Paris, where the first screening in the West took place in the Salle Pleyel in March 1950. Joris Ivens addressed his Parisian audience: 'In each of these countries I was given the greatest possible freedom with my work.'[52] A few weeks later he received a letter from Sofia informing him that even the castrated Bulgarian section – including railroad construction, new locomotive, medallions for model workers, hospital, housing construction and steel factory – could no longer be shown. Without informing Ivens beforehand, all copies were recalled from Italy, France, England, India and Hungary.[53] The Poles did not have much faith in THE FIRST YEARS either but limited themselves to a profound silence. It is unlikely that the film was ever shown in Poland.[54] West of the Iron Curtain, the film's blunt stance helped restrict it to the circles of the converted. In a letter to a deeply disappointed Marion Michelle more than a year after the first screening, Ivens observed that THE FIRST YEARS was 'an orphan with a great future, but the time of the future has not come yet'.[55]

17   The Blue Book (1950-1956)

Joris Ivens and Marion Michelle arrived in Paris impoverished and emaci-ated. Everything in Prague had been rationed, making it difficult to eat properly, and they had been paid in Eastern European currency that was worthless in France. After staying in various temporary lodgings, they found a small apartment at 14 rue Grenelle. To regain their strength they took several vacations in Raymond Leibovici's luxurious country house in St. Tropez. A well-known Parisian surgeon with a clinic on the Buttes Chaumont, Leibovici was considered one of the 'surgeons of the left and of the party',[1] and gave them free use of his summer home. He was an intelli-gent, sensitive man, who remained Ivens's physician in Paris for three de-cades and was one of the few people with whom he maintained a confidential relationship. 'I miss Raymond. Of my Paris friends, he is the one who stands out the most. Wonderful man and friend,' he once wrote.[2] Leibovici died in the 1980s.

Ivens took advantage of the break in Paris to collect his own films for the archives of Henri Langlois's Cinémathèque Française. He also studied new work by Western colleagues and re-established old contacts: with Vladimir and Ida Pozner, back from Hollywood and living in the Quartier Latin; and with film historian Georges Sadoul. For many in left-wing film circles, Sadoul's house on the Île Saint-Louis was a second home and the gentle, in-trovert Sadoul was like a father figure. But for Sadoul himself, Joris Ivens was an 'older brother'.[3] Ivens had no grounds for complaint about public in-terest in Paris. Large retrospectives of his work attracted thousands of visi-tors in 1950 and 1951.

This tranquil period came to an abrupt end on May 10, 1950, when Ivens went to the Dutch embassy in Paris to apply for an extension of his passport and discovered that the next round in his battle with The Hague had begun. The Ministry of Foreign Affairs had circulated the following letter to all Dutch missions:

'The Hague, March 30, 1950

I have the honor of informing you that, in early March 1950 in Paris, the Dutch Com-munist film director Joris Ivens publicly showed a version of his 'Zuiderzee' which he had personally augmented with a Communistic ending that changed the tenor of the film to one directed against the Dutch government.

In connection with the above, may I request that, should the party concerned ap-proach you or one of the consulates responsible to you for an extension of the validity of his passport, he only be given a laissez-passer valid for one journey to the Netherlands.

His passport should be cancelled at the same time.

The Minister of Foreign Affairs,
For the Minister,
The Permanent Secretary,
F. d'Ansembourg'

Ivens's passport had been extended for periods of three or four months since 1948, now Foreign Affairs had decided to adopt a more radical course of action. It was difficult to take the justification seriously since the film Ivens 'had personally augmented with a Communistic ending' was the ancient NEW EARTH, and the contentious augmentation was simply the last reel, which dated from 1933. The Dutch consul general in Paris had attended the premiere himself, and United States film critics had declared NEW EARTH second-best foreign film of 1936, ending and all. ZUIDERZEE was nothing more than a pretence. In the Cold War climate, Ivens's stay in Eastern Europe and the Indonesia issue weighed increasingly heavily, and any opportunity to make a case of it was more than welcome.

When Ivens arrived at the Paris embassy on May 10, his passport was seized and he was told that he had to go to The Hague to find out why. Two days earlier he had published a declaration of solidarity with the Hollywood Ten, a group of directors and scriptwriters – including several he knew personally – who had been sentenced to prison for their Communist beliefs. He must have had a definite idea of what awaited him in Holland. Why else the travel papers for a single trip to The Hague? He told the embassy that he had work to do and felt little enthusiasm for a long journey when he didn't even know what The Hague wanted to discuss.[4] He then wrote to his brother Hans for legal advice, enclosing a draft letter to the ministry requesting clarification and dealing with a number of persistent misconceptions about the events in Australia.

In his letter he defended himself against the charge that he had made INDONESIA CALLING! with government money and material, a fallacy that had even made it into the reports of the parliamentary investigative commission on misconduct during the war. Unfortunately, he weakened his case by objecting to 'the idea that I am a politician, whereas I am an artist'.[5] He obviously used his work as a vehicle for emphatic and well-considered political statements, and it was unreasonable to deny others the right to judge these statements on their merits. Nonetheless, the Passport Section of the Ministry of Foreign Affairs was not the appropriate organ for doing so.

What would have happened if Ivens had traveled to the seat of government? Were the authorities planning to follow the American example and call him to account? To try him for transgressions against a dusty, East Indian penal code, even though Holland had meanwhile recognized the Indonesian independence Ivens had pleaded for? Together with the director of Amsterdam's Stedelijk Museum, Willem Sandberg, Hans Ivens tried over the next few months to find out through contacts in the government apparatus what The Hague was really up to. They were informed that a new policy of obstructing the freedom of travel of leftists was in the offing.[6]

On October 11, the issue took an unexpected turn for the better when Ivens's passport was returned in Paris with a three-month extension. In Warsaw on February 7, 1951, he received a new three-month extension and in the years that followed he had to visit a Dutch embassy or consulate every few months in order to extend his passport. It is possible that he sometimes only received a laissez-passer, a document valid for a particular journey. On May 7, 1957, he received an extension of six months. In time this became a year, until April 26, 1961 in Paris, when he was given a passport that was valid for the normal three-year period. From then on, there were no more irregularities.[7]

Since 1948 he had been constantly forced to beg for his extensions at consulates, where the officials pointed out in passing that he was not allowed to enter the service of a foreign state. It was an odd case of harassment for reasons of state and Ivens felt deeply insulted. His sense of aggrievement went so far that he later exaggerated the affair enormously, until the story went that he had been refused a passport for ten years, that he had been forced to remain in Eastern Europe, and that he had been virtually prevented from traveling at all. Three invalid accusations that he leveled at the Dutch authorities so many times that they started believing them themselves.

In fact, throughout the period in question, he was able to move freely between East and West and did so, traveling to a variety of destinations. Between 1950 and 1957 he made countless visits to France, a number to Italy, and several to Austria. He also visited Belgium, Sweden, Finland, China and almost all of Eastern Europe. After the 1950 invitation to take a trip to The Hague, Ivens wisely avoided the Netherlands. Still he did make several advances, such as after the 1953 floods, when he offered through the embassy in Rome to make a public relations film about the disaster for the Dutch government. He also made NEW EARTH available for propaganda purposes abroad without the infamous third reel.[8] As far as is known, he received no answer.

On vacation in the South of France, early fifties. Left to right: Joris Ivens, poet-screenwriter Jacques Prévert and Ivens's doctor Raymond Leibovici. PHOTO MARION MICHELLE. COLL. MARION MICHELLE / EFJI

The French government mistrusted Ivens as well. From the moment he showed himself in Paris, he was under surveillance by agents of the DST, the French intelligence service. He found 'very curious gentlemen' waiting before his door in the mornings. 'It became very annoying and with the help of a fast car borrowed from the doctor I succeeded in losing these gentlemen,' he wrote, describing one such occasion. Marion Michelle's later husband Jean Guyard also recalled plainclothes policemen taking up position in front of their house when Ivens came to visit.[9] The sleuths were actually wasting their time as far Ivens was concerned. He commuted between East and West, occasionally had a drink with Jacques Duclos, the leader of the French Communist party, and even brought the odd letter for him, but none of this amounted to anything; there were specialists for that kind of work. Nonetheless he did use code-like names in his correspondence with Michelle, referring to his passport as 'the blue book', calling Berlin 'Lou' and 'Günther', Warsaw 'Forb', and Moscow 'the big studio'. He also sometimes signed himself 'George', a name they never used. All precautions in case the mail was opened, as it undoubtedly was.[10]

Joris Ivens and Marion Michelle had been inseparable since Australia. INDO-
NESIA CALLING!, the period in the Blue Mountains, THE FIRST YEARS – they
had been through it all together and whenever they were apart an endless
stream of letters passed between them. At such times Ivens would write: 'I
miss you so much. Really, in the end there is only one person, one real
friend, one you can count on in *any* circumstances – only one you can love.'[11]

Nevertheless, a major frustration that often spoiled Marion's Michelle's
mood had arisen between them. In California their relationship had begun
as a great passion, and after being reunited in Australia they immediately
continued in the same vein. Two months later, however, Ivens fell ill and
this marked a definitive change in their relationship. 'Have been gen. upset
because tho' J.s better – almost better than before – we have no s'life, n.y. for
the last 8 mos,' as Michelle wrote in her diary in the summer of 1946.[12] She
interpreted the lack of sexual interest as proof that their love was over and
considered returning to America. Ivens remained as tender as ever and
asked her to go to Czechoslovakia with him. She saw this as a good sign and
consented. His letters were still loving and affectionate, but nothing happened in the bedroom, and this fact gradually became intolerable for her.
She was in her thirties and unwilling to resign herself to a life of celibacy.
Medical check-ups gave Ivens a clean bill of health, and during their stay in
Prague Michelle suggested that he visit the psychotherapist L. Haas.[13] He
did so, albeit without enthusiasm; when problems arose he generally preferred to act as if they weren't there. In several sessions with Dr. Haas, he
nonetheless immersed himself in 'old ghostly influences, youth events, re-
pressed feelings' and 'cobwebs and fictions' in his head.[14] What kind of
ghostly influences could he have been referring to?

Marion Michelle had already racked her brains about the feverish
dreams he had had in Australia. He had told them to her upon awakening
and she had jotted them down. 'French woman in short shirt, black stockings, atmosphere of small French village. I had first talked to some people
and suddenly found myself sitting opposite this woman shaving me. During shaving standing sexually between my legs and twice fooling me by
suddenly cutting me across my cheek and then nose with shaving knife –
but fooling me because at these moments she used fake knife which gave
same sensation as real knife. I investigated and found it to be a sharp
wooden knife with two edges. Then the woman said, 'Let's go on with the
shaving in my house.' I knew that it wouldn't end with shaving but with
sexual relations, and then she brought me into a pretty poor house, up dark
staircases and into a dark room, in which a man rose from a bed when I entered. He looked like Groucho Marx and started to yell angrily at me to get
out. The woman said not to take notice of him because he was a crazy

Dutchman. I woke up at that moment tho' I may have yelled at him upset and angry also, because he was spoiling my fun.'[15]

Marion was unable to reach any conclusions and the sessions with Dr. Haas did not last long enough, but 'fear of bonding' could have been one of the focal points. The rapid and complete disappearance of sexual interest was a recurring theme in Ivens's relationships. His next marriage reached the same stage after just a year,[16] and both his description of his relationship with Helen as a 'fifteen-year friendship' and his remark upon returning from Spain in 1937 that their love had 'lost its vitality' point in the same direction. Whenever intimacy became too great for him and threatened to take on a permanent form, he distanced himself. He may have found erotic satisfaction in brief liaisons that occurred throughout his life. His occasional fantasies of being the father of lots of children and living in a cottage on a hilltop were romantic musings about the beauty of a foreign world. His relationships found their chief expression in collaboration on his work and revolutionary activities, and this left no place for children.

Ivens had informed his brother Hans of his intention to remarry in early 1947. When the plans began to solidify in the autumn of 1950, Marion Michelle, the bride-to-be, wrote to Dr. Haas for advice. He recommended caution.[17] Ivens had gone to Warsaw for work, and the psychoanalysis he and Haas had agreed upon had been indefinitely postponed. Ivens was counting on Michelle joining him in Poland, but she feared a resumption of their old routine and stayed in Paris. 'You could even write to Dr. H. weekly now', she wrote, 'and not just leave it at pious wishes'.[18] They did not see each other for five months and she hoped that this separation would allow them to make a fresh start.

In November 1950, Ivens and the Pole Jerzy Bossak co-directed a documentary for the Polish Documentary Film Studio. The subject was the Second International Peace Congress, which was held in Warsaw. There was good reason for concern about world peace as the Korean War had broken out that summer. After the Japanese capitulation in 1945, the Allies had divided Korea into two zones, with American forces occupying the South and the Soviet Union occupying the North. According to the Yalta agreement, the country was to be reunited after free elections, but North Korea became a Communist state and, despite elections, a pro-American autocracy emerged in democratic South Korea. Finally North Korean troops invaded the South in order to effect a violent reunification under their own conditions. America responded by sending military reinforcements to South Korea. These forces fought under the flag of the UN and were led by Ivens's old foe General Douglas MacArthur. American GIs were soon standing face to face with the soldiers of the Chinese Red Army and World War III seemed imminent, but the superpowers recoiled from escalation, and in 1953 a cease-fire that has now lasted for almost half a century was signed on the 38th parallel.

The Korean War was the focus of attention at the conference, which was organized by the International Peace Council and mainly attended by Communist delegates from numerous countries, supplemented by the inevitable celebrities. Those present in this case included Chilean poet Pablo Neruda, Brazilian novelist Jorge Amado, French scientist Frédéric Joliot-Curie, composer Dmitri Shostakovich, film director Vsevolod Pudovkin and writer Ilya Ehrenburg.

Cinematically speaking, there was little glory to be had. Bossak and Ivens's piece, entitled PEACE WILL WIN, began with skillfully edited newsreel footage about the global situation as seen from Eastern Europe. After VVVC NEWSREELS, NEW EARTH, OUR RUSSIAN FRONT and KNOW YOUR ENEMY: JAPAN, this was the kind of thing Ivens could do with one hand tied behind his back. What chiefly followed was speeches, committee meetings and cheerful delegates greeting each other. Highlight of the film was a speech by an innocent-looking North Korean, Pak Den Ai. Interrupted by shots of falling bombs and dying children, she explained that good people lived in her country and villains in America. The conclusion of this sequence was triumphantly accompanied by a part of Beethoven's Fifth fading into applause. 'One of the easy effects I can't be proud of,' remarked Ivens in the eighties. A review by Polish film historian Jerzy Toeplitz called the film 'a complete artistic triumph'. Even at the time, Ivens was unconvinced and wrote to Michelle: 'people think it is a wonderful film. Dearest, it is not.' The collaboration with co-director Jerzy Bossak had been far from smooth, and the use of Polish as the language of communication had contributed to Ivens feeling somewhat aloof from the production.[19]

During a reception at the Polish National Museum, Ivens noticed an attractive woman sitting barefoot on the stairs, deep in melancholy thought. Vladimir Pozner introduced Ivens to the dreamer, twenty-four-year-old Polish poet Ewa Fiszer. The events that followed have been lost to posterity, but a few weeks later Ivens wrote to Marion Michelle, presumably because of a half-hearted urge to honesty: 'Went for a meal at the Writers' Club with poetess and writers.'[20]

Maria Fiszer, who wrote under the name Ewa, was born on December 20, 1926 and had joined the Polish resistance as a seventeen-year-old schoolgirl. She had been a courier during the Warsaw Uprising of August and September 1944 and became active in the writers' union after the war. Her first volume of poetry *Doswiadczenia* ('Experiences') appeared in 1949, and she translated Sylvia Plath, Paul Éluard and Nazim Hikmet into Polish.

The tone of Ivens's letters to Marion Michelle did not change. He kept her up-to-date on his search for an apartment in Warsaw where they both could live, and in Holland he arranged contacts for the production of a short film she could direct there about Dutch painting, apparently for a series being launched in Eastern Europe.[21] They did not see each other again until April 1951, when they joined up for a tour of a number of Italian film clubs and visited Rome, where Ivens was guest of honor at an enormous May Day demonstration of the Italian Communist party. Michelle always looked back on their weeks together in Italy wistfully, but the hoped-for revival of their relationship did not come and Ivens, who returned to Warsaw, wrote to her: 'We tried, but a decision has to be reached.' It was a decision he had presumably already made for himself, because he added encouragingly: 'Be happy and free and jump around.'[22]

Soon after, however, he was once again 'optimistic as I think of you, of us now', and that summer he wrote: 'Miss you more than ever, in life, in work.'[23] By that time he was in Berlin for his next film, a major production about the Third International Festival of Youth and Students. Ivens asked Michelle to join him. She expected a resumption of the previous state of affairs and telephoned to tell him that she would not be coming after all. Ivens now wrote: 'I was sad – am still sad. Not only sad, very lonely... I think you did the right thing, but it hurts, even more in the future. Darling I want to be with you and you with me and we will get together.'[24]

Michelle's decision not to come may have been the last push he needed because three months later he married Ewa Fiszer, a woman Michelle had never even heard of. She had only wanted to apply pressure in an attempt to force Ivens to seriously consider their problems. But while she continued to hope that things might take a turn for the better, he had already prepared his retreat. She did not hear about his wedding in Warsaw until afterwards and was speechless. She should have known better, because the course of events was strongly reminiscent of the way he had left Helen van Dongen for her.[25]

With Peace Will Win and the film about the Berlin youth festival, Ivens was meanwhile up to his neck in an artistic morass. In The First Years he had already surrendered more control than was compatible with his status as an artist; now he had placed his work completely at the service of Eastern European bureaucracy. Communism was a major new force in the world – especially with the cooperation of the Soviet Union and China – decolonization was progressing rapidly and East and West were at war in Korea. Ivens was convinced that the decisive struggle between socialism and capitalism was imminent and that it was up to everyone to do his bit. He accepted the prospect of a career as court cineaste of Eastern Europe because he was, in his own words, 'politically satisfied' there. Despite being 'sidelined artistically', he was glad to 'be a part of this great whole'.[26]

In the early fifties, the Eastern European cultural climate reached new depths, dominated as it was by Zhdanovism, named after the Soviet Party Secretary Andrei Zhdanov, one of Stalin's confidants, who demanded rigid application of Socialist Realism and an explicit anti-Western stance. Joris Ivens toed the line as well, as Catherine Duncan and Marion Michelle discovered in early 1951 when they asked his opinion of *The Daughter of Ys*, a play they had written about life in a Breton fishing village. 'Children, this play is very far from me,' was his brusque reaction. He advised them to elevate the piece to 'the highest level of human dignity, of love, of community, of a wonderful future, of activity together', by means of '(honest to God) realism, Socialist Realism'. They needed to bring out 'the greatness of the daily life of good people'. Of course there was life and love in the play, waiting and jealousy, the sea as friend and as foe, but that wasn't enough. The fishermen 'must have heard sometime about a war, seen a warship'.[27] Duncan and Michelle carried on undaunted and several of their pieces were broadcast as radio plays by the BBC and French radio.

As victims of gruff criticism, they were in excellent company. Ivens found another expression of Western decadence: THE THIRD MAN, directed by Carol Reed with Orson Welles in one of the leading roles. Ivens mistakenly thought that the film was an American product and found it 'disgusting'. As he explained to the Belgian Communist newspaper the *Rode Vaan*: 'I wonder why directors always find it necessary to dedicate themselves to bringing out degeneration, the negative side of mankind, the blackest pessimism, in short, all the things that the peoples fought against in the last war... THE THIRD MAN presents the woman's idiotic faithfulness to the criminal as a good thing. In fact this is a glorification of evil, of wickedness. The tendency we're dealing with here is the essence of fascist art: the praise of rottenness. A solution is sought in death, in destruction. Faithfulness to the bad man, the criminal, is always preferable to the insight that one has acted wrongly. In THE THIRD MAN it is not the criminal's friend, the man who has realized how horrible his actions were, who is presented favorably, but the woman, who remains true to his memory.'[28]

The International Festival for Youth and Students, held from August 5 to 19, 1951, was an intimidating mass demonstration of Communist self-confidence on the European border where the opposition between East and West was at its most strident: partitioned Berlin. According to the organizers, two million fighters for peace from the GDR and about a hundred other countries participated. There was an atmosphere of unity in the face of a hostile outside world. During the spectacle, Soviet cineaste Ivan Pyryev and Joris Ivens directed the film FRIENDSHIP TRIUMPHS, partly in black and white, partly in color. It was a co-production of Mosfilm in Moscow and the East German DEFA Studio, with Pyryev in charge and Ivens representing the DEFA. The GDR did not have any documentary filmmakers of its own who carried any weight with the overwhelming Soviet film industry.

FRIENDSHIP TRIUMPHS became a monster production with two head directors, three directors, and six others attached to the directorial staff. There were twenty-six camera operators spread over eighteen brigades and outfitted with a jeep each. The result of these efforts was 325,000 feet of rushes: fifty-five hours of film.

Immediately upon arriving in East Berlin, Ivan Pyryev made sure that his presence would no longer be ignored. German cameramen had made the first shots in the preceding days, but Pyryev thought that the rushes lacked what he had noticed in his two days in Berlin: 'Entire streets decorated with pennants and posters, apartments sporting little flags and doves of peace, the Alexanderplatz looking magnificent, pillars with flags and banners, and so on.'[29] FRIENDSHIP TRIUMPHS shows parades, speeches, sport and folk dancing. Walter Ulbricht and Wilhelm Pieck, the general secretary and chairman of the East German Communist party, the SED, look down on their youthful followers from the stage on the Marx-Engels-Platz. Ulbricht and Pieck had been hardened by a decade in Moscow, where they had been responsible for the arrest and execution of numerous German party members living in the USSR, whom they referred to as 'scum'.[30] Among the celebrities adding luster to the festivities this time were Pablo Neruda, Jorge Amado and the Turkish writer Nazim Hikmet. Together with Joris Ivens, they became a regular team that appeared at all kinds of Eastern European congresses throughout the fifties as proof that artists supported the struggle.

Amid all this cheer, the film showed the East working on peaceful development, while the West plunged Korea into barbarism and pushed for war in Germany. In West Germany, where 'fascism was rearing its ugly head, armed with the most modern American weapons', the workers were groaning under unemployment and poverty, according to the commentary. There was also threatening language, specifically directed against West Berlin, whose existence was a thorn in the side of the GDR leaders. 'The flags of the new democratic Germany are now flying here. But they do not yet fly over all of Berlin, because the capital of our fatherland is divided. In the East, the German people rule, in West Berlin it is the American occupiers,' declared the film text. No wonder that *Junge Welt,* the magazine of the East German youth movement wrote: 'Sacred, thorny hatred against those who wish to inflict immeasurable suffering upon us, that is what the film evokes in us. And that is good.' There were also images of West Berlin. On the Kurfürstendamm you saw 'obscene slogans, fat-necked brokers, brothels for the Yanks', yes, 'filth everywhere', while in the East the August night resounded powerfully with: 'Stalin – Stalin – Stalin!'[31] Pyryev and Ivens filmed thirty thousand young people invoking their leader in one voice.

The themes and production circumstances of FRIENDSHIP TRIUMPHS cannot fail to recall that other propaganda film: Leni Riefenstahl's TRIUMPH OF THE WILL. Both films are set in stadiums and both show the individual being submerged in a crowd that submits to its leader. TRIUMPH OF THE WILL is the better film because its austere style owes much to the cinematic language of the avant-garde of the late twenties, whereas FRIENDSHIP TRIUMPHS is little more than formless stodge.

Only five years had passed since Ivens made INDONESIA CALLING! with a cranky amateur camera, and the difference spoke volumes. The earlier work had been a more or less spontaneous document made with people who were directly involved. He gave up a lucrative post to make it and did not earn a cent from the results. It was true that he had been working for the movement in Spain, China, the United States and Australia, still, he had always been able to bend the work to his personal vision. In Berlin he filmed 'endless rows of happy, determined youth'[32] with equal conviction but had been reduced to a cog in the Eastern European propaganda machine. This was compensated by the fact that, after all the setbacks in America and Australia, he was finally there where he was truly appreciated, in the socialist camp. 'I was very devoted to the party, the party made my existence possible and I felt protected by it.'[33] But those who wish to keep the party's love must be willing to serve it.

After shooting FRIENDSHIP TRIUMPHS Ivens spent ten days in Warsaw before proceeding to Moscow for the editing. He tried and failed to arrange his marriage to Ewa Fiszer during this short stopover, although the engaged couple were allocated an apartment in Warsaw. In Moscow Ivens applied to the Soviet Minister of Cinematography for four days' leave to marry in Warsaw. 'Of course, I am requesting this only when it is possible to arrange things so that the work does not suffer from this brief absence, realizing as I do that the completion of the festival film remains my primary task and responsibility.'[34] He was granted permission and Joris Ivens and Ewa Fiszer married on October 21, 1951. The bridegroom returned immediately to

Moscow and Ewa joined him several weeks later. They moved into the National Hotel opposite the Kremlin and remained in the Soviet Union for several months.

To a degree, Ivens's decision to marry was a drastic attempt to resolve his problems. He would now change and become a dedicated husband, 'take on relaxed work, live in a house with a family', take care of Ewa and 'help' her.[35] Ewa Fiszer represented the elevated world of poetry, a realm which he found especially intriguing and to which she seemed to possess the key. She was the vulnerable poetess, someone for whom the chaos of everyday reality was almost too much. Ivens wrote: 'As a woman, Ewa was terribly fragile. She was very moody and she suffered from frequent anxiety attacks. She often sank into pessimism, and then she would be critical of everything. She lived in constant fear of the insignificant aspects of life. Something simple like going to the station to buy a ticket was enough to get her into a state. If the clerk at the ticket office happened to be rude to her she would take off. Then someone else would have to do it for her.' Fiszer had never gotten over the Warsaw Uprising. Those dark days returned constantly in her poems, memories like the one of a wounded friend dying in her arms in a dark cellar when she was just seventeen. The whispering of the dead scared her at night. As he had with Germaine and Helen, Joris Ivens adopted the role of protector. Ida Pozner, who was a good friend of Ewa's for more than forty years, called her 'intelligent, charming, beautiful and impractical' and reported that Joris felt a great sense of responsibility for her, but was also afraid of her instability. He tried to make her happy; she was only satisfied when he stayed with her and did not go traveling.[36]

Ivens had not been to Moscow since early 1936 and although much had changed, many things were still the same. Nowhere had World War II cost as many lives as in the Soviet Union and reconstruction was a gigantic task. The constant factor was that Joseph Stalin was still in power and in this very period his paranoia had reached new heights, with tens of thousands again being dragged off to camps in Siberia. Foreigners were suspect by definition and Soviet citizens did not dare visit the National Hotel to see people like Joris Ivens and Ewa Fiszer. Only Nazim Hikmet, who was living in exile in Moscow, and the writer Ilya Ehrenburg dared to receive them at home. Even Ivens's old Mezhrabpom colleague Vsevolod Pudovkin avoided private contact, alhough they had met regularly at congresses and film festivals in the preceding years. At a dance he whispered the reason for not inviting them to his place in Ewa's ear: 'Too dangerous.'[37]

Dom Kino, the House of Film, organized an Ivens retrospective and the Dutch guest set about writing an article on 'Film in the Fight for Peace', in which he described how the national film industries in Western Europe were being destroyed by Marshall aid and how the silver screen was being occupied by the Americans. He criticized the 'scandalously anti-Communist film by Sartre: Les Mains Sales', but 'the greatest crime in the build up to war' had been committed by John Ford with his film This is Korea! Ivens was referring to a documentary that Ford had made for the American navy. Ivens identified another 'propagandist for the warmongers' in former colleague Lewis Milestone. He called his film Okinawa a glorification of war and despicable murder by the marines.[38] It was in fact a run-of-the-mill film about the World War II battle, and had been made by Leigh Jason and not by Milestone at all. The swipe at Milestone was particularly remarkable considering that the director of Russian Front had stuck by threatened Hollywood colleagues during the McCarthy period, something that could not be taken for granted in the Cold War climate of the day. It was as if Ivens felt obliged to explicitly distance himself from his American past now that the Kremlin had decided that the United States had not been a true ally in the Second World War, and had only set out to 'strengthen imperialism and throttle democracy'.[39]

Ivens was determined to become a good husband. He and Fiszer moved into Podwale 15M7, a two-room apartment on the first floor of a newly renovated complex in a former military museum, with a view of the old city walls of the medieval center of Warsaw. It was only a few minutes' walk to the writers' club, where they ate almost every day. Despite love and good intentions, the marriage was doomed. Ivens was soon entangled in the familiar conflict between solicitousness and a desire to escape, and the latter finally won out.

After the premiere of Friendship Triumphs in Berlin on April 30, 1952, he went looking for work closer to home. That summer he directed a color reportage of the Fifth Bicycle Race for Peace, from Warsaw to Prague via Berlin. He himself immediately classified the forty-five-minute result as 'a light film without any sophistication'.[40] More precisely, the work was drawn-out and repetitive, and Ewa Fiszer's commentary did nothing to change this. Just as with Van Dongen and Michelle, he hoped to involve Fiszer more deeply with his films, but after the bicycle-film she felt that she had enough to do with her own activities.

Ivens sought new projects in Poland. He announced plans for a film about fishery and industry on the Polish coast, and considered making a film about the Vistula River. That fall, however, he began looking further afield. He negotiated in vain with the DEFA about a film on German unity[41], and toward the end of the year he traveled to Rome, where he agreed to make a film for the PCI, the Italian Communist party, about workers in Calabria, the rugged, poverty-stricken region in the south of the country. The plan was dropped after lengthy preparations, and he began discussions with Gillo Pontecorvo and other PCI directors about a film on the River Po, another project which failed to eventuate. Ivens also wanted to make a documentary about the relationship between Italian and Dutch painting in the sixteenth and seventeenth centuries.[42] Italy continued to have a strong appeal for him and he would return there often.

His visit to Rome at the end of 1952 was not purely for business. He had a date with Marion Michelle and his letters to her had already hinted that things were not going well between Ewa and him. After their meeting in Italy he wrote to his brother Hans: 'Unfortunately, I am not terribly happy in my most recent marriage, for all kinds of reasons. Marion and I feel that we love each other deeply and belong together.'[43] It was less than fourteen months since the wedding in Warsaw. Ivens now decided to pluck up the courage to confide his deepest emotions to Ewa. After an agitated nighttime walk in the cold and rain through the streets of Rome, he wrote her a long letter in which he concluded that their marriage was a failure. He took all the blame upon himself. 'I have treated you badly and M. too', he wrote, and continued that he had not expected their marriage to be easy, but had thought that he had enough strength and love to be a good husband and take care of her while also continuing his work with greater vigor. He had been mistaken. 'I'm not the man you need. Feelings that are more permanent are needed. I see that I am weaker than I thought, in my character too. In my work I have vision and lasting trust, daring and faithfulness, but in even the closest personal relationships I lack the qualities that marriage and cohabitation require.'[44]

After three marriages and one almost-marriage, it was a moment of insight and openness. 'It is only when alone that I feel calm and able to think about my work, I'm telling you the truth.' It is uncertain whether Ivens actually sent the letter. He was no hero in such matters, and he and Fiszer remained together for another ten or so years and did not officially divorce until 1967.

Marion Michelle soon realized that the renewed intimacy in Rome had been temporary. That summer she wrote to him with uncharacteristic cynicism. 'Naturally your thoughts are toward the future and far from the past. Whatever confidences you made to me in Italy were considered only those of an old friend – as were mine – and certainly not as a betrayal of your present relationship, for which I have the greatest respect.'[45] Meanwhile she had begun a relationship with Jean Guyard, a tax officer, surrealist painter and former member of the French resistance. When Ivens visited Paris, he and

Guyard spoke man-to-man in the Tabac on the rue Vaneau. Guyard said that, as Communists, they were able to talk to each other. 'Marion is my girlfriend now', he said, 'but you're always welcome at our place'. Moved, Ivens grasped Guyard by the lapels, exclaiming: 'Jean, Jean!'[46] Marion Michelle and Jean Guyard married in April 1954 and were still together forty-five years later. Now that Ivens no longer felt the pressure and demands of an intimate relationship, a close and loyal friendship that lasted until his death developed between him and Marion.

In the summer of 1953 Ivens began a one-year contract as a director, adviser and reader in the service of the DEFA Studio for Newsreels and Documentaries in East Berlin. His job required him to live in the East German capital and he took a room in the Newa Hotel on the Invalidenstrasse, one of the few old hotels to have survived the war. With the German occupation still fresh in Fiszer's memory, she had no desire to move with him and stayed behind in their apartment on the Podwale. Ivens traveled to Warsaw regularly for weekends, and they spent their vacations at Zakopane, the Polish ski resort in the High Tatra.

Ivens felt completely at home in Berlin. Many years later he still enjoyed returning to the Newa Hotel, where he was always greeted as a regular. He was respected highly by his DEFA colleagues. Not only did his long revolutionary film career appeal to their imagination; he had also defended the studio's honor against Moscow in the co-production of FRIENDSHIP TRIUMPHS. Many of his friends and acquaintances from pre-war Berlin, Paris, Moscow and Hollywood now lived in the GDR capital. Hanns Eisler and Bertolt Brecht were back; the former Mezhrabpom boss Hans Rodenberg and Gustav von Wangenheim – director of FIGHTERS and a man Ivens regarded less highly – were top cultural functionaries; Johannes R. Becher – who had been a guest at 'Europe' s last party' as organized by Ivens and Arthur Lehning in their student days in Berlin – was about to be appointed Minister of Culture; and Dimitrov's former secretary Alfred Kurella – who had written FIGHTERS and collaborated on the Moscow version of BORINAGE – rose to the Politburo of the SED. The glory days of the Communist International lived on in East Berlin.

Joris Ivens arrived in Berlin during a dramatic period in GDR history. On June 17, 1953, 300,000 workers lay down their tools in an attempt to force improvements in working conditions and reductions in the price of food. During chaotic gatherings, the demands became more explosive: the demonstrators called for free elections and the resignation of the government. '*Schnurrbart, Bauch und Brille, das ist nicht des Volkes Wille!*' they chanted – 'Beard, glasses and fat, the people don't want *that!*' – referring to party leader Walter Ulbricht. On that same day the uprising was put down with the assistance of Soviet tanks. The GDR regime insisted that it had been an attempted fascist coup, but moderated its economic policies to reduce popular dissatisfaction. At the DEFA Ivens discussed the studio's position. In his notes he wrote: 'The populace is less politically developed than we thought... Too little trust in party and government. They don't know friends from enemies. Don't recognize provocateurs – right and left... Dissatisfaction greater than we thought. Little vigilance. Unmask fascism from Bonn. Unfortunately, many workers have not developed the necessary high-level consciousness.'[47] The conclusion was that the weekly DEFA newsreels needed to become more interesting and more attuned to the political level of the people in order to popularize government measures.

Ivens was drawn into the DEFA's routine meetings. He had to attend the sessions of the Film Trade Commission, an advisory body for the East German Ministry of Culture,[48] and was swept along by the Eastern European merry-go-round of meetings and medals, a world where old ideals solidified into bureaucratic symbolism. He routinely sent congratulatory telegrams to colleagues and functionaries who had won a prize or received some decoration, or happened to be having a birthday: 'Your work is an example to us all of how we must fight for our party and for socialism.'[49] A minor highlight was the Joris Ivens Camp on the Baltic island of Rügen, where the DEFA employees' children spent their vacation in 1955. He participated in meetings of the World Peace Council in Prague and Budapest, was a guest at a youth festival in Bucharest and at an international student congress in Prague, and in 1953 he was made a permanent member of the jury for the World Peace Prize. He was presented with this prize himself in Helsinki in 1955.

Photos from those years show Ivens in the badly-cut gray suits and boring ties that typified keen party functionaries. But as Ewa Fiszer insisted, he only looked like that on public occasions; he usually wore a casual tweed jacket with a sweater or shirt.

Ivens still saw the mass meetings, awards and prizes as expressions of a living unstoppable movement, headed for liberation. In the film SONG OF THE RIVERS, his largest production for the DEFA, he went in search of this movement's sources. It was to be another congress film, this time for the Moscow affiliated World Federation of Trade Unions. Ivens decided to play down events in the meeting hall and take the union members' daily struggles as his starting point. His links with China and Indonesia made him more interested in the Third World than was usual in Eastern Europe at that time, and he decided to construct the film around the workers' movements on six great rivers across the globe: the Volga of course, the Mississippi, the Ganges, the Nile, the Yangtze and the Amazon. In summer 1953 he wrote a scenario with Vladimir Pozner and an organization was set up in Berlin to take charge of this new megaproject. Joris Ivens called SONG OF THE RIVERS 'the most anti-bureaucratic film imaginable', referring to the fact that professional cineastes and amateurs from eighteen countries set to work with nothing more than some written instructions he sent from Berlin.[50] The management itself, however, was more bureaucratic than ever. In a sense Ivens directed SONG OF THE RIVERS from behind his desk, thousands of miles from most of the locations. 'We were elbowed off to the corner of a desk in a crowded office', wrote DEFA producer Hans Wegner, 'and composed letter after letter by hand'. Facts were dragged in about the economic and political conditions in many countries.[51] The harvest of these world-encompassing activities was supplemented with archive footage, some reenacted scenes[52] and, after all, rather a lot of shots of the World Federation of Trade Unions congress itself, held from October 10 through 21, 1953 in the Konzerthaus in Vienna.

Between shooting sessions at the Konzerthaus, Ivens and Pozner would meet in the canteen to discuss filming possibilities. Pozner described Ivens's response to his account of the deplorable conditions in Thai sugar refineries: 'Out of his pocket, Ivens pulled a stack of pieces of paper like the ones he always carried with him – old envelopes, corners of newspapers, bills, pamphlets – all covered with notes in vertical columns. With astonishing ease, as if dealing with the perfect organizational system, he pulled out the menu of a one-price restaurant in Paris that he happened to have kept for months and added 'Thailand' to a list of countries.'[53] The course of Ivens's life is recorded in partly incomprehensible key words on hundreds of notes. Marion Michelle once wrote: 'Cheri, do change your clothes once in a while – do not be too lazy to take your papers out of your jacket pocket and therefore wear the same thing months and months – wear all your clothes off and on – that keeps them aired and they do not wear out so fast.'[54]

Although SONG OF THE RIVERS can be seen as an attempt to go beyond the standard congress film, it remained a product of centralist thinking, forcing a pluralistic global reality into a simplistic framework that reduced workers to extras in a single global movement. A telling metaphor in the film is a field of waving grain, visually echoed in the following shot of a mass of workers.

Ivens and his co-workers obtained the participation of a number of well-known artists. Bertolt Brecht wrote the lyrics for several of the songs, Dmitri Shostakovitch put them to music and compiled the rest of the score from parts of his earlier work. The Russian composer later thanked Ivens for the good collaboration and especially for his 'really modest behavior'.[55] Black American singer Paul Robeson sang the songs for the English version, Ernst Busch did the same in German, and Pablo Picasso made a drawing for the cover of the book of the film. Pozner traveled to Cannes to explain the film's intentions to the painter and within a day Picasso made twenty-one sketches, from which he chose a drawing of a flower made up of six hands.

Ivens spent most of the summer of 1954 in Moscow working on the final editing of SONG OF THE RIVERS, and on September 17 the film had a spectacular premiere in the Babylon Theater in Berlin. The Politburo and the Central Committee of the SED, the GDR government and the presidium of the trade union movement were among the guests of honor. Union chairman Herbert Warnke gave a speech and an orchestra and choir provided live music. Audiences were organized on a grand scale. The film was mandatory viewing at many GDR factories, at all trade courses and in several other kinds of schools.[56]

Less than a month later, the World Federation of Trade Unions held its own international premiere in Vienna. The Italian director Guiseppe de Santis was so impressed by the film that he called Ivens 'the Garibaldi of the camera' and criticized his own neorealist masterpiece BITTER RICE for having a main character who was too distinct from the masses. The filmed evoked very different emotions in the Viennese correspondent of the Catholic Dutch daily *de Volkskrant*. He described SONG OF THE RIVERS as a film 'for complete morons' and concluded that Ivens was lost as an artist.[57] These divergent opinions emphasize that by 1954 the divide between East and West was absolute (and in Italy and France it ran straight through the country). In the East, Ivens's SONG resounded in the smallest villages, it was dubbed into eighteen languages and was apparently seen by no less than two hundred and fifty million people, including forty million Chinese. In France, on the other hand, it was only allowed to be screened after a series of cuts, and Indonesia, of all places, was one of the countries where it was banned completely. Ivens received high praise from Georges Sadoul in Paris: 'SONG OF THE RIVERS is the kind of work that a person can only create once in a lifetime and that the world itself cannot repeat too often. In its greatness the film approaches ultimate perfection.' Ivens himself was extraordinarily satisfied and basked in the applause. Twenty-five years later his enthusiasm about the adulation had cooled: 'To tell the truth, these statements can only be explained by the fact that I had become – or was becoming – the bard of advancing socialism and my films had become political instruments.'[58]

With work on SONG OF THE RIVERS in full swing, a subject other than an Eastern European congress presented itself for Ivens's following film. One day in Paris, at a lunch Georges and Ruta Sadoul had organized in the restaurant Boule d'Or opposite Notre Dame, Ivens was introduced to the French actor Gérard Philipe, the star of many films and the darling of female audiences. Philipe had recorded the French commentary of PEACE WILL WIN and was familiar with Ivens's work. Everyone present soon agreed that it would be good to make a film about Till Eulenspiegel, the main character from the novel by Charles de Coster, whose stature as a Flemish national hero was so great that it was no longer clear whether or not he had really existed. In De Coster's story Till is a cheerful buffoon who is rudely confronted with Spanish oppression when his father is burnt at the stake during the Inquisition. Ivens invited Philipe to come to the GDR for further discussions.

Gérard Philipe responded by visiting East Berlin in spring 1954, and in December they met again in Paris, where Ivens with the actor now agreed that 'he would play the role of Till under my direction at the start of 1956'.[59] TILL EULENSPIEGEL became a co-production of the DEFA and Ariane Films of Paris, and this cooperation between East and West gave the project special political significance for the GDR. The Cold War was beginning to wane a little and there were modest attempts at rapprochement. What could serve this purpose better than making a film together with a mixed cast of French and East German actors and one of France's greatest stars in the lead role?

After several failed attempts at a scenario, Gérard Philipe finally wrote a script with the writer René Wheeler. Joris Ivens was also involved, but Philipe 'reacted impatiently when I wasn't as fast at expressing and formulating my ideas as he was'.[60] It was now decided that Philipe would share directorial credits with Ivens. At the start of 1956, the crew went to a frozen lake north of Stockholm to film a number of winter scenes. Other exterior scenes were done in the GDR, and in spring they began shooting the interior sequences at Studio Victorine in Nice.

The French press followed the film crew's activities closely but only mentioned one director: Gérard Philipe. Philipe himself told everyone that it was his film and that Ivens had only been involved at the start. 'It's terrible what they are doing to Joris,' was the reaction of his friends in Paris and Vladimir Pozner wrote to him: 'We take this seriously and feel that we need to tell you. It's not just about you personally, about your name, but about everything your name stands for. Let me know if there's anything I can do.' Gérard Philipe had, however, largely told the truth and Ivens could really only accuse him of a somewhat mean-spirited attitude. During shooting it had soon become apparent that Ivens was not good at working with professional actors. 'Feel very alone and lonely these days. The people working on the film are all interested in other things, talking about women and food, and food and women. They're always acting someone other than themselves.' In contrast Philipe, an ambitious thirty-three-year-old, was in his element. He saw the film as a long-awaited chance to direct and took complete charge. Ivens answered Pozner that his friends in Paris did not need to worry and that it was good for the film when he kept a low profile. He called his co-director's working methods 'spectacular' and a 'delight to watch' and expressed understanding for the press's disinterest in the 'quiet, gray-haired gentleman who sits up on the platform and doesn't make many loud statements'.[61] He generously took the line that making the film a success came first, and his position became that of supervisor for the DEFA.

During a contemplative break in Yves Montand and Simone Signoret's country home in Autheuil – Ivens knew them from the film circles around the French Communist Party (PCF) – he concluded that fiction was not his field. 'My escapade with Till in the fiction film area was interesting,' he wrote to his brother Hans, 'but I believe that it is a question of temperament, or whatever you call it. I feel more at home with 'real' people than with actors. Documentaries give me more scope as a visual artist, more discipline in the form and more freedom as far as the content of my work is concerned.'[62] This conclusion was less contradictory than it seemed. The scenarios Ivens used for his documentaries were never as developed as a normal fiction film script. He generally limited himself to a rough sketch and otherwise simply wandered with the camera through the reality he found on location. He then created the definitive structure in the editing room. The 'reconstructions' he discussed so passionately played a subordinate role in his work. His theories about storylines and amateur actors were actually a put-up job, he had adopted them during the discussions in the Mezhrabpom Studio in 1931 and a filmmaker was expected to have a theory, but he got the best results when he ignored them and let himself be guided by his visual talents. This was the freedom he was talking about, but on the other hand there was another freedom, the freedom to create a fantasy world, which was not one of his strong points. The reality around him was his raw material, he derived the structure in his films from the processes that occurred within it, whether it was the course of a cloudburst, the construction of a dyke, or the events in a war. And when further interpretation of the facts was needed, he could always fall back on his ideology.

Despite expectations, THE ADVENTURES OF TILL EULENSPIEGEL was received fairly badly by the French critics and Ivens could now allow himself the comforting thought: 'It could have been better artistically if I had been able to be more involved.'[63] He never made another real fiction film though, despite regularly thinking along those lines.

TILL was meant to be a symbol of the reconciliation between East and West, but the date of the Paris premiere, November 7, 1956 could not have been worse. That same morning, Soviet tanks were crushing a popular uprising in the streets of Budapest. Several thousand were killed and the independently-minded Communist premier Imre Nagy, who had planned to allow a multi-party system, was later executed along with two thousand others. The events in Hungary caused great indignation in Paris. The right-wing demonstrated on the Champs Elysées and the critical left vented their fury on the offices of the Communist daily *Humanité*, where the attackers were pelted with lead type from the editorial offices and one demonstrator was reputedly put out of action after being hit with a bust of Karl Marx. Three party members died in the skirmishing. Meanwhile the PCF itself marched through the center of Paris in support of the Soviet intervention against the 'Hungarian fascists'.

After the premiere of TILL, Ivens and Philipe got mixed up in the commotion and a political breach between them became apparent. According to Ivens, Philipe 'was a genuine sympathizer, but had difficulty coping with the shock of Budapest.... It was a blow for me as well, but I didn't see things so darkly. I was of the opinion that it was a historical inevitability that had to be accepted.' In any case, Gérard Philipe should never have got mixed up with Ivens, the 'official cineaste of Eastern Europe', according to François Truffaut, one of the spokesmen for the young guard of cinema nuts centered on the magazine *Cahiers du Cinéma.* Truffaut rated TILL as the worst movie of the year.[64]

The Hungarian uprising was the highlight in a year of crucial events in Eastern Europe. At the Twentieth Party Congress of the Communist Party of the Soviet Union in February 1956, Nikita Khrushchev had launched an attack on Stalinism. Joseph Stalin had died three years earlier and Khrushchev had become leader after an internal power struggle. In a secret speech for Soviet functionaries he described a selection of Stalin's crimes and announced a less dogmatic policy. The East German and Czechoslovak leaders immediately responded that their countries had no need for de-Stalinization and took preventive action to block any attempts at liberalization. In Poland and Hungary, however, calls for greater freedom became increasingly strident. Even among Polish Communists there was a strong undercurrent of anti-Russian feelings, if only because Stalin had liquidated the Polish party's entire leadership before the war. The moderate party leader Gomulka came to power in Warsaw in the wake of the mass movement and succeeded in instigating a degree of greater independence in relation to Moscow.

In Warsaw Joris Ivens was known for his enthusiasm for the Soviet Union so Poles were not always open in their dealings with him. In Poland more than elsewhere, he was confronted with the everyday reality of 'real existing socialism' and he did not actually feel comfortable there. He believed in socialism as it should be. 'In Warsaw he lived at home, he went into shops and took the bus; in Berlin and Moscow he stayed in hotels and saw nothing. As a result he thought that everything that was wrong in Poland was the fault of the Poles and not the fault of Stalinism,' said Ewa Fiszer.[65] With her strong sense of Polish nationalism and her memories of their claustrophobic honeymoon in Moscow, she was immediately receptive to Khrushchev's criticism of Stalin. When his speech was made public, she wrote to Ivens: 'Have you read about the Twentieth Congress? One must read it. All of it.'[66] He was, however, unwilling to accept unconditionally that Khrushchev was right. 'I still think that a lot of people were bad, who we thought were bad. It's complicated,' he wrote to Marion Michelle. After the events in Budapest, he wrote to his brother: 'What a long, worrying and sometimes gruesome time it takes to reach a better world, to change an economic and social system and thus make the relationships between people better and more humane. Patience is definitely not enough. And keeping up the... our high ideals is difficult, especially keeping them up in an environment that we thought was already further down the right road.' He was not completely free of doubt, and wrote to Michelle: 'Such tragic things are going on. Things that are necessary, but sometimes I ask myself if the way in which they are done is the right one. History will show us – and confidence in all you and I believe in remains.' Nevertheless, he let her know that 'the glorification of Uncle Joe' should be cut for a Paris screening of FRIENDSHIP TRIUMPHS, referring to the sequence of thirty thousand young people shouting: 'Stalin! Stalin! Stalin!'[67]

Not everyone in Ivens's surroundings shared his almost unshakable faith. His political differences with Ewa Fiszer would grow in the coming years, until the day he told her: 'You used to be a good comrade, but not any more.'[68] Gérard Philipe signed a declaration condemning Soviet violence in Hungary and was just one of the people in Paris with whom Ivens gradually lost touch.

Although it was purely coincidental that Ivens now departed for a six-week visit to China – his first since 1938 – where he would give lectures and advise the central documentary film studio, the trip marked the beginning of a gradual shift in his political allegiance. On the last day of the turbulent year of 1956, he and Ewa Fiszer were the guests of honor at a welcome dinner in the Peking restaurant 'Happy Togetherness'.

18 Breathing Space (1957-1960)

After TILL EULENSPIEGEL it was time for Joris Ivens to slow down. Surrounded by ideological uncertainty, he awaited developments. Looking back he described it as 'a period in which I was much less militant',[1] and his work became much less political.

During the production of TILL EULENSPIEGEL, he had spent more time in Paris than in Berlin, and he now made a definitive move to the French capital. His loyalty to the GDR was undiminished, but for the time being he did not make any new commitments to the DEFA. East German friends apparently advised him to 'stay here, take a villa and move in there', but he preferred an apartment on the rue de la Bucherie, across the river from the Notre Dame. The members of a Chinese theater group who visited him there were dumbfounded. 'It was inconceivable that Ivens, an internationally renowned artist who had received the World Peace Prize two or three years earlier, was living in an attic above a little coffee shop on the bank of the Seine. His home looked like a garret in Shanghai's old city.'[2] The Chinese interpreted Ivens's home as evidence of self-effacement, but that was relative. He actually experienced possessions as ballast and hated the way they made him feel pinned down. 'He always thought that you could make a completely new start somewhere else tomorrow,' said Ewa Fiszer.[3] His attitude to domesticity had not changed in the twenty-five years since he had set up camp on two floors on Amsterdam's Singel and it never would. He reconciled himself somewhat to hearth and home in the 1980s when he had grown old and stiff, but even then there would be few things he enjoyed as much as packing his bags. 'Ha, ha, off again!' he would call out with a clap of his hands, ready to catch a plane to China or some other destination.[4] Rather than a temptation, a villa in East Berlin was a nightmare. Attempts to use such enticements to incorporate him in the established order of the GDR could only have the opposite effect.

When not traveling, he spent the following years in Paris in various apartments and hotels, mostly the Panthéon. Ewa Fiszer came over from Warsaw for a few months each year, and Ivens must have been thinking more of her than of himself when he wrote to her in 1959: 'It would be good if we could find a pied-à-terre, except that I don't know if I will ever earn enough in my life to be able to afford to buy something.'[5] The following year they found a fifth-floor apartment with an attic at 16 rue Guisarde, not far from the place Saint-Sulpice. For Ewa it became a second home, but apart from those few months in Paris and an occasional trip with Joris, she now lived alone in her apartment on the Podwale. He only showed up there once or twice a year, and then usually on lightning visits.

Ivens tried to compensate for his frequent absences with a constant stream of letters in which he wrote things like: 'I think of you often and feel alone' or 'Darling, working and seeing people allows me to vanquish my great desire to be with you.' He sometimes took the precaution of keeping a list of his correspondence, since mail from countries like China occasionally went missing. In the fifteen weeks from July to October 1958, when he was in Peking, he recorded no less than seventy-nine letters to Ewa in Warsaw; she replied with less than half that number. His outpourings did not lead to any change in his behavior and were accompanied by contradictory signals: 'I would feel more at ease if I knew that you had new friends to amuse yourself with. Of course, if you wrote telling me that you had followed my advice I would be jealous. But you know how deeply I love you and how much... eat well, rest, have fun, flirt if you feel like it... I do the same except for the flirting.'[6] It was not how Fiszer had imagined their marriage, and Ivens had begun by promising her a different future. She sometimes expressed her dissatisfaction in radio silence, and Ivens's letters regularly included complaints like (writing from Paris): 'This is my eighth letter, the west wind dominates our correspondence. I don't know anything.'[7] Things continued in this vein. He kept on sending reassuring letters, and she kept on hoping and complaining. 'She didn't make things easy for him, but she may have loved him more than anyone else,' said Ida Pozner, who observed Ivens's love affairs for more than fifty years.[8]

Marion Michelle, whom Ida Pozner called 'the second Mrs. Ivens', was still living in Paris on the rue Vaneau. She was the one who regularly ensured that his films reached their screenings on time, that the subtitles were completed, or that money was passed on to various persons. When in Paris he invariably visited her and Jean Guyard, or went for nostalgic strolls along the Seine with her alone, a tradition he also kept up with Ewa.

The idea for TILL EULENSPIEGEL had originated with film historian Georges Sadoul, who also provided Ivens's next cinematic theme. Sadoul wrote texts to accompany photo-reportages by Henri Cartier-Bresson and one of these series had been about the Seine; this gave Sadoul the idea of looking at the river from a cinematic perspective. Ivens heard of the plan and told Sadoul in late 1956 that he would like to make a film along those lines. They spent many hours walking the banks of the Seine and decided to collaborate after discovering that they viewed the world in a similar way. 'I didn't need to nudge him with my elbow', Sadoul wrote, 'when I caught sight of a child at play on the back of a barge, or a gentleman's dog obviously being walked by a servant. He spotted them the same moment I did.' According to Sadoul, they followed the example of Soviet documentary maker Dziga Vertov by using a 'shooting plan' instead of a detailed shooting script. In this case the plan was a map with the bridges over the Seine and notes all over it saying things like: 'Pont Royal, workshop girls' breakfast', an event they had presumably encountered on one of their walks.[9] Vertov may have inspired Sadoul, but Ivens was already an old hand at working without a shooting script, he almost never used one. Just as in RAIN and THE BRIDGE, the film's structure was derived from the natural course of events, in this case a river encountering all kinds of things along its route. THE SEINE MEETS PARIS became a soft-focusedportrait of the French capital as seen from the river. Georges Sadoul went abroad soon after the start of filming and left the rest to Ivens.

In 1957 a trio of friends from theater and film circles around the PCF decided to found a production company of their own, Garance Films, and Ivens's film about the Seine became their debut production. The three were actor and director Roger Pigaut; his wife, the English actress Betsy Blair, ex-wife of Hollywood star Gene Kelly; and Serge Reggiani, singer and the leading man of films like Jacques Becker's CASQUE D'OR and successful plays by Jean-Paul Sartre, among others. Ivens and his wife were good friends of Pigaut and Blair's, and Pigaut narrated three of Ivens's films.

To include the swell of the Seine in his film, Ivens filmed the banks from a fireboat. The crew concealed the camera in a crate on the banks and disguised themselves as workmen so that they could film people unnoticed from as close as ten or twelve feet. A sanitation department shed was used as a hide to film children and clochards.

The result of six weeks of shooting was a completely apolitical film, in some ways an expression of one of Ivens's main characteristics: unwavering optimism with a touch of mild melancholy. Small everyday things pass by without the filmmaker displaying any urge to delve into them more deeply: lonely fishermen, courting couples on the riverbank, workers unloading a ship, the traffic and bars along the quay, a peacefully sleeping clochard, children at play. 'The Seine hears it and flows on humming,' wrote Jacques Prévert, the great French poet and screenwriter, in the commentary Reggiani recorded. Explaining his film, Ivens nonetheless felt obliged to express a message: 'We need a romantic reaction to the excess of the *films noirs*... We have to show young people that there are good reasons for believing in life, despite the gloomy childhood we gave them with the war.'[10] *Film noir* was the American style characterized by a rather cynical view of life, with John Huston's THE MALTESE FALCON as an early example and Tay

Garnett's THE POSTMAN ALWAYS RINGS TWICE as one of the highlights of the genre's postwar boom.

In his memoirs Ivens referred to those who were directly or indirectly involved in THE SEINE as 'the reception committee'. Their support enabled him to start anew in Paris after his years in Eastern Europe. Guests at the premiere of THE SEINE MEETS PARIS on November 20, 1957 included Yves Montand, Simone Signoret, directors Marcel Camus, Chris Marker and Alberto Cavalcanti, and the writer Vercors. These PCF-linked artists felt a natural solidarity with Ivens, whom Signoret described in her memoirs as 'the purest and greatest revolutionary filmmaker of his generation'.[11]

THE SEINE MEETS PARIS was a flawless short film coming at the end of an era. With a studio-recorded commentary that was loosely connected to the images and an aloof camera feeling its way through the urban landscape, it was made in the style that had dominated the French documentary throughout the postwar decade. At the same time the New Wave, with its compulsive improvisation and aversion to the academicism of the *cinéma de papa*, was already stirring. Accordingly, some critics called THE SEINE old-fashioned,[12] but in general responses were very positive. In Cannes Ivens and Henri Gruel shared the Golden Palm for the best short film – Gruel for JOCONDE – and Ivens won the first prize at the Oberhausen Film Festival and the documentary prize at the San Francisco Film Festival.

An article about THE SEINE in the spring 1958 issue of the English film magazine *Sight and Sound* became a major preoccupation for Ivens.[13] This was hardly surprising as the reviewer, Cynthia Grenier, had cast doubt upon the artistic merit of the bulk of his oeuvre. Art had been a sore point for Ivens ever since the gravity with which it had been invoked in the Filmliga days, and in the following decades Ivens would return often to this review. Grenier praised THE SEINE as 'one of the most tender, charming, moving and accurate pictures ever made about Paris' and concluded that its maker was a romantic naturalist at heart. She found traces of this in much of his other work as well, though too little, because she believed that in many of his social and political films he had suppressed his talent in favor of easy propaganda.

Joris Ivens vigorously opposed this analysis: 'It is not so that Ivens has two guises: the leftist and the esthete. Some people say that only the purely esthetic films are artistic; the rest are not art. Others see me exclusively as a militant filmmaker. Both are incorrect. When I made THE SEINE MEETS PARIS, my views were just as left-wing as they were when making political films. With political films I have often been just as rigorous about finding the best artistic form.'[14] Of course Ivens was right in his belief that a political film could be a work of art. After all, art can take any theme as its subject. What matters is the way it is given form. Grenier had not denied this and had even cited Eisenstein as an example, but she argued that with Ivens the politics was at the expense of his creativity. She argued her case logically. In Eisenstein's films about the revolution, the theme served the director's individual creative power. For a large part of Ivens's output after 1932 the reverse was true: his political documentaries had a concrete goal, generally short term, and their form was subordinated to that goal. Ivens himself said that 'the most elevated art form has the greatest propaganda value',[15] and a film like THE SPANISH EARTH succeeded in attaining this standard, but more than once the most elevated art form was sacrificed for the practical and political necessities of the moment. THE 400 MILLION was released even though Ivens considered it poor work, there was virtually no artistic form in the diverse Eastern European films, and several of his later films were also mediocre.

The fundamental flaw in Grenier's argument was her basic premise: that Joris Ivens was *actually* a lyric poet. On the contrary, Ivens's psyche was not suited to free expression. His craftsmanship and undeniable visual talent were stymied when cut free from the service of a commission, a defined objective, political or otherwise. He had grounds for calling early films like THE BRIDGE and RAIN finger exercises. He felt they were not really about anything. As he once said: 'It rains, that's all.' They were, and still are, mileposts in documentary history, but as far as Ivens was concerned such films did not bear repetition. Later esthetic films such as THE SEINE, VALPARAÍSO and MISTRAL showcased Ivens's stylistic capabilities, but also revealed a certain shallowness that emerged as soon as his work lacked immediate purpose.

During his visit to China in late 1956, early 1957, he had been invited to return to make a film. In December 1957, he embarked on a working tour of various European capitals, then joined Fiszer in Warsaw and flew to China. She stayed there with him in a two-room suite in the Peking Hotel for a month before returning home alone. Ivens spent most of 1958 in China, where he was invited to tea by president Liu Shaoqi, premier Zhou Enlai and vice-premier Chen Yi, and by the writers Guo Muruo and Mao Dun, vice-premier and minister of Culture respectively.

In addition to his film commission and an appointment as 'general consultant' with the Central News and Documentary Film Studio in Peking, he was also officially appointed as a lecturer at the Peking Film School. He requested monthly payment in Swiss francs or pounds sterling into a French or Swiss bank account. 'Everything is submitted to me for consultation.

They have faith in me when it comes to cinema.'[16] He advised the employees of the central studio to 'create an artistic and creative ambience in the studio' to avoid an 'administrative' or 'bureaucratic' atmosphere, and to favor quality above 'hunting for the planned length of meters of films'.[17] He informed his students that they could help the inhabitants of other countries to get to know the Chinese people, 'the energetic way they take to industrializing their country, the way they develop their agriculture at phenomenal speed. The way the Communist party leads the way towards Communism.' In their search for originality, young filmmakers did not need to 'fall back into abstract experimenting, as so many documentarists in capitalist countries do. Your experiment is not abstract, but rooted in daily life.' He was seized by great enthusiasm for this country where 'the ideals are kept high in the daily concrete struggle' and where everything progressed so rapidly that the giant in seven-mile boots was a 'graybeard in slippers' by comparison. 'Here an artist feels that he is needed. There the life in ivory towers dries them up, sterilizes them. All that together is called: experimental,' as he wrote to Marion Michelle.[18]

Despite all this zeal, his most important cinematic work in China was again almost apolitical. He was to make a major documentary for the central film studio entitled SNOW, to be filmed with Chinese co-workers who would thus learn from his experience. In early 1958 he explained on Chinese radio that the film would be a spectacular panorama of China in winter, with images from the south, the north, the Gobi, and the northwest, emphasizing people's reactions to snow.[19] The plan did not eventuate and a more modest project was carried out: three short 'Letters from China', a total of thirty-eight minutes, finally distributed as a single color film under the title BEFORE SPRING – amiable impressions of rural life that only gained political meaning through the Chinese commentary.

The shooting in Inner Mongolia was done at temperatures around zero Fahrenheit. Wrapped in a thick fur coat, Ivens drove from the hotel at Hailar into the snow-covered steppe with a nomad camp as his primary destination. He advised cameraman Wang Decheng not to start filming straight away. You have to get to know the people first – but always have your camera with you to capture the unexpected.[20] On the Yangtze near Nanjing, Ivens filmed peasant life in the Dingshan agricultural cooperative, and near Shanghai he and his crew witnessed spring festivities in a fishing village.

After a summer break of six weeks in Paris, he returned in August to Peking, where he spent ten days working on THE INDIGNATION OF 600 MILLION PEOPLE.[21] This short film showed the Chinese masses crossing the screen in a constant stream, beside themselves with rage about American and British military support for Lebanon's Christian President Shamun and

King Hussein of Jordan, both of whom were resisting opposition demands that their countries join Egyptian president Nasser's United Arab Republic. No less than two million excited Chinese were said to have marched past the British embassy in Peking in two days, possibly according to the Hollywood principle for crowd scenes: those at the front rejoin at the back and march past again. The commentary began: 'Raised fist clenched in iron determination, we go forward to crush the wolfish skull of imperialism.'[22] Ivens took charge of direction and edited the work of a number of camera crews into a twelve-minute pamphlet.

The completion of BEFORE SPRING was now delayed by the Chinese authorities, who insisted that the triptych be expanded with a fourth 'Letter' in response to Chairman Mao's new call for people's communes to be formed everywhere in the countryside. The cooperatives Ivens had filmed were now politically outdated. China had been passing through an extremely turbulent period ever since Mao had launched the 'Great Leap Forward' at the start of that year with the slogan 'twenty years in one day'. Despite Ivens's enthusiasm for this gigantic movement, he did not give up his work without a fight. In a memorandum to the management of the Central Film Bureau, he replied to the authorities' wishes by saying that you could call every valuable film superfluous every time China made a new leap forward. The fourth 'Letter' would need to be followed by a fifth bringing it up-to-date, and so on, ad infinitum. He described the guidelines he had been given as 'the hardest blow' he had been subjected to 'in my thirty years creative life working for our cause'. After the squabbling over SONG OF HEROES, the Saarland film and THE FIRST YEARS, this was quite an exaggeration. The developments in China rather were a new variation on a familiar theme. Ivens hinted that the European press had already announced the release. How would he explain the delay to the journalists?

Nonetheless he saw his main argument as: 'As you know I did many films on a big scale for the international peace movement, youth movement, democratic women's movement, trade union movement. But in China not yet. Every creative artist sometimes has to catch his breath with smaller films, before returning to bigger work.'[23] The monumental Eastern European productions had exhausted him and the political uncertainty of the day had left him longing for breathing space. The authorities relented and allowed him to complete the serene BEFORE SPRING; perhaps they realized that they had little to gain from antagonizing such a faithful ally.

Meanwhile, Ivens was able to witness the Great Leap Forward at first hand. In accordance with Mao's belief that every Chinese should produce steel, the staff of his studio had set to work building clay furnaces beside the canteen. Ivens: 'At the gate of the studio I meet Ding Qiao, Editor-in-Chief

Joris Ivens and cameraman Li Zexhiang filming BEFORE SPRING (1958). CENTRAL NEWS AND DOCUMENTARY STUDIO, DUTCH FILM MUSEUM

of the studio. He jumps full of excitement out of a taxi, holding up a little piece of metal. 'It is steel,' he says. 'The metallurgical laboratory has tested it!' His whole face beams; already a procession is formed – drum, cymbals, gongs, a hastily written placard – to announce to the members of the studio the incredible result of three days' work with small primitive ovens. Through their work they are helping their country with the vital basic material for China's industrialization.'[24] Ivens was once again swept up by the enthusiasm, but the millions of mini-furnaces that arose all over the country were actually an enormous fiasco: the product was of inferior quality, the furnaces consumed all the household utensils, entire regions were deforested to feed the permanently burning fires, and people had no time left for useful employment. To make matters worse, Mao had also proclaimed 'to each according to his need' and the food supplies in the communes were being rapidly depleted. The Great Leap Forward culminated in a three-year famine that claimed an immense number of lives. Ivens preferred to believe the Chinese leaders' explanation that it was the result of a natural disaster.

The West showed little interest in BEFORE SPRING, but Ivens was convinced that his film had changed the outmoded working methods of the

Chinese documentary filmmakers and thus contributed to increasing their freedom of operation.[25] He might have been right from a technical point of view; the political situation continued unaltered.

As early as 1950, Ivens had advised the Chinese delegation at the Stockholm World Peace Congress to commission a film about Norman Bethune, a Canadian doctor *sans frontières* who had worked in the Spanish Civil War and with the Chinese guerillas, and had been one of the first to experiment with blood transfusions. In 1954 the Chinese government asked Ivens to collaborate on just such a film. Authors Ted Allen and Sydney Gordon had written a biography of Bethune, and Allen collaborated with Hollywood scriptwriter Donald Ogden Stewart on a screenplay. In 1957 Peking named Ivens as assistant producer for a film of an Allen and Gordon scenario, but little progress was made, probably because of the xenophobia of the Chinese, who wanted to limit the film to Bethune's period of under a year in their own country. It was not until 1963 that production began under director Zhang Junxiang. By this time Ivens's role had shrunk to a number of suggestions during the editing. The film was immediately shelved upon completion – according to later accounts on the orders of Mao's wife Jiang Qing – and was not shown publicly until 1977, when Mao was dead and his wife had been ousted from power.[26] In 1990 Philip Borsos's Bethune was released, a Canadian-Chinese-French co-production with Donald Sutherland in the lead role.

In Paris Joris Ivens established good relations with the Dutch embassy's cultural attaché, Sadi de Gorter, who made some contacts for him in the fatherland.[27] In the summer of 1959 the Arnhem Film Week invited Ivens to attend a screening of The Seine Meets Paris and Amsterdam's Calypso Theater planned to release the film that same week in a double premiere with Ingmar Bergman's Brink of Life. Ivens had not been in Holland since 1947, and before accepting the invitations he asked the Dutch government to guarantee that he would not be held hostage, an understandable request in the light of the peculiar attempts to browbeat him into traveling to The Hague with a laissez-passer in 1950.[28] He apparently received the requested assurance because on June 26 he attended the premiere in the Calypso. The audience greeted him with applause and the evening became a genuine triumph when at a subsequent private screening of The Seine for the Dutch Filmmakers Association, his colleagues gave an ovation in his honor and made him an honorary member. 'Even some opponents were glad,' he wrote to Ewa in Warsaw. He summed up his compatriots as 'nice people with the mentality of a little village'.[29]

Visitors came and went in his room in Hotel de l'Europe. 'I'm living in a kind of fog, the past is vague, although with many clear moments of recognition and recurring facts... seeing too many people.' He was glad to once again spend time in the artists' club De Kring and events turned full circle when a gray-haired woman of fifty-five introduced herself: Quick, his first love from Rotterdam, now Mrs. Nolthenius-De Man-Welsch and resident in Wassenaar, near his brother Hans. After five minutes, it was as if they had seen each other just the day before, but it remained an incidental meeting.[30] Quick died in 1983.

In Arnhem *Handelsblad* reporter Jan Blokker was present for the screening of THE SEINE. When the lights went up, a visibly moved Ivens stood up to accept the applause. 'He suddenly looks smaller than he really is, his gestures are somehow shy, as if he has shown his first film,' wrote Blokker. Ivens accepted the journalist's invitation to dine at his home, where the guest told Blokker's East-Indian-born wife: 'I never worked in Indonesia or under commission from Indonesia, and I would probably have not done so either, even if they had asked me... I cannot take a position against my own countrymen; and I would never have dared to eat at your table afterwards.'[31] For the moment he had forgotten about volunteering his services to prime minister Sjahrir to help set up the Indonesian Republic's film industry.

Henceforth celebrations under the slogan 'the return of the Flying Dutchman' would be held every few years in Holland, as if Ivens was always coming back for the first time. From those days in 1959 on, the Dutch film community and the majority of the Dutch dailies, including the conservative *De Telegraaf*, took Ivens's part. Only the Government Information Service and a handful of officials from the Department of Foreign Affairs, under the leadership of the minister, Joseph Luns, remained hostile toward him. Even *Het Parool*, the only newspaper to regularly publish critical pieces about Ivens in the decades to come, called THE SEINE 'enchanting' and a 'poignant cinematic ode'.[32]

While awaiting a new project in China, Ivens looked around for other work. He considered films along the lines of THE SEINE about 'The Roofs of Paris' and the Buttes Chaumont park; discussed a plan for 'The Bread of Paris' with Hanns Eisler and Vladimir Pozner; brooded over a visualization of the mistral; took steps for a documentary about Josephine Baker's children's community; revived an old plan for a film about the Po River with the Italian scriptwriter Cesare Zavattini; and discussed a film about Venice with another Italian, Giovanni 'Tinto' Brass. Almost none of these projects had any significant political implications.[33] Finally he settled on a film about the Italian oil industry.

Joris Ivens had been a familiar guest in Italy since the early fifties. At that time he had completed a successful tour and become friends with Virgilio Tosi, the leader of the Italian film club movement. In the years that followed, Ivens launched numerous film plans with Italian colleagues. He actually felt more at home there than in France, where his friendships 'were frequently crippled by ulterior motives', as he wrote in his memoirs. 'In Italy I got to know frivolity, the art of living, spontaneity, immediate friendship, all things I had naturally tended to keep at a distance.'[34] He was, in fact, perfectly suited to these relationships without ceremony or obligation.

Many of the greats of the Italian cinema maintained close links with the mighty PCI, among them Zavattini, the writer of SHOESHINE, BICYCLE THIEVES and other films by Vittorio de Sica, and the theoretician of neorealism. Zavattini believed in the evocative power of absolute realism and the application of a strict documentary approach to fiction films, which should be about ordinary people. Ivens had often pondered the usefulness of documentary techniques in fiction films and he and Zavattini had much to discuss. 'You place too much importance on life's minor details and get caught up in anecdotalism,' Ivens would say. 'We would sit there almost screaming at each other, but remained friends.'[35] When his funds were low in Rome, he would stay with director Giuseppe de Santis, who had called him 'the Garibaldi of the camera'.

Enrico Mattei was the Christian Democrat head of the Italian national oil institute, the ENI, and a fervent advocate of domestic oil production. Many doubted the existence of significant underground reserves but Mattei stuck to his guns – rightly, as it turned out – and decided to make a propaganda film supporting his vision. The story has it that he saw NEW EARTH, heard that Joris Ivens had made it and declared: 'That's the man I need.' In summer 1959 he signed a contract giving Ivens complete artistic freedom. Ivens suddenly had a job that was both well paid and socially responsible, because the film became 'an attack on imperialism, paid for by a capitalist who was a little different to the rest'.[36] The idea behind the film was that state oil production could increase Italy's economic independence and reduce the influence of American companies, a plan that was fully attuned to the PCI's goal of a 'historic compromise' with the Christian Democrats in order to maneuver the country into a more neutral position between East and West.

Ivens took on Tinto Brass, the Taviani brothers and Valentino Orsini as his co-workers for the oil film. The Tavianis and Orsini were at the start of their careers. They had worked together on documentaries and had been active in the revolutionary 'Theater of the Masses'. In September 1959 Ivens traveled the country in search of themes and then withdrew to a villa in Frascati to write the scenario. The film was to comprise three parts: the first two made under Ivens's direct leadership and the third virtually entirely the work of the Tavianis. It was given the title ITALY IS NOT A POOR COUNTRY and became a collage of extremely diverse components. Ivens was sometimes clearly working by rote, at other times he successfully experimented with new means of expression. Like Godard in BREATHLESS, he had people speak directly to the camera in order to break with the detachment of traditional documentaries. In keeping with the trends of the day, he returned to working with hand cameras, probably for the first time since INDONESIA CALLING! and the evening and night shots were done on new, highly sensitive film.[37] In a science-fiction-like experiment, he showed a dreaming boy somersaulting through the sky, and the faith in industrial progress was illustrated by a plethora of images of oil refineries and factories. One of the film's most impressive sequences dealt with the life of poor peasants in the southern region of Lucania, who saw their miserable existence threatened by an oil well before the doors of their cave homes, all this shown in images that recalled the best moments of BORINAGE.

The third part of ITALY IS NOT A POOR COUNTRY was filmed in Sicily, where, as Ivens wrote to Ewa Fiszer, it required consummate skill to steer a course between the hazards of feuding families and political factions.[38] He returned to Rome early to start editing and left the Tavianis to complete the work in Sicily. The inseparable brothers already displayed a distinctly individual style that deviated strongly from the rest of the film. They were deeply impressed by the old Dutch director who casually said things like: 'But as Sergei told me....' Meaning Eisenstein, someone they saw as a god from the early history of cinema. Later they explained that they learned a lot from Ivens, for example with the shots of a row of workers passing rocks. 'One of the men suddenly dropped a rock. Looking at the rushes in the editing room, we thought it was a shame because it disrupted the rhythm of the movement. Ivens then pointed out that of all the shots we had made there, that was the best. Because it is only when you can show that a particular rhythm has been momentarily disrupted, that you become aware of a rhythm. That is a lesson that we have applied to this day.'[39] In interviews they invariably declared that it was Joris Ivens who had pointed them in the direction of fiction films. They sent their rushes to Rome from Gela in Sicily and a few days later received a telegram from Ivens: very good material, except this is not a documentary, it's a fiction film. From that moment the brothers adopted the course that would lead to KAOS, THE NIGHT OF THE SHOOTING STARS and PADRE, PADRONE.

Fiszer came over to Italy for a few months during the work on the oil film, but the production lasted considerably longer and Ivens also arranged female company during her absence. He was entertaining the approximately thirty-year-old, blond American, Sophie Wenek, bosom friend of the wife of cineaste Jean Rouch. 'An extraordinary woman who left a lasting impression,' according to Rouch. 'We were all fascinated by her, Ricky Leacock and Pennebaker too. Someone should write a book about her.' According to Leacock she slept with anyone who made films, he even called her apartment on the rue Vernail the 'Filmmakers' Hotel'. Jean Rouch, Richard Leacock and D. A. Pennebaker were the leading figures of *cinéma vérité* and direct cinema, the new schools of documentary that emerged around 1960. Sophie wanted to become a movie actress, but according to Rouch she was not particularly photogenic, although he did give her a small part in his fiction film PETIT À PETIT. An individualistic adventurer with a pilot's license, she traveled to West Africa in the sixties with no luggage other than a blanket, perfume, nail varnish and a film camera, and stayed with the Dogon-Fulani in Niger for six months. She wrote complete novels which no one would publish. In the early seventies flying a Cessna in an air rally from the Nile to the Atlantic, she crashed and died in the Canaries because of a tornado.[40]

ENI president Mattei had intended ITALY IS NOT A POOR COUNTRY for television. By the time the film was completed, his influence had declined greatly and RAI television refused to broadcast the work in its original form. Instead, a long list of changes was presented. 'Poverty, squalor, they were things you didn't even talk about, let alone record on film. It was seen as scandalous. They demanded sweeping cuts and a new commentary,' explained Paolo Taviani. Ivens pleaded with his producer to resist the changes and appealed to Mattei. In a draft letter, he wrote: 'Don't let us down, we are loyal.' He reminded Mattei of 'the courage of his standpoint', but also observed: 'You sign a contract with a tiger and in the end you find yourself with a mouse.' 'I saw Ivens burst into tears,' said Paolo Taviani. 'Mattei was nowhere to be found.'[41] A national celebrity, author Alberto Moravia, had written the film's commentary, but this too failed to impress. A cut version of the film was finally broadcast in spring 1960 with an explanatory text negotiated by Ivens: 'Summary of an original television film by Joris Ivens.' A similarly shortened version was shown in Italian theaters.[42]

The expected work in China failed to materialize, and Ivens left for the savannas of West Africa in the spring of 1960. The Société de Cinéma Franco-Africain needed a film about the so-called Federation of Mali, which became independent on April 4, 1960. NANGUILA TOMORROW was and is one of

Ivens's least successful works: too superficial and not particularly interesting visually. As in Italy, he was dogged by bad luck in the final phases. On August 20, a few days before the film was ready, the Federation of Mali collapsed, with Mali and the more developed Senegal becoming separate states. The Société de Cinéma Franco-Africain gave Mali's Marxist president, Modibo Keita, who was oriented toward the Soviet bloc, the right of the final cut. The studio on Montmartre postponed the release until the president had studied the work, but it is unclear whether Keita ever actually turned up. At any rate, Joris Ivens had already left for another corner of the globe and when he returned to Paris several months later, the film still hadn't been shown. This situation remained unchanged. The only subsequent screenings of NANGUILA TOMORROW were at occasional ethnological conferences or solidarity meetings.[43]

In 1954 Ivens had received a letter from Henri Langlois, the driving force behind the French film archives in Paris, the Cinémathèque Française. Obsessed by cinema and capable of irrepressible passion, Langlois was convinced that a film needed to be made about the painter Marc Chagall, and in the early fifties he had visited and filmed his idol with the French documentary filmmaker Frédéric Rossif. Langlois and Rossif had fallen out and ended their collaboration. Langlois then traveled to the Soviet Union in order to make a pilgrimage of famous sites from Chagall's youth with the widow of the director Alexander Dovzhenko. In 1954 he felt able to write to Ivens that the film was in an advanced state of completion. All they needed was a director to bring the work to a satisfactory conclusion, and Langlois and Chagall agreed that, apart from the late Dovzhenko, only Ivens 'had enough commitment... to link the unreal images with the reality of our day... without losing the poetry.' They asked Ivens to supervise the film.[44]

Three years passed before Ivens had time for the project, and it was not until the summer of 1960, after the editing of NANGUILA TOMORROW, that the work could be rounded off. In Beaujolais, at the country home of Langlois's friends Jean and Krishna Riboud, they filmed Chagall's paintings on the billiards table. 'Everything is fine here', Ivens wrote to Ewa Fiszer, 'except that Henri wants to work day and night... he wants to cut and recut, and after six hours of insane work with 16mm film, oh my eyes, we go back to the starting point of my original cut'. Back in Paris Ivens was wary about returning to the Ribouds', because Henri 'wants to work when I'm there, changing 'Chagall'. The film is good. He should realize that an artist has to be able to let go of a work. He can't do it, he's an amateur and a historian.' It was August 31, 1960 and Ivens was satisfied with what he saw as the final version. Ewa Fiszer saw the film and described it: 'It was mainly paintings, that was what Chagall wanted, a succession of fantastic images.'[45] The work was never shown in Europe. Rumor has it that Langlois made the material available to the American producer Simon Schiffrin, who won the Oscar for the best short documentary in 1964 with a film entitled CHAGALL.

19   Cowboy Boots and Guerrilla Cap (1960-1964)

'The times are violent: Cuba, Congo, Mali, I don't want to stand on the sidelines like a lyric poet. I want to be a part of today's movement with my work,' Joris Ivens wrote in a letter to Ewa Fiszer in the summer of 1960. He did add that the realization of his plan for a mistral film 'about raw, violent nature' would satisfy his needs, but it was clear that he was once again focussed on militant cinema. He was about to leave for Cuba, where he wanted to film in what he called Mayakovski-style, after Soviet poet Vladimir Mayakovski, who more than anyone else had succeeded in expressing the Communist philosophy in great poetry.[1]

It was understandable that Ivens's revolutionary zeal should revive at this moment. 1960 was an important year in the process of global decolonization. A large number of African countries became independent, in others wars of liberation were raging, Fidel Castro had just seized power in Cuba – making the island a beacon for rebels all over Latin America – and China was increasingly a source of inspiration for Third World revolution. Ivens was not alone in seeing the many conflicts in Africa, Asia and Latin America as expressions of one big anti-imperialist movement and part of the global march toward socialism. He maintained his contacts throughout the Communist world, but now that Eastern Europe was becoming increasingly moderate and dull, he began shifting his interest to the south. After working as an advisor in Peking in the fifties, he now played a similar role in Cuba, South America and North Vietnam in the sixties. Of the eleven films he made in this decade, nine were shot in the Third World.

Georges Sadoul had arranged an invitation from Castro's administration. The Cubans had been hesitant at first because they had expected Ivens to demand an exorbitant salary; when this turned out not to be the case, there were no further obstacles to his arrival.[2] In the first week of September 1960, he walked into Havana's Rivièra Hotel and picked up the key to a room with a view out over the Gulf of Mexico.

The Cuban revolution appealed strongly to the imaginations of left-wing artists and intellectuals in Europe. With a group of friends, the young lawyer Fidel Castro had overthrown Batista's corrupt dictatorship and now seemed to be aiming for the establishment of a new kind of revolutionary democracy. Castro was no Communist, and this fact in particular led to high expectations, except with Ivens, who saw it as grounds for skepticism. Jean-

Paul Sartre was one of the first to come to Havana to express his solidarity, followed within a few years by a long procession of Europeans and Americans. From the film world alone: Chris Marker, Agnes Varda and Armand Gatti from France, Richard Leacock, D.A. Pennebaker and Albert Maysles from America, Roman Karmen and Mikhail Kalatozov from the Soviet Union, and Cesare Zavattini from Italy. But in 1960 Havana's José Marti Airport was also the point of arrival for Eastern European governmental and party delegations. Links with the Soviet bloc were strengthened, the United States broke off economic relations with Cuba, and in October 1960, 382 large, mostly American, companies were nationalized. In the year that followed, Castro suddenly declared himself a Marxist-Leninist, and although he continued to tug at his chains for a long time, his country slowly but surely became a Soviet satellite.

On the evening of his arrival in Havana, Ivens went straight to a large meeting of the employees of the Instituto Cubano del Arte e Industria Cinematográficos, the ICAIC, where he drew attention to the artist's responsibilities in times of revolution and discussed many technical aspects of filming. 'They said that they had never had a guest who was so inspirational and concrete at once,' he wrote to Ewa. After a screening of THE SEINE MEETS PARIS the next night, the group went on to Café 23x13, where Fidel Castro was leaning against a wall with a couple of bodyguards. ICAIC director Alfredo Guevara introduced Ivens to Castro and, despite his skepticism, Ivens was impressed. 'Fresh, straightforward, a sense of humor, sometimes convincing through a kind of innocence in his eyes,' was his first reaction. Castro talked to them for two and a half hours and thus, after two days in Cuba, Ivens was already better informed: 'You only start to understand the revolution here after meeting Fidel Castro.'[3] All the same, he still mistrusted Castro's idiosyncratic approach: 'For the stickler for orthodoxy that I was, this way of directing the revolution had so little in common with the traditional Marxist agendas that I responded somewhat coolly.'[4]

For a lover of the good life like Ivens, Havana could not fail to make a favorable impression compared to the gray reconstructed cities of Eastern Europe. He was only too happy to be swept along by this mixture of tropical sun and revolutionary leaders in their twenties with romantic beards, berets and cowboy hats. From a cinematic point of view there was also the bonus of the appealing, naive and spontaneous work of the new Cuban filmmakers. 'Forget about technical and stylistic issues... What's important now is to get life into the studios and not to become bureaucrats of the camera,' he said encouragingly.[5]

Ivens decided to make a 'film letter' about Cuba addressed to Charles Chaplin, who had always been favorably disposed toward the progressive cause. The Cuban government would follow it up with an invitation to the great artist. The short film TRAVEL NOTEBOOK was sent to Chaplin in Switzerland, where he had been living since being more or less forced out of the United States during the McCarthy period in the early fifties. A few months after the short's dispatch, however, Ivens began to doubt the appropriateness of his initiative and wrote to Chaplin: 'It was in my enthusiasm about everything I had seen and felt in Cuba and infinite admiration for your great work that I addressed you personally in this film. I hope that you can understand and forgive me my impulsiveness in this matter.' Chaplin's reaction went unrecorded.[6]

Without any great preparations, Ivens set off into the countryside with a keen Cuban crew. Their means of transport was a Cadillac, which Ivens described as cruising 'with the litheness of a big black cat'. They had already filmed over the entire island when they received a request from Castro that they interrupt their work for a film about the peasants' militia.[7] An offensive was planned against the thousand or so armed opponents of the regime still present in the dense forest of the Escambray Mountains in central Cuba.

In a military uniform, complete with cowboy boots and guerrilla cap, Ivens went up into the mountains for several weeks. The muggy Cuban climate was hard on his asthma to begin with, but in the humid air of the Escambray rainforest it was even harder for him to breathe. The expedition was a success all the same. A number of rebels were surrounded and taken prisoner, but their capture had taken place in poor light. Ivens asked the defeated insurgents to reenact their surrender at a more favorable time of day. 'Some agreed, some didn't. So we were able to reconstruct the night's events in daylight, in the same place, with the same captors and the same prisoners.'[8] He described the atmosphere as relaxed, with the prisoners calmly smoking cigarettes. He saw them as poor farmers who had been misled by Batista's people. With the exception of a few leaders, they were soon sent home. It did not occur to Ivens that they might have convictions of their own and feel like forced participants in a humiliating reconstruction. One year later Castro felt obliged to take the opposition more seriously and demanded the death penalty for every armed counterrevolutionary.[9]

The film about the militia, AN ARMED NATION, starts with peasants' touching attempts at military exercises, their clumsiness emphasizing that the defense of Cuba involved more than just the regular revolutionary army. The core of the film is the operation in Escambray and the climax is an edited sequence of marching masses intended to show that Cuba was prepared for any eventuality. This was not superfluous because on April 17, 1960 the CIA helped to land an anti-Castro force of 1,500 men in the Bay of Pigs. The invasion was defeated in two days. Ivens gave his other film, about his journey around the island, the title TRAVEL NOTEBOOK. It was the report of a political pilgrim, discovering everywhere the progress the revolution had brought to the island, something that happened to be true in several areas.

In spring 1961 he did the rounds of the socialist capitals. He first visited Moscow and Leningrad, where he showed his Cuban films among others, then stayed for a month in Peking, where he met with Premier Zhou Enlai. It was in Peking on April 12 that he heard the unimaginable news that an inhabitant of the earth had been in space for the first time and that it had been a Russian: Yuri Gagarin! Ivens saw it as confirmation of his belief that technology went hand in hand with social progress and made a note of his experiences on that historic day: 'Everyone on the street is happy. When I tell the girl in the elevator, *'Lian lo,'* the sixth floor, she answers, 'Not going any higher today?' No, not any higher, but my thoughts reach up into the cosmos. What did Gagarin see? How did he feel? This evening I have difficulty concentrating on my work: answering the Peking film school students' inquisitive and incisive questions about my experiences while making two films in Cuba: TRAVEL NOTEBOOK and AN ARMED NATION. From the broad boulevard below, I hear the sound of Chinese drums and cymbals, small groups of workers, students, carrying signs showing their vision of Gagarin, the cosmonaut, expressing their direct and spontaneous reaction to the latest and greatest success of Soviet science – a mighty Soviet victory. I can't sit still in my hotel room. I must join them. It is too much, this news. Today we have passed a new frontier in the conquest of nature.'[10] On his way back, he attended the ceremony in Gagarin's honor on Red Square, visited Ewa Fiszer in Warsaw, went to the Dutch embassy in Paris to extend his passport, and spent a week in East Berlin on a working visit to the DEFA studio.

He now began a first six-month appointment as general consultant in Cuba, where Fiszer came to keep him company for a few months in the Habana Libre Hotel, the former Hilton. After a new tour in the autumn, this time visiting the Leipzig international documentary festival, the DEFA studio, Moscow – 'to arrange many things that were going too slowly'[11] – and Prague, he returned to Cuba for two more three-month stints.

In Paris that spring Ivens had been given a passport with the normal period of validity. The Hague described this as 'erroneous', but Ivens had friends at the Dutch embassy in Paris and it is likely that they issued this passport deliberately and with pleasure. The Ministry of Foreign Affairs considered summoning him to the embassy in Havana in order to shorten the validity of his passport after all, and to take the opportunity to inquire as to his new job in Cuba. 'It is not impossible that Ivens has currently entered the service of the Cuban state without obtaining dispensation to do so.' In the end the path of least resistance was chosen and nothing was done.[12]

The officials' suspicions that Ivens had entered 'the service of the Cuban state' were closer to the truth than they could have guessed. Besides being a consultant with the ICAIC studios, he also worked for the Cuban army in 1962. After the Bay of Pigs invasion, the Cubans seriously expected another military attempt to overthrow the revolution and planned to film the following confrontation. Osmani Cienfuegos, one of the army's leaders, asked Ivens to familiarize a number of soldiers with the camera. Ivens consented but remained silent about this subject outside Cuba for twenty years.[13] If he had not, the Dutch state could have held him responsible for 'entering the service of a foreign state' or even 'entering the military service of a foreign state', the latter being strictly forbidden under Dutch law.

In Havana a story was spread that Ivens was spending time elsewhere in South America, whereas he was actually an hour's drive from the city at the Frank Paiz School, a heavily guarded hacienda that had once belonged to one of Batista's uncles. Ivens was in charge of training between forty and sixty military camera operators. Fidel Castro had explained that he wanted 'practical people who work fast. Soldiers, not artists.' Ivens had answered: 'I understand, you'll have to give me enough time.' 'How long?' 'Six months.' 'Six months?' laughed Castro. 'Out of the question. You've got a month!' They settled on a two-month training course.

The school only had one Paillard 16mm camera and hardly any other equipment, but improvisation was the trademark of the Cuban revolution. Ivens ordered a number of wooden imitation cameras and combat situations were simulated. 'They spread out over the field and filmed with their wooden cameras, one eye pressed against the hole of the viewfinder to capture the fictional images. After five or six minutes, I stopped the exercise and called everyone over. We sat down in a circle on the ground, and I questioned them all separately: 'And what did you do?' That was the most outstanding thing about this adventure. They all remembered the sequence they had filmed, and no two of them had filmed in the same way.'[14] His pupils later made army instruction films and reportages during the wars Cuban troops were involved in in Angola and Ethiopia.

Joris Ivens now felt completely at home on Cuba. 'Work and danger are pressing on all of us here, but the *Stimmung* is good. We feel strong, but it is a small island,' he wrote to Marion Michelle in Paris.[15] The new invasion never came, presumably because the USSR guaranteed Cuba's territorial integrity.

After several months in Europe, Ivens once again returned to Cuba in September 1962, only to find to his horror that most of the Cuban directors were 'in personal crisis. Surrounded by such a strong popular movement, people's courage grows along with the danger, but the ICAIC directors stand on the sidelines.'[16] The year before had already seen the 'PM affair', set off by and named after an insignificant 16mm television film about the port of Havana. PM had been banned for showing quite a few drunken Cubans who did not seem particularly determined to defend the revolution. Now, after several years of political films, a number of ICAIC directors felt a need for more personal work. They were infatuated with Alain Resnais's HIRO-SHIMA MON AMOUR and Michelangelo Antonioni's THE ADVENTURE and disgusted by the cinematic products the Soviet Union was foisting upon them.[17]

These issues were overshadowed by an international crisis that made Cuba the focus of global politics. With Castro's approval the Soviet Union had secretly installed intermediate-range ballistic missiles with nuclear warheads on the island, and these were discovered by an American U-2 re-connaissance aircraft in late August 1962. The United States felt threatened and demanded the immediate removal of the missiles. The world balanced on the edge of atomic destruction. 'The tension mounts here, the neighbor in the north is losing his head', Ivens wrote, but 'the Cubans are standing up excellently' despite 'many provocations'. The Habana Libre boasted a new view: 'From my balcony I can sometimes see one of their ships in the distance,' meaning an American warship.[18] At the end of October, Soviet leader Nikita Khrushchev backed down and announced the withdrawal of the missiles.

The army film school was not Ivens's only secret activity in Cuba. Latin America had long been marked by right-wing dictatorships, coups d'etat and the short lifespans of elected governments, and Cuba had become an in-spiration to the continent's opposition groups. This new situation made it possible for cinema to take on a more political role. At the 1960 Leipzig festi-val it had already been decided to set up an aid program for documentary filmmakers in developing countries, and the GDR had made scholarships available for six-month training courses. Participants in the scheme would also be given a free camera. The first students came from Argentina, Brazil and Peru, and the DEFA took charge of the training. In a memorandum, Joris Ivens and N. Buenauentura, central committee member of the Colom-bian Communist party, explained that these courses should be accompa-nied by a practical follow-up in Latin America for propaganda purposes in those countries. 'It is essential that an office or organization be set up in each country where they go to work in order to guarantee them legal protection, guide them politically, and finance their salaries and means of transport.' The Communist parties in the countries involved were to be informed, but a legal body should be formed whether they were interested or not.[19]

Working from a Havana villa with several assistants, Ivens began organizing the use of film as a weapon in the struggle in Latin America. It was 'a kind of semi-clandestine movement and I took on the leadership,' he wrote. 'There was no legal basis to our existence in Havana. If someone asked what I did they were given an extremely vague answer: 'Oh, Ivens is helping us film.'' He entered into one-on-one discussion with representatives from various countries, established their needs, provided equipment, arranged positions at the DEFA or ICAIC training courses, and personally bought equipment for them at a Mexico City flea market. Legal organizations as envisaged in East Berlin were established in Chile, Venezuela, Colombia and other countries. In Guatemala the contacts seemed to pass through the guerrilla movement, which was still collaborating with the pro-Moscow party at that time.

In Chile the legal cover was provided by the Instituto Cine Experimental, associated with the Cineteca Universitaria of the University of Santiago, where Sergio Bravo, Herman Valdes and Peter Chaskel were active – all members or sympathizers of the Chilean Communist party.[20] Ivens's communication with emerging director Sergio Bravo sometimes took extremely circuitous routes. At one stage Marion Michelle received news from Havana that Bravo would be visiting her in the rue Vaneau. 'He will be asking you information about his trip to his homeland... He is going to do a folklore film... The information to give to him, is that you will give him 220.000 old French francs for production costs and travel expenses. You should get this money from Geneviève.' By Geneviève, Ivens probably meant the wife of Raymond Leibovici. 'Tell him that I have sent him a camera 16mm to his country, that he should see there the writer Carlos Leon and start work immediately, and give me a report of his work. He can write me from his home via Paris, that is best. He should arrange himself a comfortable address in Paris, from where they forward his letters to me.'[21] Of course Bravo's film was not a 'folklore film' at all. In the same letter Ivens also mentioned a 'tourist film' about Spain which was actually an East German film by Jeanne and Kurt Stern about repression under Franco.

The measures to preserve secrecy were apparently successful. In June 1962 the FBI office in Miami reported: 'Selected sources have been contacted with negative results concerning the captioned subject and his activities in the Caribbean area.'[22]

From Cuba, Ivens's trips abroad included visits to Mexico, Chile and British Guiana, where in 1962 Premier Cheddi Jagan asked him to organize national film production. After Jagan was replaced by the more moderate Forbes Burnham this plan was cancelled.[23] In September of that year, in the middle of the Cuban missile crisis, Ivens flew from Havana to Chile to teach a group of students associated with Sergio Bravo at the University of Santiago. His mission to Chile seems to have had other aims as well, as evidenced by his detailed overviews of Chilean political figures of diverse plumage, and the list of '*amis personels d'Ackerman*', whom Ivens was supposed to visit in the name of this otherwise unknown figure. Ackerman's 'personal friends' were listed neatly according to political position and preferences and included a remarkable number of Christians, among them '(important) the Reverend Father Vekemans (Belgian Jesuit and *éminence grise* of Frei's party)'. Around this time, the Chilean Christian Democrats surrounding Eduardo Frei had joined the opposition to the conservative government, a fact that the Communists were naturally aware of.[24] 'Ackerman' could have been Anton Ackermann, whom Ivens had known since he had been the SED party ideologue in East Berlin in the early fifties. Ackermann became the GDR Underminister of Foreign Affairs, but was later degraded to the level of cultural functionary after internal party conflicts.

Resistance to the conservative regime in Chile grew, and Socialists and Communists worked together to gain power through the ballot box. In Chile Ivens met with an acquaintance from Cuba, the Socialist Salvador Allende, presidential candidate for the Socialist-Communist block. He was also finally able to visit the poet Pablo Neruda, an important figure in the Chilean Communist party. Ivens knew Neruda from diverse political festivals and congresses where they had taken the stage as celebrities, and Neruda had also lived for years in Paris, where he counted both Ivens and Ewa Fiszer among his friends. 'I saw Pablo and his wife Mathilde, they have invited us to visit them in Valparaiso and on Isla Negra,' Ivens wrote to Ewa, who came to Chile soon after.[25] Neruda was awarded the Nobel Prize for literature in 1971.

With all these activities, Ivens's primary goal must have nonetheless been the course at Sergio Bravo's Instituto Cine Experimentál. Ivens concentrated his lessons on a film he planned to make with his students: ... A Valparaíso. He began by asking them 'not to forget that I am a guest of your university, of your country. That is a source of obligations and limitations. My vision will be in the film, but not explicitly, not emphatically. Militant films, with criticisms, with solutions, accusations, are up to you, the young cineastes of Chile itself. It is not up to me to attack the current regime.'[26]

In mid-November Ivens began filming in the coastal town of Valparaiso with his students, but he was worried about not achieving 'a world-market quality', and asked French cameraman George Strouvé over as professional back-up. 'Valparaiso is a town, port, where the normal and the strange, the ordinary and the extraordinary, live together as if it is normal,' Ivens wrote to Marion Michelle. 'The ocean is present in the hills of the town, and on the shore you feel the hills. A town with much poverty. Dramatic town in its history: Les Corsairs who robbed the town, earthquakes, tidal waves, heavy storms, big fires, bombardments. Imagine, in 1615 a Dutch seaman (corsair, buccaneer) came to Valparaiso and robbed the people and killed many Spanish colons. His name, *Joris* Spilbergen, etc. – in 1962 etc.'[27]

Public transport on the slopes of Valparaiso was provided by some thirty cable railways. Their movement provides rhythm and structure to the film, which is closely related to THE SEINE MEETS PARIS in its impressionism, although this kaleidoscopic vision of urban life is much fiercer. In Bar Roland in the harbor an angry customer throws a bottle at a mirror, at which the film changes from black and white to color, the ominous red of blood.

Ivens edited VALPARAÍSO in Paris in spring, director Chris Marker wrote the commentary, and on June 8 the film premiered at the École Normale Superieur, the breeding ground for France's most influential intellectuals. Ivens considered the showing important for establishing his name in Paris.[28] Most French critics were positive about VALPARAÍSO and even *Cahiers du Cinéma* published a favorable review, despite the fierce opposition to Ivens from leading New Wave filmmakers. François Truffaut spoke of Ivens's 'pseudo-poetic career' and 'decorative – therefore right-wing – images, beneath which dedicated friend of the genre Chris Marker has endeavored to paste a leftist commentary in order to unify pictures that don't show anything.' In Holland photographer Ed van der Elsken had made similar noises: 'Ivens's VALPARAÍSO: which starts fantastically with the chanson *Nous irons à Valparaíso*, soon flounders when an 'artistic' voice begins exuding Chris Marker's pseudo-poetic commentary.'[29] In other words, up-and-coming young artists saw the film as old-fashioned and obsolete. VALPARAÍSO was refused for the competition at Cannes, but Ivens did win second prize at Bergamo.[30]

Ivens did not go back to Cuba to resume his Latin American coordinating work. He later stated that the Soviet Union pressured Havana to end it, which is possible, despite the network having been primarily linked to Moscow-oriented parties. The Kremlin and the pro-Moscow parties in Latin America favored the parliamentary road to socialism and were worried that Cuba might encourage armed struggle. From Paris, Ivens maintained contact with several of his South American connections into the seventies. He gave advice, arranged cameras or wrote recommendations, and made plans to return to the region himself. He hoped to make a major documentary about the social conditions in Venezuela and cherished plans for Bolivia as well; neither project came to anything. The 1964 coup in Brazil put an end to plans for a film about the peasants of the Mato Grosso.[31] He did make another film in Chile, a nine-minute 16mm short about Salvador Allende's election campaign: VICTORIOUS TRAIN. Real victory finally came for Allende in 1970. Because of commitments elsewhere, Ivens was unable to accept an invitation to attend his presidential inauguration. Three years later, Allende was murdered in the CIA-sponsored coup that brought General Augusto Pinochet to power.

Although Ewa Fiszer joined Ivens in Cuba and Chile, this did not mean that all was well with their marriage. 'What use is a documentary filmmaker to you as a husband?' asked Ivens in a letter in the summer of 1960. 'I understand your letters being full of accusations, of contempt, but if you could just once be a bit milder, if your letters could include just a few, a few friendly words, a few kind words, that would be very special to me.' In the same letter he wrote: 'I love and embrace you.' Two years later it was: 'At least give me the benefit of the doubt now and then.' In another letter, however, he revealed a change in his attitude. 'It is not only in my relationship with you that I react more intensely and better: I do it in the artistic area as well, I want to make militant films, to train militant camera operators, to be attacked, in view of the enemy.'[32] He knew where he stood again politically, and it is possible that escapades like the one in Italy with Sophie Wenek had increased his self-confidence in personal matters too.

After a long period he was once again open to a new serious relationship and in spring 1963 a candidate presented herself: Marceline Loridan. Twelve years earlier he had promised Ewa Fiszer his protective care; although unable to keep that promise, he was also incapable of simply abandoning her. It took more than a year for him to confess the truth to her, and in the summer of 1964 he wrote to her suggesting a divorce. 'What a shame,' she replied by telegram, 'been ill, love to our friends, wire your address'.[33] This laconic reply concealed her despair, and he tried to give her the bad news in small doses. In October he wrote to his brother Hans: 'I have separated from Ewa and am living with Marceline, but Ewa doesn't know that. As far as she's concerned I'm staying with Dr. Leibovici. I spoke with Ewa 1x, still not fixed up, but we're getting closer to finding a solution.'[34] Progress remained slow. She did not want a divorce and the marriage was not dissolved until 1967. Every year until his death, Ivens invited her to Paris – without an invitation from abroad, Poles were not allowed to travel to the

West – where she stayed in the apartment in the rue Guisarde. For twenty-five years they always met in the same place: Café La Mairie on the place Saint-Sulpice. In the apartment on the Podwale everything was left exactly as it was during Joris Ivens's last visit in the early sixties, and Ewa never stopped signing her letters 'Ewa Ivens-Fiszer'.

Marceline Loridan, nee Rozenberg, was born the third of five children on March 19, 1928 in Epinal in France. Her parents had emigrated from the ghetto in the Polish city of Lodz. Her father, Salomon Rozenberg, started in France as a worker in a yarn factory, began selling clothes at market, went on to become a shopkeeper, and ended up manufacturing textiles. He was a modern man. 'Even in Lodz he had defied his father, sneaking out on Saturdays, wearing modern hats and carrying a walking stick,' said Loridan.[35] At the start of World War II the family moved to the unoccupied part of France, but to no avail. Fifty members of the family were deported from Vaucluse to the German camps and few returned. Marceline Rozenberg was a girl of fifteen when she was transported to Bergen-Belsen and Auschwitz. She slept in Auschwitz-Birkenau in Barrack 27B with up to ten other women on a bunk a little over six feet long and six and a half feet wide. In the summer of 1944 'the transports arrived at a rate of eight to ten a day while there were only five crematoriums and gas chambers', she related. 'About five hundred thousand Hungarians went into them in a few weeks and we saw them lining up in rows for the gas chambers. And then that terrible smell of burnt flesh that penetrated everywhere.' She worked in the Messerschmidt factory. Forty-five years later she returned to Birkenau. 'I re-experienced all the humiliations they subjected us to: tattooing, shaving of heads and bodies, on parade for hours in rags or naked...'[36] The period in the camps marked her forever: erratic mood swings, vulnerability and insecurity, which changed into unreasonable severity at the least sign of threat.

After the war her family found a husband to give her a roof over her head. The marriage did not last long, but she kept his name after the divorce: Loridan 'was better than Rozenberg'. They lived near Saint-Germain-des-Prés, where Marceline felt at home among the children of war who gathered in the cafés and basement jazz clubs, attracted by the existentialist fashion. She was part of a 'big clan of young people who found themselves and each other. A substitute for the family.' She made a living as a pollster and studied psychology. Like the rest she was mainly searching: 'Of course I dreamed of making films, that was a preoccupation of mine in the fifties.'[37]

Shortly after the war, she joined the PCF,[38] but left the party after Khrushchev's revelations about Stalinism. Young people like her began seeing the PCF as a bastion of conservatism and conformity, and the clearest proof of this was the attitude the party took to the Algerian war of independence, which started in 1954. Until the early sixties the PCF opposed the Algerian struggle on nationalistic grounds, something that did not stop others on the left from supporting the liberation front, the FLN. From 1957 on, the so-called Réseau Jeanson was active in France, a network that provided all kinds of practical help to FLN members. Francis Jeanson had fallen out with Jean-Paul Sartre when they worked together as editors of *Les Temps Modernes*, but in 1959 Jeanson tried to gain the famous philosopher's support for his network. 'Marceline Loridan, one of the women in the organization, takes on the task. Marceline is thorough, reliable, she does not take clandestine work too lightly, she has been through a lot and her cautiousness is legendary. Furthermore, she has a very longstanding friendship with Evelyne Rey [one of Sartre's inner circle]. So Marceline asks Evelyne to gauge Sartre's availability and what he thinks of the support network.' She visited Sartre at his home and 'he immediately agreed to accompany me to Jeanson, who was in hiding at my place'.[39] At Marceline's in the rue de Chéroy, Sartre promised Jeanson his full support.

In the summer of 1960, her dreams about a cinema career became reality. Sociologist Edgar Morin had plans for a film about the atmosphere of the early sixties, and Anatole Dauman was to be the producer. Marceline knew them both and became one of the 'leading actors' in CHRONICLE OF A SUMMER. The cast included Jean-Pierre Sergent, with whom she had had a relationship for several years, and the student Régis Debray. Morin had asked cineaste-antropologist Jean Rouch to take charge of the filming, as he himself was a newcomer to the profession. CHRONICLE became an innovative film in both form and content. With the prototype of the new portable Coutant-Eclair 16mm camera with synchronized sound at his disposal, Rouch was able to achieve unprecedented mobility and immediacy. CHRONICLE OF A SUMMER led to a new concept and school in the history of film: *cinéma vérité*. Almost simultaneously, direct cinema arose in America. Both movements wanted to find truth in immediate visible reality.

CHRONICLE OF A SUMMER traces a number of friends through the summer of 1960. The jaunty pollster Marceline Loridan took to the streets with a microphone to ask passers-by 'How do you get by in life?' and 'Are you happy?' but when speaking of her own experiences in the camps she radiated enormous sadness. CHRONICLE shows the possibilities, and the limitations of *cinéma vérité*: in front of the camera the characters could not help but act out their lives and the making of the film ended up closely resembling group therapy.

Joris Ivens's attitude to this new fashion was ambiguous. As a professional, he was unimpressed; at the same time he did not want to shut out young people. The spirit of *cinéma vérité* in documentaries had a counterpart in fiction film, the New Wave, about which Ivens said: 'It is the new generation of young French filmmakers with their personal (bourgeois) problems, which they are expressing in the fiction films now conquering the screens of Paris.'[40] He recognized the beauty of the new technical possibilities; they gave you more authenticity but not necessarily more truth. Speaking to Chinese filmmakers, he explained New Wave as a bourgeois protest movement with very limited themes. It was all about eroticism, crime and the mystification of crime. The new means of expression had potential and he hoped that some of these young directors would develop further. On the same occasion he also told his Chinese colleagues something about Italian cinema, where Fellini and Antonioni unfortunately used their cinematic language to say that mankind would never understand life and was alone in the face of fate. It was all too pessimistic for Ivens. In Italy he saw Rossellini, De Santis and Pontecorvo as positive exceptions.[41]

In a skeptical article about *cinéma vérité* in the PCF journal *Les Lettres Françaises*, he posed the questions: 'Which truth? Seen by whom? Expressed by whom? Is it the whole truth or only a part of it? Which part?' He recalled that a major retrospective of his own work in Salle Pleyel in 1951 had been subtitled *Cinéma, arme de la vérité*. It was not the images themselves that expressed the truth, but their location in the context of the correct philosophy. In 1965, he again opposed the new approach by arguing for voiceover as an essential expression of the director's personal vision.[42]

These doubts did not stop him from defending the new generation at the Moscow Film Festival. He referred to Chris Marker, left-wing cineaste and maker of the archetypal *cinéma vérité* film LOVELY MAY, as 'France's leading documentary filmmaker', and told his Moscow audience that 'all these new movements and artistic endeavors by young filmmakers need to be accepted and stimulated, they have to leave the beaten track in order to explore new territory'.[43]

Accordingly, his criticism did not become a barrier to contact with his younger colleagues. Chris Marker, a quiet and reserved man, became a good friend. 'If there is one relationship that has been built on restraint and silence, this is it. When we meet each other we hardly speak,'[44] wrote Ivens, but this taciturnity was no barrier to mutual understanding. And there was also the thirty-five-year-old Marceline Loridan, who became his girlfriend, despite the fact that they seldom agreed. She believed in *cinéma vérité* and was opposed to the Soviet Union and the PCF, where Ivens was still a favorite son.

Ivens turned sixty-five that year. The older he became, the greater the difference in age between him and his female partners. Whereas Germaine was a year older, Anneke was four years younger, Helen ten, Marion fourteen, Ewa twenty-eight and Marceline thirty years younger. Ivens's character brings to mind the saying: 'If you're not a Communist at twenty, you don't have a heart. If you're still a Communist at thirty, you don't have a brain.' In his thinking, he never seemed to get any older than his twenties. Despite all the shocking things he experienced, and there were quite a few, he was averse to all kinds of skepticism, even though cynicism did creep in uninvited through the back door, because of his reluctance to face the bloody side of his own faith. He was attracted by the innocence of youth, not just by young women, but also by the young, idealistic colleagues he taught in China, Cuba and Chile. They enthused him, just as much as he enthused them.

Ivens explained later that he fell in love with Marceline the first time he saw her in CHRONICLE OF A SUMMER. Jean Rouch remembered asking Ivens to view a version of the film. During the screening Ivens had pointed at Loridan and asked: 'Who is that woman?'[45] In CHRONICLE she was precisely the kind of woman he had fallen for in the past: vulnerable, arousing his protective instincts, with a tragic past that had also made her worldly wise, and lastly, smaller than he was. A new Germaine, an Ewa, a combination of Helen and Anneke. Only Marion Michelle had been too carefree, too stable and too 'normal' to fit into this series. Later Ivens discovered Loridan's less pleasing qualities, her unpredictability and her bossiness, qualities he was defenseless against and which he automatically excused because of the sad experiences of her youth.

After Ivens's visit to Jean Rouch, however, a long time passed before he and Loridan actually met. In the spring of 1963 he was in Paris editing VALPARAÍSO, produced by Anatole Dauman's Argos Films. Another work in production at Argos Films was a documentary by the emerging filmmakers Marceline Loridan and Jean-Pierre Sergent: ALGERIA YEAR ZERO, shot in post-independence Algeria. Loridan asked Ivens to have a look at their rushes, but he was too busy and sent his editor Jean Ravel. They did not see each other again until months later at a photography exhibition on the place Saint-Germain. The middle-aged man with thick gray hair and somewhat rounded features went out for a meal with the small woman with freckles and bushy red hair, 'et voila!' according to Marceline Loridan's own account.[46] She must have seen Ivens as both father and lover, as a replacement for the security of the family she had lost. Around the end of 1964, they moved into an apartment on the sixth and seventh floors of 61 rue des Saint-

Pères, around the corner from the cafés de Flore and Aux Deux Magots. It remained their base until Ivens's death.

In the first half of 1960s, relations between the Communist superpowers, the Soviet Union and China, became increasingly strained. Moscow saw the build-up of nuclear weapons in East and West as grounds for peaceful co-existence with the capitalist world, Peking saw this as betrayal. As the Chinese party magazine *Red Flag* explained: 'If it really came to a nuclear war, this would lead to the rapid destruction of the monsters surrounding the peoples of the world, but never to the complete extermination of humanity.' While Moscow favored a peaceful road to socialism, Peking backed violent revolution. To a degree, Ivens had already been confronted with this conflict in Latin America, where the advocates of guerilla war and the pro-Soviet factions both felt an allegiance to Cuba. He saw these as subtle distinctions within one great movement, perhaps as variations in temperament. Personally he felt attracted to the struggle in the Third World – the armed struggle if necessary – and also by the zeal of China, but he did not see this as reason for distancing himself from Moscow. Even several years of public exchanges of abuse between Peking and Moscow could not destroy his belief in reconciliation.

Until 1968 Ivens's position resembled the attitude taken by North Vietnam, which he described: 'Every morning in my hotel room in Hanoi I had the right to a candy that was supposed to be part of the breakfast. One day it was a candy that had been made in the Soviet Union, the next day it was one from China, and this rule was never broken. In this way the Vietnamese expressed their faithfulness, their neutrality and their longing for independence.'[47]

Since leaving the DEFA and East Berlin in the mid-fifties, Ivens had returned with unfailing regularity for film festivals, discussions with colleagues, talks about further unspecified matters, and the occasional film production. An example of the latter was the Germans Jeanne and Kurt Stern's film about Spain for the DEFA. THE SPANISH EARTH was to be incorporated into their film and Ivens was appointed official consultant. In Moscow he discussed the project with Dolores Ibárruri, now leader of the Spanish party, and in Paris he tried to arrange filming in Spain itself through the Spanish Communist Jorge Semprun and others. The result, IN-DOMITABLE SPAIN, was released in 1962.[48]

Ivens cherished his friends in East Berlin, people like Hanns Eisler, whom he saw a few times every year in Paris or Berlin, and for the last a month before Eisler's death in 1962, when they discussed the music Eisler would write for a film Ivens was planning in British Guiana. The news of

Eisler's death reached him in Havana. 'Of course, it's a terrible shock to hear that someone who was born in 1898 has died: it's Brecht, it's Eisler, it's Eisenstein, it's Pudovkin (a bit older), Flaherty (much older). My heart could stop beating without any warning as well... One day someone in an elevator in a city somewhere in the world will say, 'Did you hear that Joris is dead?' People will be quiet. What is there to say? – That sentence doesn't depress me. I just want to live and work as well as I can.'[49]

He continued to identify with the East German state, even after it erected the Berlin Wall on August 13, 1961. Within two days the party daily *Neues Deutschland* published declarations in which Ivens's old acquaintances expressed their heartfelt support for the new measure: Hans Rodenberg, Kurt and Jeanne Stern, the filmmakers Annelie and Andrew Thorndike and Konrad Wolf (who had acted in FIGHTERS as a boy), Gustav von Wangenheim and Spanish volunteer Ludwig Renn.[50] Two years later on his birthday, Ivens himself received a letter from party leader and head of state Walter Ulbricht: 'We especially thank you for the positive attitude you publicly expressed after August 13, 1961 with regard to the protective measures taken by our Workers and Farmers' State against the aggressive ambitions of West German imperialism and militarism.'[51] It is unclear which form Ivens's public support for the Wall could have taken, but it is certainly plausible as there were no signs of his opinion having changed since his depiction of West Berlin as a hotbed of depravity in FRIENDSHIP TRIUMPHS.

The Deutschland Hotel in Leipzig must have been the only place in the world where the menu included an ice cream called the Coupe Joris Ivens. In the sixties the documentary film festival held each November in the city's Capitol and Casino theaters became a recurring highlight for Ivens, if only because it coincided with his birthday and the organizers invariably arranged a reception. Leipzig became a meeting place for the older generation of documentary filmmakers. Dziga Vertov and Robert Flaherty were dead. Flaherty's widow Frances, John Grierson, Alberto Cavalcanti, Roman Karmen, Henri Storck and the Britons Paul Rotha and Basil Wright were regular visitors to Leipzig. This gave the festival an important place in the world of documentaries, and Joris Ivens became a member of the permanent international presidium of honor.

In 1963 he attained the retirement age of sixty-five, grounds for the festival to mount a major Ivens retrospective. The celebrations were not a surprise – he traveled to Berlin several times to discuss the preparations – but they were on a grand scale. A 366-page festschrift was published, the DEFA made the documentary HE FILMED ON 6 CONTINENTS, which was broadcast on GDR television, and there was a symposium on Ivens's work chaired by Underminister of Culture Hans Rodenberg. In Berlin Walter Ulbricht presented him with the Stern der Völkerfreundschaft and at the art academy Konrad Wolf praised him as a 'Wahrheitsfanatiker', a truth fanatic.[52]

Chris Marker was awarded the festival's main prize that year for his experimental LOVELY MAY, a daring choice in GDR terms and a source of controversy. According to East German jury member Karl Gass, only the intervention of Ivens saved those involved from unpleasant consequences. In a personal meeting, Ivens managed to convince Ulbricht that Marker was a good choice for both diplomatic and political reasons.[53]

While Ewa Fiszer was not present in Leipzig in 1963, Marion Michelle and Marceline Loridan both attended. Loridan had rejected Eastern Europe years earlier and once provoked an uproar at Leipzig by fiercely criticizing Eastern European Communism and demonstratively making an early exit, leaving Ivens behind to placate their disgruntled hosts. The East Germans saw Marion Michelle as a more appropriate partner for Ivens than the critical Frenchwoman, and this preference was reflected in the seating arrangements.[54]

One of the annually recurring rituals was Ivens's visit to his own Joris Ivens Socialist Brigade, a group of turners at the Volkseigene Betrieb Bodenbearbeitungsgeräte Leipzig, a factory for agricultural machines. His arrival was a welcome diversion; they brought out chairs, sat down, poured coffee and relaxed. 'We have saved 40,000 marks in the last year,' they would say to their patron. But he preferred discussing more enjoyable subjects and asked: 'Has anyone gotten married in the meantime or have any children been born?' Yes indeed: 'The new dad's sitting here.' Ivens described his adventures of the last year, the workers presented him with photographs and a pennant, and then it was: 'Until next time.'[55]

Meanwhile, Ivens was busy arranging his come-back in Holland. Since the fifties he had kept in touch with Jan de Vaal, the director of the Dutch Film Museum, and after the successful presentation in his fatherland of THE SEINE MEETS PARIS in 1959, they had regularly consulted on the formation of an Ivens Archive, to be housed in the Film Museum in Amsterdam.[56] In time, Jan de Vaal became the chief protector of Ivens's interests in Holland. Sadi de Gorter of the Dutch embassy in Paris suggested that Ivens look for work in his own country, and by 1962 contacts had been established with Joop Landré's film production company. In the following year, the project began to crystallize. Landré, former director of the Government Information Service and future head of the radio and television broadcaster TROS, proposed a documentary about Rotterdam's port. Ivens suggested films about 'Two Cities' – Amsterdam and Venice – or 'The Clouds'.[57] The story about the clouds was very similar to the outline of a film Ivens had hoped to make in the South of France about the mistral. He also launched a third idea for a Dutch film: 'The Flying Dutchman', going back to an old idea from the Filmliga days. Besides being a film plan this was, of course, a brilliant PR idea, because Joris Ivens himself was actually the Flying Dutchman: wandering over the continents, rejected by his fatherland... For three decades the Dutch media would milk this metaphor for all it was worth.

In 1963 the Dutch authorities were faced with a promotional problem. A director needed to be found at short notice for the third part of a trilogy about Dutch coastal protection, the first two parts of which had been made by John Fernhout and Bert Haanstra. Ivens was suggested as a candidate, but the centre-right Marijnen government had no desire to allow him to make a government film and considered that 'calling in this person would unavoidably lead to entanglement in Communist propaganda and cultural events. As a means of promoting goodwill toward the Netherlands, the cabinet considered this scenario rather unattractive.'[58] Only the year before, Joseph Luns's Ministry of Foreign Affairs had refused to send a representative to the Dutch Film Days in Münster in West Germany because of the inclusion of INDONESIA CALLING! in the program.[59]

The discussion of Joris Ivens's position soon entered a more public arena when the Dutch Film Museum under De Vaal's management decided, with students of the newly established Amsterdam Film Academy, to emulate Leipzig with a major celebration of Ivens's sixty-fifth birthday. The trendsetters at the academy found their main inspiration in the French New Wave. Despite the obvious discrepancies, Ivens became their idol. There was a great need for a Dutch filmmaker who could serve as an inspiration. 'Did they actually know his work?' wondered filmmaker Jan Vrijman at the time, or in their attempt 'to rebel against the *cinéma de papa*' were they merely grasping at Ivens's 'Granddad's cinema?'[60] The sixties were dawning and the students were more impressed by Ivens's attitude than by his work. One of their leaders, the later filmmaker Pim de la Parra, summarized that attitude as 'independent, not wanting to be an asshole, standing up for what you stand for, relating to others without compromising their dignity, natural modesty, not preying on others, being concerned about what you do'.[61] On February 11, 1964 Joris Ivens arrived at Schiphol Airport for a grand reception in Amsterdam that would last a week.

The press was more than favorable in their reporting of Ivens's return. 'Let's hope that his visit to Holland will have lasting consequences,' wrote *Vrij Nederland* and this was representative of the general drift, with the *Handelsblad* adding that it was already too late, since 'Ivens now needs Holland less than Holland needs him.' *De Volkskrant* made a critical aside by calling THE FIRST YEARS a glorification of 'the people's republics imposed by Russian troops'. The reviewer felt obliged to 'place these few bitter pills among all the garlands being laid out (rightly) for Joris Ivens in these days', but he too believed that the main thing was that in the rest of his oeuvre, 'Communist and all', Ivens had maintained 'absolute artistic integrity'. As usual, only *Het Parool* was skeptical, but even it headlined an article published shortly before his arrival: 'Holland too shy of Joris Ivens.'[62]

Virtually all Dutch journalists and reviewers were enthusiastic about Ivens. After interviewing the almost legendary director, a reporter from the weekly *De Groene Amsterdammer* beautifully captured the way they felt: 'In the hours we spent talking I asked him questions. I listened and looked at him. Frankly, I scrutinized him. Well then, this man has nothing in common with doctrinaire Communists. What I heard and saw was a man with a number of honest beliefs about justice and injustice. Who might have noticed one injustice and overlooked another. But most of all, he was a man who is absorbed by his work, who loves it fiercely and wants to film and film and film again. Such great affection for the métier always radiates an irresistible charm, it makes one willing to see the mistakes he might have made in a different light, if not ignore them. I would like to go a step further: those Dutchmen who are unable to forgive Ivens for what they see as his political errors are themselves partly responsible for his having made them, because the talent that he has now used in the service of matters and struggles that many object to could have benefited our own country. Ivens is definitely not a political person first and foremost. He might not be one at all.' The journalist ended his piece with words that said it all: 'A great artist and a nice guy, or the inverse, that is Joris Ivens.'[63]

Ivens really was an extraordinarily friendly man, and virtually everyone allowed their assessment of his work and deeds to be partly or even chiefly determined by the sympathy he generated in their personal encounters. For many people, the fact that he was all three things at once, a charming man, an enthusiastic filmmaker and a Communist hardliner, went beyond their powers of imagination.

After Ivens had returned to Paris, the Minister of Education, Science and the Arts was asked in parliament if he was aware that the cineaste 'had expressed a desire to make a film in Holland' and whether the minister had not considered 'officially commissioning him to do so'. The minister answered that Ivens had stated such wishes at a press conference, and that he was therefore aware of them, but that it was up to Ivens himself to apply to the ministry for a free commission according to the procedure applicable to every Dutch director. 'The undersigned sees no grounds for deviating from this course of events with regard to Mr Ivens.'[64] The reason behind this postscript was that several film critics had pressed the ministry to commission Ivens without requiring him to first submit a request, and Ivens's future producer Joop Landré had written to the ministry a year earlier in a 'strictly confidential' attempt to tempt the ministry to commit itself without Ivens first submitting an official application.[65] The background to this squabbling was that Ivens wanted to make a film with Dutch subsidies but refused to submit an application, even after hearing from the ministry in the summer of 1963 that 'the possibilities are very favorable'.[66]

Ivens wanted public reparations from The Hague. The government had to openly admit its error, that was the line he consistently took from then on. It was true that he had been harassed about his passport for thirteen years during the Cold War, that it had been confiscated for six months, and that he had subsequently been forced to constantly renew it for short periods, but his later claim that he spent ten years without a passport was exaggerated. In Ivens's mind the issue grew out of all proportion. The Eastern European authorities had hindered him in his work far more than the Dutch government ever had, but he never uttered word of complaint about that in public. And it was of virtually no concern to him that his Polish wife had to battle through weeks of red tape whenever she wanted to set foot over the border. Despite attempts at reconciliation from the Dutch government, his attitude remained implacable for many years. More than a political issue, his feelings about the Dutch authorities were a question of psychology. All the rejection and hurt that had plagued him since the thirties now focussed on that one dot on the map of the world: the seat of Dutch government in The Hague.

In 1964 Ivens received film proposals from the Dutch company Continental Engineering and from the Royal Dutch Football Association, neither of which went to production. Through Joop Landré he finally accepted a commission from the City of Rotterdam, a project that first had to wait for more important matters overseas though: for the next three or four years the war in Vietnam had his almost undivided attention.

20 A Socialist Scoop (1964-1968)

'One day in 1958 I was lying on my back in St.Tropez looking up at the clouds.' This is how Joris Ivens described the birth of his film MISTRAL.[1] It was in the middle of his apolitical film phase, and the next year he began searching for a producer. His story about a mistral film was met with skepticism almost everywhere. 'How do you intend to make a film with an invisible main character?' everyone asked, but Jacques Prévert had provided Ivens with the perfect comeback. 'That's just like a producer saying, 'You want to make a cowboy film? Fine, but I want to see the bullets!''[2]

The financiers' reluctance was understandable. Ivens had only recently returned from Eastern Europe and the films he had made there did not augur well for the success of his wind project. The only recent work they had to go on was THE SEINE MEETS PARIS and, after 1963, VALPARAÍSO. His mistral plan was rather vague as well. In September 1963, after he had been pursuing the project for years, l'Express magazine asked him how exactly he imagined it. 'I'm not entirely sure,' he answered. 'When I make a film I never have all my ideas worked out beforehand. I let myself be carried along.' He explained that he would start in Haute-Provence, research the experiences the locals had had with the mistral, then move south to end in Marseilles, where the mistral dissipated over the Mediterranean.

'Everyone has his own wind,' he elaborated. 'Ask someone what he thinks of the wind, and his answer will reveal his character.'

'And you, what do you think of the wind?' was the interviewer's astute rejoinder.

'Me? What do I think of the...'

'Yes, of the wind, you?'

'Er... Well... It's movement. It comes from somewhere, but you don't know where from... a force of nature that purifies, that carries... You have to battle the wind, in an intelligent way, use it intelligently... and at the same time it's a mystery...'

The wind reminded him of his childhood in the Netherlands, where he had enjoyed watching the clouds as a boy. Another time he called the wind 'a sign of renewal, of rejuvenation, the wind that sweeps away all the old things'.[3] He had a vision, but was it a film?

He envisaged a complete mistral program. His own film would last three-quarters of an hour, starting in black-and-white, changing into color, and finally broadening into Cinemascope as an illustration of the growing power of the rising mistral. There would also be a cartoon by McLaren, whom he had met in Canada during the war, or else an intermezzo of ten minutes based on sayings about people trying to sell the wind. A number of Provençal amateurs would be asked to make short cinematic impressions, and a director would be sought for a twenty-minute fiction film about a love affair involving the wind.[4]

In Claude Nedjar he finally found a producer willing to take the risk. Nedjar was open to all kinds of experimentation, but the means at his disposal were modest and the project was constantly struggling with a lack of funds. In October 1963 Ivens toured Provence in search of locations and made the first shots. He already anticipated that much of the time would be taken up with waiting for the mistral to blow. 'Poor camera operators. But the arrival of the mistral is something extraordinary: in a few minutes everything is changed, the people, things, the colors, the cypresses are green torches against a beautiful hard sky, the perspectives are altered, everything is sharper and closer.'[5] More than a year later he wrote to Marion Michelle from Marseilles: 'I'm trying to make a good film but it's difficult. The mistral is still scared of our camera.' On May 17, 1965, after three periods filming in the South of France, he was finally able to inform his brother Hans that the shooting was over. It had become 'very good material', and 'we are trying to raise money for editing and mixing'.[6]

Afterwards, Ivens's faithful enemy François Truffaut, who referred to him as 'a festival freeloader', believed Ivens had actually received too much money because he had 'wasted the entire profits of the young producer of René Allio's THE SHAMELESS OLD LADY on a medium length film about the wind (!) (forty minutes for fifty million) which would never be distributed.'[7] Truffaut cited a figure of fifty million old French francs, no small amount for a documentary. Wherever he had obtained his information, his opinion was clear: the money would have been better spent on a fiction film by a New Wave director.

There was no money to make the rest of the mistral program and Ivens's own film with a length of some thirty minutes was left to stand on its own. One year after its completion he wrote to Marion Michelle: 'I don't like the film very much. It is too removed from my original conception. Text is bad and pompous. I'll try to change it.'[8] The film still won him the Golden Lion of San Marco at the 1966 documentary festival in Venice. An unbiased viewer, unaware of the maker's grandiose ambitions, saw a modest attempt to capture the mistral in creative images and was charmed for that very reason, with the underlying idea that searching is often more important than finding.

In the middle of the production of MISTRAL, Ivens suddenly disappeared on a mysterious journey. In June 1964 Marion Michelle received a letter from

Geneva: 'This time I think my decision is one of the most serious and dangerous ones I ever took. Not that I take sides completely, but everybody will think so. For the moment I keep quiet where I am going. In Paris it is only you and Marceline who know, others do not know, or guess. For everybody I am somewhere in the South of France till end of July, or on Corsica or so, without address, chasing the wind and taking some vacation. In Holland only Hans and my niece Henriet know where I am.' He was about to fly to Hanoi on the invitation of the North Vietnamese government.[9]

Since the Second World War, Vietnam had been ravaged by continuous violent conflict. Indochina had been colonized by France in the nineteenth century, and in 1945 Vietnamese nationalists under the Communist leader Ho Chi Minh had declared independence. A struggle between the Vietminh and the French colonial army ensued and did not end until the humiliating French defeat at Dien Bien Phu in 1954. An agreement temporarily dividing Vietnam along the seventeenth parallel was signed at a conference of the major powers in Geneva. While awaiting general elections, the North became Communist and the South oriented toward the West. Whereas in Korea it had been the North that had rejected free elections, now it was the South Vietnamese dictator Ngo Dinh Diem who refused to participate, with the backing of the Americans, who feared a Communist electoral victory. Under the leadership of Ho Chi Minh – for many Vietnamese the father of the nation – the guerrilla war was resumed in an attempt to force reunification. The chances of success were considerable, as the South was governed by a series of incompetent dictators. The Americans saw this last fact as further grounds for direct intervention, and by 1964 the Seventh Fleet was cruising the coastal waters and more than fifteen thousand American advisors were assisting the South Vietnamese army. 'If you see that an American *general* became ambassador in Saigon, then danger is not far,' wrote Ivens in June 1964. 'I think it will be a long game there.' Two months later the Americans commenced bombing raids on North Vietnam.[10]

After arriving at Hanoi's sleepy Giam Lam Airport, Ivens was taken to the Chien Min Hotel. Hanoi was the former colonial capital and traces of French rule were visible everywhere: in Eiffel's gigantic steel bridge over the Red River, in the stuffy colonial buildings and in the old French trams rattling down bicycle-filled streets. Ivens was introduced to his appointed interpreter and doctor, Xuan Phuong, who would accompany him on all his journeys through Indochina over the next four years. She was enthusiastic, cheerful, captivating and not easily alarmed. He would need her medical help more than once, as his asthma did not respond well to the Vietnamese climate.

His first visit to Hanoi was mainly to assess the situation. He became acquainted with the deplorable state of North Vietnamese cinema: one studio for documentaries and newsreels with a staff of some two hundred and fifty but only one editing bench on which North Vietnam's entire film production was spliced, including the odd fiction film. Everything else was in short supply as well, and even the classics of cinematic history were virtually unknown to his Vietnamese colleagues. On the positive side came their unequalled improvisational skills and great revolutionary zeal.

After returning to Paris, Ivens carefully kept his trip to Vietnam secret; the war in the former colony was a delicate issue. When making his second trip to Hanoi 1965, he again kept the journey secret outside of his inner circle. He first went to China, where he traveled the country and met with Premier Zhou Enlai, then proceeded to North Vietnam. From Peking he wrote to Marion Michelle: 'Could you do me a favor and mail the enclosed letter to Claude Nedjar... I am supposed to mail it from Caracas, Venezuela, that is better.'[11] Although one year before he had said that he would not fully take sides in Vietnam, he now saw the country as 'the point where the imperialists' attack is the heaviest' and was glad to accept the Vietnamese request to stay and teach film. He had an extensive discussion with president Ho Chi Minh. 'This time not the mistral, but the wind of history leads me.'[12]

In February 1965 the Americans began a new round of bombing of North Vietnam. On March 8 the first American combat troops landed on the beach at the South Vietnamese port of Danang. In the course of the year, the U.S. military presence in South Vietnam grew to almost two hundred thousand men. High time to inform the public in the West, thought Ivens, and in June he began a short film that ended up developing into THE THREATENING SKY, an agitational work juxtaposing two opposing worlds: the Americans in their aircraft with no direct contact with their enemies and the North Vietnamese, carrying on with their lives under the daily threat from the air. He spent weeks in a projection room going through the Vietnamese archives in search of footage to supplement his own shots. Back in Paris he skillfully welded the rather disconnected visual material into an effective whole. The French censors demanded that a number of sentences be dropped from the commentary, among them: 'Carpet bombing, that's Hiroshima on a smaller scale.'[13]

In September 1965 Ivens and Marceline Loridan traveled to Rotterdam, where the municipal commission for a short film about the harbor had been waiting for more than a year. They took rooms in the Rijnhotel and worked at high speed to shoot most of a twenty-minute 16mm film in just four weeks: ROTTERDAM EUROPORT. Cameraman Eddy van der Enden shot the rest of the film without Ivens being present. Loridan fulfilled the role of assistant to the director – with difficulty, since they were working in Dutch, a language she didn't understand.[14]

The Rotterdam film was to be about a living city growing around its port, but beyond this Ivens did not really clarify the project to his co-workers. They had no idea which direction he wanted to take the film, and he might not have really been sure himself. He was, after all, a documentary filmmaker who allowed himself to be largely guided by his impressions on the spot. What was certain was that there was to be a fictional element involving a visit to Rotterdam by the Flying Dutchman. This time the legendary mariner did not travel by sailing ship, but rounded the breakwaters at the Hook of Holland in a speedboat and decked out in James Bond garb. The hero viewed Rotterdam with seventeenth century eyes, admired the technological progress, but was anxious about the neglect of social aspects. A heavily symbolic moment was the scene in which the Flying Dutchman zoomed under the bridge over the Maas River, the subject of Ivens's first film thirty-seven years earlier.

After shooting, friction arose between Ivens and producer Joop Landré. The director had wanted to film segments in Cinemascope and was disappointed when Landré told him that the budget did not allow it. When Ivens then informed him that he needed supplementary takes, the producer answered: 'I am apparently unable to convince you that we are making a considerable loss on this commissioned film, even though we could normally expect it to yield a reasonable profit, and I am not ashamed to tell you straight out that I do not have any more money to again shoot thousands of guilders worth of new footage.' New exasperation arose when Ivens asked the Rotterdammers to come to Paris to view the working copy, an inversion of the usual practice of the filmmaker taking his work to the client. Had Ivens succumbed to the prevailing belief in Paris that Holland should be happy every time that city glanced northward? 'It might sound a little bitter, but for myself I am convinced that I could have expected a somewhat friendlier and fairer collaboration than has been the case up to now,' wrote Landré.[15]

On April 26, 1966 ROTTERDAM EUROPORT finally premiered in Rotterdam's Lumière Theater, in the presence of mayor Wim Thomassen and the director, who had brought a bottle of cognac for municipal public relations officer Ivo Blom. The film was screened the world over as part of activities promoting Rotterdam, and in Wellington, Pretoria, Bern, Buenos Aires, Sydney, Bonn and Mexico City everyone agreed: ROTTERDAM EUROPORT was quite interesting artistically but a useless publicity film.[16]

As the appearance of the Flying Dutchman suggested, Rotterdam Europort was intended as a milepost in the reconciliation between Ivens and Holland. In reality the film was little more than a distraction in the midst of Ivens's preoccupation with Vietnam. The Threatening Sky had been released that year and began playing an important role in the rapidly growing Vietnam movement. Ivens personally showed the film to workers, students and intellectuals at the most diverse locations, and in *Le Monde* and *France Nouvelle* he appealed to his colleagues to provide practical support for North Vietnam in the form of equipment and film stock. Henri Storck was one of the first to react. He donated an editing bench.[17]

Joris Ivens still had excellent contacts with the PCF and was very popular among Communist youth. The one had been a natural extension of the other, but as the sixties progressed, the PCF and its youth became increasingly hostile toward each other, with Ivens caught in the middle.

Since the fifties one of the foundations of the French youth movement had been the *cinéma parallèle*, which had expanded to become an extensive network of film clubs, union halls and student associations where films were shown that were too obscure, experimental, low budget or political for the big theaters. Before the emergence of television as a mass medium, many young people in France saw film as an essential, and the *cinéma parallèle* was both cinematic culture and a social movement. The Cinéclub Action in particular embodied the fusion of cinema and politics, and inspired a number of young people to make their own militant films. Marceline Loridan and Jean-Pierre Sergent's Algeria Year Zero was just one of dozens of shorts about Algeria, mostly of mediocre quality, to emerge from this movement.

The alternative cinema became a breeding ground for opposition to the ossification of the PCF, which was all-powerful on the left, and the Communist student movement, the UEC, also distanced itself from the mother party. Ivens was popular with the UEC because he 'sang the song of Communism the way young people liked to hear it'.[18] The radical wing of the UEC found its inspiration in the independent policies of Italian Communist leader Palmiro Togliatti, and its supporters were nicknamed Italians. This was the line Loridan followed as well. In the mid-sixties the Vietnam War became a new point of conflict for the left because whereas the PCF followed Moscow's policies by demanding 'Peace in Vietnam', the Communist student movement set up the Comité Vietnam National under the militant slogan: 'For the victory of the Liberation Front.' In 1965 the opposition within the UEC was expelled on orders from the PCF, and thereafter the party's influence among students declined rapidly. The independent

Union Nationale des Etudiants de France, the UNEF, became the leading left-wing student organization.[19]

Ivens was far from ready to break with the PCF or Moscow, but his personal allegiance to North Vietnam would not be denied. The Soviet Union gave precedence to the international balance of power and aimed for compromise in Indochina. Hanoi, on the other hand, had no intention of abandoning the struggle before Vietnam was unified under its leadership. Later Ivens referred to the 'inadmissible' PCF slogan 'Peace in Vietnam', and in the mid-sixties he undoubtedly felt more affinity for the radical line on this point. His provisional solution was to take a position between the camps. From 1965 on, he sat on the recommending committee for the annual UNEF festival, and in 1966, to his gratification, this organization mounted a major Ivens retrospective in Paris in the Musée de l'Homme and the Musée des Arts Décoratifs. In France and far beyond its borders, Ivens's Vietnam films became an almost ritual element in the programming of all kinds of student gatherings.

The apartment on the rue des Saints-Pères was adapted to the spirit of the times. One of the rooms was painted red, and between the books and cans in Ivens's study a Dutch journalist discovered 'an extensive collection by and about the Amsterdam Provos', including Dutch writer Harry Mulisch's *Bericht aan de rattenkoning.*[20] In 1966, for the first time in at least thirty-five years, he joined in public criticism of the Soviet Union, albeit criticism that came from the bosom of the PCF itself. In Moscow the writers Andrei Sinyavsky and Yuli Daniel had been sentenced to forced labor for 'the dissemination of defamatory fabrications' about the USSR, and a protest against this verdict was signed by artists and intellectuals linked to *Les Lettres Françaises*, among them Joris Ivens. However, this proved no barrier to his proposing a film production about Vietnam to the World Peace Council and the Soviet Union that same year.[21]

His more moderate friends were fond of attributing his gradual radicalization to the influence of Marceline Loridan. But even before meeting her, he had been impressed by the unflagging zeal in China and had felt perfectly at home among the Cuban revolutionaries. He also made his first trip to Hanoi without Loridan, who was not involved in THE THREATENING SKY. He placed Cuba and Vietnam on a line with the Spanish Civil War. In his search for rejuvenation, for the pure expression of the ideals he thought he remembered from the thirties, his relationship with Marceline Loridan seemed more a consequence than a cause.

Vietnam was also important to French filmmakers, and towards the end of 1966, Chris Marker brought directors Alain Resnais, Jean-Luc Godard, Wil-

liam Klein, Claude Lelouch, Agnès Varda, Joris Ivens and several others together for a combined project. Simone Signoret arranged office space at the
newspaper *France-Soir*. Chris Marker already had political films such as
Cuba Si! and Sunday in Peking to his name, and his Lovely May had
shown Parisians' reactions to the Algerian War. Most importantly, Marker
had the personal qualities needed to successfully conclude a collaboration
between these diverse directors, some of whom were distinctly lacking in
modesty. He had the tact and the professionalism to avoid the pitfalls and
draw the best out of the others. The members of his small flock had such divergent visions that the final product, Far from Vietnam, became something of a bizarre mix: Ivens's committed documentary from Hanoi, mainly
shot by Loridan; Klein's humorous account of demonstrations and counter-
demonstrations in the United States; Godard's egocentric reflections;
Resnais's images of a fretful intellectual in a moral dilemma; and several
other ingredients. The contributions by Godard and Resnais in particular
make Far from Vietnam a far-from-flattering portrait of the sixties feeling
in France and evoked a sense of embarrassment in various critics. The more
down-to-earth contributions by Ivens and Klein were, however, generally
praised. Together with Agnès Varda, Ivens traveled to the Montreal World
Film Festival, where Far from Vietnam had its world premiere on August
16, 1967.

Thanks to the famous names, Far from Vietnam ran in four Paris theaters and in many provincial towns. There was a minor sensation when the
right-wing extremist organization Occident protested by smashing show-
cases and slashing seats in one of the Paris theaters. The large-scale distribution was a failure, and in retrospect Chris Marker regretted not having
aimed straight at the target group through the *cinéma parallèle*. Nevertheless,
his work on Far from Vietnam did give birth to the Iskra film collective.
Through its documentaries about the workers' struggle, this collective centered on Marker himself played an important role in the left-wing movement in France in the following years.[22]

Joris Ivens and Marceline Loridan had been in Hanoi since mid-February
1967, with Ivens giving a course at the film school while Loridan did most of
the filming for Far from Vietnam. The Vietnamese soon suggested that
Ivens give up his teaching and make a major new film instead, something
like a Vietnamese version of Spanish Earth. Since Loridan and he did not
have the necessary equipment with them, the Vietnamese bought an
Arriflex camera and a Nagra recorder from an American journalist in Hanoi.[23] Ivens and Loridan obtained raw stock from colleagues and had their
Paris secretary, Michèle Pierret, forward film material via neutral Cambo-

dia. It was to be Ivens's first 16mm film with synchronized sound and Loridan became the sound recordist. They were most interested in the area around the seventeenth parallel, the demarcation line between North and South and the site of heavy fighting. The authorities considered this too risky and began praising a quieter area around the twentieth parallel, a little over a hundred miles south of Hanoi. According to Ivens, only one person was susceptible to his arguments, Ho Chi Minh. They were eating lunch with president Ho and prime minister Pham Van Dong, when Ho said, 'But surely *la petite* isn't going with you?' Marceline Loridan protested fiercely: 'Oh, but it's all much rougher than you might even be able to imagine. I don't know if you...' Ho suddenly noticed the number on her forearm. 'Were you in a camp?' 'Yes,' answered Loridan. 'Which one?' 'Auschwitz.' 'Really! And you came out of that chimney alive?' Whereupon Ho Chi Minh consented to her departure for the demarcation line. 'In my memories those are the kind of moments I treasure,' said Ivens.[24]

Interpreter Xuan Phuong was also present at the meeting with Uncle Ho. 'In the end they let him go, a whole team was formed to safeguard his life.'[25] Eleven-strong, the group headed south in late April 1967. Driving in three military vehicles, it was a three-hundred-mile journey over a strategic route. In addition to Ivens, Loridan and Xuan Phuong, there were two camera operators, a head of convoy, a security man, an organizer and three drivers. The road was full of military convoys, and they could only drive at night without lights. Since the permanent bridges had all been destroyed, they had to cross the rivers on small ferries or makeshift bamboo bridges. At the Ham Rong bridge they were told that the Americans had carried out four hundred bombing raids in two years. A little further along, cameraman Dao Le Binh was slightly wounded when hit in the throat by a piece of shrapnel from a fragmentation bomb, and in Ha Tinh Province, they had just crossed two dangerous ferries when the sky was lit up by magnesium flares dropped by parachute from American aircraft in order to locate targets. On that occasion Loridan suffered a knee injury when the driver bumped into a stationary truck. She could no longer walk and was left at a medical post, where she had to spend a week in bed. Cameraman Nguyen Quang Tuan kept her company while the others carried on. 'Afterwards the solidarity of the group was much greater,' said Xuan Phuong. Loridan had already partly won over the skeptical Vietnamese by the stubbornness with which she protected her recorder in difficult conditions.[26]

The route they were taking was subjected to constant bombing. 'We heard them coming from far away', wrote Ivens, 'from the South, and they approached at a constant speed, like a sound wave gaining more and more volume, until it was an enormous thundering racket over our heads. Then came a moment at which it became unbearable and that moment went on without end. Bombs fell everywhere, in front of us, behind us, on both sides of us, and it was always too much. In cases like that there was only one possibility. If the state of the road allowed it, the driver changed gear and drove as fast as he could. This being thirty miles an hour at most. If that wasn't possible we leapt out of the command car and ran into the jungle, fiercely hoping that the damned Americans wouldn't be so incompetent as to miss the road and drop their bombs in the jungle... There were bomb craters everywhere. We dived into the first one we came to. We didn't have any flashlights, we couldn't see where we put our feet, we slid into one of the holes and hugged the ground, in water up to our knees. It was lukewarm oily water and we felt things moving against our legs. Most of those craters were crawling with leeches and snakes.'[27] That year Ivens celebrated his sixty-ninth birthday.

Loridan and Ivens were firm supporters of Hanoi when they arrived, and their war experiences only strengthened their solidarity with the North Vietnamese struggle. Similarly in the South, even the most critical journalists were touched by the way American and South Vietnamese soldiers suffered at the hands of elusive guerilla units. Ivens wrote in his diary that his aim was clear: 'to take a film back to Europe, there is much to tell, especially to the revisionists.' A new word in his vocabulary: the revisionists, the Soviet Union and its allies, who deviated from revolutionary doctrine and failed to lend their full support to the armed struggle against American imperialism. 'We had to defeat our common enemy, and here they were, busy defeating him.'[28] To make a film about the war, you needed to be filmmaker and revolutionary all at once, he wrote in the magazine *Vietnam*, published in Hanoi. 'You have to closely read and study General Vo Nguyen Giap's book *People's War, People's Army*.'[29]

At the seventeenth parallel near Vinh Linh they found a lunar landscape. In the months of May and June 1967, the area around the demarcation line was the scene of a confrontation of unprecedented ferocity, later revealed as one of the preliminary skirmishes for the Tet Offensive, a large-scale military operation carried out in the South at the start of 1968 by North Vietnamese and Vietcong troops. On a hilltop on the South Vietnamese side of the border, opposite Vinh Linh, lay the small U.S. Marine base Con Thien. By the time Ivens and Loridan arrived, this advance post was already surrounded by Communist troops and the Americans were being supplied by airdrops. Six thousand marines were living there under conditions that showed a striking similarity to those Ivens and Loridan encountered in Vinh Linh. According to a *Time Magazine* reporter, the marines 'lived below ground in heavily sandbagged bunkers supported by thick wooden beams that can take all but a direct hit. In summer, when the temperature reaches 120, the camp is a swirl of choking ocher dust. In the fall, the monsoons fill the bunkers with two feet of water and mud, turn the trenches into running red rivers of sludge.' The Americans were engaged in a constant battle with thirty thousand North Vietnamese and Vietcong and were being shelled daily by heavy artillery across the border on the other side of the Ben Hai River. The Americans responded with a great show of strength. In the space of a few months, eight hundred B-52 sorties were flown and twenty-two thousand tons of bombs were dropped in the area. American reinforcements landed by sea and razed the entire region south of the Ben Hai River, driving out the remaining inhabitants.[30]

'We find ourselves in the heart of a gigantic battle of which we only perceive fragments,' noted Loridan.[31] A question she did not ask herself was why Hanoi had not evacuated the civilian population of the border villages in Vinh Linh District before commencing the battle for Con Thien. Ivens and Loridan's film, 17TH PARALLEL, gave the impression that these were peaceful villages being brutally terrorized by Americans, although an attentive viewer could see that this was not the case. Because of the extreme conditions under which 17TH PARALLEL was made, it was easy for the film to become a portrayal of the theoretical state of affairs in North Vietnam: a fully-politicized people united in a day-and-night struggle against imperialism.

Their most curious encounter was with nine-year-old Duc, hero third class of the National Liberation Front, or Vietcong, who was afraid of tigers, but not of Americans. Ivens related Duc's story in *Le Monde*. 'One day in the South near his grandmother's house he saw the Americans leveling the ground. A helicopter base was laid out. Duc calculated that he needed to put one hand behind the other fourteen times to get one meter. He then made up a game involving throwing a piece of bamboo of that length. When the 'game' is over he knows that he needs to put the piece of bamboo down 347 times to cover the distance between the helicopter base and his house and 240 times between the house and the road on the north side. 'Then', he said, 'I gave the calculations to my uncles in the army. They came with mortars and destroyed 23 helicopters on the ground.'[32] Little Duc became one of the main characters in 17TH PARALLEL.

To increase their sense of the life of the locals, the film crew set up for three weeks in a village of two thousand inhabitants on the coast, just to the north of the seventeenth parallel. A large part of village life took place below the surface. The houses, the school and the sewing workshop were all underground and connected by trenches. Joris Ivens, Marceline Loridan and Xuan Phuong stayed in an underground home with a peasant woman and her two children. A party official was also staying there, because the cadres lived with the peasants. 'This satisfies two principles', noted Loridan, 'the first is security, the other is political. Only by being bound to the masses can the party guarantee the proper development of the country and the construction of socialism.'[33] The bombing made a normal daily schedule impossible. A night's sleep ended between two and four in the morning because work on the surface had to be done in the dark, and there were still deaths every day. 'Cameraman Tuan had fallen in love with a girl', explained Xuan Phuong, 'she was called Hua. She is in the film as well. They had kissed for the first time. The next day Tuan cried, because the girl had been killed by the shock wave of a bomb. It was too much for Joris and he couldn't carry on working that day.'

Usually there was no stopping Ivens when he was at work and he had little patience when others became tired. 'Why aren't you interpreting? Go back if you're too tired,' he would say to Xuan Phuong. And when she resumed interpreting, Loridan would say: 'You're still talking, you have to be quiet when I'm recording.' Or else the exhausted cameraman would say: 'I'm not doing it anymore.' At which Ivens would ask: 'What did he say?' and Phuong would translate: 'That he's tired.' Ivens would retort: 'That's not true, he said something else.'

There was a bridge across the Ben Hai that was never used because it came under direct fire at the first signs of movement. Flags flew on both sides: on one side the North Vietnamese, on the other the South Vietnamese. Ivens asked Tuan to climb the pole to film the other side. 'Too dangerous,' said Tuan. 'You have to. Otherwise stay home and I'll do it myself,' answered Ivens, who was dressed as a peasant. 'My God, what a job,' complained Tuan while clambering up to his vantage point. The shot was a success, despite the appearance of hostile aircraft immediately afterwards. Ivens was definitely not prone to fear. During a bombing raid he calmly went up to film on the surface. 'Afterwards we were always glad that he was still alive,' explained Phuong. The crew had strict orders to protect his life at any cost. 'The party called regularly to check that he was still all right.' When things got too dangerous the Vietnamese crew simply flung themselves on top of him, while he furiously tried to throw them off.[34]

Joris Ivens became Xuan Phuong's great example. She admired his courage, his faith in the cause and his friendliness – at least most of the time. After seeing the final edited version of their work, she wrote to him that she now realized 'how deeply the artistic and revolutionary language of cinema can penetrate people's hearts'.[35] On his recommendation, she was retrained as a filmmaker, after which she made documentary reports on the Ho Chi Minh Trail, during the wars in Cambodia and Laos, and during the short war between Vietnam and China.

After about five months in Vietnam, Ivens and Loridan returned to Paris in the summer of 1967. Ivens described his time on the seventeenth parallel as the most intense experience of his life. Months later he told a journalist that he immediately looked around for shelter when he heard a plane approaching, and six months after his return he was still saying: 'You think, they're in the bomb shelters now. Will the B-52s come tonight?'[36]

Ivens had always had a fast editing style that was rich in contrasts, but this time he wanted to attain 'an almost anonymous form', with a slow pacing that connected with the speed of life of the agrarian community shown in the film – editing without ostentation. He wrestled with it for four months before starting on the sound mixing in December 1967. 17TH PARALLEL was almost two hours long and financial difficulties again arose in the final phases of production. Although the North Vietnamese government had provided material and crew, French and Dutch individuals had contributed funds, and Ivens and Loridan themselves had lived partly from a lucrative photo-reportage they had made in Hanoi for *Paris-Match*, it still wasn't enough. After taking a mortgage on their home, they were forced to seek money from Anatole Dauman's Argos production company, which demanded fifty percent of the revenues in return. The disadvantage, according to Ivens, was that 'you could no longer give the film free to a poor organization'. That was bad for the cause.[37]

During the Paris premiere on March 6, 1968 the auditorium of Studio Gît-le-Coeur was largely filled with members of the diplomatic corps. 'Chinese dignitaries, indistinguishable from welding technicians, embrace the cineaste – outside police officers swarm. Inside, flashes go off for a row of People's Republicans. There are so many of them, they could start up a Communist mini-summit all by themselves,' reported Dutch journalist Jan Blokker. Back in Holland, 'welding technicians' had featured in a recent espionage affair centered on the Chinese embassy.

Most critics were full of praise for 17TH PARALLEL. In *Le Monde* Jean Lacouture stated that no one was better able to show the reality of the Vietnam War than Ivens, PCF daily *Humanité* spoke of 'what will probably be Joris Ivens's principal work', and *Le Figaro* and other more moderate newspapers were also positive. In Holland the review in the Catholic daily *De Tijd* was representative: 'Even if we do not share Ivens's opinions and intentions, we can accept his film as a warning that things cannot go on in this fashion.'[38] *Cahiers du Cinéma*, which continued to see Ivens as a man of the old school, welcomed his use of 16mm with synchronized sound. Nonetheless there were still young Turks who found this work passé as well. In a group discussion on political film in *Positif*, cineaste Bertrand Tavernier called Ivens's editing 'obsolete'. 'Everything has been manipulated to such an extent at the level of the editing, by the way things are interrelated, the shots from below, the faces turned up to the sky, the whole picture has been taken apart and artificially reconstructed in such a way that you no longer feel a thing.' Someone else remarked that the fact that Ivens uses re-enactments in 17TH PARALLEL is not such a barrier, what is important is the way he does it. When he shows people aiming an artillery piece, you don't really believe that it's going to fire. And Tavernier added that Leacock, Pennebaker and Perrault's *verité* films had given Ivens's working methods 'the *coup de grâce*'. 'That is an indisputable fact' was the reply.[39]

The French Centre National du Cinéma awarded 17TH PARALLEL the first prize for quality. 'I think that if you believe it's worth including the major problems of life and death, of freedom and democracy in your film, then you should also have the respect to set your equipment up properly and get your lenses and editing right,' said Ivens in a discussion on the radio.[40]

At the premiere he declared that, rather than being his film, 17TH PARALLEL was actually a Vietnamese film. The audience took this as a courtesy, but there was much more to it. The filmmakers reported to the authorities in Hanoi, as in 'Report on the Work in the Area of Political Propaganda by Joris Ivens and Marceline Loridan from August 1967 to March 1968 in Europe', in which they gave a detailed account of all the activities they had developed to further the Vietnamese struggle: the various articles they had written, interviews, press conferences, posters that had been pasted up, the book *Deux mois sous la terre* about their experiences in Vietnam, and Loridan's testimony at the Russell Tribunal in Copenhagen. The report also announced that the film itself would be broadcast in at least four countries. In another report they dealt with the financing of the film, an area where the North Vietnamese actually had a right to be informed, since they had paid a large part of the costs.[41] There was also a remarkable interest in Ivens's film from the American side. Around this time, as he later told it, he received an unexpected visit from two gentlemen from the American CBS television company. A third man, whom he found 'a little suspect', was also present. They wanted to buy a number of sequences from his Vietnam film and were primarily interested in shots depicting a new heavy artillery piece of Soviet manufacture. They were not interested in Ivens's offer of picking out a few good sequences for them himself and were willing to pay twenty thousand dollars for the shots with the cannon. When Ivens responded negatively, they upped their offer: 'At which the producer went totally pale and I went totally red.' Dauman was tempted but Ivens refused outright. He had called his film of the seventeenth parallel 'a socialist scoop', and he was apparently right in more ways than one.[42]

As soon as 17TH PARALLEL was completed, Marceline Loridan left for Hanoi with a copy. The audience at the screening there included three delegates from Vinh Linh. A number of Vietnamese films were made about Vinh Linh over the years – including one which won director Mjoc Qing a prize in Moscow – 'but Joris had a better eye for the psychology, for life', according to Xuan Phuong.[43]

Marceline Loridan also began preparations for a following film, this time about workers' lives in Hanoi. This film would deal with everyday life under Vietnamese socialism. The authorities showed little enthusiasm. 'Why not another film about the war?' they said. 'My questions went too far for them,' according to Loridan. 'They touched upon secrets they didn't want to surrender. They turned against me.' She did not make herself any more popular by visiting the home of a Frenchwoman who was married to a Vietnamese in Hanoi. 'Foreigners were not supposed to do that.'[44] It is possible that the difficulties were increased by a clash of etiquette: Loridan was not particularly given to prudence. At any rate, the head of the documentary studio wrote to Ivens in Paris stating that they were impatiently awaiting his arrival: 'We're waiting until Joris is with Marceline in Thong Nhat Hotel!'[45] An appropriate name, because Thong Nhat means The Union. When Ivens arrived with Jean-Pierre Sergent in late March 1968, no progress had been made with the preparations for the new film.

The three filmmakers now proposed a trip to South Vietnam, for instance down the Ho Chi Minh Trail to the Mekong Delta, a region that was virtually unknown outside of Western propaganda. They first received permission to go to the newly conquered city of Hué; after it was retaken by the South, prime minister Pham Van Dong approved their plan for the Mekong Delta. While still in the preparatory phase, however, this expedition was also cancelled after the comrades in the National Liberation Front in South Vietnam informed them on April 26 that they were not welcome.[46] The most likely reason was that the successful Tet Offensive, which had just been concluded, had demanded such high sacrifices that the Vietcong had actually wiped itself out. In retrospect Ivens had reason to be glad this film did not go ahead, as his health was not optimal in the period that followed and the long trail through the mountains and jungles of Laos and Cambodia was much rougher than the route they had taken from Hanoi to the seventeenth parallel. One day after the South Vietnamese cancelled, Ivens noted: 'Laos is possible.' Laos it was.

This remote mountainous state west of Vietnam, a former French possession, had become independent in 1954. The king was fond of saying that his subjects were incapable of doing anything except singing and making love, but the truth was that Vientiane, the capital, was the scene of an ongoing power struggle, with coups and countercoups by rightist, neutralist and leftist factions. Since the war had flared up in Vietnam, the Communist Pathet Lao had also stepped up the guerrilla war aimed at establishing socialism in Laos. The chief opponents in the Laotian arena were two half-brothers, the princes Souvanna Phouma and Souphanouvong. The former led the government. Although he strove to maintain the country's neutrality amid the turbulence of Indochina, he was increasingly forced to rely upon American support in order to avoid being overrun by Souphanouvong's Pathet Lao.

At the start of May, Ivens's film crew left by car for the region around Sam Neua, as the crow flies only one hundred and sixty miles from Hanoi, in the mountains of Laos. On the bad muddy roads on the Laotian side of the border, they covered just thirty miles a night. Souphanouvong's headquarters was located in a cave outside Sam Neua, and Ivens and his co-workers moved into a similar mountain cave. From this base they made treks of up to twenty miles through virgin forest at hundred-degree temperatures for a few minutes' worth of shots, with a wheezing Ivens bringing up the rear. 'We realized that the Yankee planes were the biggest mosquitoes and that the biggest leeches were in the Pentagon,' he explained later, but while the insects buzzed around, the aircraft seldom appeared. 'We had a mirror to attract planes the moment we saw one in the distance, because they just didn't come,' said Xuan Phuong, who was again part of the crew. Sometimes Ivens felt too ill to go out. Then Marceline Loridan and Jean-Pierre Sergent would spend days together out filming, while he waited in the cave. 'Like a lion in a cage,' according to Xuan Phuong. 'It's the first time I've felt old age,' Ivens said.[47]

Like many others before them, the Laotians wanted to prescribe what Ivens could film. He resisted, but with their constant accompaniment and an unfamiliar local language, his possibilities were limited. 'We were manipulated a little by the Vietnamese and the Laotians,' according to Sergent. 'They showed us what they wanted to show us and said what they wanted to say.' Sergent's own contacts with the Vietnamese did not proceed altogether smoothly. Seeing him descend the airplane steps in Hanoi, Xuan Phuong had immediately taken him for '*un beau garçon Parisien*' and next to her someone had mumbled: 'We'll see whether he can do anything here.' This was despite the fact that Sergent had already made a film with the Colombian guerrilla movement. The Vietnamese camera operators found that he behaved in an authoritarian fashion, like a colonialist, and a one-day session of criticism and self-criticism was called to discuss this bad quality. 'They were right', admitted Sergent later at a sidewalk café in Paris. 'I believe that I learnt something from it and changed the way I acted.' After the *beau garçon* stood up to the conditions in the mountains, the Vietnamese finally accepted him. Ivens wrote later in his memoirs that there were also tensions between him and Sergent. The latter said that he hadn't noticed them, which is quite possible as Ivens often kept such dissatisfactions to himself.

All things considered, the journey to Laos was not particularly enjoyable, because the Vietnamese and the Laotians did not get along well either. The strict Vietnamese looked down upon their cheerful, carefree neighbors. 'It was the formality of the north opposed to the grace and friendliness of Mediterranean life,' according to Ivens. The Laotian adventure came to an abrupt end when the film crew and its protective escort of fifteen men were invited to eat with a district secretary. All fifteen members of the escort came down with food poisoning. Ivens, Loridan and Sergent were fine, but were nonetheless recalled to Hanoi for a 'medical check-up'.

In the mountains of Laos the BBC World Service had brought them the miraculous news that the revolution had broken out in Paris, and every morning at six o'clock they had sat around the radio to follow the latest developments. They also received internal news bulletins for party cadres about the events in France. 'The facts were well reported,' according to Sergent, 'but the interpretation was stupid, because that came from the PCF'.[48] Early in August 1968 they were back in France. A new era had dawned.

21   Sixty-Nine in Sixty-Eight (1968-1971)

The Paris uprising of May 1968 took Ivens and the others by surprise, despite their familiarity with the conditions in which it emerged. The conservatism of the established orders in France had become apparent during the Algerian independence struggle, and Ivens sympathized with the young people who, partly through their protests against the Vietnam War, had begun to rebel against their parents' world. The United States claimed to be fighting for Western liberties in Asia, but was unable to guarantee the freedom of its own citizens, as evidenced by the discrimination against blacks and the struggles of the civil rights movement.

Events progressed swiftly in 1967 and 1968. Left-wing youth took the fatal shooting of Martin Luther King on April 4, 1968 as a sign that the Black Panthers could be right in their belief that black liberation could only be achieved through violence. American students had been campaigning against 'the system' and 'the consumer society' for several years, and their European contemporaries were motivated by the same feelings. The German student movement, for example, cherished high expectations of an imminent social revolution. The situation in Germany began to escalate in June 1967, after Benno Ohnesorg was killed by the West Berlin police during a demonstration against the Shah of Iran. On April 11, 1968 student leader Rudi Dutschke was shot and almost killed after a smear campaign in the daily *Bild-Zeitung*. In response, a number of future members of the Red Army Faction protested by setting fire to a Frankfurt department store. On the other side of the globe, in Bolivia, the legendary guerrilla leader Che Guevara was executed by soldiers in October 1967, and Régis Debray, who Marceline Loridan and Jean-Pierre Sergent had known since CHRONICLE OF A SUMMER, had been imprisoned there for leftist activities. The whole world seemed to be changing, even the Communist countries. In Czechoslovakia Alexander Dubcek launched 'socialism with a human face' in the spring of 1968, and in China, Red Guards under Mao's inspirational leadership were establishing – so people thought – a completely new, democratic Communism.

In early 1968 Jean-Luc Godard's LA CHINOISE, a film inspired by the minuscule French Maoist movement, enjoyed a certain popularity among the more radical section of the Parisian university population. Besides being dissatisfied with the world in general, French students were becoming increasingly critical of authoritarian lecturers, crowded universities, outdated curriculums, and student homes that most resembled penitentiaries. But the uprising of May 1968 was finally set off by a series of coincidences. In March a group of Vietnam activists smashed the windows of the Paris offices of a number of American companies. When five members of the group were arrested, a protest meeting was organized at the turbulent Nanterre University, where the 'Movement of March 22' was founded. A number of Nanterre students were then called before the university's disciplinary council, among them Daniel Cohn-Bendit, who would emerge as the voice of May 1968. Students occupied the auditorium at Nanterre, and a day later the Movement of March 22 organized a meeting at the Sorbonne. There the rector fed the flames by calling in the police. General indignation arose. The movement rapidly attained mass support, and daily demonstrations followed, with the familiar demand of 'all power to the imagination'. The demonstrations spread to the provinces, and factory workers also joined in large numbers, much to the dissatisfaction of the largest union, the Communist-lead CGT.

By the night of May 10, the resemblance to the famous nineteenth-century revolutions in Paris was complete. A neighborhood south of the Sorbonne was closed off by barricades, and demonstrators battled the police until early in the morning. On May 13 seven hundred thousand demonstrators chanting 'Adieu, de Gaulle' marched from the Gare de l'Est to the Champs de Mars. Hundreds of thousands more demonstrated in the provinces, and within a week there was a general strike of close to ten million workers. Unable to ignore the facts, the CGT now placed itself at the head of the strikers and transformed the movement into a struggle for better working conditions.

President de Gaulle recovered from the initial shock and opened a counter-offensive with a radio speech mobilizing the conservative section of the population. *'Nous ne nous retirons pas!'* declared the general, and on May 30 some eight hundred thousand demonstrators over the whole country declared their support. In the vanguard of the march in Paris was an acquaintance of Ivens's, the writer André Malraux, fighter in the Spanish Civil War and the French Resistance, confirmed Gaullist since 1945 and currently minister of Cultural Affairs. A month later the Gaullists achieved a massive electoral victory. The strikes were over and the Sorbonne had been cleared by the police.

When Ivens, Loridan and Sergent returned to Paris in July, the film sector was still in turmoil and their secretary Michèle Pierret had transformed their apartment into a gathering place for radical youth.

On May 17 a thousand-strong meeting at the school for photographic and cinematic technology in the rue de Vaugirard had founded the États

Généraux du Cinéma. A telegram was immediately sent to the Cannes Film Festival calling for the festival to close in solidarity with the revolution, and delegations led by Jean-Luc Godard and François Truffaut traveled to the Riviera to encourage the festival visitors to act. Incredible but true: the festival closed early.

The États Généraux also sent out a general appeal to all filmmakers alerting them to the 'absolute necessity of placing cinema at the service of the revolution'. The amphitheater of the Sorbonne became the scene of protracted debates about the future of the medium, but with little practical result. A reasonable film about May 1968 itself would not be made until much later, and then by outsiders. By the end of the summer there were only one hundred and fifty activists involved in the États Généraux, which soon dissolved into a variety of film collectives, chiefly distinguishable by their differing interpretations of revolutionary theory.

A more general consequence of May 1968 was that left-wing radicalism came into fashion. An example of this is the metamorphosis of the film magazine *Cahiers du Cinéma*, which in the space of several years came to resemble a journal for the study of Marxism-Leninism. Now that the revolution was over, the extreme-leftist study groups, action committees and revolutionary organizations mushroomed.

Loridan and Sergent threw themselves into the fray, an option that was not available to Ivens. The exhausting journeys to Vietnam and Laos had taken their toll, and his doctor prescribed rest and convalescence. He left the completion of the Laos film to the others and set off alone for Les Diablerets in the Swiss Alps. 'It is as if I came back wounded from the front,' he wrote to Marion Michelle from the rainy health resort, and regretfully added: 'In Laos I could not always be with the shooting (first time in my career), and now I cannot be with the editing.'[1]

Health problems were nothing new. During the shooting of ITALY IS NOT A POOR COUNTRY in 1959, he had written to Michelle that he had been confined to his room for five days because of his 'annual bronchitis-asthma attack', and in spring 1962, after his return from Cuba he wrote: 'I really was run down, more than I knew.' He had needed to rest then as well, in Raymond Leibovici's house in St Tropez. But it was only after 17TH PARALLEL that his health problems began to recur so frequently that they became a constant interruption of his work. Several times in 1969 and 1970 he lost months recovering from operations, including one on a hernia and one on his prostrate. He spent most of that time in Forte dei Marmi at Villa Vittoria, the country home of the leftist Italian Countess Anna-Maria Papi.[2] The beneficent countess ran a kind of salon at her home in Florence and supported numerous artists, until finally running into financial problems of her own.

When Ivens returned to Paris from Switzerland in the last weeks of September 1968, a collective had formed around Loridan and Sergent. At meetings of the États Généraux they had met old friends who were setting up the Maoist organization Gauche Prolétarienne with student leader Alain Geismar among its leaders. Its magazine was called *La Cause du Peuple* and became famous when, after the arrest of two editors-in-chief, Jean-Paul Sartre demonstratively presented himself as the new editor and personally went out on the streets to hawk the magazine – something that did not stop him from remarking that although there were lies in the bourgeois press, there were a lot more in the radical papers. Loridan and Sergent sympathized with Maoism and felt an urgent need to compensate for having missed out on the turmoil of May. Their militant collective would complete the Laos film according to the insights acquired after May 1968.[3]

From a revolutionary point of view, Joris Ivens had an impeccable record. He had conferred with Zhou Enlai while the Chinese Communists were still a guerrilla movement, he had drunk tea with virtually the entire Chinese party leadership, had personally witnessed the Great Leap Forward, and was on first name terms with the leaders of Vietnam and Cuba. But with all his experience, he remained a gray-haired sixty-nine-year-old. The overconfident youngsters of the Laos film collective – a few film school students and others who were unburdened by any knowledge of the medium – rated their insights far more highly than the old man's. He in turn allowed himself to be swept up by the passion of the new movement, afraid as he was of being left behind now that the East Wind was blowing harder than ever.

The studio on the rue Mouffetard became the scene of endless discussions as to which cut was ideologically correct, and decisions were subsequently made by head count. 'I got a little lazy and sometimes let things slide,' wrote Ivens self-critically. He drank coffee in a café while the collective debated. 'When he saw that all those young people wanted to get involved, he left us to it,' said Sergent. Things were not always settled so calmly: there were heated clashes between Ivens and Loridan, brought on by his lagging fanaticism and insufficient aversion to the Soviet Union.[4] Nonetheless, he fully backed the collective philosophy. As late as 1970 he believed that only this egalitarian method had allowed them to tap the full wealth of their subject, and stated that 'group criticism and self-criticism' had helped him to 'bring his artistic and ideological initiative to a higher level'. It wasn't until much later that he became convinced that the collective had been dominated by 'a small-minded atmosphere' and 'intellectual terrorism'.[5]

He took to riding Maoist hobbyhorses. In the fall of 1968, he remarked that his French colleagues did not take the revolution seriously enough. He considered Jean-Luc Godard 'honestly interested' and 'a pioneer', although 'obviously too confused for my taste'. In May, Godard had 'done things the others hadn't done,' admitted Ivens, 'so courageously'. But when cineastes really wanted to become revolutionaries, they needed to do things like 'put their cinematic work aside for a few years and go to work in a factory, to really merge with the working class and learn what it means... to be a worker'.[6]

The endless debates turned the editing of the Laos film into a protracted process. It was not until July 1969 that THE PEOPLE AND THEIR GUNS was finally able to be submitted for classification, and after that it took until November for it to be released, in France at least, because an export ban was applied. Piquant detail: this stipulation originated with André Malraux's Ministry of Cultural Affairs.[7]

Since the film's political message precluded the possibility of receiving money from an ordinary producer, Ivens and Loridan produced it themselves under the name Capi-Films. They invested the proceeds from 17TH PARALLEL, took out a new mortgage on their home, discharged secretary Michèle Pierret after almost two and a half years because they could no longer afford her salary, and in November 1969 Ivens did some work in South America for French television to supplement their income.[8] Director Joseph Losey, an old friend from New York, helped out with four thousand dollars, and also encouraged a good friend to make a donation, Elizabeth Taylor, at that time Mrs. Richard Burton. 'It had not been my intention to ask you about this because it seemed too far afield', wrote Losey, 'but if you really want to do it, it would be a most marvelous thing. Joris is the dean of documentary film makers in the world and one of the best and most courageous men I have known in my life.' The film was about 'an underground village in North Laos during the constant bombardments which still go on. It is, frankly, on the guerrilla side.' Liz Taylor sent a check for three thousand dollars and Ivens thanked her '*de tout mon coeur*' as the film was now able to be completed without the involvement of commercial interests.[9]

Ivens believed that it had turned out to be a 'strong, didactic political film',[10] but it was in fact the most dogmatic tractate of his whole career, although in the light of the 'intellectual terror' it is possibly incorrect to speak of it as an Ivens film at all. THE PEOPLE AND THEIR GUNS alternated images with Maoist quotes. The film's fourth section – 'Without their Guns the People Would Have Nothing' – included titles like 'fanning hatred for the enemy in order to fight better', 'fanning hatred in order to transform it into an irrepressible

Joris Ivens in North Vietnam during the shooting of THE THREATENING SKY
(1965). DOCUMENTARY FILM STUDIO, HANOI. DUTCH FILM MUSEUM

force', and yet again, 'fanning hatred to achieve victory'. These were followed by the surprising: 'the revolution's most important promise: improving human relations'. The next sequence depicted the close bond between
peasants and soldiers: 'At the front we think of you constantly...' 'We think
of you constantly too...' 'Lately we've had many victories, you know that.
Nam Bac has been liberated. We destroyed five battalions. Laongam has
been liberated as well, and the area around Attopeu. We killed a lot of our
enemies, Mother.' 'We congratulate you.'

Jean-Pierre Sergent later stated that he had only narrowly been able to
prevent the film from ending with a call for armed struggle in France.[11]

The film magazine *Cinéma 70* published a group interview with Ivens,
Loridan and Sergent, in which they declared that they saw the Laos film as
an improvement on 17TH PARALLEL, thus underlining how much ideology
had won out over the cinematic aspects, because THE PEOPLE AND THEIR
GUNS was actually a Marxist-Leninist primer with moving illustrations, albeit some impressive images. Ivens thought that 17TH PARALLEL had
brought the public closer to the Vietnamese, but considered THE PEOPLE
more instructive; Sergent criticized 17TH PARALLEL for paying too little attention to the political work of the party; and Loridan thought that the Laos
film was better because it delineated the organizational principles of the lib-

eration movement. In mid-interview Ivens moderated his stance by adding that 17TH PARALLEL should not be underestimated.[12]

Even before THE PEOPLE AND THEIR GUNS was released by the French censors, NCRV television in Holland showed the film on October 31, 1969, at least a version adapted for television by the collective, in which all the captions were scrapped and the film's original ninety minutes was cut back to forty-five. With the growing Dutch Vietnam movement in the background, the film was sympathetically received by Dutch critics.

Thanks to the new spirit among Parisian intellectuals, THE PEOPLE AND THEIR GUNS was reviewed fairly positively in France as well. *Le Monde* saw no grounds for criticism, and Sartre's *Les Temps Modernes* went so far as to call the members of the Laos film collective 'bearers of truth'. A striking dissonant voice on the left was the film magazine *Positif*, which had maintained an independent radical course throughout the sixties and now refused to embrace the fashion for Maoism. *Positif* denounced the almost complete lack of concrete information about Laos. For instance, the film mentioned the American puppet government, but did not consider further explanation necessary. And why was it good when the Pathet Lao maintained ties with peasants, but bad when the imperialists did the same thing? *Positif* went on to ask whether the peasants in areas under Pathet Lao control handed over their produce voluntarily.[13] Ivens also met with criticism in his own circles. The film was 'Stalinist and sectarian, and it had little truth in it, and we told him so,' according to Vladimir and Ida Pozner.[14]

In Hanoi THE PEOPLE AND THEIR GUNS was screened for the Pathet Lao ambassador and his staff, together with a number of representatives of the North Vietnamese Ministry of Foreign Affairs. The Vietnamese were not impressed by the dogmatic work from Paris; the Laotians were more than satisfied.[15] A peculiar moment in the history of the showing of THE PEOPLE AND THEIR GUNS was a special screening in Brazzaville in October 1970. Congo-Brazzaville had been declared a people's republic after Major Ngouabi's coup and Ivens flew there to personally show the film. 'In the auditorium there were a lot of militants, ministers, the First Secretary of the Workers' Party (Marxist-Leninist), the ambassadors of the People's Republic of China, the Democratic Republic of Vietnam, Cuba,' he noted. 'This evening there is a screening of the Laos film for young soldiers at an army base.' Back in Paris he put together a plan for the creation of a film service in the new state.[16] THE PEOPLE AND THEIR GUNS found its way to countless political events and activists' gatherings in the Western world, and from Oslo to the occupied Coca-Cola factory in Rome, Ivens personally accompanied screenings with an inspiring introduction.

In May 1968 Paris's Quartier-Latin had witnessed a deeply symbolic meeting. The now elderly PCF cultural icon and writer Louis Aragon, a man with whom Ivens had had more or less regular contact since the early thirties, had paid a visit to the demonstrating students. Quick-witted activist Daniel Cohn-Bendit entered into discussion, or rather, wiped the floor with him, and it was obvious to all present that there was an unbridgeable gap between the Communist party and rebellious youth. Ivens too belonged to the world of Louis Aragon, but two years later he had completely turned his back on it.

Whereas he became less and less accessible to his old friends, a court of young people arose around him: leftist students who encouraged him, and emerging filmmakers seeking his support. 'Whenever you wanted to speak to Joris you always got Marceline on the telephone,' related journalist Robert Grelier, a *Positif* writer who published a book about Ivens in 1965. 'You couldn't reach him unless you called at eight in the morning, because she slept later than he did.' In Brussels Henri Storck also felt as if Loridan was trying to drive a wedge between Ivens and his more moderate friends.[17] Vladimir Pozner and Ivens continued sending each other their annual letters, but seldom met, despite living just fifteen minutes' walk away from each other. The Pozners, who remained faithful PCF members, were astonished to read in Ivens's memoirs in the eighties that their friendship had withstood 'hard ideological clashes'. It was true that they remained friends, and in the seventies they gradually began seeing each other more often again, but politics was something they almost never discussed.[18] One of the reasons for their ongoing bond was in fact Ivens's virtuoso conflict avoidance. They had been through a lot together and they liked each other – that was more important to him.

Although the Soviet Union and China had become archenemies, Joris Ivens was still a welcome guest in both Moscow and Peking. On his trips to Vietnam, he made stopovers in both cities, although in the chaotic days of the Cultural Revolution he was confined to the transit zone of Peking airport. When he and Loridan visited Moscow after filming 17TH PARALLEL, the chairman of the Union of Soviet Filmmakers, Grigori Aleksandrov, invited them to his dacha. They were astonished by their host's luxurious lifestyle. For Loridan 'his wife's bedroom was just like a bonbonnière and Mrs. Aleksandrov herself was like Chekhov's Lady with the Dog.' They had brought Vietnamese jewelry made from parts of shot-down American planes, but the Aleksandrovs showed no interest in it. The Soviet representative at the United Nations dropped in as well and made an equally poor impression in comparison to the militant comrades in Vietnam: 'A pretentious aristocratic man, who had no faith in people, only in his dog.' On his way back to Hanoi a year later, Ivens visited Moscow again, this time with Jean-Pierre Sergent. At a dinner organized by the filmmakers' union, one of the old Soviet documentarians asked Ivens why he didn't follow his example and make a beautiful film in the USSR, a nature documentary. Ivens considered it an improper suggestion at a time when the Vietnam War was raging.[19]

The Eastern Europeans might have felt their old ally slipping away from them and they went on the offensive. On May 1, 1968 a Soviet committee awarded Ivens the International Lenin Peace Prize, along with five others, among them Nguyen Thi Dinh, female commander of the Vietcong. Just one year earlier Ho Chi Minh had politely declined this same honor to avoid endangering his position with China; this time the Vietnamese laureates and Ivens accepted the prize. In a press release in Hanoi he stated that he was glad to accept such a high award and concluded that 'more than for me, this prize is a tribute to the struggle of the Vietnamese people'. His contribution had been films 'that clearly show the invincibility of the people's war'. He emphasized that 'peace would be born in the peoples' victory over imperialism'.[20]

However, between the announcement of the prize in May and the official presentation in Moscow in November, history went on, not only with the journey to Laos, the Paris student uprising and the Laos film collective, but also with Warsaw Pact tanks rolling into Czechoslovakia on August 20, 1968 to end the Prague Spring. Ivens seems to have disagreed with this punitive expedition under Soviet leadership, though there is no certainty about this, because he maintained his silence. He had the following dialogue with a journalist from *Het Parool*:

'What do you think of Czechoslovakia?'
'I don't want to talk about it.'
'Not a word?'
'Not a word. I'll leave it to history to speak.'

Speaking to the Dutch daily *de Volkskrant* he refused to go into it because: 'if we disagree with something, that's often used against everything. You can see that now in Czechoslovakia...'[21]

Ivens gave the *Volkskrant* interview in Paris, shortly before flying first class to Moscow with Aeroflot to receive the Lenin Prize at the Kremlin's Sverdlov Auditorium on November 12. The medal and diploma were presented to tumultuous applause. Ivens announced that he would use the accompanying money prize of 25,000 rubles to support a number of filmmakers in Latin America, and the ceremony was followed by a gala dinner at the Congress Palace.

A week later he was celebrated again at the Leipzig Festival, where a reception was held to mark his seventieth birthday. 17TH PARALLEL was shown, the GDR government presented him with the Fighters against Fascism medal, and Leipzig's Karl Marx University awarded him with an honorary doctorate. In his speech of thanks, he declared that the work of a committed filmmaker 'needs to be in an active interchange with the theory and must be guided by – and here at the university that bears Karl Marx's name, more than anywhere else, this can be said out loud – Marxist-Leninist ideology. In particular we must refer to the teachings of Lenin, who says that partisanship in art is of fundamental importance.'[22] These instructions must have come as a surprise to the audience; the principles had already been diluted in the GDR, and people there did not share Ivens's conviction that peace could only be attained through war against imperialism.

His swing to the radical left continued, but his alienation from East Germany only came later, not through a debate of principle but through a two-year difference of opinion about the purchase of 17TH PARALLEL. The producer Argos wanted twenty-five thousand francs for the film, and after the DEFA rejected this, the price was reduced to twenty thousand. The East Germans still considered this unacceptable, since the same film had just been sold to Hungary for seven thousand five hundred. 'DEFA Foreign Trade says rightly that your name and our close and friendly relations are being abused here in order to obtain a price which will influence all negotiations with French film sellers.' After negotiations with the DEFA came to a deadlock, the GDR tried to do business through the Leipzig Festival and the Staatliches Filmarchiv, but Paris remained intransigent.[23] The reason became apparent in autumn 1969, when Ivens received the traditional invitation with free travel and accommodation for the Leipzig Festival and answered that he would be unable to attend. In a letter to Hans Rodenberg he complained that the GDR still hadn't bought 17TH PARALLEL. 'When will our friends in socialist countries understand the difficulties faced by militant revolutionary filmmakers? It seems as if there is less understanding every year, not only in the GDR but in the other socialist countries as well. International solidarity is essential in cinema, by which I mean concrete aid. But we have understood that in our struggle on the cinematic front we now, more than in the old days, need to rely on our own resources. When it comes up in discussion, you can explain what I have written here to our friends in power.'[24] In other words, Ivens believed that a political price rather than a market price should be paid for the film.

East Berlin continued its conciliatory course. That year the GDR English-language publisher Seven Seas released Ivens's autobiography *The Camera and I*, the book he wrote with Jay Leyda in America during the Second

World War supplemented with a number of later texts. A year later a new invitation for Leipzig arrived, which Ivens again refused. The positions were not clarified until 1970, when the Dutch adaptation of *The Camera and I – Autobiografie van een filmer* – appeared. Ivens now declared that in China, 'led by President Mao Zedong, a great thinker', he had found a real longing to realize 'the new man'. Suddenly he announced that since the late fifties he had been observing flagging ideals 'in the socialist countries that adhered to a revisionism of the fundamental principles of Marxism-Leninism', in other words, in Eastern Europe. He now became *persona non grata* for the East Berlin authorities.[25]

This did not stop East Germans in the film world from trying to lure Ivens back to Leipzig after 1970; they still worshipped him. 'When you talked about him, tears almost came to their eyes,' said Marion Michelle. Hans Rodenberg called him 'a brother who has erred', and Wolfgang Klaue, director of the State Film Archives, sometimes visited Ivens when in Paris. They had known each other since the early sixties, when Klaue organized the festivities in Leipzig for Ivens's sixty-fifth birthday. Finally, in 1979, they had a long discussion in La Sarraz in Switzerland, where the fiftieth anniversary of the First International Congress of Independent Film was being commemorated. They agreed that it would be good to reopen the dialogue between old friends.[26] By this time Ivens's feelings for China were cooling.

In the Soviet Union he had had regular attention from the press over the years, and after he won the Lenin Prize moves were made to introduce him to the masses. His colleague Roman Karmen was commissioned to make a slide show entitled THE CREATIVE LIFE OF JORIS IVENS. Writing to Ivens, Karmen explained that 'slides are used on a large scale in the USSR as a means of visual propaganda in schools and institutes. They are sold in large numbers.'[27] In 1971 silence descended over the former comrade in the Soviet Union as well.

Ivens occasionally mentioned a wish to make another film in Holland. In 1966 he told Dutch television that he was thinking of a film version of Erasmus's *Praise of Folly*. He envisaged a searing indictment of modern-day stupidity, fascism, militarism and bureaucracy, inspired by Goya, but with the humor of Hieronymus Bosch. Behind the scenes, the City of Rotterdam was negotiating with Ivens and The Hague to allow him to make an Erasmus film without first submitting an official grant application. However, when the possibility was actually offered, he did not accept it, explaining in a letter to the City of Rotterdam that the world of Erasmus was not his world, and that his actual concern was 'bureaucracy, neofascism, neocolonialism and the inbreeding of kingdoms'.[28] The officials had done their best, and his answer was a slap in the face.

In spring 1968, in an interview with the Dutch weekly *Revu*, Ivens remarked that the government 'has, I believe, on occasion, indirectly said that if I had a particular proposal it would be willing to consider it'. He again mentioned *Praise of Folly*.[29] This *Revu* article prompted the head of the film section of the Ministry of Culture, Recreation and Social Work to send a memo to Minister Marga Klompé. 'My question is whether the ministry should respond to this; doing so would not only provide us with a film likely to obtain wide distribution, but would also put an end to the whining about an Ivens boycott. The government would have to come round a little, considering that it has earlier stated that he could submit an application, and that the initiative is now with the government.'[30]

In the Dutch media a paradoxical situation had gradually arisen. No other Dutch filmmaker was given as much positive coverage in the press as Joris Ivens, but these reports were invariably accompanied by remarks such as 'Dutch film prophet not honored in his own country' or 'If he returns to Holland, some way must be found to officially and unconditionally show this great countryman the honor he deserves'. The Dutch film journalists had all met Ivens, and his charm had led to the almost automatic acceptance of his own interpretation of his relationship with the authorities since 1946. It was more than a question of personal sympathy though. The ineradicable inferiority complex that afflicted and afflicts the country of Rembrandt, Van Gogh and Mondrian also played its part: people thought that Holland invariably fails to recognize its great sons.

The government's treatment of Ivens was nothing to be proud of, but the idea that his fatherland had never appreciated him was a myth.

Just as when Ivens had turned sixty-five, students at the Amsterdam film school decided to match his seventieth birthday celebrations in Leipzig with a Dutch tribute. The initiative met with loud applause. The highlight of the festivities came before the day of the tribute itself. On December 4, 1968 minister Klompé sent Ivens a letter promising to finance a short documentary, 'a cinematic vision of our own people and our own country'. Ivens was pleased, but asked: 'Why this change of course? Surely it's not just because I've turned seventy and am a well-known director.' Replying to the question as to whether he felt like an exile, he said on the radio: 'Well, let's say not in exile, no, because later too, in various matters, I have often taken a stance opposing Holland, so it's almost understandable that the Dutch government hasn't always been so pleasant in regard to me.' It was an exceptionally lenient moment, because later he returned to feeling as though he had been driven out of Holland.[31]

On December 11 Joris Ivens had a private discussion with minister Klompé in Amsterdam's Stedelijk Museum. Ivens said that he felt as if he 'was dealing with an honest partner in discussion'. There was a clear sympathy between the film director and the minister, but after the meeting Ivens's doubts returned. Speaking to the Soviet newspaper *Izvestia* – which was still writing about him at that stage – he reportedly stated that before accepting the request of the Dutch government, he needed to be sure that 'the absolute freedom every confirmed revolutionary needs' would be guaranteed. It was something you couldn't take for granted with a 'government on the other side of the barricades'.[32]

The eleventh remained a festive day. The film school screened Ivens films continuously from ten a.m. to midnight, and the reception in his honor was attended by the directors Bert Haanstra and Fons Rademakers, writer Harry Mulisch, composer Peter Schat, and numerous film industry colleagues. Also present were the Soviet ambassador and a representative from the Chinese embassy. A disgruntled *Volkskrant* reporter noted that the Dutch Ministry of Foreign Affairs was 'only' represented by a junior official; as if such birthday receptions would normally be attended by the minister himself. In the magazine *Skrien*, film school students complained that the media were good at writing beautiful commemorative articles about Ivens, but that when it came to actually doing something, it was left to them to take the initiative: 'It's only after things have built up momentum that the ministry comes up with a commission, and if we hadn't done anything, that money would have probably gone to Defense as well.'[33]

In reality the handful of Ivens adversaries left in The Hague were now fighting a rearguard action. Minister of Foreign Affairs Luns reacted to the prospect of an Ivens commission by noting: 'View this very hesitantly, which must be passed on to minister Klompé.' Luns could not even rely on his own officials. In his absence a day earlier, one of his highest ranking staff members had informed the Ministry of Culture that Foreign Affairs was considering participating in the Ivens documentary project. Other officers from the department were reprimanded for attending Ivens's tribute and press conference.[34]

In spring Ivens wrote to Klompé from Paris asking for clarification before 'definitively accepting your invitation'. He wondered whether, instead of a short documentary, a fifty or sixty minute film would be possible and proposed a new meeting. On June 12 he met with Klompé at the ministry to explain his plan for an eighty-minute fiction film about 'the legendary national figure of the Flying Dutchman, now returning to his own country'. The production would be in the hands of Pim de la Parra and Wim Verstappen of Scorpio Films. Minister Klompé granted a preparatory subsidy and promised to help seek funds for the further realization. The large amounts required for a feature film would necessitate an application to the Production Fund.

Ivens was in the middle of editing THE PEOPLE AND THEIR GUNS and the Laos collective was preparing for a subsequent production, so it is not certain whether he really wanted to make THE FLYING DUTCHMAN. Nonetheless, he might have hoped that it would eventuate, especially after the box office success of De la Parra and Verstappen's fiction film about suburban eroticism, BLUE MOVIE. De la Parra recalled that 'some people now expected us to do Joris Ivens's THE FLYING DUTCHMAN'. He also suspected that: 'After we had become millionaires', Ivens thought 'I'll go and do it with those guys'. But 'Pim and Wim' had not forgotten the criticism their other idol, François Truffaut, had published in *Cahiers du Cinéma* about the extravagant working methods Ivens had adopted for MISTRAL and his Eastern European films. 'As small-time feature makers, very low budget', explained De la Parra, 'we realized how expensive his projects were'. In short: 'It would cost us our money. He would have no trouble getting through four million on THE FLYING DUTCHMAN and that', according to De la Parra, 'wasn't our purpose in life'. The film's budget was actually less, eight hundred thousand guilders, although in practice this would naturally soon expand to somewhere over a million, at the time approximately half of the annual budget of the Dutch Production Fund. Anyway Verstappen and De la Parra had branched into fiction films and were less interested in documentaries. And for De la Parra, Ivens was 'a much older man from another era'. 'There came a time when Wim and I were no longer such big fans of Joris's, although we never dared admit it.'[35]

For Ivens, Holland disappeared behind the horizon again in 1971 when premier Zhou Enlai invited him to make a new film in the People's Republic of China.

22 The Old Steed Gallops a Thousand Li (1971-1978)

The deaths of Joris Ivens's parents and his brother Wim were in the distant past, and he was far removed from family life. In Nijmegen his sister Thea regularly received postcards from Joris from all over the world, but hardly ever saw him, and he had even less contact with his youngest sister Coba. His brother Hans, a man of the world who moved in Dutch art circles, made an effort to maintain their relationship. He had provided legal assistance with his brother's passport problem in 1950 and invariably tried to visit him when his work took him to Paris.

In the early 1970s Hans Ivens got cancer. Some four weeks before his death in The Hague on June 13, 1971, Joris visited him for the last time. They knew it was probably their final goodbye, as Joris Ivens had decided to attend a symposium for documentary filmmakers in Tokyo and accept the Chinese invitation. He received the news of Hans's death in Peking. He had lost his father, his mother, his brothers and his beloved Anneke van der Feer without being present at any of their deaths. The news always reached him from afar. At seventy-two he had only ever met death in an impersonal form, through strangers dying on the battlefield or in bombing raids. In a sense his travels had removed him from reality instead of bringing it closer.

Ivens saw his visit to China as a momentous event. Since 1966 he had come no closer to the People's Republic than the transit zone of Peking airport. In 1971 China was still dominated by bloody chaos, but within the party leadership there was an increasing desire to reduce conflict, normalize contacts with abroad, and rehabilitate moderate functionaries like the vilified Deng Xiaoping, the second 'capitalist-roader'. The country's first 'demon', deposed president Liu Shaoqi, was beyond recall: he had been dead for eighteen months without it becoming public knowledge. The elderly Liu had died in captivity from deliberate neglect and denial of medication.

Ivens and Loridan had received their invitation through the Chinese embassy in Paris and arrived in Peking on June 10. They spent three months on a very intensive tour of the country with dozens of organized visits – including trips to no less than fifteen factories, with products ranging from locomotives to ping-pong balls (the ping-pong diplomacy between China and the United States had begun). They were received by top party leaders on various occasions. On July 22, July 29 and August 1 they met with premier Zhou Enlai, and on the last-mentioned date they proceeded to a dinner with

Chairman Mao's wife Jiang Qing, followed by a visit to the revolutionary opera *The Red Detachment of Women*. After the show Jiang Qing, Joris Ivens and Marceline Loridan ascended the stage, where they were surrounded by a hundred actors, all joyfully holding up copies of *The Little Red Book*. They also went to a performance of the revolutionary ballet *Ode to Yimeng* with Jiang Qing and Swiss-Chinese writer Han Suyin, breakfasted in the Peking Hotel with Prince Norodom Sihanouk of Cambodia and attended a dinner celebrating the anniversary of the formation of the People's Liberation Army, where they were seated at the same table as Angola's president Agostinho Neto.[1]

Ivens took notes of his discussions with Zhou Enlai. He had written a report of Western cinema for the premier, who found it 'very good and politically correct'. Zhou promised to pass it on to Jiang Qing, who was in charge of the cultural sector. Ivens had also written reports for Zhou about their journey through China and about Marceline Loridan's life; the Chinese liked to know who they were dealing with. They also discussed the film Ivens would make in China in the following year. Zhou wanted it to be comprehensible for militants abroad and made 'from the perspective of foreign friends'. A pressing task was to make a film about the demoralization of the American troops in Vietnam, their drug abuse and the captured pilots. They agreed that this film should be produced from Paris, but nothing came of this. They also discussed the imminent visit to Peking of the French journalist Jean Lacouture. Ivens and Loridan saw Lacouture as an opportunist who did not recognize the Soviet threat. 'Comrade Zhou asked me to be present at his interview with Lacouture, so as to be able to later take on a corrective role if necessary (a delicate mission).'[2] Lacouture's interview took place on the twenty-ninth, in the presence of Ivens, and appeared in the daily *Nouvel Observateur* without any intervention being deemed necessary.

After their trip, Ivens and Loridan were euphoric about the Cultural Revolution. Ivens had even worked in a locomotive factory for four days to come closer to the workers,[3] and everywhere they had found an intense revolutionary atmosphere that even extended to kindergartens. It was not easy to return to Paris. Instead of vast Chinese panoramas, they had to make do with the same-old view of the École Administrative on the other side of the street. Ivens explained to a visiting Dutch journalist that the French capital had come as a 'mental blow'. Romanticizing a communal life he had always avoided, Ivens explained that 'you realize how far apart from each other people are here, how tense they are, how aggressive'. He said that he had never seen a society as relaxed as the Chinese.[4]

In a glowing article about education in China, he and Loridan reported to French readers on their findings in the People's Republic. The Chinese schools were successfully run by revolutionary committees of workers, peasants and soldiers, so that the children would be educated to continue the revolution. 'Pupils of about ten years old put on an especially moving show for us,' they wrote. 'Dancing with cardboard pens that are twice their size, they sing: 'We have pens to do battle with the four Obsolescences: obsolete morals, obsolete ideologies, obsolete habits, obsolete customs. With the pens we write wallposters. The working class is guiding the pens now. It will never relax its vigilance. Oh, how nice our uncles the workers are!' Nowhere else in the world had there ever been such socially-minded children as in the China of the Cultural Revolution, they continued. The population was so socially involved that police were unnecessary. 'A group of comrades within the revolutionary committee is responsible for security and is supported by the revolutionary committees of the streets, which are in turn supported by people who are responsible for the separate blocks. They are elected by the residents at every level, they are all representatives of the masses. Everyone participates in guaranteeing security...' For *Cahiers du Cinéma* they wrote an exultant piece about the Chinese studios: 'When the working class does not seize power in the arenas of literature and art, when authentic proletarian art is not created in the service of the great masses, then the bourgeoisie will do it.'[5]

At an Amsterdam press conference in the Film Museum in October 1971, Ivens praised a ten-minute Chinese film entitled THE PHILOSOPHY OF KEEPING TOMATOES FRESH, which showed how Mao's teachings helped Chinese farmers to improve their way of storing tomatoes. 'The workers noticed that the tomatoes on the top of the basket were riper and redder than the ones at the bottom. A quick look in Mao, and – lo and behold – on the basis of the *Little Red Book* a method was found to get all the tomatoes as red as the book,' noted the reporter from *De Tijd*. A journalist from *De Telegraaf* wrote: 'The usual Marxist-Leninist and Maoist terms alternated in Ivens's speech, making it dry and impersonal. But, as always in Holland, Ivens's audience remained attentive and, on the surface, very believing. This is extremely deceptive for the man, because in the break and afterwards you always hear large numbers of the listeners taking a very different tone than in their contact with him. Evidently, considerations that Ivens is a nice man and a celebrity, and getting on in years, restrain many of these people from adopting the same critical frankness in direct confrontation with him.'[6] At that time there was nonetheless one incisive and even piquant interview with the director. Piquant because the interviewer was his nephew Urias Nooteboom, Thea's son.

'I see China as an example of the purity of a socialist state,' said Ivens. 'Power is back in the hands of the masses. There is a genuine dictatorship of the proletariat.'

'But,' Nooteboom asked, 'what are the possibilities for people in China who don't want to believe in either Mao Zedong or the Cultural Revolution?'

Ivens: 'The masses, that is the workers, the peasants and the soldiers of the people's army, help the people who can't believe. It is never a case of repression or force. The Chinese say that repression is a sign of political weakness. They try to convince people until the very end. They still let people who have done terrible things work in the factories 'under the control of the masses'. The workers don't exclude someone like that, instead they try to draw him in.'

Nooteboom: 'They contain – or encapsulate – him. That could be very disagreeable.'

Ivens: 'That depends. If the man involved is really criminal and betrayed Communists to Chiang Kai-shek's Kuomintang regime during the war, for example, and perseveres in his deviant opinion, then he is sent to prison.'

Nooteboom: 'Where is this so-called renegade [Liu Shaoqi]?'

Ivens: 'He has been deposed and is probably living somewhere in a village, under house arrest. As far as that is concerned the Chinese party is very different from the Russian party. The Chinese leadership has never had people executed for political reasons.'[7]

Although the interview appeared in the provincial *Eindhovens Dagblad*, it was now clear to everyone that Joris Ivens had been reborn. For a long time he had more or less reconciled himself to socialism's tendency to stagnate in Eastern European style bureaucracy; in China he had seen for himself that pure socialism was possible after all. His radicalization reached an apex and remained at dizzying heights for five more years. 'When you spoke to people there, they believed in it,' said Marceline Loridan, looking back on their journeys to the East. 'A lot of people spoke of serving the people and the struggle against egoism. You started believing that something was really happening, that it couldn't possibly all be propaganda. We didn't like the cult of Mao, but you ended up trying to justify everything.'[8] In the West many others shared Ivens and Loridan's belief in China's New Man. Ivens was an exception in only one regard: he was virtually the only Westerner who had lived through the entire history of Soviet socialism and yet still had such an uninhibited belief in Maoism.

The effects of May 1968 could still be felt in early seventies Paris. The Maoist group Gauche Prolétarienne broke into delicatessens and distributed the proceeds among the poor, forged metro tickets when the fares were increased, and tried to establish itself among the workers in major industries. When the security of the Renault car factory shot the young Maoist Pierre Overnay dead in 1972, Ivens was one of two hundred thousand mourners. An alternating group of leading figures became known as *les pétitionneurs*. Among them were Simone Signoret, Yves Montand, Costa-Gavras, Jean-Paul Sartre, philosopher Michel Foucault, the political intellectuals Régis Debray, Maurice Clavel and Claude Mauriac – son of writer François Mauriac – and Joris Ivens. The name they were given was naturally derived from the many petitions and declarations they signed in support of all kinds of leftist causes. Their name or physical presence at a demonstration could be a reason for it to be reported in the press; fame had become a weapon in the class struggle.

Often it was Gauche Prolétarienne that mobilized the celebrities for these kind of activities. The *pétitionneurs* themselves were hardly uniform in their convictions. They were all left-wing opponents of the PCF, but whereas Costa-Gavras and Yves Montand had just made THE CONFESSION, a film indicting the Stalinist persecution in Eastern Europe and indirectly the Stalinism of the PCF, Ivens believed that the party had lost the faith and betrayed its old principles.

Gauche Proletariènne dissolved in 1972, but everywhere in the West small parties and organizations based on Mao's ideas remained. Despite Ivens's ideological affinity, he did not join any of these groups. 'They all say that they're the only true revolutionaries,' he explained to a radical leftist audience at the film and television school in West Berlin. 'That's something a lot of people can do without.' He believed that the groups first needed to unite in the struggle. At the same time he saw himself as something of a grand old man of the radical left. In 1976 he felt called upon to point out to the activists that 'you cannot be a revolutionary militant unless you are armed with the theory of Marxism-Leninism' and to warn against 'strong tendencies in France to liquidate Marxist-Leninist principles or simply forget them'.[9]

Ivens maintained numerous contacts with Dutch activists, among them the Cineclub film collective. The Dutch distributors of THE PEOPLE AND THEIR GUNS, Cineclub was also involved in local campaigns in Amsterdam. Through them, Ivens sent a message of solidarity to the Nieuwmarkt Action Group, which opposed the construction of a subway line. Organizations such as the leftist theater group Proloog, the Association for Dutch-Chinese Friendship and the Medical Committee Netherlands-Vietnam could count on Ivens's support, and he also visited the headquarters of the Dutch Communist Party/Marxist-Leninist. At times another manifestation of the spirit of the times also reached out to him in letters from Holland: 'Mayken just told me that she was intensively involved with you during this acid trip she just took and that she got some inspiration for her book... She's currently into horoscopes, she says she'll cast yours for you if you pass on your hour, date and place of birth.'[10]

In Paris the peace talks between North Vietnam and the United States dragged on until January 1973, when Le Duc Tho and Henry Kissinger reached an agreement. Once the last American combat troops had pulled out of South Vietnam a few months later, it was only a matter of time before the final defeat of the South Vietnamese army. Communist troops took Saigon on April 30, 1975, and the South was placed under the administration of Hanoi.

Through personal contacts and receptions at the embassy in Paris, Ivens had maintained his excellent relationship with the North Vietnamese and felt able to state confidently 'that the agreements made in Paris are violated daily by the American and South Vietnamese government (Saigon). In contrast, the peoples of Vietnam, the government of the Democratic Republic of Vietnam and the Provisional Revolutionary Government of South Vietnam do take these agreements seriously.'[11] In September 1974, however, a very unwelcome letter arrived at the rue des Saints-Pères, sent by Debbie Litt of Detroit:

'Dear Mr. Ivens,

I am writing you for information about a picture that you took in Hanoi, North Vietnam in 1967. This picture is of an American pilot, Lt. Ron Dodge of the United States Navy, being escorted by North Vietnamese soldiers. It first appeared in the French magazine *Paris-Match* on September 9, 1967. It also appeared on the cover of *Life* magazine in 1972, and various other publications here in the United States. Despite the signing of the Vietnam peace agreement, the North Vietnamese and Viet Cong have not provided a complete and accurate accounting of the men whom they were believed to have been holding.

There are still over 50 Americans of whom there is proof of capture, (such as picture taken in captivity, enemy propaganda broadcast, etc.), but who were not released or accounted for by the enemy. Lt. Dodge is one of these men. The picture that you took in Hanoi is evidence that he was at one time in enemy hands. Even so, the North Vietnamese deny any knowledge of him.

I am active in the MIA [Missing in Action] issue here in the US and I believe that you have some information that would help me get *all* the MIA's accounted for.'

After a series of questions about the conditions in which Ron Dodge was being held in North Vietnam, Debbie Litt continued:

> 'Mr. Ivens, I hope this questioning doesn't seem rude or offensive. You see, Ron Dodge is somewhat special to me. Even though I have never met him, he is like a brother. Although I am working for all the MIA's, I must admit that I am working for Ron in particular, and I would be forever grateful to you if you could possibly answer, to the best of your ability, the questions asked above... My last question to you is whether or not there is anyone whom you are familiar with, who witnessed Lt. Dodge's capture. If so, could you please give me an address where I might write to this person?'

This letter worked like fly paper: once you'd touched it, you could no longer shake it off, and the more you tried to get rid of it, the more it stuck. How should Ivens reply? Ron Dodge was a prisoner, and since, as he himself stated, the North Vietnamese kept their agreements, Ron would have to be produced. The obvious next step was to write to prime minister Pham Van Dong in Hanoi – he still sent Ivens a card each New Year's – or at least to raise the issue with the ambassador at the next Vietnamese reception in Paris. Instead Ivens did neither and wrote to Debbie Litt: 'I received your letter in which you are asking me information about an American pilot, Lt. Ron Dodge. The picture you are referring to is a blow up of a frame of a motion picture made by a film operator of Vietnam and I included it in a film I made in 1967 in Vietnam.'

Debbie Litt did not accept this answer and she or her friends called at the rue des Saint-Pères seeking more information. 'These people came by and we explained to them that the shot was made by a Vietnamese cameraman and that we neither spoke to him nor know his name,' noted Ivens in 1980 on his copy of the letter to Detroit.[12]

It was probably true that he himself had not filmed the shot of the captured pilot in THE THREATENING SKY,[13] but a letter or a telephone call to his colleagues in Hanoi would have been enough to identify the cameraman. What prevented him from promoting compliance with the Geneva Convention now that it was a North Vietnamese violation? He presumably wanted to avoid difficulties with Hanoi, and knew in the back of his mind that their public claims about keeping their promises were not entirely true. Seven years later, in July 1981, after pressure from America, the Vietnamese government handed the remains of Ron Dodge over to the United States after all. He had died in captivity, but no information as to the date or circumstances was provided. The only thing that could be said with certainty was that he had been dead for a very long time.[14]

North Vietnam protested ignorance of the whereabouts of American pilot Ron Dodge, but his capture had been shown in Ivens's THE THREATENING SKY. A still from the film made the cover of *Life*. TIME/LIFE

Ivens's European activities in this period were intermezzi in years of work on a monumental project in China. From fall 1971 he had given lectures about his trip to China in Holland, Belgium and Italy, while Loridan took care of France. They took note of two hundred questions from the floor and used these as starting points for their new film, which premiered four years later as a twelve-hour film cycle entitled HOW YUKONG MOVED THE MOUNTAINS. The title was inspired by one of 'three articles by Chairman Mao that were always to be reread', as they were known in China. In 'The Foolish Old Man Who Removed the Mountains' Mao referred to the legend of an old man who decided with his two sons to begin the impossible task of shoveling away two mountains that obstructed his path. They worked day and night. 'God was moved by this', according to Mao, 'and he sent down two angels, who carried the mountains away on their backs. Today, two big mountains lie like a dead weight on the Chinese people. One of them is imperialism, the other is feudalism.' [15]

Malicious tongues whispered that Ivens and Loridan's film was being financed by the Chinese authorities but, just as with the Vietnam films, the reality was more complex. The French Centre National du Cinéma provided three advances against the receipts of YUKONG, and these paid for 16mm equipment, film and laboratory costs. The Central Studio for News and Documentary Films in Peking made a Chinese crew available, and in return Ivens trained its members in modern film techniques. Travel costs and accommodation were presumably met by the Chinese government.

Ivens and Loridan arrived in China to start work on their film on March 19, 1972. The Peking Hotel, near Tiananmen Square and the Forbidden City, became the base from which they spent several months finding locations and making preparations at the Central Studio. Ivens's colleagues informed him that he was expected to provide professional and political leadership, but that he should remain a 'simple fighter' in the collective and apply the 'line of the masses', by seeking the opinion of the people.[16] This boiled down to a somewhat dogmatic formulation of his normal working methods and did not require any major compromise on his part. On the job, he decked himself out in a blue Mao suit and cap.

The vast chasm between European and Chinese working methods became apparent when shooting began at Peking's Tsinghua University. Twelve years after the first *cinéma vérité* films, 16mm with synchronized sound was still unknown in China. There was only 35mm filmed in an extremely static style. Ivens and Loridan were determined to exploit the possibilities of *cinéma vérité* in YUKONG, and it took cameraman Li Zexiang months to get the hang of it. This was not the only Chinese convention that needed to be overcome. 'We felt the hesitation of our man to take close-ups, we had to convince him that the close-up has the same beauty as the landscape,' according to Ivens. Li Zexiang explained the differences of opinion at the university by saying: 'Ivens obviously wanted to reflect real school life through natural details, while I considered his demands naturalistic. Real life was not necessarily what I intended to film. The classroom was for serious teaching and concentrated listening. I felt that was the true situation in our schools.'[17] In time, however, Li became enthusiastic about the unprecedented possibilities of the Éclair camera, which had already inspired a generation of French filmmakers to develop in new directions. Four and a half months after Ivens's arrival in China, the shooting at Tsinghua University was finally completed.

On 26 August the crew moved on to the Xingjiang-Uygur Autonomous Region in the extreme west of China, where new difficulties presented themselves. In his memoirs Ivens described endless negotiations with local party functionaries, who patiently tried to explain how he should make his film. The authorities of Kashgar were the most shameless. In this city close to Tadzhikistan, Afghanistan and Pakistan, actually part of the Islamic world: 'I was allowed to make the most sumptuous directorial decisions of my entire career. There was a time, while I was vegetating in Hollywood, that my friends at the William Morris Agency wanted to make me first adviser for crowd scenes.' According to Ivens they would have been astounded by what Kashgar had to offer. 'At seven o'clock in the morning, an intersection and whole streets enlivened with hundreds of extras: men and women, all smiling, dressed in immaculate blue; and school children, each wearing a brand-new apron...' Various scenes that emphasized aspects of the political line had been set up here and there along the film crew's route. Among them: 'the mosque with several men sunk in prayer to show that there really was freedom of religion; a tradesman in a working class neighborhood – a tinker – to convince us that individual enterprise really did exist in China; and as the climax of this astonishing display, a large store with happy citizens filing through it and picking products at will from fully stocked shelves.'[18] Leaving the city, the crew was escorted by five or six carloads of accompanying officials. Many of the shots from the far west were unusable as a result, but Ivens did notice that his 'lungs were very happy with the dry air of the desert'.[19] A decade later he took advantage of this knowledge and filmed part of A TALE OF THE WIND in this same Taklamakan Desert.

They returned to Peking just in time for the celebration of the founding of the People's Republic on October 1. In a letter to Marion Michelle, Ivens wrote: 'Peking became a great park with happy people. Wonderful – the whole city was relaxed, celebrating – buying in the shops, (3 days off!), eating in the restaurants or at home, families together.' Nonetheless, he was unable to ignore the fact that in more than half a year in China they had only managed thirty-seven days of filming. Perhaps because of the stress, he now came down with bronchitis and high fever and was forced to spend three weeks in hospital to avert pneumonia. On urgent medical advice he abandoned plans to film in the freezing north, and Shanghai now became the next destination.[20] To prevent the recurrence of the problems they had encountered in the far west, they were assigned a new escort, party man Chen Li-jen, whose task was to ensure better communication between the directors and the local cadres.

In January 1973 the crew arrived in Shanghai where they filmed impressions of the city, everyday life in a pharmacy, and the work in a generator factory. They visited the pharmacy regularly for a month before starting filming, and in the factory they followed the same procedure.[21] In Nanjing, a couple of hundred miles to the west, they filmed in a barracks, and that summer they were in Shandong at the fishing commune Da Yu Dao on the Yellow Sea. With the winter over, they were now able to leave for Manchuria and the Daqing oilfields. During the Cultural Revolution these oilfields were considered an exemplary production site and every Chinese knew the slogan 'In industry, learn from Daqing.' In Peking they filmed a physicist, Professor Chen, who related before the camera how Red Guards had roughly, but to his satisfaction, taught him that he was not a good scientist, even though he had always thought he was. He had studied in Canada and was very well-known in his field, but after being confronted with the question 'What good are all those books?' and working in the countryside, he realized how wrong he had been. 'The party and the revolutionary forces are tremendously patient with the older generation,' observed Ivens.[22]

At the end of 1973, after some twenty months in China, he and Loridan returned to France with one hundred and twenty hours of exposed film in their baggage. Around July 1974 a rough cut with a length of some thirty hours had been made on three editing benches, and the work was almost completed by the end of the year. All they needed was some supplementary material in China about the latest political developments. When the rushes they had requested from cameraman Li Zexiang arrived in Paris, however, they turned out to be unusable. After a more moderate period in 1971-1973, the radicals in China had launched a counter-offensive in the form of a campaign 'against Lin Biao and Confucius'. Lin Biao had been poised to succeed Mao and had died in a mysterious plane crash two years earlier. The philosopher Confucius had died in 479 BC. The fiercely anti-Western movement's slogans included: 'Criticize Beethoven! Condemn Confucius!' One of the more peculiar victims was the Italian film director Michelangelo Antonioni, who had worked in the People's Republic at the same time as Ivens and Loridan. Altough his film, CHINA, had initially been favorably received in Peking, it had been condemned from one day to the next as a 'wild provocation against the Chinese people'.[23]

The Chinese embassy in Paris asked Ivens to publicly disassociate himself from Antonioni, but he had little desire to do so, and in an interview he did not go any further than to remark that his colleague 'had not seen that he was in a country where something collective was being born'. Loridan was less reticent: 'The Chinese he shows us, and with which he confirms the inaccurate image Westerners have of China, are fearful, smile stupidly or are simply aggressive.' She found Antonioni's attitude to his subject 'extremely unpleasant. Because I really don't like pinning people up like butterflies, whether it's in China, Japan or in the Ardèche. It is a violating camera and we, we tried to do the opposite.' She saw the roots of Antonioni's failure in the fact that his work 'is film of the crisis, the ideological crisis in Western society'.[24]

Ivens and his friends were surprised by the formal shots Li Zexiang had sent them and did not understand that he too was battling with the same adverse winds as Antonioni. Unprepared for trouble, Ivens and Loridan left for Peking in the summer of 1975 to film their own supplementary material. They were received with great respect by vice-premier Zhang Chunqiao,[25] confidant of Mao's wife Jiang Qing, and housed on the sixteenth floor of the new wing of the Peking Hotel – with air conditioning and lots of glass and marble and only open to foreigners and high-level party functionaries. Despite appearances, however, the reception was cool. They had brought a number of completed parts of YUKONG with them and screened them for a group of leading cinematic and cultural representatives, as well as a number of people the authorities had brought to Peking from the various locations. As Ivens and Loridan were refused permission to return to these locations, there was little chance of supplementary material. After the screening the criticism was 'so rigid and formal that it was like a lesson the people had learnt off by heart', said Ivens.[26] A functionary from the Ministry of Culture read out a list of sixty-one suggestions for the removal of scenes or the provision of new commentary.

They decided to waste no time before returning to Paris, and their faithful friends were at the airport to see them off. 'Our entire crew was there,' according to Ivens. 'In Peking they had become 'the people from YUKONG' and in all my life I have never experienced such a moving farewell. Is it imaginable? In socialist China? Forty Chinese jostling at the foot of the stairs, as far as they were allowed to go. They all hugged us and kissed us. The majority of them were crying, and it wouldn't have taken much more to set me off either.' The Parisian guests left without properly understanding what had actually happened in the political snake pit of Peking and without realizing that this was the practical reality of the Cultural Revolution their film was praising. One of those waving goodbye was Sidney Shapiro, an American who had been living in China since the forties, and Ivens wrote to him as soon as he was back in Paris: 'As you can imagine we were very moved by the send-off by all our friends at the airport. The first hour Marceline and I did not say much... We felt that all of you knew that we were in for a hard time, with difficult tasks to fulfill, but we felt that you had confidence, and that gives us the force to deal with tough businesspeople... The way you and Huimin helped [Situ Huimin, underminister of Culture] Marceline and me in a complicated situation has given us strength and direction to act as we did.'[27]

After negative reactions from French distribution companies, they decided to release YUKONG themselves through their production company Capi-

Films. This took up virtually all their time over the following years. Making contacts, distributing publicity material, designing posters, everything was organized from the rue des Saints-Pères. With the Association for Sino-French Friendship pasting up posters, How Yukong Moved the Mountains premiered on March 10, 1976 in four small theaters on Paris's Left Bank. Ivens personally visited the theaters to check the copies and box-office receipts.

Normally Loridan arranged business, handled negotiations and resolved conflicts, tasks Ivens preferred avoiding. 'All screenings, programming and interviews with television stations in all countries are concentrated with Mrs. Loridan, Capi Films,' he once wrote in answer to a letter addressed to him. 'Negotiations about prices and programming are not carried out by me, but by Capi Films.'[28] Capi's business address was their own home address, and Marceline could very well have been sitting beside him while he wrote.

Considering the documentary and political character of Yukong and its exorbitant length, the public interest was far from disappointing. According to Ivens's figures, three hundred thousand people saw the film in French theaters, of which one hundred and thirty thousand in Paris,[29] where Yukong drew larger audiences than any other film for the two weeks following its premiere. It is not entirely clear how these calculations were made, as four tickets were required to see all twelve parts. After the screenings Ivens and Loridan entered into discussion with the audience and these sessions often went on until late at night.

Yukong was released at the right moment. Maoism was still popular with the left, and there had also been a warm interest for China on the right since President Richard Nixon's official visit to Mao in 1972. The Chinese leaders were more fiercely anti-Soviet than the American hawks. The China trend would reach even greater heights after 1976, when Mao Zedong died and the leadership in Peking passed into the hands of more moderate figures who began discovering positive aspects of capitalism. China had been closed off for decades and there was an enormous desire for information about it. How Yukong Moved the Mountains finally gave its audiences a sense of being able to peep behind the scenes in this distant country.

Leading French newspapers such as *Le Monde, Le Nouvel Observateur, Le Figaro, Libération* and the film magazines were positive. The general response was that the filmmakers had penetrated deeply into ordinary day-to-day life in China without placing their own political sympathies in the foreground. Readers of *France-Soir* were even able to attend a special preview. The newspaper recommended that 'to gain an impression of the whole, you need to see all the films being shown, in other words, you need to visit all four of the theaters in question'.[30] In retrospect, the success of YUKONG can be fully attributed to the circumstances of the day because anyone who watches the film now, cannot fail to recognize that the judgement of the *International Herald Tribune* was more accurate: 'The film itself is not distinguished by any cinematic artistry and never rises above the newsreel-level, but as a screen reportage it is an achievement crowded with valuable information.'[31]

YUKONG was exceptional for the simple reason that China was closed to most Western cineastes, although leftist journalists such as Felix Greene had been allowed to film there. Ivens had supported the Chinese revolution for more than thirty years. Peking gave him almost complete freedom of movement because they knew he would never cast a negative light upon the People's Republic. Some Western critics believed that he had been misled by the authorities, that everything had been staged, or that he himself was a co-conspirator. In fact the picture he gave of the superficial public face of everyday life in China was doubtlessly authentic. Except, what did that mean with such strong social control, with revolutionary committees in every street, mass meetings where anyone could be dragged through the mire, ideological control from above, and police interventions when required? In a sense, Chinese citizens were always acting in an attempt to live up to an ideal image, even those who did not ascribe to that ideal. Still, the filming of YUKONG had been much less spontaneous than was first suggested. When Guangdong Television interviewed a number of characters from 'The Pharmacy' for a documentary about Ivens in 1996-1997, they related that Ivens himself had asked them to do some scenes ten or twelve times.[32] The main objection, however, remained that YUKONG gave a false picture because it did not probe beneath visible reality, did not penetrate to the underlying mechanisms of Chinese society. The danger of *cinéma vérité* that Ivens had once warned about, that it only showed the exterior, infected his own film to the core.

Joris Ivens was seventy-seven when YUKONG premiered, and the years were beginning to weigh increasingly heavily. In the summer of 1974, during the editing, he had spent ten days in the French Alps recovering from bronchitis, and in the months after the film's release, he twice spent three weeks at La Clusaz, in the Savoy Alps near Mont Blanc. His respiratory system caused him more and more problems, and in February of the next year he spent four weeks in a Peking hospital with bronchial pneumonia. In the following years he invariably visited La Clusaz or Les Diablerets in Switzerland once or twice annually to flush out his lungs and regain his strength – and enjoy being alone, because he reserved these mountain vacations for himself. 'Long walks, mountains, the outlines of mountains, clouds, colors, pine trees, wind – plus not thinking about anything and feeling good,' as he wrote on a postcard to an acquaintance in the Netherlands. He told a *Le Monde* journalist: 'I never get bored – which is not to say that I'm a thinker. Even now, when I come back from three weeks away, Marceline Loridan says to me: 'Where have you been? What did you think about?' I didn't think about anything. I walked. I noticed that the same bird is always singing in a particular spot.'[33] He was as much of a loner as he had been on the Joris Fen.

On January 5, 1977 after a relationship of almost fourteen years, Joris Ivens and Marceline Loridan married in a private ceremony. Their life together had been set in hotels, Vietnamese huts or Laotian caves, and in between times in the apartment on the rue des Saints-Pères. Despite sharing his love for hotels – with their absence of household chores and everyday worries – Loridan was the first woman since his mother to succeed in instigating some kind of domesticity in Joris for longer than six months. Even the fact of having had the same address since 1964 was unprecedented, although his advanced age and increasing physical limitations played a role in this.

They had worked together on films without interruption for some ten years, and Ivens called their union 'a marriage of image and sound', referring to the division of labor on 17TH PARALLEL and YUKONG.[34] Loridan can hardly have been happy with this characterization of the nature of their collaboration. In a 1977 interview with the German magazine *Filmfaust* she said: 'It was only through the women's movement after May 1968 that it became clear to me that as a woman I had to earn a place for myself as opposed to men... I have expressed and proven myself in the work – but not publicly. Every time a film was finished, I didn't think it worth the trouble of signing my name because I knew that they would only speak about Joris Ivens anyway and not about Marceline Loridan.' Ivens had also realized that things could not go on like that, she added, and they had agreed to agitate for their acceptance as equal partners. Something not everyone was willing to do. Despite their declarations in Europe that they were the co-directors of YUKONG, the Chinese did not take this seriously and continued to consistently refer to them in publications as 'film director Ivens' and 'film worker' Loridan. Even underminister of Culture Situ Huimin, a longstanding personal friend of Ivens's who had worked in Hollywood after the war, expressly referred to Loridan in an article as Ivens's 'assistant'. The Chinese were not alone in refusing to grant her an equal position. 'In Italy for example', she said, 'a country where the men are still very phallocratic, I simply do not exist when it comes to our films'. In another interview she remarked

During the filming of How Yukong Moved the Mountains. Joris Ivens wearing cap, Marceline Loridan with microphone (China, 1972-1974).
NEW WORLD PRESS

that she was thinking about making films by herself, not because of any breach with Ivens, but because 'I am a woman and have a different perception of things, a different sensibility.'[35] This did not go beyond being a resolution.

The Ivens-Loridan home was full of things Chinese. In Ivens's study there were statues of Chinese warriors in battle, the walls were hung with Chinese landscapes on rice paper, there were Chinese carvings on the mantelpiece, and the bookcase was filled with works about China. 'Mao's philosophy is the primary truth,' explained Ivens to a Dutch reporter he received there.[36]

Peking greeted the Paris premiere of Yukong with a steely silence. A fierce power struggle had erupted after the eternal man of the party center, Zhou Enlai, had become seriously ill in 1975. Much to the dissatisfaction of the radicals, the experienced moderate Deng Xiaoping was called back into the leadership to fill the vacuum. A 'Criticize Deng' campaign was launched. After Zhou's death in January 1976, the path seemed clear for the leftists and Deng was again stripped of all his posts. But in September Mao

Zedong died as well, and in the space of a few weeks the internal party conflict reached an unexpected denouement with the arrest of the so-called
Gang of Four around Mao's widow Jiang Qing.

By sheer chance, Joris Ivens and Marceline Loridan were being interviewed by journalists from *Filmfaust* in October 1976 when the news of the
arrest of the Gang of Four reached Paris. Ivens had just expressed a number
of dogmatic opinions about several issues related to the Communist line. In
response to the Germans' criticism of Stalinism, he had claimed that things
had been very good in Eastern Europe at the time he had worked there. 'I do
not agree with what you're saying about Stalinism... Many Germans see Stalinism the wrong way... I myself need to thoroughly think this issue through
before giving a clear answer. This issue is much too important for a superficial treatment.' The gist of his future conclusions was indicated by his remark: 'I considered Khruschev's speech against Stalin at the Twentieth
Party Congress of the CPSU to be totally ridiculous.'

In 1956, Ivens had not been pleased with Khruschev's speech, but it had
set off doubts in his mind, and in practical terms he had followed the Eastern European change of course without argument. Now he said that 'within
a few months' after Kruschev the Chinese 'had produced a much more lucid
analysis'. The Great Helmsman had pronounced that Stalin had been 'seventy percent good and thirty percent bad', and the Chinese party leadership
took pride in seeing themselves as continuers of Stalin's work. By 1976 Ivens
too had come full circle to a renewed appreciation for the Soviet leader.
'When Stalin died it was an enormous shock, something like the death of
your father. Stalin was so rooted in me. He had stood at the head of something in which I was a firm believer. There were so many emotional aspects
related to Stalin. He was a hard leader, but honest... Khruschev was a
kitchenmaid, an insignificant minor statesman with a concierge's criticisms
of his predecessor.'[37] Speaking to *Filmfaust* he went so far as to say of The
Seine Meets Paris: 'I can hardly bear to look at that myself.' He found it too
apolitical.[38]

Even members of the inner circle around Ivens and Loridan were concerned
about how radical they were becoming, among them family friend Jean-
Pierre Sergent. 'When Joris and Marceline came back from China after making Yukong, Marceline was totally Maoist,' he explained. 'I had already
given it up. I had difficulties communicating with Marceline – which upset
me, because I loved them both. With Joris it was different, he was a friendly,
quiet old man.' When Yukong was launched, Sergent and his friend Jean-
Marie Doublet interviewed Ivens and Loridan for a press release for publicity purposes. Sergent: 'We had great difficulties formulating it in a way that

would be acceptable to French journalists. They were too involved, too Maoist. They didn't know how to speak to the press. A lot of magazines quoted the end of the interview, which I had written myself, completely, both questions and answers.'[39]

And then Mao's widow and three of her faithful supporters were arrested. In Ivens's presence, the *Filmfaust* interviewers asked themselves how they should interpret this. 'In any event, let's wait for the reports from the Chinese press itself before we judge,' suggested Ivens.

Almost three months later he wrote to Marion Michelle: 'Our Chinese film friends would dearly like to see both our films and us in the new period of their creative film work. So they've invited us, very unexpectedly and at very short notice, that is, we leave for Peking on Monday January 11 and return on February 10. I am very happy to be going there and Marceline is too, now that everything seems to be in a state of constant change after the death of Mao.'[40] For the first time the completed YUKONG cycle was now shown in China, in private clubs and at the French embassy – where the Peking diplomatic corps appeared in large numbers – and also in Shanghai at the generator factory and in the locomotive factory in Peking.

On February 9 the Association for Friendship with other Peoples organized a screening for delegates from the art world. Poor health prevented Joris Ivens from attending, but Marceline Loridan read a speech he had written. She attacked the Gang of Four and explained: 'Since our arrival here we have not only seen that their conception is irreconcilable with ours in the field of art, we have also discovered the damage they have caused in all other fields.' Two weeks later they were received by the vice-chairman of the Central Committee, General Ye Jiangjing, who had played a leading role in overthrowing the Gang of Four. 'You have done a great deal of work. I am glad to meet you,' declared the elderly soldier before sitting down to a banquet together.[41] Another journey to Peking followed in late 1977, and on December 29 the official Chinese premiere of How YUKONG MOVED THE MOUNTAINS was held, a year and ten months after the first screening in Paris. The Minister of Culture gave a speech and the Dutch ambassador was present. In January Ivens and Loridan were received by Mao Zedong's successor as party chairman, transitional figure Hua Guofeng, who was replaced some time later by Deng Xiaoping. In 1978 Ivens visited Deng for tea.

Ivens and Loridan followed the change of course closely. They stayed in China for several months each year as guests of the government and had an undeniable interest in maintaining friendly relations with the Chinese leaders, but it was also true that Ivens's character had more affinity with party cadres from the center like Zhou Enlai and Situ Huimin than with the radicals. He was open to 'pure' ideals but was no hysteric. Decades earlier, jour-

nalist Martha Gellhorn had noted a striking resemblance between Ivens and
Zhou in terms of their appearance and 'their charms and quiet intelligence'.
She even went so far as to describe Zhou as 'the Chinese version of Ivens'.
Gellhorn had known Ivens since the Spanish Civil War and had met Zhou in
China in 1941.[42]

Until summer 1978 Ivens and Loridan were preoccupied with the international promotion of YUKONG. Television networks in Holland, Germany,
Belgium, Italy, Finland, England, and Canada broadcast the film in whole
or in part, and its makers spent some time as guests in virtually all these
countries, speaking to the press and monitoring the dubbing. Ivens was
thoroughly insulted by the attitude of French television. He considered it
'scandalous' that only the third network was willing to broadcast YUKONG,
and even then only a limited number of sections totaling just four hours.[43]

He preferred the generous American television station that, after his first
visit to the United States in thirty-two years, flew him home by Concorde:
New York to Paris in three hours and nineteen minutes. This was not the
only time YUKONG brought Loridan and Ivens to America. The Museum of
Modern Art in New York hosted YUKONG's American premiere on February
7, 1978, and the guests at the celebratory party on Park Avenue included the
actress Shirley MacLaine, former Frontier Film members Willard van Dyke
and Leo Hurwitz, *New York Times* journalist Harrison Salisbury, and Robert
Capa's son Cornell. In April they crossed the Atlantic again to attend
screenings at Berkeley and in the World Theatre in San Francisco's Chinatown, where the audience was largely Chinese. 'It was a good feeling to
strike different emotional chords with our film than we do with the people
who usually see it. Deep memories, nostalgia. Refreshing forgotten childhood experiences from their own country, China. Tremendous success in
numbers too. The first night packed (1,200 seats) and outside a queue of a
thousand people wanting to get in!' wrote Ivens on the plane to Montreal.[44]
Invitations from Spain, Austria, England and Hong Kong led to more flights
abroad.

Since leaving Eastern Europe in the fifties, Ivens had not known such intense international interest, and the change was largely attributable to television. In the words of *American Film*, he had 'reemerged from the obscurity
of the film history books'.[45]

Holland was – along with Italy, Canada and Finland – one of four countries
to show YUKONG on television in its full length. The ratings in the country of
his birth were impressive and polls showed that the film met with equal approval from viewers on the right and the left.[46] Contrary to Ivens's expecta-

tions, the reactions from the press were predominantly positive across the political spectrum. A conservative weekly like *Elseviers Magazine* declared resolutely: 'China epic flawless' and called Ivens 'a man of the left, in as much as honesty and anti-dictatorial emotions are often confused with being left-wing.' There were some critical rumblings. One of the most remarkable reactions came from Renate Rubinstein in the weekly *Vrij Nederland*. She thought she recognized the guide who had accompanied her during her own five-day visit to China in the section about the pharmacy. Except that this guide was now playing the role of expropriated pharmacist. Another story that circulated independently suggests that Rubinstein might have been right. In the late seventies, the Canadian National Film Board made three documentaries in China. The Chinese authorities strongly recommended a 'farmer' for the main character and the Canadians took photos of this man back to Canada with them. In the studio he was recognized as Ivens's pharmacist.[47]

Ivens mainly remembered the few Dutch critics who made negative comments: 'I regretted several miserable little articles and lies about my work. Unfortunately Holland is good at that. In all other countries the reviews are better, deeper and more interesting, and it is seen as an important event in cinema history and also as a political event. That old saying about a prophet in his own country is unfortunately applicable to me,' he wrote to an old acquaintance in Holland. As far as the Netherlands was concerned, Ivens still had his old tendency of working himself up to a completely negative image. Just two months later, he wrote from China: 'the people recognize themselves in our films – and the top leaders also show their interest. The minister of Culture gave the opening speech at the Peking premiere and then Marceline and I addressed the audience. This shows up the official reaction in the Netherlands to a cinematic work of this greatness: politically and artistically. The reviews by Dutch television critics were in general miserable. How is it possible that people writing about an international film like this can be so bitter, lazy, immodest and contemptuous?'[48]

The recipient of Joris Ivens's outpourings was a mysterious lady in Bilthoven, whom Ivens almost invariably visited for an hour or so when in Holland. For some, she was the subject of wild speculation. Was she the mother of an illegitimate child of Ivens's? Tineke de Vaal, wife of the director of the Dutch Film Museum, always drove Ivens there and waited outside in the car while he went in. The lady was Miss A.B. van Zomeren, a septuagenarian who had never married. Where had they met? Their correspondence began in the late sixties, and the salutation of the letters Ivens wrote to her for at least sixteen years was generally 'Dear Miss van

Zomeren', with occasional variants like 'Chèr Madame van Zomeren'. He never used her Christian name. According to her 'foster daughter' – she had two, both with identifiable biological parents – Miss van Zomeren was the kind of person who personally approached artists she admired and 'wasn't easy to shake off'. In photos she comes across as a resolute no-nonsense woman.

Miss van Zomeren had been an executive secretary at Philips when Joris Ivens filmed PHILIPS RADIO there in the early thirties. Was she the unknown woman who had helped Ivens to keep Mark Kolthoff awake in their Eindhoven hotel? In any case, in 1969 she began sending Ivens frequent packages of newspaper clippings to keep him up-to-date with events in Holland. In their correspondence they called this the 'paper camera'. She took out subscriptions for this purpose, and he expressed his gratitude and assured her that he was aware of 'how much work it was: reading, selecting, categorizing, sending'. She sent gift packages to Paris for the feast of St Nicholas and even began saving money for the film Ivens planned to make about the Netherlands, THE FLYING DUTCHMAN. By 1978 the balance of a special account in Ivens's name in Amsterdam had risen to twelve thousand guilders, all deposited by Miss van Zomeren. Whenever he was in the newspapers or on television, she telephoned her acquaintances to alert them to the fact.

She was a demanding admirer who expected to receive regular answers from Ivens. If he had visited and been somewhat cool, she would recall the occasion with slight offense in her next letter, after which he would reassure her that he still felt an unaltered friendship for her. Ivens regularly excused himself for not having written and occasionally made an extremely polite request that she might contain the quantity of clippings. All in all, Miss van Zomeren received more mail from him than his sister Thea did and the clippings and donations really were welcome in Paris.[49]

Despite the strange ongoing formality between them, Ivens's relations to Miss van Zomeren were somewhat comparable to those in several of his marriages. He actually felt himself to be the stronger party but was afraid of hurting the other person, and this led to a compliance that in turn made him vulnerable to browbeating. The weaker the other person supposedly was, the more powerless his attitude. Joris Ivens was virtually the fulfillment of Miss van Zomeren's life. She died six months after him.

As part of the festivities for his eightieth birthday, the Dutch minister for Overseas Development, Jan de Koning, presented him with the Dick Scherpenzeel Prize for services to the promotion of development issues on November 13, 1978. The jury believed that the laureate had placed his life 'in the service of the struggle for independence and development'. He had 'never hesitated to take sides', but as a filmmaker he had 'never lapsed into the blunt realism of propaganda'. The jury cited How YUKONG MOVED THE MOUNTAINS as the pinnacle of Ivens's work. De Koning was not particularly happy with the left-wing jury's choice, but manfully praised Ivens's thorough approach and his filming of development in China. He did insist on a note stating that 'whereas Ivens primarily pleads for a system of collectivization, minister de Koning's vision focuses on building up a democratic society'. In his speech of thanks Ivens concluded that: 'The minister clearly thought it necessary to distance himself for political reasons.' Later he described it as a 'ridiculous situation', which led to the reaction in *Het Parool*: 'He had absolutely no problems picking an ideological path through Mao's China, but in democratic Holland he is lost. He doesn't realize how nice it is that a minister allows a jury that he disagrees with, or only partly agrees with, to go its own way.' [50]

The Scherpenzeel Prize represented the start of the activities centered on Ivens's eightieth birthday. On the initiative of the Dutch Film Museum, Tineke de Vaal, film historian Bert Hogenkamp, and museum employees put together a major exhibition entitled '50 Years World Cineaste', accompanied by an extensive Ivens retrospective that began in Amsterdam and then traveled on to Rotterdam, Modena, Florence, London, Paris and Peking.

By the summer of 1978, the promotion of YUKONG was largely behind him, and in both autumn 1978 and autumn 1979, Ivens worked as a consultant to studios in the People's Republic. There was another big birthday celebration on November 18, 1979, this time an enormous banquet in the Peking Hotel, where all his old Chinese film friends had gathered and Zhou Enlai's widow was seated next to him. The year that followed saw the Ivens retrospective in Peking, accompanied by the Amsterdam exhibition. Although those present did not realize it, these festivities amounted to the farewell to an era. Ivens's relations with the Chinese leadership remained extremely cordial, but the shine was fading. They changed, and so did he.

The preface of the Chinese book published in conjunction with the exhibition drew on an old Chinese proverb to compare Ivens to 'an old steed in the stable' that 'still aspires to gallop a thousand li'. [51] It was true that despite his advanced years, Ivens had galloped at high speed through China in the seventies, and the saying would also prove prophetic, because in the decade to come the old steed would indeed cover another thousand li through the Middle Kingdom, this time under completely new social circumstances and, increasingly, step by step.

23 An Arduous De-Stalinization (1978-1985)

After the death of Mao Zedong and the fall of the Gang of Four, Ivens began to doubt his old certainties. For thirteen years he had been making distinctly political films, now he seriously considered a project without any political constraints, a film about Florence. There was a notable similarity to the course of events in 1956. After that year of upheaval in Eastern Europe, he had begun work on THE SEINE MEETS PARIS. That film had been followed by a new period of total revolutionary commitment; this time the break would be final.

Ivens was no stranger to Florence. Countess Ana Maria Papi, the patroness of successful and destitute artists, including Ivens, lived on the via Gino Capponi, and the city was also home to Aristo Ciruzzi, whom Ivens had counted as a friend since his first Italian tour in 1950. Above all, he had been a regular and popular guest at Florence's annual, PCI-inspired Festival dei Populi since the sixties.

On the invitation of the region of Tuscany and the municipality of Florence, Ivens and Loridan began preparations in late 1979 for a film about the city. In late 1980 they moved for three months into an apartment on the Arno, near the Ponte Vecchio, to write a scenario and immerse themselves in Florence present and past. The following May Ivens informed his sister Thea: 'Finally, finally we have reached an agreement about the conditions, the contract for our film, with the authorities of the City of Florence, the RAI-[Italian Television] and a producer in Rome. Incredible bureaucracy in Italy... And after a final meeting of the parties here in Paris we agree. But the Italian television asks for just 40! days to arrange all the contracts. So we'll start in early June, which is too late. June and July are terribly hot in Florence, impossible for me to work intensively. The sun is too high as well... so now there's a plan to start in mid-August.'[1] Rather than the end, this turned out to be the start of their tribulations. Due to disagreement between the Italian partners, and elections that altered the political balance, there was still no contract two years later. On January 15, 1983 the commissioning bodies and the filmmakers finally gathered for a meeting where the project was given the *coup de grâce*. The Italians withdrew all their promises and Ivens declared that Florence was definitively off.[2]

Apart from some film royalties, he had not worked for payment for three years. He drew a Dutch old-age pension and Loridan received a French allowance as a victim of the war. This led, and not for the first time, to a schizophrenic situation in which they could make all kinds of trips to film festivals and other official occasions where the host organizations paid their expenses, while Ivens still needed to be grateful when Miss van Zomeren sent him another thousand guilders from Bilthoven. 'I shall use it to buy a pullover in Stockholm,' he wrote back.[3]

Besides frustration, all that remained from the plans for Florence was a scenario. The film had been planned at eighty minutes, and was to be an encounter between an old man and an ancient city, between Joris Ivens and Florence. Approximately one quarter of the film was planned as a dialogue between a television journalist and Ivens about his life and work, alternating with images from his films. This meeting would be fitted into a search through Florence, in which Ivens would become acquainted with the city's people, its art and its history. The story was one of filmmaker and city falling in love with each other.[4] Ivens and Loridan later elaborated on this idea in their Chinese film A TALE OF THE WIND, this time with a meeting between Joris Ivens and China, in which the hero wanders through the history and culture of the Middle Kingdom while looking back on his work.

The Florence scenario represents a remarkable change in Ivens's orientation. Since WIGWAM in 1912 he had not appeared in his own films, let alone as a main character, and even his freest films had given few insights into his psyche. Now, however, he began seeing life differently. He was over eighty, many of his old friends had died, he himself was suffering all kinds of physical ailments. His own mortality became part of his everyday reality and gave birth to an urge to present a vision of himself in one of his last films. He touched upon death with his nephew Urias Nooteboom, who visited him in the rue des Saints-Pères. Nooteboom dropped by at six o'clock in the afternoon: 'Joris opens the door... slippers, dark-blue socks, pajamas, light-blue bathrobe, yellowish-gray hair, sideburns roughly shaved off, long hair combed back... hug. He's looking good. He has more of a belly than last time... pulls the bathrobe tighter now and then. The apartment looks smaller, so does he... 'Would you like a whiskey? I always drink an Irish whiskey around this time of day. I always have it in the house.' Giving me a small glass, he says: 'Put some water in for me'... His left index finger is curled up, so is his little finger... There are actually very few books in the study. 'I have to get rid of them every time,' he explains. A five-foot row about Florence.' Sipping from his glass, Ivens raises the subject of mortality. 'I'm not afraid of dying, but I don't want to die yet... But what I am afraid of is that dying could become a long-term issue. I would find that unpleasant for the people around me. Being ill for several years. Needing constant care. A narrowing perspective. Tying people to you, becoming senile. That isn't good. But on the other hand, I'm too much of an optimist to commit suicide.'[5]

Loridan already had a hard task caring for her husband, who was thirty years her senior and plagued by a whole battery of complaints. In his correspondence with Miss van Zomeren, Ivens gave a detailed account of his health problems, the perfect subject for an exchange of thoughts with an elderly lady. He had been admitted to hospital several times each year since 1980. Despite two weeks' rest at Flims in Switzerland in spring 1980, he suffered asthma attacks 'more severe than any in the last decade'. After being treated in hospital, he was no longer capable of working at night and felt 'like an old gent who is withdrawing from his activities'. During a trip to China that same year he was admitted to a Shanghai clinic for a pulmonary infection and heart problems. His hip had been playing up for some time and he reported: 'Now walking with a stick, pant when I have to climb a few steps.' The following summer he spent a few weeks with the writer Robert Destanque in the South of France, but had to be rushed to the resuscitation department of the Montpellier hospital because of complications arising from bronchitis and asthma. Back in Paris, tests established that only one third of his lungs was functioning. 'I have a new dictator inside me, the care for my health, something I'm not used to... the doctors tell me that I've overtaxed my lungs too often.' On New Year's Eve in 1981 he had to be admitted to hospital in Paris for cardiac problems and twice more in the months that followed, this time for stomach problems as well. Thereafter he visited a clinic for breathing exercises every second day. 'Walking in the Jardin de Luxembourg. There are lots of benches to sit down on when I get tired.' Ivens befriended a lung specialist, Dr. Even: 'My friend has now said that I can work a maximum of three to four hours a day.' The Chinese sent a doctor to the rue des Saints-Pères to check on him.

Meanwhile the arthritis in his hip had become unbearable. He was dependent on painkillers and needed two sticks to walk. Without an operation he would have been ultimately confined to a wheelchair, and in 1983 his doctors finally gave in to his persistent demands. 'The alternative is unacceptable for my active mind and body.' After the operation Ida and Vladimir Pozner laughed heartily when he performed a triumphant imitation of Charlie Chaplin, twirling the cane he could now, for the time being, do without. 'Typical Joris,' they thought. At the end of that year new problems arose. This time it was his kidneys. His bronchitis began playing up dangerously again, and his back was so weak that he had new difficulty walking. 'Buying a newspaper and mailing a letter are real chores. Used to take three and five minutes – now fifteen and thirty. With resting here and there, sitting on the hoods of cars parked in the street, because there aren't any benches in the street, unfortunately.' As his back was inoperable, he returned to using a stick.[6]

All this did not mean that he started taking things any easier than was strictly necessary. His doctor, Jean-François Masson, who had become a personal friend, recalled his meetings with Joris and the French-Chilean painter Roberto Matta, who was over seventy. The two had probably met in 1978 when they both received honorary degrees from the Royal College of Art in London. Masson was around forty, but could hardly keep up with the other two in nighttime drinking sessions that lasted until three in the morning. What did they talk about until so late? 'Joris could listen. It's fantastic if you're old and can talk about your experiences and adventures, but no. Someone who is almost ninety who spends a lot of time with you and listens to you, that is rare. So I told him about the problems in my life, my profession, emotional problems. He always gave me good advice.'[7]

In 1979, while waiting for the work in Florence to eventuate, Ivens decided to start new memoirs. The autobiography he had written in the forties, *The Camera and I*, had been published ten years earlier but much had happened since then, and his ideas about a number of matters had been changing, and not just politically. There had been almost no references to his personal life in *The Camera and I*. Even the fact that Helen van Dongen was not only his 'long-term collaborator' but also his lover and later wife was withheld. This time he would hesitantly tell more about his private life.

Ivens had successfully maintained control over the books that appeared about him for decades. In 1950 Pierre Boulanger, assistant at the Cinémathèque Française, started work on an Ivens biography with the collaboration of the main character himself. Boulanger worked on the book for a year and traveled with introductions from Ivens to the Netherlands and elsewhere for research. 'We are very busy developing his notes,' wrote Ivens. We! After Boulanger had completed a number of chapters, the work was continued for obscure reasons by Marion Michelle and Catherine Duncan. Duncan, who had worked with Ivens and Michelle on INDONESIA CALLING! and was now living in Paris, then took over the writing and invested a large amount of work in the book. Because of her own marital situation, she was initially reluctant to begin the project. Ivens wrote to Marion Michelle: 'Now Cathy – tell her not to be an ass... She has the best thing she can have. The book about my work, my life... With or without all personal difficulties, no person, not Roger, nor anybody else who loves her, has the right to take her away from this human and political responsibility. I am counting on her... It puts her right in the middle of international attention.' But after being given five chapters to read, he was less than charmed by her unconditionally loyal, but light and humorous approach. He informed her that he would now write an autobiography instead. Though the relationship between Duncan and Ivens remained amicable, their friendship was blemished. 'I found his behavior improper,' said Duncan. 'One doesn't create one's own image, you can't impose it. I could never fully accept what happened with that biography.'[8]

In the mid-fifties it had briefly seemed that Jay Leyda would succeed in arranging publication of *The Camera and I*, but Ivens was too busy to become involved and the publication was delayed until 1969. New prospective authors presented themselves. In 1960 the young French journalist Robert Grelier approached Ivens with a plan. Grelier published in leftist magazines about film, culture and politics, and was active in the Paris Film Club movement. Ivens was negative about his proposal at first. Grelier began anyway and Ivens eventually granted him access to an array of documents and became an active participant. In one letter he mentioned 'Grelier, who is writing a biography about me'. At the same time, another biography was being written in the GDR by Ivens's friend and co-worker from SONG OF THE RIVERS, Hans Wegner, whom Ivens provided with numerous documents. Monitoring all these activities, however, Ivens again concluded that he would be better off writing a book himself. 'At a remove it won't be as good, especially with writers like Grelier and Wegner. The former is too small-minded and lacks the imagination and creative power... the latter is too methodical and orthodox... The danger is that these two authors, or others, will place their own direction or perspective in the foreground, and thus give a false picture and put the emphasis on the wrong things.' He now gave Grelier an ultimatum. 'Either he stops completely and gives me all his notes and summaries, or else he writes a small book about a period from my career... without his own evaluations. Either way he has promised not to publish anything without showing it to me... He's a nice guy and dedicated, but I have no choice.'[9]

He retrieved his documentation from Grelier and made it available to A. Zalzman, a Colombian student at the IDHEC film school, a protégé of film historian Georges Sadoul and future head of Colombian radio and television. 'I have stopped the Grelier book for the moment,' noted Ivens. After being read by Ivens and thoroughly corrected by Sadoul, Zalzman's text was published in Paris in 1963. Grelier's publisher decided to cancel as a consequence and his book appeared two years later with another publisher.[10] Around this time the soundest and most comprehensive of the three biographies was published in East Berlin, Hans Wegner's *Joris Ivens. Dokumentarist der Wahrheit* ('Truth's Documentarian').

Joris Ivens and Marceline Loridan on their balcony on the rue des Sts.-Pères
(Paris, 1978). PHOTO MARION MICHELLE. COLL MARION MICHELLE / EFJI

As Ivens had predicted, each author had his own perspective. Grelier
wrote an essay, supplemented by an overview of facts and dates and a number of existing texts by and about Ivens. Zalzman produced a transcription
of Ivens's own manuscripts for *The Camera and I*, making his book a preview
of the book that Ivens himself would publish six years later. Wegner had
written a real biography, albeit an orthodox one, that is, one that conformed
to the GDR line on cinema and history. In one crucial regard, however, all
three shared the same approach: they based their work on information supplied by Ivens himself; they worked almost under his personal supervision;
and they did not deviate essentially from his interpretation.

Ivens was also involved with the content of a fourth book to appear
around this time, the Festschrift in honor of his sixty-fifth birthday that was
presented to him at the Leipzig Festival.[11]

A new publication did not appear until 1970, this time in Holland: Han
Meyer's *Joris Ivens. De weg naar Vietnam* ('The Road to Vietnam'). The first
half of this book is once again a virtually literal reproduction of texts that
would appear in *The Camera and I* and which Ivens himself had supplied to
the author. Meyer only came to an interpretation of his own for the period

from the late forties on, years either ignored or scanned in Ivens's book. Meyer localized his subject in a Cold War context in which East and West were so diametrically opposed that, in his view, it was virtually impossible for a committed person to make a balanced choice. It was almost pre-ordained that Ivens would end up in the Soviet Bloc, with all the one-sidedness this choice brought with it. As far as the facts were concerned, Han Meyer too based his work almost entirely on information provided by Ivens.

Joris Ivens was not averse to vanity and saw a biographer's duty as highlighting the grandeur of his life and work. And so he worked industriously on his own myth. The image he wished to convey was of an intensely involved but independent filmmaker, who was always there where injustice was being fought.

In 1979 Ivens thus began work on a second version of his memoirs, which would be given the title: *Joris Ivens ou la mémoire d'un regard* ('Joris Ivens, A Vision Remembered'). At first Ivens was to be assisted by family friends Jean-Pierre Sergent and Robert Destanque, but Sergent withdrew after being offered a job as editor-in-chief of the popular science magazine *Ça*. An old friend of Loridan's, Destanque had been indirectly involved in THE THREATENING SKY in the mid-sixties and had made dozens of films on commission for the French government and television. Loridan had worked with him on several of these in the early sixties. Later he settled in the countryside near Montpellier and began writing detective novels.

The new uncertainties had led Ivens to question his interpretation of his own life, and Destanque believed that Ivens asked him to collaborate on the autobiography because of his ability to identify the problems. During the many sessions they held over a period of more than two years, mainly in the rue des Saints-Pères but sometimes at Destanque's home in the Herault, Destanque did not hesitate to ask incisive and painful questions. Loridan participated in the discussions until it became too much and Destanque snapped at her: 'It's going to be Joris's book, not yours.' Her criticism of the past was probably sharper than Ivens's. He had, after all, been involved for several decades more and needed to wrack his brains over a half century of history with friendships and loyalties, personal sympathies and shared experiences that weighed heavily for him. Talking about an intimate meal with Ho Chi Minh, he said: 'If one of those young neo-thinkers were to say to me now, 'But Joris, that's impossible! Pay attention to this! Look at that! Communism never produced anything worthwhile.' How could I get him to understand that my memory and sensitivity work very differently to his? Just because of a lunch like that, which sealed a kind of contract between

Marceline and me, and because of that old man who had dedicated his life to the struggle for the independence of that country.'[12]

It was later claimed that Ivens and Destanque had written the book as equals and that it remained unclear as to what Ivens himself actually thought, but Destanque emphatically opposed this vision. Everything Ivens said was recorded on tape and the book was merely an adaptation. Destanque described it as made up 'exclusively of statements by Joris Ivens'. 'In no way at all, did I interpret or comment upon Joris's words... Joris would have immediately intervened to correct minute deviations by me, because he knew exactly what he wanted to say.' Ivens corrected the final text – which was written in the first person – in its entirety.[13] They were the memoirs of Joris Ivens and nothing else.

The results, published in Paris in 1982, reveal that he was in a state of great confusion during the writing, torn between the desire to be honest and concern for his image, between attempts to reach new insights and the stubbornness of his old beliefs. Ivens was not a great thinker, and Destanque's assistance was not enough to reach a deeper explanation of his life.

He stated that he was 'the opposite' of 'the kind of Communist and revolutionary who is locked up within a system', meaning perhaps that he was no theoretician, meanwhile he also said that 'once the party had spoken, you believed and accepted that. Our commitment was based entirely on this belief in the party.'[14] The contradictions began in the introduction, where he wrote: 'For us, born together with the century, the Bolshevik revolution was a source of hopeful expectation and Lenin was a great man. But the teeth of time are sharp. The state we so passionately wanted to see disappear has returned, and since then there is a chasm between the socialism I joined a half century ago and that which still adorns itself with the original attributes.' But Communism had not begun 'as a flower' only to be 'suffocated by weeds' later, as he still believed.[15] Even when he had joined the movement fifty years earlier, the Soviet state had imposed itself more than the Tsarist state at its peak, and the reality of Communism was dictatorship, a permanent dictatorship with which Ivens aligned himself practically and psychologically. At the root of it all, particularly in the early days, was the doctrine that anything was permissible in the struggle to achieve utopia, a concept he fully supported in the Soviet Union and in Spain in the thirties. This was only one of the countless contradictions in his book.

Sometimes there was something touching about the entanglement of Ivens's old obsessions and his desire for change, for example, when he said that socialism needed renewal; 'that is not to say' that it should 'become revisionist', adding: 'I do not wish to be identified with the principles of the Second International'. It was all terminology from a bygone era.[16]

Ivens did not mention in his memoirs that he had been a long-term party member. Only in 1971 had he once let slip the thruth. That was in an interview with comrades from the Dutch Communist Party/Marxist-Leninist, and virtually no one took the brochure in which it was published seriously. As late as 1982, in an interview with Urias Nooteboom, he stated that he 'had clearly never been a member' of the Communist party. In 1985, however, he admitted in an unpublished interview that his period of membership had lasted 'for a few years'.[17] Why was he so reluctant to admit the facts?

It is plausible, and even likely, that the CPH had decided that he should conceal his membership in order to increase his influence on non-party artists and intellectuals. For many years the party had a similar agreement with the Dutch historians Jan and Annie Romein. In time it presumably became more important for Ivens himself that he wished to be seen as an independent artist, loyal to the movement but autonomous in his work. Neither his membership nor the fact that he had made several of his films within the structures of the Communist International were consistent with this image. In Münzenberg's Mezhrabpom Studio, where he went to work in late 1931, any autonomy was short-lived, and his unwillingness to draw attention to having been a member in the USSR under Stalin was understandable.

Despite the contradictions, Ivens's alienation from Communism was clearly visible in *Joris Ivens ou la mémoire d'un regard*, although he himself preferred to see it as a logical progression rather than a breach with the past. He claimed that his course had remained essentially unchanged: 'The historical development moves in a certain direction, you think you're following it correctly, it changes course, or a hidden undercurrent becomes stronger and sweeps everything along with it. What does this all mean? That I've looked beyond all this turbulence and opted for a direction I believe in, and to which I will remain true. Namely, people struggling for their freedom and liberty.' Only occasionally did he see that there was a great contradiction between this ideal and his Communist ideas. Then he wrote: 'I had fitted man into a doctrine and he was to submit to its laws. I gradually became a different person, until I realized with certainty that every human being has the fundamental right to never be limited in his life's expression.'[18]

With his advancing years and the long duration of his political involvement, it is scarcely surprising that he never succeeded in resolving these problems; the seriousness of his attempt testifies to some degree of courage. With all its confusion, *Joris Ivens ou la mémoire d'un regard* definitely shows a desire to be honest. As is usual in memoirs, the book still contained all kinds of major and minor untruths, and considering the strange twists of memory, it is very possible that Ivens believed them himself. He incorrectly pre-sented things as if he had already broken with the Soviet Union in the early sixties,[19] and above all, the picture of his relations with Holland was dis-torted to mythical proportions. Since BORINAGE he had been an outcast in Holland, on returning in 1947 he was a pariah, and was thus forced to settle behind the Iron Curtain, from which he was hardly allowed to travel be-cause the Dutch government withheld his passport from 1948 to 1957. The absolute low was the claim that the Ministry of Foreign Affairs had made it impossible for him to attend his mother's funeral. As shown above, some thirty percent of his accusations were true; seventy were pure invention.

More than the confused content of his memoirs, a peculiar event showed most clearly how vigorously Ivens was searching for a new place in society. The issue was who would publish the Dutch translation of his book, *Aan welke kant en in welke heelal* ('On which Side and in which Universe'). The well-respected Amsterdam publisher Rob van Gennep was very interested, but heard to his astonishment that Ivens considered him too left-wing. The book was published by Meulenhoff and Van Gennep never forgave Ivens his 'hypocritical attitude'.[20]

Practically speaking, Ivens's political reorientation suffered from the law of delayed response. As far as international issues were concerned, he contin-ued almost without exception to follow the Peking line until the mid-eight-ies. Like the Chinese, he believed that the USSR was preparing for war. 'There is cause for concern,' he wrote. 'If the Russian party and government clique is not stopped by a combined effort from Europe and America, I fear the worst. All of Europe could one day become a kind of Finland.'[21] It was virtually a literal rendering of what could be read weekly in the *Peking Re-view*. When Vietnam invaded Kampuchea in 1979, because of self-interest, but also to put an end to the murderous Pol Pot regime, Ivens, with pain in his heart, made a clear statement of condemnation. That same year he sym-pathized with China's attack on Vietnam in support of its Khmer Rouge al-lies. Vietnam had aligned itself with the Soviet Union and thus belonged to the enemy camp.

Even within the film world, Ivens was able to exercise influence along these lines. In autumn 1983, he was one of the chairmen at the world con-gress of filmmakers on Madeira. Among those present were Costa-Gavras, Turkish director Yilmaz Güney and Dutch filmmaker Wim Verstappen. 'It was in danger of becoming a fiercely anti-American occasion,' according to Verstappen. 'The Greek Communists submitted a motion stating: 'The cruise missiles threaten humanity and thus cinematography.' There were a lot of Communists from France, Greece and Italy. I stood up to oppose the motion, because a completely anti-American world congress of filmmakers is absurd, considering America's role in cinema. The audience response was hostile. Then Joris took the floor and spoke out against the motion as well. That was the end of that.'[22] What Verstappen did not realize was that Ivens's motivation was very different to his own: Ivens was not pro-American, he was simply anti-Russian. In 1985 he could still surprise the Dutch left-wing with his position that it was good to install cruise missiles, because 'all of Europe has to build itself up tremendously against a possible Soviet invasion...'[23]

One of the few international political issues on which he disagreed with Peking was that of the Polish union Solidarity. Ivens saw it as an encouraging development that could lead to more freedom for the Poles, whereas the Chinese party leadership saw clearly that it set a precedent for similar opposition in China itself. Beyond this, Ivens also objected, and according to his own information in Peking as well, to China's rapid recognition of the Pinochet regime in Chile, which had gained power through a bloody coup whose victims included Ivens's old acquaintance president Salvador Allende.

He was less convinced by China's domestic policies. 'In China, unfortunately, things are not going very well. Much confusion,' he wrote in 1982. And in that same year: 'I keep in close touch with China and my friends there, although I have my reservations about their policies.'[24] Setbacks in the democratization in China disappointed him, and he became active for artistic freedom, supporting Chinese writers and the Association Internationale du Defense des Artistes, AIDA, including its campaign for the Georgian director Sergei Paradzhanov who had been declared an 'ex-cineaste' by the Soviet government. In the mid-eighties Ivens described the situation in China: 'Even now it remains a socialist country where the party is in control. They do say that art needs to be free, but in practice you are faced with tensions between the authorities, the people and art. The people with power and money apply limitations to artists in all societies. But in Western countries there is more freedom than in the Soviet Union and China. The power in socialist states is greater because it is based upon one ideology, whereas in capitalist countries different ideologies and religions live side by side.'[25]

A half year after its completion, Ivens and Loridan began to realize that YUKONG was already a political anachronism. The arrest of the Gang of Four had cleared the way for criticism of the Cultural Revolution the film presented so positively. It did not take long before the new Chinese leaders were calling the Cultural Revolution 'an unimaginable disaster', and in 1982 Loridan remarked in an interview that in private she and Ivens called

YUKONG 'a monster' and 'madness'. Later she even said that she 'just wanted to die' after having sat through the twelve parts again. 'To think that I believed it all, the things that were said in those films!' She concluded that it had been the work of two Westerners who filmed a dream, which later turned out to be utopian. 'We might have cheated people in our innocence.'[26] As usual, Ivens refrained from definite statements. Costa-Gavras met with him occasionally and once, when they touched upon China, Ivens said, without further explanation: 'I've had enough, they make major mistakes.' That was all. 'Then I knew that he had changed his mind about it,' said Costa-Gavras. In 1978 Ivens and Loridan invited Jean Rouch to a viewing of YUKONG in the Cinématèque. Afterwards Rouch remarked: 'I now know what I don't want for my children.' Loridan wanted to react fiercely, but Ivens said: 'No, Marceline, he could be right.' Some time later Ivens did tell Rouch that he was right. 'Do you know what my next film will be about? About Florence, about love.'[27] The degree to which YUKONG had become a thorn in their side became obvious in March 1985 when they ordered the Dutch Film Museum to stop making the film available for screenings.[28] This step undoubtedly satisfied the wishes of the authorities in power in Peking, but Deng Xiaoping's criticism of Mao Zedong had also opened the door to more fundamental criticism of Communist ideology, and Ivens and Loridan did not stop where Deng had drawn the line.

Imminent death and ideological uncertainty moved Ivens in unexpected directions. As early as late 1978 he made an extremely uncharacteristic statement to a journalist from *Le Monde*: 'I was born on November 18. Scorpio... Do you believe in that? I believe in all that.'[29] Among friends he became also fond of discussing being a Scorpio, even though he can't have taken this way of thinking too seriously, as he did not even know Loridan's sign. It was part of a new, nonspecific, vague fascination for magic and mysticism. In interviews in the eighties he showed an unaltered optimism about the world, which was 'moving towards something better'. In a letter to Miss van Zomeren he sounded less sure of himself: 'You write that you are sometimes unable to take any more of the horrors of our 'bleeding' world; we all feel that way. But at the same time, it is no longer possible for us to take the entire weight of the uncertain conditions of our world too heavily upon us. As individuals we are more powerless than in years gone by, so more concentration on our immediate surroundings, on family, friends, ourselves, is our only option... Humanity is going through difficult years, but did so in the past as well... It's important to stay close to nature.' He no longer concentrated on the social struggle of the day, and turned to the timeless, the metaphysical, 'the great stream, upon which humanity moves forward, independent of the smaller streams, of empires, of fascism, of civilizations in decline'.[30]

24 Unfavorable Winds (1985-1989)

Joris Ivens was developing a new image, both for himself and for the world. He was planning a new China film, about which he said: 'If I ever make THE ROOF OF THE WORLD, fans of 'Ivens as militant filmmaker' will have reason to pose themselves questions and answer them as they see fit.' THE ROOF OF THE WORLD would be 'the most lyrical film of my entire career', yes, 'a fantastic, epic film showing both the infinity of the universe and the scope of a civilization moving from cave dwellers to socialism'.[1] His words sounded somewhat aggrieved, although he himself had naturally provided abundant grounds for his reputation as a militant filmmaker. Henceforth, however, he had other concerns. In his new vision of a lifetime making films, he had been, above all else, a poet.

Asked in 1987 for a top ten of his favorite films, he listed:[2]

Alberto Cavalcanti – ONLY THE HOURS

Robert Flaherty – NANOOK OF THE NORTH

René Clair – THE ITALIAN STRAW HAT

The abstract films of Walter Ruttman and Viking Eggeling

Vsevolod Pudovkin – STORM OVER ASIA

Sergei Eisenstein – STRIKE and THE BATTLESHIP POTEMKIN

René Clair – EIFFEL TOWER

Luis Buñuel – LAND WITHOUT BREAD

The silent films of Charles Chaplin

The films of D.W. Griffith

With the exception of Buñuel's 1933 documentary LAND WITHOUT BREAD, all these works dated from the second and third decades of the century. An old film director was recalling his early period, but there was more to it. After fifty years of viewing his own early films as style exercises in preparation for his real work, Ivens had begun reassessing his avant-garde work. His youthful concentration on form was now in perfect harmony with his desire to distance himself from the revolutionary film.

'I suppressed the poet within me for a time,' he said in 1986, and shortly before his death the transformation was complete. 'I don't believe that I have ever been a documentary filmmaker in the traditional sense,' he explained. 'I have always been interested in both, reality and fantasy.'[3] With this he went so far as to deny the greatest achievement of his filmmaking career, because along with leading figures such as Flaherty, Vertov and Grierson, he was actually one of the pioneers of the documentary. He had contributed to the definition of the 'traditional' documentary and had played an indisputable role in the development of cinematic realism, but in retrospect this did not please him and he suddenly produced the old cinematic conjurer Georges Méliès as a great source of inspiration. His picture of himself now concentrated on the poet he had aspired to become. He wanted to confound the skeptics by placing his whole oeuvre in a new light by making THE ROOF OF THE WORLD.

In his memoirs in the early eighties, Ivens provided a general sketch for this film, which later proved to be the first steps toward the film that was released in the theaters in 1988 as A TALE OF THE WIND. He would fly over China in an airplane and dive down through the clouds in various places for a closer view of various facets of the country's history. He already mentioned mythological Chinese figures who would later take the stage in A TALE OF THE WIND, such as the Moon Fairy and the Monkey King, and he appealed to Chinese and French sinologists to gather documentation for the project.

Ivens's ideas solidified after the French cineaste Juliet Berto asked him to act in her fiction film HAVRE (1986). A few years earlier the Taviani brothers had wanted Ivens to take the role of old man in KAOS, and only circumstances had prevented this from going ahead.[4] Juliet Berto had been La Chinoise in Jean-Luc Godard's eponymous film, she had acted in films by Jacques Rivette and had co-directed several others. In the words of one critical appraisal, HAVRE included 'superficial esotericism and obscure exaltation',[5] but in the role of Dr. Digitalis Ivens demonstrated that his furrowed features and white mane made him exceptionally photogenic. This success revived the old idea from the Florence scenario of appearing as an actor in one of his own films. During the filming of HAVRE, Ivens also met Berto's co-writer, twenty-five-year-old Elisabeth D. A member of a generation that had not consciously experienced the sixties and early seventies, she had never heard of Joris Ivens. On her first visit to the rue des Saint-Pères, Ivens and Loridan showed her a scenario for A TALE OF THE WIND. It still had a real documentary character, according to D., and she proposed a number of changes to introduce a fiction element. This lead to numerous sessions in which the three of them further developed the script, and at home Elisabeth D. noted the outcome of each discussion. 'We never talked about politics. Sometimes you could see that Joris was still concerned about it, but no more than five percent.'[6]

According to their plan, the film would include two visions, two perspectives, Ivens's and Loridan's, 'each separate and both together, apart and simultaneous'. The synopsis, presented to potential financiers under the working title THE WIND, included two separate parts elaborated under the headings: 'Section to be realized by Joris Ivens' and 'Section to be realized by Marceline Loridan'. One would work with a Chinese crew to chase the wind, the *véhicule visuelle* that carried with it impressions of China's culture and history; the other would observe this quest with a French team.[7]

The start of shooting in China was originally planned for April 1984, then put forward to the summer. Despite innumerable preparatory trips to China, the first test footage in the Taklamakan Desert was not shot until the following spring.

The financing of THE WIND still had to be finalized. The Chinese contributed in their own way. 'They are open-minded and give me everything I need', wrote Ivens, 'but no French francs or dollars, they have to come from France'.[8] China probably paid for part of the manpower, and the travel and living expenses within the country. The filmmakers received a considerable advance on receipts from French film foundations, and the producer La Sept invested around 330,000 guilders. A major portion of the budgeted 4.3 million guilders still had to be raised, when salvation was at hand.

In Utrecht the 1985 Dutch Film Days had decided to award Ivens with a Golden Calf. The jury report observed that Ivens was one of the founders of the documentary. 'For any jury, including the board of the Dutch Film Days, this fact alone would be more than enough reason to award the Prize to Joris Ivens.' But the jury went further: 'As long as film and television have existed, bureaucracies, ruling cliques and politicians have tried to control the medium. Joris Ivens has resisted this pressure all his life. He has suffered outrageous libel and deep humiliations for filming what he saw.'[9]

Shortly before, at the Venice Film Festival, Ivens had told Dutch journalists that, after all that Holland had submitted him to, he would only accept a Calf if the minister of Welfare, Health and Cultural Affairs, Elco Brinkman, brought it to him personally.[10] The Lubbers cabinet decided that it was time for the minister to bend his knee, and on Wednesday September 11, 1985 Brinkman flew to Paris with a number of staff members. In that morning's *Volkskrant* he could already read the ominous words: 'Since he knows that his mission will be a failure if he has even the slightest reservations about handing over the prize and the considerable amount of money to Joris Ivens, he will need to first formally make up for years of scandal and repay a debt of honor. Ivens will not accept anything from a representative of the government unless told in so many words that Holland has been unjust to its greatest film director for almost forty years.'[11] Brinkman had nothing to fear; Ivens had read his speech in advance.

The great event Ivens had been looking forward to for so long took place that evening in the Parisian Institut Néerlandais. The Mitterrand government had made him a Commander of the Legion d'Honneur the year before; in Madrid he had received a golden medal for services to art; and, together with the Dutch cineaste Fons Rademakers, he had been named a Knight Commander of the Order of Merit of the Italian Republic. These tributes to the last remaining grand old man of the early documentary, the oldest living director – this said in a whisper – were now being followed by a public admission of guilt from the Dutch government. In Paris Elco Brinkman spoke to Joris Ivens: 'Although your professional colleagues can outline your qualities as a filmmaker better than I can, I would like to dwell on one aspect of your work. Namely the strong social conscience and the political commitment that have characterized your work through the years. From your involvement with the subject of your documentaries, you derived a capacity, sometimes far ahead of others, to recognize the historical significance of political and social developments and capture it on film. This involvement and commitment have added a dimension to your work that has definitely contributed to the genuinely exceptional position that you, as a Dutch filmmaker, occupy in the world... Shortly after the war, your support of Indonesia's right to self-determination and your film INDONESIA CALLING! brought you into conflict with the Dutch government. Now that we have the opportunity to meet each other, I do not want to ignore the past. The Netherlands raised diverse obstacles to your work as a filmmaker. I can say now that history has come down more on your side than on the side of your adversaries. As minister of Culture I propose that we now shake hands and I hope that you will accept this offer.'[12]

Brinkman handed Ivens the Golden Calf and promised him one hundred thousand guilders for the administration of his archive at the Dutch Film Museum, and three hundred thousand guilders for the completion of THE WIND from the Production Fund for Dutch Films. Moved, Ivens took Brinkman's hand. 'Thanks to you, I am now reunited with my fatherland,' he said. 'Tonight I really feel happy. The road has been cleared. I don't know how to thank you.' Fifty years of frustration had been lifted as if by magic. The general delight grew even more when the Dutch broadcaster, the NOS, stated that it would make a further three hundred thousand guilders available for THE WIND.[13] For Ivens there was only one blemish on the evening: in an interview he gave soon after he refuted Brinkman's assertion that his films were most remarkable for their political commitment.[14]

The ceremony of reconciliation in Paris was greeted in Holland with almost universal satisfaction. The only dissenting voice was a controversial article in *Intermediair*, a weekly for academics. The authors protested against 'the declaration of sainthood' for Ivens, since he 'had provided propagandist assistance to two major and numerous minor mass murderers'. A rectification of Brinkman's speech and especially of the report of the jury of the Dutch Film Festival was in fact justified, because there was definitely a suggestion that Ivens had always had right on his side.[15]

Five weeks later Ivens and Loridan flew back to Peking to put together a technical crew for THE WIND. In the months that followed, they were scarcely able to do any actual filming. They were due to return to Paris a week before Christmas, when on the morning of departure Ivens came down with severe pneumonia. His condition was so critical that there was no time for a trip to the operating theater, and an operation was performed on the spot, after first disinfecting the room. An incision was made in his windpipe and he spent five days unconscious in Intensive Care. Marceline slept on a camp bed beside him while he lashed out deliriously at the hoses and machines.

In the rue Madame in Paris, Dr. Jean-François Masson's telephone rang. It was Marceline Loridan in Peking. 'Joris is dying!' she exclaimed. Masson worshipped Joris Ivens and had promised to come to China if necessary. 'I arrived in Peking at Christmas. It was freezing cold. When I arrived at the hospital in the middle of the night, Joris was unconscious. He really was dying, but he felt that I was there. The monitors showed immediate improvement in his heart and breathing, he calmed down... He had great faith in me, I don't know why, he just did. There are plenty of doctors who are better than I am. He told me what you always hear from people with a near-death experience. That he was floating above his bed, that he had seen me enter the room, even though he was unconscious.'[16]

The Dutch ambassador visited Ivens in hospital and several Paris specialists arrived in Peking a few days after Masson. They decided to take the patient straight back to France with Mondial Assistance, an organization that usually transports accident victims but made an exception for the occasion, probably at the insistence of the French minister of Culture, Jack Lang. At thirteen degrees below zero, Ivens was lifted by elevator into an Air France airliner from which a number of seats had been removed. After an eighteen-hour flight and five or so days in Laënnec Hospital in Paris, he was sent home with twenty-four hour nursing care. Some time later Loridan returned alone to China and the waiting technical crew.

Scarcely recovered, Ivens dragged himself to a filmmakers meeting in January. He explained to Dr. Masson that his lung disease made him optimistic: one moment you felt like you were dying, and a few days later it was over again. Marceline Loridan thought that Ivens was far too optimistic about his physical state and in mid-March he had another relapse. He made several more trips to China for THE WIND, but after falling seriously ill again he remained in Paris and left the work in China to Marceline Loridan. Ivens himself took the leading role in the film, so his absence forced Loridan to change a number of scenes and sometimes use a Chinese stand-in. She conceived the studio sequence about the Chinese mini-society, in which the Monkey King silences a party functionary by pulling out the plug of his microphone. Later the Monkey King turns out to be Joris Ivens, at least his stand-in. She also found inspiration in Ivens's near-death experience. 'I felt very cruel, because I was on the point of filming Joris's passing. I phoned him every day and he kept on asking me whether I had found any solutions. I told him I had, but not which... When I came back to France, I didn't dare to tell him at first, but I warned him when he came to view the rushes. It hurt him deeply. He didn't want to incorporate the scenes in the film... but I convinced him that they were essential to the internal structure.'[17]

With the expansion of Loridan's directorial role came a shift in the concept of THE WIND. According to the plan, Ivens was to be a cineaste in search of the wind and Chinese culture, and Loridan's crew would simply observe him at work. It now became a film about Joris in search of the wind, made by Marceline. Ivens explained the film by calling the wind a 'metaphor for rage and rebellion' and explained that he used the wind to 'express that rigid systems like Marxism and Leninism are outdated and need to be replaced by something new'.[18] In the film there were few traces of any relationship between the wind and these philosophical considerations. They remained words, while on the screen Ivens sat on a chair waiting for the wind to blow, or was carried up a mountain on a sedan so that he could test the currents of air with a microphone. In his condition this was a great effort. The Chinese authorities had good reason for having a doctor permanently on hand with a truck full of medical supplies. Meanwhile, the film's visuals were largely the work of Loridan, not only those in which Ivens appeared on screen, also many others that she filmed while he was in Paris.

The encounters with Chinese culture in THE WIND were virtually all placed in the context of Ivens's life. His visit to a Tai-Chi master referred to his asthma, negotiations with Chinese bureaucrats referred to his own earlier experiences, and the Chinese poetry related directly to him. The Moon Fairy recites:

> Don't you see that the glittering mirrors
> in the upper room
> are saddened by your white hair?
> At daybreak it was dark silk
> by twilight it is white as snow.

Nothing could be more obvious than the suspicion that the fairy is speaking for Marceline Loridan. A hint is given in the description of an ancient Chinese poet: 'One drunken night, when he wanted to embrace the moon, a rebellious poet drowned. And now for a thousand years, rice has been fed to the fish on the day of his death to stop them from devouring him.' Present throughout the film is the cavorting Monkey King, the hero of the ancient Chinese legend *The Journey to the West* and here Ivens himself. There is a famous story in which the Monkey King sits in the palm of Buddha's hand boasting about his knowledge and insight. After Buddha asks him to show him how wise he is, the monkey sets out in search of the end of the world and pisses on one of the five pillars he finds there. He returns to Buddha and confidently tells him that he found the end of the world, whereupon Buddha says: 'You pissed on one of my fingers.'

Ivens had organized in-depth preparatory research into Chinese mythology, and the Monkey King's appearance in the film can be seen as evidence of his new perspective on the revolutionary struggle he had dedicated so many years to.

The biographical character of A TALE OF THE WIND meant that audiences without any insight into Ivens's life could only partly understand the film. On top of this came the references to a mythology that was unfamiliar to most Westerners. These things made it hard to see the tragedy behind the images on the screen: the tour de force of an old man who wants another chance and attempts a final leap for freedom, who wants to be a poet after all, but already feels the wind of death; his imminent end captured in his own film against his objections; the story of an old filmmaker who, despite all his efforts, no longer succeeds in keeping a firm grip on his work; the strange interchange between him and his wife that results...

On February 21, 1988, in Gaumont-Ambassade on the Champs Elysées, a preview of A TALE OF THE WIND was organized by the Fondation Danielle Mitterrand, in the presence of Mrs. Mitterrand herself. A number of colleagues and close friends were invited and all present agreed that the film included beautiful images. Ivens's older friends in particular however found it difficult to grasp what they saw. 'INDONESIA CALLING! seemed a long time ago,' noted Catherine Duncan. 'Is it possible to divorce Joris from his revolutionary past? Are we to think of him as a reformed Red, now devoted to the wider issues of art? Do we return to RAIN, THE BRIDGE, BREAKERS, as our points of reference, to which perhaps should be added the French films on the Seine and the mistral? Setting aside all the major films (and quite a number of the minor) as the aberrations of a young idealist?' His fifty years of revolutionary activity were virtually missing in A TALE OF THE WIND and Duncan pointed out that 'the Joris we knew is almost absent from the film'. In her view it was 'an official portrait for posterity', and she wondered whether 'posterity won't be left with a question rather than an answer' about who Joris Ivens was.[19]

After seeing the new work, Henri Storck, his old friend from Brussels, had mixed feelings. It was a beautiful lyrical film, that was true, but 'under Marceline's influence Joris suddenly wanted to become a philosopher. And he thought that he was a god, the god of the wind. In that film he says: 'I can tame you, if I want to.' I consider that exaggerated. Perhaps he will be recognized as a god some time, but in general the gods don't say it of themselves.'[20]

Others also found that he had become too vain. Martha Gellhorn had nothing but good memories of their time in Spain and America. In *Travels with Myself and Another* she described Ivens as a treasure of a man. When she visited him in the eighties at the rue des Saints-Pères she was disappointed. He was not as much fun as he had been and had adopted the airs of an old maestro. 'Shortly before his death he seemed to have received all kinds of awards, then you get that kind of thing of course, and at least he wasn't as bad as a lot of others.'[21] A visiting niece noticed that Ivens was taking himself more seriously than ever. She wanted to put on his Legion d'Honneur for a joke, but he wouldn't let her. He thought it a display of a lack of respect.

Joris Ivens ninetieth birthday was approaching, and eighteen months before the date feverish preparations began in Nijmegen, which had not been able to lay claim to such a famous son since the days of Charlemagne. Holland began a new round of tributes. On January 26, 1989 Ivens opened the eighteenth Rotterdam Film Festival in the Luxor Theater with the Dutch premiere of A TALE OF THE WIND. 'The audience greeted Ivens as if he were a pop star,' wrote a reporter. 'A surge of applause, stamping feet and shrill whistling accompanied Ivens's entrance into the auditorium in the company of Queen Beatrix. Afterwards he was given a standing ovation.' At long last George Henri Anton Ivens had followed his father in receiving a royal decoration. That afternoon he had been named a Knight in the Order of the

Dutch Lion. A large headline in *De Telegraaf* read: 'Flying Dutchman meets his queen.' Speaking to that same newspaper, he said: 'It's good that it has all turned out well. But you have to live a long time.'[22]

Marceline Loridan had provided a list with practical requests for the Rotterdam ceremony. Joris was old, so the car had to be heated, smoking was not allowed and there were other, similar considerations. That night, after the official ceremonies were over, Ivens sat in a smoky cellar surrounded by twenty girls who all wanted to hold his hand. 'He didn't care what was good or bad for him,' said Dr. Masson. 'That was a good lesson for me. How could someone live so long and with such vigor? He ate what he felt like and sometimes he hardly slept, but he had a tremendously strong will to live. He lived like a child, with joy and delight.'[23]

Wolfgang Klaue of the GDR State Film Archives witnessed a comparable scene. He saw Ivens in 1988 during a reception at a congress of the international federation for film archives, the FIAF. 'Whenever beautiful women went by he would stop talking to watch them. Almost ninety! I'll never forget that. We were the last ones left. Eventually they came to us saying: 'You have to go, we're switching off the elevator.' He was already in the car, then he got out again to hug me one more time, as if he knew that it would be our last meeting. And it was.'[24]

Joris Ivens had been knighted by the Dutch queen, he had been decorated in various countries, and in 1988 he had also received a Golden Lion at the Venice Film Festival for his oeuvre. A TALE OF THE WIND was finished and only required administrative activities and tiring presentations in various countries in the hope that the investment could be recovered. On April 19, 1988 he had already written: 'I have decided that THE WIND is my last film.'[25] Although he changed his mind a few months later, the writing was on the wall. He no longer had a clear goal to arouse his energy.

His niece Annabeth Ivens, daughter of Hans Ivens, visited him in spring 1989. 'He was already far gone,' she found. 'Communicative, but impersonal.' Ivens wrote about another visit around the same time: 'We had a fine conversation for an hour, then I try to forget my tired head for a moment and listen attentively, to be interested and push aside my permanent (unwanted) indifference to the outside world.'[26] The circumstances were not favorable. His view of the world was literally darkening. On doctor's orders he had to stay inside and the view from his windows was all gray; the building was being renovated and on both sides the scaffolding was covered with gray plastic to protect the workers from the elements. Ivens was deeply disappointed by the reception of A TALE OF THE WIND in Paris. The reviewers were friendly; the theaters dropped the film after just a week or two because of a lack of public interest.

In May 1989 he broke out for one last time to visit the Cannes Film Festival. There, one hundred and twenty European directors founded yet another organization, this time under the device 'Cinéma et Liberté'. Older and more fragile than ever, Joris Ivens gave a speech leaning on a cane. His voice trembled so much that many of his words were impossible to understand. What mattered to the audience was the presence of a legend from film history. On May 15 he returned home exhausted, and the next day he anxiously composed a letter of no less than twelve closely-written pages to historian Eric van 't Groenewout of Leiden. Van 't Groenewout had written a thesis about the INDONESIA CALLING! affair, in which he had cleared Ivens of the criticism of his behavior in Australia. Ivens had been very grateful, and Van 't Groenewout had now informed him of his desire to make a documentary about the same subject. 'It is important to consider whether a film about INDONESIA CALLING! made now would be important,' wrote Ivens. 'I believe that that is not the case. You have given the matter a thorough, well-documented, historical and scientific treatment in your thesis. This resulted in a reconciliation between me and the Dutch government (not a rehabilitation, that was not necessary because I had done nothing illegal)... At that time I personally told Minister Brinkman that, as far as I was concerned, we should just 'forget about it', in other words, that both sides would drop it... For me, that is dignified and correct. As you know, I have stuck to that. When articles appeared in the press or elsewhere about my political position in 1945, I have not responded. I consider the matter closed, it doesn't need to be done to death yet again in the last years of my life, bygones and all that.' He added that other injustices had been much more significant. 'An Indonesian victim at that time weighed a thousand times heavier than taking away a filmmaker's passport' and compared to some of his colleagues he had nothing to complain about, because 'how many cineastes have been killed or wounded carrying out their work? How many have spent years in prison for making 'forbidden films'. They suffered more than I did.' Brinkman's Golden Calf and being decorated by Beatrix had given him peace of mind in his old age. 'I would like to ask you to let INDONESIA CALLING! rest for the time being, the few years ahead are very precious to me, I need all my energy for a new major film with Marceline... Leave it for what it is.' His extreme concern was proven beyond doubt when he sent a second, similar letter of five pages the next day.[27]

Plans for a new film did indeed begin to take shape, and there were also negotiations with the Dutch municipality of Zaanstad, which had asked him to make a film about a new bridge being built there. On July 15, 1989, however, Ivens informed Zaanstad that he saw no possibility of fulfilling such a commission. In a newspaper interview Loridan said that she hoped that they would be able to make one more film together, whereupon Ivens boldly said: 'Why just one?' But an interview with Germany's ZDF television around the same time left no room for doubt. The couple were seated on a bench at their country home La Troque. 'Our last film was about the wind, the next one will be about fire,' said Marceline Loridan. Joris Ivens raised his hands hesitantly and said: 'Yes.'[28] He could not have convinced anyone.

On June 4, the Chinese army brutally suppressed the student democracy movement in Tiananmen Square, Peking's 'Square of Heavenly Peace'. 'When Joris phoned me after the bloodbath in Peking he sounded tired and said that he had cried,' wrote Eric van 't Groenewout at the time.[29] The image of a tank being halted by a single demonstrator must have especially touched Ivens, as it was made from inside the Peking Hotel, where he had stayed so many times. He now abandoned his forgiving attitude to the Chinese party leadership, and he and Loridan sent a telegram of protest to the chairman of the People's Congress: 'The students and the hundreds of thousands who supported them deserve respect and admiration at an international level for their courage and unbounded dedication during their nonviolent demonstrations. We add our voices to the international condemnation of this blind and brutal attack; an attack on a peaceful demonstration of a people who asked only for a democratic dialogue with their government.' On June 21 *Le Monde* published a manifesto of the Committee against the repression in China, whose signatories included Henri Cartier-Bresson, Bernhard-Henri Lévy, Michelangelo Antonioni, Bernardo Bertolucci, Alberto Moravia, Steven Spielberg, Edgar Snow's widow, and Joris Ivens and Marceline Loridan. When Chinese students in Paris mounted a demonstration near the Trocadero, Ivens delighted everyone by putting in an appearance. It was a highly symbolic final political act.

Soon after, on the evening of Wednesday June 28, 1989, Joris Ivens died of renal failure in Paris's Laënnec Hospital. 'With the passing of time I was no longer able to imagine Joris dying of anything', related Dr. Masson, 'this time I knew it was over. In hospital he was always angry, aggressive and authoritarian, but this time he had less mental energy. He died peacefully.'[30]

At quarter to five in the afternoon of July 6, hundreds of people gathered at the gates of Montparnasse cemetery. The hearse carrying the coffin set off and was followed by Marceline Loridan, supported by Simone Veil, her friend from the concentration camps. That evening Loridan would give a long emotional speech at a memorial gathering in the Palais Chaillot. Among the many mourners in the funeral procession were Marion Michelle, Henri Storck, Jean-Pierre Sergent, Jean Rouch, Costa-Gavras, Claude Lanzmann, Bernhard-Henry Lévy, Jan and Tineke de Vaal, the Dutch filmmaker Johan van der Keuken, the mayor of Nijmegen Ien Dales, and a representative of the Dutch Ministry of Culture. Also present were the ambassador and cultural attache of the People's Republic of China and a delegation of democratic Chinese students in Paris. Both groups of Chinese were bearing wreaths: the representatives of the state had a large one; the students' was smaller. 'Let he who has never erred, throw the first stone,' said Costa-Gavras. The former director of the Dutch Film Museum, Jan de Vaal admitted to a journalist that some of the accusations leveled at Ivens 'had not been unjustified... We have to see him as a man with faults and good qualities. That speaks for itself. But he was a good man, I can testify to that.'[31] In clammy heat, with a storm brewing, flowers were laid quietly around the grave.

Acknowledgements

This book would have been impossible without the kind help of many people. Firstly, I am most grateful to Joris Ivens's widow Marceline Loridan-Ivens of Paris, who gave me permission to use two extensive collections of documents, in Amsterdam and Berlin. I am equally grateful to Ivens's ex-wife, the now deceased Ewa Fiszer from Warsaw, and his former partner Marion Michelle in Paris, who both placed numerous documents at my disposal. All three tolerated days of my questioning. At the last moment, however, and without having read a word of my book, Marceline Loridan-Ivens became convinced that my work was 'very polemic' and 'destructive', and consequently requested that I refrain from using the interviews she had granted me. Although there was no legal compulsion to do so, I have taken her wishes into account.

One former spouse is missing here: Helen van Dongen (now Durant) of Brattleboro (Vermont). She had no desire to dedicate another word to Joris Ivens. The wounds were too deep. I would like to thank Helen Durant for her permission to listen to the recordings of the conversations she had with Dutch film editor Hans van Dongen in preparation for his documentary DOUBLE EXPOSURE.

I am especially grateful to the Ivens family: Joris Ivens's now deceased sister Thea Nooteboom-Ivens, who repeatedly gave me a warm welcome in Nijmegen, his nephew Urias Nooteboom of Vught, now also deceased, and his nieces Annabeth Ivens and Henriet Nooteboom in Amsterdam.

All the others who were so kind as to spare the time to answer my questions can be found in the list of interviewees. It is saddening to see how many of them are no longer with us.

Film historian Bert Hogenkamp gave me his undivided support from the beginning and historian/journalist Eric van 't Groenewout made a considerable amount of research material available. I would also like to thank my Dutch publisher Jan Mets and his collaborators for years of fruitful cooperation.

During my research I was grateful for the assistance of: Winifred van Alphen-Kaldewaaij (Blaricum), Odet Bies (Moscow), Mardoeke Boekraad (Amsterdam), Jan van de Broek (Groningen), Lou Brouwers (Berlin), Femke van Doorn (Amsterdam), Gerrit van Elst (Amsterdam), Germaine Krull Stiftung (Wetzlar), Geert Groot Koerkamp (Moscow), Joep Haffmans (Utrecht), Maarten Hin (Haarlem), Marc Jansen (Amsterdam), Mieke Lauwers (Amsterdam), Arthur Lehning† (Amsterdam), Miryam van Lier ('s Hertogenbosch), Herbert Marshall† (Carbondale, Ill.), Merel Mirage (Amsterdam), the Dutch embassy (Washington DC), Dobromila van Ree (Amsterdam), Erik van Ree (Amsterdam), Pieter-Jan Smit (Rotterdam), Arian van Staa (Rotterdam), André Stufkens (Nijmegen), Gerrit Voerman (Groningen), Astrid Vorstermans (Amsterdam), Edith Wäscher (Berlin), Rudi Wester (Amsterdam), Levien Wielemaker (Kapelle), Froukje Wiersma (Crespières) and many others.

It is impossible to give the names of all the helpful staff members of the archives and institutes found in the following list of abbreviations. Nonetheless, I would like to specifically thank Bettina Berndt, Helmut Morsbach and Undine Völschow from the German Bundesarchiv/Filmarchiv; Kees Bakker and Eugène Geldof from the Europese Stichting Joris Ivens; Ivo Blom, Daan Hertogs, Jeroen van der Meij and Sonja Snoek from the Dutch Film Museum and Ton van Zeeland from the archives of the Dutch Ministry of Foreign Affairs.

Bart van der Boom, Tineke Daniëls and Bert Hogenkamp read my manuscript. Their critical comments and suggestions were a great help, but I remain the only one who can be held responsible for the final product.

I would especially like to thank Sibylle Rauch in Rhöndorf and Anneloes van Staa of Rotterdam for many years of moral support.

Archives and Document Collections

With abbreviations as used in the notes:

AI	Collection Annabeth Ivens, Amsterdam.
AdK/HEA	Akademie der Künste der ehemaligen DDR, Hanns Eisler Archiv, Berlin.
ARA-II	Algemeen Rijksarchief – Tweede Afdeling, The Hague.
AVZ	Collection A.B. van Zomeren, Blaricum.
BA/FA	Bundesarchiv/Filmarchiv, Berlin. - Coll JI = Collection Joris Ivens (SW = Schriftwechsel. RuA = Reden und Aufsätze. F= Filme. G = Grußberichte). - Folders Leipzig, folders JI etc. are documents outside the JI Collection.
BVD	Archief Binnenlandse Veiligheidsdienst, The Hague.
BZ	Archieven Ministerie van Buitenlandse Zaken, The Hague.
CCF	Archief Centrale Commissie voor de Filmkeuring, The Hague.
CIN	Collection Cineclub, Amsterdam.
EF	Collection Ewa Fiszer, Warsaw.
EHC	Ernest Hemingway Collection, John F. Kennedy Library, Boston.
EVTG	Collection Eric van 't Groenewout, Leiden.
FBI	U.S. Department of Justice, Federal Bureau of Investigation, Washington DC. Dossier George Henri Anton Ivens.
FL	Collection Last family, Amsterdam.
GA/HSA	Gemeentearchief, Hendrik Scholte Archief, Amsterdam
GARF	State Archives of the Russian Federation, Moscow.
IfGA/ZPA	Institut für Geschichte der Arbeiterbewegung, Zentrales Parteiarchiv, Berlin.
JHA	Jan Hin Archief, Haarlem.
JIA	Europese Stichting Joris Ivens (European Foundation Joris Ivens), Joris Ivens Archief, Nijmegen.
JIA/MBG	Europese Stichting Joris Ivens, Collection Miep Balguérie-Guérin, Nijmegen.
KB/HMA	Koninklijke Bibliotheek, Hendrik Marsman Archief, The Hague.
LM/JLA	Letterkundig Museum, Jef Last Archief, The Hague.

MM	Collection Marion Michelle, Paris.
MVJ	Archieven Ministerie van Justitie, The Hague.
NFA/JFA	Nederlands Foto Archief, John Fernhout Archief, Rotterdam.
NFM/HVDA	Nederlands Filmmuseum (Dutch Film Museum), Helen van Dongen Archief, Amsterdam.
NFM/LJA	Nederlands Filmmuseum (Dutch Film Museum), L.J. Jordaan Archief, Amsterdam.
OCW	Archieven Ministerie van Onderwijs, Cultuur en Wetenschappen, The Hague.
PCA	Philips Company Archives, Eindhoven.
RTsChIDNI	Russian Center for the Preservation and Study of Documents relating to Recent History, Moscow.
TNI	Collection Thea Nooteboom-Ivens, Nijmegen
UB/HSA	Universiteitsbibliotheek Amsterdam, Henrik Scholte Archief.
UN	Collection Urias Nooteboom, Vught.

The archive situation described above was accurate when I concluded my research in the autumn of 1995. Since then much has changed. Some collections or parts of collections have been or will be transferred to the Europese Stichting Joris Ivens in Nijmegen: AI, BA/FA (Ivens collection), EF, MM, TNI, UN. The notes refer to the situation in the autumn of 1995.

People Interviewed

Santiago Alvarez†, Havana
Eva Besnyö, Amsterdam
Mies Bouhuys, Amsterdam*
Costa-Gavras, Paris
Elisabeth D., Paris
Andries Deinum†, Portland (Or.)*
Catherine Duncan, Paris
Ewa Fiszer†, Warsaw
Martha Gellhorn†, London
Frenny de Graaff, Philadelphia
Robert Grelier, Paris
Jean Guyard, Paris
Annabeth Ivens, Amsterdam
Joris Ivens†, Paris
Wolfgang Klaue, Berlin
Mark† and Hetty Kolthoff, Laren
Marion de Koning-Beunders, Leiden
Michel Korzec, Amsterdam
Piet Kruijff, Amsterdam
Richard Leacock, Paris*
Lou Lichtveld (Albert Helman)†, Hilversum
Marceline Loridan-Ivens, Paris
Jean-François Masson, Paris
Marion Michelle, Paris
Emiel van Moerkerken†, Amsterdam
Henriet Nooteboom, Amsterdam
Urias Nooteboom†, Vught
Thea Nooteboom-Ivens†, Nijmegen
Pim de la Parra, Amsterdam
Arie van Poelgeest, Amsterdam*
Ida Pozner†, Paris
Vladimir Pozner†, Paris
Florrie Rodrigo†, Amsterdam
Jean Rouch, Paris
Jean-Pierre Sergent, Paris
Henri Storck†, Brussels
Henny de Swaan-Roos†, Amsterdam
Jan de Vaal, Culemborg

Tineke de Vaal, Culemborg
Wim Verstappen, Amsterdam
Theun de Vries, Amsterdam*
Xuan Phuong, Ho-Chi-Minh City

* Interviewed by telephone.

For reasons of privacy some interviewees wished to remain unnamed.

Notes

Notes to Chapter 1

1 JI interviewed by Urias Nooteboom, 5 July 1981 (typescript). UN.
2 Family data is derived from genealogical research carried out by Hans Ivens in 1939-1940. UN.
3 Ingeborg Th. Leijerzapf, 'Wilhelm Ivens: een leven in de fotografie in Nijmegen', *Numaga*, September 1988, 73-79.
4 Kees Ivens, Schemering en schemeringstijden III (Diary), entry 17 May 1938. UN.
5 Urias Nooteboom and André Stufkens, 'De bron' in: André Stufkens, Jan de Vaal and Tineke de Vaal, eds., *Rondom Joris Ivens, wereldcineast. Het begin, 1898-1934*, Nijmegen 1988, 14.
   JI interviewed by Urias Nooteboom, 5 July 1981. UN.
6 Nooteboom and Stufkens, 'De bron' in: *Rondom Joris Ivens*, 19.
7 Nooteboom and Stufkens, 'De bron' in: *Rondom Joris Ivens*, 16.
8 Kees Ivens, Schemering en schemeringstijden III, entry 17 November 1939. UN.
9 JI interviewed by the author, 16 April 1986.
10 Thea Nooteboom-Ivens interviewed by the author, 23 October 1992.
   JI interviewed by Urias Nooteboom (typescript), 8 May 1982. UN.
11 Dora Ivens-Muskens writing to JI, 2 August 1939. Undated, BA/FA Coll JI SW 1.
12 Kees Ivens, Diary (manuscript). Gemeentearchief Nijmegen.
13 Joris Ivens and Robert Destanque, *Aan welke kant en in welk heelal. De geschiedenis van een leven*, Amsterdam 1983, 237.
14 Joris Ivens writing to Miep Balguérie-Guérin, 17 September 1922. JIA/MBG.
15 Ivens and Destanque, *Aan welke kant*, 24.
16 Joris Ivens, Preface in: *Joris Ivens en Nijmegen*, Nijmegen 1987.
17 Ivens and Destanque, *Aan welke kant*, 20, 24.
18 JI interviewed by Hans Wegner (transcription tape 1), BA/FA Coll JI RuA 3.
19 George Zorab writing to JI, 5 January 1975. JIA, pl. no. 96.
20 Ivens and Destanque, *Aan welke kant*, 27.
   Diary Marion Michelle, 10 February 1945. MM.
21 Reports G.H.A. Ivens, 1911-1917. Archief Stedelijke Scholengemeenschap Nijmegen.
22 Thea Nooteboom-Ivens interviewed by the author, 17 May 1991.
23 JI interviewed by Hans Wegner (transcription tape 1).
24 Frank van der Maden, 'Een wemeling van galops en helse achtervolgingen. Joris Ivens' eerste filmavontuur', *Numaga*, September 1988, 81.
25 Van der Maden, 'Een wemeling van galops' in: *Numaga*.
26 Nooteboom and Stufkens, 'De bron' in: *Rondom Joris Ivens*, 30.
   Ivens and Destanque, *Aan welke kant*, 30.
27 Kees Ivens, Schemering en schemeringstijden III, entry 19 January 1938. UN.
28 JI interviewed by Hans Wegner (transcription tape 1).
29 JI interviewed by Hans Wegner (transcription tape 1).

30 Arthur Lehning, 'Herinneringen aan een vriendschap' in: *Rondom Joris Ivens*, 34.
31 Thea Nooteboom-Ivens interviewed by the author, 17 May 1991.
32 Ivens and Destanque, *Aan welke kant*, 23, 38.
33 JI interviewed by Eric van 't Groenewout, 1985.

Notes to Chapter 2

1 Joris Ivens and Robert Destanque, *Aan welke kant en in welk heelal. De geschiedenis van een leven*, Amsterdam 1983, 41.
2 JI writing to Miep Balguérie-Guérin, undated (1922?). JIA/MBG.
3 JI writing to Miep Balguérie-Guérin, 1 November 1922, 19 July 1922 and undated (1922). JIA/MBG.
4 Ivens and Destanque, *Aan welke kant*, 42.
5 JI writing to Miep Balguérie-Guérin, undated (July 1922?). JIA/MBG.
6 JI writing to Miep Balguérie-Guérin, 20 August 1922. JIA/MBG.
7 George Zorab writing to JI, 5 January 1975, JIA, pl. no. 96.
8 Claire Devarrieux, *Entretiens avec Joris Ivens*, Paris 1979, 70.
9 JI writing to Miep Balguérie-Guérin, undated (January 1925). JIA/MBG.
10 'Marsman en het expressionisme' in: Arthur Lehning, *De draad van Ariadne. Essays en commentaren 1*, Baarn 1979, 27.
11 JI interviewed by Eric van 't Groenewout, 7 February 1988 (recording).
12 Lehning, 'Herinneringen aan een vriendschap' in: André Stufkens, Jan de Vaal and Tineke de Vaal, eds., *Rondom Joris Ivens, wereldcineast. Het begin, 1898-1934*, Nijmegen 1988, 41.
   Wolfgang Hauch ed., *Franz Pfemfert. Ich setze diese Zeitschrift wider diese Zeit. Sozialpolitische und literaturkritische Aufsätze*, Darmstadt 1985, 19-47.
13 Rudolf Herz and Dirk Halfbrodt, *Revolution und Fotografie. München 1918/19*, Berlin 1988, 68-72, 297.
14 Germaine Krull, *La vita conduce la danza*, Florence 1992, 101-116.
   Ida Boelema, 'La vie mène la danse. De vroege jaren van Germaine Krull volgens haar memoires', *Jong Holland*, no. 3, 1995, 31-40.
15 Krull, *La vita conduce la danza*, 127-128.
16 Germaine Krull writing to Hendrik Marsman, no. 11, 1 April 1924. KB/HMA.
   Ivens and Destanque, *Aan welke kant*, 46.
   A detailed article by Ida Boelema about the Krull-Marsman correspondence appeared in *Jong Holland* number 4, 1990, 2-11.
17 Ivens and Destanque, *Aan welke kant*, 46.
18 Devarrieux, *Entretiens avec Joris Ivens*, 36.
   Ivens and Destanque, *Aan welke kant*, 49.
19 Petra Lataster, 'Gespräch mit Joris Ivens' in: Klaus Kändler, Helga Karolewski and Ilse Siebert eds., *Berliner Begegnungen. Ausländische Künstler in Berlin 1918 bis 1933*, Berlin (GDR) 1987, 133.
   JI and Hendrik Marsman writing to Arthur Lehning, 14 September 1924 quoted in: *Rondom Joris Ivens*, 39.

20 Lehning, 'Herinneringen aan een vriendschap' in: *Rondom Joris Ivens*, 39.
    Rudolf Leonhard, 'Aphorismen' in: Otto F. Best ed., *Theorie des Expressionismus*,
    Stuttgart 1982, 96.
21 Joris Ivens, *The Camera and I*, New York 1969, 17.
22 Annie Grimmer writing to Arthur Lehning, 29 May 1923, quoted in: *Rondom Joris
    Ivens*, 202.
    Joris Ivens, curriculum vitae (typescript), September 1927. JIA.
    JI was registered as a chemistry student from 19 October 1921 to 7 July 1925, but did
    not graduate. Technical University Berlin writing to the author, 27 July 1993.
23 Joris Ivens, curriculum vitae, September 1927. JIA.
    JI interviewed by Hans Wegner (transcription tape 1), undated (1950s). BA/FA Coll
    JI RuA 3.
24 Petra Lataster, 'Gespräch mit Joris Ivens' in: *Berliner Begegnungen*, 135.
25 Germaine Krull writing to Hendrik Marsman, no. 4, undated. (September-October
    1924). KB/HMA.
26 JI interviewed by Urias Nooteboom, 8 May 1982 (typescript). UN.
    Thea Nooteboom-Ivens interviewed by the author, 17 May 1991.
27 JI writing to Miep Balguérie-Guérin, undated (January 1925). JIA/MBG.
28 Kees Ivens writing to the Hellemans family, 2 December 1924, quoted in: Kees Ivens,
    Schemering en schemeringstijden III (Diary in manuscript), UN.
29 André Stufkens, 'De avant-garde rond Joris Ivens' eerste films' in: *Rondom Joris Ivens*,
    58, 203.
30 Lehning, 'Herinneringen aan een vriendschap' in: *Rondom Joris Ivens*, 39, 41.
31 Yve-Alain Bois, *Arthur Lehning en Mondriaan. Hun vriendschap en hun correspondentie*,
    Amsterdam 1984, 18.
32 Germaine Krull, 'Einstellungen. Autobiographische Erinnerungen' in: *Germaine
    Krull. Fotografien 1922-1966*, Bonn 1977, 117-127.
    Annick Lionel-Marie and Alain Sayag eds., *Eli Lotar* (Catalogue from the Centre
    Georges Pompidou), Paris 1993, 13.
33 Henri Storck interviewed by the author and Bert Hogenkamp, 28 November 1990.
    Lou Lichtveld interviewed by the author, 18 November 1992.
34 Germaine Krull writing to Hendrik Marsman, no. 5, undated (spring 1927).
    KB/HMA.
35 Krull, *La vita conduce la danza*, 136-146.
36 Ville de Paris, Extrait des minutes des actes de mariage.
    In *Aan welke kant en in welk heelal* JI incorrectly gave date as 1929.
37 Ivens and Destanque, *Aan welke kant*, 82.
    Germaine Krull writing to Hendrik Marsman, no. 14, 31 October 1926; no. 5, undated
    (spring 1927); no. 15, 11 April 1927; no. 16, 21 May 1927; no. 17, 11 July 1927.
    KB/HMA.

Notes to Chapter 3

1 Hendrik Marsman writing to Elisabeth de Roos (1926), quoted in André Stufkens, Jan de Vaal and Tineke de Vaal eds., *Rondom Joris Ivens, wereldcineast. Het begin: 1898-1934*, Nijmegen 1988, 50-51.
2 Fons Grasveld, *Een rapport over Mannus Franken, mens en kunstenaar*, Amsterdam 1976, 6.
3 L.J. Jordaan, *50 jaar bioscoopfauteuil*, Amsterdam 1958, 125-126.
   Jan Heys, 'Inleiding' in *Filmliga 1927-1931* (reprint), Nijmegen 1982, 12.
4 Henrik Scholte, Diary, 225-227, GA/HSA.
5 *Filmliga*, undated (September 1927).
6 Joris Ivens and Robert Destanque, *Aan welke kant en in welk heelal. De geschiedenis van een leven*, Amsterdam 1983, 67.
7 Jordaan, *50 jaar bioscoopfauteuil*, 139.
8 Henrik Scholte, Diary, 46.
9 Joris Ivens, 'Filmtechniek' in *Filmliga*, undated (September 1927), 7.
10 JI interviewed by Eric van 't Groenewout (recording), 7 February 1988.
11 Scholte, Diary, 235, 237.
12 'De Vliegende Hollander' in: H. Marsman, *Verzameld werk*, Amsterdam 1979, 183-185.
13 According to Ivens the Zeedijk film and other material disappeared during World War II when the Germans 'annexed' the Capi store in the Kalverstraat. JI interviewed by Urias Nooteboom, 8 May 1982 (transcription). UN.
14 Ivens and Destanque, *Aan welke kant*, 73.
   Piet Kruijff interviewed by the author, 19 July 1991.
   JI interviewed by Eric van 't Groenewout, 7 February 1988.
   De Tribune, [?] February 1929.
15 Menno ter Braak, 'Un auteur de films Hollandais: Joris Ivens', *Variété* no. 12, 1929, 651-653.
16 Jef Last, 'Die Strasze' (manuscript in notebook), LM/JLA.
17 F.J. Haffmans ed., *Geest, kolzuur en zijk. Briefwisseling van Erich Wichman*, Westervoort 1999, 47-51, 292-296.
   Hans Schoots, 'De stad is ziek, de stad is rot. De opmerkelijke vriendschap tussen Erich Wichman en Joris Ivens', *Vrij Nederland*, 25 September 1999.
18 Hans van Meerten, 'Ik-film' in *Filmliga*, January 1928, 6-10.
   JI writing to editors *Filmliga*, 30 December 1927. NFM/LJA.
19 Joris Ivens, 'Ik-film', *Skoop*, March 1964, 44.
20 Joris Ivens, 'Technische opmerkingen over de Ik-film', *Filmliga*, April 1928, 6-8.
21 Han Meyer, *Joris Ivens. De weg naar Vietnam*, Utrecht 1970, 51.
   Joris Ivens, 'Films te Berlijn', *Filmliga*, undated (October 1927), 8.
22 JI interviewed by Hans Wegner (transcription tape 1), undated. BA/FA Coll. JI RuA 3.
23 Béla Balázs, *Der Film*, Vienna 1961, 180-181.
24 Joris Ivens, 'Amateurfilm-Bericht von Joris Ivens' in: Michael Kuball, *Familienkino Band I, 1900-1930. Geschichte des Amateurfilms in Deutschland*, Reinbek bei Hamburg, 1980, 72-73. (Taken from *Film für Alle*, February 1929, 34-38).
   Joris Ivens, 'De brug', *Cinema en theater*, July 1928.

25 Ivens, 'Amateurfilm-Bericht' in *Familienkino I*, 73.

26 Jordaan, *50 jaar bioscoopfauteuil*, 147.

27 JI interviewed by Hans Wegner (transcription tape 1). *Filmliga*, May 1928, supplement.

28 Menno ter Braak, ' 'Branding' als mislukking en als resultaat' in *Filmliga* March 1929, 65.
Menno ter Braak, 'Un auteur de films Hollandais: Joris Ivens' in *Variété* no.12, 1929, 651-653.
L.J. Jordaan, *Joris Ivens*, Amsterdam 1931, 11.

29 L.J. Jordaan, 'Onze elfde en twaalfde matinee', *Filmliga*, August 1928, 9.

30 Anonymous typescript quoted in: *Rondom Joris Ivens*, 60.

31 Nieko van de Pavert, Jef Last tussen de partij en zichzelf (thesis), Nijmegen 1982, 97.

32 L.J. Jordaan, 'In de filmkraamkamer II', *De Groene Amsterdammer*, 25 August 1928.

33 Jordaan, 'In de filmkraamkamer II', *De Groene Amsterdammer*, 25 August 1928.

34 Joris Ivens, 'M. Franken en Joris Ivens filmen 'Branding'', in program supplement with *Filmliga*, February 1929.
De Nieuwe Rotterdammer, 5 October 1929.

35 Ter Braak, ' 'Branding' als mislukking en als resultaat', *Filmliga*, March 1929, 65-68.

36 JI interviewed by Eric van 't Groenewout, 7 February 1988.

37 Anneke van der Feer writing to JI, undated (ca. 1949). BA/FA, Coll JI SW 4.

38 Igor Cornelissen, *De GPOe op de Overtoom. Spionnen voor Moskou 1920-1940*, Amsterdam 1989, 101, 104, 114-117, 155-158.

39 Koninklijk Besluit 5 March 1923, no 55. ARA-II.

40 Helen van Dongen, 'Ik kwam Joris Ivens tegen', *Skoop*, November 1978.

41 Urias Nooteboom, 'Het verborgen leven van de jonge Joris Ivens', *De Tijd*, 10 November 1978, 53.
Claire Devarrieux, *Entretiens avec Joris Ivens*, Paris 1979, 36.

42 Koninklijk Besluit 8 March 1929, no. 35. ARA-II.

43 *De nood in de Drentsche venen*, Titel list with censorship report, 28 February 1929. CCF.

44 Bert Hogenkamp, 'Joris Ivens, vijftig jaar wereldcineast', *Skrien*, November 1978, 24.
'Kou en armoe op de Drentse heide', *Het leven*, 2 March 1929, 274-278.
In 1935 the CPH changed its name to the CPN.

45 Anatoli Loenatsjarski, 'Conversation with Lenin' in: Richard Taylor ed., *The film factory. Russian and Soviet cinema in documents 1896-1939*, London 1988, 57.

46 Ger Harmsen, *Nederlands kommunisme. Gebundelde opstellen*, Nijmegen 1982, 86-87.
Bert Hogenkamp, ' 'Hier met de film' Het gebruik van het medium film door de communistische beweging in de jaren twintig en dertig' in: Bert Hogenkamp and Peter Mol, *Van beeld tot beeld. De films en televisieuitzendingen van de CPN, 1928-1986*, Amsterdam 1993, 20-23.

47 Leo van Lakerveld interviewed by Eric van 't Groenewout (recording), 4 April 1985.

Notes to Chapter 4

1   Willem Bon interviewed by Bert Hogenkamp, Edith Taekema and Herman de Wit (recording), 6 November 1987.
2   Kees Ivens, Schemering en schemeringstijden I (Diary in manuscript). UN.
3   JI writing to Arthur Lehning, 8 June 1927, quoted in André Stufkens, Jan de Vaal and Tineke de Vaal eds., *Rondom Joris Ivens, wereldcineast. Het begin: 1898-1934*, Nijmegen 1988, 41.
4   JI interviewed by Eric van 't Groenewout (recording), 8 and 9 May 1986.
5   Helene van Dongen in: Wolfgang Klaue, Manfred Lichtenstein, Hans Wegner eds., *Joris Ivens*, Berlin (GDR) 1963, 42-43.
    André Stufkens, 'De avant-garde rond Joris Ivens' in: *Rondom Joris Ivens*, 71.
6   Thea Nooteboom-Ivens interviewed by the author, 17 May 1991.
7   JI interviewed by Urias Nooteboom, 8 May 1982 (transcription). UN.
8   Dan van Golberdinge, 'Eva Besnyö, fotografe' in: *Rondom Joris Ivens*, 112.
9   Lou Lichtveld interviewed by the author, 18 November 1992.
10 Hans Keller, interview with Helen van Dongen-Durant, *NRC Handelsblad*, 26 January 1984.
11 Ben Achtenberg, 'Helen van Dongen: an interview', *Film Quarterly*, winter 1976-1977, 48.
    Helen van Dongen, 'Ik kwam Joris Ivens tegen', *Skoop*. November 1978.
12 Quote from correspondence that remains anonymous at the request of the owner.
13 Joris Ivens and Robert Destanque, *Aan welke kant en in welk heelal. De geschiedenis van een leven*, Amsterdam 1983, 93.
14 Paul Rotha, *The Film Till Now. A Survey of World Cinema* (with a supplement by Richard Griffith), Feltham 1967, 613.
    Richard Barsam, *The Vision of Robert Flaherty. The Artist as Myth and Filmmaker*, Bloomington 1988, 93.
15 Ageeth Scherphuis, interview with Helen van Dongen-Durant, *Vrij Nederland*, 28 September 1985.
16 Mark and Hetty Kolthoff interviewed by the author, 30 August 1990.
17 'Gesprek met John Fernhout', *Skoop*, March 1964, 14.
18 Helene van Dongen stated that she also edited this material into several archive films, *De Zuiderzeedijk* and *Nieuwe polders*, for the Rijksarchief and the archives of the Maatschappij voor de Uitvoering van de Zuiderzeewerken. In 1993-1994, however, these films could not be located in these or related archives.
19 Helen van Dongen, 'Ik kwam Joris Ivens tegen', *Skoop*, November 1978.
    There is a photo of Helene van Dongen at De Vlieter. NFM/HVDA, folder 41-42.
20 *Het Volk*, 4, 6 and 10 January 1930.
21 JI writing to Mannus Franken, 19 and 25 October 1927, quoted in: Fons Grasveld, *Mannus Franken, mens en kunstenaar*, Amsterdam 1976, 75-76.
22 Henrik Scholte, Diary, 49. GA/HSA.
23 Bibeb, 'Joris Ivens: een dialoog met het publiek over een groot ideaal', *Vrij Nederland*, 22 February 1964, 5.

24 Ed Pelster writing to Mannus Franken, 26 February 1928 and Mannus Franken writing to Ed Pelster, 28 February 1928, quoted in: Grasveld, *Mannus Franken*, 76.

25 Ivens and Destanque, *Aan welke kant*, 79.

26 JI writing to Mannus Franken, undated (spring 1928), 1 October 1928 and 15 June 1929, quoted in: Grasveld, *Mannus Franken*, 77, 79.
De Nieuwe Rotterdammer, 15 October 1929.

27 JI writing to Mannus Franken, 22 and 27 April 1929, quoted in: Grasveld, *Mannus Franken*, 77-78.
Filmliga, November 1929, 22.

28 *Nieuwe Rotterdamsche Courant*, 11 February 1930.

29 *De Nieuwe Rotterdammer*, 5 October 1929.
Nieuwe Rotterdamsche Courant, 10 February 1931.

30 L.J. Jordaan, *50 jaar bioscoopfauteuil*, Amsterdam 1958, 149.
L.J. Jordaan, *Joris Ivens*, Amsterdam 1931, 16-17.
Henrik Scholte, 'Joris Ivens', *Filmliga*, December 1929, 22-23.
Close-up, 'Een oordeel over Joris Ivens', *Filmliga*, April 1930, 95-97.
Lou Lichtveld interviewed by the author, 18 November 1992.

Notes to Chapter 5

1 Hans Richter in: Fritz Mierau ed., *Russen in Berlin. Literatur, Malerei, Theater, Film 1918-1933*, Leipzig 1991, 498.

2 W. Pudovkin, 'Vortrag, Filmliga Amsterdam 10 januari 1929', *Filmliga*, February 1929, 54-57.

3 JI writing to J. Malzev, 17 May 1929. GARF, R-5283 inv 5.

4 Correspondence between JI and VOKS, 1929. GARF, R-5283 inv 5.
(Anton) Struik, Conclusion regarding comrade Joris Ivens. 5 June 1936. RTsChIDNI 495-244-99.

5 Vsevolod Pudovkin, 'Joris Ivens', *Filmliga*, May 1930, 102-104.

6 Ivens showed Mannus Franken's Jardin du Luxembourg, Willem Bon's Stad, J.C. Mol's Uit het rijk der kristallen and Andor von Barsy's Hoogstraat. Cf.: Joris Ivens's arrival in the USSR (typescript). GARF, R-5283 inv 5.
Hans Wegner, *Joris Ivens, Dokumentarist der Wahrheit*, Berlin (GDR) 1965, 31.

7 *Nieuwe Rotterdamsche Courant*, 6 April 1930.

8 'Joris Ivens', *Kino i Zjizn*, 1930 no. 5.
Vetsjernaja Moskva, 5 February 1930.

9 Showing Dutch films (typescript), 30 January 1930. GARF, R-5283 inv 5. The text is in the third person because the interpreter's translation went into the minutes.

10 Resolution passed after the screening of the films of the Dutch director Joris Ivens in the communal hostel The Builder, 6 February 1930 (typescript). GARF, R-5283 inv 5.

11 Joris Ivens's arrival in the USSR. Undated (March 1930). GARF, R-5283 inv 5.

12 JI writing to Millman, 26 February 1930. GARF, R-5283 inv 5.

13 Dzherzhanin writing to Millman, Report on Joris Ivens's stay in Leningrad, 18 February 1930. GARF, R-5283 inv 5.

14 L.J. Jordaan, 'Uit het land van Poedovkin. Een gesprek met de Nederlandse cineast Joris Ivens', *De Groene Amsterdammer*, 12 April 1930.

15 Joris Ivens, draft for *The camera and I*, Chapter 4 (manuscript), undated (1941-1944). EF.

16 JI writing to Millman, 26 February 1930. GARF, R-5283 inv 5.

17 Jordaan, 'Uit het land van Poedovkin', *Groene Amsterdammer*, 12 April 1930.

18 *De Tribune*, 22 April 1930.
JI interviewed by Pim de la Parra and Wim Verstappen, *Skoop*, March 1964, 4.
JI interviewed by Hans Wegner (transcription tape 3), undated BA/FA, Coll JI Kiste 11 Akte VII.

19 Lou Lichtveld interviewed by the author, 18 November 1992.

20 *De Tribune*, 20 March 1931.
Bert Hogenkamp, ''Hier met de film'. Het gebruik van het medium film door de communistische beweging in de jaren twintig en dertig' in: Bert Hogenkamp and Peter Mol, *Van beeld tot beeld. De films en televisieuitzendingen van de CPN, 1928-1986*, Amsterdam 1993, 26-28.

21 Piet Piryns, 'Joris Ivens over de Leica en de revolutie', *Vrij Nederland*, Supplement 15 May 1976, 17.

22 Lou Lichtveld interviewed by the author, 18 November 1992.

23 Joris Ivens's arrival in the USSR. GARF, R-5283 inv 5.
Notes Jan Hin; JI writing to Jan Hin, 1 May 1930 and 6 May 1930. JHA.

24 JI writing to Otto Katz, 13 February 1931. JI writing to Schumann and Ilyinskaya, 14 April 1931. JI writing to Millman, 20 May 1931. JI writing to Mezhrabpom, 26 May 1931. GARF, R-5283 inv 5.

25 *Nieuwe Rotterdamsche Courant*, 7 and 10 February 1931.

26 Mark Kolthoff interviewed by Bert Hogenkamp (recording), 20 November, 1979.
Mark Kolthoff interviewed by the author, 30 August, 1990.

27 *Nieuwe Rotterdamsche Courant*, 31 May 1931.

28 Karel Dibbets, *Sprekende films. De komst van de geluidsfilm in Nederland, 1928-1933*, Amsterdam 1993, 241.

29 *De Tribune*, 29 September 1931.
JI writing to Jan Hin, 13 August 1929. JHA.

30 *Het Volk*, 29 September 1931.

31 JI interviewed by Pim de la Parra and Wim Verstappen, *Skoop*, March 1964, 3.
Nieuwe Rotterdamsche Courant, 7 February 1931.

32 JI interviewed by Eric van 't Groenewout, 8 and 9 May 1986.
Communiqué quoted in *Filmliga*, November 1931, 17.
Philips writing to Commission for Film Censorship, 5 August 1933 and 18 April 1934. CCF.

33 See extensive correspondence 1931-1932 in dossier Philips Radio. PCA.
'Philipsfilm en auteursrecht' in *Filmliga*, January 1932, 50.

34 Joris Ivens, 'Monolog auf Hanns Eisler', *Sinn und Form. Eisler Sonderausgabe*, 1964, 38.

35 See also the filmography produced in consultation with Ivens for the Dutch Film Museum brochure *Joris Ivens, 50 jaar wereldcineast*, Amsterdam 1978, appendix 1, 6.
Claude Guiguet and Emmanuel Papillon, *Jean Dréville. Propos du cineaste. Filmographie. Documents*, Paris 1987, 54-55.

Jean Dréville interviewed by Claude Brunel in: Claude Brunel ed., *Joris Ivens*, Paris 1983, 36.

Wolfgang Klaue, Manfred Lichtenstein and Hans Wegner, eds. *Joris Ivens*, 44. Berlin (GDR),

Algemeen Handelsblad, 27 January 1932.

Van Dongen's involvement in the editing is seen from a letter from her to Jan Hin, 15 September 1931. JHA.

36 *Nieuw Weekblad voor de Cinématografie*, 5 December 1930.

JI interviewed by Eric van 't Groenewout, 7 February 1988.

Mark Kolthoff interviewed by the author, 30 August 1990.

Helene van Dongen in: Klaue, Lichtenstein and Wegner, *Joris Ivens*, 43.

37 Kees Ivens, Schemering en schemeringstijden I (diary), 9 September 1935 and undated (1935). UN.

38 JI interviewed by Eric van 't Groenewout, 8 and 9 May 1986.

39 (Anton) Struik, Conclusion regarding comrade Joris Ivens, 5 June 1936. RTsChIDNI, 495-244-99. The facts concerning Ivens's party membership were confirmed by a letter from Ivens to Samsonov, 3 November 1935, printed in *Filmblatt* Fall 1999, 36-37.

40 Lou Lichtveld interviewed by the author, 18 November 1992.

41 Mark Kolthoff interviewed by the author, 30 August 1990.

Arie van Poelgeest in telephone conversations with the author, 9 May and 28 June 1990. Cf.: Interview with Arie van Poelgeest, *Provinciale Zeeuwse Courant*, 25 March 1989.

42 Kees Ivens, Schemering en schemertijden I, opening pages and 9 September 1935. UN.

43 Joris Ivens and Robert Destanque, *Aan welke kant en in welk heelal. De geschiedenis van een leven*, Amsterdam 1983, 125.

44 Kees Ivens, Schemering en schemeringstijden III, undated. UN.

Jaarverslag NV Capi, 1939. BA/FA, Coll JI SW 1.

Kees Ivens writing to JI, 4 May 1940. BA/FA, Coll JI SW 1.

45 Ivens and Destanque, *Aan welke kant*, 99.

46 Joris Ivens, Lezing aan de Volkuniversiteit Rotterdam (manuscript), 1930. JIA, pl.no. 288.

Oprechte Haarlemsche Courant, 15 April 1930.

47 Joris Ivens, 'Quelques réflections sur les documentaires d'avant-garde', *La Revue des Vivants*, October 1931.

Notes to Chapter 6

1 *Die Welt am Abend*, 16 October 1931.

2 Mark Wlolozki and Juri Sjvirjov, 'Korte inleiding bij de films van de Mezhrabpom-filmstudio', *Filmmuseum Cinematheek Journaal 21*, February-March 1978, 6.

3 J.A. Lvoenin, 'Mezhrabpom en de Sovjet-film (1921-1936)', *Filmmuseum Cinematheek Journaal 21*, 12.

4 This issue of *Vechernyaya Moskva* is absent from diverse Moscow archives. The quotes from it were printed in *De Tribune*, 11 November 1931.

5 Capi writing to Philips, 20 November 1931.
   Report of converstation with Kees Ivens by Dr. N.A. Halbertsma, 22 December 1931. Both: PCA.
   De Tribune, 15 December 1931.

6 JI writing to Henrik Scholte, undated (December 1931). UB/HSA.

7 Joris Ivens, Vor dem Film 'die Brücke' (typescript), undated (autumn 1934). JIA.

8 Herbert Marshall, *Masters of Soviet-Cinema. Crippled Creative Biographies*, London 1983, 12-13.
   Herbert Marshall, Preface in: *Immoral Memories. An Autobiography by Sergei M. Eisenstein*, Boston 1983, xx.

9 Joris Ivens, Notes for reading on 24 January 1933 at the Film collective at Rotterdam. JIA.

10 Joris Ivens, Zur methode des dokumentarischen Films, im besondern – des Films 'Komsomol' (typescript), undated (late February, early March 1932). JIA.

11 *Experimental Film*, no 20, 1931 quoted in: Marshall, *Masters of Soviet Cinema*, 30.

12 Joris Ivens, Mein Film über den Komsomol (typescript) undated (spring 1932). BA/FA Coll JI RuA 1.

13 Joris Ivens, Mein Film über den Komsomol.

14 Jef Last, *Het stalen fundament. Reportage over 2500 K.M. zwerftochten door de Oeral*, Amsterdam 1933, 58.

15 Last, *Het Stalen fundament*, 69.

16 Joris Ivens and Robert Destanque, *Aan welke kant en in welk heelal. De geschiedenis van een leven*, Amsterdam 1983, 107.

17 A.K. Martinova, 'Magnitogorsk: its year and vicissitudes', (publication for an exhibition at the Local History Museum of Magnitogorsk, originally in Russian), Magnitogorsk 1992.
   John Scott, *Behind the Urals. An American Worker in Russia's City of Steel*, Bloomington 1989, passim.
   Stephen Kotkin, *Magnetic Mountain. Stalinism as a Civilisation*, Berkeley 1995, passim.

18 Ivens and Destanque, *Aan welke kant*, 106.

19 G. Dmitrin, 'Inspired by meeting inhabitants of the Urals': *Rifej* (Ural literary folkloric magazine, originally in Russian), 1980.

20 Joris Ivens, *Autobiografie van een filmer*, Amsterdam undated (1970), 54.

21 'Proletarskoye Kino Editorial: We are continuing the struggle' and 'Party Central Committee Decree: The reorganisation of literary and artistic organisations' in: Richard Taylor ed., *The Film Factory. Russian and Soviet Cinema in Documents*, London 1988, 321-322, 325.

22 Ivens, Zur Methode des dokumentarischen Films, im besondern – des Films 'Komsomol'.

23 Joris Ivens, 'Kentering in de Russische film I', *Filmliga*, 20 January 1933, 66.

24 F. C. W(eiskopf)., 'Bei Joris Ivens in Magnitogorsk', *Moskauer Rundschau*, 19 June 1932.

25 Sergej Tretjakow, *Gesichter der avantgarde. Porträts, Essays, Briefe*, Berlin 1991, 484.

26 Ivens, Zur methode des Dokumentarfilms, im besondern – des Films 'Komsomol'.

27 Joris Ivens, 'Monolog auf Hanns Eisler', *Sinn und Form, Eisler Sonderausgabe*, 1964, 35.
    Sergei Tretyakov writing to Hanns Eisler, 22 November 1932 in: Tretjakow, *Gesichter der Avantgarde*, 398.

28 Stephanie Eisler and Manfred Grabs, Gespräch mit Joris Ivens über seinen 'Monolog auf Hanns Eisler' (typescript), 21 January 1967. AdK/HEA.

29 Sergei Tretyakov writing to Hanns Eisler, 13 November 1932. AdK/HEA.

30 S. Drobashenko, *Kinorezisser Joris Ivens*, Moscow 1964, 46.

31 JI in telephone conversation with the author, 22 May 1989.

32 *Nieuwe Rotterdamsche Courant*, 13 January 1933.
    Het Volk, 13 Januari and 1 July 1933.

33 Minutes of the meeting of the Vereniging 'Nederlandsch Fabrikaat' and the advisory commission for 'Made in Holland' promotion, 3 January, 7 February and 26 May 1933. Archives of the Vereniging 'Nederlandsch Fabrikaat'. ARA.

34 Joris Ivens, Film in dienst van de klassenstrijd (manuscript), undated (February-March 1933); 2e les M.A.S. Film in dienst van de klassenstrijd (manuscript), 14 March 1933. Both: BA/FA, Coll JI RuA 1.

35 Links richten tussen partij en arbeidersstrijd 2 (collective thesis project group literary sociology), Nijmegen 1975, 398-404.
    Bert Hogenkamp, 'Ideologie, cultuur of koopwaar? De boycot van Duitse films in 1933', *GBG-Nieuws*, summer 1994, 22-35.
    JI interviewed by Eric van 't Groenewout, 8 and 9 May 1986.

Notes to Chapter 7

1   Hans Sluizer, 'Parijse brief', *Filmliga*, 20 March 1933, 130.

2   Joris Ivens, Mijn lezing in Parijs (typescript with accompanying letter by Helene van Dongen), 11 April 1933. UB/HSA.

3   Vladimir Pozner interviewed by the author, 6 February 1990.

4   Arthur Koestler, *The Invisible Writing. The Second Volume of an Autobiography: 1932-1940*, London 1969, 369-372.

5   Henri Storck in a telephone conversation with the author, 11 August 1990.

6   Hanns Eisler, *Fragen sie mehr über Brecht. Gepräche mit Hans Bunge*, Darmstadt 1986, 101.

7   Eisler, *Fragen sie mehr über Brecht*, 101.
    Hanns Eisler writing to Bertolt Brecht, 10 August 1933. AdK/HEA.

8   Joris Ivens, *The Camera and I*, New York 1969, 96.
    JI interviewed by Pim de la Parra and Wim Verstappen, *Skoop*, March 1964, 5.
    Hanns Eisler writing to Bertolt Brecht, 10 August 1933.

9   Joris Ivens, 'Monolog auf Hanns Eisler', *Sinn und Form, Eisler Sonderausgabe*, 1964, 37.

10 Petra Lataster, 'Gespräch mit Joris Ivens' in: *Berliner Begegnungen. Ausländische Künstler in Berlin 1918 bis 1933*, Berlin (GDR) 1987, 130-131.

11 Eisler, *Fragen Sie mehr über Brecht*, 101.

12 Links richten tussen partij en arbeidersstrijd 2 (collective thesis project group literary sociology), Nijmegen 1975, 475.

13 Ida Pozner interviewed by the author, 6 February 1990.
    Babette Gross, *Willi Münzenberg. Eine politische Biographie*, Leipzig 1991, 253-254.
    Richard Gyptner, Über die Internationale Arbeiterhilfe (IAH) und Münzenbergs
    Apparat 1933-1935 (typescript), 1 March 1963. Archive Richard Gyptner. IfGA/ZPA.
14 Joris Ivens, 'Monolog auf Hanns Eisler', *Sinn und Form*, 37.
15 Martin Schouten, *Rinus van der Lubbe, 1909-1934*, Amsterdam 1986.
    Fritz Tobias, *Der Reichstagsbrand. Legende und Wirklichkeit*, Rastatt 1962.
    Even within the GDR the conclusion was reached that Van der Lubbe had acted
    alone. Cf.: Ger Harmsen, *Nederlands kommunisme. Gebundelde opstellen*, Nijmegen
    1982, 331.
16 Jef Last, memoirs (typescript). FL.
    Freek van Leeuwen, *De deur op een kier. Levensherinneringen van Freek van Leeuwen*, The
    Hague 1981, 105-108.
17 *Braunbuch über Reichstagbrand und Hitlerterror*, Basel 1933, 52.
18 Henri Storck, 'Chronologie van de produktie van de film' in: Bert Hogenkamp and
    Henri Storck eds., *De Borinage. De mijnwerkersstaking van 1932 en de film van Joris Ivens
    en Henri Storck*, Amsterdam 1983, 23.
19 *Nieuwe Rotterdamsche Courant*, 21 August 1933.
    Mark and Hetty Kolthoff interviewed by the author, 30 August 1990.
20 Henri Storck, Notes 7 August through 17 September 1933, 'Chronologie' in:
    Hogenkamp and Storck, *Borinage*, 23-24.
21 Henri Storck, 'Herinneringen aan de Borinage' in: Hogenkamp and Storck, *Borinage*,
    34.
22 Storck, Note 29 September 1933, 'Chronologie' in: *Borinage*, 26.
23 Jan Fonteyne, 'Diverse aantekeningen met betrekking tot de Borinage-film' in:
    Hogenkamp and Storck, *Borinage*, 37.
24 Storck, 'Herinneringen aan de Borinage' in: *Borinage*, 33-34.
    Fonteyne, 'Aantekeningen' in: *Borinage*, 38.
25 Joris Ivens and Robert Destanque, *Aan welke kant en in welk heelal. De geschiedenis van
    een leven*, Amsterdam 1983, 124.
    Joris Ivens, Ideas in documentary films. Outline of chapters. Undated (1943). BA/FA,
    Coll JI RuA 1.
26 Storck, 'Herinneringen' in: *Borinage*, 35.
27 To make things more confusing the title Borinage was used in the advertising for the
    premiere, for the next screening in Brussels, however, it was back to Misère au
    Borinage.
28 Film historians Eric van 't Groenewout and Bert Hogenkamp concluded this inde-
    pendently after research in the archives of the Centrale Commissie voor de
    Filmkeuring, The Hague.
29 Henri Storck interviewed by the author and Bert Hogenkamp, 28 November 1990.
30 *Het Volk*, 15 March 1934.
31 *Het Volk*, 15 March 1934 and 5 July 1937.
32 *Nieuwe Rotterdamsche Courant*, 8 March 1934.
33 *De Groene Amsterdammer*, 17 March 1934.
34 *Algemeen Handelsblad*, 16 December 1933.
    Het Volk, 21 December 1933.
    De Telegraaf, 17 December 1933.

35 *De Tribune*, March 1933.
36 Henrik Scholte, 'Joris Ivens 'Komsomol'', *Filmliga*, October 1933, 309-310.
37 Dr. Hans van Loon, 'Ivens als betoger', *Filmliga*, year 7 no. 1, 1934.
38 Ivens and Destanque, *Aan welke kant*, 124-125.
    JI made similar statements in an interview with the author, 16 April 1986.
39 *Algemeen Handelsblad*, 5 October 1929.
40 Vsevolod Poedovkin, 'Joris Ivens', *Filmliga*, May 1930, 102-104.
41 Joris Ivens, 'Quelques réflections sur les documentaires d'avant-garde' in: Robert
    Grelier, *Joris Ivens*, Paris 1965, 142-144. (Taken from *La Revue des Vivants*, October
    1931.)
42 Joris Ivens, Speech at the International Congress for Photography, Leipzig (manu-
    script), 1932. JIA.
43 Interview with Joris Ivens and Henri Storck, *Documents 34*, January 1934.
44 Joris Ivens, Vor dem Film 'die Brücke' (typescript) undated (autumn 1934). JIA.
45 Gustav Regler, *Das Ohr des Malchus. Eine Lebensgeschichte*, Cologne 1958, 267.
46 Joris Ivens, Notizen über russische Filme (manuscript), undated (autumn 1934). JIA.
    Printed in: Wolfgang Klaue, Manfred Lichtenstein and Hans Wegner, eds., *Joris Ivens*,
    Berlin (GDR) 1963, 265-266.
    Karl Radek, 'Die moderne Weltliteratur and die Aufgaben der proletarischen Kunst'
    in: H.J. Schmitt and G. Schramm eds., *Sozialistische Realismuskonzeptionen. Dokumente
    zum 1. Allunionskongress der Sowjetschriftsteller*, Frankfurt/Main 1974, 140-213.

Notes to Chapter 8

1   Piet Piryns, "Joris Ivens over de Leica en de revolutie", *Vrij Nederland*, Supplement 15
    May 1976, 17.
2   JI interviewed by Eric van 't Groenewout (recording), 8 and 9 May 1986.
3   *Cinemonde*, 28 December 1933 and 18 January 1934.
    Het Volk, 15 March 1934. *Intransigeant*, 14 May 1934.
4   *Intransigeant*, 14 May 1934.
    Passport George Henri Anton Ivens, issued Paris 28 June 1933<$]FIGS>. STAMPED 13
    APRIL 1934 BASEL AND AUSTRIA, 14 APRIL 1934 BRECLAV, VISA USSR 15 APRIL 1934.
    JIA, PL.NO. 629.
5   Helene van Dongen writing to Jan Hin, 24 June 1934. JHA.
6   Doc. 1303, about Anneke van der Feer, undated (1935). RTsChIDNI, 495-244-101.
7   Helene van Dongen writing to Jan Hin, 7 December 1931. JHA.
8   Anneke van der Feer writing to Joris Ivens, 28 February and 22 April 1940. Anneke
    van der Feer writing to Helene van Dongen, 19 March 1941. All: BA/FA, Coll JI SW 1.
9   Hanns Eisler writing to Bertolt Brecht, 14 May 1934. AdK/HEA.
    Helene van Dongen writing to Jan Hin, 24 June 1934.
10 Joris Ivens and Robert Destanque, *Aan welke kant en in welk heelal. De geschiedenis van
    een leven*, Amsterdam 1983, 201-202.
11 Herbert Marshall, *Masters of the Soviet Cinema. Crippled Creative Biographies*, London
    1983, 215.

Jean Lacouture, *Malraux, une vie dans le siècle*, Paris 1976, 158.

Deutsche Zentral-Zeitung (Moscow), 15 June 1934 and 8 July 1934.

12 See note 3 and Ivens and Destanque, *Aan welke kant*, 132.

13 *Arbeiterzeitung* (Saarbrücken), 13 December 1934, quoted in: Ralph Schock, *Gustav Regler – Literatur und Politik (1933-1940)*, Frankfurt/Main 1984, 91.

14 JI interviewed by Saarlander Rundfunk, quoted in: Schock, *Gustav Regler – Literatur und Politik*, 91.

15 Gustav Regler, *Das Ohr des Malchus. Eine Lebensgeschichte*, Cologne 1958, 264-267.

16 Gustav Reglers notebook from 1937, quoted in: Schock, *Gustav Regler*, 605.

     Regler, *Das Ohr des Malchus*, 387.

17 Regler, *Das Ohr des Malchus*, 289, 300.

     Arbeiterzeitung (Saarbrücken), 13 December 1934, quoted in Schock, *Gustav Regler*, 91.

18 JI in telephone conversation with the author, 22 May 1989.

19 Marshall, *Masters of the Soviet Cinema*, 92.

20 John Willett, *The Theatre of Erwin Piscator. Half a Century of Politics in the Theatre*, London 1978, 129-130, 140.

     Maria Hilgenbach, *Kino im Exil. Die Emigration deutscher Filmkünstler 1933-1945*, Munich 1982, 66-67.

     Petra Lataster, "Gespräch mit Joris Ivens" in: *Berliner Begegnungen. Ausländische Künstler in Berlin 1918 bis 1933*, Berlin (GDR) 1987, 129.

21 Joseph Zsuffa, *Béla Balázs, The Man and the Artist*, Berkeley 1987, 226.

22 David Pike, *Deutsche Schriftsteller im sowjetischen Exil 1933-1945*, Frankfurt/Main 1981, 465.

     Regler, *Das Ohr des Machus*, 290.

     Alfred Kurella, *Ich lebe in Moskau*, Berlin 1947, 109.

23 Henri Storck interviewed by the author and Bert Hogenkamp, 28 November 1990.

24 Francesco Misiano writing to Samsonov, undated RTsChIDNI, 538-3-175.

25 JI writing to Babitski, 24 September 1936. Archive Hans Rodenberg, IfGA/ZPA.

26 Ivens and Destanque, *Aan welke kant*, 130-131.

27 Reinhard Müller, ed., *Die Säuberung. Moskau 1936: Stenogram einer geschlossenen Parteiversammlung*, Reinbek bei Hamburg 1991, 323-326, 295.

28 Müller, *Die Säuberung*, 323-326, 295 and passim.

29 Ivens and Destanque, *Aan welke kant*, 131.

30 Richard Taylor, ed., *The Film Factory, Russian and Soviet Cinema in Documents*, London 1988, 358-369.

31 Gustav von Wangenheim, "Über die Entstehung des Films 'Kämpfer'(9)", *Junge Welt*, 28 March 1963.

32 Henri Storck, "Chronologie van de produktie van de film" in: Bert Hogenkamp and Henri Storck, *De Borinage. De mijnwerkersstaking van 1932 en de film van Joris Ivens en Henri Storck*, Amsterdam 1983, 27.

     JI writing to Boris Shumyatsky, 24 September 1936. Archive Hans Rodenberg, IfGA/ZPA.

33 Production plan 1935 (typescript). RTsChIDNI, 538-3-175.

     Maxim Gorki writing to Alfred Kurella, 29 January 1935. Partially printed in *Sonntag* (Berlin (GDR)) no. 8, 1963.

Alfred Kurella, Bemerkungen des Genossen Gorki zu dem Manuskript "Kämpfer", 9 April 1935 (typescript). BA/FA, Folder "Kämpfer".

34 Francesco Misiano writing to Narkomindel, 4 April 1935. RTsChIDNI, 538-3-172.
35 Müller, *Die Säuberung*, 416.
36 *Deutsche Zentral-Zeitung*, 24 June 1935.
   Julius Hay, *Geboren 1900*, Munich 1980, 217.
37 "The work has been finished for weeks," writes the *Deutsche Zentral-Zeitung*, 4 June 1936.
   Gustav von Wangenheim, "Über die Entstehung des Films 'Kämpfer'(conclusion)", *Junge Welt* (Berlin (GDR)), undated (late March, early April 1963).
38 Müller, *Die Säuberung*, 414.
39 Pike, *Deutsche Schriftsteller im sowjetischen Exil*, 91-95.
40 (Anton) Struik, Conclusion regarding comrade Joris Ivens, 5 June 1936. RTsChIDNI, 495-244-99.
41 Joris Ivens interviewed by Eric van 't Groenewout, 8 and 9 May 1986.
42 Cf.: Müller, *Die Säuberung*, 9, 555-556, 562-564 and passim.
43 Letter JI to Boris Shumyatsky, 24 September 1936. Archive Hans Rodenberg, IfGA/ZPA.
44 Report JI for Boris Shumyatsky, 24 September 1936. Archive Hans Rodenberg, IfGA/ZPA.
   Gustav von Wangenheim, "Über die Entstehung des Films 'Kämpfer'"(conclusion), *Junge Welt*, undated (late March, early April 1963).
45 JI writing to Boris Shumyatsky, 24 September 1936.
   JI writing to Hans Rodenberg, 13 August 1936. Both: Archive Hans Rodenberg, IfGA/ZPA.
46 Doc. no. 1803 ref. Anneke van der Feer, undated (1935-1938). RTsChIDNI, 495-244-101.
   Cf. correspondence Anneke van der Feer and JI between 1940 and 1948. BA/FA Coll JI SW 1.
47 Ivens and Destanque, *Aan welke kant*, 130.
48 "Dokument nr. 6" (Interrogation Gustav von Wangenheim on 1 June 1936, from KGB-archives) in: Müller, *Die Säuberung*, 560-562.
49 Schock, *Gustav Regler – Literatur und Politik*, 538-539.
50 Willett, *The Theatre of Erwin Piscator*, 141.
51 Pike, *Deutsche Schriftsteller im sowjetischen Exil*, 204, 256, 440-441, 456, 493.
52 Hans Olink, *De vermoorde droom. Drie Nederlandse idealisten in Sovjet-Rusland*, Amsterdam 1993.
   JI acquaintance with Sebald Rutgers and his wife Bartha is clear from a letter from JI to Anneke van der Feer, undated (1945). BA/FA, Coll JI SW 1.
53 JI in conversation with Marion Michelle (recording), 21 March 1988.
54 Claire Devarrieux, *Entretiens avec Joris Ivens*, Paris 1979, 59.

Notes to Chapter 9

1   JI in conversation with Marion Michelle (recording), 21 March 1988.
2   Joris Ivens and Robert Destanque, *Aan welke kant en in welk heelal. De geschiedenis van een leven*, Amsterdam 1983, 134.
3   Letter JI to Boris Shumyatsky, 24 September 1936. Archive Hans Rodenberg, IfGA/ZPA.
4   Report JI to Boris Shumyatsky, 24 September 1936. Archive Hans Rodenberg, IfGA/ZPA.
5   Joris Ivens, 'Notizen für eine Vorlesung an der Universität New York, 16 April 1936' in: Wolfgang Klaue, Manfred Lichtenstein and Hans Wegner eds., *Joris Ivens*, Berlin (GDR) 1963, 266-269.
    William Alexander, *Film on the Left. American Documentary Film from 1931 to 1942*, Princeton 1981, 122.
6   Alexander, *Film on the Left*, 113.
7   Report JI to Boris Shumyatsky, 24 September 1936.
8   Leo Hurwitz interviewed by Jan Heys, *De Groene Amsterdammer*, 30 November 1983.
    Alexander, *Film on the Left*, 121-123.
    Thomas H. Waugh, *Joris Ivens and the Evolution of the Radical Documentary, 1926-1946*, Ann Arbor 1981, 238.
9   Alexander, *Film on the Left*, 215.
10 Hans Wegner, *Joris Ivens. Dokumentarist der Wahrheit*, Berlin 1965, 60-61.
    Findings of Ivo Blom and Bert Hogenkamp during the restoration of this film at the Netherlands Film Museum.
11 Joris Ivens, 'Notes on Hollywood', *New Theatre*, October 1936.
12 Larry Ceplair and Steven Englund, *The Inquisition in Hollywood. Politics in the Film Community, 1930-1960*, Berkeley 1983, 106.
    John Russell Taylor, *Strangers in Paradise. The Hollywood Émigrés 1933-1950*, London 1983, 111-112.
13 Joris Ivens, 'Notes on Hollywood', *New Theatre*, October 1936.
14 Ivens and Destanque, *Aan welke kant*, 138.
15 Report JI to Boris Shumyatsky, 24 September 1936.
16 Joris Ivens, 'Notes on Hollywood', *New Theatre*, October 1936.
17 Malcolm Cowley, *The Dream of the Golden Mountains. Remembering the 1930's*, Harmondsworth 1981, 303.
    Allen Churchill, *The improper bohemians. Greenwich Village in its heyday*, New York 1959, 235, 240.
18 Vladimir Pozner interviewed by the author, 6 February 1990.
19 Churchill, *The improper bohemians*, 236.
20 JI writing to Hans Rodenberg, 13 August 1936. Archive Hans Rodenberg, IfGA/ZPA.
21 Report JI to Boris Shumyatsky, 24 September 1936.
    Joris Ivens and Helen van Dongen, 'Apres-midi d'un faune', breakdown, first draft, July-August 1936. NFM/HVDA, folder 41.
    The Boston Symphony Orchestra collection does not include such a film.
22 JI interviewed by L.J. Jordaan, *Haagsche Post*, 25 December 1937.

23 Michel Ciment, *Conversations with Losey*, London 1985, 66-67.
24 Ivens and Destanque, *Aan welke kant*, 141.
25 Alexander, *Film on the Left*, 150-151.
    Carlos Baker, *Ernest Hemingway. A Life Story*, Harmondsworth 1972, 455.
26 Report JI to Boris Shumyatsky, 24 September 1936.
27 See Chapter 11.
28 Daniel Aaron, *Writers on the Left. Episodes in American Literary Communism*, New York
    1961, passim.
    Russell Drummond Campbell, *Radical Cinema in the United States, 1930-1942. The
    Work of the Film and Photo League, Nykino and Frontier Films*, Evanston 1978, 217-219.
29 Jeffrey Meyers, *Hemingway. A Biography*, New York 1985, 312.
    William Wright, *Lillian Hellman. The Image, The Woman*, London 1987, 136.
    Waugh, *Joris Ivens and the Evolution of the Radical Documentary*, 242.
    Class Eleven. Department of Fine Arts – Columbia University (typescript memos
    from reading JI), 13 December 1939, 16. BA/FA, Coll JI RuA 1.
30 JI writing to John Fernhout, 12 December 1936. NFA/JFA.
    JI writing to Contemporary Historians, 15 July 1937. EHC.
    JI writing to John Fernhout, 16 December 1936. JIA.

Notes to Chapter 10

1   Autorisation Buñuel, 15 January 1937. JIA.
    John Baxter, *Buñuel*, London 1995, 163.
2   A letter from JI to Hemingway, 28 January 1938, EHC, infers that both men met
    Münzenberg ('M') on their way to or from Spain.
3   JI interviewed by Robert Grelier, *Cahiers de la Cinémathèque*, January 1977, 36.
4   Joris Ivens, 'Brief aan de Groene', *De Groene Amsterdammer*, 25 December 1937, 10.
5   Claud Cockburn, *In Time of Trouble*, London 1956, 258-259.
6   Margaret Hooks, *Tina Modotti. Photographer and Revolutionary*, London 1993, 229.
7   Pierre Broué, *L'assassinat de Trotsky*, Brussels 1980, passim.
    Burnett Bolloten, *The Spanish Revolution. The Left and the Struggle for Power during the
    Civil War*, Chapel Hill 1979, 457, 537.
    John Costello and Oleg Tsarev, *Deadly Illusions*, London 1993, 287-292.
    Hooks, *Tina Modotti*, passim.
    Dorothy Gallagher, *All the Right Enemies. The Life and Murder of Carlo Tresca*, Rutgers
    1988, passim.
8   Gillo Pontecorvo writing to JI, May (1953 or 1954). JI writing to Vittorio Vidali (April-
    May 1969). Vittorio Vidali writing to JI, 22 April 1971. JIA, pl.nos. 46, 68, 435.
9   Joris Ivens, *The Camera and I*, New York 1969, 115.
10 JI interviewed by Robert Grelier, *Cahiers de la Cinémathèque*, January 1977, 41.
    Algemeen Handelsblad, 13 March 1937.
11 Archibald MacLeish writing to Ernest Hemingway, 8 February 1937. EHC.
12 Carlos Baker, *Ernest Hemingway. A Life Story*, Harmondsworth 1972, 451.

13 Joris Ivens and Robert Destanque, *Aan welke kant en in welk heelal. De geschiedenis van een leven*, Amsterdam 1983, 151-154.
14 Jeffrey Meyers, *Hemingway. A Biography*, New York 1985, 303.
  Martha Gellhorn interviewed by the author, 15 July 1995.
15 Virginia Spencer Carr, *Dos Passos: A Life*, New York 1984, 365.
16 Spencer Carr, *Dos Passos*, 366-367.
17 Martha Gellhorn interviewed by the author, 15 July 1995.
18 Jef Last, *De Spaansche tragedie*, Amsterdam 1938, 94.
  John Fernhout interviewed by *Alkmaarse Courant*, June 1937.
19 Salvoconducto para circular por la zona de vanguardia. NFA/JFA.
  Ernest Hemingway, 'The heat and the cold' in: Valentine Cunningham ed., *Spanish Front. Writers on the Spanish Civil War*, Oxford 1986, 206-207.
20 Gustav Regler, *Das Ohr des Malchus, Eine Lebensgeschichte*, Cologne 1958, 388.
  Hemingway, 'The heat and the cold' in: Cunningham, *Spanish Front*, 208.
21 JI interviewed by Robert Grelier, *Cahiers de la Cinémathèque*, January 1977, 37.
  Joris Ivens, 'Brief aan de Groene', *De Groene Amsterdammer*, 25 December 1937, 10.
22 JI interviewed by Bob van Dam, *Wereldkroniek*, 18 July 1959.
23 Ernest Hemingway, 'NANA Dispatch 6', 9 April 1937, *The Hemingway Review*, spring 1988, 25.
24 Regler, *Ohr des Malchus*, 388.
  Martha Gellhorn interviewed by the author, 15 July 1995.
25 JI writing to Ernest Hemingway, 26 April 1937. EHC.
26 Joris Ivens interviewed by William Braasch Watson, quoted in: William Braasch Watson, 'Joris Ivens and the communists: bringing Hemingway into the Spanish civil war', *The Hemingway Review*, autumn 1990, 13.
27 Ernest Hemingway, *For Whom the Bell Tolls*, New York 1940, 230.
28 Spencer Carr, *Dos Passos. A Life*, 370.
  John Dos Passos, *Journeys between Wars*, New York 1938, 385-389.
  New York Times, 25 July 1937.
29 Carlos Baker, ed., *Ernest Hemingway. Selected Letters, 1917-1961*. London 1981, 461.
30 Ernest Hemingway writing to Mrs. Paul Pfeiffer, 2 August 1937 in: *Hemingway. Selected Letters* 461.
  Ernest Hemingway, 'Vorwort' in: Gustav Regler, *Das grosse Beispiel*, Frankfurt/Main 1978, 9 (The earlier English-language publication was *The Great Crusade*, New York 1940).
  Joris Ivens, 'Brief aan de Groene', *De Groene Amsterdammer*, 25 December 1937, 10.
31 Carol Schloss, *In Visible Light. Photography and the American Writer 1840-1940*, Oxford 1987, 170.
32 Meyers, *Hemingway*, 308.
33 JI writing to Ernest Hemingway, 26 April 1937. EHC.
34 JI writing to Ernest Hemingway, 27 January 1938. EHC.
35 JI writing to Ernest Hemingway, 28 January 1938. EHC.
36 Ivens and Destanque, *Aan welke kant*, 153.
37 Spencer Carr, *Dos Passos*, 372.
38 Spencer Carr, *Dos Passos*, 372.
39 *New York Times*, 25 July 1937.

40 Ivens and Destanque, *Aan welke kant*, 159.
41 Helen van Dongen interviewed by Hans Keller, *NRC Handelsblad*, 26 January 1984.
42 Meyers, *Hemingway*, 312.
43 Orson Welles, 'A trip to Quixoteland', *Cahiers du Cinéma*, November 1966, 42.
44 Meyers, *Hemingway*, 313.
45 Baker, *Hemingway*, 477.
    Joris Ivens, Notes Writers Congress, undated (June 1937). BA/FA, Coll JI RuA 1.
46 *Hemingway. Selected Letters*, 460.
47 Ivens and Destanque, *Aan welke kant*, 164.
48 Ernest Hemingway writing to Mrs. Paul Pfeiffer, 2 August 1937 in: *Hemingway. Selected Letters*, 460.
    News Chronicle, 22 July 1937. *World Telegram*, 10 July 1937.
49 Rede nach Vorführung von Spanische Erde Haus v. Fredric March (typescript), undated. (12 July 1937). BA/FA, Coll JI RuA 1.
50 *New York Times*, 25 July 1937.
    Hans Helmut Prinzler, ed., Von Joris Ivens lernen. Ein Protokoll (Report of Ivens's visit to the Deutsche Film und Fernsehakademie), Berlin 1974, 10.
51 Kenneth S. Lynn, *Hemingway*, London 1987, 451.
    Ivens and Destanque, *Aan welke kant*, 166.
52 Anthony Powell, 'A reporter in Los Angeles – Hemingway's Spanish film', in: Cunningham, *Spanish Front*, 208-211.
    New York Times, 25 July 1937.
53 JI writing to John MacManus, 30 August 1937. BA/FA, Coll JI SW 1.
    Joris Ivens, Lecture New York University (manuscript), January 1940. BA/FA, Coll JI RuA 1.
54 Thomas H. Waugh, *Joris Ivens and the Evolution of Radical Documentary, 1926-1946*, Ann Arbor 1981, 356.
55 Censor's report, 17 November 1937 with supplement from 20 November 1937. CCF.
56 The excerpt cut out in the GDR was sent to the Netherlands Film Museum in a can with the misleading label 'Ivens in Poland'. Bert Hogenkamp, 'Oude glorie', *Dagkrant* International Documentary Festival Amsterdam, 12 December 1994, 6.
57 JI writing to Ernest Hemingway, 28 January 1938. EHC.
58 JI writing to Hemingway, 28 January 1938.
59 Nieko van de Pavert, Jef Last tussen de partij en zichzelf, (thesis), Nijmegen 1982, 215, 303.
    Volksdagblad, 24 July 1937.
60 Jef Last, *Mijn vriend André Gide*, Amsterdam 1966, 136-151, 171.
61 JI writing to Martha Gellhorn, undated (April 1939?). BA/FA Coll JI RuA 3.

Notes to Chapter 11

1   Catherine Duncan, 'China – the great compromise' (typescript), undated (ca. 1951). MM.

2 Joris Ivens, Rede nach der Vorführung von 'Spanische Erde' Hause von Fredric
   March (typescript in English). BA/FA, Coll JI RuA 1.
3 M.T. Yuan writing to Helene van Dongen, 26 January 1937. BA/FA, Coll JI SW 1.
4 Joris Ivens and Robert Destanque, *Aan welke kant en in welk heelal. De geschiedenis van
   een leven*, Amsterdam 1983, 176-177.
5 Martha Gellhorn interviewed by the author, 15 July 1995.
6 JI writing to Ernest Hemingway, 28 January 1938. EHC.
7 Vladimir and Ida Pozner interviewed by the author, 6 February 1990.
8 JI writing to Hemingway, 28 January 1938.
9 Babette Gross, *Willi Münzenberg. Eine politische Biographie*, Stuttgart 1967, 197-198.
10 Kees Ivens, Schemering en schemeringstijden III (Diary). UN.
11 Ivens and Destanque, *Aan welke kant*, 198.
   Kees Ivens, Schemering en schemeringstijden III, entries October and November
   1938. UN.
12 JI writing to Hemingway, 28 January 1938.
13 K.C. Li writing to JI c/o David Kung, Central Bank of China, 19 March 1938. JIA, pl.
   no. 247.
14 JI writing to Hemingway, 28 January 1938.
15 JI writing to Ernest Hemingway, 22 or 23 December 1937, EHC. (EHC inaccurately
   dated this letter November 1937, albeit with a question mark.)
16 JI writing to Ernest Hemingway, 30 March 1938, EHC.
17 Carlos Baker, *Ernest Hemingway. A Life Story*, Harmondsworth 1972, 540-542.
   JI interviewed by Bibeb, *Vrij Nederland*, 22 February 1964, 5.
18 Marion Michelle interviewed by the author, 14 February 1990.
   Mary Hemingway writing to Staatliches Filmarchiv der DDR, undated (1963)
   BA/FA, Folders Leipzig 1963.
19 Kees Ivens, Schemering en schemeringstijden III, entry 19 January 1938. UN.
20 JI writing to Miep Balguérie-Guérin, 24 January 1938. JIA/MBG.
   Miep Balguérie-Guérin writing to JI, 28 June 1938. BA/FA, Coll JI SW 1.
21 JI interviewed by Urias Nooteboom, 5 July 1981 (transcription). UN.
   In October 1937 the 'Hawaiian Clipper' disappeared in the Pacific.
22 Joris Ivens, 'Today is Tomorrow. Diary of a Motion Picture Director in China' (typescript), undated (1938). NFM/HVDA, folder 9.
23 W.H. Auden and Christopher Isherwood, *Journey to a War*, London 1973, 43.
24 Babette Gross, *Willi Münzenberg*, 198, 239.
   Janice R. MacKinnon and Stephen R. MacKinnon, *Agnes Smedley. The Life and Times of
   an American Radical*, Berkeley 1988, 117-118.
25 Joris Ivens, Chapter VI – China, in draft for *The Camera and I* (typescript), undated
   (1941- 1944). EF.
26 Barbara W. Tuchman, *Stillwell and the American Experience in China 1911-1945*, New
   York 1971, 234.
27 Ivens, Chapter VI – China, in draft for *The camera and I*.
28 W.H. Auden and Christopher Isherwood, *Journey to a War*, 55.
29 Ivens, Chapter VI – China, in draft for *The Camera and I*.
   Richard Whelan, *Robert Capa*, 134.
30 Joris Ivens, Chapter China and Chapter Ohio in draft for *The Camera and I* undated
   (1941-1944). EF.

31 Cf. Jay Leyda, *Danying. Electric Shadows. An Account of Films and the Film Audience in China*, Cambridge (Mass.) 1972, 111-112, passim.

32 Auden and Isherwood, *Journey to a War*, 43-44.

33 Joris Ivens interviewed by (Hinman?) (transcription), 30 January 1942. BA/FA, Coll JI RuA 1.

34 Anneliese Wang writing to JI, 28 June 1956, BA/FA, Coll JI SW 3.
    Harvey Klehr, John Earl Haynes and Fridrikh Igorevich Firsov, *The Secret World of American Communism*, New Haven 1995, 60-70.

35 Evans Fordyce Carlson, *Twin Stars of China. A Behind-the-scenes Story of China's Valiant Struggle for Existence by a U.S. Marine who Lived and Moved with the People*, New York 1940, 139, 142.

36 Carlson, *Twin Stars*, 147.

37 Robert Capa writing to Peter Koestler, 17 April 1938, quoted in: Richard Whelan, *Robert Capa*, London 1985, 137-138.

38 Ivens, 'Today is Tomorrow. Diary of a Motion Picture Director in China'.

39 *The New York Times*, 28 August 1938.

40 Ivens, Chapter VI – China in draft for *The Camera and I*.

41 Joris Ivens (untitled manuscript), 15 May 1938. JIA.

42 Joris Ivens, Plan for shooting film of 8th Army (manuscript). JIA.

43 Hollington Tong and J.L. Huang writing to JI, 11, 12 and 21 May 1938.
    JI writing to Hollington Tong and J.L. Huang, 11 May 1938. JIA.

44 Joris Ivens, Notes on Borinage, in draft for *The Camera and I* (typescript) undated. (1941-1944). EF.

45 *New York Times*, 28 August 1938.

46 A. Zalzman, *Joris Ivens*, Paris 1963, 66-67.
    JI writing to Herman Shumlin, undated (Winter 1938-1939). JIA.

47 *New York Times*, 28 August 1938.

48 Joris Ivens, 'How I filmed The 400 Million' in: *Joris Ivens and China*, 29.
    William Alexander, *Film on the Left. American Documentary Film from 1931 to 1942*, Princeton 1981, 190.

49 JI writing to Shumlin, undated (winter 1938-1939).

50 Alexander, *Film on the Left*, 194.

51 *Het Volk*, 15 April 1939. *Nieuwe Rotterdamsche Courant*, 18 April 1939. *Pour Vous*, 24 May 1939.

52 Kees Ivens, Schemering en schemeringstijden III, entry April 1939. UN.

53 Annekavapiet (Anneke van der Feer, Eva Besnyö, Piet Huisken) writing to JI, 26 April 1940. BA/FA, Coll JI SW.
    Filmex N.V. writing to Centrale commissie voor de filmkeuring, 10 November 1939. Censor's report, 21 September 1945. Both: CCF.

Notes to Chapter 12

1   Erik van Ree, *Bloedbroeders. Stalin, Hitler en het pact*, Amsterdam 1989, 75.

2 Margarete Buber-Neumann, *Gevangene van Stalin en Hitler. Een vrouw tussen rode en bruine terreur*, Haarlem 1979.
   Harald Wessel, *Münzenbergs Ende. Eind deutscher Kommunist im Widerstand gegen Hitler und Stalin. Die Jahre 1933 bis 1940*, Berlin 1991, 217.
3 Nancy Lynn Schwartz, *The Hollywood Writers' Wars*, New York 1982, 146.
4 Joris Ivens and Robert Destanque, *Aan welke kant en in welk heelal. De geschiedenis van een leven*, Amsterdam 1983, 199.
5 Ernest Hemingway, Preface in: Gustav Regler, *Das große Beispiel*, Frankfurt/Main 1978, 10.
   JI writing to Ernest Hemingway, 21 February 1940. BA/FA, Coll JI SW 1.
6 David Caute, *The Fellow-Travellers. A Postscript to the Enlightenment*. London 1972, 195.
   Schwartz, *Hollywood Writers' Wars*, 147.
7 Albrecht Betz, *Hanns Eisler. Musik einer Zeit, die sich eben bildet*, Munich 1976, 152.
8 Joris Ivens, Chapter Ohio, in draft for *The Camera and I*, undated (1941-1944). EF.
   Class eleven. Department of Fine Arts – Columbia University (Notes from a lecture by Joris Ivens), 13 December 1939. BA/FA, Coll JI RuA 1.
9 Thomas H. Waugh, *Joris Ivens and the Evolution of the Radical Documentary, 1926-1946*, Ann Arbor 1981, 441.
   Larry Ceplair and Steven Englund, *The Inquisition in Hollywood. Politics in the Film Community, 1930-1960*, Berkeley 1983, 116.
   Het Volk, 15 April 1939.
10 Robert L. Snyder, *Pare Lorentz and the Documentary Film*, Norman 1968, 121-123.
   A detailed synopsis in Ivens's handwriting is dated 'June 1939 Hollywood'. EF.
11 Helene van Dongen writing to JI, 27 June 1940. EF.
12 Pare Lorentz interviewed by Snyder, 28 July 1961, quoted in Snyder, *Pare Lorentz*, 125-126.
   Floyd Crosby interviewed by Snyder, February 1962, quoted in ibidem, 126.
13 Joris Ivens, 'Collaboration in documentary', *Films*, spring 1940, 32.
14 Snyder, *Pare Lorentz*, 125.
15 Pare Lorentz writing to JI, quoted in Snyder, *Pare Lorentz*, 127.
16 Joris Ivens, 'Collaboration in Documentary', *Films*, spring 1940, 36.
17 Class eleven. Department of fine arts – Columbia University, 13 December 1939.
18 Ivens, *Autobiografie van een filmer*, 144-145.
19 'Bip' Parkinson writing to JI, undated (late 1940). EF.
20 Pare Lorentz, *FDR's Moviemaker, Memoirs and Scripts*, Reno 1992, 152.
21 JI writing to his parents, 22 April 1940. AI.
22 REA picture. Cost summary: April 11, 1940.
   JI writing to Helene van Dongen, undated (20-27 May 1940). Both: EF.
23 Richard Meran Barsam, *Non Fiction Film, a Critical History*, New York 1973, 96.
   Snyder, *Pare Lorentz*, 188.
24 Draft scenarios in German among Ivens's papers indicate that Herzfelde was involved in writing them. Cf. various documents undated (spring 1940). EF.
25 Outline of blocks of ideas for Frontier Film (typescript), 22 March 1940. EF.
   JI writing to Hemingway, 21 February 1940.
   JI interviewed by Hans Wegner (transcription of recording, Tape 6) undated BA/FA, Coll JI RuA 3.

26 Scenario quoted in Hans Wegner, *Joris Ivens, Dokumentarist der Wahrheit*, Berlin (GDR) 1965, 99.

27 William Alexander, *Film on the Left. American Documentary Film from 1931 to 1942*, Princeton 1981, 264.

28 Alexander, *Film on the Left*, 265-266.
Waugh, *Joris Ivens and the Evolution of the Radical Documentary*, 477.

29 Ivens and Destanque, *Aan welke kant*, 212.

30 JI interviewed by Gordon Hitchens on 20 November 1968, *Filmculture*, spring 1972, 205.
Richard Barsam, *The Vision of Robert Flaherty. The Artist as Myth and Filmmaker*, Bloomington 1988, 84.

31 Andries Deinum in telephone conversation with the author, 31 October 1994.

32 Andries Deinum writing to JI, 10 April 1956. BA/FA, Coll JI SW 1.

33 Schwarz, *The Hollywood Writers' Wars*, 162.

34 JI writing to Archibald MacLeish, 8 May 1940, return MacLeish to Ivens, undated
Archibald MacLeish writing to JI, 16 January 1941. Both: BA/FA, Coll JI SW 1.

35 Kees and Dora Ivens writing to JI, 8 December 1940. Other correspondence from Ivens's parents dates from: 30 May, 31 May, 6 June, 18 June, 7 July, 25 July, 6 September, 18 September, 24 October 1940.
Kees and Dora Ivens writing to Helene van Dongen, 18 September and 15 October 1940. All: BA/FA, Coll JI SW 1.

36 JI writing to his parents, 5 July 1941. AI.

37 Script oil for alladinns lamp. EF.

38 Draft for *The Camera and I*, undated (1941-1944). EF.
Claire Devarrieux, *Entretiens avec Joris Ivens*, Paris 1979, 45.

39 JI writing to the responsible Bolivian minister 19 January 1941, printed in: Joris Ivens, *The Camera and I*, New York 1969, 236.
Notes on Joris Ivens. FBI.
Donald Ogden Stewart, Jimmy Jones – Good neighbour (typescript), undated (1940-1941). BA/FA, Coll JI RuA 1.

40 Donald Ogden Stewart, *By a Stroke of Luck! An Autobiography*, New York 1975, 257.

Notes to Chapter 13

1 Annabeth Ivens interviewed by the author, 26 February 1992.
Kees Ivens writing to JI, 4 May 1940. BA/FA, Coll JI SW 1.
De Gelderlander, 29 August 1941.

2 JI writing to his parents, 5 July 1941. AI.

3 JI writing to Dora Ivens, 5 October 1941. AI.

4 Dora Ivens writing to JI, 7 November 1941. BA/FA, Coll JI SW 1.

5 Joris Ivens and Robert Destanque, *Aan welke kant en in welk heelal. De geschiedenis van een leven*, Amsterdam 1983, 212.
Joris Ivens, Notes for Australian and Indonesian chapter, (manuscript) 2 December 1946. MM.

6 Note JI, undated (September 1944). EF.

7 Joris Ivens. Memorial article for Robert Flaherty (typescript), August 1964. JIA, pl. no. 143.

8 Joris Ivens, Notes for meeting 29 October 1941.
   JI writing to Lewis Milestone, 30 October 1941. Both: EF.

9 Joris Ivens, Notes for diary (manuscript), undated (mid-November 1941). EF.

10 Joris Ivens, Notizen zur Vorlesung über die Entwicklung des Dokumentarfilms in Russland vor und während des Krieges, 22 March 1943, University of Southern California (German translation of English original). BA/FA, folders Leipzig 1963.

11 Edward C.Carter (National Committee of Russian War Relief) writing to David R. Faries (Hollywood Committee of Russian War Relief), 26 October 1941. EF.

12 Joris Ivens, Notes for diary (manuscript), undated (November 1941).
   Joris Ivens, Notes for meeting, 29 October 1941. Both: EF.

13 Artkino writing to JI, 28 November 1941. EF.

14 Nick Napoli writing to JI, 28 November 1941. JI writing to Lewis Milestone, 21 November 1941.
   JI writing to Edward C. Carter, 22 November 1941. All: EF.

15 Arthur L. Mayer (Rialto Theatre) writing to Harry Rathner, 17 February 1942. BA/FA, Coll JI SW 1.

16 Joris Ivens. Memorandum to Mr. Archibald MacLeish, 31 December 1941. BA/FA, Coll JI SW 1.
   Untitled scenario (Letter to the President from Bill Grant, railroad engineer), undated (1941-1942). EF.

17 New York File 100-49157, Report 31 July 1943. FBI.

18 Without date or place. FBI.

19 U.S. Department of Justice, Federal Bureau of Investigation, FOIA-Section writing to the author, 14 May 1990.

20 JI writing to Frank Judson, 27 December 1941. BA/FA, Coll JI SW 1.

21 JI writing to Frank Judson, 27 December 1941. Frank Judson writing to JI, 14 January 1942. Both: BA/FA, Coll JI SW 1.
   Bill Hagens, 'The Vital Post', revised script, 29 March 1942. EF.

22 JI (probably writing to National Film Board), 31 July 1942. EF.

23 Joris Ivens, Note (handwritten), undated EF.
   Hans Wegner, *Joris Ivens, Dokumentarist der Wahrheit*, Berlin (GDR) 1965, 106.

24 Joris Ivens, Notes from Canada diary, undated (second half of June 1942). EF.
   JI (probably writing to the National Film Board), 31 July 1942. EF.

25 Joris Ivens, Notizen zur Abschlussvorlesung über die Dokumentarfilmproduktion in den USA, England, der Sowjetunion und Kanada, 26 March 1943, University of Southern California
   (German translation of English original). BA/FA, Folders Leipzig 1963.

26 Ivens, Notizen zur Abschlussvorlesung, 26 March 1943.

27 Peter Morris, ed., *The National Film Board of Canada: The War Years. A Collection of Contemporary Articles and a Selected Index of Productions*, Ottawa 1965, 27.

28 Notes on Joris Ivens, quoted in: Los Angeles file no. 100-18730, Report 24 May 1943. FBI.
   Joris Ivens, RE: Data concerning application for Re-entry Permit. MM.

29 Andries Deinum in telephone conversations with the author, 31 October and 16 November 1994.
    Jean Renoir, *Mein Leben und meine Filme*, Munich 1980, 148.
30 Joris Ivens, Notes (manuscript), undated (lecture at the University of Southern California, 18 March 1943). BA/FA Coll JI RuA 1.
31 Joseph McBride, *Frank Capra. The Catastrophe of Success*, New York 1992, 481.
32 Joris Ivens, 'Dokumentarfilm und Bewußtsein. Aufzeichnungen für ein Dokumentarfilmseminar am 28 Oktober 1943' in: Wolfgang Klaue, Manfred Lichtenstein and Hans Wegner eds., *Joris Ivens*, Berlin (GDR) 1963, 300.
33 Hans Burger writing to Helen van Dongen and Joris Ivens, 10 July 1943. BA/FA, Coll JI SW 1.
34 Los Angeles File 100-18730, Report 11 December 1944. FBI.
35 McBride, *Frank Capra*, 480
36 JI interviewed by Gordon Hitchens, 20 November 1968, *Filmculture*, spring 1972, 209-210.
37 Marion Michelle, 'Aufzeichnungen über Ivens' aufenthalt in den USA' in: Klaue, Lichtenstein and Wegner, *Joris Ivens*, 217.
38 Joris Ivens and Helen van Dongen, Synopsis *Know your enemy: Japan* in: Joris Ivens, *The Camera and I*, New York 1969, 239-240.
    Production # 19 *Know your enemy: Japan*, 23 November 1943. JIA, pl. no. 636.
39 State Department Memorandum, May 1943 quoted in Dr. L. de Jong, *Het Koninkrijk der Nederlanden in de Tweede Wereldoorlog* 11b, II first half, The Hague 1985, 118.
40 De Jong, *Het Koninkrijk der Nederlanden*, 11b, II first half, 117.
41 McBride, *Frank Capra*, 499.
42 Supplement in the *Nederlands Filmmuseum Cinematheek Journaal 23*.
43 Nancy Lynn Schwartz, *The Hollywood Writers' Wars*, New York 1982, 182-184.
    Larry Ceplair and Steven Englund, *The Hollywood Inquisition. Politics in the Film Community, 1930-1960*, 180.
44 Schwartz, *Hollywood Writers' Wars*, 192-194.
    Joris Ivens, Notes for four lectures Writers School Hollywood (manuscript), 11 June, 18 June, 25 June, 2 July 1943. BA/FA, Coll JI RuA 1.
45 Brian Neve, *Film and Politics in America. A Social Tradition*, London 1992, 74.
46 Hans Wegner, *Joris Ivens, Dokumentarist der Wahrheit*, Berlin (GDR) 1965, 109.
47 JI interviewed by Marcel Martin, *Cinema 69*, February 1969.
48 Ceplair and Englund, *The Hollywood Inquisition*, 186-189.
    Schwartz, *Hollywood Writers' Wars*, 192-194, 198-202.

Notes to Chapter 14

1   Standard Certificate of Marriage, Los Angeles, 1 January 1944. State of California, Department of Health Services, Sacramento.
    Andries Deinum in telephone conversation with the author, 31 October 1994.
2   Helen van Dongen interviewed by Ageeth Scherphuis, *Vrij Nederland*, 28 September 1985, 16.

3 Copy Inschrijvingsformulier Joris Ivens, undated (second half 1950s). BA/FA, Coll JI SW 3.
4 The exact date is given in Marion Michelle's diary, 3 January 1945 and 3 January 1946. MM.
5 Marion Michelle interviewed by the author, 14 February 1990.
6 Frenny de Graaff interviewed by the author, 28 May 1990.
7 Correspondence left anonymous at the request of the owner.
8 Marion Michelle interviewed by the author, 20 January 1993.
   Germaine Krull writing to JI, 12 November 1945. Max Horkheimer Archiv, Frankfurt/Main.
   Passport Germaine Krull, issued by the Dutch embassy in Bangkok, 1961. Fotografische Sammlung, Folkwang Museum, Essen.
   JI writing to Dora Ivens, 22 August 1946. AI.
9 Michelle interviewed by the author, 14 February 1990.
10 Michelle, Diary, 26 January 1945. MM.
11 Marion Michelle interviewed by the author, 14 February 1990.
   Paul Strand writing to Xavier Icaza, 26 March 1941. MM.
12 Andries Deinum in telephone conversations with the author, 31 October and 16 November 1994.
   Harvey Klehr, John Earl Haynes and Fridrikh Igorevich Firsov, *The Secret World of American Communism*, New Haven 1995, 277, 259-286.
   Alfons Söllner, ed, *Zur Archäologie der Demokratie in Deutschland. Analysen politischer Emigranten im amerikanischen Geheimdienst, Band 1: 1943-1945*, Frankfurt/Main 1982, 7-37.
13 Michelle interviewed by the author, 14 February 1990.
14 Minutes of the craft problems of the realistic film seminar meeting, 11 January 1944. BA/FA, Coll JI SW 2.
15 *Los Angeles Daily News*, undated (April 1944).
   Joris Ivens, Notes on Australian and Indonesian chapter. MM.
   Anonymous text, without date or place. BA/FA, Folders Leipzig 1963.
16 Neve, *Film and Politics in America*, 79.
17 *Los Angeles Daily News*, undated (April 1944).
18 Salka Viertel, *Das unbelehrbare Herz. Ein Leben in der Welt des Theaters, der Literatur und des Films*, Hamburg 1970, 403-404.
19 Viertel, *Das unbelehrbare Herz*, 404.
   · Joris Ivens interviewed by Hans Wegner (transcription of tape recording, Tape 6), undated BA/FA, Coll JI RuA 3.
20 JI writing to Lester Cowan, 19 April 1944. EF.
21 John Grierson writing to JI, 22 May 1944. EF.
22 JI writing to Dora Ivens, 22 August 1946. AI.
   Joris Ivens, Draft telegrams, undated (May 1944). EF.
23 Statement from Joris Ivens regarding Garbo film (typescript), 14 July 1944.
   Statement from Vladimir Posener regarding Garbo film (typescript), 14 July 1944. Both: EF.
   Viertel, *Das unbelehrbare Herz*, 405.
24 Marion Michelle interviewed by the author, 29 November 1993.
   Diary Marion Michelle, 14 January 1945. MM.

Larry Ceplair and Steven Englund, *The Inquisition in Hollywood. Politics in the Film Community, 1930-1960*, Berkeley 1983, 95-96.

25 Statement from Vladimir Posener regarding Garbo film, 14 July 1944. Statement from Joris Ivens regarding Garbo film, 14 July 1944. EF.

26 *Hollywood Week*, undated (July 1944).
   Viertel, *Das unbelehrbare Herz*, 405.

27 JI writing to Lester Cowan, 3 and 4 July 1944. EF.

28 Joris Ivens and Robert Destanque, *Aan welke kant en in welk heelal. De geschiedenis van een leven*, Amsterdam 1983, 216.
   Viertel, *Das unbelehrbare Herz*, 405.

29 Vladimir Pozner and JI writing to Greta Garbo, undated (July 1944). EF.

30 Eric van 't Groenewout, Indonesia Calling. Het verhaal van de schepen die niet uitvoeren (thesis), without date or place. (Leiden 1988), 34-35, 73.

31 Van der Plas writing to JI, 28 September 1944. Dossier 823.39, Joris Ivens 1955-1964. BZ.

32 JI writing to Office of War Information, 18 October 1944. JI in radio interview (transcription) 8 January 1945. Both: BA/FA, Coll JI RuA 2.
   Hollywood Reporter, 19 October 1944.
   Motion Picture Herald, 28 October 1944.
   San Francisco Chronicle, 1 January 1945.
   People's World, 5 January 1945.

33 JI writing to Marion Michelle, undated (November 1944). MM.
   Joris Ivens writing to Slotemaker de Bruine, 31 October 1944. Arsip National Republik Indonesia, Jakarta.

34 Joris Ivens, Data concerning application of Re-entry Permit. Undated. (March 1945). MM.

35 R. Hood, SAC Los Angeles to Director, 13 May 1944, Los Angeles File 100-18730. Stamped: Report made at Los Angeles, 24 February 1945, Los Angeles File 100-18730. Both: FBI.

36 Cf. Serial Removal Charge National Security Surveillance File, Subject Joris Ivens, 22 September 1976.
   Hoover writing to SAC Los Angeles, undated (December 1944).
   FBI-teletype Hood to Director, undated (late December 1944).
   All: FBI.

37 Office Memorandum 40-6917, M. Ladd writing to The Director, 15 March 1945. FBI.

38 Joris Ivens, Data concerning application of re-entry permit.

39 The Director writing to SAC, Miami, 16 May 1962.
   Office memorandum 40-69173, M. Ladd writing to The Director, 15 March 1945.
   Letter (author and addressee blacked out), 19 November 1946. All: FBI.
   In an index about part of the FBI Ivens dossier dd. 24 February 1945 the Communist party in California is mentioned 24 times. All the pages concerned are absent from the released dossier.

40 Telegram from: cg usafe sgd macarthur to: australia base section, cite U 21592. Dossier Joris Ivens no. 2035832. BVD.

41 Wolfgang Kießling, *Brücken nach Mexiko. Traditionen einer Freundschaft*, Berlin (GDR) 1989, 302.

42 Office memorandum, SAC San Francisco writing to The Director, 5 March 1945. FBI.

43 James K.Lyon, *Bertolt Brecht in America*, London 1982, 260-261, 265-279.
44 Vladimir and Ida Pozner interviewed by the author, 6 February 1990.
45 Meetings of Brecht and Eisler with Kheifetz were documented by the FBI. Cf: John Fuegi, *The Life and Lies of Bertolt Brecht*, London 1994, 441, 448.
    Eric Bentley, ed., *Thirty Years of Treason. Excerpts from Hearings before the House Committee on Un-American Actvities, 1938-1968*, New York 1971, 56, 214, 235, 29, 241-242, 775.
    Lyon, *Bertolt Brecht in America*, 298, 331.
46 Pavel Soedoplatov et al., *Special Tasks. The Memoirs of an Unwanted Witness – a Soviet Spymaster*, London 1994, 57, 84-85, 174-175, 185, 188.
47 Bentley, *Thirty Years of Treason*, 242-244.
48 Vladimir Pozner, *Se souvient...*, Paris 1989, 125, 130-131.
49 Van Boetzelaar writing to Charles van der Plas, 4 June 1945. Archief Van Mook 2 21 123, ARA-II.
50 Los Angeles File 100-18730, Report, 24 February 1945. FBI.
51 Marion Michelle, Diary, 20 and 21 January, 16 February 1945. MM.
52 Vladimir and Ida Pozner interviewed by the author, 6 February 1990.
53 Los Angeles File 100-18730, Report 20 April 1945. FBI.
54 John Edgar Hoover writing to SAC Los Angeles, 9 December 1944.
    San Francisco File 100-24793, Report 18 April 1945. Both: FBI.
55 Los Angeles File 100-18730, Report 20 April 1945. FBI.
    Marion Michelle, Diary, 12 March 1945. MM.

Notes to Chapter 15

1 Memo Luitenant-Generaal L.H. van Oyen, 4 April 1945. Joris Ivens Dossier no. 2035832, BVD.
    Memo, San Francisco 14 May 1945, Algemene Secretarie Batavia I-XXIII-67-1, ARA-II.
    Joris Ivens, Notes for Australian and Indonesian chapter (manuscript), 2 December 1946. MM.
2 Joris Ivens, Time schedule for film project, undated (early March 1945).
    JI writing to Marion Michelle, 9 April 1945. Both: MM.
    Eric van 't Groenewout, Indonesia Calling. Het verhaal van schepen die niet uitvoeren (thesis), without date or place (Leiden 1988), 61.
3 C. van der Plas writing to H. van Mook, 18 April 1943. Archief Algemene Secretarie Batavia I-XXIII-67-1, ARA-II.
4 Telegram: cg usaffe sgd macarthur to: cg australia base section. cite u 21592, 20 April 1945.
    Secret persoonlijk verbaal Onderwerp security Joris Ivens No. EP 3/13537/6 (Spoor writing to army commander Van Oyen), 24 April 1945.
    Telegram cg absec ap nine two three to: cg usaffe apo five zero one, 25 April 1945.
    Telegram cg usaffe sgd macarthur to: cg absec u 22699, 27 April 1945.
    All: Dossier Joris Ivens no. 2035832, BVD.

5 Memo, San Francisco 14 May 1945. Archief Algemene Secretarie Batavia I-XXIII-67-1, ARA-II.
6 Joseph R. Starobin, *American Communism in Crisis, 1943-1957*, Berkeley 1972, 55.
   Fernando Claudin, *The Communist Movement. From Comintern to Cominform*, New York 1975, 395-396, 406-407 and passim.
   Marion Michelle interviewed by Bert Hogenkamp (recording), 26 January 1986.
7 JI writing to H. van Mook, 17 July 1945. MM.
8 S.H. Spoor writing to Military Commander in the East, 2 July 1945. Dossier Joris Ivens no. 2035832, BVD.
9 JI writing to Helen van Dongen, 30 April, 2 May, 14 June 1945. Helen van Dongen writing to JI, 5 May 1945. All: MM.
10 Helen van Dongen writing to JI, 4 April 1946. BA/FA, Coll JI SW 1.
11 *New York Times*, 1 December 1972.
   Louis Fischer, *Men and Politics. An Autobiography*, New York 1941, 300.
12 Helen van Dongen, 'Ik kwam Joris Ivens tegen', *Skoop*, November 1978.
   Helen van Dongen interviewed by Hans van Dongen (recording), summer 1984.
   Helen van Dongen interviewed by Ageeth Scherphuis, *Vrij Nederland*, 28 September 1985, 16.
13 Marion Michelle, Diary, 29 March, 6 July and 1 August 1946. MM.
14 Marion Michelle, Diary, 31 August 1945. MM.
15 Anonymous text without date or place. BA/FA, folders Leipzig 1963.
   Catherine Duncan and Marion Michelle interviewed by Bert Hogenkamp (recording), 26 January 1986.
16 Catherine Duncan interviewed by Bert Hogenkamp, 26 January 1986.
17 Anonymous text without date or place. BA/FA, Folders Leipzig 1963.
   JI writing to Dora Ivens, 22 August 1946. AI.
18 C.J. Warners writing to JI, 24 September 1945. MM.
19 JI writing to C. Van der Plas, 23 August 1945.
   Marion Michelle, Diary, 25 September 1945. Both: MM.
20 L. de Jong, *Het Koninkrijk der Nederlanden* 11c, 595, 631-632.
21 Marion Michelle, Diary, 23 September to 18 October 1946. MM.
22 JI writing to Helen van Dongen, 12 October 1945. MM.
23 Joris Ivens, Notes for Australian and Indonesian chapter. MM.
   Rupert Lockwood, *Black Armada*, Sydney 1975, 138.
24 Ivens, Notes for Australian and Indonesian chapter.
   Joris Ivens, Production schedule, Sydney, 28 October 1945.
   Marion Michelle, Diary, 24, 27 and 30 October 1945. All: MM.
25 Lockwood, *Black Armada*, 173-174.
26 Ivens, Notes on Australian and Indonesian chapter.
   Marion Michelle, Diary, 5, 7, 9, 11 and 16 November 1945. MM.
27 Ivens, Notes on Australian and Indonesian chapter.
28 G. van Rijn writing to Government Information Service, Batavia, 24 November 1945.
   Supplement: Manderson Report, 23 November 1945. T 16 Joris Ivens C-G Sydney, BZ.
29 JI writing to Helen van Dongen, undated (November-December 1945). BA/FA, Coll JI SW 2.
   JI interviewed by Bert Hogenkamp (recording), 22 March 1986.

30 JI writing to Dutch East Indies government, Batavia, undated (21 November 1945). MM.

31 JI writing to Charles van der Plas, 21 November 1945. Archief Van Mook, no. 2 21 123, ARA-II.

32 Marion Michelle, Diary, 21 November 1945. MM.

33 Andries Deinum interviewed by the author, 31 October 1994.

34 JI writing to Bondan, 21 January 1947. MM.

35 Slotemaker de Bruine writing to Van der Plas, 11 June 1945. NIB New York Box 15, no. 176, BZ.

Bert Hogenkamp, 'Een artiest tussen de ambtenaren. John Fernhout filmt de bevrijding van Nederland in dienst van de RVD, 1944-1945', *GBG-Nieuws*, spring 1994, 4-13.

36 JI writing to (Helen van Dongen?), undated (spring-summer 1946). BA/FA, Coll JI RuA 2.

37 Eva Besnyö interviewed by the author, 19 September 1990.

38 History Today Inc. writing to John Ferno, 11 January 1938. NFA/JFA.

39 Eva Besnyö interviewed by the author, 19 September 1990.

40 JI writing to Van der Plas, 12 Februari 1946. MM.

41 Press release A. Schuurman. Archief Consulaat-Generaal Sydney T 16 Joris Ivens. BZ.

42 Manderson rapport, 23 November 1945.

O.W.P. Mohr writing to A.Z., 21 January 1948. 823.39, Joris Ivens, 1945-1952, inv.no. 29, box 4. BZ.

Mr. Kroon (head Dutch information in Australia) writing to Ministry of Foreign Affairs, 9 February 1948. Dossier Joris Ivens P3/49, MVJ.

Aantekening over het ontstaan van de film 'Indonesia calling' van Joris Ivens (part of A.Z. No 9639), undated, Dossier Joris Ivens P3/49, MVJ.

Ivens did not use the Kinamo with which he filmed *De brug* in Sydney, this camera was in New York. George L. George writing to JI, 1 December 1950. BA/FA, Coll JI SW.

43 Memorandum J.B.D. Pennink, 1 December 1945.

J.B.D. Pennink writing to the Envoy Extraordinary and Authorized Minister in Melbourne, 26 November 1945 and 13 December 1945.

W.H. Sturrock writing to J.B.D. Pennink, 8 December 1945.

All: Archief Consulaat-Generaal Sydney T 16 Joris Ivens, BZ.

44 JI writing to Helen van Dongen, 7 December 1945.

W.F. Gonggrijp writing to JI, 10 December 1945.

Ivens, Notes on Australian and Indonesian chapter.

JI writing to Gonggrijp, 2 January 1946. All: MM.

45 Marion Michelle, Diary 10 and 11 January 1946. MM.

46 JI writing to Tom Brandon, 15 September 1946. MM.

47 Lockwood. *Black Armada*, 161-163.

48 Ivens, Notes for Australian and Indonesian chapter.

49 Marion Michelle, Diary, 8 January, 31 January, 1 and 2 February 1946. MM.

50 JI writing to Dora Ivens, 22 August 1946. AI.

51 Marion Michelle interviewed by the author, 29 November 1993.

52 Marion Michelle, Diary, 8 August 1946. MM.

Michelle interviewed by the author, 29 November 1993.

53 JI writing to Hans Ivens, 3 February 1947. AI.
54 JI writing to Brandon, 15 September 1946.
   JI writing to Eddy Allison, 15 September (1946). Both: JIA.
55 JI writing to Helen van Dongen, 29 July 1945. MM.
56 Dora Ivens writing to JI, 23 March 1946. Dora Ivens writing to Helen van Dongen, 21 March, 1 July and 9 September 1946. Helen van Dongen writing to JI, 4 April 1946. All: BA/FA, Coll JI SW 1.
57 JI writing to Dora Ivens, 22 August 1946. AI.
58 Dora Ivens writing to JI, 15 September 1946. BA/FA, Coll JI SW 1.
59 Jitske van de Berg writing to JI, 6 October 1946. BA/FA, Coll JI SW 1.
60 *The Sunday Times*, 18 August 1946. *Examinor*, 7 August 1946.
61 JI writing to Bondan, undated (March 1946) and 12 January 1947.
   Marion Michelle, Diary, 1 November 1946. All: MM.
62 Joris Ivens, Book, 'Otranto' (manuscript, notes for autobiography), undated (January 1947).
   JI writing to Bondan, 12 January 1947. Both MM.
63 Joris Ivens, Book, 'Otranto'.
   JI writing to Bondan, 12 January 1947.
64 JI writing to Bondan, 12 and 21 January 1947. MM.

Notes to Chapter 16

1 *De Waarheid*, 25 February 1947.
   Elseviers Weekblad, 1 March 1947.
2 Joris Ivens and Robert Destanque, *Aan welke kant en in welk heelal. De geschiedenis van een leven*, Amsterdam 1983, 237.
3 Marion Michelle interviewed by the author, 20 January and 29 November 1993.
   Thea Nooteboom-Ivens interviewed by the author, 17 May 1991.
4 Anneke van der Feer writing to JI, 25 September 1946. BA/FA, Coll JI SW I.
5 JI writing to Hans Ivens, 3 February 1947. AI.
6 JI writing to Eddy Allison, 7 February 1947. JIA.
   JI writing to Hans Ivens, 3 February 1947. AI.
7 Elizabeth Sussex, *The Rise and Fall of British Documentary. The Story of the Film Movement founded by John Grierson*, Berkeley 1975, 175-176.
8 *De Waarheid*, 3 and 7 March 1947.
   Het Vrije Volk, 3 March 1947.
9 *Het Vrije Volk*, 3 March 1947.
   Marion Michelle interviewed by the author, 13 December 1989 and 20 January 1993.
10 Theun de Vries interviewed by the author, 8 September 1993.
11 *De Waarheid*, 22 and 25 February 1947.
   Algemeen Handelsblad, 25 February 1947.
   Het Parool, 22 February 1947.
   Het Vrije Volk, 22 and 25 February and 3 March 1947.
12 JI writing to Dora Ivens, 3 August 1947. AI.

13 Ministry of Foreign Affairs writing to the Ministry of Justice, 9936 BZ, 5 February 1947. Dossier Joris Ivens no. P3/49, MVJ.

14 JI writing to Dora Ivens, 4 April 1947. AI.

15 JI writing to Dora Ivens, 5 January 1948. AI.

16 JI writing to Eddy Allison, 2 June 1947. JIA.

17 Joseph Zsuffa, *Béla Balázs. The Man and the Artist*, Berkeley 1987, 354, 502.

18 Lubomir Linhart, 'Seit eh und jeh mit Joris Ivens' in: Wolfgang Klaue, Manfred Lichtenstein and Hans Wegner eds., *Joris Ivens*, Berlin (GDR) 1963, 59-67.

19 Ivens and Destanque, *Aan welke kant*, 242.

20 'De geboorte van een film', *Politiek en Cultuur*, 1948, 64-65.
   Politika (Belgrade), 27 November 1947.

21 Joris Ivens, Notes (manuscript), 31 October 1947. JIA, pl. no. 633.

22 Marion Michelle interviewed by the author, 14 February 1990.

23 JI writing to Dora Ivens, 12 December 1947. AI.
   Anneke van der Feer writing to JI, 25 September 1946 and undated (early 1948?). BA/FA, Coll JI, resp. SW 1 and SW 4.

24 Marion Michelle writing to Elmar Klos, 18 January 1948. JIA, pl. no. 499.

25 Hans Magnus Enzensberger, ed., *Europa in Trümmern. Augenzeugenberichte aus den Jahren 1944-1948*, Frankfurt/Main1990, 239-250, 281-294.

26 *De Waarheid*, 16 July 1948.

27 Thea Nooteboom-Ivens writing to JI, 12 and 18 May 1948.
   JI writing to Thea Nooteboom-Ivens, 25 May 1948. Thea Nooteboom-Ivens writing to JI, 28 May 1948.
   All: BA/FA, Coll JI SW 1.

28 Ivens and Destanque, *Aan welke kant*, 246.

29 Claire Sterling, *The Mazaryk Case. The Murder of Democracy in Czechoslovakia*, Boston 1982, 250.

30 Michelle interviewed by the author, 14 February 1990.

31 JI writing to Dora Ivens, 10 March 1948 and 3 August 1947. AI.

32 JI writing to Marion Michelle, undated (10 June 1949). MM.

33 Michelle interviewed by the author, 14 February 1990.
   Catherine Duncan interviewed by the author, 5 February 1990.

34 'Gegevens inz. Joris Ivens', Majoor Kies, NEFIS, writing to Ministry of Justice, undated, Dossier Joris Ivens no. P3/49, MVJ.

35 Ministry of Justice writing to Ministry of Foreign Affairs, 1 May 1948.
   Ministry of Foreign Affairs writing to Ministry of Overseas Territories, 28 September 1948. Both: Dossier Joris Ivens no. P3/49, MVJ.

36 J. Schaap, Dutch consul Bern, writing to Management Information Abroad, 8 July 1948. 823.39, Joris Ivens, 1945-1952, inv. no. 29, box 4. BZ.
   De waarheid, 22 July 1948.

37 The consul writing to Minister of Foreign Affairs, no. T.11-6336/717, 29 October 1948. 823.39, Joris Ivens, 1945-1952, inv. no. 29, box 4. BZ.

38 M.J. Rosenberg Polak writing to Ministry of Foreign Affairs, 22 November 1948.
   Ministry of Foreign Affairs writing to A. Merens, Consul in Prague, 21 December 1948. Both: Dossier Joris Ivens no. P3/49, MVJ.
   JI writing to Hans Ivens, 11 May 1950. AI.

39 Directorate Chief, Ministry of Foreign Affairs writing to A. Merens, Consul in
    Prague, 12 November 1948. 823.39, Joris Ivens, 1945-1952, inv. no. 29, box 4. BZ.
    Dossier Joris Ivens no. 2035832, BVD.
40 Illegibly signed document to head of the Second Section, 3 October 1947.
    Letter Ministry of Foreign Affairs to E.N. van Kleffens, 7 February 1948. Both: Dossier
    Joris Ivens no. P3/49, MVJ.
41 D. Engelen. *Geschiedenis van de Binnenlandse Veiligheidsdienst*, The Hague 1995, 178-
    181.
42 JI writing to Eddy Allison, 2 June 1947. JIA.
43 Joop Morriën, *Indonesië los van Holland. de CPN en de PKI in hun strijd tegen het
    Nederlandse kolonialisme*, Amsterdam 1982, 160-165.
44 Morriën, *Indonesië los van Holland*, 162.
    Joris Ivens, 'Ansprache auf der internationalen Filmkunsttagung in Perugia, Septem-
    ber 1949' and 'Einführung zu Indonesia Calling!' in: Klaue, Lichtenstein and Wegner,
    Joris Ivens, 311, 157.
45 JI writing to Zhou Enlai, 5 August 1948. BA/FA, Coll JI SW 1.
46 JI interviewed by Stephen W. Pollak, BA/FA, Coll JI RuA 2.
    JI writing to Dora Ivens, 4 May 1948. AI.
    JI writing to Catherine Duncan, 22 February 1948. BA/FA, Coll JI SW 1.
    JI writing to Marion Michelle, undated (June 1949). MM.
47 *De Waarheid*, 16 July 1948.
48 JI interviewed by *Filmfaust*, December 1976, 19-20.
49 JI writing to Marion Michelle, various letters, undated (June 1949). MM.
50 Joris Ivens, Entwurf Rede Prague '49 (manuscript), undated BA/FA, Coll JI RuA 2.
51 Jay Leyda, *Kino: A History of the Russian and Soviet Film*, Princeton 1983, 398.
52 Joris Ivens, 'Intervention à la Salle Pleyel, Paris 1950' in: Jean Loup Passek, ed., *Joris
    Ivens. 50 Ans de cinéma* (catalogue Centre Georges Pompidou), Paris 1979, 63.
53 JI writing to Czechoslovakian State Film, 29 April 1950. JIA, pl. no. 499.
54 Polish film historian Jerzy Toeplitz was convinced that 'The First Years' was never
    shown in his country. Toeplitz interviewed by Bert Hogenkamp and Miryam van
    Lier (transcription), May 1991.
    Michelle interviewed by the author, 14 February 1990.
55 JI writing to Marion Michelle, 6 February 1951. MM.

Notes to Chapter 17

1 Marion Michelle interviewed by the author, 29 November 1993.
2 JI writing to Marion Michelle, 14 February 1951. MM.
3 Georges Sadoul in: Wolfgang Klaue, Manfred Lichtenstein and Hans Wegner eds.,
   Joris Ivens, Berlin (GDR) 1963, 77.
4 JI writing to Hans Ivens, 11 May 1950. AI.
5 JI writing to Hans Ivens, 11 May 1950.
   JI writing to Ministry of Foreign Affairs, 4 August 1950. BA/FA, Coll JI SW 1.
6 Hans Ivens writing to JI, 5 September 1950. BA/FA, Coll JI SW 1.

JI writing to Hans Ivens, 11 May and 17 October 1950. AI.

7   Paris embassy to Ministry of Foreign Affairs, 14 November 1951. 823.39, Joris Ivens, 1945-1952, inv. no. 29, box 4. BZ.
    Warsaw embassy to Ministry of Foreign Affairs, 15 January 1951. JIA, pl. no. 672.
    Notes Joris Ivens (manuscript), 7 February 1951. BA/FA, Coll JI SW 1.
    Extract No. 457/82, Warsaw, 12 February 1952. JIA, pl. no. 672.
    Note Joris Ivens (manuscript), 21 March 1952. BA/FA, Coll JI SW 2.
    JI writing to Hans Ivens, 17 February 1953. AI.
    W. Sandberg writing to JI, 30 November 1955. BA/FA, Coll JI SW 3.
    Note Joris Ivens 'Mercredi 28 nov '56' (manuscript), undated (late December 1956). JIA, pl. no. 49.
    Consular section of the Dutch embassy to JI, 7 May 1957. JIA, pl. no. 608.

8   JI writing to Hans Ivens, 17 February 1953. AI.

9   JI writing to Ewa Fiszer, undated (1954). EF.
    Jean Guyard interviewed by the author, 30 November 1993.

10 Marion Michelle interviewed by the author, 14 June 1991.

11 JI writing to Marion Michelle, 11 June 1949. MM.

12 Marion Michelle, Diary, 25 June 1946. MM.

13 Marion Michelle interviewed by the author, 29 November 1993.

14 JI writing to Marion Michelle, 13 February 1951. MM.

15 Marion Michelle, Diary, 18 April 1946. MM. (Slightly edited).

16 JI writing to Ewa Fiszer (draft letter), without place or date (Rome, February 1953). BA/FA, Coll JI SW 4.
    JI writing to Ewa Fiszer, undated (May 1963). EF.

17 Dr. Haas writing to Marion Michelle, 7 November 1950. MM.

18 Marion Michelle writing to JI, undated (autumn 1950). BA/FA, Coll JI SW 4.

19 JI writing to Marion Michelle, undated (late February 1951). MM.
    Jerzy Toeplitz, 'Der Friede besiegt den Krieg' (translated from *Kwartalnik Filmovy*, no. 1, 1951) in: Klaue, Lichtenstein and Wegner, *Joris Ivens*, 167.

20 JI writing to Marion Michelle, 25 January 1951. MM.

21 JI writing to Marion Michelle, 3 February 1951. MM.

22 JI writing to Marion Michelle, undated (early May 1951). MM.

23 JI writing to Marion Michelle, undated (May 1951), 21 May 1951 and 9 July 1951. All: MM.

24 JI writing to Marion Michelle, 27 July 1951. MM.

25 Marion Michelle interviewed by the author, 29 November 1993.
    Vladimir and Ida Pozner interviewed by the author, 6 February 1990.

26 Joris Ivens and Robert Destanque, *Aan welke kant en in welk heelal. De geschiedenis van een leven*, Amsterdam 1983, 248.

27 JI writing to Marion Michelle, undated (late February 1951). MM.

28 JI interviewed by *De Rode Vaan*, 3 March 1950.

29 Besprechung bei Herrn Pyrjev (typescript), 26 July 1951. JIA, pl. no. 42.

30 Reinhard Müller, ed., *Die Säuberung. Moskau 1936: Stenogramm einer verschlossenen Parteiversammlung*, Reinbek bei Hamburg, 1991. 568-570, passim.

31 *Junge Welt*, 3 May 1952.
    Neue Berliner Illustrierte, Sonderausgabe, August 1951.

32 Joris Ivens, Aus der Praxis und Thematik des Dokumentarfilms (typescript), undated (1952) BA/FA, Coll JI RuA 2.

33 Ivens and Destanque, *Aan welke kant*, 249.

34 JI writing to the Soviet Minister of Cinematography, 15 October 1951. BA/FA, Coll JI SW 1.

35 JI writing to Ewa Fiszer (draft letter), undated (February 1953). BA/FA, Coll JI SW 4.

36 Ivens and Destanque, *Aan welke kant*, 247.
   Ewa Fiszer, *Trzecia rano* [*Three in the Morning*], Warsaw 1982, passim.
   Ida Pozner interviewed by the author, 22 January 1993.

37 Ewa Fiszer interviewed by the author, 12 October 1990.

38 Joris Ivens, Film in the fight for peace (manuscript), January 1952. BA/FA, Coll JI RuA 2.

39 Declaration of the Cominform congress 1947, quoted in: Fernando Claudin, *The Communist Movement. From Comintern to Cominform*, New York 1975, 391.

40 JI writing to Marion Michelle, 7 October 1952. MM.

41 *L'Écran Français* no. 327, 1952.
   Ewa Fiszer interviewed by the author, 12 October 1990.
   Joris Ivens writing to Günther (Klein), 19 October 1952. BA/FA, Coll JI SW 2.

42 Press and Propaganda Management Partito Communista Italiano on the Press and Propaganda Section of the Central Comittee of the SED, 5 December 1952 and 18 March 1953. BA/FA, Coll JI SW 2.
   Gillo (Pontecorvo) writing to JI, undated (May 1953 of 1954); JI writing to Gillo Pontecorvo, 30 July (1953 of 1954); W. Sandberg writing to JI, 7 March 1953. All three: JIA, pl. no. 46.

43 JI writing to Hans Ivens, 17 December 1952. AI.

44 JI writing to Ewa Fiszer (draft letter), February 1953. BA/FA, Coll JI SW 4.

45 Marion Michelle writing to JI, 24 July (1953). BA/FA, Coll JI SW 3.

46 Jean Guyard interviewed by the author, 30 November 1993.

47 Joris Ivens, notes, undated (summer 1953). BA/FA, Coll JI RuA 2.

48 Anton Ackermann, Hauptverwaltung Film, writing to JI, 17 September 1954 and 10 January 1955.
   Günther Klein writing to JI, 4 June 1955. All: BA/FA, Coll JI resp. SW 2, SW 3 and SW 3.

49 JI writing to Paul Wandel (Central Committee member SED), 15 February 1955. BA/FA, Coll JI SW 3.

50 Ivens and Destanque, *Aan welke kant*, 252.

51 Hans Wegner, *Joris Ivens. Dokumentarist der Wahrheit*, Berlin (GDR) 1965, 147-148.

52 Ida Pozner interviewed by the author, 22 January 1993.

53 Joris Ivens and Vladimir Pozner eds., *Lied der Ströme*, Berlin (GDR) 1957, 20-21.

54 Marion Michelle writing to JI, undated (November-December 1950). BA/FA, Coll JI SW 4.

55 Dmitri Shostakovich writing to JI, 26 November 1954. BA/FA, Coll JI SW 2.

56 *Volksstimme*, 21 September 1954.
   Hans Wegner writing to JI, 25 August 1954. BA/FA, Coll JI SW 2.

57 *L'Information Syndicale Mondiale*, 15-31 October 1954.
   de Volkskrant, 16 October 1954.

58 Georges Sadoul, 'Das wahre Lied der Welt' in: Klaue, Lichtenstein and Wegner, *Joris Ivens*, 197.

Ivens and Destanque, *Aan welke kant*, 254.

59 JI writing to Anton Ackermann, 22 December 1954. BA/FA, Coll JI SW 2.

60 Claude Roy, ed., *Gérard Philipe. Souvenirs et temoignages receuillis par Anne Philipe*, Paris 1960, 323.

61 Vladimir Pozner writing to JI, 26 March 1956. BA/FA, Coll JI SW 4.

JI writing to Marion Michelle, undated (spring 1956). MM.

JI writing to Vladimir Pozner, 2 April 1956. Collection Pozner, Parijs.

62 JI writing to Hans Ivens, 26 July 1956. AI.

63 JI writing to Hans Ivens, 10 December 1956. AI.

64 Pierre Cadars, *Gérard Philipe*, Paris 1984, 108-109.

Ivens and Destanque, *Aan welke kant*, 256.

65 Ewa Fiszer interviewed by the author, 10 October 1990.

66 Ewa Fiszer writing to JI, undated (1956). BA/FA, Coll JI SW 4.

67 JI writing to Marion Michelle, undated (spring 1956). MM.

JI writing to Hans Ivens, 24 November 1956. AI.

JI writing to Marion Michelle, 27 November and 18 December 1956. Both: MM.

68 Ewa Fiszer interviewed by the author, 12 October 1990.

Notes to Chapter 18

1 Von Joris Ivens lernen. Protokoll der Diskussion vom 22 Februar 1974 in der Deutsche Film und Fernsehakademie Berlin (typescript), 73. NFM/Library.

2 Xia Yan, 'An Old Steed in the Stable still Aspires to Gallop a Thousand Li' in: *Joris Ivens and China*, Peking 1983, 9.

3 Ewa Fiszer interviewed by the author, 25 May 1991.

4 Marceline Loridan-Ivens interviewed by the author, 22-23 November 1991.

5 JI writing to Ewa Fiszer, 1 June 1959. EF.

6 JI writing to Ewa Fiszer, undated (spring 1957), 9 August 1958, undated (July 1958?). EF.

List from JI (manuscript) concerning correspondence with Ewa Fiszer, 30 June-15 October (1958). JIA, pl. no. 593.

7 JI writing to Fiszer, 1 June 1959.

8 Ida Pozner interviewed by the author, 6 February 1990.

9 Georges Sadoul in: Wolfgang Klaue, Manfred Lichtenstein and Hans Wegner eds., *Joris Ivens*, East Berlin 1963, 81-82.

10 A.Zalzman, *Joris Ivens*, Paris 1963, 90.

11 Simone Signoret, *Nostalgia Isn't what it Used to Be*, New York 1978, 162.

12 JI writing to Marion Michelle, 1 January 1958. MM.

13 Cynthia Grenier, 'Joris Ivens: Social Realist versus Lyric Poet', *Sight and Sound*, spring 1958, 204-207.

14 JI interviewed by the author, 16 April 1986.

15 JI in the East German television documentary by Alfons Machalz, *Menschen am Pulsschlag der Zeit*, 1963.

16 JI writing to Fiszer, 1 June 1959.
Note JI about his contract with China, undated (1957-1958). JIA, pl. no. 608.

17 Joris Ivens, Lecture about theme of doc. film (manuscript), undated (1958). JIA pl. no. 607.

18 Joris Ivens, Lecture Film Academy 27 September 1958. BA/FA, Coll JI RuA 3.
JI writing to Marion Michelle, 4 May and 18 August 1958. MM.

19 Joris Ivens, 'Return to China (1958)' in: *Joris Ivens and China*, 74.
Joris Ivens, Memorandum to Central Film Bureau, undated (late September-early October 1958). BA/FA, Coll JI RuA.

20 JI writing to Ewa Fiszer, undated (early 1958). EF.
Wang Decheng, 'What I Learned from Joris Ivens, Co-producing Early Spring' in: *Joris Ivens and China*, 125-134.

21 The Chinese translated the title as The Indignation of 600 Million People. Cf. *Joris Ivens in China*, 7 and 142. In documents from 1958 the film is called 'The Roar of 600 Million and also China Roars'. Cf. Joris Ivens. Lecture 27 September 1958 and Memorandum to Central Film Bureau. BA/FA, Coll JI RuA 3.
Ivens himself later used the English title '600 Million with You'.

22 Commentary text in English of China Roars. JIA, pl. no. 600.

23 Joris Ivens, Memorandum to Central Film Bureau, undated (late September-early October 1958). BA/FA, Coll JI RuA 3.

24 Joris Ivens, 'Making Documentary Films in China' in: *China Reconstructs*, January 1959, 19.

25 JI writing to Ewa Fiszer, 9 August 1958. EF.
JI writing to Marion Michelle, 4 November 1959. MM.

26 *Joris Ivens and China*, 7. Jay Leyda, *Dianying. Electric Shadows. An Account of Films and the Film Audience in China*, Cambridge (Mass.) 1972, 315-316.
Régis Bergeron, *Le cinéma Chinois 1949-1983*, part III, Paris 1984, 101.
Correspondence JI-Ted Allen, JI-Chinese Ministry of Culture, JI-Sydney Gordon. BA/FA, Coll JI SW 3 and 4; JIA, pl. nos. 590, 607, 608.

27 JI writing to Ewa Fiszer, 1 June 1959. EF.

28 Van der Molen writing to Ministry of Culture, 14 March 1968. OCW.

29 JI writing to Ewa Fiszer, undated (autumn 1959). EF.

30 JI writing to Fiszer, undated (autumn 1959).

31 *Algemeen Handelsblad*, 4 July 1959.

32 *Het Parool*, 24 June 1959.

33 JI writing to Marion Michelle, 14 March 1959. MM.
JI writing to Ewa Fiszer, 1 June 1959 and undated (June 1959). EF.
Het Parool, 24 June 1959.
Joris Ivens, 'Monolog auf Hanns Eisler', *Sinn und Form, Eisler Sonderausgabe*, 1964, 42-43.

34 Joris Ivens and Robert Destanque, *Aan welke kant en in welk heelal. De geschiedenis van een leven*, Amsterdam 1983, 259.

35 Ivens and Destanque, *Aan welke kant*, 260.

36 Ivens and Destanque, *Aan welke kant*, 263.

37 Hans Wegner, *Joris Ivens. Dokumentarist der Wahrheit*, Berlin (GDR) 1965, 194.

38 JI writing to Ewa Fiszer, undated (early November 1959). EF.

39 Paolo and Vittorio Taviani interviewed by Pieter van Lierop, *Utrechts Nieuwsblad*, 31 March 1988.

40 Jean Rouch in interview and telephone conversation with the author, 29 July 1990 and 25 April 1994 resp.
    Richard Leacock in telephone conversation with the author, 27 April 1994.

41 Paolo Taviani interviewed by Joyce Roodnat, *NRC Handelsblad*, 23 November 1990.

42 Anonymous (Faleschini), Osservationi sui tre documentari L'Italia... (typescript), 19 February 1960.
    JI writing to Fédérigo Valli, 20 February 1960.
    Notes JI for letter to Enrico Mattei, undated (spring 1960).
    'Tinto' Brass writing to JI, undated (spring 1960). All: JIA, pl. no. 428.

43 JI writing to Ewa Fiszer, undated (August-September 1960 and autumn 1960). EF.
    JI writing to Marion Michelle, undated (August-September 1960). MM.

44 Virginia Haggard, *7 Jahre der Fülle. Leben mit Chagall*, Zürich 1987, 194-195.
    Henri Langlois writing to JI, 26 August 1954. JIA, pl. no. 50.
    JI writing to Marion Michelle, undated (March 1957), 1 January and 18 August 1958. MM.
    Marc Chagall writing to JI, 1 August 1957. BA/FA, Coll JI SW 4.

45 JI writing to Ewa Fiszer, undated (August 1960), 31 August 1960 and undated (late August-early September 1960). EF.
    Ewa Fiszer interviewed by the author, 24 May 1991.

Notes to Chapter 19

1 JI writing to Ewa Fiszer, undated (August-September 1960). EF.

2 JI writing to Ewa Fiszer, undated (summer 1960). EF.

3 JI writing to Ewa Fiszer, 8 September 1960. EF.

4 Joris Ivens and Robert Destanque, *Aan welke kant en in welk heelal. De geschiedenis van een leven*, Amsterdam 1983, 271.

5 *Cine Cubano* no. 3, 1960, 33.

6 JI writing to Ewa Fiszer, undated (September 1960). EF.
   JI writing to Charles Chaplin, 12 May 1961. JIA, pl. no. 421.

7 JI writing to Ewa Fiszer, undated (autumn 1960). EF.

8 Joris Ivens, *The Camera and I*, New York 1969, 230.

9 *Neues Deutschland*, 1 December 1961.

10 Joris Ivens, Quelques impressions d'un voyage (various manuscripts and a type-script, somewhat divergent), April 1961. JIA, pl. no. 424.

11 JI writing to Marion Michelle, 17 December 1961. MM.

12 DAZ/JZ writing to Chef DAZ, 6 July 1961 and DAZ/JZ-89901/228, 7 July 1961. Both: 823.39, Joris Ivens, 1955-1964, cover 1754, box 156. BZ.

13 No sources other than JI's own information are as yet available about this episode. Cf.: Thomas Waugh, 'Joris Ivens' Work in Cuba', *Jump Cut*, May 1980, 26-27; Michael

Chanan, *The Cuban Image. Cinema and Cultural Politics in Cuba*, Bloomington 1985, 158-159;
Ivens and Destanque, *Aan welke kant*, 278-282.

14 Ivens and Destanque, *Aan welke kant*, 278-279.

15 JI writing to Michelle, 17 December 1961.

16 JI writing to Ewa Fiszer, 11 September 1962. EF.

17 Michèle Firk, 'Naissance d'un cinéma', *Positif*, no. 53, 1963, 13-16, and 'Cuba polémiques', *Positif*, June 1965, 75-91.

18 JI writing to Marion Michelle, 10 September 1962. MM.
JI writing to Ewa Fiszer, undated (September 1962). EF.

19 Joris Ivens and N. Buenauentura, Documentaires pour l'Amérique Latine (type-script), 1961. JIA, pl. no. 374.
Willi Zahlbaum writing to JI, 2 January 1961. JIA, pl. no. 426.

20 *P.E.C. Politica, Economia, Cultura*, June 1963.

21 JI writing to Marion Michelle, 17 December 1961. MM.

22 SAC Miami writing to director FBI, 29 June 1962. FBI.

23 Note JI from 1962. JIA, pl. no. 426.
Sunday Chronicle (Georgetown), 18 March 1962.

24 Note JI: 'A voir d'Ackerman (amis personels)'. Undated (1962-1963).
Address book and notes concerning contacts in Chili. JIA, pl. no. 142, 145, 374.
Orlando Millas, 'New trends in catholicism and the policy of Chilean communists' in: Luis E. Aguilar, ed., *Marxism in Latin America* (revised edition), Philadelphia 1978, 226-230.

25 JI writing to Ewa Fiszer, 2 October 1962. EF.

26 JI writing to Ewa Fiszer, 11 September and 5 October 1962. EF.
Joris Ivens, Quelques pensées sur la réalisation du film de Valparaiso (manuscript), 11 November 1962. JIA, pl. no. 138.

27 JI writing to Marion Michelle, 4 November 1962. MM.

28 JI writing to Ewa Fiszer, undated (May 1963). EF.

29 'Entretien avec François Truffaut', *Cahiers du Cinéma*, May 1967, 20-21.
Algemeen Handelsblad, 15 February 1964.

30 JI writing to Ewa Fiszer, undated (spring 1963). EF.

31 Cf. Correspondence JI and Carlos Rebolledo 1964-1965. JIA, pl. nos. 141, 185, 374.
JI interviewed by *L'Express*, 26 September 1963, 33.
A. Zalzman, *Joris Ivens*, Paris 1963, 99

32 JI writing to Ewa Fiszer, undated (July-August 1960). EF.
JI writing to Ewa Fiszer, undated (September 1962). EF.

33 JI writing to Marion Michelle, 8 September 1964. MM.

34 JI writing to Hans Ivens, 4 October 1964. AI.

35 'Marceline Loridan: Retour sur les camps', *Passages*, April 1991, 70.

36 *Passages*, April 1991, 71.

37 Marceline Loridan interviewed by Peter van Bueren and Philip Freriks, *de Volkskrant*, 20 January 1989.
Mareline Loridan interviewed by the author, 12 December 1990.

38 Marceline Loridan interviewed by Serge Daney, Thérèse Giraud and Serge Le Peron, *Cahiers du Cinéma*, May 1976, 10.

39 Annie Cohen-Solal, *Jean-Paul Sartre. Zijn biografie*, Amsterdam 1988, 418-419.

40 JI writing to Marion Michelle, 18 April 1959. MM.

41 Notes JI for a speech at a conference of Chinese cineastes (manuscript), 1963. JIA, pl. no. 181.

42 Joris Ivens, 'Vive la Cinéma-vérité', *Les Lettres Françaises*, 21 March 1963.
    JI interviewed by Guy Gauthier, *Image et Son*, no. 187, 1965, 41-43.

43 Speech of Joris Ivens on the forum of the III International Festival of Moscow on: film and progress (typescript), 12 July 1963. BA/FA, Coll JI RuA 3.

44 Ivens and Destanque, *Aan welke kant*, 354.

45 Jean Rouch interviewed by the author, 29 July 1990.

46 Marceline Loridan in interviews with the author, 12 December 1990 and 22-23 November 1991.
    Marceline Loridan interviewed by Claude Brunel in: Claude Brunel, ed., *Joris Ivens*, Paris 1983, 75.

47 Ivens and Destanque, *Aan welke kant*, 301.

48 Contracts JI with DEFA as 'Berater Spanienfilm', 7 and 24 March 1961. BA/FA, Coll JI SW 1-2.
    JI writing to Ewa Fiszer, undated (March-April 1961). EF.
    Ricardo Muñoz-Suay, 'Archive et memoire (Un projet inédit de Joris Ivens sur l'Espagne)', *Cahiers du Cinematique*, January 1977, 105-108.

49 JI writing to Ewa Fiszer, undated (September 1962). EF.

50 *Neues Deutschland*, 13, 14, 15 August 1961.

51 Walter Ulbricht writing to JI, 18 November 1963. BA/FA, Coll JI G.

52 Telegrams in BA/FA, Coll JI G.
    Ansprache von Nationalpreisträger Konrad Wolf auf einer Festveranstaltung der Deutschen Akademie der Künste im Filmtheater 'Kosmos' in Berlin, 26 November 1963. BA/FA, Folders JI.

53 Peter Zimmermann, ed., *Deutschlandbilder Ost. Dokumentarfilme der DEFA von der Nachkriegszeit bis zur Wiedervereinigung*, Constance 1995, 105-106.

54 Jan and Tineke de Vaal interviewed by the author, 18 December 1991.
    Marion Michelle interviewed by the author, 29 November 1993.

55 *Freiheit* (Halle), 25 November 1961.

56 See e.g. JI writing to Marion Michelle, 1 January 1960. MM.

57 Joop Landré writing to J. Hulsker, Ministry of Education, Culture and Science, 9 April 1963. Archive Arts, box 323a, no. 54.17.88, OCW. Landré quotes a letter to him from Ivens.

58 G.J. van der Molen writing to permanent secretary Van de Laar of Ministry of Education, Culture and Science, draft answer with background to parliamentary questions by J.J. Voogd. 15 April 1964. Archive Arts, box 323a, no. 54.17.88. OCW.

59 *de Volkskrant* and *Algemeen Handelsblad*, 25 July 1963.

60 Jan Vrijman, 'Filmers en critici in Holland', *Podium*, January 1964, 179.

61 Pim de la Parra interviewed by the author, 8 February 1994.

62 Rob du Mee, 'Wat we van Ivens' films te zien kregen', *Vrij Nederland*, 22 February 1964,
    Algemeen Handelsblad, 13 February 1964.
    de Volkskrant, 21 February 1964.
    Het Parool, 14 December 1963.

63 Jac. van der Ster, 'Wie is Joris Ivens?' *De Groene Amsterdammer*, 4 juli 1959, 3.

64 *Aanhangsel tot het Verslag van de Handelingen der Tweede Kamer. Zitting 1963-1964*, The Hague 1964, 307.
65 Van der Molen writing to Van de Laar, 15 April 1964. OCW.
66 Joop Landré writing to JI, 9 May ('sent 16 July by error') 1963. JIA, pl. no.588.
   Cf. Landré writing to Hulsker, 9 April 1963. OCW.

Notes to Chapter 20

1 JI interviewed by Madeleine Chapsal, *L'Express*, 26 September 1963.
2 JI writing to Marion Michelle, 6 June 1959. MM.
   JI writing to Ewa Fiszer, undated (June 1959), undated (August 1959) and undated (August-September 1960). EF.
   L' Express, 26 September 1963.
3 *L' Express*, 26 September 1963.
   JI interviewed by Pim de la Parra and Wim Verstappen, *Skoop*, March 1964, 7.
4 *Skoop*, March 1964, 7.
5 JI writing to Marion Michelle, 22 September 1963, 8 November 1963 and undated (February 1964). MM.
   L' Express, 26 September 1963.
6 JI writing to Hans Ivens, 17 May 1965. AI.
7 'Entretien avec François Truffaut', *Cahiers du Cinéma*, May 1967, 20,23.
8 JI writing to Marion Michelle, 11 September 1966. MM.
9 JI writing to Marion Michelle, 24 June 1964. MM.
10 JI writing to Michelle, 24 June 1964.
11 JI writing to Michelle, 7 June 1965.
12 JI writing to Marion Michelle, 7 June 1965. MM.
   Literaturnaya Gazeta, 3 August 1965.
13 Commission de Contrôle des Films writing to JI, 3 March 1966. JIA, pl. no. 60.
   J.C. Ulrich (Chris Marker), 'Le ciel, la terre (commentaire)', *Positif*, June 1966, 62.
14 Marceline Loridan in interviews with the author, 12 December 1990 and 22-23 November 1991.
15 Joop Landré writing to JI, 23 December 1965, 5 January and 6 February 1966. All: JIA, pl. no. 578.
16 Resumé beoordelingen 'Rotterdam-Europoort', undated JIA, pl. no. 574.
17 JI interviewed by Guy Gauthier, *Image et Son*, October 1965.
18 Robert Destanque interviewed by Mardoeke Boekraad (transcription), 18 October 1989.
19 Jean-Pierre Jeancolas, *Le cinéma des Français. La V e République*, Paris 1979, passim.
   Freddy Buache, *Le cinéma Français des années 60*, Lausanne 1987, passim.
   Patrick Seale and Maureen McConville, *French Revolution 1968*, London 1968, passim.
   Cinéma d'Aujourdhui, March-April 1976, Special: 'Cinéma militant, histoire, structures, méthodes, idéologie et esthétique'.
20 *Haagse Courant*, 20 January 1967.

21 Joris Ivens, Projet de film sur le Vietnam pour le Conseil Mondial de la Paix (typescript), 20 September 1966. JIA, pl. no. 187.

22 Jeancolas, *Le cinéma des Français. La Ve République*, 167.
Han Meyer, *Joris Ivens. De weg naar Vietnam*, Utrecht 1970, 9.
Cinéma d'Aujourdhui, March-April 1976, 35-36.

23 Marceline Loridan interviewed by Claude Brunel in: Claude Brunel, ed., *Joris Ivens*, Paris 1983, 75-76.

24 Joris Ivens and Robert Destanque, *Aan welke kant en in welk heelal. De geschiedenis van een leven*, Amsterdam 1983, 307.

25 Xuan Phuong interviewed by the author, 10-11 May 1990.

26 Marceline Loridan, 'Deux mois sous la terre' in: Marceline Loridan and Joris Ivens, *17e parallele. La guerre du peuple*, Paris 1968, 24-37.

27 Ivens and Destanque, *Aan welke kant*, 309-310.

28 Joris Ivens, Diary 28 April to 20 May 1967. JIA, pl. no. 60.

29 Joris Ivens, 'Some Reflections on the Film 'The 17th Parallel – The Peoples War'', *Vietnam* (Hanoi), July 1968. 16-17.

30 Stanley Karnow, *Vietnam. A History*. New York 1983. 538-539.
'The Bitterest Battlefield', *Time Magazine*, 22 September 1967, 30.

31 Loridan and Ivens, *17e parallèle. La guerre du peuple*, 43-45, 60-63.

32 *Le Monde*, 17 August 1967.

33 Marceline Loridan 'Deux mois sous la terre' in: Loridan and Ivens, *17e parallèle. La guerre du peuple*, 84.

34 Xuan Phuong interviewed by the author, 10-11 May 1990.

35 Meyer, *Joris Ivens*, 20.

36 JI interviewed by Urias Nooteboom, *Limburgs Dagblad*, 16 November 1967.
Meyer, *Joris Ivens*, 20.

37 Joris Ivens and Marceline Loridan, Dans quelles conditions financières fut produit en France le film '17eme Parallèle. La guerre du peuple' realise par Joris Ivens. undated (March 1968). JIA, pl.no. 60.
Paris-Match, 9 September 1967.
Hans Helmut Prinzler ed., Von Joris Ivens lernen. Protokoll der Diskussion vom 22 januar 1974 in der Deutsche Film- und Fernsehakademie Berlin, 31. NFM/Library.

38 *De Tijd*, 12 March 1968. *Le Monde*, 5 March 1968. *Humanité*, 28 February 1968. *Le Figaro Litteraire*, 11-17 March 1968.

39 *Positif*, February 1970, 17.

40 Radioserie 'De onvergetelijken' (transcription), undated (October 1971). JIA, pl. no. 463.

41 Joris Ivens and Marceline Loridan, Rapport de travail dans le domaine de la propagande politique de Joris Ivens et Marceline Loridan du mois d'aout 1967 au mois de mars 1968 (7 mois) en Europe, apres un sejour de 5 mois au Nord-Vietnam, 7 April 1968. JIA, pl. no. 53.
Ivens and Loridan, Dans quelles conditions financières. JIA, pl.no. 60.

42 Prinzler, Von Joris Ivens lernen, 32, 58.

43 Xuan Phuong interviewed by the author, 10-11 May 1990.

44 Marceline Loridan interviewed by the author, 22-23 November 1991.

45 (Le Huan) writing to JI, 10 March 1968. JIA, pl. no. 60.

46 Rapport adressé au camarade Nguyen Van Tien de la part de Joris Ivens, Marceline Loridan et Jean-Pierre Sergent (typescript), 5 April 1968. JIA, pl. no. 585.
Rapport de Joris Ivens sur les préparations du départ du groupe des cinéastes sur le sud (typescript), 15 April 1968. JIA, pl. no. 60.
JI writing to Le Huan, 27 April 1968. JIA, pl. no. 62.

47 Xuan Phuong interviewed by the author, 10-11 May 1990.
Jean-Pierre Sergent interviewed by the author, 23 March 1990.

48 Xuan Phuong interviewed by the author, 10-11 May 1990.
Sergent interviewed by the author, 23 March 1990.

Notes to Chapter 21

1 JI writing to Marion Michelle, 18 August 1968. MM.

2 JI writing to Marion Michelle, 18 August 1968, 4 November 1959, 31 May 1962, 21 November 1967, 5 August and 9 September 1969, 30 July, 14 August and 4 October 1970. MM.
JI writing to Hans Rodenberg, 21 November 1967 and 28 October 1969. IfGA/ZPA, NL 204/54.

3 Jean-Pierre Sergent interviewed by the author, 22 February 1990.
Robert Destanque interviewed by Mardoeke Boekraad (transcription), 18 October 1989.

4 Sergent interviewed by the author, 22 February 1990.
Destanque interviewed by Boekraad, 18 October 1989.

5 Joris Ivens and Robert Destanque, *Aan welke kant en in welk heelal. De geschiedenis van een leven*, Amsterdam 1983, 321.

6 JI interviewed by B.J. Bertina, *de Volkskrant*, 16 November 1968.

7 JI writing to Hans Rodenberg, 28 October 1969. IfGA/ZPA, NL 204/54.
E. Michelet writing to Société Capi-Films, (3?) November 1969. JIA, pl. no. 435.

8 JI writing to Rodenberg, 28 October 1969.

9 Joseph Losey writing to Mrs. Richard Burton, 30 January 1969.
JI writing to Mrs. Richard Burton, 17 March 1969. Both: JIA, pl. no. 441.

10 JI writing to Rodenberg, 28 October 1969.

11 Sergent interviewed by the author, 22 February 1990.

12 Joris Ivens, Marceline Loridan and Jean-Pierre Sergent interviewed by Guy Hennebelle, *Cinéma 70*, February 1970, 81-89.

13 *Le Monde*, 10 October 1969.
Christian Zimmer, 'Dans la nuit de Marguerite Duras', *Les Temps Modernes*, February 1970, 1313.
Paul-Louis Thirard, 'Deux films 'maoïstes'', *Positif*, March 1970, 1-4.

14 Vladimir and Ida Pozner interviewed by the author, 6 February 1990.

15 Xuan Phuong interviewed by the author, 10-11 May 1990.

16 JI writing to Marion Michelle, 31 October 1970.
Various proposals for the establishment of a film service in Congo-Brazzaville, several dates including 26 November 1970. JIA, pl. no. 470.

17 Robert Grelier interviewed by the author, 1 December 1993.
   Henri Storck interviewed by the author and Bert Hogenkamp, 28 November 1990.
18 Ivens and Destanque, *Aan welke kant*, 359.
   Vladimir and Ida Pozner interviewed by the author, 6 February 1990.
19 Marceline Loridan interviewed by the author, 12 December 1990.
   Sergent interviewed by the author, 22 February 1990.
20 Joris Ivens, Press release (typescript), 5 May 1968. CIN.
21 JI interviewed by B.J. Bertina, *de Volkskrant*, 16 November 1968.
   JI interviewed by C.B. Doolaard, *Het Parool*, 11 December 1968.
22 Joris Ivens, Speech of thanks at the Karl Marx University, Leipzig (typescript in German), undated (18 November 1968). BA/FA, Coll JI RuA 3.
23 Wolfgang Harkenthal writing to JI, 4 June and 3 September 1969, 20 October 1970.
   JI writing to Wolfgang Harkenthal, 22 October 1969. JIA, pl.no. 440.
24 JI writing to Rodenberg, 28 October 1969.
25 Joris Ivens, *Autobiografie van een filmer*, Amsterdam undated (1970), 161-162.
   Wolfgang Klaue interviewed by the author, 15 January 1992.
26 Wolfgang Klaue interviewed by the author, 15 January 1992.
27 Roman Karmen writing to JI, 25 February 1969. JIA, pl. no. 68.
28 Bax writing to JI, 6 July 1966. JIA, pl. no. 192.
   JI writing to Bax, 11 July 1966. JIA, pl. no. 186.
29 *Het Parool*, 9 June 1966.
   JI interviewed by Trix Betlem, *Revu*, 9 March 1968, 11.
30 Van der Molen writing to Minister Klompé, 14 March 1968. Dossier Joris Ivens. De Vliegende Hollander, no. 1.854.17. OCW.
31 Minister Klompé writing to JI, 4 December 1968.
   JI writing to Minister Klompé, (late) May 1969.
   6-12-1968, Hilversum III, Joop van Tijn, 12.03 hours (transcription).
   All: Dossier Joris Ivens. De Vliegende Hollander, no. 1.854.17. OCW
32 Minister Klompé, Kort verslag van een gesprek met de Heer J. Ivens op woensdag 11 december 1968, 19 December 1968. Dossier Joris Ivens. De Vliegende Hollander, no. 1.854.17. OCW.
   Izvestia, 18 December 1968.
33 *de Volkskrant*, 12 December 1968.
34 Memo 33/68, Head DCV writing to S, 3 December 1968.
   Memo 45/68, Head DCV writing to S, 16 December 1968. Both: 823.39, Joris Ivens, 1965-1974, cover 6863. BZ.
   Note CRM writing to hr DGC. Dossier Joris Ivens. De Vliegende Hollander, no. 1.854.17. OCW.
35 Pim de la Parra interviewed by the author, 8 February 1994.

Notes to Chapter 22

1 Notes JI from 22 and 29 July 1971. JIA, pl. no. 466.
   Renmin Ribao, 30 July and 2 August 1971. *De Tijd*, 4 August 1971.

JI writing to Norodom Sihanouk, 10 July 1971. JIA, pl.no. 466.

2   Notes JI from 22 and 29 July 1971.

3   JI interviewed by Urias Nooteboom, *Eindhovens Dagblad*, 20 October 1971. Anonymous (Koos van Zomeren), *Joris Ivens. Een revolutionair met een camera*, without date or place (Rotterdam 1972), 31.

4   JI interviewed by P.J. Kat, *NRC Handelsblad*, 15 October 1971.

5   Joris Ivens and Marceline Loridan, 'L'éducation en Chine', *Pourquoi?*, January 1972, 12-28.
Joris Ivens and Marceline Loridan, 'La Révolution Culturelle dans les studios en Chine', *Cahiers du Cinéma*, March-April 1972, 67-75.

6   *De Tijd*, 20 October 1971. *De Telegraaf*, 22 October 1971.

7   JI interviewed by Urias Nooteboom, *Eindhovens Dagblad*, 20 October 1971.

8   Marceline Loridan interviewed by the author, 12 December 1990.

9   Hans Helmut Prinzler ed., Von Joris Ivens lernen. Protokoll der Diskussion vom 22. Februar 1974 in der Deutsche Film- und Fernsehakademie Berlin (typescript), 39-44. NFM/Library.
Joris Ivens, 'Les trois yeux du cinéaste militant', *Cinéma d'Aujourdhui. Nouvelle Serie*, March-April 1976, 9.

10 Simon de Jong writing to JI, undated (ca. 1970). JIA, pl.no. 463.

11 Declaration JI for the study group Film voor Vietnam of the Medisch Comité Nederland-Vietnam (manuscript), 20 April 197(3?). JIA, pl.no. 88.

12 Debbie Litt writing to JI, 26 August 1974.
JI writing to Debbie Litt, undated (1974 or 1975) Both: JIA, pl.no. 60.

13 Cf. Bui Dinh Hac writing to JI, 8 August 1967. JIA, pl.no. 53.

14 3. National League of Families of American Prisoners and Missing Persons, Washington DC, in telephone conversation with the author, 16 June 1995.

15 Mao Zedong, *Quotations of Chairman Mao*, Peking 1966 (Chinese and English edition), 379.

16 Ivens and Loridan, *Cahiers du Cinéma*, March-April 1972, 67-75.

17 JI quoted in: Robert Sklar, 'Joris Ivens. The China Close-up', *American Film*, June 1978, 63.
Li Zexiang, 'The style and characteristcs of Ivens' films' in: *Joris Ivens and China* (Edited by the Chinese Film Archives and the editors of the New World Press), Peking 1983, 119.

18 Ivens and Destanque, *Aan welke kant*, 337-338.

19 JI writing to Marion Michelle, 25 October 1972. MM.

20 JI writing to Marion Michelle, 25 October and 22 November 1972. MM.

21 JI's diary 1973, entries from 8 January to 16 April 1973. JIA, pl.no. 321.

22 JI interviewed by Klaus Kreimeier in: Klaus Kreimeier, *Joris Ivens. Ein Filmer an den Fronten der Weltrevolution*, West Berlin 1976, 125-126.

23 Régis Bergeron, *Le cinéma Chinois 1949-1983, III*, Paris 1984, 29-32.

24 JI and Marceline Loridan interviewed by: *Cinéma 76*, April 1976, 62; *Cahiers du Cinéma*, May 1976, 8; Kreimeier in: *Joris Ivens. Ein Filmer an den Fronten der Weltrevolution*, 124.

25 *Brabants Dagblad*, 16 September 1975.

26 Ivens and Destanque, *Aan welke kant*, 344.

27 Ivens and Destanque, *Aan welke kant*, 346.

JI writing to Sidney Shapiro, 28 September 1975. JIA, pl. no. 89.

28 JI writing to Klaus Kreimeier, 11 February 1976. JIA, pl. no. 88.

29 Hennie van de Louw, 'Joris Ivens, wereldcineast', *De Nieuwe Linie*, 15 November 1978, 11.

30 *France-Soir*, 10 March 1976.

31 *International Herald Tribune*, 22-23 May 1976.

32 This documentary was shown on Chinese television in 1997-1998. In spring 1997 the author viewed a rough cut at Nederland Wereldomroep in Hilversum, which collaborated with Guangdong Television on the project.

33 JI writing to A.B. van Zomeren, July 1974. AVZ.
   Claire Devarrieux, *Entretiens avec Joris Ivens*, Paris 1979, 59.

34 Marceline Loridan interviewed by the author, 22 and 23 November 1991.
   Devarrieux, *Entretiens*, 58.

35 Situ Huimin, 'Joris Ivens: Master Filmmaker, and China', *China Reconstructs*, November 1980, 26.
   Marceline Loridan interviewed by Alexandra Kluge and Bion Steinborn, *Filmfaust*, December 1977, 41-42.
   Marceline Loridan interviewed by Els Naaijkens, *Skrien*, October 1977.

36 JI interviewed by Pier Jan Kat, *De Nieuwe Linie*, 14 January 1976, 3.

37 JI interviewed by Alexandra Kluge and Bion Steinborn dd. 11 and 12 October 1976, *Filmfaust*, December 1976, 23-26.
   JI interviewed by Kat, *De Nieuwe Linie*, 14 January 1976, 3.

38 *Filmfaust*, December 1976, 35-37.

39 Jean-Pierre Sergent interviewed by the author, 22 February 1990.
   The interview was made available to the press in various languages and later printed in: Jean-Loup Passek, ed., *Joris Ivens. 50 ans de cinéma* (Catalogue Centre Pompidou), Paris 1979, 90-92.

40 JI writing to Marion Michelle, 10 January 1977. MM.

41 Hsinhua press release, 10 February 1977 (Cf. JI writing to Marion Michelle, 7 March 1977. MM.)
   Hsinhua press release, 23 February 1977.

42 Martha Gellhorn interviewed by the author, 15 July 1995.

43 Ivens and Destanque, *Aan welke kant*, 348.

44 JI writing to A.B. van Zomeren, 24 April 1978. AVZ.

45 *American Film*, June 1978, 59.

46 Hans Wentholt, Hoe Yoekong de bergen verzette. Kijkgedrag en reakties van het publiek op een serie televisieprogramma's over de Volksrepubliek China, January 1978. JIA, pl. no. 93.

47 Dutch filmmaker Nico Crama provided this information. At that time he was working for Tom Daly, producer of the involved films, entitled NORTH CHINA COMMUNE (1979), NORTH CHINA FACTORY (1980) and CHINA: A LAND TRANSFORMED (1980). Direction was by Tony Ianzelo and Boyce Richardson.

48 JI writing to A.B. van Zomeren, 25 November 1977 and 22 January 1978. AVZ.

49 Mrs. van Alphen-Kaldewaay (a 'foster daughter' of Miss van Zomeren) interviewed by the author, 5 January 1993.
   Correspondence JI to A.B. van Zomeren, 1973-1985, incl. 30 May 1978, 26 March 1978, 4 August 1978. AVZ.

Declaration A.B. van Zomeren regarding her employ by Philips from 1 June 1926 – 31 January 1934. PCA.

50 Jury report Dick Scherpenzeel Prize 1977 and press release 13 November 1978. NFM/Library.

Trouw, 14 November 1978. *Het Parool*, 14 November 1978.

De Groene Amsterdammer, 15 November 1978.

Het Parool, 16 November 1978.

51 Xia Yan, 'An Old Steed in the Stable Still Aspires to Gallop a Thousand Li' in: *Joris Ivens and China*, 5-13.

Notes to Chapter 23

1 JI writing to Thea Nooteboom-Ivens, 4 May 1981. TNI.

2 JI writing to Van Zomeren, 11 January, 16 February, 20 March 1983. AVZ.

3 JI interviewed by Urias Nooteboom (typescript), 8 May 1982. UN.
   JI writing to Van Zomeren, 28 April 1980. AVZ.

4 Marceline Loridan kindly gave me access to this scenario.

5 JI interviewed by Urias Nooteboom (typescript), 8 May 1982. UN.

6 JI writing to Van Zomeren, 4 March and 9 October 1980, 15 March, 10 September and 27 November 1981, 12 January, 29 March and 23 April 1982, 20 March, 22 May and 17 November 1983, 6 February 1984. All: AVZ.
   JI interviewed by Nooteboom, 8 May 1982.

7 Jean-François Masson interviewed by the author, 24 March 1990.

8 JI writing to L.J. Jordaan, 2 April 1950. JI writing to Hans Ivens, 30 April and 11 May 1950. Both: AI.
   JI writing to Marion Michelle, 19 February and 21 May 1951. MM.
   Catherine Duncan interviewed by the author, 5 February 1990.

9 Robert Grelier writing to JI, 29 August 1960. JIA.
   JI writing to Robert L. Snyder, 1 August 1962.
   JI writing to Marion Michelle, 4 November 1962. Both: MM.

10 JI writing to Ewa Fiszer, May and June 1963. EF.
   George Sadoul writing to JI, 1 October 1963. JIA.
   Robert Grelier interviewed by the author, 1 December 1993.

11 JI writing to Ewa Fiszer, (summer) 1963. EF.

12 Joris Ivens and Robert Destanque, *Aan welke kant en in welk heelal. De geschiedenis van een leven*, Amsterdam 1983, 308.

13 Robert Destanque writing to the author, 21 November 1990.

14 Ivens and Destanque, *Aan welke kant*, 18, 202.

15 Ivens and Destanque, *Aan welke kant*, 9, 62.

16 JI interviewed by Ton Regtien, *De Waarheid*, 23 October 1982.

17 Anonymous (Koos van Zomeren), *Joris Ivens. Een revolutionair met een kamera*, without date or place (Rotterdam 1972), 35.
   Claire Devarrieux, *Entretiens avec Joris Ivens*, Paris 1979, 39
   JI interviewed by Urias Nooteboom (transcription), 8 May 1982. UN.

JI interviewed by Eric van 't Groenewout (recording), 1985.
18 Ivens and Destanque, *Aan welke kant*, 350, 143-144.
19 Ivens and Destanque, *Aan welke kant*, 270, 288.
20 Rob van Gennep, statement to the author, 2 December 1992.
21 JI writing to Van Zomeren, 28 April 1980. AVZ.
22 Wim Verstappen interviewed by the author, 2 February 1994.
23 *Utrechts Nieuwsblad*, 17 September 1985.
24 JI writing to Van Zomeren, 29 March and 1 November 1982. AVZ.
25 JI interviewed by the author, 16 April 1986.
26 Marceline Loridan interviewed by Claude Brunel in: Claude Brunel, ed., *Joris Ivens*, Parijs 1983, 76.
    Marceline Loridan interviewed by Peter van Bueren and Philip Freriks, *de Volkskrant*, 20 January 1989.
27 Costa-Gavras interviewed by the author, 20 February 1990.
    Jean Rouch interviewed by the author, 29 July 1990.
28 JI interviewed by the author, 16 April 1986.
    Database Dutch Film Museum, Amsterdam.
29 Claire Devarrieux, *Entretiens avec Joris Ivens*, Paris 1979, 22.
30 JI writing to Van Zomeren, 22 May 1983. AVZ.
    JI interviewed by the author, 16 April 1986.

Notes to Chapter 24

1   Joris Ivens and Robert Destanque, *Aan welke kant en in welk heelal. De geschiedenis van een leven*, Amsterdam 1983, 292-293.
2   Note Tineke de Vaal from telephone conversation with JI. The question was put to Ivens in preparation for the ceremony in Nijmegen in October 1988.
3   Joris Ivens interviewed by the author, 16 April 1986.
    Joris Ivens interviewed by ZDF television, spring 1989.
4   Paolo and Vittorio Taviani interviewed by Joyce Roodnat, *NRC Handelsblad*, 23 November 1993.
5   René Prédal, *Le cinéma Français depuis 1945*, Paris 1991, 520.
6   Elisabeth D. interviewed by the author, 27 July 1990.
7   JI writing to Gerry van der Ven, 30 January 1985, with outline 'Le vent'. JIA/GvdV.
8   JI writing to A.B. van Zomeren, 10 November 1984. AVZ.
9   Rapport Cultuurprijs 1985 Nederlandse Filmdagen. JIA, pl. no. 655.
10 *NRC Handelsblad*, 11 September 1985.
11 *de Volkskrant*, 11 September 1985.
12 Speech Minister Brinkman on the presentation of the Culture Prize on 11 September 1985, *Cinematheek journaal*, October 1985, 5-6.
13 *NRC Handelsblad*, 12 September 1985, *de Volkskrant*, 12 September 1985, *Algemeen Dagblad*, 16 September 1985.
14 JI interviewed by Rudolph Bakker (typescript) undated (September 1985).

15 Michel Korzec and Hans Moll, 'De heiligverklaring van Joris Ivens', *Intermediair*, 4 October 1985, 1-10.

16 Jean-François Masson interviewed by the author, 24 March 1990.

17 Marceline Loridan interviewed by Piet Adriaanse, *Dagkrant* International Documentary Festival Amsterdam, 14 December 1994, 6.

18 JI interviewed by Serge Toubiana, *Cahiers du Cinéma*, May 1989.
Eric van 't Groenewout, 'Der alte Mann und der Wind', *Blimp*, spring 1989, 24.

19 Catherine Duncan. Notes on the preview of Une histoire de vent on 21 February 1988 (English typescript). MM.

20 Marion Michelle interviewed by the author, 14 February 1990.
Henri Storck interviewed by the author and Bert Hogenkamp, 28 November 1990.

21 Martha Gellhorn interviewed by the author, 15 July 1995.

22 *Het Parool*, 29 June 1989. *De Telegraaf*, 20 January 1989.

23 Jean-François Masson interviewed by the author, 24 March 1990.

24 Wolfgang Klaue interviewed by the author, 15 January 1992.

25 JI writing to the City of Zaanstad, 19 April 1988, quoted in *Zaanse Gezinsbode*, 4 July 1989.

26 Annabeth Ivens interviewed by the author, 26 February 1992.
JI writing to Eric van 't Groenewout, 29 April 1989. EG.

27 JI writing to Eric van 't Groenewout, 16 and 17 May 1989. EG.

28 JI and Marceline Loridan interviewed by Erwin Leiser, *Frankfurter Allgemeine Magazin*, 23 June 1989, 10.
Aspekte, ZDF, July 1989.

29 Eric van 't Groenewout, 'De Chinese studenten op het plein, dat was de wind', *Film en tv maker*, September 1989, 24.

30 Jean-François Masson interviewed by the author, 24 March 1990.

31 *de Volkskrant*, 7 July 1989. *NRC Handelsblad*, 7 July 1989.

Bibliography

This overview is limited to publications in book, thesis or brochure form.

I. By Joris Ivens

Ivens, Joris, and Vladimir Pozner, *Lied der Ströme*, Berlin (GDR) 1957.
- and Marceline Loridan, *17e Parallèle. La guerre du peuple (deux mois sous la terre)*, Paris 1968.
-, *The Camera and I*, Berlin (GDR) 1969.
-, *Autobiografie van een filmer*, Amsterdam undated (1970).
-, and Robert Destanque, *Joris Ivens ou la mémoire d'un regard*, Paris 1982.
-, and Robert Destanque, *Aan welke kant en in welk heelal. De geschiedenis van een leven*, Amsterdam 1983.

II. About Joris Ivens

Bakker, Kees, ed., *Joris Ivens and the Documentary Context*, Amsterdam 1999.
Barbian, Jan-Pieter and Werner Ruzicka, eds., *Poesie und Politik. Der niederländische Dokumentarfilmer Joris Ivens (1898-1989)*, Luxembourg 2000.
Bertina, B.J., *Joris Ivens, Revolutionair*, Amsterdam 1969.
Bleeckere, Sylvain de, *Une histoire de vent*, Kampen 1997.
Böker, Carlos, *Joris Ivens, Filmmaker. Facing reality*, Ann Arbor 1978.
Brunel, Claude, ed., *Joris Ivens* (catalogue Centre Georges Pompidou), Paris 1983.
Caffarena, Attilio, *Il Ponte di Joris Ivens....*, Genoa 1976.
Cassiers, Willem, Joris Ivens; het filmmedium als politiek uitdrukkingsmiddel, (thesis), Brussels 1974.
Costa, José Manuel, *Joris Ivens*, Lisbon 1983.
Delmar, Rosalind, *Joris Ivens: 50 Years of Film-making*, London 1979.
Devarrieux, Claire, *Entretiens avec Joris Ivens* (collected interviews with *Le Monde*), Paris 1979.
Drobashenko, S., *Kinorezisser Joris Ivens (Film Director Joris Ivens)*, Moscow 1964.
Foto's uit de eerste films van Joris Ivens, Baarle-Nassau 1981.
Grelier, Robert, *Joris Ivens*, Paris 1965.

Groenewout, Eric van 't, Indonesia Calling. Het verhaal van de schepen die niet uitvoeren (thesis), without date or place (Leiden 1988).

Hiller, Norbert, Ein Dokumentarfilm im Auftrag der Industrie – Joris Ivens und sein Film 'Philips-Radio' (thesis), Cologne 1983.

Hogenkamp, Bert, and Henri Storck, De Borinage. De mijnwerkersstaking van 1932 en de film van Joris Ivens en Henri Storck, Amsterdam 1983.

Jordaan, L.J., Joris Ivens, Amsterdam 1931.

Joris Ivens, 50 jaar wereldcineast (catalogue Dutch Film Museum), Amsterdam 1978.

Joris Ivens and China (edited by the Chinese Film Archives and the editors of the New World Press), Peking 1983.

Joris Ivens en Nijmegen, Nijmegen 1987.

Klaue, Wolfgang, Manfred Lichtenstein and Hans Wegner eds., Joris Ivens (festschrift), Berlin (GDR) 1963.

Kreimeier, Klaus, Joris Ivens. Ein filmer an den Fronten der Weltrevolution, West Berlin 1976.

Meyer, Han, Joris Ivens. De weg naar Vietnam, Utrecht 1970.

Passek, Jean-Loup, and Jacqueline Brisbois eds., Joris Ivens. 50 Ans de cinéma (catalogue Centre Georges Pompidou), Paris 1979.

Reijnhoudt, Bram, The Difficult Road to the Restoration of the Films of Joris Ivens (NFM Thema Serie 28), Amsterdam 1994.

Saaltink, Hans, Joris Ivens 65 jaar, Amsterdam 1964.

Schoots, Hans, Gevaarlijk leven. Een biografie van Joris Ivens, Amsterdam 1995.

Stufkens, André, Jan de Vaal and Tineke de Vaal eds., Rondom Joris Ivens, wereldcineast. Het begin, 1898-1934, Nijmegen 1988.

Stufkens, André, ed., Passages. Joris Ivens en de kunst van deze eeuw, (Catalogue Museum Het Valkhof), Nijmegen 1999.

Tendler, Silvio, La rélation cinéma et histoire vue a travers l'étude de l'oeuvre de Joris Ivens (thesis), Paris 1976.

Terzi, Corrado, Zuiderzee, Milan 1945.

Waugh, Thomas H., Joris Ivens and the Evolution of the Radical Documentary, 1926-1946, Ann Arbor 1981

Wegner, Hans, Joris Ivens. Dokumentarist der Wahrheit, Berlin (GDR) 1965.

Zalzman, A., Joris Ivens, Paris 1963.

(Zomeren, Koos van), Joris Ivens, een revolutionair met een kamera, without place of publication (Rotterdam) 1972.

III. Further Literature

Aaron, Daniel, *Writers on the Left. Episodes in American Literary Communism*, New York 1961.

Abusch, Alexander, *Der Deckname. Memoiren*, Berlin (GDR) 1981.

Alexander, William, *Film on the left. American Documentary Film from 1931 to 1942*, Princeton 1981.

Andrews, Christopher, and Oleg Gordievsky, *KGB. The Inside Story of its Foreign Operations from Lenin to Gorbachev*, London 1990.

Arbeid, Annette, and Teun van den Berg, eds., *Op de Kring. Zeventig jaren kunstenaarsleven in beslotenheid*, Amsterdam 1992.

Aub, Max, *Conversaciones con Buñuel*, Madrid 1984.

Auden, W.H., and Christopher Isherwood, *Journey to a War*, London 1939.

Baker, Carlos, *Ernest Hemingway. A Life Story*, Harmondsworth 1972.

Balázs, Béla, *Der Film*, Vienna 1961.

Barsam, Richard Meran, *Non Fiction Film, a Critical History*, New York 1973.

–, *The Vision of Robert Flaherty. The Artist as Myth and Filmmaker*, Bloomington 1988.

Baxter, John, *Buñuel*, London 1994.

Bentley, Eric, ed., *Thirty Years of Treason. Excerpts from Hearings before HUAC, 1938-1968*, New York 1971.

Bergeron, Régis, *Le cinéma Chinois 1949-1983, parts I, II, III*, Paris 1983-1984.

Berlijn-Amsterdam 1920-1940, wisselwerkingen, Amsterdam 1982.

Bertin, Célia, *Jean Renoir*, Paris 1986.

Best, Otto F., ed., *Theorie des Expressionismus*, Stuttgart 1982.

Betz, Albrecht, *Hanns Eisler. Musik einer Zeit, die sich eben bildet*, Munich 1976.

Bohn, Thomas William, *An Historical and Descriptive Analysis of the 'Why we Fight' Series*, New York 1977.

Bois, Yve-Alain, *Arthur Lehning en Mondriaan. Hun vriendschap en correspondentie*, Amsterdam 1984.

Bolloten, Burnett, *The Spanish Revolution. The Left and the Struggle for Power during the Civil War*, Chapel Hill 1979.

Boode, Arij de, and Pieter van Oudheusden, *De 'Hef'. Biografie van een spoorbrug*, Rotterdam 1985.

Bool, Flip, and Jeroen de Vries, *De arbeidersfotografen. Camera en crisis in de jaren '30*, Amsterdam 1982.

Boost, Charles, *Van Ciné-Club tot filmhuis. Tien jaren die de filmindustrie deden wankelen*, Amsterdam 1979.

Brandenburg, Angenies, *Annie Romein-Verschoor 1895-1978, Leven en werk, deel 1 en 2*, Amsterdam 1988.

Brandt Corstius, J.C., *De dichter Marsman en zijn kring*, The Hague 1980.

Braunbuch über Reichstagsbrand und Hitlerterrror, Basel 1933.

Brederoo, Nico J., *Charley Toorop, leven en werken*, Amsterdam 1982.

Broué, Pierre, *L'assasinat de Trotsky*, Brussels 1980.

Buache, Freddy, *Le cinéma français des années 60*, Lausanne 1987.

Buber-Neumann, Margarete, *Als Gefangene von Stalin und Hitler*, Stuttgart 1978.

Buchsbaum, Jonathan, *Cinema Engagé. Film in the Popular Front*, Urbana 1988.

Buñuel, Luis, *Mon dernier soupir*, Paris 1982.

Burg, Fenna van den, *De Vrije Katheder 1945-1950. Een platform van communisten en niet-communisten*, Amsterdam 1983.

Cadars, Pierre, *Gérard Philipe*, Paris 1984.

Campbell, Russell Drummond, *Radical Cinema in the United States, 1930-1942. The Work of the Film and Photo League, Nykino and Frontier Films*, Evanston 1978.

Capra, Frank, *The Name Above the Title: An Autobiography*, New York 1971.

Carlson, Evans Fordyce, *Twin Stars of China: A Behind-the-Scene Story of China's Valiant Struggle for Existence by a US Marine who Lived and Moved with the People*, New York 1940

Caute, David, *Communism and the French Intellectuals, 1914-1960*, London 1964.

–, *The Fellow-travellers, A Postscript to the Enlightenment*, London 1972.

–, *Joseph Losey. Revenge on Life*, London 1994.

Ceplair, Larry, and Steven Englund, *The Inquisition in Hollywood. Politics in the Film Community, 1930-1960*, Berkeley 1983.

Chanan, Michael, *The Cuban Image. Cinema and Politics in Cuba*, Bloomington 1985.

Charley Toorop 1891-1955 (catalogue Centraal Museum), Utrecht 1982.

Churchill, Allen, *The Improper Bohemians. Greenwich Village in its Heyday*, New York 1959.

Ciment, Michel, *Conversations with Losey*, London 1985.

Claudin, Fernando, *The Communist Movement. From Comintern to Cominform, parts 1 and 2*, New York 1975.

Cockburn, Claud, *In Time of Trouble*, London 1956.

Cohen-Solal, Annie, *Sartre, 1905-1980*, Paris 1985.

Coppens, Jan, *De bewogen camera. Protest en propaganda door middel van foto's*, Amsterdam 1982.

Cornelissen, Igor, *De GPOe op de Overtoom. Spionnen voor Moskou 1920-1940*, Amsterdam 1989.

Costello, John, and Oleg Tsarev, *Deadly Illusions*, London 1993.

Cunningham, Valentine, ed., *Spanish Front. Writers on the Civil War*, Oxford 1986.

D., Elisabeth, *Les mots de la tribu*, Paris 1986.

Dankaart, Hans, et al., *De oorlog begon in Spanje. Nederlanders in de Spaanse burgeroorlog 1936-1939*, Amsterdam 1986.

Desneux, Richard, *Yves Montand. L'artiste engagé*, Lausanne 1989.

Dibbets, Karel, *Sprekende films. De komst van de geluidsfilm in Nederland 1928-1933*, Amsterdam 1993.

–, and Frank van der Maden ed., *Geschiedenis van de Nederlandse film en bioscoop tot 1940*, without place of publication 1986.

–, Karel, et al. ed., *Jaarboek Mediageschiedenis 5*, Amsterdam 1993.

Dick, Bernard F., *The Star Spangled Screen. The American WW II Film*, Lexington 1985.

–, *Radical Innocence, a Critical Study of the Hollywood Ten*, Lexington 1989.

Diepraam, Willem, *Een beeld van Eva Besnyö*, Amsterdam 1993.

Dittmar, Linda, and Gene Michaud eds., *From Hanoi to Hollywood. The Vietnam War in American Film*, New Brunswick 1990.

Dongelmans, Maarten J.M., *Nijmegen Toen Ter Tijd*, Nijmegen 1988.

Dos Passos, John, *The Fourteenth Chronicle. Letters and Diaries*, Boston 1973.

–, *Journeys between Wars*, New York 1938.

Eisenstein, Sergei M., *Immoral Memories. An Autobiography*, Boston 1983.

Eisler, Hanns, *Fragen Sie mehr über Brecht. Gespräche mit Hans Bunge*, Darmstadt 1986.

–, *Muziek en politiek*, Nijmegen 1972.

–, and Theodor W. Adorno, *Composing for the Films*, New York 1947.

El Campesino, *Morgen ist ein anderer Tag. Memoiren*, Frankfurt/Main 1978.

Engelen, D., *Geschiedenis van de Binnenlandse Veiligheidsdienst*, The Hague 1995.

Enzensberger, Hans Magnus, ed., *Europa in Trümmern. Augenzeugenberichte aus den Jahren 1944-1948*, Frankfurt/Main 1990.

Fischer, Louis, *Men and Politics. An Autobiography*, New York 1941.

Fiszer, Ewa, *Trzecia rano* [*Three in the Morning*], Warsaw 1982

Fleischer, Alette, and Alexander Valeton eds., *De maaltijd der vrienden. Kunstenaars in Bergen 1930-1935*, Amsterdam 1994.

Friedrich, Otto, *City of Nets: A Portrait of Hollywood in the 1940's*, New York 1988.

Fuegi, John, *The Life and Lies of Bertolt Brecht*, London 1994.

Gallagher, Dorothy, *All the Right Enemies. The Life and Murder of Carlo Tresca*, Rutgers 1988.

Gaßner, Hubertus, and Eckhart Gillen, *Zwischen Revolutionskunst und Sozialistischem Realismus. Dokumente und Kommentare. Kunstdebatten in der Sowjetunion von 1917 bis 1934*, Cologne 1979.

Gellhorn, Martha, *Travels with Myself and Another*, Cambridge 1978.

Guiguet, Claude, and Emmanuel Papillon eds., *Jean Dréville. Propos du cinéaste, filmographie, documents*, Paris 1987.

Guillaume-Grimaud, Geneviève, *Le cinéma du Front Populaire*, Paris 1986.

Grasveld, Fons, *Een rapport over Mannus Franken, mens en kunstenaar*, Amsterdam 1976.

Gross, Babette, *Willi Münzenberg. Eine politische Biographie*. Stuttgart 1967.

Haffmans, F.J., *Geest, koolzuur en zijk. Briefwisseling van Erich Wichman*, Westervoort 1999.

Haggard, Virginia, *Seven Years of Plenty – My Life with Chagall*, New York 1986.

Hamilton, John Maxwell, *Edgar Snow. A Biography*, Bloomington 1988.

Hans Richter, 1888-1976. Dadaist. Filmpionier. Maler. Theoretiker (catalogue Akademie der Künste), Berlin (GDR) 1982.

Harmsen, Ger, *Nederlands kommunisme. Gebundelde opstellen*, Nijmegen 1982.

Hay, Julius, *Geboren 1900. Aufzeichnungen eines Revolutionärs. Autobiographie*, Munich 1977.

Hazeu, Wim, *Slauerhoff. Een biografie*, Amsterdam 1995.

Heijs, Jan, ed., *Filmliga 1927-1931* (reprint with introduction), Nijmegen 1982.

Hekking, Sybrand, *Cas Oorthuys. Fotograaf. 1908-1975*, Amsterdam 1982.

Hemingway, Ernest, *For Whom the Bell Tolls*, New York 1940.

–, *Selected Letters, 1917-1961*, London 1981.

Herz, Rudolf, and Dirk Halfbrodt, *Fotografie und Revolution. München 1918/19*, Berlin 1988.

Hilgersbach, Maria, *Kino im Exil. Die Emigration deutscher Filmkünstler 1933-1945*, Munich 1982.

Hogenkamp, Bert, *De Nederlandse documentaire film 1920-1940*, Amsterdam 1988.

–, *No pasaran! Film en de Spaanse burgeroorlog*, Amsterdam 1986.

–, and Russell Campbell, *Film en de Amerikaanse arbeidersbeweging 1910-1942: het ontbrekende hoofdstuk. De Film and Photo League*, Amsterdam 1985.

–, and Peter Mol, *Van beeld tot beeld. De films en televisieuitzendingen van de CPN, 1928-1986*, Amsterdam 1993.

Hollander, Paul, *Political Pilgrims. Travels of Western Intellectuals to the Soviet Union, China and Cuba, 1928-1978*, Oxford 1981.

Honnef, Klaus, ed., *Germaine Krull. Fotografien 1922-1966*, Bonn 1977.

Hooks, Margaret, *Tina Modotti. Photographer and Revolutionary*, London 1993.

Jeancolas, Jean-Pierre, *Le cinéma des Français. La Ve République (1958-1978)*, Paris 1979.

Jong, L. de, *Het Koninkrijk der Nederlanden in de tweede wereldoorlog, 11b en c, Nederlands -Indië II en III*, The Hague 1985-1986.

Jordaan, L.J., *50 jaar bioscoopfauteuil*, Amsterdam 1958.

Karnow, Stanley, *Vietnam. A History*, New York 1983.

Kändler, Klaus, Helga Karolewski and Ilse Siebert eds., *Berliner Begegnungen. Ausländische Künstler in Berlin 1918 bis 1933. Aufsätze – Bilder – Dokumente*, Berlin (GDR) 1987.

Keuken, Johan van der, *Zien, kijken, filmen. Foto's, teksten en interviews*, Amsterdam 1980.

Klehr, Harvey, John Earl Haynes and Fridrikh Igorevitsch Firsov, *The Secret World of American Communism*, New Haven 1995.

Kießling, Wolfgang, *Brücken nach Mexiko. Traditionen einer Freundschaft*, Berlin (GDR)1989.

Klein, Wolfgang, *Schriftsteller in der französischen Volksfront. Die Zeitschrift 'Commune'*, Berlin (GDR) 1978.

Kline, Herbert, ed., *New Theatre and Film, 1934 to 1937. An Anthology*, San Diego 1985.

Koch, Stephen, *Double Lives. Spies and Writers in the Secret Soviet War of Ideas Against the West*, New York 1994.

Koestler, Arthur, *The Invisible Writing. The Second Volume of an Autobiography: 1932-1940*, London 1954.

Kotkin, Stephen, *Magnetic Mountain: Stalinism as a Civilisation*, Berkeley 1995.

Krull, Germaine, *La vita conduce la danza*, Florence 1992.

Kuball, Michael, *Familienkino Band 1, 1900-1930. Geschichte des Amateurfilms in Deutschland*, Reinbek bei Hamburg 1980.

Kurella, Alfred, *Ich lebe in Moskau*, Berlin (GDR) 1947.

Lacouture, Jean, *Malraux, une vie dans le siècle, 1901-1976*, Paris 1973.

Langer, Elinor, *Josephine Herbst. The Story She Could Never Tell*, New York 1984.

Last, Jef, *De Spaansche tragedie*, Amsterdam 1938.

–, *Het stalen fundament. Reportage over 2500 K.M. zwerftochten door de Oeral*, Amsterdam 1933.

–, *Mijn vriend André Gide*, Amsterdam 1966.

Leeuwen, Freek van, *De deur op een kier. Levensherinneringen van Freek van Leeuwen*, The Hague 1981.

Lehning, Arthur, *De draad van Ariadne. Essays en commentaren 1*, Amsterdam 1966.

Leyda, Jay, *Kino. A History of the Russian and Soviet Film*, Princeton 1983.

–, *Dianying. An Account of Films and the Film Audience in China*, Cambridge (Ma.) 1972.

Lichtenstein, Manfred, and Gerd Meier eds., *American Social Documentary. Beiträge zur Geschichte des Dokumentarfilmschaffens in den USA bis 1945*, Berlin (GDR) 1981.

Liebmann, Rolf, Evelin Matschke and Friedrich Salow eds., *Filmdokumentaristen der DDR*, Berlin (GDR) 1969.

Liehm, Mira, *Passion and Defiance. Film in Italy from 1942 to the Present*, Berkeley 1984.

Links Richten tussen partij en arbeidersstrijd. Materiaal voor een theorie over de verhouding tussen literatuur en arbeidersstrijd, deel 1 en 2 (collective thesis project group sociology of literature 1), Nijmegen 1975.

Linssen, Céline, Hans Schoots and Tom Gunning, *Het gaat om de film! Een nieuwe geschiedenis van de Nederlandsche Filmliga (1927-1933)*, Amsterdam 1999.

Lionel-Marie, Annick, and Alain Sayag eds., *Eli Lotar* (catalogue Centre Georges Pompidou), Paris 1993.

Living films. A Catalogue of Documentary Films and Their Makers Published by the Association of Documentary Film Producers, Inc., New York 1940.

Lockwood, Rupert, *Black Armada*, Sydney 1975.

LoBianco, Lorraine, and David Thompson eds., *Jean Renoir. Letters*, London 1994.

Lorentz, Pare, *FDR's Moviemaker. Memoirs and Scripts*, Reno 1992.

Ludington, Townsend, *John Dos Passos. A Twentieth Century Odyssey*, New York 1980.

Lynn, Kenneth S., *Hemingway*, London 1987.

Lyon, James K., *Bertolt Brecht in America*, Princeton 1980.

MacCann, Richard Dyer, *The People's Films. A Political History of US Government Motion Pictures*, New York 1973.

MacKinnon Janice R., and Stephen R. MacKinnon, *Agnes Smedley. The Life and Times of an American Radical*, Berkeley 1988.

Mackinnon, Lachlan, *The Lives of Elsa Triolet*, London 1992.

Maelstaf, R., *Henri Storck. Mens en kunstenaar*, Ghent 1971.

Marshall, Herbert, *Masters of the Soviet Cinema. Crippled Creative Biographies*, London 1983.

Marsman, H. *Verzameld werk*, Amsterdam 1979.

Matthews, Herbert L., *A World in Revolution. A Newspaperman's Memoir*, New York 1971.

Mayenburg, Ruth von, *Hotel Lux. Das Absteigequartier der Weltrevolution*, Munich 1978.

Meyers, Jeffrey, *Hemingway. A Biography*, New York 1985.

McBride, Joseph, *Frank Capra. The Catastrophe of Success*, New York 1992.

Mierau, Fritz, ed., *Russen in Berlin. Literatur, Malerei, Theater, Film, 1918-1933*, Leipzig 1991.

Morrien, Joop, *Indonesië los van Holland. De CPN en de PKI in hun strijd tegen het Nederlandse kolonialisme*, Amsterdam 1982.

Morris, Peter, ed., *The National Film Board of Canada: The War Years. A Collection of Contemporary Articles and a Selected Index of Productions*, Ottawa 1965.

Mückenberger, Christiane, and Günter Jordan, *'Sie sehen selbst, Sie hören selbst...' Eine Geschichte der DEFA von ihren Anfängen bis 1949*, Marburg 1994.

Müller, Reinhard, ed., *Die Säuberung. Moskau 1936: Stenogramm einer geschlossenen Parteiversammlung*, Reinbek bei Hamburg 1991.

Münzenberg, Willi, *Erobert den Film! Winke aus der Praxis für die Praxis proletarischer Filmpropaganda*, Berlin 1925.

Neve, Brian, *Film and Politics in America. A Social Tradition*, London 1992.

Neruda, Pablo, *Confieso que he vivido: Memorias*, Santiago 1974.

Nollau, Günther, *Die Internationale*, Cologne 1959.

Olink, Hans, *De vermoorde droom. Drie Nederlandse idealisten in Sovjet-Rusland*, Amsterdam 1993.

–, *Nico Rost. De man die van Duitsland hield*, Amsterdam 1997

Oltmans, Willem, *Vogelvrij*, Amsterdam 1992.

Orbanz, Eva, ed., *Helen van Dongen: Robert Flaherty's 'Louisiana Story'*, Constance 1998

Pavert, Nieko, Jef Last tussen de partij en zichzelf (thesis), Nijmegen 1982.

Pelikán, Jirí, ed., *The Czechoslovak Political Trials, 1950-1954, The Suppressed Report of the Dubcek Government's Commission of Inquiry, 1968*, Stanford 1971.

Pells, Richard H., *Radical Visions and American Dreams. Culture and Social Thought in the Depression Years*, New York 1973.

Pfemfert, Franz, *Ich setze diese Zeitschrift wider diese Zeit. Sozialpolitische und literaturkritische Aufsätze*, Darmstadt 1985.

Pike, David, *Deutsche Schriftsteller im sowjetischen Exil 1933-1945*, Frankfurt/Main 1981.

Platt, David, *Celluloid Power. Social Film Criticism from The Birth of a Nation to Judgement at Nuremberg*, Metuchen 1992.

Pozner, Vladimir, *Se souvient*, Paris 1989.

Prédal, René, *Le cinéma français contemporain*, Paris 1984.

–, *Le cinéma français depuis 1945*, Paris 1991.

Prox, Lothar, ed., *Borinage 1934/1984*, Cologne, undated, (1984).

Ree, Erik van, *Bloedbroeders. Stalin, Hitler en het pact*, Amsterdam 1989.

Reggiani, Serge, *La question se pose. Autoportrait*, Paris 1990.

Regler, Gustav, *Das Ohr des Malchus. Eine Lebensgeschichte*, Cologne 1958.

–, *Das große Beispiel*, Frankfurt/Main 1976 (In English 1940: *The Great Crusade).*

Renoir, Jean, *Ma vie et mes films*, Paris 1974.

Richter, Hans, *Köpfe und Hinterköpfe*, Zürich 1967.

–, *Der Kampf um den Film*, Vienna 1976.

Robins, Natalie, *Alien Ink. The FBI's War on Freedom of Expression*, New York 1992.

Rollyson, Carl, *Nothing Ever Happens to the Brave. The Story of Martha Gellhorn*. New York 1990.

Rosenthal, Alan, ed., *New Challenges of Documentary*, Berkeley 1988.

Rotha, Paul, *The Film Till Now. A Survey of World Cinema* (revised and extended version with an additional section by Richard Griffith), Feltham 1967.

–, *Documentary Diary*, London 1973.

Roud, Richard, *A Passion for Films. Henri Langlois and the Cinémathèque Française*, New York 1983.

Roy, Claude, ed., *Gérard Philipe. Souvenirs et témoignages recueillis par Anne Philipe*, Paris 1960.

Salles Gomes, P.E., *Jean Vigo*, Berkeley 1971.

Sapasnik, Tatjana, and Adi Petrowitsch, *Wsewolod Pudowkin. Die Zeit in Großaufnahme. Aufsätze, Errinerungen, Werkstattnotizen*, Berlin (GDR) 1983.

Schebera, Jürgen, *Hanns Eisler. Eine Bildbiographie*, Berlin (GDR) 1981.

Schmitt, H.-J., and G. Schramm, *Sozialistische Realismuskonzeptionen. Dokumente zum 1. Allunionskongreß der Sowjetschriftsteller*, Frankfurt/Main 1974.

Schock, Ralph, *Gustav Regler – Literatur und Politik (1933-1940)*, Frankfurt/Main 1984.

Schwartz, Nancy Lynn, *The Hollywood Writers' Wars*, New York 1982.

Seale, Patrick, and Maureen McConville, *French Revolution 1968*, London 1968.

Shloss, Carol, *In Visible Light. Photography and the American Writer: 1840-1940*, New York 1987.

Signoret, Simone, *La nostalgie n'est plus ce qu'elle était*, Paris 1976.

Sklar, Robert, *Film. An International History of the Medium*, New York 1993.

Snyder, Robert L., *Pare Lorentz and the Documentary Film*, Norman 1968.

Snow, Edgar, *Red Star over China*, London 1937.

Söllner, Alfons, ed., *Zur Archäologie der Demokratie in Deutschland. Band 1: 1943-1945. Analysen politischer Emigranten im amerikanischen Geheimdienst*, Frankfurt/Main 1982.

Spencer Carr, Virginia, *Dos Passos: A Life*, New York 1984.

Stange, Maren, ed., *Paul Strand. Essays on his Life and Work*, New York 1990.

Starobin, Joseph R., *American Communism in Crisis, 1943-1957*, Berkeley 1972.

Sterling, Claire, *The Masaryk case. The Murder of Democracy in Czechoslovakia*, New York 1969.

Stewart, Donald Ogden, *By a Stroke of Luck! An Autobiography*, New York 1975.

Stott, William, *Documentary Expression and Thirties America*, New York 1973.

Sudoplatov, Pavel, et al., *Special Tasks. The Memoirs of an Unwanted Witness – a Soviet Spymaster*, London 1994.

Suid, Lawrence H., *Guts & Glory. Great American War Movies*, Reading 1978.

Surmann, Rolf, *Die Münzenberg-Legende. Zur Publistik der revolutionären deutschen Arbeiterbewegung 1921-1933*, Cologne 1983.

Sussex, Elizabeth, *The Rise and Fall of British Documentary. The Story of the Film Movement Founded by John Grierson*, Berkeley 1975.

Taylor, Richard, ed., *The Film Factory. The Russian and Soviet Cinema in Documents 1896-1939*, London 1988.

Taylor, John Russell, *Strangers in Paradise. The Hollywood Émigrés, 1933-1950*, London 1983.

Thomas, Hugh, *The Spanish Civil War* (revised and extended edition), Harmondsworth 1977.

Tobias, Fritz, *Der Reichstagsbrand. Legende und Wirklichkeit*, Rastatt 1962.

Tresca Memorial Committee, ed., *Who Killed Carlo Tresca?*, New York 1945.

Tretjakow, Sergej, *Gesichter der Avantgarde. Porträts, Essays, Briefe*, Berlin 1991.

Tuchman, Barbara W., *Stilwell and the American Experience in China, 1911-45*, New York 1971.

Uitert, Evert van, and Jacobien de Boer eds., *De kunst van Mark Kolthoff. Van realisme tot abstractie. Aspecten van het Nederlandse kunstleven in de periode 1930-1980*, Rijswijk 1986.

Veen, Adriaan van der, *Vriendelijke vreemdeling*, Amsterdam 1969.

Vernon, Kathleen M. ed., *The Spanish Civil War and the Visual Arts*, Ithaka 1990.

Verrips, Ger, *Dwars, duivels en dromend. De geschiedenis van de CPN, 1938-1990*, Amsterdam 1995.

Viertel, Salka, *Das unbelehrbare Herz. Ein Leben in der Welt des Theaters, der Literatur und des Films*, Hamburg 1970.

Weintraub, Stanley, *The Last Great Cause. The Intellectuals and the Spanish Civil War*, New York 1968.

Weringh, Koos van, and Toke van Helmond, *Joseph Roth in Nederland*, Amsterdam 1979.

Wessel, Harald, *Münzenbergs Ende. Ein deutscher Kommunist im Widerstand gegen Hitler und Stalin. Die Jahre 1933 bis 1940*, Berlin 1991.

Whelan, Richard, *Robert Capa. A Biography*, London 1985.

Willett, John, *The Theatre of Erwin Piscator. Half a Century of Politics in the Theatre*, London 1978.

Willy Kessels, fotograaf. Geheugenverlies, verantwoordelijheid en collaboratie, Brussels 1997.

Wit, Cor de, *Johan Niegeman. Bauhaus, Sowjet Unie, Amsterdam*, Amsterdam 1979.

Wright, William, *Lillian Hellman. The Image, the Woman*, London 1987.

Würzner, M.H., Antoine Bodar, Nico J. Brederoo et al. eds., *Aspecten van het interbellum.*

Beeldende kunst, film, fotografie, cultuurfilosofie en literatuur in de periode tussen de twee wereldoorlogen, The Hague 1990.

Wijk, Kees van, *Internationale Revue i10*, Utrecht 1980.

Zimmermann, Peter, ed., *Deutschlandbilder Ost. Dokumentarfilme der DEFA von der Nachkriegszeit bis zur Wiedervereinigung*, Constance 1995.

Zsuffa, Joseph, *Béla Balázs, The Man and the Artist*, Berkeley 1987.

Filmography Joris Ivens

prod. = producer; dir. = director; ed. = editor, scen. = scenarist; cam. = camera; com. = commentary writer; v.o. = voice-over; act. = actor; adv. = advisor

Official English titles given where they exist. Unofficial titles in brackets.

DE WIGWAM – WIGWAM, 1912, scen. act. (Kees Ivens, dir.)
'T ZONHUIS, 1925. (home movie)
'T ZONHUIS, 1927. (home movie)
THEA'S MEERDERJARIGHEID ZONNELAND, 1927, dir. cam. (home movie)
Various film experiments in Amsterdam, 1927.
Takes for a fiction film with Charlotte Köhler, 1927, dir. cam.
ZEEDIJK-FILMSTUDIE – FILMSTUDY ZEEDIJK, 1927, dir. cam.
De zieke stad – (The Sick City), 1927-1928, dir. (with Erich Wichman), cam.
   (uncompleted)
ÉTUDES DE MOUVEMENTS – STUDIES IN MOVEMENT, 1928, dir. cam. ed.
DE BRUG – THE BRIDGE, 1928, prod. dir. scen. cam. ed.
BRANDING – BREAKERS, 1929, cam. ed. (Mannus Franken, dir.)
Ik-film experimenten – I Film experiments 1929, dir. cam.
SCHAATSENRIJDEN – (SKATING), 1929, dir. cam.
DE NOOD IN DE DRENTSCHE VENEN – (POVERTY IN THE BOGS OF DRENTHE),
   1929, cam. ed. (Leo van Lakerveld, dir.)
REGEN – RAIN, 1929, prod. dir. (with Mannus Franken), cam. ed.
WIJ BOUWEN – WE ARE BUILDING, 1930, dir. scen. cam. ed.
(various sections of WE ARE BUILDING were also released separately: HEIEN
   – PILE DRIVING; NVV-CONGRES; JEUGDDAG; NIEUWE ARCHITECTUUR;
   CAISSONBOUW; AMSTERDAMSE JEUGDDAG; ZUIDERZEEWERKEN –
   (ZUIDERZEE WORKS); ZUID-LIMBURG)
JEUGDDAG VIERHOUTEN, 1930, dir.
ZUIDERZEE, 1930, dir. scen. cam. ed.
FILMNOTITIES UIT DE SOVJETUNIE – NEWS FROM THE SOVIET UNION, 1930, dir.
   cam. ed.
BREKEN EN BOUWEN – (CONSTRUCTION AND DEMOLITION) 1930, ed. (Mark
   Kolthoff, dir.)
Various VVVC-JOURNAALS – (VVVC NEWSREELS) 1930-1931, ed.
DONOGOO-TONKA, 1931, cam. ed.
PHILIPS RADIO, 1931, dir. scen. cam. ed.
CREOSOOT – CREOSOTE, 1931, dir. (with Jean Dréville)

Pesn o gerojach (Komsomol) – Song of Heroes (Komsomol), 1933, dir. ed.

Nieuwe gronden – New Earth, 1933, dir. scen. cam. v.o.

Misère au Borinage/ Borinage, 1934, dir. (with Henri Storck), scen. cam. ed.

Borinage, Russian version, 1934, dir. cam. ed.

Saarabstimmung und Sowjetunion – (Saar plebiscite and Soviet Union), 1934, dir. (with Gustav Regler)

Compilation film on the 'Schutzbündler', 1934 or 1935, dir.

Kämpfer/Bortsy– Fighters, 1936, dir. (with Gustav von Wangenheim)

The Russian School in New York, 1936.

The Spanish Earth, 1937, dir. scen.

The 400 Million, 1939, dir.

Power and the Land, 1940, dir. scen.

New Frontiers, 1940, dir. scen. (production ended during shooting)

Oil for Alladinn's Lamp, 1941, dir.

Our Russian Front, 1941, adv. dir. (with Lewis Milestone)

Action Stations!, 1943, dir. scen. ed. (short version given the title Corvette Port Arthur)

The New Earth, 1944 (A Dutch government adaptation of Nieuwe gronden)

Know Your Enemy: Japan, 1945, dir. scen. (completed without Ivens's participation)

The Story of GI-Joe, 1945, adv. (William Wellman, dir.)

Indonesia Calling!, 1946, dir. scen. ed.

The First Years, 1949, dir. ed.

Pokoj zwyciezy swiat – Peace will Win, 1951, dir. (with Jerzy Bossak)

Freundschaft siegt! – Friendship Triumphs, 1952, dir. (with Ivan Pyrjev)

Wyscig pokoju Warsawa-Berlin-Praga – Peace Tour 1952, 1952, dir. scen.

Lied der Ströme – Song of the Rivers, 1954, dir. scen.

Les aventures de Till l'Espiegle/Die Abenteuer des Till Eulenspiegel – The Adventures of Till Eulenspiegel, 1956, adv. (Gerard Philipe, dir.)

Mein Kind – (My Child), 1956, adv. (Alfons Machalz and Vladimir Pozner, dir.)

Die Windrose – (The Compass Card), 1957, adv. (Alberto Cavalcanti, Gillo Pontecorvo et al, dir.)

La Seine a rencontré Paris – The Seine meets Paris, 1957, dir.

Before Spring, 1958, dir.

THE INDIGNATION OF 600 MILLION PEOPLE/600 MILION WITH YOU, 1958, dir. ed.

L'ITALIA NON É UN PAESE POVERO – ITALY IS NOT A POOR COUNTRY, 1960, dir. scen. ed.

DEMAIN À NANGUILA – NANGUILA TOMORROW, 1960, dir. com.

MARC CHAGALL, 1960, cam. ed. (Henri Langlois, dir.)

CARNET DE VIAJE – TRAVEL NOTEBOOK, 1961, dir.

PUEBLO ARMADO – AN ARMED NATION, 1961, dir.

UNBÄNDIGES SPANIEN – (INDOMITABLE SPAIN), 1962, adv. (Jeanne and Kurt Stern, dir.)

... À VALPARAÍSO, 1963, dir. scen.

LE PETIT CHAPITEAU – (THE LITTLE CIRCUS), 1963, dir.

LE TRAIN DE LA VICTOIRE – VICTORIOUS TRAIN, 1964, dir.

AAAH... TAMARA, 1965, act. (Pim de la Parra, dir.)

POUR LE MISTRAL – MISTRAL, 1965, dir. scen.

LE CIEL, LA TERRE – THE THREATENING SKY, 1966, dir. v.o.

ROTTERDAM-EUROPOORT – ROTTERDAM EUROPORT, 1966, dir. scen.

LOIN DU VIETNAM – FAR FROM VIETNAM, 1967, collective work together with Alain Resnais, Jean-Luc Godard, William Klein, Claude Lelouch and Agnès Varda, headed by Chris Marker.

17E PARALLÈLE, LA GUERRE DU PEUPLE – 17TH PARALLEL, 1968, prod. dir.

LE PEUPLE ET SES FUSILS – THE PEOPLE AND THEIR GUNS, 1970, prod. collective work together with Marceline Loridan, Jean-Pierre Sergent et al.

RENCONTRE AVEC LE PRÉSIDENT HO CHI MINH – (A MEETING WITH PRESIDENT HO CHI MINH), 1970, prod. dir. (with Marceline Loridan)

LE SOULÈVEMENT DE LA VIE – (ELEVATING LIFE), 1971, cam. (idea: Maurice Clavel)

COMMENT YUKONG DEPLAÇA LES MONTAGNES – HOW YUKONG MOVED THE MOUNTAINS, 1976, prod. dir. (with Marceline Loridan) Sections: AUTOUR DU PÉTROLE: TAKING; LA PHARMACIE NO. 3: CHANGHAI; L'USINE DE GÉNÉRATEURS; UNE FEMME, UNE FAMILLE; LE VILLAGE DES PÊCHEURS; UNE CASERNE; IMPRESSIONS D'UNE VILLE: CHANGHAI; HISTOIRE D'UN BALLON: LE LYCÉE NO. 31 À PÉKIN; LE PROFESSEUR TSIEN; UNE RÉPÉTITION À L'OPÉRA DE PÉKIN; ENTRAÎNEMENT AU CIRQUE DE PÉKIN; LES ARTISANS.

LES KAZAKS, MINORITÉ NATIONALE, SINKIANG – THE KAZACHS, NATIONAL MINORITY, SINKIANG, 1977, prod. dir. (with Marceline Loridan)

LES OUIGOURS, MINORITÉ NATIONALE, SINKIANG– THE OUIGOURS, NATIONAL MINORITY, SINKIANG, 1977, prod. dir. (with Marceline Loridan)

HAVRE – (HAVEN), 1986, act. (Juliet Berto, dir.)

UNE HISTOIRE DE VENT – A TALE OF THE WIND, 1988, act. prod. dir. (with Marceline Loridan)

Index